D0787913

*Socialist Europe and revolutionary Russia: perception and prejudice* 1848–1923 analyses perceptions and images of Russia held by European socialists in the period between the revolutions of 1848 and firm establishment of the Soviet regime in the early 1920s. Professor Naarden investigates in detail the sometimes pernicious influence of the age-old Western image of Russia on the ideological outlook and actions of the largest organised political movement in Europe. Whereas the history of socialism has been largely written from a national point of view, or within a national framework, this survey of a major pan-European theme permits an alternative perspective on contemporary East–West relations, and on numerous important aspects of nineteenth-century socialism, not least the powerful role in its development of a number of Russian writers, whether as protagonists or opponents. The recent resurgence within the Soviet Union of alternative, non-Leninist political traditions gives much of this book, in which the Mensheviks assume special significance, considerable topical relevance at the present time.

# SOCIALIST EUROPE AND REVOLUTIONARY RUSSIA: PERCEPTION AND PREJUDICE 1848–1923

# SOCIALIST EUROPE AND REVOLUTIONARY RUSSIA: PERCEPTION AND PREJUDICE 1848–1923

## BRUNO NAARDEN

*Professor of Russian History and Director of the Institute for*
*Russian and Eastern European Studies at the University of Amsterdam*

CAMBRIDGE
UNIVERSITY PRESS

Published by the Press Syndicate of the University of Cambridge
The Pitt Building, Trumpington Street, Cambridge CB2 1RP
40 West 20th Street, New York, NY 10011-4211, USA
10 Stamford Road, Oakleigh, Victoria 3166, Australia

First published 1992

Printed in Great Britain by Bell and Bain Ltd., Glasgow

*A cataloguing in publication record for this book is available from the British Library*

*Library of Congress cataloguing in publication data*
Naarden, B., 1940–
Socialist Europe and revolutionary Russia: perception and
prejudice 1848–1923/Bruno Naarden.
p. cm.
Includes bibliographical references.
ISBN 0 521 41473 3 (hardback)
1. Socialism – Europe – History – 19th century.
2. Socialism – Soviet Union – History – 19th century.
3. Soviet Union – Foreign public opinion, European.
4. Revolutions – Soviet Union – History – 20th century.
5. Soviet Union – Politics and government – 19th century.
6. Soviet Union – Politics and government – 20th century.
I. Title.
HX238.N33  1992
324.1'7'094 – dc20   91–33995   CIP

ISBN 0 521 41473 3 hardback

AS

# CONTENTS

# INTRODUCTION

For a long time the Iron Curtain has been seen as the main obstacle to the normalization of relations between East and West. Since it disappeared in 1989 the contrast between the prosperous and politically stable nations in Western Europe and their less endowed counterparts in the East has turned out to be far more marked than we thought. Although mutual contacts have become more intensive and diverse, the continuing dissimilarity between the two halves of Europe in many ways precludes the establishment of normal relations. The disastrous situation in Central and Eastern Europe is largely the result of communist dictatorship. It is still worth while to study the history of communism since it continues to exert its influence even in the post-communist era. Nevertheless, we should be careful not to blame every manifestation of abnormality in our present and future connections with Central and Eastern Europe on its communist period. It is also possible that a more remote past is still playing tricks on us. There is a substantial amount of historical literature proving that the relationship between Russia and Europe has hardly ever been 'normal' and that the cause of this had nothing to do with Soviet communism.

In this book the sometimes pernicious influence of traditional Western attitudes towards Russia is studied in detail and over a long period. It deals with perceptions and 'images' of Russia held by European socialists in the years 1848–1923. Its aim is to put the 'Russian question' in the Western labour movement of this period in a wider and more historical context. It throws a different light on a number of developments in both Russian and Western socialism but is also meant as a contribution to a better understanding of contemporary relations between East and West. When I started my research it seemed useful to study one particular problem which had been an important subject of discussion within the socialist movement as a whole and throughout almost all of its history. Until then the history of socialism had been written mainly from a national point of view, or within a national framework. At the same time I wanted to give special attention to the history of non-Bolshevik Russian socialism, and especially to Menshevism, because this topic had not been studied exhaustively in the West and had been neglected in the Soviet Union. By studying Russian social democracy not exclusively as a purely Russian matter but as an element in the development of European socialism I also hoped to get a better understanding of certain events in the history of the Internationals and of the socialist parties of the West.

This was not the only or even the principal reason for the writing of this book. The material I studied revealed a European image of Russia and a European Russian policy behind which lay a definite pattern of prejudiced opinions: a mental framework which was evidently extremely resistant to change. It reminded one of the *prisons de longue durée* in which, according to Braudel, human thought and behaviour can be fettered for centuries.[1] The scholarly world since the Second World War has been intensively engaged in social and political judgements. It has become established that stereotyped thought about the behaviour of other groups of people is not something particularly Western, but a universal human trait. The same is true of the human tendency to form a mental image of the world in which people have to orientate themselves by means of a sort of mental map. On this map each different area has its own emotional colour. Ethnocentrism, the tendency to emphasise the excellence of one's own community, is likewise something encountered all over the world.[2] In the relations between the West and the rest of the world such large groups of people are involved that the term 'macro-ethnocentrism' has been coined. However, the social scientists have not been very active in this subject.[3]

Nevertheless, we know very well that many of these 'old-fashioned' prejudices about nations and peoples die hard. We are also to some extent conscious of the fact that prejudices cannot be totally eradicated because our knowledge of reality remains incomplete. The need for an opinion, even if it is an irresponsible generalisation about matters of which we know little, will always exist. Unavoidably these opinions adopt standardised forms determined by culture and history and become fossilised into prejudices. These prejudices endure because they not infrequently contain something of the truth and are apparently validated by observations from reality. It is more rarely appreciated that prejudices have a chameleon-like character and, after they have been hunted down and rejected as untrue, can reappear in a new form. 'The adequate record of even the confusions of our forebears', wrote A. O. Lovejoy, 'may help, not only to clarify those confusions, but to engender a salutary doubt whether we are wholly immune from different but equally great confusions.'[4] And indeed not only our parents were 'mistaken' about Russia. Our forefathers were equally mistaken. These errors did not only emanate from disdain for non-Western backwardness and lack of civilisation. We have also projected our aspirations on to foreign peoples, and admired or even venerated them. The world outside Europe has been our mirror.

The practitioners of the social sciences have thought up the term 'negative ethnocentrism' for this phenomenon, but they have not paid it much attention. It is, however, something which confronted me very frequently in the historical material I was studying. A few historians and sociologists have already gone into this problem. David Caute and Paul Hollander have each devoted a book to the enthusiasm of fellow-travellers and political pilgrims for Soviet Russia.[5] But the explanations given by these authors for the existence of the curious opinions about Russia, China, Cuba, and so on, are not completely satisfactory. According to Caute the glorification of 'leftist' dictators by 'leftist' intellectuals is an after-effect of the ideals of the eighteenth century. He therefore gave his book the subtitle *A postscript to the Enlightenment*. Hollander rejects this thesis in imitation of the American philosopher Lewis Feuer. In his view the explanation must be sought in the 'alienation' or 'estrangement' of the Western intellectual in the twentieth century. There is no need to take up a stand either for or against one of these two interpretations. In no way do they rule each other out, but rather they complement each other. In my opinion they are not incorrect, but inadequate.

In the last half-century there have, after all, always been intellectuals who have refused to embrace 'socialist' dictators. Men like Raymond Aron or Albert Camus cannot be discounted as reactionaries or accomplices of the establishment. There is little reason to suppose that the ideals of the Enlightenment had no hold over them, or that the alienation phenomena that can be the result of an intellectual attitude passed them by. The glorification of 'leftist' despotism was, moreover, definitely not the preserve of intellectuals. It is barely necessary to mention the average member of a Western communist party here. The fellow-travellers and the political pilgrims who visited Soviet Russia after 1917 included many who were neither communists nor intellectuals. The same is true of the Europeans who aired comparable opinions about the Third World. In the beginning of the nineteenth century, in fact, tsarist Russia was glorified by *conservative* intellectuals, who had every reason to feel alienated and displaced in Western society. Of equal importance is the fact that 'leftist' Europe has never agreed about Soviet Russia since 1917. Opinions were very much divided. Finally, the eighteenth century has possibly been of decisive importance for various forms of thought which have had great influence in this century, but the origin of our attitude to the non-European world does not lie there. Its roots can be traced back deep in classical Antiquity. Beside a tradition which has stood firm for so many centuries and through so many generations of Europeans, comparatively modern concepts such as Enlightenment or alienation lose much of their value as explanatory interpretations.

In short, we are dealing with a complicated and comprehensive phenomenon which not only profoundly modified our emotions towards the non-Western world in the past but which continues to do so at the present time. It is impossible to offer the one and only correct explanation for this. But since historians such as Léon Poliakov and Norman Cohn have made us aware that the most barbaric expressions of hatred of the Jews possibly originated in very old myths that were deeply anchored in our culture, we have no need to be greatly surprised at the antiquity, the intricacy, the range and the timelessness of Western

European ethnocentrism.[6] If we are ready to acknowledge this, then the question emerges as to how it should be studied. Naturally I do not pretend to have found the correct approach or method for this. But it remains of importance to know more about the subject and for that purpose this book may offer certain advantages. By devoting attention to a period in which the ideological opposition between capitalism and communism did not yet exist in the form we became used to after 1917, the ethnocentric background of the East–West antithesis can more easily be laid bare. The book analyses the attitudes of a large group of people in Europe and over a long period. It shows how their opinions about Russia proceeded from particular historical developments and how these views in their turn influenced those developments.

A great advantage of the period chosen is that a number of Russians who gave their own views unmolested and had no obligations to a dictatorial state, play the most important role in this account, both as fellow players and as opposite numbers. East–West relations within the socialist world can, in this way, be illuminated from both sides, whereas for a later period this would be impossible. Of course this study has its limitations. It is certainly not a complete inventory of the relationships between Russian and Western socialists. To achieve that end one would need to write a much more extensive work than this already substantial book. The emphasis is upon those people and matters which in my view provide the most insight into the 'Russian question'. In doing this the Mensheviks receive more attention than the Bolsheviks or the Bundists and the Russian social democrats more than the Russian anarchists or the socialist revolutionaries. For the same reason more information will be found about German social democracy than about British or Belgian socialism. This is meant to be a book about a specific part of the historical background of big movements like Russian socialism or main events like the October revolution. These important movements and events themselves are therefore only summarily dealt with.     Finally, in more than a merely geographical sense Russia has always been a part of Europe. Between 1945 and 1989 Central Europe disappeared from the political map and we understood the expressions East and West and Eastern and Western Europe somewhat differently than before the Second World War. Now we start again to make new distinctions between the different parts of our continent. Terms which I have frequently used in this book, such as Europe, the West or Western European, have here for the most part a global meaning only in contrast to words like Russia and Russian. As a Dutch historian I am well aware of the problems connected with the idea of Europe. Diversity far more than unity seems to be Europe's characteristic feature, and when words like Europe or European are used in a general way they always seem to imply generalisations which can only be justified to a certain extent. Perceptions of Russia of course also differed in different parts of Europe. But at the same time they had something in common which allowed this book to be one on European history.

Without the assistance of many people and institutions this book would never have been completed. In the original version of this book I thanked many Dutch friends and colleagues. In the English edition I want to express my appreciation for the help I got from abroad. I want to thank Terence Emmons for his warm hospitality and the staff of the Hoover Institution for its assistance in the early stage of my research. I am deeply grateful to Margaret Vaughan who made the English translation. I was greatly helped by the remarks, criticisms and corrections I received from Marc Raeff, Abraham Ascher, David Kirby and André Liebich. The translation of the Dutch text was financed by NWO, the Netherlands Organisation for Scientific Research. I want to pay homage to the late Anna M. Bourguina and the late Boris M. Sapir, both archivists of the Menshevik movement, who so kindly shared their knowledge and experience with me.

# I

# THE WESTERN EUROPEAN IMAGE OF RUSSIA

What significance should be attached to the occurrence of the October revolution in Russia rather than in a Western European country? What is the importance of the fact that the first social revolution propagated by socialists took place in a backward, rural country on the periphery of European civilisation, whilst socialism was an intellectual legacy of the French revolution and a typically Western reaction to the modernisation and industrialisation of Europe? Even now it is impossible to give a conclusive and universally satisfactory answer to these questions. Although the differences between Russia and Europe have fascinated us since the sixteenth century and continue to determine our attitudes of mind towards Eastern Europe to this very day, we still cannot agree about the weight to be attached to Russia's dissimilarity. This discussion still brings colour and excitement to Western historiography about the Russian revolution. In the years immediately after 1917 this revolution formed one of the most acute problems facing Europeans. They were forced to take a stand, whilst the only information available about the situation in Russia was totally inadequate, so that feelings, suppositions and preconceptions had the widest possible scope.

It is understandable that the most deeply rooted prejudices within the European consciousness were those which had the most influence. In the past, too, Russia had aroused powerful emotions in Europeans. If we look back, we can see how these emotions united to form a clear and ever-recurrent pattern which became a permanent component of the richly coloured tapestry of our cultural history. Stereotyped ideas about Russia have been in existence for centuries, and the most remarkable thing about them is that their content has changed so little. Only the form in which they were expressed was modified to suit the intellectual fashions and political climates of each period. Anyone who needed to could create a Russia to his own taste with the help of clichés handed down to him. If the situation demanded it, negative elements could be replaced by positive ones and vice versa. At certain times when Europeans felt they were going through a crisis in the history of their part of the world which had some connection with Russia, these old images came vigorously to the fore and, because of their conflicting content, they intensified political dissension. In this respect the period after 1917 has much in common with those after 1812 and 1945.

The socialist who after 1917 very deliberately steered clear of the, in his view, too critical manner in which the 'bourgeois' European presented Soviet Russia, kept his own counsel but remained nevertheless within the traditional framework. This furnished sufficient scope for very divergent interpretations of Russian events while at the same time offering opportunities for mystifications which had little in common with Bolshevik reality. The European image of Russia certainly did not determine the reactions to Bolshevism from A to Z. There were, after all, in the opinion of Europeans, very substantial, concrete and immediate issues at stake in the struggle for or against communism. However, time-honoured ideas about Russia were continually present in the background and these influenced the formation of opinions often unremarked, but unremittingly. They also provide us with a partial explanation for the intensity of the feelings of antipathy, apprehension and admiration for Russia. These were emotions which hit Europe like a tidal wave shortly after 1917, afterwards ebbing somewhat but never disappearing and from time to time reviving tempestuously.

Unless one has some insight into the continuity of the Russian image one can scarcely visualise its impact. Its origins and the persistence with which it held its own are in any case difficult to explain. Historical writing has habitually been concerned with the problem of the forming of images of other nations, but has never tried to research this systematically from one specific point of view. Up to now there have only been impressionistic essays[1] and well-founded monographs about incidental and limited subjects.[2] A compendious and explanatory survey of the inception and development of the Western image of Russia has never appeared.

The image of Russia originated from West European convictions with regard to barbarism, which have to a large extent determined our relations with non-Western peoples. Stereotypical concepts about Russia are thus tributaries of a wider current in our cultural history, the source of which must be sought deep in classical Antiquity. Western attitudes towards the outside world have been contradictory from time immemorial. Contempt has always existed, but fear, curiosity, amazement and admiration for the barbarians also occurred. This very contradiction can be seen as something typically European. Other civilisations have sometimes given the impression that they reacted to their surroundings in a less ambivalent way. Europeans have never cut themselves off from contact with non-Europeans such as the Japanese. European ethnocentrism was also usually distinct from the egocentric self-satisfaction displayed by the Chinese for a long period of their history. The inhabitants of Europe have probably never been entirely deprived of contacts with the inhabitants of Africa or Asia. There are no known instances of totally ignorant Europeans who hailed visitors from other parts of the world as gods. Such a reception did indeed fall to the lot of European travellers as they first set foot on land in America or other places where a white man had never before penetrated. Although we readily consider ourselves as 'civilised' and call others 'savage' and 'barbaric', the word 'man' in European languages referred to all the people in the world, and was not, as in the case of the Ancient Egyptians or the Navaho Indians, exclusively reserved for their own ethnic group.

It is questionable whether one can venture to assume from information of this kind that Europe's reactions to the outside world would from the start have been different from those of non-European peoples. But one can safely argue that Europe's growing position of authority in the world since the sixteenth century has achieved very distinct changes in the way in which Europeans and non-Europeans look at each other. Certainly, the master–servant relationship which existed between them from the nineteenth century onwards was not only characterised by feelings of superiority on one side and inferiority on the other. But the substantial real inequality in their mutual relationship was certainly of paramount importance. The European's self-satisfaction did not necessarily deteriorate into arrogance, although this was frequently the case. In principle he was free to behave in the opposite manner if he chose to do so. In the case of the non-Europeans there was scarcely any possibility of a comparable freedom. They, too, showed contempt, fear, curiosity and admiration; but these feelings caused tension because they were combined with insecurity, frustration, envy and hatred. These last emotions were virtually unknown to Europeans in their contacts with non-Europeans and were certainly not fostered. Only their attitude towards the Russians was somewhat exceptional in that respect.

This inequality, and the sentiments it awakened in both parties, likewise played a significant role in the relationships between Russia and Europe. This was not strictly logical, for Russia's position was totally different from that of the colonies. She was indeed backward in various fields. Around 1900 she was economically so dependent on the West that one could speak of her 'semi-colonial' status. But the country was never occupied or dominated for any length of time by a Western state. It was not only an independent, but also an expansionist and later an imperialistic nation. Since the eighteenth century Russia cannot be seen otherwise than as a great European power. Around 1900, as far as the extent of her territories was concerned, she was the largest state in the world. Russia was, moreover, the first country to carry out large-scale reforms with a view to overtaking the West, and in so doing she achieved striking results that compelled respect there, arousing panic but also engendering admiration. It is remarkable that precisely because of this, the Western image of Russia became dominated, in a far more extreme way than was expressed in our ideas about other areas, by the strange ambivalent feelings that the 'civilised' West has cultivated towards 'barbarian' peoples ever since the days of the Ancient Greeks. An unbroken line cannot however be drawn from the concept of barbarians in Antiquity to the Western image of Russia, which only came into being in the sixteenth century, but which from then onwards followed the classical example more and more closely. For this reason, in what follows not only do we briefly consider the relationship between Greeks and barbarians, but the route along which this cultural legacy probably penetrated our ideas about Russia is also indicated.

## FROM ANTIQUITY TO THE SIXTEENTH CENTURY

It was Homer who first used the word 'barbarian', without attaching any unfavourable meaning to it. On the contrary, he characterised the barbarian tribe of the Albii as 'the most right-eous among men' (*Iliad*, XIII, 5–6). Later generations assumed that he was referring to the Scythians, a nomadic people who lived in the steppes to the north of the Black Sea. The word barbarian was, however, later to arouse different associations. At the time of the Persian Wars in particular, it acquired an extremely pejorative meaning. Barbarians were ungainly, coarse, stupid, ignorant, superstitious, antisocial, uninhibited, perverse, violent, cruel, greedy, mendacious, unreliable, submissive, slavish, and so on. There has been no lack of expert correction to this caricature either in Antiquity or later. But the need to experience one's own ethnical, national or cultural unity by looking down upon all that was foreign was stronger. Under-estimation of the barbarians could, however, quite easily give way to overestimation. The barbarians were then no longer seen as cowardly, but as aggressive. Fear that the barbarian hordes, led by despots worshipped as gods, would conquer the civilised world hardly contributed to a balanced and realistic judgement.

Favourable appraisals of the barbarians did not however disappear. Eight centuries after Homer, the geographer Strabo alluded to the poet in describing the Scythians as 'noble savages'.[3] The Scythians were not usually felt by the Greeks to be a threat. They showed respect for this nation that had defeated the Persians. The Greeks were interested to note the criticism levelled at their religious observances by prominent Scythians. The judgements of the fabulously wise Scythian king Anacharsis, who had travelled around Greece, strengthened the scepticism with which the Greeks sometimes regarded their own civilisation. In Strabo's view the less agreeable qualities of the Scythians were a sign of decadence and resulted exclusively from the corrupting influence which emanated from their contact with the superior Hellenistic civilization. In this way what was unpleasant in their own culture projected itself into the illusion of an originally unspoilt and natural barbarian way of life. But there was yet another form of glorification of the barbarian. The Asiatic despots who had huge towns, palaces, temples and mausoleums built, or who were able to follow their own caprice or wisdom by carrying through large-scale social reforms, were regarded by the Greeks with amazement, but sometimes also with jealousy or admiration.[4]

The foundations of the Greeks' image of barbarians, rich as it was in contrasts, thus lay as much in contempt as in fear and glorification, and we find this again in the Western image of Russia. There, too, glorification sometimes takes the upper hand and leads to the opinion that things which were no longer possible in weary, overcivilised Europe could be accomplished only in Russia. Thus the Eastern tyrants' bent towards megalomania did not awake amazement and admiration in the free Greek citizen alone. The equally freedom-loving French philosophers of the eighteenth century deliberately joined in with this tradition by naming Catherine II of Russia the Semiramis of the North. The great respect shown in the West even by non-communists for Lenin and Stalin is akin to this. The traditions of classical geography were just as tenacious and were still detectable in the nineteenth century. The later Slav inhabitants of Russia were even then still occasionally described as Scythians and this could be interpreted as favourable or unfavourable.[5] In this century after all, there were Russians who bore the name Scyth with pride.[6] Western admiration in the nineteenth and twentieth centuries for 'barbarian' Russian art and literature, the Russian 'soul' and Russian piety point however towards the kind of glorification that the Greeks had entertained for the Scythians and other 'primitive peoples'. The Greeks' fear of the Persians was to live again in the terror of the Russian hordes to which civilised Europe was subject.

If we try to follow the adventures of the barbarian image in Antiquity, it becomes apparent that the attitude of the Romans towards the barbarians was mostly determined by fear and contempt. But the glorification of primitive peoples remained a beloved theme in literature, where the Scythians retained a conspicuous place.[7] It is significant for the more recent image of Russia that the pitiable collapse of the Roman Empire under barbarian assault was to remain indelibly engraved on the minds of the later Europeans. The tradition of classical learning gave comparisons between Antiquity and one's own age an air of natural truthfulness,[8] and – sometimes to the dismay of serious scholars – great political influence.[9] In the first half of the nineteenth century many intellectuals had been spell-bound by Gibbon's *Decline and Fall*, above all because in reading it they had at the same time to think of the Russia that had defeated Napoleon. Gibbon blamed Rome's downfall primarily on internal weakness. Many of his readers believed likewise that Europe had lost its vitality and was thus ripe for barbarian conquest. The comparison between the fate of the ancient civilisation and the possible future Russification of Europe became such a cliché that people spoke of 'the great parallel'.[10] The fact that the eastern part of her empire endured for another millennium did not in their view detract from the drama of Rome's downfall. The end of Byzantium ultimately came about in a similarly tragic manner.

For the medieval Byzantines themselves barbarism was a permanent trauma. They believed their empire to be an island of culture in a sea of incivility and prayed daily for the victory of their emperor over the warring barbarians, amongst whom they also not infrequently included the Christian nations of Western Europe. But around the year 1000 the Russians were especially feared. They had shown themselves to be formidable military opponents and according to tradition had been identified with the Scythians, the classical prototype of all that was barbaric. Great then was the Byzantines' joy that the Slavs had been successfully won over to Christianity. It was regarded as a miracle from God that even the most savage tribes had allowed themselves to be converted to brotherly love and chastity. The emperor commended Cyril the missionary for transforming the Scythians from wolves into lambs.[11] The Byzantines had plenty of opportunity via their intensive contacts with the Russia of the time, the empire of Kiev, to form a balanced image of the Russians. Their initial enthusiasm for the metamorphosis of savage heathens into Christians was based on an underlying belief in the malleability of the barbarians' nature that we can find again later in Western Europe. There, many were enraptured by the reforms of Peter the Great and Catherine II as if the barbaric

Russians could have been changed into civilised Europeans at the touch of a wand. In the present century the belief that 'a new man' was coming into being in communist Russia was to gain support.

In the middle ages Western Christendom was familiar with the literary tradition which regarded the Scythians as heathen barbarians and noble savages, and followed in its footsteps. But the empire of Kiev was at the time usually considered as a distant but flourishing Christian empire that was no less important than Poland or Hungary. The relationships maintained with it, though not intensive, were based on mutual respect and equality. When, however, Kiev was conquered by the Mongols in the thirteenth century, it almost totally disappeared from West European awareness. Only Novgorod and southern Russia remained susceptible to Western influences. The rise of Muscovy went unnoticed in Europe. The memory of the Christian civilisation of Kiev-Rus faded and contributed nothing to the formation of the Russian image.[12] Therefore it was indeed relevant that during the middle ages – thus long before the East–West problem had manifested itself in the form in which we know it – Europe was faced with a political and ideological division into an Eastern and a Western camp. The West was not only confronted with the threatening power of Islam in this period, but the unity of the former Roman Empire was never again restored and after the schism of 1054 Christianity likewise became divided into an Eastern and Western church. Relations with Byzantium remained strained. The fact that Russia adopted the Eastern Orthodox rite was later to prove of fundamental significance. In the middle ages, fear of the 'Eastern' threat was stimulated by the German *Drang nach Osten* and the acute danger from the Mongols. Under the pressure of these circumstances Christian Europe formed an image of itself in the surrounding world which was later also to determine its attitude with regard to Russia as soon as it was discovered afresh by the West.[13]

The lengthy process of violent conquest and peaceful co-operation that characterised the relationship of the Germans with the peoples living to the east of them, led in the nineteenth and twentieth centuries to nationalistic interpretations of medieval history which intensified German–Slav opposition prodigiously. On the German side expansion in an easterly direction was presented as civilisation making great strides into barbarian territory. In the middle ages many Germans saw the heathen Slavs as savage, ferocious and unreliable, but at the same time there were also Germans who thought the Slavs were peaceful, hospitable and even chivalrous people who, if they had become Christians, could only have been held up as an example to their fellow believers.[14] The classical view of the barbarians can thus be recognized in the medieval image of heathens. This is the case, for example, with the medieval barbarians *par excellence*, the Mongols, who proved to be unconquerable because of their perfidious cunning and atrocious inhumanity and thus inspired apocalyptic views about a struggle between Christendom and the empire of barbaric darkness. A number of elements in medieval ideas about the Mongolians can be rediscovered in an attenuated form in the Western image of Russia in the sixteenth and seventeenth centuries.[15]

Latin Christendom was able to make use of classical literature to typify the Greeks of Byzantium as undeniably well-spoken and intelligent, but also cunning, proud, decadent, effeminate and cowardly.[16] Antiquity, however, had no anchorage to offer for a coherent opinion about Islam. For medieval Europe it remained inexplicable that a non-Christian religion, disseminated with such zeal and aggression, had developed in so short a time into a power and civilisation that was in so many respects superior to everything the West had to offer. Only when the Islamic world became Turkish did the West feel itself to be of equal stature in a spiritual sense, though the military threat had not thereby been diminished. The misunderstanding and incomprehension about Islam remained. Certain supposed characteristics such as sexual immorality labelled the Muslims as barbarians. The same was true of the exotic power of their sultan. Because of this, in the sixteenth and seventeenth centuries the Turks were a popular object of comparison with that other uncivilised nation in Europe, the Russians.[17]

## FROM THE SIXTEENTH TO THE NINETEENTH CENTURY

An image of Russia only came into being in the sixteenth century, after first the Italians and then the Germans and the English had 'discovered' Muscovy for Europe. These new contacts were extremely advantageous both for Russia and for Europe. Russia was an important supplier of vital raw materials for Western industry and formed a potential, and sometimes even an actual, ally in the struggle against the Turks. Europe supplied Russia with knowledge and many products that she herself could not yet manufacture. But the relationship between East and West was, from the outset, in many respects abnormal, paradoxical and utterly unbalanced, and has remained so to this day. Between 1500 and 1700 diplomats, merchants and all kinds of skilled workers visited Russia for short periods or stayed there for years. Most of them were, however, glad to be able to leave the country again. Their impressions were almost without exception extremely unfavourable. They scarcely even noticed the visible aspects of Russian culture, such as the icons and the architecture.

In the sixteenth and seventeenth centuries Russia was regarded as a partly or completely Asiatic country with wholly barbaric manners and customs. The sort of esteem for 'the noble savage' in which sixteenth-century Europe held the South American Indians did not extend to the Russians. They were regarded as servile, suspicious, cunning, mendacious, deceitful, thievish, corrupt, ill-mannered, violent, cruel and indifferent to the lot of their fellow men, with a tendency towards drunkenness, and a passion for gambling, gluttony and the most perverse forms of vice. Naturally many travellers there substantiated their opinions about the Russians with glaring examples. These stories were mostly anecdotal in character and frequently recur in the travel literature. The total image they conjured up showed a clear affinity to the unfavourable image of barbarians and heathens which had been created in Antiquity and the middle ages. The blame for this can be laid at the door of the classical upbringing shared in those days by every educated Westerner, and the feeling of superiority with regard to the rest of the world which came into being in the middle ages and was strengthened by European expansion.[18]

Of course the characterisation of the Russians by Western travellers has been dismissed as a valueless caricature by the eminent Russian historian Klyuchevsky.[19] But he also noted that many of these travellers to Russia were nevertheless good observers and have therefore been valued and utilised by prominent modern Russian historians.[20] Moreover Western ideas about Russia changed gradually. Peter the Great was the first Russian about whom not only bad, but also good, qualities were reported;[21] though the image of his subjects did not alter until the beginning of the nineteenth century. Later certain elements of Russian culture such as literature and the aspects of 'the Russian man' considered to be favourable, even became a subject for glorification.[22] But whatever people in the West later thought about Russia, they continued to see the country through the tinted spectacles of their own prejudice. The unfavourable image was moreover only partially superseded by the favourable one. Indeed in the twentieth century much occurred to strengthen the Europeans' conviction that Russia was a backward, uncivilised and barbaric country to which no Western standards could or should be applied.

In the sixteenth and seventeenth centuries it was taken for granted that a barbaric nation deserved a despotic government. Here too, the parallel with Antiquity was indisputable. One of the most influential travellers to Russia, Olearius of Holstein, quoted as self-evident Aristotle's statement on tyranny among barbaric peoples and that of the prophet Daniel about the king of Babylon in characterisation of the Russian monarchy.[23] In Western opinion the Russians, because of their servility, were only suited to living under a tyranny. If they rebelled against it – Western Europeans were also witness to the large-scale civic and peasant revolts which ravaged Russia in the seventeenth century – they showed such savagery in the process that this seemed to justify the tsar's omnipotence over his subjects.[24] However, not all Western observers judged that the Russians were only happy in slavery. The imperial envoy Sigismund von Herberstein, who more than anyone else gave shape to the Russian image of the time, had already raised the question which was to fascinate people of later centuries: 'I am not at all sure', he wrote in his 1526 book, 'if this merciless people needs such a tyrant as ruler, or whether it has only become so harsh and cruel as a result of princely tyranny.'[25] In the political tracts of the sixteenth and seventeenth centuries the Muscovite autocracy was mostly considered, in imitation of Aristotle's characterisation of Persian kingship, as an Eastern despotism, a form of government which otherwise only occurred in Turkey, China and Africa and was foreign to and incompatible with Western political traditions. Supporters of absolute monarchy sometimes showed appreciation for the unlimited sovereignty of the tsar. But the realisation that they were fortunately not slaves but subjects of a ruler mostly ensured that their satisfaction about their own freedom and political civilisation was even more warmly felt.[26]

The West had scarcely any appreciation of the individual character and historical background of the Russian state, nor of the limitations imposed by tradition, religion and geographical-climatological circumstances on the power of the tsar.[27] Because of this, bewilderment also prevailed concerning Russia's significance for European politics. The question of whether Muscovy was only a colossus with feet of clay, or whether it would in the future flood Europe with its barbaric hordes like a tidal wave, had already been asked in the sixteenth century, but seldom realistically answered then or later. Initially, Western observers in Russia did not consider the tsar's ill-equipped army as being capable of much. But when Ivan the Terrible conquered Narva on the Baltic Sea in 1558, many European courts gave way to quite groundless panic. Emperor Ferdinand wrote to the pope that the tsar not only wished to annexe the Baltic lands, but was also aiming at Germany, England and the Low Countries. Even thirteen years later the duke of Alba was not only afraid for the Low Countries he ruled, but also for the lot of 'all of Christendom'.[28] Muscovy threatened to be a danger greater than the Turks, and the comparison with the Scythians and the Huns pervaded all the stories about Russian atrocities in Livonia which was then still a German territory.

The Reichstags of 1559 and later years however, because of the Turkish problem, proved unprepared to make great sacrifices in defence of Europe. In the north this duty was left to the Poles and the Swedes, who discharged it purely out of self-interest. At the same time Rome was looking forward to the eradication of Protestantism in the areas occupied by Russia, and English and Dutch merchants profited from the great advantages of a Russian port in the Baltic to the disadvantage of the Danes and the Germans. In Moscow, the Mongol khan of Kazan, subdued and held captive by Ivan IV, spat in the faces of the German prisoners of war and shouted at them that the European peoples had brought destruction on his empire by helping the Russians to procure modern weapons. They were now to get their just deserts by soon undergoing the same fate. The German emperor did indeed impose a weapon embargo on the Russians in 1560, but because of the opposition of the Hanseatic town of Lübeck this remained a paper measure only. Lübeck pointed out that if the Russians, as a result of the ban on trade, were to go into shipping themselves, they would soon become an even greater military danger.[29]

This first manifestation of Russophobia was of short duration, for Ivan IV lost Narva to Sweden in 1581 and soon afterwards Muscovy ran into such internal difficulties that plans were laid in England and Germany for the subjection of Russia. But the Narva episode gave a foretaste of what was to follow and of the reactions in Europe towards future Russian expansion. Until 1700 it seemed easy to use Russia for their own ends and at the same time to keep her ostentatiously out of the concert of European nations. Poland and Sweden formed a sort of *cordon sanitaire* by means of which any Russian disruption of the European balance of power could be frustrated. But after 1700 it appeared that both these nations, which should have served as a bulwark against the barbarians, had been undermined and weakened. Russian and European interests were at the same time so intertwined and Russia had become so much more powerful that she could no longer be harnessed to the European cart. She would have to be accepted as a full member of the Western community of states. But this acceptance was not wholehearted and continued to meet with stubborn resistance.[30]

The image of Russia was in any case altered by the new situation. It was henceforth no longer exclusively determined by disparagement and antipathy. Russia was to command respect because a former fear was realised: under Peter the Great she became a formidable military power. Fear was to play an increasingly important role. Thus in European awareness Russia performed a different function from that of other non-European territories. After all, no one was afraid of the native populations of America, Asia or Africa. This meant that the image of Russia became more and more like the classical barbarian image, which had been largely determined by fear. On the other hand, admiration, which had also constituted an essential element in it, was a completely different matter. Up till now the Russians had only been admired for their exceptional excellence at chess. And of course there were marvels in that exotic, immeasurable country. Fantastic stories about strange peoples in its high north and far east were in circulation.[31]

By the end of the seventeenth century a few people in Europe had begun to believe that Russia was destined to fulfil special expectations of salvation. The famous religious fanatic Quirinus Kuhlmann, under the influence of Jacob Boehme and Commenius, became convinced that the foundation of the kingdom of God could brook no further delay. After initially trying his luck in the Low Countries and attempting in vain to persuade the crowned courts of Europe to abdicate their power voluntarily, he travelled full of expectation to Russia, where his zeal was rewarded by being sentenced to be burned to death. Thus Kuhlmann died in the first year of Peter's reign. In Pietist circles despite Kuhlmann's death, Russia was still seen as an important missionary area. August Herman Francke's institute at Halle in Germany became the first centre in Europe for Russian and Slavic studies.[32]

Even before Peter had started his reforms, some Western scholars tried to win the tsar over to their ideas, for his extensive and uncivilised country seemed such fertile soil for large-scale political, educational, economic and social experiments. The Englishman Francis Lee made an elaborate and extremely impracticable proposal of this kind to the tsar during his stay in England in 1698.[33] It was in fact the great Leibniz who incorporated Russia into a new vision of the future of the world and tried to interest the tsar in this. Because of her geographical situation between the two most prominent centres of civilisation, Europe and China, Russia occupied a special place amongst the remaining nations. Barbarian Russia was seen by Leibniz as a *tabula rasa*. It should have been possible, in Russia, for an energetic tsar like Peter to combine the best of both these high-principled cultures into a nobler synthesis. When Peter actually began the reform of his country in earnest, Leibniz became more and more convinced that Russia could be a new Europe free from the sins and faults of the old.[34] 'Momenta temporum pretiosissima sunt in transitu rerum. Et l'Europe est maintenant dans un état de changement et dans une crise, où elle n'a jamais été depuis l'Empire de Charlemagne', he wrote in 1712.[35]

Such a point of view was rather exceptional at that time.[36] Although books like Montesquieu's *Lettres persanes*, which also appeared in 1712, did something to differentiate Europe's view of foreign peoples, public opinion about Russia hardly changed.[37] Still Leibniz was not to remain an exception. Many intellectuals after him lived likewise with the depressing belief that they were witness to a profound crisis in European civilisation. Therefore a number of them – certainly not every cultural pessimist showed this tendency – looked towards Russia as a future that was already in sight, as a younger and more vital successor to Europe, or simply regarded that country as a piece of the frozen past, in which values already lost in the West would be protected against further destruction. From the time of Leibniz until after the Second World War, Russia, or rather the idea in which it was embodied, had always been for certain people a noble and beloved unknown quantity which they would happily have exchanged for the depravity of Europe. This phenomenon was perceptible for such a long period that it could be described as an ingrained habit, but not as a deep crisis, for Europe did not suffer from a lack of self-confidence at this time. We are dealing here with an undercurrent of dissatisfaction with one's own society which was continuously present, though not always of equal strength, and which manifested itself in a completely conventional manner by the projection of its own desires on to a suitable object.

In that respect the eighteenth century is a crucial period in the development of the Western European image of Russia. According to Leibniz God had given Russia a special destiny, and people continued to believe this until well into the twentieth century. On the other hand, in our time, a far larger group came into being for whom Russia was the country of the revolution. Both the religious expectations of salvation, and also the belief that the future would be conquered with violence in the East, and could be designed according to plan, had their roots in the classical barbarian image. But Pietism and the Enlightenment infused these old thoughts with new life. It was probably of great importance that in the eighteenth century Russia underwent a very radical metamorphosis, which appealed to the didactic missionary zeal of the Enlightenment. In England Aaron Hill wrote in 1718:

> Britons and Russians differ but in name,
> In nature's sense all nations are the same,
> One world, divided, distant brothers share,
> And man is reason's subject – everywhere.[38]

Although people had for a long time enlarged on the differences between Europeans and Russians, Russia became the equal of the Western European nations because she could be identified with rationality and progress. Tsar Peter, the cause of this miracle, was a legend in his own country as well as in the West. His popularity was not wholly spontaneous, for the practical tsar was clearly aware of the need for propaganda in his affairs, abroad as well as at home.[39] Even Catherine II's fame would to a large extent be the result of a campaign in which the empress played upon the fashionable intellectual tendencies in the West with great refinement.

These attempts to exert an influence were only partially successful. Both rulers met with large-scale opposition from their subjects and in the West mistrust was more evident than enthusiasm. British writers about Russia such as William Richardson saw through the game that Catherine was playing with the French *philosophes* and remained firmly opposed to autocracy. In England, where no one had ever harboured the slightest fear of the Russians and Russia had been considered from of old as a useful trading partner and a willing ally against France, even the statesmen became more and more apprehensive. After her victories over the Swedes, Poles and Turks, Russia assumed the pretensions of a great power and exhibited sympathies which were in conflict with British interests. It was embarrassing that, during the American War of Independence, St Petersburg adopted an unfriendly attitude towards England, which the English had to accept because without Russian raw materials they could not wage war. All the elements of a traditionally nascent Russophobia, such as gross overestimation of Russia's military power and nervous presentiments about a repetition of the invasions of the Goths and the Vandals in Europe, now came to the forefront in England. It is remarkable that at the end of the century this disparaging attitude towards Russia had come to belong to the fixed traditions of one political group. The Whigs, and later the Liberals, proved themselves to be Russian-haters and ardent supporters of the oppressed Poles. However, the Tories, who continued the well-tried policy of friendship with Russia, had the upper hand for the time being. It was not until the nineteenth century that an important section of British public opinion was overcome by a virulent form of Russophobia, and this was why the British were so enthusiastic about England's participation in the Crimean War.[40]

In France, which had always been a political ally of Turkey and Poland, the increase of Russian power was regarded with the utmost possible suspicion and the two countries remained at daggers drawn during the eighteenth century. Thus it was not unnatural that the very people who proclaimed themselves as a 'leftist' opposition should defend Russia. But the *philosophes* did not form a political party which, like the Whigs in England, advocated a separate foreign policy, though this intellectual pressure-group did have great influence on public life. The *philosophes'* glorification of Russia was different in essence from that of the deeply religious Leibniz. They did not believe in a European spiritual crisis, but in the triumph of reason. They were not disquieted, but indignant, that their own country conformed so little to the model they had designed of an ideal society. They felt themselves to be Frenchmen and at the same time citizens of the world, though they were not genuinely interested in foreign countries, unless they could provide them with suitable arguments in their struggle against the French establishment. They were against tyranny, obscurantism and injustice, which in France they perceived in the intolerance of the church, the arrogance of the aristocracy, the censoriousness of the *parlements* and the misuse of power by a fossilised royal absolutism. Thus they wondered if the Turks who experienced religious tolerance, or the Chinese who were ruled by wise mandarins, were not as happy as, or happier than, the French.

What then was so objectionable about Eastern despotism when, in Russia, it was evidently capable of civilising a barbaric people by intelligent law-giving and rational reforms?[41]

It was Voltaire who gave definite shape to the *miracle russe* in his *Pierre le Grand*, a commission from the Russian court which he had coveted for some time. Voltaire probably had, since his remarkable friendship with Frederick II of Prussia, no illusions at all about the true nature of despotism, nor did he show any profound interest in Russian history and geography or in the Russian people.[42] His book was packed with factual inaccuracies which the author corrected barely or not at all when Western and Russian scholars pointed them out to him. The great tsar was in his view a mere demonstration model for his own ideology and with this fashionable hagiography he achieved the ends he hoped for among his readers. Not all his fellow *philosophes* agreed with him, however. Montesquieu doubted if reforms carried out on such a large scale and at such a rapid tempo, without taking the nature of the country or the people into account, really contributed anything to the happiness of mankind. Rousseau was to continue to hold this view all his life and moreover to worry greatly about the lot of the Poles and the possibility that Europe would soon be dominated by a power which had out-grown its barbarity only in appearance.

Jean Jacques remained adamant in the face of Russian offers and Catherine II forbade his *Emile* as a dangerous book. But a number of *philosophes* relented when she set up her plans for reform in total agreement with their ideas, and the empress offered them opportunities for publication and financial support unprecedented in France. In exchange for her patronage they overwhelmed her with praise. It is not at all clear who was making most use of whom in this play-acting. Political motives and intellectual ambitions were at stake on both sides and vanity and insincerity played a role. In these respects Voltaire and Catherine II were a perfectly matched pair. Diderot, who owed his financial security entirely to the tsaritsa, was probably being honest when he wrote: 'It is in France, in the country of polite-ness, the sciences, the arts, of good taste and of philosophy that we are persecuted, and it is from the depths of barbaric and frozen regions that a hand is held out to us.'[43] But this was also the message that they hammered home to their public regardless of the lack of freedom of their 'Cateau's' subjects. They were also her confederates in the suppression of adverse information about Russia in France. They glossed over her *coup d'état* and the murder of her husband and defended her aggression against Poland and Turkey. 'She sent forty thousand Russians to preach tolerance, with bayonets at the ends of their muskets', wrote Voltaire in all seriousness about the Russian campaign against Poland.[44] The division of Poland was also justified with a reference to the Poles' inability to rule themselves: 'Unfortunate Poles ... you will henceforth be fortunate despite yourselves.'[45] Against the Turks, whom he had once fervently supported against Western prejudice, he practically preached a crusade, and he urged the empress not to make peace before she had conquered Greece and Constantinople. And Diderot wrote to the sculptor Falconet who was working in St Petersburg: 'Inform me immediately of the massacre of 50 or 60,000 Turks, if you want to make me jump for joy.'[46]

The historian Talmon, amongst others, points out that with the Enlightenment we stand at the fountain-head of modern totalitarianism. The *philosophes* appeared fully prepared to accept total lack of freedom in the name of an all-embracing abstract ideal of freedom. Eighteenth-century rationalism thought it could construct the ideal state. They embarked on a slippery slope when they gave up the old-fashioned trial-and-error principle, which up till then had been reckoned as the highest political wisdom. The word-magic which they suffused with meanings like humanity or progress, laid the basis for a new secular faith. This *Wort- und Namenaberglaube* (word and name superstition), as A. H. Koppelmann once called it, was in this century to link large groups of people together emotionally and render them defenceless against totalitarian temptation.[47] There is indeed a striking resemblance between the *philosophes* and the socialists and left-wing intellectuals in the twenties and thirties who embraced communism partially or totally, both with regard to their critical attitude towards their own society, and their vision of the future or their opinion of the regime in Russia. Voltaire, Diderot and their followers were the first fellow-travellers. But this very comparison can put us on our guard against describing the connection between the Enlightenment and modern totalitarian democracy in oversimplified terms.

One of Talmon's ideas was that the ideals of the Enlightenment cleared the way for an omnipotent state, because they were worldly and freed mankind from the moral restrictions of Christianity.[48] However, the fight against heresy and the religious wars show that religious fanaticism, too, is bound by few limitations. Calvinistic Geneva can indeed be seen as a precursor of the totalitarian state.[49] Talmon's concept stands or falls above all on the presumption that the *philosophes* and their nineteenth- and twentieth-century heirs took their ideas absolutely seriously and were prepared to accept all the consequences. Their views about Russia show that this was certainly not always the case and that their glorification of an ideologically based despotism proceeded from quite other motives than from a fanatical belief in that ideology. Like most *communisants* of this century most *philosophes* kept at a safe distance from Russia. Voltaire was not keen to exchange his freedom and tranquillity at Ferney for a precarious courtier's existence at a St Petersburg Sanssouci. D'Alembert refused three times running to become tutor to Catherine's son Paul. There were too many bloodthirsty palace revolutions in Russia for his taste. And his last illusions were dispelled when Catherine flatly refused his request for the repatriation of French officers who were imprisoned in Poland, despite either his appeal to 'philosophy' or his affirmation of the value of such a regal gesture as propaganda. The unworldly Diderot, after much hesitation, did go to Russia, but came back discouraged and convinced beyond doubt that the exercise of power ought to be subject to strict laws and supervision by the people.[50]

The *philosophes* reserved their doubt, disappointment and scepticism for their mutual correspondence – at least in so far as they trusted each other – or for their personal notes, but this was not intended for the public eye. How many Frenchmen who shared their ideological inspiration, accepted their image of Russia without criticism? How important was 'philosophy' in this? Possibly the many references to Antiquity with which the eulogies of Peter and Catherine were larded contributed a great deal towards the spread of this myth. 'The Scythians will become our masters in everything', wrote Voltaire, and he compared Tsar Peter's journey to the West with the journeys of King Anacharsis in Ancient Greece.[51] Thus he appealed to an old tradition to which the civilised eighteenth-century public was not insensitive. The *philosophes* certainly did not win it over completely to their point of view. The majority of the information available in France was far too much influenced by former images of Russia for that. The almost exclusively unfavourable accounts by Frenchmen who had visited the country and the frequently dissolute behaviour of Russian aristocrats in Paris strengthened the ever-present adverse impression of the Russians 'who have beautiful ruffles, but no shirts'.[52] After Voltaire and Diderot's deaths, Catherine, whose love for 'philosophy' had cooled, no longer wished to favour second-class French men of letters. The French Revolution caused a hundred-year-long severance of the links between aristocratic Russia and progressive France. The tsaritsa rallied to the counterrevolutionary camp and turned away from France in disgust. Russia became a refuge for royalist émigrés. For the Jacobins the Semiramis of the North had become the Messalina of the North. After this everyone in Europe who considered himself liberal, revolutionary or socialist was anti-Russian. The glorification of Russia was from then onwards left to their ideological opponents.

## THE FIRST HALF OF THE NINETEENTH CENTURY

When the Russian troops marched into Paris to celebrate the defeat of Napoleon, Tsar Alexander I had become the incomparable hero of all the adversaries of the revolution in the West. His idea of the Holy Alliance was welcomed as the ultimate victory of Christian and royal principles over the pernicious and undermining forces of democracy and atheism. Not everyone concurred with those who glorified Russia. Castlereagh thought the Holy Alliance was mystical nonsense. In the footsteps of the conservative thinker Edmund Burke, who saw Russia as a threat to the European balance of power, the British remained somewhat insensitive to the ideological background noises of the settlement of 1815. French traditionalists such as Bonald and de Maistre also did not want to believe that the half-civilised, orthodox (and thus non-Catholic) Russia, led by a despot who philandered with constitutional ideas, could be the instrument chosen by Providence to save Christian civilisation in Europe. After the Polish uprising of 1830 and the oppression of non-orthodox Christians by the Russians, the pro-Russian attitudes of many conservative and Catholic Frenchmen were reversed.[53]

In Germany the Russophilia was mainly a reaction to the Russophobia in progressive circles. But the sympathy for Russia proved to be a more powerful and permanent phenomenon there than in France. Many conservative aristocrats embodied their romantic longings in an idealised feudal society, in the stable values and norms of the *ancien régime* in the Russia of Alexander I and Nicholas I. Leibniz's ideas and eighteenth-century Pietism with its belief in the new Kingdom of God in the East became involved and were given an extra impulse by international events. Herder's idyll of the Slavs as peaceful farmers and future exponents of European culture – so completely within the classical tradition of glorification of the barbarian – strengthened the tendency to see Russia as a utopia. Novalis, the poet, was genuinely convinced that the tsar was the only obvious figure to restore Christian solidarity in Europe and thus liberate the world from further revolutionary turbulence. The leader of the German revivalist movement, Jung-Stilling, and his followers saw Napoleon as the Antichrist and Alexander as the angel of the Apocalypse. One of the most prominent Catholic thinkers of his day, Franz von Baader, exulted in Russian Orthodoxy as a branch of belief predestined to bridge over the painful contrasts between faith and reason, Protestantism and Catholicism, in Western Christendom. This was a thought that the Russian Slavophiles gratefully adopted. Their ideas also ran parallel to those of the conservative nobleman von Haxthausen, who, in 1843, made a study of Russian society with the support and supervision of the tsarist government. He came to the conclusion that the *mir*, the Russian village community with its collectively owned land and despotic rule by elders of the village, was the best guarantee against revolution, atheism and democracy that a country could wish for. In this Russia possessed an institution that provided her society with the harmonious coherence so painfully lacking in the West. The *mir* and other forms of Russian collectivism found their natural complement in autocracy and orthodoxy. Russia had no impoverished industrial proletariat and no dangerous socialist utopias, but enjoyed an age-old, Christian, patriarchal form of socialism, which could well be held out as an example to the West.[54]

Despite von Haxthausen's conservative intentions, his *Studien über die innern Zustände Russlands* also struck a responsive chord in Russian and Western progressives such as Herzen, Bakunin and Michelet. The idea that Russia was already socialist in essence, and could also be a beacon along the road to a socialist future, was later to become the starting-point of a new kind of glorification of Russia in the leftist camp.[55] But, in the first half of the nineteenth century, this was preparing itself for a life-and-death struggle with a Russia that was seen as the most important bulwark of reaction. All the unfavourable clichés about the barbaric country of 'knout and terror', 'the hyperborean colossus' and its inhabitants 'the Huns of our time', were habitually used to depict Russia as the kingdom of darkness.[56] Exaggerated enthusiasm and political poetry about Poland completed the picture.[57] The 1812 campaign had already been represented by Napoleon's propaganda apparatus as a war that was necessary to save European civilisation. For this a forged document was used, the so-called 'Testament of Peter the Great' in which the Russian struggle for dominion of the world was expounded. This 'Testament' was for a very long time to remain a component of European Russophobia.[58] In the first half of the nineteenth century this hatred of Russia was sometimes to assume bizarre forms; the murder of Kotzebue in 1819 by the student Karl Sand is one of them. Kotzebue, a well-known playwright who had defended Russia against Western attacks, was regarded as a spy because of his relationship with the Russian government. Sand was executed for his deed. Handkerchiefs dipped into the blood of this martyr to the good cause were later sold for high prices. In 1848 the revolutionaries were still convinced that the future of democratic Europe could only be kept safe by means of a successful war against Russia. That would make the definitive decision as to whether despotism or freedom would prevail. Ferdinand Freiligrath described 'the last battle ventured by the East against the West' in a visionary poem.[59]

Between the two extremes of aggressive adversaries and passive glorifiers of Russia lay a group of pessimists who expected little good from the East but at the same time thought that the tsar's sovereignty over the whole European continent was inescapable. To this group belonged quite dissimilar personalities like the philosopher Hegel and his left-wing follower Bruno Bauer, the poet Heinrich Heine and French publicists like de Tocqueville and Montégut. The German Orientalist Fallmerayer impressed on his fellow countrymen that they should seriously consider the possibility of a Russian conquest, given that so far all attempts to hold back the tsar had failed. 'We are, to be sure, more cultured than the Russians, but the Ancient Greeks also succumbed to the peasant-boys of Latium.'[60]

Astolphe, marquis of Custine, also pointed emphatically to the danger of Russia, which was not so much caused by Russian superiority as by the weakness of Western power and morals. His travel book *La Russie en 1839* was a great success, probably because, though an aristocrat and Catholic, he clearly demonstrated that Russophobia was not the privilege of democrats and socialists. In it he repeated all the old arguments brought forward by anti-Russian French publicists ever since the Revolution and in this way offered every Russia-hater something he was delighted to read.

Custine's narrative has tempted our contemporaries to make curious generalisations. For example Tibor Szamuely, in his compelling interpretation of the Russian past, drew his readers' attention to the striking similarities between Herberstein, Custine and André Gide's 1936 *Retour de l'URSS* and saw this principally as a proof of continuity in Russian history.[61] Bedell Smith, American ambassador in Moscow in Stalin's time, wrote in his introduction to the translation of Custine by Phyllis Penn Kohler (the wife of another US ambassador in Moscow): 'I could have taken many pages verbatim from his journal and, after substituting present names and dates for those of a century ago, have sent them to the State Department as my own official reports.'[62]

George Kennan, the diplomat and connoisseur of Russia, who had likewise been American ambassador to the Soviet Union, devoted attention to this curious problem in his book about

Custine. He pointed out that *La Russie en 1839* appeared before the period of internal reforms and before the existence of the Russian revolutionary movement. Custine's travel account was an exaggerated but understandable response to the reactionary despotism of the tsar who as 'policeman of Europe' also inspired fear in the West. Only in this way could a mediocre book about the time of Nicholas I seem to be an excellent book about Stalin's Russia. This is nevertheless hardly a plausible explanation for this anachronistic paradox. Kennan himself acknowledges that Custine quoted, with approval, Herberstein's famous statement about the relationship between the coarseness of the people and the cruelty of the tsar. Despite all the similarities between dictatorships of every time and country, such differences persist between the regimes of Ivan III, Nicholas I and Stalin, that the striking resemblance between Herberstein, Custine and Bedell Smith can be better explained as a result of the continuity of the Western image of Russia than of the continuity of Russian history.[63]

The situation after 1945 was certainly not the same as that after 1815, though there was a certain similarity in the way the people in these widely separated periods experienced the relationship with Russia. In both cases, fear of the Russians was so intense and widespread that there was little room left for critical and detached reactions to this kind of emotion. Moreover in the first half of the nineteenth century Russia made such an overwhelming impression alongside a defeated France, a divided Germany, a weak Austria and an inward-looking England, that it hardly seemed necessary to consider if a permanent Russification of Europe, whether for military, economic or political reasons, was indeed a possibility. There were nevertheless people then, too, who disagreed with prevailing opinions. In 1835 Richard Cobden, while he was still an unknown English manufacturer, opposed the anti-Russian outbursts of his fellow countryman Urquhart with the argument that the development of modern weaponry made an invasion by savage hordes from the East impossible. Frenchmen like the writer Victor Hugo or Ambaylard and Germans like the economist List were too convinced of the superiority of their own people and civilisation to fear the Russians.[64] In this group there were also people who were inclined to see Russian autocracy merely as an imposing façade which was skilfully kept upright by Russian diplomats. The tsar's actual power was assailed by incompetence and corruption. Moreover the Decembrist revolt had proved that the country was much less safe against revolution than had been believed in the West. The nationalistic German author Buddeus, who had worked as a journalist in Russia, depicted the Russian intelligentsia as a 'noble proletariat' which would create the same social unrest as the factory workers of the West had done. In a small country such as Holland, which was more likely to feel threatened by the great Western nations than by Russia, with whom it in any case had dynastic ties, violent emotions against Russia were non-existent in this period.[65]

These were exceptional opinions. The choir which continued to sing, in every possible key, the old trusted tunes of terror, loathing and admiration, drowned out all other sounds. Russia thus held a special place in the thoughts of Europeans. Of course the French had peculiar views about the Germans and the British cherished odd ideas about the Italians, and so on. But even in that time of insidious nationalism the prejudices of the European nationalities about each other never dispelled a feeling that they all belonged to one family and one civilisation. Not only their image of Russia but also their notions about America were products of this shared inheritance. That country, too, was both admired and despised, though it posed no real threat. Because of this, ideas about it were not so divided and it fulfilled a different function in European consciousness than was the case with Russia.[66] This was to an even greater extent true for China, which had been such a beloved idol in the eighteenth century. In the next century this chinoiserie was to disappear rapidly. Thereafter China was regarded as the prototype of Asiatic stagnation until, after 1895, terror of the 'yellow peril' assumed hysterical proportions.[67] Russia meanwhile remained a special case.

## AFTER THE CRIMEAN WAR

In the second half of the nineteenth century the image of Russia changed in character. It was in this period that the assurance with which Europeans, unhindered by real knowledge, had dared to express their prejudices about Russia disappeared to a large extent. The causes for this lay in the outcome of the Crimean War, the internal reforms, the rise of a revolutionary movement and the flourishing of Russian literature and art. The humiliating defeat of Russia in a war which was greeted with such enthusiasm by all the friends of Poland and haters of Russia aroused serious doubts. Was Russia after all, as had frequently been maintained, merely 'a colossus with feet of clay'? The heavy-handed suppression of the Poles in 1863, the conquests in Asia and the Russo-Turkish War showed that the Russian bear still had claws and teeth. But Russia was no longer the policeman of Europe and it was not until 1945 that, in her relations with our part of the world, she once again assumed a position of power comparable to that in the period after the Napoleonic Wars. No one felt totally freed from the Russian threat after 1856, but even the tsar's fiercest opponents had to recognise that his country, because of its benevolent neutrality, rendered possible revolutionary revisions of the map of Europe. The Second Empire's Italian policy and Bismarck's unification of Germany would have had far less chance of success without Russian backing. Russia proved that she could be a reliable ally. But how strong was she in fact? Uncertainty about this persisted until 1914, and even during the First World War was a source of great tension and nervousness for friend and foe.

Another problem shaped the evaluation of the internal situation in Russia. Was the country moving in the direction of a Western, industrialised state ruled by parliament or was it falling into an increasing state of disintegration and chaos? In Germany, where so many conservatives had been numbered among the friends and admirers of Russia, a choice was made after 1871 by an influential group of liberal and right-wing publicists for the second of these alternatives. They predicted an easy victory of Pan-Germanism over Pan-Slavism. With extreme nationalists like Constantin Frantz, Victor Hehn, Theodor Schiemann, Paul Rohrbach, Johannes Haller, Johannes Scherr and others, we can rediscover the time-honoured image of the Russians as barbaric and inferior beings. They would for their part pass on this stereotype unchanged to the national socialists. After the unification, a somewhat moderated form of contempt for Russia was widespread in Germany. At the same time, however, there was also a vague but persistent fear of the arrival of the Cossacks. Intellectual celebrities like Nietzsche still believed in the possibility of a Russian conquest of Europe. The spectre of the steamroller from the East crushing everything before it was to have a fatal impact on the decisions of German socialists and generals in 1914.[68]

France was the only country in Europe where, after 1870, an anti-Russian attitude was replaced by enthusiasm among the general public. Fear of Germany played a significant role in this. It was logical for French revanchists and Russian Pan-Slavists to see the advantages of an alliance between the two countries. But the fact that this treaty came into being in 1891 and that five years later during his visit to France Tsar Nicholas II was cheered, was remarkably enough also largely thanks to the great esteem for Russian culture which had come into being in Europe. In England too, a real sympathy with Russia grew up everywhere because of it. But Russophobia did not completely disappear in either country and uncertainty about Russia increased rather than decreased.[69]

After 1900 liberals and socialists in England and France retained very strong objections against the alliance with an Asiatic tyranny. They were torn between their contempt of tsarism and their admiration for the heroic Russian revolutionary movement. It is striking that English and French diplomats and governments contributed little to improve Russia's image. They supported the alliance with Russia as a military interest, but generally had no admiration for the country or the people to whom they were allied. The setback against Japan and the revolution of 1905 made them fear the worst for the survival of Russian power, though this shaken trust was somewhat restored in the last years before the outbreak of the First World War.[70]

Only a few scholars and journalists have made an effort to build up a better understanding of Russia. In England these were, amongst others, Donald Mackenzie Wallace of *The Times*, the historian Bernard Pares and the literary journalist Maurice Baring; in France, the linguist Louis Leger, the historians Rambaud, Leroy Beaulieu and Haumant, and the diplomat and man of letters de Vogüé. In Scandinavia this role was filled by the critic Georg Brandes, and in Germany the historians Hoetsch and Brückner, the economist M. Sering and the Berlin professor Holl occupied a similar position. It was the intention of these people to furnish reliable information about Russia based on profound study and objective observation. With their often pioneering work they laid the basis for modern Western Russian scholarship, although they themselves were not free from nationalistic feelings and the tendency towards broad generalisations which was so much a part of their time. It is mainly thanks to the activities of some of these writers that Russian literature suddenly gained enormous popularity in this period.[71]

In Europe, there has never been anything exceptional about respect for the literary achievements of another country. It was certainly not only the classics and the greatest national authors who were and are read by an international public. But the intense interest, not infrequently transformed into idolatrous veneration, which was conferred on Russian literature at the end of the nineteenth century and which endured for decennia, was a special phenomenon. The discovery of Russian prose – in translation, of course – coincided with the discovery of 'the Russian soul'. By labelling all that was Russian as mysterious, the prevailing uncertainty about Russia could be expressed, but so could the admiration, aversion and terror which had defined the image of Russia from of old. Thus originated the tenacious habit of seeing Russia as a mystery. In 1939 Winston Churchill was still able to describe Russia as 'a riddle wrapped in a mystery inside an enigma'.[72]

It seemed to Western readers of Russian novels that these books gave access to the deepest stirrings of the human soul. Did the Russian possess a real self-knowledge because he was exposed to a barbaric climate and subject to a barbaric regime and was thus purified by suffering? And was that why that country could produce such brilliant writers? There was a strong tendency to answer these questions in the affirmative, and admiration for Russian literature can therefore be partly seen as a new form of that glorification of the barbarian which has been an element in our culture since the days of the Ancient Greeks. It remains striking that Russian novels, and especially those of Dostoyevsky, were considered not only as 'the heroic literary phenomenon of modern times' but also as a photographically exact reproduction of Russian reality. Little attention was paid to criticism levelled at this gullibility by certain prominent Russian and Western writers. Dostoyevsky was considered the most Russian, for he was barbaric and primitive, a 'genuine Scythian', who in his cruelty and tenderness united the sensually tangible with the abstract in a kind of mystic realism.[73]

The admiration was of course also based on the intrinsic quality of this literature. The rising interest in psychiatry also played an important role among the readers of Dostoyevsky. For Nietzsche, Dostoyevsky (and to a lesser extent Tolstoy as well) was a revelation, which profoundly influenced not only his ideas about psychology but also about Christianity and the Christian image. Nietzsche's friend Lou Salomé made a pilgrimage to Russia with the poet Rilke, during which they visited Tolstoy on his estate Yasnaya Polyana. Rilke's introduction to the Russian people's faith, which he felt was barbaric, that is to say primitive and childish, betokened an artistic breakthrough for him. For a number of other men of letters and artists a journey to Russia likewise meant a religious rebirth and liberation from narrow-minded, bourgeois Europe, tainted by money and technology.[74]

The need to regard the Russians as allies who were at least equal to, or even superior to, the Germans clearly existed in England, where the Dostoyevsky cult reached its peak during the First World War. Remarkably enough England was the country where the Dostoyevsky cult caught on the most. But enthusiasm there, too, ebbed again quickly after 1921 and came to a dignified end with E. H. Carr's sober and sobering biography of the great writer in 1931. On the continent veneration of Russian literature and the Russian people was kept alive.[75] The horrors of the World War gave many intellectuals there occasion to regard the decline of Western civilisation as an indisputable fact and the Russian Revolution as a new beginning. Thomas Mann wrote in 1921: 'In fact there are two experiences which brought the son of the nineteenth century, the bourgeois epoch, into relationship with modern times, protected him from torpidity and intellectual death and built a bridge for him into the future, namely that of Nietzsche and of the Russian being ... They are both of a religious nature, – religious in a new vital and forward-looking sense.'[76] Such thoughts were also cherished by one of the most prominent ideologists of the anti-democratic movements in the Weimar Republic, Arthur Moeller van den Bruck, the author of *Das dritte Reich*, who worshipped Dostoyevsky.[77] Many Europeans came to believe that the confused feelings to which they were subject at this time, had already best been interpreted earlier by Russian literature. Dostoyevsky, wrote Thomas Masaryk, 'would have seen in Bolshevism the proof in support of his theory and of his *Possessed'*.[78]

It was evidently no simple matter to free oneself from the stunning effect of Russian literature. The Englishman Edmund Gosse, who had presented *Crime and Punishment* to the English public in 1887 as a 'masterpiece of psychological study', had done it with success. In 1926, shortly after the appearance of Gide's study of Dostoyevsky, he wrote to the Frenchman: 'May I venture to wish that you would release yourself from your bondage to the Russians and particularly to Dostoyevsky? We have all in turn been subjected to the magic of this epileptic monster ... He is the cocaine and morphia of modern literature.'[79] Still Gide had first to go through a pro-communist phase in his life and to return deeply disappointed from a journey to the Soviet Union in 1936, before he could free himself from the Russians. It is nevertheless striking how many Western authors of the interwar years have to be counted among the fellow-travellers and it is not implausible that their political preference was to a large extent inspired by their love for classical Russian novels. This was taken up by the Bolshevik regime which had Maxim Gorky explain, during the first congress of Soviet writers in 1934 and in the presence of many prominent foreign guests, that Dostoyevsky had been the writer who had best described the intellectual decay of the bourgeoisie. A few years later the writer Heinrich Mann and the American journalist Walter Duranty consulted Dostoyevsky in order to explain human behaviour during the great purge trials and to justify Soviet jurisprudence.[80]

Admiration for Russian literature and the veneration for Russia and the Russian people which arose from it held its own without being coupled with sympathy for communism. It is remarkable how the eighteenth-century Pietist tradition of seeing Russia as a source of Christian inspiration survived until well into this century and was combined with interest in the

Russian novel. The atheism of the Bolshevik regime barely affected this notion. At the beginning of the nineteenth century Baader had already written: 'And if such a nation in fact fully de-Christianises itself, it will nevertheless to its own damnation never again wholly free itself from that character.'[81] This thought reverberated in this century in, for instance, Toynbee's idea of Bolshevism as a diabolical Judaeo-Christian heresy. The belief that the Russian man, because of his plasticity, simplicity, creativity and piety, is an example to the Western man had the good fortune to live a long life.[82]

This survey of the Western European image of Russia must, given the available literature, remain sketchy and incomplete. But it does offer a framework within which we can situate and understand the developments to be described in the chapters which follow. Western socialists had their own ideas about Russia and these rubbed off on to the opinions of their contemporaries, who persisted in other political ideas as well. But disagreement about Russia, as we have already seen, was nothing exceptional. Differences of opinion have constituted an essential part of the Western image of Russia ever since the eighteenth century. In the second half of the nineteenth century the socialists were to become more and more fascinated by Russia. The former ideas of Russia as a barbaric reactionary power remained for them a reality which they condemned and detested in the same way as many people in our days demonstrated their abhorrence of the regimes in South Africa or Chile. Gradually, nevertheless, the Russian revolutionary movement, and the revolutions of 1905 and 1917 in particular, aroused great hopes and extravagant expectations.

All that had of old been most valued in socialism – faith, dedication, self-sacrifice, perseverance, martyrdom, militancy and revolutionary *élan* – were personified in the Russian 'heroes'. These were qualities which, according to many, were increasingly lacking in the Western movement. In the long term it was no longer believed that a revolution would ever be achieved without the Russians and this was somewhat embarrassing. The fact that the Russians were also inclined towards a radicalism and a violence which had always been strongly opposed in their own movement, was not overlooked. But – it was thought – other criteria applied to the Russians who lived under 'barbarian' conditions. It was only through their 'elemental' strength and courage that the fetters of feudalism and capitalism, which the new socialist society still kept imprisoned and hidden, could be broken. The revolution was to come from the East, and so it did. *Ex oriente lux*! The Russian workers became an example of this and a model for their Western comrades.

## 2

---

# RUSSIAN AND EUROPEAN SOCIALISTS

Russia has been undergoing a process of Westernisation since the end of the sixteenth century, while Europe on the other hand has never been Russianised. The influence of the West on Russia is undeniably great and has been much greater than the other way round, but has continually met with resistance. The opposition to Peter the Great's reforms and the debate carried on in Russia since then about the significance of this turbulent period in Russian history are striking evidence of this. There have always been Russians who pointed out the greatness and national exclusivity of Russia to their fellow countrymen and warned them against pernicious foreign influences. In the nineteenth century these nationalist ideas were linked by Danilevsky to the expectation of an apocalyptic struggle against the hostile outside world. Yet, during his lifetime and afterwards until 1917, his fatherland could probably count more defenders and followers of Western civilisation than ever before. The fundamental question at issue of whether the differences between Russia and the West should be considered as a curse or a blessing has always dominated Russian intellectual life.

Russian preoccupation with the West and the less general, but nevertheless often passionate way in which the West became fascinated by Russia, acted as mirror images of each other. Russians and Europeans, though often for opposite reasons, were happy to compare Western sins with Russian virtues or Western civilisation with Russian backwardness. The existence of traditional concepts on one side or the other did not however work wholly detrimentally on the imagination. Contacts between Russians and Europeans could be extremely productive. Prejudices were seldom totally suppressed, though they were weakened and changed. Contempt could change into admiration. The history of socialism is an example of this.[1]

Initially Russian socialism was a product of the ever-advancing process of Westernisation in Russia, but in spite of this it left its mark on developments within the European labour movement, even before 1917. Russian socialists have been troubled by existing prejudices in the West about Russia, but they have also profited from the special place made for them because of these prejudices within international socialism. On the other hand, it was extremely difficult for these Russians to free themselves from the preconceived opinions which they themselves cherished about Europe and European socialism. The development of socialist thought displays a singularity which gives a notable cachet to the Russo-European antithesis and makes it clear that Russia's 'difference' cannot be simply translated as 'backwardness'. For in Great Britain, the most industrialised country in Europe with the largest factory proletariat, socialist thought never rose to an impressive height, whereas in the still extremely agrarian France of pre-1848 it flourished. But immediately afterwards French socialism encountered competition in this field from Germany, which was certainly no more developed economically. The attempts on the German side to establish a sort of ideological supremacy met with stubborn resistance from a country which during the eighteenth century had outdone England in certain sectors of industrial production, but which after 1800 rapidly dropped behind the rest of Europe, namely Russia. Marx and Engels were to find Herzen, Bakunin and Lavrov alongside and opposite them as socialist leaders and thinkers and were increasingly forced to acknowledge the Russian impact on the Western labour movement.

Herzen and Bakunin were the most prominent representatives of a Russian political emigration which first came into being in the West during Nicholas I's reign. From the beginning these exiles were to be the source of an endless series of difficulties and conflicts, not only between the emigrants and an awakening revolutionary movement in Russia, but also within Western socialism. The misunderstanding on both sides between Russians and Europeans was considerable and partly ineradicable. In 1847, when Herzen arrived from Russia in Paris, in those days the Mecca of revolution, he was embarrassed by the servility of his Russian companions in adversity towards the great figures of Western socialism. 'It was painful to see how our compatriots queued up for inspection by those matadors of rhetoric who flooded us with words, sentences and platitudes spoken at *vitesse accélerée*. And how, the more modestly the Russians behaved and the more they blushed and tried to veil this clumsiness (as loving parents or proud spouses would have done), the worse the others posed and put on airs towards these hyperborean Anacharses.'[2] For some of the European socialists the same impression was very persistent although they drew contrary conclusions from it. Karl Marx was to write to Kugelmann as late as 1868:

It is an irony of fate that the Russians, against whom I have struggled unremittingly for twenty-five years, and not only in the German language but also in French and English, were always my 'protectors'. In Paris in 1843–4 the Russian aristocrats there made much of me ... The Russian aristocracy is brought up in its youth in German universities and at Paris. It always pursues the greatest extremes the West can supply ... That does not stop these same Russians becoming blackguards as soon as they join the civil service.[3]

Despite Marx's and Herzen's persistent tendency to exaggerate, their words nevertheless well reflect the peculiar relationship between Western and Russian socialists. The image of the rich, French-speaking, eccentric Russian nobleman had been an established one since the eighteenth century, and in the middle of the nineteenth century there still existed a Russian colony in Paris which answered admirably to this description. The dividing line between these often extravagant aristocrats who moved in the highest French political and cultural circles and those who, living in enforced or voluntary exile, opposed the Russian autocracy, could not always be clearly drawn. Marx in fact met Russians in Paris and Brussels who were little inclined to connect their interest in radical ideas to its evident consequences. Besides, at the time it was not always a simple matter to make out whether one was dealing with a genuine Russian socialist or an *agent provocateur* of the tsar.

It is not surprising that the suspicious and vindictive Marx, ridden with all sorts of prejudices about Russia, should now and then regard Herzen and Bakunin as political spies. They were in no way his inferiors in odd behaviour, moved in the Western socialist environment with aristocratic nonchalance, and exhibited their Russian chauvinism and disdain for 'bourgeois' Europe. The fact that they translated these feelings into socialist ideas must have stirred up bad blood. Their greatest antipathy was reserved for Germany. The characterisation which Herzen gave of the German revolutionaries living in London after 1848 was one of the most brilliant, sarcastic and unjust passages in his famous autobiography. Bakunin's Germanophobia, sometimes mixed with a generous dose of anti-Semitism, was equally conspicuous. Right from the beginning, the antithesis between Russia and Europe within international socialism manifested itself most strongly between the Germans and the Russians, and this was to remain so until long after the Russian Revolution. The history of the sometimes bizarre attitude of Marx and Engels towards the Russian revolutionaries is therefore of much more than symbolic significance for later developments within the European labour movement.[4]

It is characteristic that Herzen and Bakunin, who in Russia were reputed to be *zapadniki*, or convinced supporters of the West, had in Europe tried to disseminate highly Slavophile ideas. Von Haxthausen's book about Russia inspired both men to the elaboration of the notion that the Russian village commune ought to be the one and only starting-point for a socialist reform of Russia and Europe and that the Russian peasants were the future liberators of mankind. As fervent opponents of Russian despotism and supporters of Polish freedom they were accepted by the Western revolutionaries as equals, though this did not mean that their ideological message was accepted, for an extremely anti-Russian disposition continued to hold sway in these circles. Bakunin aroused more admiration through his active participation in the revolution of 1848 and his twelve-year imprisonment in Russia and the exile which followed than through his writings.[5]

Herzen made his name as a writer, but he had far more influence in Russia than in the West, where his books and articles could be freely printed. His collaboration with the well-known

French socialist Proudhon in the publication of an international periodical in 1849, financed by the wealthy Herzen, rapidly came to grief. Proudhon's social ideas had a special appeal for Herzen just as much as for Bakunin. But Herzen soon suspected that Proudhon, who had been weaned on political radicalism, would consider his contributions too biased with 'barbaric fervour' and was afraid that his readers would be frightened off by the audacity of 'a Scythian'.[6] Herzen did win the friendship and esteem of the great liberal historian Jules Michelet, but he could not convince the patriotic Frenchman of the truth of his Russian messianism.[7] Herzen met with unexpectedly overt approval only from Coeurderoy, a somewhat hysterical French revolutionary who wrote a pamphlet in 1854 with the enthusiastic title: *Hurrah!!! Ou la Révolution par les Cosaques.*[8] Another eccentric, though a famous one, the historian Carlyle, likewise supported him because he thought he had understood from Herzen's work that the Russians were still at least acquainted with the old-fashioned virtue of obedience 'which is out of vogue in other quarters just now'.[9] These were tokens of appreciation with which Herzen could not have been very happy.

The criticism levelled at Herzen by Western socialists and radicals was often extremely caustic and mostly came from the German side. The famous left-wing Hegelian Arnold Ruge accused him of having 'tempted' Bruno Bauer to write one of his idolising books about Russia – totally unjustly, for Bauer had been inspired only by von Haxthausen.[10] In 1840 Ruge himself had defended the notion that a war between Europe which was free, progressive and animated by a Latin-Germanic spirit, and Russia which was inhibited, stagnant and devoid of history, was unavoidable and necessary.[11] Around 1854 he made an extraordinarily vehement attack on Herzen's ideas in a letter to him. 'Suppose you won over the whole world with your propaganda for Russia and for the Russian peasant communes, you would be the most dangerous enemy of the human race.'[12] More balanced and friendly in tone was the criticism levelled by Moses Hess, who, before 1848, like all left-wing Hegelians had expressed himself about Russia in roughly the same way as Ruge. But it is evident from his letters too how seriously Herzen's ideology was felt to be a threat to Western socialism.

In contrast to Bauer, Ruge and Hess did not wish to give way to pessimistic opinions, even though the revolution of 1848 had such a disappointing outcome and the situation thereafter offered little chance of a revolutionary victory over autocratic Russia. They refused to despair for the future of Europe and resisted the paralysing influence which emanated from the evocative 'great parallel' with the barbarian raids of Antiquity. Now especially, this comparison was exploited by Herzen to praise Russian socialism. Hess was of the opinion that 'collective social democratic freedom' could not be provided by Russia. What Europe needed was not an invasion from outside, but one from within, of its own barbarians: the factory workers. He reproached Herzen for having no understanding of economics and for basing his philosophical theories on so much hot air. Only the British workman should be considered the true 'master of socialism', not a handful of intellectuals from France, Germany or Russia. But if Herzen really wanted to understand what was going on in Europe he ought to read the writings of Marx, 'this incontrovertibly most brilliant man of our party'. Hess did immediately admit that Marx was not satisfied with the recognition which fell to his lot, 'but who appears to demand a personal acquiescence which I at least would never have vouchsafed to any individual'.[13]

This passage about Marx was deleted by Hess, but Herzen did not need such a warning. Nothing indicates that he ever read anything by Marx and he never met him, though both men lived in London and moved in the same circles. Herzen openly admitted his aversion to the German socialist and his supporters whom he called 'Marxites'. There is no doubt that these feelings were mutual. But Marx and Engels did read Bakunin and Herzen's publications. They considered the Russians' productions as frivolous romanticism and misplaced chauvinism. Intellectually speaking that kind of writing was not to be taken seriously, though according to Marx and Engels it did constitute a political danger. Disillusion after 1848 was intense and many revolutionaries were inclined to wash their hands of Europe. They could then choose between the two alternative Europes which sprung to mind as a matter of course: America, where many emigrated, and Russia. That country had always been designated by revolutionaries as the bulwark of reaction, and glorified only by conservatives, but the Bauer case proved how irresistible the Russian temptation could be. Herzen's ideology was an attempt to raise up the Slavonic East as an ideal acceptable to every socialist. Marx and Engels saw this as little else than a manoeuvre to sell reactionary contraband under the democratic and socialistic flag.[14]

This, they thought, deserved vigorous counteraction. Like Custine, they believed that Western indolence and passivity rather than Russian power and vitality had fed the tsarist empire's unceasing desire for expansion. Now with Herzen and Bakunin a similar sort of situation threatened to arise in their own camp. A genuine revolutionary mentality could only be shown by tenaciously holding on to the anti-Russian convictions of pre-1848. Marx's numerous articles about international politics at this time also display an intense hatred of Russia, which blinded him to the intentions of European statesmen. Thus he believed that the British minister Palmerston and many other Western politicians and diplomats were paid agents of the Russian government and that the Crimean War was nothing more than a sham. Marx and Engels mostly went reasonably deeply into the material about which they wrote. But it was still chiefly those highly cliché-ridden and unrealistic elements of their image of Russia which were able to turn the republication of these articles in different editions in the 1950s into a current political event. Although one was by then somewhat accustomed to the sway of anti-Russian propaganda, the Russophobic writings of Marx and Engels during the time of the 'Cold War' made very spicy reading.[15]

But in fact their opinion on Russia was not only negative. Their reactions to both Russian socialists was most characteristic. Herzen, whom they did not know personally, was naturally numbered as one of the enemy camp. But it was more difficult to adopt such an attitude towards Bakunin.[16] Many people were fascinated by his exuberant and disarming personality. Marx, who had known him since 1844, was probably also somewhat susceptible to it, especially because Bakunin admired him and in general was far less anti-European than Herzen. Marx and Engels followed a strange zig-zag course in their verdict on Bakunin. They light-heartedly spread the news that he was a tsarist agent and later easily accepted him again as a friend.[17] At the same time Engels took the trouble to learn Russian in 1852, in order to resist Bakunin's influence more effectively. This, in his own words, also enabled him to get to know 'the details of the social institutions' of the country that was the principal enemy of revolutionary Germany.[18]

But a year earlier he had written to Marx that the European powers were out to keep Germany divided, and that therefore she had only one ally, namely 'Russia, on condition that a peasant revolt took place there'. This was a thought that could equally well have been voiced by Bakunin or Herzen. In the same letter, Engels, who like all Western radicals otherwise regarded himself as a supporter of Polish freedom, called Poland 'a worthless nation' in comparison with which Russia stood out as a vital state which had shown itself able to assimilate other peoples and had managed to make use of Western industrial techniques.[19]

The idea of a revolution in Eastern Europe which could turn the political constellation in the West upside down, thus creating the possibility of a socialist upheaval, haunted Marx and Engels. Because of this, their image of Russia became more and more Janus-like. According to them the country was still the great conservative force which, even after the loss of the Crimean War, continued to determine relationships between the remaining European powers. This point of view, which was based much less on insight into international politics than on an exaggerated fear of the Russians, brought them round to the opinion that the downfall of the Russian autocracy would unleash an avalanche which would carry everything with it. A revolution in Russia led them to expect a repetition in true barbaric style of the events in France in 1789 and 1793. The tsar's attempts to save his regime by freeing the peasants and making constitutional concessions could only lead to a Grande Peur and revolutionary terror on a gigantic scale. The preposterous result of all this violence would be that in Russia 'a real and general civilisation' would replace 'the sham and show introduced by Peter the Great', according to Marx in the *New York Tribune* of January 1859.[20]

The Russian revolution would thus not only form the driving force for a European upheaval, but also bring the country itself into the circle of Western civilisation. In Marx's view it was impossible that the Russian peasants could constitute a shining example for Western socialism, as Herzen and Bakunin maintained. Moreover Russia was not the only smouldering fuse which could reignite the extinguished European revolution. Marx and Engels studied in detail all the phenomena which could have produced this effect, whether they were economic crises or troubles in Spain or Ireland. But in the midst of the many revolutionary scenarios which they designed and then often rejected again, they still continued to expect the most from the performance of the Russian spectacle. The period of reform under Alexander II, which for many Europeans led to a change in their views about Russia, occasioned these speculations. Marx and Engels followed this development closely and read everything about it they could lay their hands on, even the publications of the odious Herzen.

Their already easily elated revolutionary feelings were heated to fever pitch by the Polish uprising in 1863, for they hoped that this would spread to Russia and afterwards to the West. They were certainly not the only ones to hold these views. Bakunin, who had escaped from Siberia two years before, had even tried unsuccessfully to join up with the struggling Poles. The Poles had not the ghost of a chance against the tsar's armies. Influenced by these disappointing experiences, Marx and Engels came to the conclusion that the period of reforms had led only to a reinforcement of autocracy and that Alexander II could now, as his father had done before the Crimean War, once more act as the policeman of Europe.[21]

The discovery of Russia as a society on the move did not cause Marx and Engels to qualify their opinion that Russia constituted an extraordinarily dangerous Asiatic force. For them there were only additional reasons to contend with that country. This in their view also naturally remained the task of all socialists and workers. In order to convince them of this duty all the old arguments were good enough. In their writings during those years Marx and Engels made no precise distinction between the Russian state, Russian society and the Russian people. They had in fact no genuine sympathy for anything Russian, and therefore they had no difficulty in uniting utterly cliché-ridden statements with an extensive knowledge of facts into an extreme political position. Even the racialist argument that the Russians stemmed from the Mongols and should thus possess the qualities associated with them – which Marx and Engels did not themselves believe – was employed by them if it was convenient.[22]

Their main sphere of action in these years was the First International, which was set up, not by chance, in the year after the failed Polish uprising of 1863. Since 1830, when an earlier attempt at undoing the Russian dominance in Poland had failed, Polish émigrés had done their very best to keep the sympathy for their homeland alive in the West. This had been highly successful especially in France, where ever since the days of Napoleon there had been a kind of reverence for the brave Poles.[23] The 1863 rebellion thus led as a matter of course to protest meetings in a number of countries, but in this case also to contacts between French and British workers who, by means of a co-ordinated endeavour, hoped to induce their governments to intervene in the Polish question. Their plan was doomed to failure from the start, but at least it was an explicit gesture. Moreover these talks were followed by the setting up of the International Workers' Association, later better known as the First International.

When the First International was set up in September 1864 the Polish question was clearly much less in the limelight, despite all the efforts of the remaining Poles in London. The situation was different within the board of the organisation, the General Council, where Marx rapidly took a dominant role and also enlisted supporters. He tried to translate his indignation about the behaviour of the major powers into a policy of the international proletariat.[24] In the first declaration of principles or *Address* of the association written by Marx, Russia was once more the principal target: 'the immense and unrestricted encroachments of that barbarous power, whose head is at St Petersburg and whose hands are in every cabinet in Europe, have taught the working classes to master themselves the mysteries of international politics.'[25]

It was therefore not surprising that at the first conference of the International in 1865 'The Muscovite invasion of Europe and the re-establishment of an independent and integral Poland' was the only political question raised. This item on the agenda, however, provoked a spirited debate at the meeting in London. The Belgian de Paepe and the Frenchmen Vésinier and Lassassie saw the opinion of the Council as a sort of selective protest. In their opinion there were other tyrannies and oppressed peoples in Europe. Given the place of the meeting, the comparison between England and Ireland was an obvious one. And had not Russia freed her peasants and opened up Asia for Western civilisation? Russian peasants and students were fighting as socialists for freedom. Herzen and Bakunin were praised as their champions by Vésinier and he accused Marx of a 'Russophobic monomania'. Moreover what guarantees were there that the desired freedoms in an independent Poland would benefit the people and not merely the nobility and the clergy?[26]

This was entirely in the spirit of Marx's former opponent Proudhon, who had repeatedly spoken out against a denunciation of Russia and had regarded the freedom-loving Poles with scepticism. As Marx wrote to Engels: 'The fellows have all joined Proudhon-Herzen Muscovitism.' Therefore Engels wrote a special pamphlet about this entitled *What Have the Working Classes to Do with Poland?* But this was to no avail, for at the first congress of the Association in September 1866 it was again evident that many of those present refused to see the Russian danger as the central issue in European politics. Changes in the Western European image of Russia after the Crimean War thus soon influenced the debate within the International.[27]

By 1866, however, it turned out that Russophobia had not yet disappeared on the French left. Alexander II's state visit to France was disturbed by demonstrations and a failed assassination attempt on the tsar. The General Council of the International was naturally pleased with this action against the 'Asiatic and barbaric power'. As usual, the administration of the International lent its assistance to a polite British tea party in January 1867, at which the band of musical instrument makers played Polish hymns alongside waltzes and quadrilles, and traditional anti-Russian resolutions were passed. But Marx's scheme of giving greater unity to the extremely heterogeneous and varied company of the First International by making use of the anti-Russian feelings which dominated public opinion in England, failed. It is difficult to make out to what extent Marx himself was ruled by emotions of this kind or if he mainly used them to augment his influence in the Association. During a meeting of the General Council in November 1869 he indirectly agreed with the opponents of an exclusively anti-Russian course of action. He declared that England was not Russia's superior when it came to treatment of political prisoners.[28]

It is certainly true that Marx's ideas about Russia went through a definite evolution in these years. Just because, in contrast to many of his liberal and socialist contemporaries, he had few illusions about the salutary effects of the tsar's reforms, he was susceptible to the ideas of Russian radicals who shared his scepticism. An extremely important factor here was that these men, to his utter amazement, were interested in his magnum opus *Das Kapital* which, when it was published in Western Europe in 1867, had occasioned no sensation. The Russians even made a translation of it. While Marx had managed to value Bakunin only temporarily, for the rest of his life he would foster great respect for the two translators of the book, Lopatin and Danielson, with whom he had been in contact since 1868.

Danielson sent Marx his compatriot Flerovsky's study of *The State of the Working Class in Russia* which regenerated his zeal for Russia's revolutionary potential. Marx was so enthusiastic that he started to learn Russian. Engels, too, brushed up his knowledge of the language. For it was evident from Flerovsky 'that the current situation in Russia is no longer stable ... that a frightful social revolution is imminent'. Marx rejected Flerovsky's ideas about 'the perfectible perfectibility of the Russian nation'.[29] That smacked to him too much of Herzen's recipes for the welfare of mankind. Later he was to reconsider his opinion on this point. However, Flerovsky's more sober, detailed and therefore shocking analysis of Russia's social actuality was to make a great impression. In Marx's eyes the book compared very favourably with the mystical veneration of Russian agrarian relations in the style of von Haxthausen and his conservative and socialist followers in Russia and the West. Of course, in Marx's view, Bakunin belonged with them as well, for after Marx, in 1869, had come to the conclusion that the Russian wanted to play first violin in the International, all the negative associations which the word 'Russian' awoke in him became bound up with Bakunin's name.

The conflict between Marx and Bakunin can well be described as a struggle between two socialist Titans about the diametrically opposed principles of 'authoritarian' Marxism and 'libertarian' anarchy with power over the International at stake. But it is also possible to see the conflict as a rather pointless quarrel between two extremely different but dominating personalities who tried in vain to impose their views on an organisation which because of its heterogeneous composition was in any case doomed to disintegration. Of course the problem is not whether there are any great differences to be found in the theoretical concepts of Marx and Bakunin, for they are obvious, but rather how much importance should be attached to these differences anyway. Like all radical socialists of their time both men found it unnecessary to offer an effective solution to the problem of the exercise of power after a socialist revolution. Neither Marx's dictatorship of the proletariat nor Bakunin's secret societies and anarchy offered any guarantee against the misuse of power. Bakunin's comments about the dangers to freedom which lay hidden in Marx's theory are so global and take so little account of the changes and nuances in the outlook of his opponent, that their prophetic nature should not be valued too highly. For there is little point in saddling Marx and Engels exclusively with fathering later totalitarian forms of socialism. Revolutionary socialists who are completely convinced of the necessity of a speedy and total social revolution are seldom inclined to worry about its political and ethical legitimacy. Of course this was equally true for Bakunin.

Initially Marx had certainly manoeuvred carefully within the General Council, but when after a number of years this had not had the desired effect, and moreover Bakunin threatened to undo what had already been achieved, his suspicion overcame his tact. He triumphed over his supposed enemies, but sealed the fate of the Association in the process. The result of his actions was that the International ceased to exist. Marx seemed to have thrown away the baby with the bathwater. Bakunin was an incorrigible romantic, not devoid of cunning, but as a very unpractical person totally unsuited to leading a complex body such as the International – something to which, as an anarchist, he did not actually aspire. Because of this the way in which the conflict was fought out was just as important as its background of differences in principle. Both Marx and Bakunin were so afraid of each other's potential ruling influence that they also availed themselves of very rough methods of combating their adversary and presented the outside world with only a caricatural image of each other's views; though it can be said in Bakunin's favour that he was too fickle to do this with regard to Marx as thoroughly as Marx deemed necessary with regard to him.

Hardly surprising, but very striking, is the weight they attached to the propagation of national resentment. It continually appears from Marx's correspondence that he saw Bakunin as a danger mainly because he was a Russian and must thus be an untrustworthy schemer and Pan-Slavist: an opinion which Engels entirely shared and which was also to take root in social democratic circles.[30] In the socialist press their acquaintances like Moses Hess summoned up the spectre of a secret Russian party under Bakunin's leadership, which was prepared to stir up a social war which would give these northern barbarians the chance to rebuild Western civilisation to their own taste. As secretary of the General Council, Marx wrote confidential letters in the same vein to deprive Bakunin of the chance of qualifying as head of the rebellious sections of the International.[31]

A piquant fact was that Marx could only be informed of the details of Bakunin's activities from the Russian side. Here his contacts with Lopatin and Danielson were not alone in their usefulness. Radical representatives of the revolutionary student movement in Russia who had had to flee from the Russian police to Switzerland, were evidently very interested in the International. For Marx it was important that these young people thought Herzen too liberal to be acceptable as leader and that some of them had quarrelled with Bakunin as well. In 1870 these students formed a Russian section in the International and asked Marx very politely to be their representative in the General Council.[32] He wrote to Engels not without perverse delight: 'What a droll position for me to act as representative of young Russia! A man never knows what he can achieve and what kind of strange fellowship he may have to endure.'[33] Within the Russian section Nikolai Utin in particular emerged as a zealous confederate of Marx in the struggle against Bakunin.

There was little more that Bakunin could do about the war of slander being waged against him except complain to his

friends. They, however, had formed anything but the secret sect
of which Marx was so afraid. More serious was the fact that he
tried to explain his enemies' campaign. All his slanderers, Marx,
Borkheim, Hess and Utin, were after all Jews. Assisted by this
coterie of members of his race, Marx was obviously making an
attempt to subject the International and thereafter the whole
world to German-Jewish power.[34] According to Bakunin, the
German influence on Russian history had even been so great
that the Germans could be held responsible for the most unsatis-
factory features of the Russian state which he regarded as a
'knouto-Germanic empire'. This was a case of the Russian pot
calling the German kettle black, for to us, Bakunin seems to
have been just as prone to ridiculous exaggeration as Marx who,
after all, until shortly before had seen Prussia as nothing other
than Russia's servile ally.[35]

Marx challenged Bakunin in a way which was later to become
general practice amongst Bolsheviks and communists. From
1868 onwards an extravagant campaign was carried out which
put all the opposing groups within the International into the
defendant's seat, while the General Council played the role of
the innocent victim. No trouble was spared in the collection of
incriminating material with which, by twisting the facts, Bakunin
could be presented as a prospective usurper of the International.
Meanwhile the General Council high-handedly extended its
jurisdiction. By manipulation it gained itself a majority at the
congress in The Hague in 1871. In this way the 'Bakuninist'
minority could be excommunicated and the organisation
purified, with the result that the International was split and
completely emasculated.

From the 'Nechayev affair', which was to play such an important role in Bakunin's removal from the International, it once
more emerged how much both great socialists were inclined to
apply different ethics to their friends than to their enemies. The
young Russian revolutionary Nechayev had, together with a few
members of a secret society he led, murdered a comrade named
Ivanov in 1869. Nechayev gave as his motive that Ivanov was a
police spy and thus worthy of execution as a traitor. The real
reason was that Ivanov had dared to cast doubts on the indubit-
able and absolute authority with which Nechayev ruled over this
group of youths. This spectacular crime became a *cause célèbre*

in the history of the Russian revolutionary movement and inspired Dostoyevsky to write his novel *The Possessed*. It was to show that political radicalism can also lead to the use of violence between revolutionaries themselves, to 'violence done to brothers' as Camus was to write later, or in the words of the historian Confino, to 'violence within violence'.[36]

Bakunin was already completely under Nechayev's spell before Ivanov's murder, and remained so for a long time afterwards. He became friendly with him in Switzerland and co-operated with him intensively. According to Bakunin the revolution in Russia ought to be led by youthful fanatics of this sort. There is no evidence that he ever doubted, or wanted to doubt, Nechayev's version of Ivanov's death. Other Russian exiles likewise stuck to the fiction of a political murder against their better judgement, because they believed that higher interests were served in this way. Bakunin broke with Nechayev in 1870 when it became evident that the youngster had betrayed and robbed him. In a long letter he dissociated himself from the immoral practices and political views of his former friend which had proved to be more Jacobin, statist and authoritarian than those of his enemy Marx. At the same time this letter made it clear that all forms of trickery, guile and violence remain justified at all times in the strife against the established order.[37]

Utin and Marx did not hesitate to exploit Bakunin's connections with Nechayev to the full. Naturally they saw Bakunin as the principal and not as a fairly defenceless victim of the young Russian. To some extent it was Bakunin's own uncontrollable inclination for mystification which facilitated this interpretation. On the other hand, the warnings of some Russian informants not to jump to conclusions were also thrown completely to the winds. Utin and Marx went to ridiculous extremes when they declared, at the conference of the Association in London in 1871, that secret societies were superfluous in Russia given the fact that individual freedom ruled there to such an extent that everyone could safely join the International. Engels wrote the official report of the split in 1873 in the same spirit.[38] In this the Nechayev question was once more explained in full and Bakunin's ideas about a peasant revolution in Russia, provoked and led by a vanguard of youths from the intelligentsia, were made to look ridiculous. Actually there may well have been reason enough for this merciless criticism. There were after all Russian revolutionaries too, who disagreed fundamentally with Bakunin. But in the long run the hopes of Marx and Engels themselves were also fixed on a spontaneous and exceptionally violent uprising of the Russian peasantry and it was soon to become clear that they too were not averse to the elitist, patronising role that the intelligentsia could play in this.

The Russian revolutionary movement was to experience more affairs like the Nechayev case which showed that the boundaries between idealism and crime could become blurred. Nechayev's deed was rejected by most Russian revolutionaries as criminal and perverted. After the conflict between Marx and Bakunin this affair was still used by socialists in the East and the West to demonstrate the perfidy of anarchy. In the case of the later 'affairs' this rejection was sometimes less widespread. Western socialists were also to have more trouble later in condemning this kind of Russian lapse as vigorously as had happened in the Nechayev case, especially after 1917.

## MARX AND RUSSIAN POPULISM

After the fall of the Paris Commune and the collapse of the International, the chance of a speedy revolutionary breakthrough in the West evaporated. The threat of an armed conflict between the German empire and revanchist France that could unite with autocratic Russia hung over Europe. According to Marx and Engels it was not very likely that these international tensions would give socialists the opportunity to seize power. More probably they would be unable to prevent a war because the workers would be sensitive to chauvinist propaganda. The socialist movement would then be doomed to impotence for decades. The immediate outlook thus seemed somewhat bleak, unless a revolution were to break out in Russia. Then not only would the international situation be drastically altered, but the Western proletariat would also be given the necessary impulse to take action. Marx's and Engels's image of Russia thus still had the appearance of a head of Janus: on one side the grim visage of the European policeman, and on the other the face of the young revolutionary as the only one capable of giving the decisive thrust for the liberation of mankind. The fear and

admiration which barbarism had always conjured up in the West
also determined their thoughts about Russia. But it was just in
this last period of their lives that their appreciation of all that
was Russian overcame their contempt.[39]

This reversal in their thoughts was characteristic of the spirit
of the time. As we have seen, the Crimean War, the internal
reforms and the revolutionary disturbances brought about a
shift in European political opinion about Russia. For conservatives it had become a much less attractive country; for those on
the left of the political spectrum it was no longer the country
of 'knout and terror'. For a long time Marx and Engels had
taken a stand against a positive approach to Russia in the socialist
milieu, but they did not maintain it. One of the reasons was of
a personal nature. Their former Russian opponents had been
eliminated. Herzen died in 1870, Bakunin was no longer involved and was to die in 1876. 'As to the Russians in general . . .',
wrote Engels to Becker in 1872, 'there is a tremendous difference
between the noble, aristocratic Russians like Herzen and
Bakunin, all of them swindlers, who came to Europe earlier on,
and those arriving now, who rose out of the *people*. Among these
are some who in talent and character unquestionably belong to
the very best in our party, men whose stoicism, firmness of
character and abstract intellectual grasp are amazing.'[40] From
the very mouth of Engels, who remained much more strongly
convinced than Marx of the superiority of Western civilisation,
this undisguised admiration for the Russian revolutionaries was
remarkable, especially since he so quickly accepted that their
exceptional qualities were linked to their social origin. For within
the radical Russian intelligentsia, which as a whole remained
separated from the broad mass of the people by an unbridgeable
gulf, the fact that someone was a noble hardly counted.

Marx's and Engels's appreciation of their Russian friends was
seldom uncritical. With Lopatin, who perhaps more than anyone
had served as a model for Engels's characterisation of the young
Russian revolutionary, the relationship was sometimes tense. For
like numerous other socialists he regretted that the unity of the
labour movement had been sacrificed to a pointless and
extremely sordid quarrel with Bakunin. This was also the
opinion of Lavrov, one of the most distinguished ideologists of
Russian populism, who fled to Paris in 1870 and was one of

Marx's principal informants about the Commune. Marx's and Engels's long and heartfelt friendship with this man remained coloured by a certain condescending disdain. This appeared very strongly when in 1874 Engels meddled in a debate which took place between Lavrov and Tkachov.[41]

Lavrov, a scholarly recluse who became a revolutionary, was an idol of radical Russian youth because of his *Historical Letters* which appeared in 1868–9. He thought that the people ought to free themselves. The intelligentsia should take upon itself the role of educator of the people. Revolutions had to be thoroughly prepared. Propaganda was the keyword. There is probably no Western socialist to be found who pointed out the dangers of revolutionary impatience and dictatorial tendencies which unavoidably emerge in the movement more clearly than Lavrov did. Tkachov was indeed a very definite representative of the Jacobin-Blanquist tradition within the Russian revolutionary movement. Later historians saw him as a forerunner of Lenin.[42] In 1874 Lavrov emphatically pointed out to him the results of a *coup d'état* by a minority.

> History proves to us, and psychology convinces us, that every unlimited power, every dictatorship, demoralises the best men, and that even geniuses who think they are proving a boon to the people with their decrees, are not in a position to do this ... In the struggle of a party for power, in the tension caused by public and secret intrigues, a new necessity to maintain power is awakened every moment and a new impossibility to give it up. A dictatorship can only be torn out of the hands of the dictators by a new revolution.[43]

Engels on the other hand considered Lavrov's reaction as a form of philosophising about the revolution which was about as valuable as 'the investigations of a scholastic into the Virgin Mary'. He reproached 'friend Peter' again with refusing, at that time, to take up a position in the conflict with Bakunin. Engels also experienced some malicious joy now that the kind-hearted Lavrov had become embroiled in a polemic with Tkachov. In his view the latter was merely a copy of Bakunin in pocket form, 'a green grammar school student of remarkable immaturity'. If anyone believed that a revolution could immediately be made in Russia and thought it was only a question of daring, then he should begin it himself. But everything indicated that Tkachov was only a man of letters and an intriguer who was seeking his own glory and therefore deserved the same treatment as Bakunin or Nechayev. The Russians should accommodate themselves to the fact that from now on their movement would be under the control and supervision of Europe. That was only in their own interest.[44]

When Tkachov reacted resentfully to Engels's article, Engels, on Marx's advice ('keep striking heartily, in a cheerful way'[45]), put him through the wringer once more. If Tkachov thought that a socialist revolution would be easier in Russia than in the West because that country had no proletariat or bourgeoisie, then this simply proved that he 'still had to learn the ABC of socialism'. As he had done in earlier attacks on Herzen and Bakunin, Engels repeated that the survival of earlier forms of collectivism in Russia such as the *mir* and the *artel* simply indicated backwardness and not an exceptional aptitude for socialism. Isolated village communities such as the *mir* had always formed an ideal foundation for Asiatic despotism, of which Russian autocracy was also an example. Moreover, the communal ownership of land in Russia was being undermined by economic development. Only a proletarian revolution *in the West* could save the *mir* from certain doom. Only then could that institution, at least if it were capable of thorough modernisation, become the point of departure for a socialist reorganisation of Russian society.

Thus Engels no longer entirely rejected the Russian populists' beloved idea that their country had at its disposal a unique road to socialism. But his criticism of Tkachov would have lost its point if he had embraced that ideal heartily. So he kept several options open. He believed, like Marx, that Russia was on the eve of a great revolution. The situation there, they liked to claim, was similar to that in France in the second half of the eighteenth century. What the Russian revolutionaries thought was therefore not so important: they had to act. Engels did not share Lavrov's concern about the consequences of the Blanquist coup. Blanqui was after all the only French revolutionary for whom he and Marx had any respect. Russia was probably waiting for a kind of bourgeois revolution, which could only assume socialist characteristics with Western, proletarian help. *Mutatis mutandis* this was the model for a revolution in two stages which Marx and he had designed for Germany in 1848. In 1848, only a revolutionary France could have provided for a socialist element in the German 'bourgeois revolution'. Now, a quarter of a century later, the entire West could render Russia a service of this nature.[46]

About ten years later Plekhanov was to present this idea as *the* Marxist blueprint for the future Russian revolution, including the two stages and the possibility of a reduction in the period between the bourgeois and the socialist phases thanks to Western intervention. Until 1917, this remained the axiom of all Russian social democrats including Lenin. But for them, as for Marx and Engels in 1848, the proletariat was the only true revolutionary class. It was not very consistent of Engels that, in his piece against Tkachov, he still ended up with the *mir*. In his utterly critical assessment of it he echoed the great Russian social thinkers more than he himself realised. Practically no one in Russia believed that the *mir* in its present state formed an ideal basis for socialism or that this could be achieved without Western knowledge and technology.[47] Whilst he, with Western arrogance, was carrying on a controversy with Tkachov, Engels tacitly accepted Herzen's notion that Russian backwardness was concealing the possibility of a socialism without capitalism, without bourgeoisie and without proletariat.

For Marx, who had once expressed himself so contemptuously about 'the idiocy of peasant life', the thought of a specifically Russian dialectic of progress had almost become an obsession. Since Marx had read Flerovsky and Chernyshevsky, his correspondence with Russians had borne witness to an unceasing interest in Russian agrarian relationships. In December 1872 he confided to Danielson that he was planning to go into them in great detail in the second part of *Das Kapital*. His Russian translator was himself an expert in that field with a declared opinion, and he was interested in winning Marx over to his views. In long letters, sometimes running to dozens of pages, he gave an account of the debate about the past, present and future of the *obshchina*, the Russian village commune, which occupied people's minds in his country. He regularly sent a parcel of books to London, so that Marx could read the subject up in detail. Danielson tried to convey the message to Marx that the government's attempts to modernise Russia were doomed because they were at the expense of agriculture, the basis of economic life. The results for the peasants were disastrous. In his book Marx had described British capitalism as a result, as necessary as it was spontaneous, of certain social circumstances and a long historical development. It would not be displeasing to Danielson if Marx were to show, in the second part of his book, that Russian capitalism was merely an artificial product of a corrupt, incompetent and dictatorial government. In this way the Russians, who maintained that it was evident from *Das Kapital* that capitalism was something unavoidable in Russia as well, would be deprived of a telling argument.[48]

Marx had after all cried out to the German reader in his foreword:

> *De te fabula narratur!* ... The country that is more developed industrially only shows, to the less developed, the image of its own future ... Alongside of modern evils a whole series of inherited evils oppress us, arising from the passive survival of antiquated modes of production, with their inevitable train of social and political anachronisms. We suffer not only from the living, but from the dead. *Le mort saisit le vif!* [The dead grasps the living!] ... And even when a society has got on the right track for the discovery of the natural laws of its movement – and it is the ultimate aim of this work to lay bare the economic law of motion in modern society – it can neither clear by bold leaps nor remove by legal enactments the obstacles offered by the successive phases of its normal development.[49]

According to some reviewers of *Das Kapital* in Russia, not only Germans but Russians, too, ought to take these words to heart. The populists, however learned some of them may have been, appear to have understood nothing about economics if they thought that the backwardness of their country could be an advantage. N. I. Sieber (Ziber), the liberal professor at Kiev university who could be reckoned as a passionate defender of Russian capitalism, was full of praise for Marx. Sieber believed that in his country one would only be able to understand where one was going 'if the Russian *muzhik* was boiled up in a factory kettle'.[50] Marx was delighted at the interest in his book in Russia and mentioned Sieber by name in the foreword of the second German edition in 1873. It was not until 1877 that he came to realise because of Danielson's communications that his book was being used in Russia as an apologia for capitalism.

1877 was, however, the year of the Russo-Turkish War, and Marx and Engels expected more from it than from theorising. Of course they hoped that Russia would lose the war, which would make a revolution there unavoidable. Marx explained to Sorge why this crisis was 'a new turning-point' in European history. 'All the strata of Russian society are economically, morally and intellectually in complete decay. This time the revolution is beginning in the East, the hitherto invulnerable bastion of the counter-revolution and headquarters of its reserve army.'[51] But all their sympathy was with the Turks, much to Lavrov's fury, who wrote to Lopatin:

> Today I was with Marx. Inwardly I was annoyed by him .... He spoke about socialism and the Turks' superb qualities, a small number of pashas notwithstanding: notwithstanding! 'The Turks as a whole, as a people', he said, 'were naturally less dissolute than the ...' (he paused, I thought he was going to say: Russians, but he probably considered that would be dreadfully rude and finished the sentence:) ... 'than, for instance, the French peasants.'[52]

Marx also wrote to Liebknecht that the Turkish peasants were among the 'most competent and moral' in Europe. These letters were attached in the same year to an essay by Liebknecht in an *Exhortation to the German People* that gave the point of view of the German Social Democratic Party about the war under the title *On the Eastern Question or Will Europe Become Cossack?* The still young Kautsky took exception to this one-sided anti-Russian view which disguised the Turkish oppression of the Balkan peoples. The German socialist Levy also took up the cudgels against Liebknecht in a pamphlet entitled *On the Eastern Question or Will the Socialist Workers' Party Become Turkish?* In the debate Liebknecht, who was not yet embarrassed by his Russophobia like Marx, maintained in opposition to Levy that 'the average Turk' was 'undoubtedly superior in culture to the average Russian'. Until then Marx had seen no reason for the glorification of the Russian peasants and that of the Turkish quickly evaporated when they lost the war. After all, they had neglected to make a revolution.[53]

Meanwhile in 1877 Danielson had sent Marx some material which showed how powerfully *Das Kapital* had influenced the discussion about Russia's future. Marx did not react until November 1878 after a worried letter from Danielson. He had indeed received an article by Sieber and one by someone else, 'I think Michailov', both published in the magazine *Patriotic Notes*. There was no mention of the content. After Marx's death Engels found, among his friend's belongings, a letter directed to the editor of this Russian magazine in which the piece by Mikhailovsky was examined in detail. This author, whose name Marx could not manage to remember properly, was one of Russia's most important essayists who had an even greater influence on the intelligentsia than Lavrov. He regarded Marx as an especially prominent Western economist, but on moral grounds he resisted the idea that *Das Kapital* was a reflection of Russia's future. Did Russian socialists really have to watch with folded arms while workers, women and children were swallowed up by the capitalist Moloch because this was the necessary, unavoidable sacrifice in order to be able to enter the socialist paradise?[54]

In his letter, Marx defended himself firstly against Mikhailovsky's accusation that it was evident from a vicious remark about Herzen in *Das Kapital* that he actually did not concede the possibility of a separate economic development to the Russians.[55] He had after all expressed himself full of praise for the Russian social critic Chernyshevsky in the 1873 second edition of his book. Marx did not admit that the very fact that he had left out this thrust at Herzen in the second German edition, and replaced it with praise for Chernyshevsky, proved how much his views about Russia had evolved. Instead he claimed that no insight concerning Russia's future could be extracted from his book. The historical process outlined in it *only* related to Western Europe. Since 1861 Russia had taken a great deal of trouble to become a capitalist nation after the Western model. If she continued to do this 'the best opportunity that history has ever offered a nation to evade the disastrous vicissitudes of the capitalist regime would be lost'. Marx thus thought that if a country had the opportunity of being contented without capitalism, it should not let this chance go by.[56]

Why was this letter never sent? According to Engels, Marx must have thought that he would endanger the survival of the magazine *Otechestvennye Zapiski (Patriotic Notes)*. In 1878 Marx wrote to Danielson under the pseudonym Williams. A correspondence with Marx, who had become notorious far and wide because of the International, could according to Russian friends have had harmful consequences for Danielson. D. M. Wallace, the British journalist and Russian expert who later became famous, was in fact arrested in 1873 in St Petersburg suspected of being Marx.[57] But in spite of this the Russian translation of *Das Kapital* was passed by the censor and the lively discussion about the book in the press was not obstructed by the authorities. Moreover Lopatin and Lavrov in the West and even Engels also knew nothing about the letter. In 1906 Lopatin still stated: 'Marx has not expressed himself to me either in a categorical or in a clear-cut way, as to whether he hoped that the Russian village commune could help Russia to avoid the capitalist stage. *I do not think* that he believed it even for a minute.'[58] Was there a serious reason for this mysterious performance?

In this letter of 1878 Marx proclaimed that social developments ought to be studied in their concrete historical context. In his view no real insight could be gained from 'the universal key of a general theory of philosophical history whose greatest virtue is to be above history'. This fragment is willingly quoted as proof of the subtlety of a great thinker, who prided himself, after all, on not being a Marxist. But Marx's qualified viewpoint raised more questions than it supplied answers. Why should the whole of Western Europe have to submit to the 'Caudine yoke' of capitalism which was invented by the British, while Russia alone did not? Why should that yoke be heavier in Germany because there were heavier burdens of backwardness to bear there than in England, while in Russia an even greater backwardness could be a blessing? On the face of it Marx had become imprisoned by his image of Russia. If he did not respond to Mikhailovsky, he would be implicitly agreeing with the Russian 'liberal' economists who maintained that the old agrarian attitudes were simply impeding the modernisation of Russia and should therefore be cleared away. In that case there was no fundamental difference whatsoever between Russia and Germany and this was in conflict with Marx's image of Russia as a semi-Asiatic nation, the antipodes of the civilised West. At the same time it meant that he would have to join the Western socialists who judged Alexander II's reforms favourably, and that was certainly not his intention, all the more so because his radical Russian acquaintances were even less prepared to do so.

Marx's hope for a Russian revolution as a condition for a socialist uprising in the West and his admiration for the courage and intellectual stature of some Russian socialists left no room for lukewarm indifference. But joining the camp of the glorifiers of Russia, whom he had always opposed so bitterly, was indeed a substantial step. He nevertheless took this step in his letter by pointing out the advantage that Russia's lack of civilisation could provide: a route to socialism without the pain and trouble which the West had to undergo for it. His old enemies von Haux-thausen, Herzen and Bakunin were thus proved right. After the conservatives and the Christians, now socialists, too, could point to Russia as a unique utopia in the history of mankind. This must have been a little too much for Marx. The idea of a barbarian mass of peasants elected to socialism had always aroused his disgust. He was sensitive to the scholarly slant in the argumentation of the Russian populists. In his letter he had written that 'the expropriation of the agricultural producers, of the peasants' formed 'the foundation of the whole process' of the capitalist accumulation of wealth.[59] This could mean that the basis of a Western capitalism was lacking in Russia because the peasants there had never experienced individual ownership of land. Everything turned on the fact that even in this unfruitful soil a sort of weed was shooting up everywhere which was difficult to call anything else but capitalism. By keeping this letter in his portfolio Marx secretly admitted that, like so many others in Western Europe, he actually did not know what to do about Russia in the period after the Crimean War. The former preju-dices and prototypical impressions were no longer satisfactory as a definition, but it was extremely difficult to arrive at a new evaluation.

The pressure to take a public stand increased in the last years of his life. In the first place the second part of *Das Kapital* was anxiously awaited in Russia because this was to contain a special study of the Russian agrarian situation. Danielson continued to send long letters and other material. Moreover in 1880 he wrote an elaborate essay on this subject. Danielson did argue once more that the Russian economy was caught up in a vicious circle. Forced industrialisation could only be paid for by overcropping in agriculture, which would make the population too poor to buy industrial products, while Russia as an industrial newcomer would produce too expensively and inefficiently to be able to compete on the world market. National bankruptcy, permanent famine and the total collapse of economic life were inescapable unless the policy were reversed and the tempo of modernisation slowed down by means of socialist planning with the ancient collective social institutions as a starting-point.

Marx was enthusiastic about this piece, which he called 'original in the best meaning of the word'. But he did not show to what extent he shared the point of view of the author. He had informed Danielson a short time beforehand that the second part of his book would have to wait, partly because he still had so much Russian material to study. In December 1881 he wrote that he still wanted to finish the book as quickly as possible. But nothing was to come of this. Engels, who had warned his friend that the manuscript would never be finished if Marx buried himself in Russian affairs, after his death found two cubic metres of Russian material and many excerpts from it. But practically all the fragments of any coherence in Marx's handwriting dated from the sixties, and to the great disappointment of Danielson and many of his compatriots, none were about Russian attitudes.[60]

It is strange that on 19 February 1881 Marx sang Danielson's praises for his essay but did not breathe a word about its content. A few months earlier the organisation of terrorists in St Petersburg, which as the whole world knew was hunting down the tsar, had asked him to shed some light on the future of Russia. Marx had promised a pamphlet but had left this work on one side. Three days before he answered Danielson, another request of this kind reached him. This time it was from Vera Zasulich, who in 1878 had become a European celebrity because of her pistol shot at the governor of St Petersburg, her acquittal by a jury which followed, and her miraculous escape abroad. She politely asked Marx for his opinion of the *mir* because this was a matter 'of life and death' for every Russian socialist. Marx now decided to answer, and the tenor of his short letter was the same as that to the editor of *Oteshestvennye Zapiski*. The content of *Das Kapital* did not allude to Russia and he explained plainly that the Russian village commune could be 'the fulcrum of social regeneration' if it were offered the opportunity of a spontaneous development.[61]

Marx drew Zasulich's attention to the fact that his letter was not intended for publication, and from this it is already evident that he was still undecided, despite his clear, sharp formulation and decisive tone. The point in time had an important role to play in this. Marx was convinced that the revolution in Russia could break out at any moment. Five days after Marx answered Zasulich, Tsar Alexander II was assassinated by terrorists. Nevertheless, the letter was a product not of opportunism, but of deep reflection. His aversion to the Russian miracle propagated by Herzen and Bakunin had been so great that the need for an adequate rationalisation of his altered opinion made itself felt very forcefully. Both he and Engels had, in the past, expressed themselves derisively about the conservative von Haxthausen, who had praised the Russian village commune as something unique. In their opinion this social structure had after all existed earlier throughout the world, and at the beginning of the nineteenth century there were rudiments of it in Germany: for example, in the area round Trier, Marx's birthplace, they were still perceptible. Since then Marx had delved deeply into the history of this phenomenon, not only by becoming acquainted with historical studies of the Russian *obshchina*, but also through the work of the leading ethnologists of his day. It was probably mainly the American Lewis Morgan's book *Ancient Society* which made it possible to place the glorification of the *mir* by the Russian populists in a wider scholarly framework and made it more acceptable to Marx. Morgan's romantic vision of the prehistory of mankind as a primeval communist society, which formed both a primitive pre-echo and at the same time an image of the future for the modern world, was an expression of the enthusiasm for lack of civilisation, naturalness and absence of property that had remained so characteristic of the Western attitude with regard to the barbarian peoples and therefore fitted in so admirably with Marx's thoughts about Russia.[62]

This however only became evident when as many as four drafts of the short letter to Zasulich were found among Marx's effects after his death. Basing himself on a quotation from Morgan, Marx argued that Western capitalism was in a crisis that would first end in socialism, that is to say, in the 'return' of modern society to the 'archaic' prehistoric social prototype in a higher form. In Russia this archaic social prototype had remained essentially intact. Therefore the country was in an absolutely unique position which had no historical precedent. The centuries-long cultural isolation which the survival of the *mir* had ensured had now been breached. Russia was, however, not a colony but a very great independent state. She was thus free to choose her own way of making use of Western civilisation. She could go ahead as she was now doing, with the adoption of the Western capitalist system. Marx pointed out – following Danielson – that Russian capitalism was a forced greenhouse plant which could only grow at the expense of agriculture. Soon most of the peasants would be property-less proletarians, while only a small minority would be able to maintain themselves as an agrarian middle class. This disastrous process could only be stopped by a revolution. The fall of tsarism would make it possible to profit from the blessings of Western technology and learning without capitalism and its accompanying misery and exploitation. Russia would be able to transform its archaic collectivism into something of a higher order, and without going through the stage of capitalism, become the equal of a socialist Western Europe.[63]

It is evident from Marx's wrestling with the Russian problem that an extremely negative approach to it could be reversed, if he retained the notion that the differences between Russia and the West were fundamental in nature. Only then would the possibility diminish and the need disappear for the application of Western standards to Russia. For Marx this meant that he gave up the claim to a universal validity for his theory on behalf of a country to which he had always so ostentatiously confessed his aversion. This was reason enough for triumphant satisfaction among his foes, confusion and disappointment among his friends, but also for doubt and reserve for Marx himself.

### TERRORISM IN RUSSIA

Evaluation of the Russian revolutionary movement and the

methods it employed in the struggle against the tsar, sworn enemy of the whole of left-wing Europe, raised fewer problems. Admiration for the Russian terrorists was here pretty general. Vera Zasulich was a fêted celebrity, and Hartman, who had taken part in a failed attack on the tsar in 1879 and had been arrested in France, became one likewise. The French socialists and radicals, among them Victor Hugo, incited by Lavrov and Kropotkin, waged a campaign to prevent his extradition to Russia. When Hartman was deported to England, Marx and Engels organised a banquet in his honour and drank *Bruderschaft* (brotherhood) with him. The leadership of the Russian terrorist organisation the People's Will (Narodnaya Volya) asked Marx to take care of Hartman in a letter full of expressions of praise for him. Marx stood by him in word and deed and Engels supported him financially. Other Russian terrorists too, like Morozov and Stepnyak, constantly received their hospitality.[64]

The standpoint of Marx and Engels on violence and terror was ambivalent. In their early years they had opposed the romantic glamorisation of the revolution in the spirit of Buonarroti and Babeuf. The Russian Annenkov had seen how Marx attacked the tailor and workers' leader Weitling in 1846 for this. 'Look', he added, pointing suddenly towards me with an angry glance, 'there is a Russian among us. In his country, Weitling, you could play your role. There alone, indeed, can alliances between senseless prophets and senseless disciples be forged and held together. In a civilised country like Germany', continued Marx, 'people without positive teaching can accomplish nothing . . .'[65] But when the revolution of 1848 miscarried, Marx for a short time preached revolutionary terror in order to hasten the downfall of the old society, proving himself to be a supporter of Jacobin and Blanquist views. Still later, in 1870, Engels spoke slightingly about the Jacobins: for the most part they were 'vile little philistines who wetted their pants' and practised terrorism out of fear.[66] At about the same time Marx praised the Paris Commune because it had been such a peaceful rebellion, and he seems to have been convinced that a non-violent development towards socialism was also possible for democratically governed countries like England. But he admired the Irish freedom fighters, who were also an inspiring model for the Russian terrorists. The Russian scholar Kovalevsky was visiting Marx in

1878 when the news of the failure of Dr Nobiling's attack on the German emperor reached him. 'Marx reacted to this report by cursing the unsuccessful terrorist, explaining that there was only one thing to expect from his criminal attempt to accelerate the course of events – new reprisals against the socialists.'[67]

However, he put a different complexion on the struggle of the Russian terrorists. N.A. Morozov, a member of the Executive Committee of the People's Will, visited Marx in 1880 and discussed their activities with him. 'Marx was especially interested, and said that our struggle against autocracy appeared to him and all Europeans as something completely fantastic; as something only possible in whimsical novels.'[68] After the Western press had come out in 1880 in huge headlines with the sensational news of the explosion in the Winter Palace which resulted from an unsuccessful bomb attack on the tsar by the People's Will, Hartman wrote: 'Marx sees in this event a sign of the approaching revolution and of the exclusive virtue of the terrorist party. He even asked me to tell Lavrov and the Russian socialists in his name that he considered the Russian terror to be the only logical and the only practically possible and useful concern in Russia at this moment.'[69] After Alexander II had been killed in March 1881, Marx wrote to his daughter Jenny that the behaviour of the heroic terrorists at their trial was 'strikingly different from the schoolboyish ways of people like Most and other childish cry-babies who preach tyrannicide as a 'theory' and 'panacea' . . . On the contrary they endeavour to inform Europe that their *modus operandi* is a specifically Russian and historically inevitable one, and that there is just as little in it to moralise about – for or against – as there is in the earthquake on Chios.'[70]

Although the exploits of the People's Will made a great impression on all Russian revolutionaries – even Lavrov and Mikhailovsky put their objections against revolutionary violence temporarily aside – this by no means meant that all of them too, like Marx, considered terrorism as something typically Russian or as the only effective method for the Russian revolution. The revolutionary organisation Land and Freedom (Zemlya i Volya) broke up in 1878 precisely over this question. Besides the People's Will, the Black Partition (Chorny Peredyel) made its appearance, concentrating on propaganda among the peasants.

But the police made no distinction between them, and members of the People's Will as well as of the Black Partition found themselves forced to flee abroad.[71] Marx, probably influenced by Hartman, spoke very slightingly of the Black Partition in a letter to Sorge: 'As against the terrorists who were risking their lives, its members – most (but not all of them) people who have left Russia *voluntarily* – form the so-called Party of Propaganda. (To make *propaganda* in *Russia*, they head for *Geneva*! What a *quid pro quo*!)' The boring doctrinairianism of these people reminded him of Bakunin.[72]

Thus there was veneration for the Russian terrorists, contempt for Western socialists like the Most mentioned by Marx who found that the Russian example deserved to be followed, and contempt, too, for Russian revolutionaries who did not praise terrorism as the only cure for Russia's complaints. In this way was laid down the fundamental attitude towards the Russian revolutionary movement which was to remain characteristic of a large number of Western socialists and radicals until long after 1917. It was a position made possible by the classic Western European image of Russia. Here too it was true that an absolute character was conferred on the differences between Europe and Russia. In this way one acquired an excuse for not making any attempt to change society in one's own country in the same way as advocated by some Russians one wanted to admire. Revolutionary violence continued to exercise a great fascination on people who longed for a social revolution, even if they realised that the treatment could be worse than the complaint. This was a form of playing with fire which people were glad to watch with bated breath from a safe distance. Russians who thought that the results could be just as detrimental for their country as for any other European country only aroused resentment, while Europeans who tried to set their own country on fire with Russian matches were considered stupid or dangerous.

The years 1878–81 differed in this respect from the period when Marx and Bakunin were at loggerheads. Marx detested Bakunin because he was a Russian. Bakunin, however, was not followed by the anarchists because of their admiration for Russian radicalism. But now things were different. The terrorist activities in Russia coincided with a series of attacks on other heads of state. This was the time when Western anarchists were perpetrating the 'propaganda of the deed', when the three emperors of Europe consulted each other on anti-terrorist measures, and when Bismarck submitted his anti-socialist laws to the Reichstag. The construction of an organised and large scale socialist movement was still in a critical preliminary phase and the dissatisfaction of the workers also found expression in deeds of violence. Precisely because the situation in Russia was in a number of respects comparable with that in large parts of Europe, the successes of the Russian terrorists were an inspiration to anarchists in France, Austria and Italy; and not only to anarchists. Some German social democrats and workers were not much taken with the extremely cautious politics of the German Social Democratic Party (Sozialdemokratische Partei Deutschlands or SPD), which wished above all to prevent its supporters from being tempted by Bismarck, the police or *agents provocateurs* into disastrous actions. One of these opponents, the SPD representative Hasselmann, protested his solidarity with the Russian terrorists during a speech in the Reichstag in May 1880 at the top of his voice above an uproar from the right-wing members of parliament. He promised his audience that the German workers would act in the same way, and regretted that some of his party colleagues had distanced themselves from the Russian revolutionaries. The German socialist Most propounded the same point of view in the paper *Freiheit (Freedom)* which he edited from London. This had many avid readers in Germany, and could count on substantial interest in Austria too.[73]

Kautsky described how great the expectations from the Russian wonder were. In March 1881, with the Russian Plekhanov, he attended a meeting in Paris at which Louise Michel, the heroine of the Commune who had returned from exile shortly before, spoke. 'As fascinated as we all were, she too awaited the dawning of a new era as a result of the killing of Alexander II.'[74] In London, Most was sentenced for a lyrical article about the Russian events to sixteen months' imprisonment and hard labour because the British authorities, after some wrestling with the German language, came to the conclusion that the use of the word *krepieren,* to die like an animal, with reference to the death of a tsar, was a form of *lèse-majesté.* The

Russian example also made itself felt at the international congress of anarchists in London in 1881. By a resolution there, the workers were recommended to study chemistry, even though Kropotkin pointed out to the participants at the congress that this was not such a simple science, and that the Russian comrades had made use of experts in this field for the manufacture of explosives.

After 1881 enthusiasm for the Russian terror ebbed quickly away, among the broad public, too, who could satisfy their appetite for reading thanks to the publication of a large number of articles and books about the sensational developments. The anarchistic 'propaganda of the deed' in the West did not have any lasting result. And even earlier the Russian miracle had turned into a nightmare. The Russian state was now once again in a position to rule out the revolutionary intelligentsia as a political factor for the coming decade. In that country too, terrorism had the effect about which Western socialists had constantly warned their own followers.[75]

Just as the Narva episode in the sixteenth century had all of a sudden revealed the entire gamut of negative views about Russia which were to remain in force until our time, so the years of Russian terrorism disclosed the patterns of Western socialist reaction to the Russian revolutionary phenomenon. This proved most apparent in the politics of the German Social Democratic Party. Most and Hasselmann were expelled in August 1880 without being given the chance to defend their viewpoint before a party forum. This was how members who linked consequences for Western socialism with their admiration for the Russian revolutionaries were dealt with. For them as for the anarchists the rules of fair play did not apply. To take the wind out of the sails of Most's *Freiheit*, the SPD leadership had started an illegal paper *Der Sozialdemokrat* in Switzerland in 1879. In it the Russian terrorists were indeed exhaustively praised, but the differences between Russia and Germany were also emphasised at length. 'In a country in which a tyranny like that in Russia holds sway ... where every possibility for the peaceful improvement of a situation which has become intolerable is excluded ... even poison and the dagger, the revolver and dynamite are valid means of bringing the sanguinary despotism to an end.'[76]

Marx refrained from open support for the terrorists because he too feared being involved with bomb-throwing liberals rather than socialists. But Bebel and Liebknecht, who had also distanced themselves publicly from the terrorists with this argument, were given a lecture. Marx's daughter Jenny wrote to her husband describing how Liebknecht received a lesson in Russia-glorification during a visit to London:

> If Bebel and Liebknecht have shown less sympathy for the Russian nihilists this is because they had altogether false conceptions of the matter and had the misfortune to meet a pack of Russian swindlers who even called themselves nihilists, with whom the continent is swarming. Fortunately Liebknecht's eyes have now been opened by papa and Hartmann; they have aroused his profound interest and pointed out to him the meaning of the Russian movement and the incomparable greatness of the true nihilist heroes.[77]

Marx had been angry because the SPD leaders received their information about Russia mainly from Russians like Plekhanov, Deutsch, Akselrod and Zasulich. They all belonged to the Black Partition and were consequently dubbed by Marx 'mere doctrinaires' and 'confused anarchist-socialists'. They were certainly not the cause of the tension within the SPD. Even the moderate defence of Russian terrorism by the party journal gave the opponents of the SPD in parliament ample opportunity for attack. Some socialist deputies therefore resented the 'radical' stand of the *Sozialdemokrat* led by the young Eduard Bernstein who was befriended with Akselrod.[78] This time the disagreements about Russian terrorism between the left and right wing of the party could easily be settled because the powerless Russian revolutionary movement for a number of years after 1881 could not cause much trouble for the Germans.

The Russian problem, however, was not resolved. Since Russia had become the revolutionary example *par excellence*, the revolutionaries of 1905 and 1917 would once more and on a far greater scale occasion violent differences of opinion among the German socialists. The same was true of the other European socialist parties. In the twentieth century too, the debate about Russia was defined by standpoints which had already emerged in the discussion about Russian terrorism. From this it became apparent that later opinions were to a great extent dictated by a relationship between socialist ideals and traditional modes of thought about Russia already laid down in the past.

## ENGELS AND THE FUTURE OF RUSSIA

The accession of Alexander III to the throne brought about a change in the political climate of Russia which directly affected the revolutionaries. While their hopes for a speedy revolution or a constitution went up in smoke, they awaited the death sentence, imprisonment or exile. A protracted twenty-year period ensued during which the opposition to tsarism slowly regrouped into three movements: the liberals, the socialist revolutionaries and the social democrats. In this respect Russia was not noticeably behind many European countries, where the formation of the modern political groupings took place at the same time. But there was one absolutely fundamental difference: the Russian autocracy remained powerful enough up to 1917 to prevent the coming into being of large-scale and tightly organised parties which elsewhere in Europe were already forming a significant element in national politics before the First World War.

It was precisely this difference which caused an especially serious problem for the Russian social democrats. Although they were completely orientated towards the West, they could in no single respect measure up to the Western socialist leaders who in the course of time acquired the backing of large parties and trade unions. It was doubly poignant that in countries with comparable political and social systems, such as the German and Austrian empires, the socialist movement contrived to develop powerfully in the teeth of repression. For the other Russian parties these problems were not so serious. The Russian liberals could console themselves with the thought that their ideals were not by any means everywhere in the West buttressed by large-scale parties. The socialist revolutionaries would continue the agrarian, anti-industrial and terrorist traditions of nineteenth-century populism. Their belief in a separate Russian road to socialism made their party the odd man out in the international labour movement and the living confirmation of the prejudices about Russia existing there. The Russian social democrats formed the living negation of this perception of Russia. They could only justify their existence by convincing others that Russia's metamorphosis into a Western, capitalist country was merely a question of time.

It was no simple task to fight against the powerful currents of opinion which labelled Russia as something unique. Nor were the Russian social democrats particularly successful here. This was partly because they could make neither themselves nor others aware that a Western-type labour party was a self-evident possibility in Russia. Those leaders of the Black Partition who were in the West, and who set up the first Russian social democratic organisation in 1883, likewise found this difficult. Plekhanov, Akselrod, Deutsch and Zasulich had not rejected the *putsch*-like terrorism of the People's Will on moral grounds, but because as followers of Lavrov and Bakunin they judged that this was not the right way to carry out a social revolution. The terrorists' actions had however opened their eyes to the importance of the political struggle. They too began to realise that a people without political freedom was in no position to change social relationships. As soon as the Black Partition distanced itself from its anarchistically slanted ideal and it had become impossible for the People's Will to engage in terrorism, there was every reason to restore unity between the two groups. But the attempts to do this failed. Among most Russian revolutionaries there was little respect for the parliamentary-reformist course of action of the German socialists. But Plekhanov and his associates who had lost their faith in the Russian peasants were impressed by the large-scale, well-organised and disciplined power formed by the SPD. In their view such a labour party was a revolutionary instrument which they ought to have at their disposal in their own country in order to combat autocracy effectively.[79]

Before anything of this kind was possible, however, it was clear that Russia would first have had to expand into a capitalist, industrial nation. Moreover the existence of this possibility was denied with great expertise by populists such as Danielson and Vorontsov. If they were right, the Russian revolutionaries ought to have been satisfied with the peasants even if sufficient reasons existed to cast doubt on their socialist qualities. The members of the Black Partition had awaited Marx's reaction to Zasulich's question about the future of the *mir* with excitement. Plekhanov's reaction to Zasulich's and Deutsch's joke was characteristic. On 1 April 1882 they let him know that Marx was with them nearby in Switzerland and that he was expecting a visit from Plekhanov. 'Georgy Valentinovich [Plekhanov] dressed up as smartly as possible and set out in the company of his friends. On the way he touched upon a series of questions which he planned to discuss with the master; among them figured one that lay nearest to Georgy Valentinovich's heart, the question of the Russian village commune.'[80] It had naturally been a disappointment to them that Marx was so non-committal and above all declared that *Das Kapital* was not relevant to Russia. However, it was Plekhanov who despite his subservient reverence for Marx had first overcome his uncertainty. As he wrote later in 1881, he nevertheless believed he had found in the works of Marx and Engels 'the Ariadne's thread' which could rescue the Russian revolutionaries from 'the labyrinth of contradictions' in which they were imprisoned.[81]

It was the *Communist Manifesto* which made Plekhanov realise that there were no differences in principle between Russia and Western Europe and that the tactics of the Russian socialists should be the same as those which Marx and Engels had recommended to the German communists in 1848. So he started in 1881 with a translation of the manifesto. At the same time he wrote to Lavrov that he considered the question of Russian socialism decided. Russia had already started on the road that prescribed 'the natural law of her development'.[82] The well-known foreword of *Das Kapital* was cited here in a peculiar and erroneous way, but Plekhanov was obviously using it to mean that capitalism was unavoidable for Russia. It is doubtful that Lavrov shared this opinion. But he did write to Marx and Engels to say that one of their 'most industrious pupils' had made a translation, and asked them for a foreword to the new Russian edition.[83]

This foreword shows clearly that Marx and Engels wanted to be less Marxist with regard to Russia than Plekhanov. They were still glowing with enthusiasm for an immediate Russian revolution. In 1848, when the *Communist Manifesto* came out, they had described Russia as still 'the last great reserve of European reaction'. Now that country formed 'the vanguard of the revolutionary movement in Europe'. The tsar, once the policeman

of the civilised world, was now a prisoner of war of the revolutionaries and was hiding in his country palace at Gatchina.
A more optimistic presentation of the facts was scarcely possible.
And on this they based their hopes that the *mir* would be able
to maintain itself in spite of 'the rapidly prospering capitalist
swindle'. 'If the Russian revolution is to become the signal for
a proletarian revolution in the West, so that each complements
the other, then present-day Russian communal ownership of
land will be able to serve as the point of departure for a communist development.' This last sentence from the foreword
betrayed the hand of Engels, who was probably its principal
author. Marx after all, without his friend's knowledge, believed
in a more autonomous development towards a specific Russian
socialism, while Engels thought this impossible without the help
of the Western working classes, who were superior to the Russian
peasants.[84]

The foreword was first published by the People's Will and
Engels was proud of this, while the terrorists naturally saw a
confirmation of populist principles in the text. After Marx's
death too, Engels remained convinced that their tactics were
right. As against Lopatin he let his opinion be known that it was
the revolutionaries' task to create so much confusion that both
state and people would be forced into social reforms: a chaos
created by revolutionaries as a basis for the revolution. This was
a recipe worthy of Bakunin. Lenin and Trotsky were to bring
it into effect in 1917. Engels also maintained, against Plekhanov
and his friends who in 1883 presented themselves as Marxists
and social democrats with a new organisation called the Liberation of Labour Group (Gruppa Osvobozhdenie Truda), that
Russia was a volcano that could erupt again at any moment.
Russia would acquire freedom of the press sooner than Germany. In vain Zasulich pointed out to him that he was deluding
himself. According to her the terrorists could well every now
and then kill 'one or two gendarmes' but were 'in no position
to strike an effective blow against despotism'.[85]

For this reason she tried to interest Engels in the propaganda
for Marxism in Russia given out by the Liberation of Labour
Group and particularly for Plekhanov's polemic against the
populists. Engels certainly was impressed by Plekhanov's theoretical considerations. He remarked to Kautsky that he found
the work brilliant but considered every attack on members of

the People's Will altogether wrong. Engels wrote to Zasulich that he was proud that a Marxist party had emerged among Russian youth which joined battle with anarchic and Slavophile trends. 'Marx's historical theory is in my opinion the basic condition of all *coherent and consistent* revolutionary tactics; to discover these tactics one needs only to apply the theory to the economic and political circumstances of the countries concerned.' Engels gave the interpretation of the little word 'only' in the rest of the letter: 'If ever Blanquism – the fantasy of turning over an entire society through the action of a tiny group of sworn conspirators – had a certain *raison d'être* it was undoubtedly in Petersburg.' According to Engels it mattered little who was to make the hole in the dike which would allow the tidal wave of revolution to flow over the country. 'The people who prided themselves in having *made* a revolution have however always seen on the day after that they did not know what they were doing, that the revolution actually *made* was nothing like the one they wanted to make. Hegel calls this the irony of history . . .'[86]

True words, but, in that case, what was the function of the carefully laid down revolutionary tactics based on Marx's historical theory? It must have been baffling for the Liberation of Labour Group that Engels now seemed to maintain the opposite of what he had argued ten years before in his criticism of the Blanquist Tkachov. For, together with the foreword to the Russian edition of the *Communist Manifesto*, these articles formed the only public pronouncements about Russia from the two fathers of 'scientific socialism'. And precisely because of Engels's polemic with Tkachov the Russian social democrats had felt themselves supported from behind, for it was argued there that in Russia too a socialist revolution must be sustained by a social class and could not be achieved by a handful of intellectuals. Engels once more created the impression that he considered the outbreak of a Russian revolution so essential for Europe that he did not wish to apply the same standards to it as to a revolution in the West.[87] Zasulich could only write to Engels that in Russia 'nowadays even the most ardent Blanquist can do nothing other than make propaganda'.[88] But she apparently realised that she would not be taken seriously by Engels. Akselrod best expressed the group's disappointment in words: 'I am convinced that even the most fervent opponents of Bakuninism and Blanquism

among the [Western] social democrats are ready to be reconciled
to the one thing or the other in Russia and even to greet the
devil enthusiastically if he could only succeed in making them
believe in his power to have done with Russian absolutism and
to relieve the civilised world from this bulwark of reaction.'[89]

All the same, Engels was to change his mind too. The Russian
revolution failed to occur, and he became increasingly concerned
about an impending European war which, according to the
confident conviction of the socialists, could not be averted.
Moreover he had never to the same extent as Marx been taken
with the idea of a separate Russian road to socialism. The
vigorous industrial growth which Russia experienced in the
1880s and 1890s also in his eyes made such a thing extremely
improbable. He put this view forward more and more overtly
in the exhaustive and courteous correspondence he took up
after Marx's death with Danielson, who also translated the
second volume of *Das Kapital* brought out by Engels. According
to Engels the huge increase in the forces of production in
countries that had until recently been purely agricultural, was
one of the most remarkable developments of the last thirty years.
Russia was in this way caught up in a world-wide process and
no longer formed an exception. Danielson, who stuck to his old
opinions, was naturally not in agreement. But Engels brushed
aside his remark about Russia's poor competitive position on
the world market with a reference to the protectionist policy of
the German government. Russia could do the same. Marx had
said that the *mir* would be sentenced to death if capitalism
obtained a firm foothold in Russia. 'I fear that we must regard
the *obshchina* as a dream about a past never to return and reckon
for the future on a capitalist Russia.' And in the event progress
was thereby served, thought Engels.[90]

Danielson refused to understand this remark. Capitalism
possessed no basis for an autonomous development in Russia.
He referred Engels to Marx, who had, after all, regarded it as
a blessing that Russia had at her disposal the possibility of
skipping capitalism. According to Engels, however, his friend
had only believed in the possibility on condition that capitalism
in the West was destroyed and Russia would experience this
change in the European economy as 'a jolt from the outside'.
Engels did recognise that capitalism had caused even greater
misery in Russia than in the West. 'But history is after all the

most cruel *vsech bogin* [of all goddesses] and she drives her victory chariot over mountains of corpses ...'[91]

Engels's standpoint had in effect come very close to that of the Liberation of Labour Group. Nevertheless, the Russian social democrats had up till then been obliged to manage with virtually no support from Engels, although for a decade they had devoted themselves unreservedly in the most difficult possible circumstances to the dissemination of Marxism in Russia. In this they had not so far registered much result. Engels did admit to Zasulich in 1890 that populism – the belief in the specific destiny of a people – ought to be challenged. But to another Russian correspondent he complained that 'passages from Marx's writings and letters have been interpreted by different groups of Russian emigrants in a most contradictory way, exactly like the texts of the classics or the New Testament'.[92]

While Engels complained about the 'exaggerated belief in recognised authorities'[93] of the Russians, he was chiefly irritated by the constant bickering between the populists and the Marxists. He would have nothing to do with the pedantic tournament Plekhanov was conducting using Marxist dogmas. He thought him just as much a troublemaker as the British Marxist Hyndman and feared that the Russian Marxists, just like the British, would remain an impotent little group of sectarians. In a lengthy article he once more expounded his old standpoint that the pernicious and powerful influence in Europe of tsarist Russia – bent on world rule – was still strong enough to prevent the final triumph of the working classes. Russia was the main source of international tensions that could lead to a European war the outcome of which no one could predict but which would surpass all earlier wars in carnage and scope. The Russian revolution remained a sort of *conditio sine qua non* for a socialist Europe. Engels presumably thought that such an important affair could not be handed over to the current generation of quarrelling Russian revolutionaries. On the other hand, he was afraid that a public choice by himself for one group or the other would weaken the movement rather than strengthen it.[94]

The Russian social democrats could, however, with reason complain to him that their work was hampered to a considerable extent because populists like Danielson also appealed to Marx. Not until the years following the famine of 1891, which shook the opposition movement awake again, did a generation of

Marxists emerge in Russia which could alter the anti-capitalist mentality of the intelligentsia. The signs of the times had become so apparent in the last years of the nineteenth century that belief in a Russian capitalism could no longer be undermined. But in Engels's lifetime this outcome was not yet certain.

The Russian social democrats continued their efforts to get Engels on to their side. Engels still refused to do so openly. He congratulated Danielson in a friendly way on his success with a book about the impossibility of Russian capitalism and even negotiated plans for a German translation.[95] In these years Plekhanov prepared a major philosophical treatise against populism. Engels's articles against Tkachov especially, proved their worth here. Plekhanov cleverly pointed out to Engels how right he had been at the time. Nowadays populism was only a reactionary philosophy. Even populists like Danielson based their hopes for the practical implementation of their economic ideas on the Russian authorities. 'Socialism created by Russian *ispravniki* [police inspectors] – what a chimera!'[96] It was precisely now that influencing the generation growing up in Russia had a good chance of success. Because of this it was exasperating that people like Danielson could pose as Marxists and that writers like Mikhailovsky misused Marx's well-known letter, which had been put about in Russia thanks to Engels, as a banner for his cause.

Engels acknowledged that there was nothing to be done about Danielson. 'It is absolutely impossible to carry on a controversy with the generation of Russians to which he belongs and which in spite of everything believes in a spontaneous communist mission which will distinguish the true *Svyataya Rus* [Sacred Russia] from other, untrustworthy, peoples.'[97] Meanwhile Zasulich had translated his old articles against Tkachov and Engels declared himself ready to add an epilogue to them. This was Engels's last publication about Russia, but here too he refused to make a choice between populists and social democrats. He did not hazard a judgement on the meaning of the *mir*. It did not matter so much either, he thought, whether Russia attained socialism via the village commune or via capitalism. In either case a Russian revolution would bring nearer the victory of the modern industrial proletariat in the West, without which any form of Russian socialism was inconceivable.[98]

Naturally Engels could not proclaim that the differences between Russia and Europe would disappear in the foreseeable future without publicly abandoning Marx. Probably he himself was not fully of this opinion, because it had some most unattractive aspects. The possibility of a speedy Russian revolution was lost. If Russia was to develop peacefully from a barbaric country into a normal one like Germany, then it would also be increasingly unlikely that the signal for the liberation of the Western proletariat would be given from the East. The possibility of a gradual modernisation of Russia was by preference not seriously contemplated by Western socialists and Russian revolutionaries because that would entail cancelling all the accounts they had to settle with the future. Now the idea that Russia could make up for her lost ground with a single jump had lost much of its force, Engels could again give outspoken expression to Western European feelings of superiority. But on the other hand the future, if autocracy continued in existence, looked so sombre that he also dared not reject the populist scenario for the overthrow of the political and social order in Russia as entirely outdated and unworkable.

Uncertainty thus defined in large measure Engels's judgement of Russia and that had also been true for Marx, whose expectations had been pitched even higher. Precisely for this reason his pronouncements are always regarded as something special. Subsequent generations of Marxists have been irritated by them or tried to play them down. Opponents of communism and of the Soviet state have played them out triumphantly. Still others particularly admired 'the revolutionary pragmatism of a man ever ready to re-think his basic views in the light of practical developments', and saw in it support for their view that Russia had always been different and would have to go her own way after 1917 too.[99] If one views the variegated series of pronouncements of Marx and Engels as an isolated phenomenon, then some of them can hardly be interpreted otherwise than as meaningless aberrations from the core of their thinking or as remarkable manifestations of their versatility of mind. But when they are placed, as we have attempted here, in the framework of their time and of the traditional European way of thinking about Russia, then they lose much of their originality and seem characteristic rather than exceptional.

After Marx and Engels socialists, who hardly knew their work, would still believe with many of their contemporaries that tsarist Russia formed a permanent and serious threat for the civilised world. At the same time people expected much from Russia. Not only in the speculations of socialists, but also in those of numerous politicians, diplomats, army officers and intellectuals Russia formed the great, uncertain, mysterious and unknown factor on which so infinitely much could depend. Socialists, through their high social ideals, could more easily follow in the footsteps of the eighteenth-century Pietists, Leibniz or the French *philosophes*. As soon as turbulent events in Russia provided the occasion, the idea that an ideal society could more easily be brought into being in this primitive country than in the extremely complex society of the West acquired enormous canvassing power. Socialists were then also prepared to declare their solidarity with Russian revolutionaries, who used methods which were rejected as criminal in the West. The twentieth century was in this respect to be no different from the nineteenth.

# 3

# RUSSIAN AND WESTERN SOCIAL DEMOCRACY 1890–1905

The fact that the tsarist autocracy, after a short democratic intermezzo of eight months' duration, was followed in 1917 by a new dictatorship, never aroused much surprise in the West. European political freedom did not fit into one's image of Russia. What did seem to be a paradox was that the Bolshevik regime had elevated Marxism into a guiding principle, for Marx's teaching was after all, in many people's view, pre-eminently a theory about social revolution in the Western industrialised world, and not about that in the poor, backward agrarian East. If one wanted to deny the existence of such a paradox it was possible to argue that Marx's work contained solid elements which facilitated the formulation of a Marxist strategy for a developing country. This last idea had of course been disseminated from the very beginning by the first Russian social democrats. But they felt they were continually being forced on to the defensive by socialists in and out of Russia who refused to believe that there was room for such a Western phenomenon as a social democratic party in that country.

The endless discussions of this problem among Russian social democrats, both between themselves and with their Western and Russian critics, also influenced the views of later historians who wrote about this movement. Their main conclusion was that, independently from the ideas of the socialists of the time, one could actually point out objective causes which had made the introduction of Marxism into Russia more difficult. Leonard Schapiro summed these up in his *History of the Communist Party of the Soviet Union*. Firstly, even in comparison with the Western Europe of 1848, Russian capitalism around 1890 was still in its infancy. The number of workers was small, even negligible in proportion to the overwhelmingly large peasant masses. It would be a long time before a proletarian majority had built itself up, this being according to Marx a prerequisite for a social revolution. Secondly, the peasants were not interested in socialism but in land. Giving it to them in order to gain their co-operation in the revolution was in conflict with its principal aim: the nationalisation of the means of production. Thirdly, in contrast with Germany or England around 1890, there were no middle-class parties or political freedoms in Russia. The opportunity to organise the proletariat was therefore more or less totally lacking. Moreover, supposing Russian capitalism were indeed to create a kind of political liberalism, would social democracy then have to wait passively until this middle-class party had completed something like a 'bourgeois revolution'? Or would the socialists have to try, with all the risks of such an action, to join battle with the liberals and autocracy at the same time?[1]

On further consideration it is doubtful whether these circumstances were so uniquely Russian and whether, in comparison with the situation in Western Europe, they did seriously hinder the spread of Marxism. In 1914 Russia had already outstripped France in important sectors of industrial production, while in 1848, with the exception of England and Belgium, an economic revolution had occurred virtually nowhere.[2] Moreover it is not certain that workers are always more enthusiastic for socialism than peasants. The Belgian labour party, at its foundation in 1885, carefully avoided mentioning the word socialism. In any case the agricultural situation in Spain, Italy, Finland or Hungary had much in common with that in Russia, and parties with Marxist-tinged programmes came into being in those countries, too. Even in Germany and Holland relations with the farmers had become a source of acute differences of opinion between socialists. Co-operation with the 'bourgeois' parties was everywhere one of the greatest problems of socialist politics before 1914. The 'bourgeois revolution', that is to say the setting up of a parliamentary democratic republic, had not yet been accomplished in most European countries. Socialists often had to fight a dogged struggle for the universal franchise and battle against all kinds of obstacles which stood in the way of the free development of a socialist labour movement within a state and society which was still partly 'feudal'. These difficulties constituted just as much a stimulus as an impediment to socialism, which now embodied the social protest against the existing order and was preaching its overthrow. The opposition which socialists encountered confirmed that their point of view was right, and was not infrequently a prerequisite for the success of their movement.[3]

Because of this the proposition that the absence of civil freedom and industrial development hindered the growth of Marxism and socialism has been reversed under the motto 'no feudalism, no socialism'. America seems to be a living proof of this, though of course this point of view has also been opposed. It has even been asserted that conditions for the workers in the United States were no better and social mobility was no greater than in Europe, yet socialist ideas found acceptance in the New World and were to some extent realised. This did not occur via a socialist party, but the struggle for the social welfare state in Europe had never been an exclusively socialist field of activity, either. It remains a fact, however, that the sanguine expectations about American socialism which were alive amongst European socialists were never fulfilled.[4] The future has nowhere actually become what the socialists imagined. They had just as much reason for amazement about what did not happen in America as for what did happen in Russia. But the vicissitudes of socialism and Marxism in Western Europe were fundamentally no less remarkable. Our part of the world had been the cradle of these 'isms' and the Western socialists believed with rock-solid confidence that their ideals could first be realised there. Perhaps this was why they were challenged by their political opponents with such fearful intensity. Nevertheless, around 1900 Western socialism gave no grounds for grave concern. In fact the situation was at the time nowhere such that immediate danger threatened of a revolution led by a socialist party.

England had served as a model for *Das Kapital* and had thus already made it clear to the world how much social misery an industrial revolution could cause. The ideal of equality had never been elevated there, as it was in America, into a national dream which could supplant the idea of socialism. But to the dismay of Marx and Engels the British workers proved somewhat insensitive to the socialist gospel. The class-ridden society of

Britain offered optimal prospects for them to be organised. But the members of the powerful British trade unions were politically orientated rather towards liberalism or even conservatism. The Labour Party developed exceptionally late and slowly into an independent current in British politics and in 1914 held only 42 of the 670 seats in the House of Commons. Not until 1918 did this party have a programme which could be called socialist. Naturally this was never realised in full. Marxism seemed to be a non-starter in England. It was even rejected by the most prominent socialist intellectuals, who proudly called themselves Fabians. Hyndman's Social Democratic Federation never outgrew the stature and mentality of a sect and still less did it make any original contribution to Marxism. This was while, in the period before 1914, very large groups of workers were repeatedly involved in unofficial strikes and appeared to be averse to social pacifism.

In France, which economically speaking was behind England, but which besides the universal franchise had a glorious revolutionary and socialist tradition, things were in no better shape. Hyndman's kindred spirits Guesde and Lafargue were certainly Marxists of somewhat greater stature and they were more successful. But the SFIO (Section Française de l'Internationale Ouvrière), the unified French socialist party into which their faction was absorbed in 1905, was never Marxist and before 1914 had never more than 90,000 members. This party did not gain its greatest following from the workers. The French proletariat, in so far as its inclinations were socialist and revolutionary, did not take kindly to politics and joined the revolutionary syndicalist trade union movement. In short, in countries where, in comparison with Russia, social democrats were in an ideal situation to organise the proletariat, other circumstances evidently existed which reduced the influence of Marxism almost to nil. Already in 1905, when the revolution broke out in Russia, every Marxist in France or England had good reason to be jealous of the barbaric East where Marxism had such sway over socialist theory and praxis.

They could of course also be envious of the Marxist Sozialdemokratische Partei Deutschlands or SPD, which in this period appeared to control the international socialist stage in a majestic fashion. The Germans did indeed distinguish themselves from their French and British comrades by their *Gründlichkeit* (thoroughness) and *Tüchtigkeit* (efficiency). In 1914 their party formed an impressive ideological and organisational unit with a million members supported by 2 million trade union members. Thanks to 4 million voters, the SPD was the largest political group within the Reichstag. So on the face of it, the empire of Kaiser Wilhelm, that peculiar mixture of old and new, where an archaic power structure maintained itself thanks to hyper-modern industry and technology, appears to have been the ideal breeding ground for a social democratic movement. Every worker in Germany had good reason to feel himself a pariah and to seek refuge in socialism. Nevertheless, the success of the SPD was to a large extent nothing but show. Many critics of the socialist scene indicated at the time that the influence of the SPD, in view of the impotence of the German parliament, was not impressive. Perhaps more important still was the fact that even the large electorate of the party constituted only about a third of the German 'working class', which as a whole made up not much more than a quarter of the population. The workers who voted for the party were by and large skilled artisans from small businesses in small towns. The greatest Marxist party in the world did not outgrow these provincial and artisan surround-ings before 1914. It was not capable of mobilising the 1,200,000 workers who could be counted as the 'real' factory proletariat in the big cities and who were thus, according to its own teaching, the salt of the earth.[5]

In other words, not only in Russia, but elsewhere as well, Marxists were faced with insurmountable difficulties whenever they tried to organise 'the' proletariat into the revolutionary power of the future. Whatever their expectations may have been for their own country or abroad, the chance of uniting a pro-letarian majority of the population under the Marxist banner in fact existed nowhere. This situation throws a curious light on the function of Marxist ideology. Political parties were the result of socio-economic changes and of the intellectual climate of the nineteenth century, in which comprehensive views of mankind played an important role. The more insignificant the influence of a particular party was, the greater its need for ideological legitimisation. Socialist parties were moreover no ordinary politi-cal parties, but emancipation and opposition movements.

Socialists wanted to change the world totally. They gave the impression that they wanted to take over power in order never to have to relinquish it. It was understandable that, around 1890 when most socialist parties were being set up, Marxism possessed something irresistible. It professed after all to provide not only a complete world view, but also the analytical apparatus with which history (and thus the future) could be fathomed. In this way it seemed possible to determine the strategy of the movement in a scientific manner. At the same time, however, Marxism was such an abstract, complicated and obscure theory, full of concepts with a magical sound, that its truth or falsity could only with difficulty be demonstrated. It was a kind of secular faith which was not challenged by the vast majority of Western social democrats, but not passionately acknowledged either. Life was mostly stronger than this teaching which was more often used to justify a practice than to determine it. When a few decades later the principal maxims of Marxism had, in the eyes of many people, lost even the appearance of being tenable, it was silently dismissed by Western European social democracy.

The creation of Marxism as a party ideology was the work of a tiny group of Marx's and Engels's followers. The most important of these was Kautsky, who found the SPD a fertile area of activity because its most distinguished leaders likewise considered themselves pupils of Marx and Engels. But it is doubtful if Marxism contributed more to the SPD than the jargon for certain theoretical discussions. Members of parliament and other officials of the party or the trade union repeatedly made their contempt for theorising apparent and thus did not much care for doctrine. For the average party member Marxism was heavy and indigestible fare. The Scandinavian parties and those of Holland, Switzerland, Italy, Austria, Finland and Hungary, which had accepted the SPD programme set up by Kautsky as their ideological guideline, did not give the impression that Marxism had become the indispensable leaven of socialist politics. The predominantly reformist trend of these parties could if necessary certainly have been made legitimate by Marxism, but one did not really need Marxism to do this. The number of Western socialists who were Marxist to the bone and were able to express this in an original way remained very small. It was only in Kautsky's native Austria, and to a lesser extent in

Holland, that intellectual currents of any scope which tried to develop Marxism further came into being.[6]

In comparison with this, the introduction of Marxism into Russia was a resounding success. The Liberation of Labour Group saw the chance of winning almost an entire generation of young revolutionaries to Marxism. Here, anyway, it could be claimed, the differences between Russia and Europe were of decisive importance. The striking phenomenon of an intellectually brilliant though socially rootless cultural elite was seen by contemporaries and historians as a product of Russia's backwardness. This view lost its cogency when in the 1960s characteristics typical of the Russian revolutionary intelligentsia reappeared among youthful radicals in modern welfare states under tolerant, democratic governments. Nor was the Russian intelligentsia unique in the nineteenth century, which had experienced a Young Italy and a Young Germany. Young intellectuals were to play an important role in the rise of socialism and anarchism in the West. There too the antithesis between the workers and the 'gentlemen' who offered to lead and civilise them was ubiquitous.

Yet the differences between Russia and Europe in this case were indeed an important factor, though this was chiefly because of the specific manner in which they were experienced by Russian intellectuals. For it was only in Russia that the intelligentsia could have the feeling that the acceptance of Marxism was a definitive and decisive choice for a Western future for their country. This choice forced them to give up their hope for a specific Russian socialism. The Russian Marxists no longer believed that immediate solutions for Russian problems existed, although these were far greater and more urgent than in any other European country. This gave their decision to become Marxist a significance which it could not have for any one else in Western Europe.

Such a fanatical belief in a distant future would have unexpected results for the founders of Russian Marxism. In 1917 Plekhanov, Akselrod and Zasulich were shocked to see how the concept of 'the dictatorship of the proletariat' was turned into a tyranny over the Russian workers by their former pupils. But in fact they themselves had twenty years before created the wind that was to blow up into this revolutionary storm. Marxism was something that could only be made use of by intellectuals. Workers not only in Russia but everywhere else as well would never manage to make much of it. Marxism in the view of Plekhanov and his friends was exclusively a means of awakening the consciousness of the proletariat. Nevertheless, the intellectuals were the public for whom they were writing and whom in the first instance they wished to convince. Since populism determined the thoughts of the Russian revolutionaries, Russian Marxism developed out of a debate of many years' standing with this ideology. Russian Marxism was in the first place Plekhanov's brainchild and it was thanks to his passionate temperament and biting pen that it acquired such voluntarist and maximalist traits. These were foreign to Kautsky's ideas but still very reminiscent of the populist way of thinking from which Marxism had cut itself off so firmly and dogmatically.

This defined the peculiar character and originality of Russian Marxism. The Liberation of Labour Group, unlike most European Marxists, could not fall back on the templates constructed by Kautsky, for these were not yet there. The group was set up in the same year as *Die Neue Zeit* was founded (1883). Kautsky's periodical was only after some time to be recognised as the authoritative forum for international Marxism. The SPD first became a Marxist party in 1891 thanks to the Erfurt programme designed by Kautsky, and as such the great example for social democrats elsewhere. Russian Marxism was thus an independent creation. The Liberation of Labour Group, however, was not proud of this. The group wanted its Marxism to be accepted as an orthodox creed. Both in the West and in Russia the fact that something like a doctrine could only with the greatest difficulty be distilled out of the works of Marx and Engels was glossed over. The opposition in Russia had always fought the government with foreign doctrines and had a definite need to lean on Western authorities. In no single country in Europe was Kautsky to gain so much influence as in Russia.

The Russian social democrats were glad to emphasise to the Western public the similarities between their movement and those in the West. They could do so because the writings of the Russian Marxists remained to a large extent unread in the West. Marx and Engels had taken the trouble to learn Russian, their followers in general neglected to do so. The Liberation of Labour

Group did not boast of the success of Marxism in Russia; after all, it was concerned with the conversion of workers, not intellectuals. Moreover the intellectual quality of Russian Marxism revealed itself primarily in an endless stream of conflicts and quarrels with the populists and among themselves. The Russian social democrats were soon to notice that their Western comrades did not automatically opt for Russians who presented themselves as the most orthodox Marxists. As far as Russia was concerned the European socialists like their contemporaries did not easily supersede traditional preferences and sympathies.

## RUSSIAN SOCIAL DEMOCRACY HAS TO PROVE ITS RIGHT TO EXIST

The Russian social democrats were repeatedly to discover that their party would not be accepted as a self-evident component of European socialism. The first occasion when this problem arose on an international scale was the foundation of the Second International in 1889. Engels had asked the Liberation of Labour Group through Lafargue to attend the congress to be held in Paris with this end in view. This was actually to teach Lavrov a lesson, for he had refused to make his contribution to the struggle which had immediately broken out to put the new International under Marxist supervision.[7] Plekhanov, and probably Akselrod as well, were thus witness to the laborious reunification of European socialism which took place exactly a century after the storming of the Bastille. Plekhanov contributed to the symbolic significance of the moment by opening up a prospect on the Russian revolution in a short, but from a propagandist point of view, subtle speech. He referred to the familiar image of Russia as the reactionary policeman of Europe and once more advanced the old thesis that the victory of the Russian revolutionary movement would also herald the liberation of the European workers. Then he tried to convince his audience that his country was no European China in which economic life was at a standstill. Whatever the populist economists had to say on the subject, it was certain that the *mir*, which had also become an object of unbridled mystification in the Western socialist press, was being destroyed by capitalism. A 'schwärmerisch' (romantically enthusiastic) student youth could not form a rev-

olutionary movement. 'Finally I repeat and emphasise: the revolutionary movement in Russia will be victorious as a workers'
movement or it will never be victorious.'[8]

According to Liebknecht, the editor of the German congress
proceedings, Plekhanov's words were received with great
enthusiasm and he left the podium 'to deafening applause'.
However, Lavrov had spoken before him to 'repeated boisterous
acclamation' and Plekhanov's argument had been undermined
by the appearance of the populist Bek on behalf of the People's
Will. Lavrov proved at the congress that he was still the most
authoritative Russian socialist, who for this reason was also elected into the presidium and the council of the congress. His
speech was published in Benoît Malon's *La Revue Socialiste*, a
more authoritative paper than the still illegal *Sozialdemokrat* in
which Plekhanov's address was printed. Moreover in 1890 the
German paper published an attack by Bek on the Russian social
democrats. When after the abolition of the anti-socialist legislation *Vorwärts* was able to appear as the official organ of the SPD,
Liebknecht as general editor passed over the Russian Marxists
and secretly asked Lavrov and his kindred spirit Rusanov to be
anonymous correspondents for Russian affairs. Only a quick-
tempered youngster, Clara Zetkin, expressed indignation about
this.[9]

The socialist press in the West continued to show a preference
for typically Russian subjects such as nihilism and literature both
of which gained ample attention. It was very characteristic that
the important French paper *La Revue Socialiste* never devoted
any attention to the Russian Marxists. In 1892 it did publish an
interview with a Russian 'nihilist' which was surrounded by the
appropriate aura of romantic secrecy. It was explained that
Russian nihilism and Western anarchy had nothing to do with
each other. This belief was also readily put forward by the British
Marxist Hyndman. His hero was the Russian emigrant Stepnyak,
then in England, who had killed Mezentsev, the head of the
Russian security police, with a dagger. Stepnyak became widely
known for his books about the revolutionary movement and the
peasants.[10]

The Austrian party leader Victor Adler did translate into
German one of Stepnyak's books, which had originally appeared
in Italian. The book was published with Kautsky's help by Dietz.
Kautsky himself gave Stepnyak the opportunity to explain his

point of view about terrorism in *Die Neue Zeit*, although he must have known that his good friend Akselrod held different views on this question. Stepnyak took it for granted that terrorism resulted from a lack of political freedom. Therefore in the West it was the wrong weapon, while in Russia it could be used daily with impunity. Only after Stepnyak did the Russian Marxists get their chance in Kautsky's journal. Bebel, however, wrote to Kautsky that Plekhanov's articles did not increase the topicality or the popularity of the *Die Neue Zeit*. *Vorwärts* likewise ignored the contributions of Russian social democrats in *Die Neue Zeit* or attributed them with deliberate carelessness to Lavrov.[11]

Victor Adler, in his introduction to Stepnyak's book about the Russian peasants, did however place himself behind Plekhanov. But Kautsky wanted to revise this text. In his view Plekhanov had never maintained that the liberation of Russia could only be accomplished by the workers. 'My conviction is that the revol.[-utionary] intellectuals, the lower middle class and the peasantry must work together in the next revolution, the proletariat is too weak to accomplish it alone (in a certain sense this is also true for the whole of Europe, apart from England).'[12] Kautsky showed more insight into the nuances of Russian Marxism than Adler. The peasants and the *petite bourgeoisie* were not, however, essential categories in Plekhanov's revolutionary sociology.[13] Kautsky was later repeatedly to show that he would not always let himself be convinced by his Russian friends. Adler on the other hand had reproduced the essence of their propaganda, but his remarks about the 'rapidly developing, class-conscious and revolutionary proletariat' in Russia must have almost embarrassed them.[14] In their publications they had indeed created the impression that the Russian workers had adopted Western social democratic principles as their own. But the Liberation of Labour Group had had to abandon its participation in the Brussels congress of the International in 1891 because it could produce no Russian mandate whatever. In spite of this Plekhanov nevertheless decided to go to the next congress in 1893, even though he had to appear there as a delegate for a couple of sympathisers in New York.[15]

Plekhanov's qualities as a theoretician had already been wholeheartedly recognised by Engels and Kautsky, but via the congress of Zürich in 1893 he was to achieve recognition in a wider circle as an adversary of anarchism. The battle of the International with these heretical comrades went on unabated and the inclination to depict one's personal opponent as a sort of anarchist was fairly general in socialist circles. The Liberation of Labour Group was no exception to this. It had deeply offended the Russian populists by reporting to the Brussels conference of the International that the *narodniki* were still under the spell of Bakunin. The Polish social democrats were depicted in the same vein. Its leader Jogiches, an arch-manipulator, had aroused Akselrod's and Plekhanov's aggression to such an extent, that he was described by them in a letter to Engels as a 'Nechayev in miniature'.[16] Rosa Luxemburg, who also belonged to this group, could not be accused of anarchism because she rejected the idea of Poland's independence with strictly Marxist arguments. But Plekhanov united himself with the nationalist Polish socialists in order to exclude her from the congress. Plekhanov and Akselrod had their doubts about the patriotism and anti-Semitism which cropped up among these Poles. But the traditional pro-Polish sentiments of the Western socialists were not to be underestimated and the Russian Marxists did not wish at any price to be branded as Russian chauvinists.[17]

This was again clearly evident when Plekhanov took up the cudgels at the congress against Domela Nieuwenhuis. The Dutch socialist leader, who in recent years had presented himself more and more as an anarchist, had, because of his merciless criticism of the SPD's parliamentary reformism, brought the anger of Bebel and Liebknecht upon himself. His suggestion of responding to the outbreak of a European war with a general strike was now under discussion at the congress. As representative of the preliminary committee Plekhanov pointed out that Nieuwenhuis's concept could only have occurred to the inhabitant of a small country with no military tradition worthy of mention. In France and Germany a general strike would lead to an immediate suppression of all protestors for peace. And suppose, argued Plekhanov, that such an action should unexpectedly succeed, then the war would be won by the country with the weakest labour movement. That country would of course be Russia. The European 'civilised nations' would be delivered up to the Russian Cossacks. 'Russian despotism would sweep away our entire culture, and in place of the freedom of the proletariat for which the military strike ought to be a glorious beacon, the Russian

knout would hold sway.' Plekhanov therefore welcomed the
resolution introduced by the Germans, in which they only made
generalisations and nothing concrete was suggested, as 'truly
revolutionary' and in the interests of 'freedom, civilisation and
the revolutionary proletariat'. In this way he did the Germans'
dirty work for them, but at the same time created the impression
that the Russian workers, whom he wrote and spoke about in
such enthusiastic terms, were in absolutely no fit state to undertake anything against Russian autocracy.[18]

Domela Nieuwenhuis's response did indeed prove how little
the Dutch understood the fears of the inhabitants of large nations
which manifested themselves in the image of Russia, and how
easily they were able to appoint themselves as the promoters of
international interests. Nieuwenhuis showed that 'Hollanditis'
was an old disease. Plekhanov's scaremongering with Russia (and
Bebel according to Nieuwenhuis had expressed himself in a
similar way in the Reichstag) 'is like frightening a small child
with the bogeyman'. Germany had despots exactly like those in
Russia. 'Is it not laughable to call Russia the stronghold of
brutality and barbarism, as if Germany were a stronghold of
education and gentility?' One only needed to ask the French
for their opinion of Germany. A Cossack invasion would not be
all that bad if the capitalist bourgeoisie were to suffer from it.
This kind of language had not been heard since the days of
Coeurderoy; and the Pole Mendelsohn, Liebknecht and Adler
assaulted Nieuwenhuis with a torrent of words in which,
however, not a single new argument emerged. In the end it was
evident that the majority of the French delegation supported
the Dutch proposal. Plekhanov asked them haughtily whether
they so greatly underestimated the Russian danger that they,
like the French bourgeoisie, could lend a helping hand to the
tsar, 'the murderer of Poland'.[19]

This was very strange reasoning and it is not surprising that
the French reacted with a thorough disruption of the meeting.
Even the non-socialist press in France resented Plekhanov's
words. The campaign especially in the paper *Le Temps* led to a
trial and the deportation of Plekhanov and Zasulich from France
where they then lived. But at the congress the German resolution
was accepted and Plekhanov had earned for himself the esteem
of Bebel and Liebknecht. Liebknecht let him know that every-

thing he wrote would be published in *Vorwärts*. Adler, too, asked him for contributions for *Arbeiterzeitung*. At the beginning of 1894 Richard Fischer, the German social democrat, asked Plekhanov to write a leaflet against anarchy. This pamphlet, which was printed by the publisher of *Vorwärts* under the title *Anarchismus und Sozialismus* and soon afterwards translated into English, French and Italian, definitively confirmed Plekhanov's fame as a Marxist theoretician.[20] All this did not mean that the Liberation of Labour Group's image of Russia also gained acceptance. After Plekhanov's appearance Liebknecht had explained in Zürich: 'Given Russian circumstances in Germany, there would be nothing left for our German social democrats but the tactics of the nihilists'[21] – this at a time when Plekhanov had several months earlier in an open letter very explicitly tried to show him the necessity of a social democratic movement in Russia. Even after the congress, *Vorwärts* carried another enthusiastic report about a paper which had been brought out in London by a group of youthful supporters of the People's Will. Akselrod therefore thought that Plekhanov ought to try to make it clear to 'the old man', namely Liebknecht, that in this way he was giving moral support to 'our miniature Nieuwenhuises, Mosts and all possible intriguers'.[22]

The absence of spectacular manifestations of workers' protest and of a workers' movement in Russia induced the Russian Marxists to write articles about social, economic and cultural processes which in their opinion would undermine the feudal structure of their country and hasten the downfall of autocracy. In *Die Neue Zeit* Akselrod drew attention to the progressive Westernisation of the Russian bourgeoisie and the sharply increasing demand for knowledge even in the lowest strata of the population, which had been met by the circulation of cheap literature. This sympathetic interest in the emergence of moderate liberal movements in Russia indicated a change in the political orientation of the Liberation of Labour Group which was to have far-reaching consequences. The Russian social democrats in determining their tactics would continually have to consider what significance this gradual evolution of Russia towards a Western society could have. It was self-evident that here was a source of serious misunderstandings, and this soon became apparent. In the West the Europeanisation of Russia was primarily a problem which held the interest of the right wing of the political spectrum. The left was still waiting for sensational, revolutionary events, and analyses like those of Akselrod caused no amazement.[23]

The joy of the Liberation of Labour Group was undoubtedly great when something seemed to be happening in Russia. In May 1896, 30,000 textile workers in St Petersburg stopped work. To a modest extent this strike was the result of agitation by the social democratic combat leagues in the capital with which the emigrants were in contact. The violent industrial disorders led to some reduction of the extremely long working hours. Potresov, one of the young social democrats from the capital who was temporarily resident in the West, wrote an enthusiastic article for *Vorwärts* about the strike which in his view showed how deeply revolutionary feelings had penetrated the masses. Nihilism had come to an end and been replaced by a modern labour movement. In *Arbeiterzeitung* Victor Adler devoted words of equal import to the news from Russia. Vera Zasulich, who was then living in England, met with great sympathy for the Russian strikers from Eleanor Marx and the trade unions. The British also took a great deal of trouble to help them actively by means of collections. Zasulich, who, like so many foreign socialists before and after her, was disconcerted by the complete lack of revolutionary zeal among the British workers and thus tempered the Liberation of Labour Group's initially unbridled veneration of the Western proletariat, now wrote a joyful letter to her friends on the continent.

The behaviour of the British trade union leaders, who at the close of a meeting drank champagne with her at the bar to the welfare of the Russian workers, was indeed in sharp contrast to Liebknecht's cautious attitude. His paper devoted quite as much attention to a Russian student protest at the St Petersburg senior school of forestry against the coronation of the tsar as to the strike. Liebknecht had promised Plekhanov he would do everything for the strikers, but an appeal for financial support in *Vorwärts* was formulated in such a way as to preclude almost any inclination to give. And hardly any money was forthcoming. Liebknecht, who once, standing before a map of Europe, had confided to Akselrod his fears about the pressure of the gigantic land mass of Russia upon Germany, told him frankly some time later that the workers' strikes in Russia had been in vain. He saw more benefit in student riots, the expressions of Russian protest more familiar to Western socialists.[24]

But the congress of the Second International in London in 1896 recognised for the first time the importance of Russian social democracy. The seven-man-strong Russian delegation had proudly armed itself with mandates from Russia, and was able to draw the congress's attention to the progress of their movement. Akselrod solemnly had this fact established in a resolution formulated by him which at his request was submitted by the Swiss and was accepted by the congress. The last sentence of it read: 'The congress sees in the organisation of the Russian proletariat the best guarantee against tsarist power, which forms one of the last pillars of European reaction.' Moreover the fear that the *narodniki*, with support from the members of the SPD in sympathy with them, would have occasion during the discussion of the agricultural problem once more to recommend the Russian *mir* as the solution to the social problem, proved groundless. The definitive expulsion of the anarchists, for which the British congress leaders simply summoned the police – even a good-natured man like Kropotkin was excluded – also provided the opportunity to put the *narodniki* out of action. Nonetheless, out of courtesy, a letter from Lavrov was read aloud. Volkhovsky, the populist well known in Britain through the Free Russia Committee, complained in the Independent Labour Party's paper about the treatment of his sympathisers at the congress, but to no avail.[25]

Although Rosa Luxemburg could now, as a fully-fledged Polish delegate, be present at the congress, her resolution denying the usefulness of Polish independence had no ghost of a chance. Kautsky had indeed accepted her talented articles about this problem for his paper, but he did not leave them unchallenged. He admitted that the Polish question no longer had the same significance as at the time of the First International. Above all the emergence of the revolutionary movement in Russia had fundamentally altered the situation. The notions 'Russia' and 'reaction' were no longer completely synonymous. But he refused to see Polish nationalism as an outdated affair. Tsarism was still the most dangerous enemy of European civilisation. Opposition in Poland was dependent on support from elsewhere. When the International backed the struggle of the Polish socialists this gave no support to bourgeois chauvinism, which was injurious to the international solidarity of the labour movement. Nor did Luxemburg get any help from Vaillant, whom she had tried to lobby in Paris. Adler, who as an Austrian social democrat eschewed all extremism in the thorny problem of nationalities, was infuriated by her 'extremely inopportune views' and called her a 'doctrinaire goose'. The congress avoided a painful debate about Poland and declared itself only in general terms an advocate of the right of self-determination.[26]

Rosa Luxemburg's Marxist logic ricocheted off a wall of traditional beliefs. Even the socialists, who personally showed little susceptibility to that sort of sentiment, realised that their supporters did do so and that they must take this into account. Luxemburg was to remain a prominent opponent of the prejudices which clung to the image of Russia, but she was to earn little credit for this. The majority of Polish socialists tried to make the most of the fear and contempt of barbaric Russia and the admiration for everyone who opposed her. This also applied to the *narodniki*, who soon presented themselves once more and with great success as socialist revolutionaries in the West. The Russian Marxists were in two minds. They knew that their horror of tsarism was shared by their political sympathisers in the West and Plekhanov had repeatedly appealed to it and did not shrink from its propagandist effect. But at the same time they had to arouse understanding in the West for the non-barbaric side of Russia, for her European and modern facets. In this way their message lost eloquence. As Russian revolutionaries they could rely on respect, but as leaders of a working class *in statu nascendi* modesty was expected of them. The role of 'poor relations' of Western socialism did not suit them at all, but it could not be completely avoided.[27]

Sometimes this was painful. At a congress in Zürich in 1897 about social legislation the Russian delegation had borne itself as far as possible in a manner consistent with the 'youth and relative weakness' of the Russian labour movement. But Akselrod was not allotted sufficient speaking time by the Germans and Austrians to be able to bring the special position of the Russian workers who had 'just arrived on the battlefield' to the attention of the congress. He finally published the speech he had wanted to give there in *Die Neue Zeit*.[28] Moreover the founding of the Russian social democratic workers' party (shortened in Russian to RSDRP) in 1898 was hardly noticed in the West. The news that a number of social democratic groups had amalgamated in Minsk to form a party reached the Liberation of Labour Group by means of a newspaper sent to the West, in which an account was given of the congress by placing dots under certain letters. The police in Russia were, however, well informed and arrested 500 social democrats in different Russian towns. Only the manifesto of the Minsk congress, written in triumphant tones, was published in *Vorwärts*. Rosa Luxemburg wrote to Jogiches with malicious joy about the small amount of attention the new party had been given in the socialist press: 'As a result of this there will certainly again appear in *Die Neue Zeit* 'an unspoken speech' or 'unthought thoughts' by Akselrod.'[29]

Akselrod had indeed just published a long article in Kautsky's paper under the pregnant title 'The historical justification of Russian social democracy'. As is evident from the above, the Russian workers' movement and Russian social democracy were not yet familiar concepts in the West. Even in Russia itself, according to the Liberation of Labour Group, they were much misunderstood. Akselrod, supported by the prestige of *Die Neue Zeit*, hoped to be more able to correct certain ideological tendencies in the Russian movement which caused him and his friends some anxiety. But it was also his intention to remove 'a certain scepticism' towards Russian social democracy which was 'pretty widespread' among Western labour parties.[30] This article was the first comprehensive publication on this subject in the West and it contained subtle and well-thought-out sociological Marxist analyses. Kautsky was delighted with the article which in his opinion was full of food for thought. 'It contains much that is worthy of consideration not only for Russia, but also for Germany and Austria, which after all in a certain sense form a link between Russia and the West, which is represented to the greatest degree by England.'[31] Akselrod and Plekhanov, too, no longer believed that the principles of the Western labour movement could simply be applied to Russia. Akselrod therefore emphasised certain differences between his country and the rest of Europe. But at the same time he clearly wanted to place the emphasis otherwise than was usual in traditional ideas about

Russia. Western and Russian critics had always impressed on the Russian Marxists that the proletariat could not form the true revolutionary power in Russia. A practicable socialist labour movement could only be the product of a liberal capitalist environment and thus not a force that could produce this new order by itself. Moreover tsarism showed itself to be the guardian angel of the rising class of capitalists, who thankfully accepted this protection. Thus in Russia the revolutionary contrast between a feudal *ancien régime* and the bourgeoisie, characteristic of Europe in the period 1789–1848, did not exist.

Akselrod did not challenge this simplification by referring to England, where this contrast had never existed in the classical Marxist form. Still less did he point out, though it would have been more natural, the co-operation between capitalists and Junkers in Prussia. From this union between 'grain and iron' it was likewise evident that the modernisation process could also in the West deviate from the Marxist blueprint. He simply admitted that, in contrast to Marxist theory, the capitalist bourgeoisie in Russia did not show itself to be liberal. In Russia the initiatives for a modern society, the germs of a revolutionary epidemic, were formed in a different way. In large sections of the country nobility and the middle-class intelligentsia, freedom-loving tendencies had gained the upper hand. These groups belonged to the thinking section of the nation without which no state whatsoever could function. But they could only with difficulty wrest themselves free from their environment and were in no fit state to take a hard line against the autocracy. That could only occur if they were prepared to make a treaty with the class which had suffered the most from capitalist exploitation and tyrannical suppression. Not the peasants, but the factory workers, were the appropriate shock troops of the revolution, because of their numerical strength, their concentration in the towns, their essential position in the production process and their 'native strength'.[32]

For the future new society a social base was thus also laid down in Russia, which, just as formerly in the West, had a strongly radical-liberal slant. But meanwhile in Europe the situation had altered radically. There liberalism had lost its progressive character. In Russia where the chance of self-development was denied to every social category, the liberation of society had become the goal of every progressive human being irrespective of his or her social origin. Since there could be no question at that stage in the development of society of the taking over of power or the introduction of socialism by the proletariat, there existed in Russia no unbridgeable antithesis between liberalism and social democracy. On the contrary, the common aim demanded 'continuous, energetic, mutual support'.[33]

Akselrod was not thinking here of a fusion of liberalism and socialism and certainly not of anything like the British 'lib–lab' collaboration, either. In Russia too, liberals and social democrats each had their own ideology, their own social base and their own sphere of activity. The proletariat had to make use of the political dissension among the other social classes by assuming the leadership of the revolutionary movement and stirring up the remaining opponents of the tsar into adopting as radical a position as possible. This concept of the 'hegemony of the proletariat' was part of the nucleus of the ideology which the Liberation of Labour Group had developed in the foregoing period. It was an original idea, but it did to some extent have the character of an intellectually desperate measure and was therefore little suited to reducing Russian or Western sceptics to silence. The Russian workers would lead the revolution and afterwards would have to hand back the power they had seized to the bourgeoisie, and thus had to have at their disposal not only unbridled revolutionary energy but also exceptional self-control towards their economic exploiters. Of course Akselrod himself saw that there were serious problems here. In order to provide the proletariat with the exemplary upbringing necessary for the success of the revolution, sustained paternal care of the workers by the radical intelligentsia was a primary requisite. However, according to Akselrod, grave dangers likewise went with this patronage.[34]

Without leadership there was a chance that the workers' movement 'would not be able to escape from the rut of mere struggles for wages and other conflicts with employers'.[35] This would also occur if the social democratic intelligentsia identified itself too closely with the economic interests of the workers. Akselrod wrote that the continued existence of the tsarist regime in itself was already offering a sufficient guarantee against this danger. But in fact the Liberation of Labour Group was very worried about the first signs of reformism within their movement. Even Russia now seemed to be somewhat infected with this typically

Western malady. The recent publications by Akselrod's great friend Bernstein were characteristic of a developing demand in Europe for a thorough revision of Marx. This denoted a serious crisis which could have had an extremely adverse effect on the Russian situation. This too was one of the reasons why Akselrod now, in contrast to earlier, wanted to accentuate the peculiarity of the Russian situation. Western socialism was no longer in all respects an example that deserved indiscriminate imitation. The indifferent attitude of the French Marxists around Guesde in the Dreyfus affair had also greatly shocked him.[36]

Akselrod's greatest concern, however, was that in the history of Russian and Western socialism worse developments had taken place in the past which must at all costs be prevented from recurring. He was thinking of the tradition of radical populism with its mesmerising effect on Western socialism. Nothing would be more disastrous than the Russian workers' movement falling under the spell of the Bakuninist or Blanquist schools of thought which would have staked everything on carrying out an anarchist or communist revolution immediately. Then the workers' movement would exhaust itself in senseless actions. It was the 'cursed duty and obligation' of the Russian social democrats to prevent this from happening.[37] These words were to prove prophetic, but to many Akselrod merely gave the impression that he was fighting against ghosts from the past.

Akselrod's carefully composed articles were rather attempts to conjure up the future with the help of Marxist formulas than to analyse reality. In his view the Russian workers would never be capable of achieving the historic task allotted to them as long as they remained poor and ignorant. It was absolutely vital that they should first become participants in European culture before they could free mankind from tsarism. Intensive contacts with the progressive part of the Russian intellectual elite and with the Western labour movement were necessary not only for their own emancipation, but also in order to keep the revolutionary process both in Russia and in the world on the right track. The Russian proletariat, the Russian intelligentsia and the European socialists would have to comply with Akselrod's strict standards to prevent history resulting in something which was the opposite of his highest ideal. There were not many people who shared his anxiety to this extent. In the inaugural manifesto of the RSDRP it was bluntly postulated that the Russian proletariat was standing completely alone. 'The further to the East one goes in Europe, the weaker, the more cowardly and the nastier the bourgeoisie is and the greater the cultural and political tasks the proletariat must undertake. The Russian working class shall and must carry the burden of the conquest of political freedom on its own strong shoulders.'[38] Obviously the revolutionary potential of the Russian workers cast the qualities of their Western fellow sufferers into the shade. Thus the thesis of the hegemony of the Russian proletariat could mean different things to different social democrats. Readers of *Vorwärts* could still shrug their shoulders about this in 1898. But in 1905 many of them were to become convinced that the Russian workers were something truly exceptional. How simple it proved to be a few years later to project the wonderful qualities which in the West had been attributed to the Russian man and his soul on to the Russian proletariat!

Akselrod remained faithful to the ideas he had taken so much trouble to formulate, and thus it is not difficult to recognise the later ideologist of Menshevism in the author of *The Historical Justification*. The intellectual development of others frequently proceeded more capriciously. The 28-year-old Lenin in 1899 agreed entirely with Akselrod's evaluation of the role of the revolutionary intelligentsia.[39] It was already evident that Lenin valued Russian liberalism less highly than Akselrod did. But they were both well aware of its importance. The discovery and evaluation of yet more new aspects of the process of modernisation and Westernisation to which tsarist Russia was being subjected, sometimes had radical consequences for others. P. B. Struve, the framer of the inaugural manifesto of the RSDRP, in which such contempt was expressed for the Russian bourgeoisie, changed within a few years from a promising social democrat into one of the ideological leaders of liberalism. He was certainly not the only Russian intellectual for whom Marxism possessed merely a passing attraction.[40]

## REVISIONISM

Not everyone who objected to Plekhanov's ultra-revolutionary and hyper-dogmatic version of Marx became a liberal. There were also activists in the RSDRP who refused to see the struggle for higher wages and better working conditions as something which was completely subordinate to the higher goal, the overthrow of autocracy. These views were soon labelled as 'Economism' within the RSDRP, and their proponents branded as 'Economists'. It was very difficult for subsequent historians to describe this conflict purely in terms of opposing principles. It was tempting to see it mainly as a struggle for power in which the ever-present personal animosities were easily sublimated into fundamental ideological principles.[41] It went without saying, however, that a dogmatist like Plekhanov saw an immediate connection between this Russian dissident trend and the Bernstein affair, the most sensational case of apostasy ever to take place in Marxist circles.

It is indeed possible to see a connection. Like the Russian 'Economists' Bernstein had a more optimistic and evolutionary view of the future of socialism than his friends who remained faithful to Marxism. The struggle between Plekhanov and his followers and the 'Economists' was about the assessment of the most recent history of their fatherland. Which fact was more important for the future: the skill with which the autocracy had managed to maintain itself after 1861, or the economic and social changes which were taking place at top speed? Strangely enough the Marxists appeared to attach a greater importance to the political factor. Similarly in Germany, Bernstein's opponents attached more value to the reactionary characteristics of the political regime in Germany than to the rapid economic development which had taken place under it. Thus it was not only in Russia that the discussion about the strategy of a socialist party was to a large extent determined by the moot question of how Western, in the sense of modern and advanced, the country actually was. As had already been evident from Kautsky's reaction to Akselrod's article, most Marxists, like many other intellectuals around 1900, were thinking of a sort of sliding scale of values which should be applied to Europe. Western European England formed one extreme here, and Eastern European Russia the other. East and West met in Central European Germany. The conflict with Bernstein was to a large extent imperceptibly determined by the question of whether Germany should be seen through English or Russian spectacles.[42]

Doubts in fact existed among Western socialists not only about the viability of a social democratic movement in Russia: the same applied to England, though for other reasons. A number of

Marxists believed, as had Marx and Engels before them, that in countries with the most democratic governments – which were also as it happens the most Western – the workers would be able to gain power without violence and revolution. A logical result of this admission was that a preponderance of reformist tendencies and a weak position for Marxism and social democracy in England and France had to be accepted as a reality. If, however, not only Russia but also these other countries deviated from the classical Marxist pattern, then Germany alone among the great nations actually remained a normal country.

But Germany too was becoming continually more troublesome to accommodate into a simple schema of development. The success of German social democracy had at the beginning of the 1890s led to overconfident thoughts about a rapid collapse of Kaiser Wilhelm's empire. Even Engels had dreamed aloud of a conquest of the state by means of electoral victories.[43] But the striking vitality of Bismarck's creation had a sobering effect. The leaders of the SPD came to realise that no real power could result from the ballot-box in their country. They knew moreover that the masses who followed them had no chance against the strongest and most modern military and police forces in the world. In normal times there could be no thought of revolutionary adventures. A reformist policy was the maximum attainable and a dire necessity. Bernstein now suggested making a virtue of this necessity, but the party was not willing to follow him in this. This was understandable. The atmosphere and the harmony within the SPD, and likewise the proletarian character of the party, were determined by the emotional conviction of its members that there was an unbridgeable gulf between the workers and the Junker empire and capitalists. It was to this that the party owed its success as a political unit. This feeling was strengthened and kept alive by the stirring rhetoric of socialist propaganda and was consolidated by numerous unpleasant experiences in the political and social structure of Germany around 1900.

For Bebel, Liebknecht and Kautsky it went without saying that Bernstein had lost contact with German reality during his long stay in England. His suggestion that this reactionary regime should be peacefully undermined by means of a gradual 'growing together' of democracy and socialism was in their view absurd. Co-operation with the liberals, which would have had to be the driving force behind the developments which Bernstein wished for, was likewise an illusion. The German bourgeoisie was not liberal and regarded the socialist movement as an un-German, un-Christian and therefore undesirable element. In Germany liberalism could not become a strong movement capable of democratising and reforming society. This task fell to the SPD.[44]

Bernstein reproached his friends for not wanting to co-operate with the liberals. Their ideological preoccupations were forcing the party into a sterile isolation. The German social democrats – with Bebel in the forefront – still cherished fantastic expectations of a great *Kladderadatsch* or 'bang', a quick and total collapse of the established order. According to Bernstein this mystique of 'collapse' was in strange contradiction to the reformist practices of the party. 'The doctrine is not realistic enough for me, it has as it were lagged behind the practical development of the movement. It may possibly yet be suited to Russia ... but in Germany in its old form it is out of date.'[45] While Marx and many after him had maintained that his theory did not apply to Russia but to Western Europe, Bernstein came to the conclusion that Marxism in its old-fashioned form, that is to say with the glorification of revolutionary violence it had derived from the Blanquist tradition, was still only appropriate in the least civilised country in Europe. This was nothing more than a passing remark in a letter in which at the same time Bernstein observed with satisfaction that even in the Russian movement there were people who were nearer to him than to his greatest opponent Plekhanov. But the view that socialism could be achieved in Russia by revolution and violence, while for Western and Central Europe a peaceful and gradual route lay open, followed logically from Bernstein's standpoint. In 1905 he would forcefully make the same claim and then it would become clear how many agreed with him.

This was of course a sensitive issue in 1899 too. Germans, not excluding social democrats, liked to see their country as an important – if not the most important – representative of European civilisation. Moreover Kautsky was in complete agreement with Bernstein that romanticising violence should form no part of Marxism.[46] But neither he nor Bebel believed that a democratic republic could replace the German empire without a cataclysm. In view of the catastrophic course of German history between 1914 and 1945 the German Marxists showed more realism in this respect than Bernstein and his associates. This meant, however, that they were forced to represent their country as less civilised and Westernised than Bernstein and other revisionists or reformists claimed. For instance, in 1904 at the Amsterdam congress of the International, Bebel was to defend himself against Jaurès's attack on the SPD with the remark that Germany 'with the exception of Russia and Turkey' had 'possibly the most reactionary government of any country in Europe'.[47] But at the same time the Russian Marxists had done their level best for years to convince the German comrades that Russia lay less far to the East than was believed in Europe. Finally, in his polemic with the populists, Plekhanov had openly rejected Blanquist putschism as incompatible with Marxism earlier than had Bernstein or Kautsky.

As in the days of Marx the idea of revolution in Central Europe still remained ultimately linked to that of revolution in Russia. For every Marxist the German state, like the other two military monarchies, Russia and Austria, was a historical freak, a relic of feudalism that was condemned to death by the further development of capitalism. The ever-increasing international tensions in Europe made it even easier to imagine the eclipse of the three empires as a disastrous collapse. This prospect was as pleasurable as it was alarming. Perhaps unique chances for the realisation of socialist ideals would come into existence, possibly also unknown dangers for the survival of the labour movement. Around 1900 the Austrian state seemed to be already in an advanced state of decay and few were more cynical about the capacities of the Habsburg monarchy than Victor Adler. But the policies of the Austrian socialists were determined by the fear that the royal house as it fell would sweep away their movement too. If the empire were to disintegrate into various national states, social democracy would likewise be spread over the different nationalities. The weak Austrian party dared not undertake anything that would hasten the fall of the Habsburg house. Adler could thus label his party as 'the only upholder of the state' and jokingly call himself the *Hofrat der Revolution* or court councillor of the revolution.[48] The SPD was much larger and stronger than the Austrian party but felt itself to be no match for Kaiser Wilhelm's state. A radical breakthrough out of this frustrating situation could only be expected from Russia. Tsarist Russia formed the greatest threat to the continued existence of the German and Austrian monarchies. Bebel and Adler now thought it even less likely than Marx and Engels had earlier that the international proletariat would be able to prevent a war. Moreover Bebel thought that German socialists should defend their country against the Cossacks. Kautsky, too, considered this right. As soon as the danger arose that 'this government by knout would become all-powerful in Europe, then German social democracy should not delay for a moment in sending its representative to the ministry charged with the organisation of the national war'.[49] The spirit of 1848 had thus remained alive and would continue to do so until the fatal month of August 1914. Revolution in Russia was a most attractive alternative to war. The Russian socialist movement had no impressive mass organisations to be proud of, but was thereby also more free to engage in a life and death struggle with the regime. All the actions of the Russian comrades were perforce illegal and revolutionary. The fall of the tsar would undermine the thrones in Germany and Austria and perhaps offer the socialists the opportunity to fight out the definitive struggle for power without their movement bleeding to death in the process. These rarely expressed uncertainties and pipe dreams also formed part of the background against which the discussion about Bernstein took place. An important result of it was that the German and Austrian parties remained exceptionally sensitive to Russian developments and showed great readiness to help their Russian comrades.

For their part the Eastern European Marxists realised only too well that Bernstein was threatening to cut through the ideological link between them and the Western socialists. The prospect of having to live as a revolutionary *rara avis* in a reformist and revisionist Europe was very depressing. To some extent it was, however, all too true. 'The most distressing thing of all', wrote Plekhanov to Akselrod in 1898 in a sharply negative reaction to Bernstein's latest article, 'is that in a certain sense Bernstein is right. For example, one cannot of course count on an immediate realisation of the socialist ideal.' Akselrod wrote back that he saw Bernstein's essays above all as a sign of a widespread *manque de foi* in mankind and progress.[50] Now that the West no longer seemed to be living up to his expectations, Akselrod found himself in a crisis comparable to that of Herzen half a century earlier after the 1848 revolution. But he lacked Herzen's brilliant literary talent and still less did he excel in debate. He was only capable of influencing people in direct personal contact and through his articles. He did not take action in public against Bernstein, who as a person was dearer to him than his fellow combatant Plekhanov. For Kautsky, too, his close friendship with Bernstein, and the uneasy feeling that Bernstein was not entirely wrong, formed an obstacle to going over to the attack. Victor Adler likewise turned vehemently against any action which could lead to the denunciation and excommunication of such a beloved and prominent political associate.[51]

The struggle to preserve Europe for the revolution was therefore launched by three Eastern European Marxists living in the West, who were surpassed by no one in intellect, ambition and polemical talent: Plekhanov, Luxemburg and Parvus. They were to learn that attempts to teach socialist Europe a lesson would raise just as intensely negative reactions as they had done in the days of Herzen. The thunderstorm which they unleashed into the rarefied atmosphere of Marxist abstractions proved that Marxism was a form of wishful thinking presented as scholarship, an economic and sociological scholasticism which, because of its inaccessibility, was to a large extent excluded from adjudication by the uninitiated. Bernstein, according to almost all the representatives of this diligent and conscientious generation of Marxists, had gone to work in a superficial and slovenly way and had produced too few numerical data to corroborate his assertions. He gave his Eastern European opponents ample opportunity to jeer at him.[52]

For tactical reasons this was probably not unwelcome to Bebel. Something had to be done about Bernstein, who had infringed in an inadmissible way the emotional and intellectual codes which had grown up with the party. Both he and Liebknecht therefore thanked Plekhanov for his article against revisionism. Parvus and Luxemburg were also protected. But actually the leaders of the SPD made skilful use of these foreigners. After these Eastern European theoreticians had done their 'duty' they could go away. Afterwards Bebel, together with Kautsky whom he at first had to spur on repeatedly, could pose as the moderate defenders of the old familiar teaching, with its – for Germans – more acceptable, less adventurous, almost *gemütlich* idea of the revolution. It was *the* way to assure themselves of an easy victory in the party. Parvus and Luxemburg, however, found it hard to endure a number of party congresses at which it emerged repeatedly how appalled many in the SPD were about the behaviour and writings of these 'literary ruffians'. The populist Shidlovsky had the opportunity to state in the *Sozialistische Monatshefte* that Plekhanov was 'the most inflexible, orthodox Marxist in the entire world'. This paper was to become Bernstein's mouthpiece after *Die Neue Zeit* had been closed to him. However, for Parvus and Luxemburg it would for some time be very difficult to get anything published in the German socialist press. Even Kautsky refused to accept their contributions. Rosa Luxemburg lost her post as general editor of the *Sächsische Arbeiterzeitung*; despite the prominent position she had earned in the SPD, she would always remain an outsider.[53]

Akselrod had warned Plekhanov that the pretentious tone of his polemic was 'a diplomatic fault', with which he antagonised the 'influential element' within the SPD and just 'created a favourable, sympathetic atmosphere for our [Russian] home-made caricatures of social democrats'. Moreover, wrote Akselrod, who was capable of following Plekhanov on his philosophical excursions? Swiss socialist intellectuals still said to Akselrod: 'We can understand nothing of it!' Akselrod himself had great difficulty with it, and indeed Bernstein had confessed to him that he did not understand Plekhanov. 'In the whole of international social democracy there are hardly a dozen men to be found who are capable of following these serious debates, let alone taking part in them.' Akselrod also drew Plekhanov's attention to Victor Adler's emotional outbursts in the Viennese *Arbeiterzeitung* against pointless theoretical discussions, without knowing that Adler, in his letters to Bebel and Kautsky, expressed himself even more cuttingly. There he depicted Plekhanov as 'frightfully arrogant' and his articles and those of Parvus and Luxemburg as 'preposterous priestly rubbish'.[54] The Russian socialists had the reputation among their Western comrades, who were themselves not conspicuous for their great forbearance, of being a belligerent little tribe. This impression was greatly strengthened by Plekhanov's crusade against Bernstein. The Germans were ready to help the Russian social democrats, but much less inclined to listen to them for long. Misconception and ignorance about Russia and the Russian revolutionaries thus remained abundantly alive and this was also later partly to be blamed on the Russians themselves.

## ISKRA

The sectarian intolerance of the leading Russian social democrats had particularly disastrous results for their own party. The RSDRP bore no resemblance to her great German model. In fact there was not even a party. There were many small fluctuating groups of predominantly very youthful intellectuals, working illegally in the Russian towns, in forced exile in Siberia and studying or living in Europe as political outcasts. Their revolutionary inclination cannot easily be called in question, their Marxist convictions even less so. But the Marxism of the Russian intelligentsia was, as a concerned Russian social democrat wrote, 'a fashionable theory that everyone continually has in mind, that everyone always talks about, that everyone counts on, and against which everyone measures his views and tastes'. The Marxism of these youths was vague and elusive, still miles removed from a programme of action or a party ideology.[55] No wonder words like 'organisation' and 'party discipline' acquired such special import in a fragmented party harassed by the police in which the impossibility of developing normal political activities was compensated for by heated debates about the form which must be given to the future.

In all socialist parties the problem existed of how utopian ideals, which were mostly propagated by intellectuals, should be harmonised with the daily needs and practical interests of the workers. Bernstein had thought up a solution to this proletarian squaring of the socialist circle. But the adage which even he himself did not mean literally, 'The goal is nothing, the movement is everything', had above all aroused indignation in Germany and was a meaningless statement for Russia,[56] where, after all, there was hardly anything that resembled a movement. Tsarism suppressed all reformist tendencies in society with great

vigour. During this period the security police for a time successfully experimented with taking the wind out of the socialists'
sails via the trade unions it protected. No Western form of
socialist reformism thus had the slightest chance and not a single
Russian social democrat was an outspoken advocate of it. The
gulf between the workers and the intelligentsia was and
remained wide and the history of the RSDRP could be described
as a series of hopeless attempts to close this rift. It goes without
saying that some of these 'Economists' sought inspiration from
Bernstein for a time or put forward ideas which with a bit of
goodwill or ill will could be construed as Bernsteinian.

The accusation by Plekhanov and others that they were deliberately neglecting the revolutionary and political aims of the
RSDRP was largely groundless. Neither he nor Akselrod had
much understanding of the fact that their young comrades in
or outside Russia were only trying to find their own way. The
generation gap created regularly recurring conflicts in every
socialist party, even in the disciplined SPD. But the position of
leaders like Bebel was so unassailable that they did not need to
undertake anything drastic against their youngsters.[57] Akselrod
and Plekhanov were in a much less favourable situation and
despite the warnings of Vera Zasulich were dragged into a series
of sordid emigrant conflicts. The result was that the 'Economists'
seemed to get the upper hand. The old guard of the Liberation
of Labour Group were in danger of becoming completely isolated from their fellow members.[58]

What was distressing in this was that Bernstein in his book
*The Preconditions for Socialism*, in which he defended himself in
detail against Plekhanov, prided himself on his Russian adherents. Plekhanov thought the struggle between 'Economism' and
'Bernsteinianism' in the Russian movement was therefore 'the
most vital question of the moment'. It was 'a fight not for life
but for death, I repeat, it is a matter of who will bury whom:
Bernstein social democracy, or social democracy Bernstein'.[59]
He regarded each young fellow party member with so much
suspicion that he had great difficulty in accepting the help of
three highly talented social democrats from Russia. Lenin, Martov and Potresov approached Zasulich, Akselrod and Plekhanov
with the proposition that they should edit a periodical together.
By means of this paper, called *Iskra* (*The Spark*), which would

be printed in the West, and the necessary organisation for its illegal circulation in Russia, a large-scale attempt would be made to unite the party once more under the banner of Marxism. Zasulich and Akselrod needed all their diplomatic talents and the youths all their patience to reach an agreement with Plekhanov. The result was that six people appointed themselves as leaders and placed the party under their guardianship as if it were a problem child. They were determined to impose their will on all dissidents in the RSDRP and to take up arms against Bernsteinian heresies. They did not realise that in this way they were mainly fighting against phantoms floating about in their own heads. On the other hand, they were perfectly well aware that their plans could not be realised without generous material and personal support from the German sister party.

This had peculiar consequences. The SPD could in no way be considered as a bulwark of revolutionary Marxism. But the revisionism and reformism within it could not be attacked by the editors of *Iskra* as fiercely as similar tendencies in the Russian movement. This was to have clear repercussions on the position that the 'Iskrites' were to occupy in the international arena. Just before the first issue of *Iskra* appeared, the International met in Paris in September 1900. Plekhanov had attended the preparatory conference in Brussels the year before with the intention of opening up the hunt for revisionists in that gathering too. It was probably partly at his instigation that the problem of the socialists' assumption of power was placed on the agenda of the congress. Because of the admission of the French socialist member of parliament Millerand into the Waldeck–Rousseau cabinet, this question had become a currently burning issue. Guesde, who knew Plekhanov well, had begged him to come to Paris. The French Marxist was afraid that the opponents of socialist participation in bourgeois governments would be in a minority. Plekhanov shared this fear chiefly because, if he and his friends did not come, the Russian delegation would largely consist of 'Economists'. There was a good chance that they would follow Jaurès, who had accepted Millerand's conduct with the argument that the French republic ought to be defended against monarchical and reactionary forces. However, Plekhanov was still *persona non grata* in France and for this reason had been unable to attend Lavrov's funeral at the beginning of the year.

He therefore wrote to his closest companions to persuade them to visit the congress. But Zasulich, too, was afraid of problems with the Sûreté and the Parisian department of the Russian security police. Eventually, ironically enough, Jaurès and Millerand saw to it that the Russians experienced no problems.[60]

In this way as a large group equipped with a number of mandates from Russia they were able to appear at the congress. The greater part of the delegation, however, consisted of social democrats with whom Plekhanov and his associates had quarrelled. There were besides a few populists present, amongst whom were Rubanovich and Shidlovsky who were highly respected by the French. These compatriots were treated in such a way by the social democrats that they – just as the *narodniki* had once done at the congress in London – complained about it to the organisers, and this time also in vain. But the Iskrites did not have everything their own way either. The 'Economist' Krichevsky was chosen as chairman of the delegation and Plekhanov had to be satisfied with the post of secretary. They both took places in the newly formed Bureau of the International. Thus the differences of opinion within the Russian party acquired their permanent character in a world-wide framework. According to Vera Zasulich, Krichevsky merely aroused amusement and embarrassment with his statements, but nothing of this appears in the congress report. The peculiarity of Plekhanov's behaviour was much more striking, for he did not come forward as a fervent supporter of Guesde, who together with the Italian Ferri demanded from the International an absolute ban on socialist participation in bourgeois governments. Instead Plekhanov tried to give a somewhat less elastic character to Kautsky's flexible resolution, which permitted the socialists to assume the responsibility of government in cases of emergency. Here therefore the situation which had occurred at the Zürich congress seven years before (in 1893) was to some extent repeated. Then, too, Plekhanov had supported a not very revolutionary proposal against a radical one from Domela Nieuwenhuis in order to please the Germans.[61]

For his amendment, which made the participation of socialist ministers in a 'bourgeois' government dependent on the explicit consent of their party, Plekhanov was thanked by the Belgian Vandervelde with a deep bow to his qualities as a theoretician.

Kautsky's resolution was accepted by the congress with Plekhanov's supplementation. But the prominent German socialist Auer rightly wondered afterwards whose permission Millerand should have asked, in view of the mutual disagreement among the French socialists. (Millerand had in fact asked for and obtained the approval of the socialist members of parliament.) Plekhanov's intervention was of little relevance and could not conceal the fact that the Russian crusader against revisionism dared not oppose Jaurès directly in the French conflict. His change of course was probably a manoeuvre to prevent Krichevsky and his friends from becoming too influential. The newly formed editorial staff of *Iskra* could not allow itself to be pushed out of favour with the German social democrats by this group.[62]

Thanks to the intellectual talents of the editorial members and the organisational skills of Lenin, *Iskra* was to become one of the best socialist periodicals ever to appear. But since the activities of the Russians had to remain secret from the German police, which was co-operating fully with the Russian, the help of dozens of German comrades for the solution of problems raised by housing, printing, storage, circulation, and so forth, was indispensable.[63] Owing to this dedication on the German side the Iskrites were also able to carry out their intention to win over the party in reality. After two years of intensive work, plans were already being made for a congress that would lay down the ideological direction and the organisational structure of the RSDRP according to the opinions of *Iskra*. The behaviour of the editors was, however, rather aggressive. A number of prominent party leaders and important organisations were quite prepared for a compromise but not for the unconditional submission that was demanded of them. They would take their revenge at and after the Second Party Congress in 1903, when it turned out that the Iskrites were divided amongst themselves and thus totally incapable of giving definite form to Russian social democracy. *Iskra*'s claims to power, moreover, were not confined to their own party, but extended over the whole Russian opposition movement. The liberals and the social revolutionaries who at that time were organising themselves into separate groups had no thought of accepting the hegemony of the social democrats as a matter of course. The initial benevolence of *Iskra* towards both currents quickly changed into open enmity which precluded both co-operation on an equal basis and united action by the Russian opposition against autocracy.

Since the Western social democrats could not read Russian, they were largely spared these venomous disputes. But the Iskrites could see no chance of winning them over to their point of view. Their paper was meant to provide detailed information about the European socialist movement. Although Vandervelde, Jaurès, Guesde, the Swiss Greulich and Victor Adler's son Fritz were asked to contribute, they produced no articles. The SPD executive committee, which two years before had subsidised the Dutch Social Democratic Labour Party (SDAP) with ten thousand marks for the publication of *Het Volk* and had donated a thousand marks to the Pole Daszynski for a similar purpose, refused to give *Iskra* a thousand marks in 1901. The excuse given was that there were so many small Russian groups: a strange argument, for the Dutch and the Poles did not form single units either. Akselrod, offended, wrote to his friend Kautsky that the group to which he belonged was regarded even by its Russian opponents as the intellectual elite of the party.[64]

Kautsky was in full sympathy with the work of his old Russian friends, but even he sometimes annoyed Axelrod. The information in *Die Neue Zeit* about the Russian movement was carefully selected even at the expense of truth. According to Kautsky too much indiscretion would endanger the survival of both Russian and German periodicals. This was also the opinion of Dietz, the socialist publisher who printed for the Russians and also produced *Die Neue Zeit*. German press laws were strict and Dietz simply refused to publish anything which could indicate a link with illegal activities. When confronted with angry Russians he would appeal to Bebel and Singer of the party board, who were equally afraid that recklessness on the part of the party publisher could have unfortunate results for the SPD. Lenin especially was enraged by this 'censorship', called Dietz 'a capricious gentleman' (*kaprizniy barin*) and wondered when the Russians would be able to free themselves from the 'guardianship of these *Dreckgenossen* (companions in filth)'. Of course the Iskrites were not pleased that Dietz also published *Osvobozhdenie* (*Liberation*), the paper of their liberal opponent Struve, and that this was accidentally introduced as a social democrat newspaper by *Vorwärts*.[65]

They were also at a loss about Kautsky's request to write an article in *Die Neue Zeit* about the student riots in Russia at the time. There had been disturbances in Russian universities through the whole of the second half of the nineteenth century, but the years 1899–1902 formed an unprecedented peak. The student protest was unusually spectacular but had no real power. Thus the continued existence of autocracy was not threatened, but the government acted harshly and punished the rebellious youths severely. Precisely because of this the attention of the European public was focused upon Russian events, which were also reported in detail and analysed in *Iskra*. The social democrats did not believe, as their emigrant 'Economist' opponents noisily insisted, that the time for the decisive battle with autocracy had come. Moreover they were afraid that under the intelligentsia there would be a regression to the cult of individual heroism from the days of the People's Will. The successful assassination of the minister of education pointed in that direction.[66]

Situations like this faced the Russian social democrats yet again with the same problem. When things happened in Russia which appealed to the traditional image that Western socialists and liberals had of that country, then the Russian social democrats felt called upon to temper European sympathy for Russian revolutionary phenomena, which they themselves needed so badly, with subtle distinctions, for which as they knew from experience there was little understanding. At the instigation of Italians like Turati, Bissolati and Ferri, the Bureau of the International was occupying itself exhaustively with the Russian situation. The Italians, who excelled in enthusiasm without much knowledge of affairs, had spoken of the 'grandeur of the awakening of the Russian proletariat which is suddenly entering modern history'. The Bureau's Appeal to the socialist parties revealed the influence of Krichevsky and spoke of a 'turning-point in the history of the tsarist empire'. The document also contained the usual clichés about Russia such as 'the brutal forces', 'the brutal conspiracies', 'the odious and barbaric acts' and 'the despotism' of the autocracy. The Bureau called upon the affiliated parties, as had already happened in some countries, to hold demonstrations of solidarity with the Russian students. It was difficult to criticise this well-meant if somewhat naive Western propaganda for Russian affairs. The same was true for the 'demonstration of sympathy' which Kautsky personally wrote because the Iskrites had not managed to produce any contributions to his paper.[67]

Kautsky emphasised that students in Russia took up a totally different position from those in the West. In Europe, too, the class war needed scholarly leadership, but from 'mature thinkers' not from students. In Russia, unlike the West, the students were not the green, intellectual recruits of the labour movement, but the real 'champions' of socialism. He explained this fact with the usual references to the absence of a radical liberal bourgeoisie in Russia, the lack of revolutionary zeal among the peasants, the cultural barbarism in which the majority of the population lived and above all, of course, the weakness of the autocracy. What probably reconciled the Iskrites to Kautsky's superficial and traditional opinion was that he devoted a great deal of attention to the support which the students had obtained from the workers' side. This moreover proved in his view that Bernstein's political supporters, who had believed that the proletariat was not mature enough for political action, were wrong. More important, Kautsky opposed terrorism and rejected it as an outdated and harmful weapon even for Russian revolutionaries. Kautsky nevertheless wrote to Akselrod that his article did not make a Russian contribution superfluous, but what was the point of throwing cold water on all these warm feelings for Russian insurgency?[68]

The Iskrites evidently thought it more important to prevent their opponents from building up too much power within Western socialism. Martov attacked the 'Economist' Krichevsky who, as the Parisian correspondent of *Vorwärts*, had written articles about the aftermath of the Millerand affair which had been rather sympathetic towards Jaurès. The result was a pointless tit for tat squabble in the columns of the party paper which must had found few interested readers. It was a fruitless effort to condemn a lax attitude towards revisionists. The Iskrites tried to win Kautsky, Luxemburg, Parvus, Bebel and Guesde over to their point of view but this was only partially successful. Only the leader of the Blanquists, Vaillant, and the Guesdist Bracke showed themselves to be openly pleased with Russian support in their quarrel with Jaurès and his followers. Luxemburg was in complete agreement with them from a political point of view, but she was amazed at the 'clumsiness' of the Russians' behaviour in the international arena and the poor German of their articles.[69]

The results of Martov's action were pathetic and, given Plekhanov's support of Kautsky's resolution at the Paris congress, they must also have been barely comprehensible to the Germans. Within the SPD people continued to think that Russian social democracy consisted of a number of rival groups and *Iskra's* point of view was not acknowledged as the only right one. The attempts by Akselrod and F. I. Dan – a correspondent for *Iskra* who was helping Kautsky with the publication of Marx's manuscripts – to interest German and Austrian party leaders in a single letter from Russia from a real worker sympathetic to *Iskra* was naturally of no avail. Rosa Luxemburg had taken cursory note of Lenin's diatribe against the 'Economists' which had appeared in Russian in 1902 under the title *Chto Delat'* (*What Is To Be Done*). But she was not at all impressed by it, since in her view it was written in the style that was so characteristic of the group around Plekhanov. Dan's idea that this kind of polemic was important enough to be translated into German, she thought ridiculous. 'I have convinced them', she wrote to Jogiches, 'that no German would read it.' It would be two years before Luxemburg felt it incumbent upon her to react to *What Is To Be Done* in *Die Neue Zeit*. Later still this document in which Lenin had set down his organisational views was to be regarded as the theoretical foundation of Bolshevism.[70]

In view of the scanty prestige possessed by the group around *Iskra* in the West, Akselrod was not keen to attend the SPD congress in Munich in 1902, unless he could appear there as the delegate of a large number of party committees in Russia and thus be authorised to declare that 'the actual and formal unification of Russian social democracy is looming much nearer than outsiders think'. Otherwise he would simply figure as 'a poor relative in the midst of uncharitable, rich kinsmen, without a shadow of authority or a chance of any attention'. It was just as it had been formerly with Engels or Liebknecht (who had died in 1900) or even worse, wrote Akselrod. The proud SPD leadership had few principles where Russia was concerned and they sympathised just as much with the Russian supporters of terrorism as with the liberals. Evidently Akselrod did not succeed soon enough in boosting his importance as a delegate of the RSDRP with an impressive number of Russian mandates, for he did not go to Munich. *Iskra* simply sent a telegram to the congress and it was Luxemburg who there asked for and obtained from the party a declaration of solidarity with the Russian revolutionaries. Akselrod was not even invited to the Austrian party congress and, although he knew Victor Adler well, he still thought it humiliating to have to ask him for an invitation.[71]

In the West *Iskra* met with hardly any response. But the activities of the editorial staff were directed in the first place towards Russia and their own party and the results of this exceeded their own expectations. In any case the Iskrites were devoting most of their time to the reconciliation of the vehement differences of opinion within their own circle, so that they could present a unified front at least outwardly. Nevertheless, they did realise that they could never really win their case in Russia without the support of Western socialist opinion. Both in Russia and in the West there was a feeling among socialists of intense mutual dependence. In an article written for *Iskra* in March 1902 Kautsky had once more focused attention on the importance that was attached in Europe to the Russian revolutionary movement. In 1848 the Slavs had frozen the budding revolution with a cold blast; 'now perhaps they are predestined to become a storm which will melt the ice of reaction'. Kautsky even hoped that Western socialism would be freed from the mindless fossilisation in which it appeared to be imprisoned by the Russian revolutionary movement and the proletariat behind it. In a comment on Kautsky the *Iskra* editorial staff had maintained that the labour movement in the whole world was ready to consider the struggle being carried out in Russia as its own. 'In a confederation like that with support like that, we shall indeed be invincible.' At the end of 1902, however, the Iskrites had very few facts at their disposal to indicate that the vague Western enthusiasm for the Russian revolutionary movement also carried with it an ideological like-mindedness between Western and Russian social democrats.[72]

Vera Zasulich took the opportunity to promote this when Kautsky asked her in 1902 to give a description for *Die Neue Zeit* of the different revolutionary currents in Russia. The article, which came out in 1903, was, following Akselrod's of 1898, a second attempt to vindicate Russian social democracy in the eyes of Western socialism. The title 'The terrorist movement in Russia' was well chosen. For it was Zasulich's intention to show that the terrorism which had recently been preached and perpetrated again by the socialist revolutionaries was to a far lesser degree an obvious product of Russian circumstances than many Western socialists were prepared to believe. Earlier, in the *Leipziger Volkszeitung*, Rosa Luxemburg, too, had condemned the systematic terrorism in Russia as ineffective. The Polish socialist felt that the socialist press should exercise great caution in its coverage of terrorism. In Germany this was generally the case. The SPD was afraid of being provoked and did not wish to risk coming into conflict with the authorities because of its alleged collaboration with Russian murderers. Otherwise they could not defend the interests of the Russian socialists who remained in Germany against the German police and justices who sometimes acted as if they were receiving their orders from St Petersburg.[73]

This was nevertheless not the same thing as a complete rejection of terrorism and all the revolutionary heroism which clung to it. Among the Iskrites Akselrod was probably the fiercest opponent of revolutionary violence. Some time later at the Second Party Congress of the RSDRP in 1903, he was to submit a resolution which was also accepted by the meeting, in which it was said of the socialist revolutionaries that they were in fact not socialists but bourgeois democrats whose terrorist activities harmed the proletariat and the struggle against autocracy. The absurdity of an accusation like this struck only a few of the participants at the congress. The resolution had undoubtedly been so clearly formulated because successful terrorist actions did not leave the Russian social democrats unmoved either. Hatred of the regime was simply one of their principal motives. Earlier in *What Is To Be Done* Lenin had thrown vitriol over people who supported social democrat ideas and at the same time defended terrorism. Nevertheless, there were still people in the RSDRP who refused to condemn terrorists so severely and did not want to preclude co-operation with them. Among the European socialists there was no one to be found who rejected the socialist revolutionaries because they were not socialists and not revolutionaries.[74]

In the writing of her article Zasulich gave due consideration to these feelings. 'Kautsky remarked about my article', she wrote to Akselrod, 'that I had been involved in the revolution for more than a generation (I am thus evidently 80 years old or so [Zasulich was 53 at the time – B.N.]), but that I had never yet taken up even half such an unprejudiced position towards it.'[75] Zasulich made a careful distinction between incidental terrorism by a few isolated persons and organised terrorism by the Party of Socialist Revolutionaries (PSR). For individuals who tried to free themselves from a smothering oppression by means of a heroic flight forward, the social democrats had great sympathy. They even felt themselves partly responsible for these deeds of despair. Their party, because of its inadequate organisation and internal differences of opinion, was not in a position to guide these people's hatred of the regime and sacrificial zeal on to the right track. The rise of the socialist revolutionaries too, in the midst of the increasing social and political unrest in Russia was facilitated by the temporary lack of coherence among the social democrats. The new-style populists had also profited from the so-called crisis within international Marxism. Their ideas were a sort of hotch-potch of Marx's and Lavrov's body of knowledge. Of course, wrote Zasulich, the socialist revolutionaries presented themselves as the true followers of the People's Will (*Narodnaya Volya*). According to the socialist revolutionaries terrorism was an indispensable weapon in the hands of the revolutionaries for the protection of the people's movement against the hydra of tsarism and the utter arbitrariness of the tsar's ministers.

Zasulich challenged this emphatically by pointing out that the regime had sufficient people at its disposal to fill the gaps in its ranks which had been opened up by the terrorists. The minister of the interior, Sipyagin, who had been moderate in everything, was assassinated and succeeded by Pleve, notorious for his cruelty. Moreover terrorism had its own dynamism. It swallowed up all the energy of a revolutionary group and led to total exhaustion and moral decline. Self-sacrificing people now ought to take their places in the midst of the masses and control their emotions. The socialist revolutionaries even dared to accuse the social democrats of not being truly revolutionary in their propaganda and agitation and in their struggle to organise the workers. Demonstrations and strikes according to these revolutionaries delivered the workers up to the Cossacks. Zasulich in contrast suggested that this was in fact the only way in which 'the new Russia' could join battle with the autocracy. It was no less brave or dangerous than terrorism, which brought people to the gallows.

Zasulich's portrait of the socialist revolutionaries was not unfair. She avoided, for instance, drawing the reader's attention to the striking similarities shared by anarchists and socialist revolutionaries in the field of fighting methods and organisation. Nor was the socialist and revolutionary character of this party proposed for discussion. Zasulich did point out that the socialist revolutionaries were as scatter-brained as their populist predecessors because they made no distinction between the peasants and the workers. She forgot to mention that in 1902 there had been a number of peasant uprisings behind which the government suspected the social revolutionaries. This omission was not fortuitous. The Russian social democrats might not have thought much of the peasants, but Zasulich knew that the Western socialists were not inclined to write off the Russian peasants as a revolutionary factor. In this – as Zasulich very well knew – they were thinking wholly in the spirit of Marx. It was moreover unfair of Zasulich to saddle the PSR (Party of Socialist Revolutionaries) with the accusation that they had no detailed theoretical programme. The RSDRP also had none and Lenin and Plekhanov were fighting like two tigers over every paragraph of the draft that *Iskra* was going to submit to the coming party congress. Zasulich and the others had their hands full to prevent a split in the editorial staff.

The later history of the PSR was to confirm the accuracy of Zasulich's ideas about terrorism. But even though the ideology and the tactics of this party were primitive and backward in Marxist eyes, the PSR was soon to form a political force which would prove to be at least the equal of the social democrats. The Iskrites themselves on the other hand constituted the living proof that lavish attention to theory and ideological dialectic safeguarded the socialists even less from illusions. Further developments within Russian social democracy would in a distressing fashion give the lie to the optimism that Zasulich displayed in this article about the future of her own party. She naturally emphasised the fact that the crisis experienced by the social democrats had been more or less surmounted. There were still a few groups of émigrés who opposed *Iskra*, such as Krichevsky and others, but these had no backing in the mother country any more. Now that there was substantial unanimity in the ideological field, the first task for the social democrats was to organise their party as efficiently as possible.

Zasulich left it in no doubt that the independence of the local party committees would have to come to an end. A revolutionary party could never react quickly to developments in its favour unless unanimous decisions were taken and implemented. The vital importance of a guiding organ, a central committee to which the local sections would be subordinate, was universally appreciated, though there were differences of opinion about its character. The Iskrites were, however, convinced that the tsar's 'regime of absolute despotism' only offered socialism one way of organising itself. 'It will be an organisation of select 'illegal' revolutionaries; an organisation consisting of people who have so to speak made the revolution into their only profession, who devote themselves exclusively to revolutionary work and as a result are in a position to change not only their names but their circumstances and thus escape persecution, while they continue to serve their cause and their cause alone.'[76]

Thus the organisational model which Lenin had worked out in *What Is To Be Done* was taken over in full and for the first time presented to the outside world as the only one possible. It has amazed historians that the remaining members of the *Iskra* editorial staff voiced so little fundamental criticism of Lenin's ideas and that it was only a year later, at the 1903 Second Party Congress, that irreconcilable differences of opinion were found to exist which were the source of a definitive split in the RSDRP. However, the real problem was that there was no attractive alternative for the organisation of social democracy in Russia. There was indeed criticism of Lenin's obstinacy, his minimal interest in moral problems, his verbal extremism and his inability to conform to the judgement of others. But Plekhanov's autocratic tendency caused similar problems. Moreover Lenin was the only one in the group who understood the art of organisation. His ideas about it were not original and were derived directly from the People's Will. The Liberation of Labour Group had also always thought that the word 'party' meant an organisation of this kind. The People's Will, wrote Zasulich, had always consisted of generals without an army. Now there was the proletariat, and the RSDRP guaranteed 'that soon the illegal cadres would be at hand which in Russian circumstances are necessary to mobilise this army'.[77]

The socialist revolutionary Rusanov was one of the few who reacted to Lenin's document. He had criticised Lenin's negative attitude towards trade union work, but had praised the author because his remarks about the importance of conspiratorial activities by a small minority came so close to the Blanquist views of the People's Will.[78] Rusanov got to the heart of the matter here. But the Iskrites had always seen terrorism and 'Economism' as two sides of the same coin, as a result of the glorification of 'spontaneity' in the behaviour of workers and revolutionary intellectuals. In their opinion the co-ordinated action of the two groups ought to be a result of the right social democratic 'consciousness' which could only be conferred on the movement by Marxist ideologists. This was of course true not only for Russia but for every socialist workers' party. Lenin had made an emphatic reference to a quotation from Kautsky for this, though he could just as well have based himself on a statement by Plekhanov or Akselrod.

For Lenin, however, there was no distinction in principle between 'the mobilisation' and the 'inspiring with consciousness' of the working class. He was one of the rare intellectuals who meant what he wrote literally. But for the other Iskrites too, the word 'mobilisation' was more than just a militant metaphor. With the exception of Plekhanov, they were soon to realise that they had not seen through Lenin, and that they themselves, during the dogged struggle against every adversary, were temporarily blinded to the dangers caused by an ultra-centralised and authoritarian party organisation. However, it was not only their Jacobin inclinations or Russian circumstances which were playing tricks on them: contacts with the Western labour movement, which in its own opinion should have been the great guide for the Russian proletariat, had above all given these émigrés a feeling of impotence and frustration. There was also a certain anxiety that as Russians they would not be taken seriously unless, during a period of social unrest in their fatherland, they presented themselves as the most militant and disciplined revolutionaries. Only then perhaps would their criticism of the terrorists be accepted. Their ostentatious preference for forceful power and authority is understandable if one pays attention to the functioning of their Western examples, the SPD and the parties which followed in its wake. Western social democracy remained, as it had in many respects originally been, a sharply negative reaction to the social radicalism of the first half of the nineteenth century. A massive following, a democratic party organisation, a 'scientific' ideology and a socialist delegation in parliament were the answers of modern socialism to the utopian dogmatism and the conspiratorial sectarianism of the 'old movement'. Therefore at first sight it seems amazing that Russian social democracy could only become 'presentable' by introducing itself as an old-fashioned secret society that had to lead a backward proletariat to the promised land. In fact, however, the contrasts between East and West were much less distinct and the SPD could remain the party which mirrored the RSDRP, not only as a model for the distant future but even for immediate practice. The actual balance of power within the SPD and its Western sister parties was after all to a large extent determined by the presence of domineering leaders and by an expanding party bureaucracy. The Western socialist parties displayed conspicuously populistic traits. As in Russia, the mobilisation of the masses for ends desirable to the leaders was easier and more natural than the painful process of training and educating workers into perfect representatives of their class. The dangers for the Russian revolutionary movement which Lavrov and Akselrod had pointed out, also existed in another form in the West. Nor were critics, especially from the anarchistic side, lacking there either.

Authoritarian leadership continued to be a normal phenomenon within the socialism of both East and West. The Russian professional revolutionary found his counterpart in the Western salaried party official. Apart from the revolutionary intermezzo in 1905, the situation in both halves of Europe remained fairly stable until 1914. Everywhere, the social democrats were obliged to take on routine activities while waiting for the great day which was never to come. The stability of the executive elite and a somewhat relentlessly optimistic view of the future prevented the socialists as a whole from becoming aware of what dangers the normal ins and outs of party life brought with it for its continued existence as a bulwark of socialism. After 1914 it would become apparent how wide the gulf between ambition and reality was and how little these leaders and this professional executive were capable of dealing with the problems raised by war, revolution and totalitarianism. Around 1900, however, it was not surprising that the Russian social democrats tried to impress their foreign comrades with a strong leadership and a strict organisation. The SPD leadership had every sympathy with this, not only because it was characteristic of their own party, but mainly because their image of the Russian situation seemed to justify extreme measures.

### MENSHEVISM AND BOLSHEVISM

Perhaps in this way the Iskrites could have earned for themselves the abiding respect of Western socialists. But this did not succeed, because they soon became hopelessly divided. As a result the socialist revolutionaries continued to reap the benefit of the Western esteem which the traditional European image of Russia and Russian revolutionaries could supply. It is well known that the RSDRP split into Mensheviks (members of the minority) and Bolsheviks (members of the majority) at the Second Party Congress in the summer of 1903. Although this congress was held in Brussels and, because of the disturbing interest of the Belgian and the Russian police, was continued in London, it went unremarked by Western socialists. Not only did no single foreigner attend any of the many lengthy sittings, but the usual telegrams, letters and so on with which socialists on these occasions gave evidence of international solidarity were also absent. Since the deplorable results of the congress were disconcertingly confusing, Western socialists could not make head or tail of it subsequently. They would also have preferred not to have got mixed up in these Russian vendettas. But they had to, for they had the fearful suspicion that these quarrelling Slavs were the ones chosen to lead a revolution which might perhaps offer the one and only chance of realising socialism in the West within the foreseeable future.[79]

At the congress the comparison between Russia and the West formed the backcloth against which a number of the most violent debates took place. It was almost symbolic that one of the delegates who was appearing as an opponent of the *Iskra* school of thought had chosen the name of the Belgian socialist de Brouckère as her political pseudonym. The opposition to *Iskra*, which consisted of a couple of 'Economists' who had been allowed into the congress and a few representatives of the Bund, the Jewish social democratic labour movement, was doomed to failure from the start. It was only natural that this small group should appoint itself as the defender of more democratic, more Western attitudes in the party in so far as Russian circumstances allowed. The Bundists and 'Economists' therefore also supported Martov and his adherents when this group of Iskrites proved defenders of similar ideas, and got into a hopeless conflict with Lenin and his followers about it. This new 'Menshevik' trend at the congress, which did not yet possess a clear vision and which tactically speaking was acting extremely clumsily, did not thank the 'Economists' and the Bundists for their support. The old animosities still proved to be more powerful than the newly born ones between Bolsheviks and Mensheviks. The Iskrites continued to form one block against their former enemies. Consequently the opponents of *Iskra* felt themselves obliged to leave the congress, with the result that Lenin afterwards had control of a majority and the congress ended with a series of decisions which sealed the split in the party.

Thus these Bundists and 'Economists', and especially Akimov their principal spokesman, were the first to point out the fatal consequences of the decisions the congress was making. There was enough to complain about. The congress was not representative of the party as a whole. A number of organisations and groups had not been invited or were under-represented. The Iskrites had, often by unseemly methods, built up a secure majority. The proposed party organisation left hardly any room for initiative from the lower ranks and likewise seemed to be directed towards the muzzling in advance of all future opposition. The party programme left much to be desired with regard to clarity on the most essential points, and the explanation of some congress-goers made one fear the worst. Plekhanov shed a strange light on the concept 'dictatorship of the proletariat', which the RSDRP was the only party in the world to mention

in its programme. Under the motto *salus revolutionis suprema lex*
he declared that the revolutionaries should be prepared to tear
apart every parliament where there was no co-operative majority
to be found. Akimov did his best to convince his fellow party
members, by pointing out the practices and programmes of
Western social democracy, that there were reasonable alternatives. He believed that it was bureaucratic centralism itself, combined with haziness of ideology and programme, which left
room for dictatorial tendencies and the craving for political
adventurousness within the RSDRP.

The congress would not listen to him. Subsequent history
consolidated Akimov so firmly in the role of a socialist Cassandra
that he even acquired a historian who was able to estimate his
merits as a prophet of doom at their full value.[80] But Akimov
shared this honour with a number of figures from the Russian
socialist or communist movement who were praised by other
historians for similar reasons, such as Plekhanov, Akselrod,
Martov, Tsereteli, Luxemburg, Trotsky and Bukharin. Not only
in the historiography of the Russian revolution but also in that
of socialism, a great deal of attention has been given to people
who at a given moment were on the margin of the movement
or completely outside it, who could perhaps have warded off
disasters if they had only been able to carry out their policies
or if their warnings had not been disregarded. Even Lenin,
because of his critical remarks about Stalin in his political testament, qualified for this tradition. There is therefore reason for
some restraint in the posthumous distribution of prophets'
mantles, for the history of socialism in fact includes too many
Cassandras for every instance to be taken seriously. These people
were of course nearly always right, but this was not so much a
result of their prophetic gifts as of the utopian nature of socialism
itself.

Moreover, however disturbed a socialist in 1903 might have
been about less democratic practices and ideas amongst his
comrades and the dictatorship to which these could lead, he did
not have the faintest suspicion of the totalitarian monster which
we would meet in the twentieth century, and which has so
profoundly determined *our* understanding of democracy. There
is therefore some point here in pausing to consider the problems
of revolution and morality and of democracy and dictatorship

as they occurred around 1900. Every socialist in East and West had great expectations of democracy. They did not realise that political democracy would be not much more than a continuation of the age-old game of ruling elites gaining and then losing power, with the voter's capricious favours as the only new regulatory mechanism. This was a democracy which not only Plekhanov or Lenin, but also Bernstein and Jaurès would have emphatically rejected. Their ideals extended much further. After all, they wanted to conquer power in order never to lose it again.

When Akimov pointed out the moderation of Western socialism to his fellow party members, he was well aware that this did not need to conceal itself behind illegality and emigration, those unhealthy breeding grounds for suspicion and fanaticism. But he was oblivious of the fact that in the European parties, too, there were considerable differences of opinion which were by no means always fought out in an honest, open and strictly democratic manner. Political parties simply do not function like that. In so far as Western socialism displayed moderation, this was not completely natural but to some extent enforced. In countries less autocratically governed than Russia there were many more opportunities for all sorts of different influential groupings to mobilise political opinion against socialism, and these were extensively used. Therefore it was the duty of socialist parties not only to spread a radical message, but also to demonstrate their political decency and trustworthiness. This had become second nature to Western socialist leaders, while the Russians did not even recognise the problem. Nevertheless, it was evident time and time again, for instance from the extreme reactions to people like Millerand and Bernstein who had broken out of the self-appointed isolation of socialism, that the old ideals still possessed great emotional force. Even someone like Jaurès did not expressly exclude revolution and violence. Western socialist parties around 1900 had no need of the concept 'dictatorship of the proletariat', but after 1917 it was to become evident how fascinating a term like this could still be for many people who belonged to these parties.

Amoral radicalism was not a typically Russian phenomenon. It was a general and permanent problem of socialism. The authoritarian character of certain leaders could be a significant factor in the development of such ideas. But it is wrong to attribute Lenin's disastrous role in the subsequent history of Russia and socialism solely to the circumstance that this man was a sort of twentieth-century Machiavelli or a criminal *realpolitiker*. There were other forces at work as well. Social reality, the misery which many workers had to undergo, led over and over again to the contemplation of radical solutions in which violence and dictatorial power played an important role. The socialist utopia also provided sufficient authority to carry out fairly ruthless actions. Likewise Marxism with its emphasis on historical inevitability made the age-old question about the morality of methods less relevant. Only after his split with Marxism could Bernstein once more urgently ask for attention to this problem. But we have already seen that for Bernstein Russia lay outside the usual norms of decency and morality. Consequently, in his opinion, events in that country were of scarcely any concern to the West.

Other Western social democrats, however, who had a following to lose and who bore genuine responsibilities, began to realise that socialist policy was a curious kind of compromise between dream and action. The clichés of the socialist image of Russia suited them well. In internal politics they had insufficient power to be able to realise drastic reforms. Both the fierce aversion to tsarist autocracy and the glorification of revolutionary heroism in Russia offered them an outlet for the idealism and revolutionary emotions which had accumulated within Western socialism. This was the exact opposite of the situation for the only critics of Bolshevism in the years to come, the Mensheviks. They were to see Russian circumstances more and more as an impediment to the expansion of their longed-for social democracy. For them, Western example and Western support became more and more important. Thus there arose a curious mutual dependence between moderate socialists in East and West. In Europe the glorification of Russian radicalism was used as a sort of safety valve with which to let off surplus revolutionary steam. On the other side the Mensheviks tried to utilise the moderation of the Western movement as a sort of brake to prevent the Russian movement from rushing into disastrous revolutionary adventures. In the course of time it was to become evident that moderate socialism in the West would not and could not fulfil this function.

But here we are going ahead of our story, for 1904, the first year after the RSDRP's Second Party Congress, gave the Mensheviks little occasion for sombre thoughts. Lenin, who had made use of his small majority at the end of the congress to occupy the administrative body of the RSDRP with his personal followers, was to gain little profit from this coup. On the contrary, his machinations only made it clear how easily the party could be delivered up to the dictatorship of an individual. And this was something from which even his own followers temporarily recoiled. Their hesitation enabled the Mensheviks to isolate Lenin, but not for good. Lenin was to fall out or quarrel with almost everyone in his environment. His mind and character permitted little understanding of divergent opinion or for the independence of comrades who were able to stand up to him to some extent. He was always ready for a split at a moment he considered right. His pedantry and the blunt straightforwardness of his argumentation nowadays turn the reading of his works, which consist mainly of polemic, into an exercise in boredom. Nevertheless, this man possessed the charm and talent to be able constantly to unite new groups of followers to himself or to reconcile himself with former enemies. In using people for his own ends Lenin was not only almost indiscriminate but also utterly practical and not without subtlety. But it should be emphasised again that it was not only Lenin's personality which made him such a formidable opponent. He was also able to take full advantage of the youthful inexperience of his adepts, of the essentially conspiratorial character of his party and of every emancipatory opposition movement's need for strong leadership.

The Mensheviks could of course change little of this. Nevertheless, it was not until after 1917 that Lenin was able to withdraw the Russian workers' movement definitively from their influence, and then only by making use of state power and state terrorism. Before the October revolution Bolshevism and Menshevism more or less balanced one another out, and which of the two currents could temporarily impress its seal with more force on to Russian social democracy was primarily dependent on fairly fortuitous circumstances. From this it became evident that the Menshevik strife for a Western-type labour movement under Russian circumstances was much more than just vain effort and that the differences between Russia and Europe hardly justified platitudinous generalisations. The Mensheviks' success is all the more remarkable because it was initially extremely difficult for them to give business-like and intellectually satisfying content to their ideological offensive against Lenin. From the beginning it was evident that the Marxist conceptual apparatus was more of a hindrance than a support in the search for an explanation of the Leninist phenomenon.

Of course after the party congress the Mensheviks opened fire upon Lenin's practices and concepts. But they could not do this without admitting that they had perpetrated and adhered to a somewhat less extreme form of these themselves. They were thus compelled to recognise that the critics of *Iskra*-policies in the party had to a large extent been right. But in doing this they also gave Lenin the chance to redirect to their address all the old accusations of opportunism and Bernsteinism which had been unloaded on to the 'Economists' by *Iskra*. How were they to explain that Lenin's centralism was wrong and Menshevik centralism was something good? It was hardly convincing when Martov, reacting to Plekhanov's undemocratic remarks at the congress, declared that he could not believe that the proletariat could ever end up in a situation in which it would have to suppress political rights such as freedom of the press. It was even less impressive that Plekhanov, whose Jacobin temperament had brought him to Lenin's side at the congress, a few months later dissociated himself from Lenin on the grounds that he seemed to be a sort of Robespierre. The Mensheviks ought to show that 'scientific socialism' had a different logic at its disposal in Russia, too. The only person who felt himself called upon to do this was Akselrod. In the long years before the congress he had lived in the shadow of Plekhanov, who was a sharper thinker and a better polemicist than he was. Now he stepped forward as the *spiritus rector* of Menshevism.

It was characteristic of Akselrod that in his analysis of Leninism he directed himself emphatically towards the whole party and did not even mention Lenin's name. The Second Congress, in his view, had marked the triumph of revolutionary thinking over the other ideological currents in the social democratic camp, but at the same time showed what a gulf there was between the intellectual aspirations and the practical transactions of the party.

The entire *Iskra* persuasion had wanted to have done with the amateurish organisation of the independently operating local party committees. The bureaucratic centralism which was held out to the whole party as a prescription for this complaint nevertheless bore witness to a much more amateurish mentality. Everything had been concentrated on the construction of an elaborate administrative apparatus in which the ordinary party members were tiny cogs in the wheel, which was set in motion by an all-powerful party leadership. But ultimately this machinery had been set in motion for one purpose: the creation of a unified social democratic party, by which the whole Russian proletariat could be united into one self-assured, emancipated group. But now, everyone had to realise that the means and the end were not in harmony.

Akselrod blamed the fact that this insight came so late on typically Russian circumstances. In the West, the social democrats had far more possibilities at their disposal for attracting the proletariat into political life in an active and independent manner. The European political system and the constitutional state were the result of a revolutionary struggle led in the past by the bourgeoisie. The struggle for freedom and democracy had a long tradition which had also influenced the workers. From a cultural and political point of view, they were already to some extent prepared for their future task, and because of this more susceptible to the socialist message. In this way they were also in a position to maintain and develop themselves as a separate group in a hostile capitalist environment. But the Russian proletariat was walking in darkness and its path had to be lit by the radical intelligentsia. The intellectuals, however, had to learn again and again to withstand the temptation of treating the proletariat as the cannon fodder of their future revolutionary battles. A Jacobin revolutionary zeal of this kind only bore witness to their bourgeois background. And now their very task was to guard the workers from bourgeois paternalism. This was especially important in Russia. A socialist revolution, the establishment of a proletarian dictatorship, was after all not in order there. It was more a matter of eliminating tsarist autocracy and establishing a bourgeois, democratic republic. The workers would not only have to form the decisive force behind this revolution, but also be able to show themselves to be an independent and oppositional factor in political life after-wards. Therefore it was of vital importance for the social demo-cratic intelligentsia to understand that its initial task was one of service and education and not one of leadership.[81]

In a brief summary, Akselrod's balanced, stately Marxist gen-eralisations acquire an almost banal casualness. But for his sym-pathisers in the party who had lost their ideological compass amongst the intrigues and feuds of the faction struggle, he was the first man to have put the Menshevik creed into words. His ideas were enthusiastically embraced and later, too, the Men-sheviks were constantly to wonder whether their standpoints were indeed *po Aksel'rodu* (à la Akselrod), that is to say whether the emancipation of the proletariat and the growth of an as Western as possible socialist movement were being promoted by them. But Akselrod had not stated how this strife should be put into practice. Moreover he had drawn heavily on the work-ers' will to elevate themselves into self-confident proletarians. This was an extremely difficult task, even in the West, at which Akselrod was once more looking through somewhat rose-coloured spectacles.

Lenin reacted furiously to Akselrod's article, which in his opinion represented a denial of everything that had been brought about in the *Iskra* period. According to the Bolshevik leader Akselrod had written a sort of Bernsteinian apologia for the Menshevik rebellion against the lawful decisions of the Second Party Congress and Lenin answered this with a pamphlet of at least two hundred pages in length entitled *One Step Forward, Two Steps Backwards*. Lenin was of course incapable of seeing his organisational ideas as a model for a personal dictatorship, for he was driven by a socialist ideal of great simplicity and not by a pathological thirst for power. He simply could not under-stand – as his opponents certainly could – that the results of both impulses could now and then be identical. In his view the workers would have no trouble in reconciling themselves to strict revolutionary discipline. They had after all been brought up in the severe training school of capitalist exploitation and factory work. It was the intellectuals, wrapped in cotton wool, who refused to subject themselves to the laws and norms which were necessary to control a social democratic movement. In *What Is To Be Done* of 1902 Lenin had excluded the proletariat from the party and placed it under the control of the intelligentsia.

In *One Step Forward, Two Steps Backwards* of 1904 he freed the party from the disastrous influence of the intellectuals. If he had had his way, there would have been nothing left but a compact underground organisation which could have been put in motion by its leader at any moment and which would not shrink from any method of winning over and making use of the masses.

Within a year the fundamental differences between Bolshevism and Menshevism had made themselves clearly manifest. Bolshevism was proudly acclaimed by Lenin as *true* social democracy, as the twentieth-century form of Jacobinism. The Mensheviks were, in contrast, the fickle Girondists of this century. Lenin naturally did not think of really identifying himself with an eighteenth-century revolutionary movement. In his historical comparison there was nevertheless an important grain of truth. The Mensheviks were not averse to violence and power, for they firmly held on to the class war, the revolution, the dictatorship of the proletariat and the hierarchical party structure. Their ideology was thus characterised by the same kind of ambivalences as those with which Western social democracy was struggling. In Lenin's view the emphasising of a *humane* class war, a *decent* revolution or a *noble* dictatorship was irrelevant. Power was power and violence was violence; the end would justify the means. The advantages of straightforward, ice-cold logic were his, but so were the consequences.

## *DIE NEUE ZEIT* AND RUSSIAN PARTY DISPUTES

However, the hysterical fanaticism with which Lenin attacked his opponents went against all reason. He simply denied that they were social democrats and put them on a par with Western revisionists and reformists. As before he sought recognition and support from the German social democrats, who could never with the best will in the world be regarded as Jacobins. In *What Is To Be Done* he had defended the authoritarian relationship between the professional revolutionaries and the working masses by pointing out the continuity of leadership in the SPD. In *One Step Forward, Two Steps Backwards* he appealed to Kautsky's authority to prove that the 'organisational opportunism' of the Mensheviks was evidence of a reformist mentality. In *Die Neue Zeit* Kautsky had indeed sided with the SPD leadership when, in a couple of cases, it had curtailed the freedom of action of chosen members of parliament and union leaders by appealing to the higher interests of the party.[82] The organisational relationships within the SPD were indeed under pressure and came up for discussion at party congresses. Lenin was right in stating that the centralising trend was increasing. Kautsky was not opposed to this in itself, but he was somewhat disturbed by the increase in officialdom and bureaucracy which accompanied it. For Parvus and Rosa Luxemburg this was a veritable spectre. This was also one of the main reasons why Lenin, who besides bureaucracy also propagated a sort of German *Kadaver- und Schafsgehorsam* (mechanical discipline and sheep mentality), aroused their disgust. It went without saying that Kautsky was more sensitive to their judgement about Lenin than to Lenin's judgement about old comrades of long standing such as Plekhanov and Akselrod. He found it impossible to believe that these people had suddenly become followers of Bernstein.[83]

The Mensheviks had of course been trying to influence Kautsky for a long time. Dan as well as Akselrod had expressed every sort of criticism of Lenin in correspondence. Akselrod, however, neglected to send Kautsky a translation of the article in *Iskra* in which he ranked the party disputes as being more than just a quarrel about personal and organisational matters. Kautsky thus did not know exactly what was happening, and experience had convinced him that Russian socialists were always quarrelling and that as an outsider one was better off not involving oneself. The timing of this most recent disagreement was, however, particularly unfortunate. In the second half of 1903 the world had been rudely awakened by the threat of war in the Far East, and after the outbreak of the Russo-Japanese War in January 1904 the hope for a socialist breakthrough in Europe thanks to a revolution in Russia was revived in many socialists.[84]

In 1904 Kautsky devoted an article in *Die Neue Zeit* to Europe's revolutionary prospects. Once more he drew attention to the unlikelihood of a revolution breaking out in Germany. 'The German government is still today the most powerful in the world', he observed soberly. The Russian situation was described with the usual rhetoric: 'On the other hand there is no other government in the whole of Europe, with the possible exception of Turkey, as feeble as that of Russia ...' And Russia now had a proletariat which 'plunges itself into battle in defiance of death when it is still at the stage in which it has nothing to lose but its chains and a whole world to win'. If the war were to lead to a 'violent conflagration of the revolutionary movement' and the fall of tsarism, then this would have large-scale repercussions in the West. This splendid prospect of course assumed that the future leaders of the Russian revolution would not fritter their time away in bickering amongst themselves.[85]

Kautsky did not mention this complication to his readers, for that would have thoroughly undermined the effect of his argument, but he urged unity on his Russian friends. In the course of time the whole Western socialist movement would exert very great pressure on the Russian socialists of all persuasions to lay down their mutual differences and harmoniously devote themselves to their most important task. But initially no one knew anything about these problems, and the few socialists who were informed showed a minimal interest in this typical emigrants' quarrel. The day before the outbreak of the Russo-Japanese conflict the Bureau of the Socialist International met and congratulated the RSDRP on the results of the Second Congress. In the presence of Plekhanov, Kautsky and Luxemburg, who were evidently careful to remain silent, the meeting recorded *avec une joie bien vive* that the Russian social democrats were now once more united.[86] However, shortly afterwards, Kautsky was forced to take up a position, because Mandelshtam, one of Lenin's adjutants, offered him an article for *Die Neue Zeit* in which the party dispute was analysed from a Bolshevik point of view. This contribution was refused, but Kautsky, for politeness' sake, did explain this decision in a letter to Mandelshtam. To avoid misunderstandings he sent a copy of it to the Mensheviks.

Mandelshtam came to hear that his article would not be published because the German workers were so strongly ruled by the desire for unity that they hated a party in which quarrels took place. This did not only apply to the Russians but also to the French. However, at this moment it was of the utmost importance that the Russians should be given the most wholesale suport possible by the Germans. Publication of the split in the RSDRP, for as long as the chance of restoration of unity existed, was therefore in no one's interest. Kautsky sided with the Mensheviks, however. He referred to the historical example of the SPD, which at the time of the anti-socialist legislation had likewise not found it necessary to create an organisation of the Leninist type. He blamed Lenin to a large extent for having robbed Akselrod, Zasulich and Potresov of their important positions as editors of the party paper at the Second Party Congress.

From this statement it is evident how poorly informed Kautsky was. The comparison between the RSDRP and the SPD of the time of Bismarck would not stand up. After all socialist delegates could then, because of universal suffrage, certainly be elected to parliament in Germany. The editorship of Akselrod, Zasulich and Potresov was not extended by a majority of the delegates at a party congress which they themselves accepted as lawful. Moreover, after the Mensheviks had eased Lenin out of the editorial staff, they were restored to their former positions. Kautsky underestimated the seriousness and the nature of the conflict by making the suggestion to both sides that they should have a cooling-off period. In his view Russian social democracy would take on a heavy responsibility if, because of personal and organisational problems, it let 'the one valuable, never to be repeated opportunity to strike at Russian absolutism' slip past. He deprived himself of every chance of having this proposal accepted by the Bolsheviks when he added: 'Lenin, however, would have to take responsibility for having begun this disastrous dispute.' Lenin had, after all, just as much right to claim that the other party had begun it.[87]

The Mensheviks were of course delighted with this reaction and they asked permission to print the letter in *Iskra*. After the appearance of Lenin's *One Step Forward, Two Steps Backwards* they were in an aggressive mood. Only Parvus had repeatedly insisted that unity should be restored in view of the situation in Russia. But Akselrod now actually made up his mind that there was no place for Lenin in the party and that steps should be taken to rule out his becoming party leader. Were this to meet with resistance from the Bolsheviks – and that went without saying – then the question should be brought before the Bureau of the International and prominent socialists such as Bebel and Kautsky should have access to all the relevant documents and publications. But according to Potresov mental attitudes would first have to be made ripe for this. As soon as he had Kautsky's permission to publish his letter to Mandelshtam, he wrote to Akselrod: 'So, the first bomb has been made and with God's help will blow up Lenin ... if we explode it, then let it be completely, methodically and according to plan ... However, the problem is how we should defeat Lenin. Firstly, I think, we should set the authorities on him, Kautsky (who has already done his duty), Rosa Luxemburg and Parvus.'[88]

Kautsky was somewhat surprised that he had evidently analysed the problems of his Russian friends so aptly. He had the feeling, he wrote to Akselrod, that behind the organisational problems other, deeper differences of opinion lay concealed. But with a little tact it should nevertheless be possible to restore unity 'over Lenin's head'. He therefore refused, despite Akselrod's repeated insistence, to dissociate himself publicly and as a matter of principle from Bolshevism.[89] But since he saw the elimination of Lenin as the quickest solution to the difficulties, he did publish in *Die Neue Zeit* an article by Rosa Luxemburg, which she had originally written for *Iskra* at the request of Potresov. The Russian party disputes, which had been so carefully kept secret from the outside world, were then proclaimed from the mountain tops. That was a disadvantage which had to be accepted into the bargain.

In order to dispel the impression that Luxemburg's article was no more than a hostile reaction from one of Lenin's opponents, Kautsky wrote by way of introduction in *Die Neue Zeit* that the problems it raised were also under discussion 'of the most lively kind' at the moment within the SPD. But Rosa's verdict on Lenin's ideas was devastating. His 'ultracentralism' was 'of its very nature not the product of a constructive and creative, but rather of a sterile, night-watchman, mentality'. Russian social democracy was on the eve of 'a great revolutionary battle for the overthrow of absolutism'. For this it would have to appeal to the inventiveness, the improvisational skills and the initiative of the revolutionaries and there was no room whatsoever in Lenin's organisation for that. In Germany too, there was a good chance that the SPD, because of its exclusive concentration on parliamentary tactics, would not have a revolutionary answer at its disposal if the situation were to demand it.[90]

The reformism and revisionism in the Western movement, which in Luxemburg's view was rightly called 'opportunism' by Lenin, was in her opinion a product of middle-class parliamentarianism and the growth of the labour movement. In Russia this problem did not arise. In other words, according to Rosa the Mensheviks were not opportunists, as Lenin claimed. But she went a step further: 'Even from the standpoint of Lenin's apprehensions of the dangerous influences of the intelligentsia on the proletarian movement, his own concept of the organisation constituted the greatest danger for Russian social democracy.' Therefore Lenin, in Luxemburg's view, was more comparable with former socialist leaders like Blanqui or Lasalle than with the leaders of modern social democracy. Kautsky added an editorial note to the effect that the non-social-democratic Fabians in England, and especially the Webbs, were the most diligent advocates of bureaucratic centralism and opponents of democratic organisations in which the proletarian masses could make their influence felt. According to Luxemburg, Lenin's aversion to the socialist intelligentsia could be found again in the *Méfiez-vous des politiciens!* of the French syndicalists or the suspicion of the British trade unions for socialist 'visionaries'.[91]

One important fact was to emerge from these remarks, namely that dictatorial inclinations within socialism should not necessarily be identified exclusively with Bolshevism or with Russia. For the rest Luxemburg, in her very characteristic way, had made things easy for herself. She devoted little attention to the differences between Russia and Europe, to which Lenin's personal leadership and organisation were in a number of respects a logical answer, and which certainly did not, as she claimed, exclude tactical manoeuvrability. In her view political terrorism and the absence of political freedom in Russia were of subordinate importance: 'in Russia too the mass movement had known how to overrun the restraints of the absolutist 'constitution' and create its own, even though crippled, 'constitution' of 'street disturbances'. It will know how to do this henceforth until its final victory over absolutism.'[92]

This certainly rather naive and therefore also dubious glorification of the spontaneity of the masses which came clearly to the forefront for the first time in this piece, was later to become Luxemburg's hallmark. It also proved how far removed she was – in theory at least – from Bolsheviks, Mensheviks and most social democrats, and how her viewpoint was approaching that of anarchists and syndicalists. Luxemburg's theory of spontaneity was in the first place the reaction of an outsider to the passivity and immobility that she thought she observed in the SPD. In her own small Polish party, which like the RSDRP consisted chiefly of intellectuals, Rosa was not very concerned about the application of her principles, and her friend Jogiches proved himself in those years to be a shrewd manipulator who, devoid of scruples, threw his weight about as a party leader of the Leninist type. Luxemburg had no real respect for the Mensheviks and her article was partly a revenge on Lenin, who had frustrated the affiliation of her party to the RSDRP by laying down very harsh conditions.[93]

Thus the fundamental significance of Luxemburg's intervention should not be estimated too highly; its practical results were likewise negligible. Kautsky refused to publish Lenin's rejoinder, but Lenin did not allow this to cause him to lose ground. Although he had temporarily lost power over the administration of the party, he nevertheless had at his disposal a number of followers who enabled him to carry on his fight against the Mensheviks as if he were still followed by a majority. On the other hand, the Mensheviks, just because they had found a willing ear in Kautsky, Parvus and Luxemburg, had increasingly to take account of Western yearning for the restoration of unity. So they did not persevere with their plans to excommunicate Lenin, who was not impeded by scruples of this kind. He began to make plans for another congress at which he would be able to expel the Mensheviks from the party. Thus Kautsky's clumsy and partisan intervention was counterproductive.

### THE WESTERN PARTIES AND RUSSIA.
### THE AMSTERDAM CONGRESS

Within the Western socialist movement which was now preparing to attend the congress of the International in Amsterdam in the summer of 1904, disagreement was so rife that the problems of the RSDRP, which practically no one knew or understood, could easily be overlooked. However, Russia had everyone's attention. The role of the International Socialist Bureau (ISB) in this was remarkable. In the eyes of the advocates of a forceful central administration of the International this institution was not much more than a letter-box. But that was enough to spread the anti-tsarist emotions or actions of one group or party over the whole International and all affiliated parties. The common aversion to tsarist Russia and solidarity with the Russian revolutionary movement could thus form an important connecting link between socialists of different nationalities and ideological orientations. We shall give below some examples of the various ways in which these parties became involved with Russia, beginning with an episode from the history of the Italian party.

In 1900 Italy had broken itself off from Germany and Austria by means of a treaty with France. The Italian socialists had applauded this for they saw French rather than German socialism as their example. However, the Italian government hoped to complete its new orientation in foreign policy by an approach to Russia, and that met with socialist opposition. Some leaders of the PSI realised that this development, in view of the international balance of power, had a certain inevitability and that the socialists, in so far as they felt themselves to be Italian, could not actually go against it. For the left wing, however, the arrest of the socialist revolutionary M. R. Gotz in Naples in March 1903 was a welcome occasion for attesting to its anti-Russian convictions. Gotz was the member of the Central Committee of the Party of Socialist Revolutionaries (PSR) who had the special task of supervising the terrorist activities of the combat detachment (*boevaya organizatsiya*) of the party. This section was led by Gershuni and Azeff. The latter was later to prove to be an *agent provocateur*. After consultation with Gotz, Gershuni had decided to organise an attack on the Russian minister of the interior, Sipyagin. This task was afterwards successfully carried out by their fellow party member Balmashev, whose trial attracted the attention of the world press. The PSR had publicly accepted full responsibility for this deed. The Russian government demanded from the Italian authorities the arrest and extradition of Gotz as accessory to murder.[94]

The socialist revolutionary Rubanovich, who lived in France, travelled to Rome to advise the Italian socialists who had already decided to do their best for Gotz's release. Since the PSR was not yet represented in the International, Plekhanov at the same time requested the Bureau to draw the attention of the European proletariat to this case, which it did by means of a circular to all the associated parties. There followed an extensive campaign in the Italian socialist press supported by questions in parliament. During his trial Gotz was defended by the socialist barrister Ferri, the editor-in-chief of the party paper *Avanti*. Gotz's release was celebrated as a great triumph for socialism.[95]

There was even more excitement when it was announced that the tsar intended to visit Italy. The socialist delegate Morgari informed parliament that the tsar would receive only catcalls from the Italian people. Ferri wrote to Victor Servy, the secretary of the International at the time, that the Bureau ought to support this action. But it soon became evident that not everyone was enthusiastic about this affair. Both the reformist leader Turati and the left-wing syndicalist Labriola wondered if such a blatant manifestation against the tsar could not be interpreted as a demonstration in favour of the Triple Alliance, the former treaty with Germany and Austria. Jaurès had similar qualms. He too sought a balanced judgement on the relationship with Russia. The ISB eventually did side with Morgari's idea, but was certainly not whole-heartedly enthusiastic about it. The Italian party's action against the tsar continued nevertheless and the government in St Petersburg abandoned the state visit. This was applauded in the socialist world as a great victory over Russian autocracy and tribute was paid to the PSI for this achievement in *Iskra*. Well over a year later, at the Amsterdam congress of the International, a proud Ferri reminded the socialists present of this Italian triumph and was rewarded with an 'explosion d'applaudissements'.[96]

In the same excited way the socialists reacted to the pogrom of Kishinev. The ISB, at the request of the Russian socialists, of course asked for a strong socialist protest against this outburst of anti-Semitism in Moldavia under the watchful eye of the tsarist authorities. But it was ridiculous that the Bureau pointed out to the European workers that with this pogrom tsarism above all was 'pursuing the extermination of the self-conscious proletariat'.[97] The co-operation between the police and justices of a number of Western countries and the Russian authorities also roused the anger of socialists and added an extra dramatic accent to the daily struggle between government and socialist opposition. Especially in France the socialists had got into the habit of posing as the guardians of Western civilisation while they accused their government of being in league with a barbaric power and of having themselves adopted its barbaric methods of combating revolutionaries.[98] The socialist revolutionaries made the utmost political capital out of events like this. Rubanovich, who was a French citizen and thus less vulnerable, started publication in

1904 of *La Tribune Russe*, a newspaper which came out every two weeks and in which the Western public was informed about the Russian revolutionary movement. The terrorism of the PSR was as constantly defended in it as the alliance between France and Russia was attacked. The paper was a great success and not only in France.[99]

In Germany the most spectacular events took place. Since the student uprisings in Russia and the assassination of the minister of education Bogolepov in 1901, the Russian students studying in Germany were kept under careful surveillance by order of Wilhelm II. Regular house-to-house searches were carried out, revolutionary texts were confiscated and students expelled from the country. The German police, thanks to their spies, knew very well which of the Russian students were members of revolutionary organisations and what contacts they maintained with the SPD. To the relief of the authorities the German students proved to have no revolutionary tendencies.

The SPD devoted a great deal of attention both in *Vorwärts* and in parliament to the authorities' 'licking the boots of tsarism' as Bebel expressively put it. Because of this the government tried to obtain proof that the German socialists were lending a helping hand to Russian 'terrorists, murderers and anarchists'.[100] Although the SPD outwardly continued to show its solidarity with the Russian social democrats, the party leadership was anxious. The Russian comrades were still being given generous assistance with the distribution of illegal literature. The cellars of the *Vorwärts* building were even serving as a storage space. 'I received a letter full of complaints from Bebel', wrote Parvus to Potresov.

> The public propaganda for a violent revolution by Russian social democracy is damaging to all German parliamentary tactics. Naturally there is nothing to be done about this, and I have written to him to that effect. But it should not be forgotten that the German government is only seeking an opportunity to accuse the social democrats of preparing for armed revolt in order to be able to justify the introduction of political repression at the same time. Therefore the editorial staff of *Iskra* must strive to avoid anything that the German government could consider to be formal grounds for advancing false accusations against the German social democrats ... Bebel has threatened amongst other

things to change the party's tactics towards the Russian social democrats. One should not lose sight of this.[101]

The climax of this sparring match between SPD and government was the *Königsberger Prozess* in July 1904. Nine party members stood trial for the smuggling of illegal literature. At the same time they were accused of attempted high treason, insulting the tsar and having dealings with unlawful secret societies. The party saw this as a repetition of the manoeuvres which had led to the introduction of the anti-socialist laws under Bismarck. The accused were defended by socialist attorneys, among them Hugo Haase and Liebknecht's son Karl, who had given legal aid to many Russian socialists in the preceding period. They successfully convinced the tribunal that Russian social democracy was an active opponent of all forms of revolutionary terrorism, with the result that the judges dropped the main points of the charge. However, what could have been regarded as proof of the existence of a German *Rechtsstaat* and of the moderation of Prussian judicial power, was triumphantly seen by some in the SPD as a 'blood trial over Russia and Prussia', indeed even as a 'collapse of Russian absolutism'.[102]

In July, the month in which the Königsberg trial was held, the socialist revolutionaries succeeded in killing the Russian minister of the interior, Pleve. Pleve was universally hated, even in Russian government circles. It is possible that the organiser of the attack, Azeff, acted not only in consultation with Gotz and the Central Committee of the PSR, but also with the tacit foreknowledge of some of the Russian authorities. In any case the assassination had a disruptive effect on public opinion in and out of Russia. 'I can remember', wrote the Menshevik Garvi in his memoirs more than forty years later, 'how the paper boys ran through the streets of Paris as they shouted out this sensational news and how the passers-by tore the newspapers out of their hands.' The news was received with jubilation in the entire Russian revolutionary and opposition camp. Liberals like Struve and social democrats like Plekhanov temporarily forgot their objections to terrorism.[103]   Plekhanov, who shortly beforehand, on behalf of the German comrades in Königsberg, had spoken out quite openly and in principle against terrorism, appears even to have suggested to the leadership of his party that this method should be recognised as an appropriate weapon in certain circumstances and that an agreement be made with the socialist revolutionaries. At this, Akselrod and Martov threatened to resign immediately and Plekhanov evidently quickly changed his mind. In an article for *Vorwärts* he argued that the work of a socialist agitator or propagandist in Russia was weightier and more difficult than the most daring attack. In his view Western socialists often forgot this. Even when they were against terrorism in principle, they still wrote about terrorists as if they were illustrious heroes. Plekhanov was referring here to editorial comments which had appeared in *Vorwärts*.[104]

The editorial board of *Vorwärts* defended itself by remarking that even though social democracy dissociated itself from terrorism, it could not help admiring revolutionaries who risked their lives in heroic sacrifice. Kautsky wrote to Plekhanov that one should not try to change the opinions of the *Vorwärts* editorial board, for it consisted of 'confused emotional socialists' and not of true-born Marxists. However, *Vorwärts*, in its recognition of terrorism, had taken a stand which was shared by practically the entire international socialist press and also many liberal newspapers. The opinion of *The Times* or the *Berliner Tageblatt* scarcely differed from that of the Dutch socialist newspaper *Het Volk*, the Viennese *Arbeiterzeitung*, the French *l'Humanité* or the Belgian socialists' paper *Le Peuple*.[105]

The socialist revolutionaries were triumphant. They did not realise that they had unwittingly handed over their terrorist organisation, which was virtually uncontrollable and had cost the party a fortune, to an *agent provocateur*. *La Tribune Russe* proudly reported reactions in the Western press. In an *Appel du Comité Central* of the PSR 'aux citoyens du monde civilisé' it was emphatically stated: 'Yes, citizens, the bloody act of justice which has just been accomplished by the Combat Organisation of our party, and for which the Central Committee does not hesitate to take upon itself full and total responsibility in the face of history and the conscience of civilised peoples, this act is neither an isolated fact, nor is it the action of an individual.'[106]

In this way in 1904 the socialist revolutionaries successfully dominated the image of the Russian revolutionary movement which the socialist world was trying to visualise. In Italy and France they were extraordinarily popular. The Russian social democrats were scarcely known there. In Germany and Austria too, they counted as people who at least did something. They evidently quarrelled less than the Russian social democrats, with whom, with some difficulty, solidarity was affirmed but who, as soon as they passed themselves off as labour leaders, continued to be regarded as children who had not yet learned to walk. The socialist revolutionaries repeatedly appealed to the statements of Marx and Engels about Russia and populism in order to dispel objections on the social democratic side to their programme and tactics. The PSR had already requested a seat on the BSI in 1903. It was evident that the party would take its place in the Socialist International at the following congress and that protests against this from Akselrod and Plekhanov would be to no avail.[107]

The congress of the International in Amsterdam, which was held in August 1904, took place in the shadow of the Russo-Japanese War. Before this war broke out the ISB had already expressed the fear that France, Germany and England would also become involved in the conflict and had called upon the socialists to do everything to prevent this. This request was complied with in various ways. General feeling in the socialist world was so anti-Russian that many saw the war as the struggle of moderation and progress as embodied by Japan against naked Russian reaction and aggression. The reformist *Sozialistische Monatshefte* expressed itself thus:

> Must the dominion over Eastern Asia devolve upon a nation which is in essence akin to the Eastern Asiatic peoples, but which is talented enough to spread the achievements of European culture over Eastern Asia within the foreseeable future, or must its new extension fall to the lot of an economically and politically backward regime, which is only capable of expansion but can in no way be considered as a modern power, and through which the rise of Japan will be arrested?

Kautsky, Arturo de Labriola and many other Western socialists commented in the same spirit. In this Hyndman found himself in harmony with public opinion in England, which was allied to Japan by a treaty. In France, however, opinion was strongly pro-Russian and only the socialists showed great concern about the possible consequences of France's solidarity with the tsar. Jaurès and his friends did not express themselves too critically about the Franco-Russian treaty which they still continued to see as a guarantee of France's security. They only hoped that the fall of tsarism would give France the assurance in the future that she would not be involved in the imperialistic adventures of her Eastern ally. The Guesdists and the Blanquists did, however, speak at the time of 'une alliance monstrueuse'.[108]

The Russian social democrats behaved as unpatriotically as possible, but the sympathy with Japan felt by many Western socialists was not shared by them. Their lack of patriotism did not go to the extent of reacting to the proposals of the Japanese government, which was prepared to place money and weapons at their disposal. Other Russian revolutionaries had fewer scruples. During a meeting of the ISB in Amsterdam in preparation for the congress it was established with approval that Plekhanov and the Japanese socialist Katayama could get on very well together. It was decided that they, together with the Dutchman Van Kol, would preside over the opening session of the congress. In his welcoming address to the congress Van Kol once more expressed his great appreciation of socialist love of peace and the international solidarity exhibited by the Japanese and the Russian.[109] The scene which followed is most charmingly described by the American Daniel de Leon.

> Plekhanov had been watching for his chance. The moment it came he seized it. He rose, stretched his arm across Van Koll's wide girth and took Katayama's hand. Katayama took the hint; he also rose and, symbolically, the Russian proletariat was shaking hands with their Japanese fellow wage slaves. It was a well thought out demonstration, the work of a flash of genius ... rousing the Congress from the languor it was drooping into, and driving it to frenzied applause ...[110]

This was a splendid beginning for Russian social democracy. The Mensheviks had done their best to present themselves as well as possible. Dan had written a report for the participants at the congress about the achievements of his party. In it he criticised the other Russian opposition parties such as the liberals and the socialist revolutionaries, but the conflict within the RSDRP was not mentioned.[111] The entire official delegation of the party consisted of Mensheviks: Plekhanov, Akselrod, Zasulich, Dan and Deutsch. The last of these was a former member of the Liberation of Labour Group, and his newly published book about the years of his exile in Siberia had been greeted very favourably in the West.[112] Lenin did not appear because he was ill, but he had sent Krasikov and Mandelshtam to Amsterdam. Lenin was furious about Dan's report, and Mandelshtam had therefore written a brochure specially for the congress about the party disputes. But the Bolsheviks were not admitted into the official delegation by the arrogant Plekhanov.[113]

The Bund also appeared with an eight-man-strong delegation which represented 23,000 Jewish workers in Russia. In its report to the congress the Bund also spoke about the problems within the RSDRP. The Bund had resigned from the party at the Second Party Congress because the congress had left it no room for independent organisation. The present quarrel between the Bolsheviks and the Mensheviks had brought all party activities to a standstill and threatened the RSDRP with total collapse. The Bund therefore asked to be allotted one of the two votes which the International had granted to each country.[114] The socialist revolutionaries, however, also demanded one. In their communications to the congress there was mention of the wrong interpretations of Marxism and the economic determinism of the Russian social democrats, who demonstrated 'an almost peasant-phobic mentality'. The PSR moreover defended 'direct revolutionary fighting', in other words terrorism, which could only be understood 'by studying the situation particular and special to Russia, the situation which tsarist reaction has created and for which it is and will remain responsible before history and humanity'.[115]

The monopoly position which Plekhanov and with him also the Mensheviks had recently enjoyed within the International – Krichevsky had not put in an appearance at the Bureau since 1902 – was now threatened from three sides. The pragmatic Victor Adler had, at the first meeting of the ISB in Amsterdam, suggested giving Russia three or four mandates, instead of the usual two. Adler was well aware of the fact that the Bund was the only workers' organisation of any significance in the entire Russian empire. Rosa Luxemburg had, however, tartly told the Austrian party leader in reply that Russia was not an 'ethnographical museum'. Most members of the Bureau, with the exception of Plekhanov of course, thought that the PSR should

F

have a seat in any case since they represented a different school of thought from the Mensheviks, the Bolsheviks or the Bundists, who were all social democrats. This was the decision made and with it a socialist grouping was admitted in Amsterdam which employed the same fighting methods as the anarchists, who had been excluded more and more rigorously from previous congresses.[116]

The Bundists could thus do little else than seek admission into the Menshevik delegation. But this was refused. The Mensheviks had been pleased to see that the two seats were divided between them and the Bundists. They had no wish to share their own seat with them. Whereupon the Bund once more put their case before the Bureau. Kautsky and Luxemburg tried to mediate, but came up against the indomitable Plekhanov. Kautsky did compel the Mensheviks to accept into their midst the two Bolsheviks who had also complained to the Bureau about Plekhanov. This proves that Kautsky shared the implacable viewpoint of his Russian friends much less than they had thought, and remained primarily intent on the restoration of unity.[117]

At the congress little was put forward against the Bureau's decisions. The Bundists remained outside the Bureau and had to be satisfied with the acceptance by the congress of a resolution they put forward against the anti-Semitic policies of the Russian government. Jaurès did refer to the acceptance of the PSR in a speech in which he put up a fight against an unusually harsh attack on Millerand. He considered that circumstances in European countries differed too much to justify generalising statements about socialist tactics. If the congress really thought it ought to denounce the behaviour of some socialists in the French republic, then it ought also to speak out about Russian terrorism and Plekhanov's criticism of it. Plekhanov replied that it would only be necessary to ask if a terrorist belonged to a socialist party when he had bowed before the tsar and accepted a ministerial seat like Millerand. With this polemic dexterity he certainly won some laughter, but at the same time let the only opportunity for a fundamental debate about terrorism slip by.[118] Rubanovich could safely explain that 'Russian revolutionary terrorism has always been surrounded by socialist sympathy. If an international congress had condemned it we would have hung our heads.'[119] Rubanovich defended terrorism once more during a massive open-air meeting in the Linnaeuspark. The only person in Amsterdam who openly turned against terrorism was the Romanian socialist Rakovsky. When Akselrod at the next meeting of the ISB made a vague allusion to the bourgeois and non-socialist character of the PSR and Rubanovich flared up about it, Vandervelde, the chairman, explained that the very fact of the admission of socialist revolutionaries into the Bureau of the International permitted no doubt about the socialist character of their party.[120]

There did prove to be a certain anxiety at the congress that Russian methods and modes of thought might find acceptance in the West. In one of the debates Clara Zetkin angrily accused the socialist revolutionary Ustinov of wanting to connect the issue of the general strike with Russian terrorist practices. Jaurès warned the congress against neglecting democratic and republican principles for the benefit of socialist ones. It was evidence of a dangerous partiality when Russian revolutionaries claimed under the influence of 'our eminent friend' Plekhanov that 'this triumph of democracy will replace the intelligent egoism of a monarch with the free egoism of the bourgeois class monopolising the emancipation movement'. The Belgians Anseele and Furnémont also explained that it was quite easy for the Russians not to fall out over the issue of co-operation with bourgeois parties and participation in the government.[121]

Adler said he found it remarkable that the two countries which cried out the loudest for international unity, France and Russia, were themselves the most divided. When Plekhanov interrupted this with: 'Not the Russian Marxists!', Adler reacted: 'Yes, if you throw out the undesirable elements from the party it is not difficult to achieve unanimity of tactics!' This incident caused merriment. The congress had indeed spent a great deal of time on the reconciliation of differences between socialists and had also taken a resolution in which it was stated that there was only one proletariat in each country and therefore there should be only one socialist party and 'the disastrous results of the continuation of splits' were mentioned. The different French socialist parties had under this pressure decided to co-operate and this was to lead to the formation of the SFIO (Section Française de l'Internationale Ouvrière).

For the Russians the matter was far more difficult. Rubanovich had openly declared that he could not vote for the resolution of unity since no merger was possible with the Russian social democrats. Nevertheless, the congress remained optimistic, the leading German social democrats in particular believing that they had achieved something by working on old friends like Plekhanov and Akselrod. A month later Bebel said at the SPD congress in Bremen: 'Another gratifying fact is that the Amsterdam congress also had a very salutary influence on the different Russian groups, so that some of them who came to Amsterdam as enemies recognised that it is of vital importance to present a united front to the common foe'. He was soon to realise that he was mistaken and that even the outbreak of a revolution could not compel the Russian socialists to unite.[122]

# 4

## 1905: A FAILED REVOLUTION
## IN RUSSIA

A large question mark can be placed against the revolutionary inclination of Western socialism after 1900, and contemporaries and historians have not neglected to do this. Certainly when seen in retrospect, the so-called emancipation of the working class proved in practice to amount to nothing more than a gradual integration into capitalist society. And thanks to this development the rudiments of an essentially nineteenth-century revolutionary tradition were slowly but surely eroded. Thus everything to do with making a revolution seemed to belong to the romanticism and rhetoric of socialism. However, such an interpretation does too little justice to the importance of social protest as a permanent theme in the history of Western Europe, which has simply never experienced a harmoniously integrated society. Movements like socialism, which set themselves up as spokesmen and representatives of resistance to the existing order, were then seldom or never capable of a complete revolutionary destruction of it. Thus they were confronted with the problem of having to canalise this social and political dissatisfaction. The leadership could not let itself at the slightest provocation become involved in one kind of adventure or another. The moment for a meeting, a demonstration, a strike or an uprising had to be carefully chosen. On the other hand, the leadership had to give due consideration to the emotions which dominated the lowest regions of its own movement. The members could after all leave the organisation *en masse* because it no longer represented their current interests.

The usual answer to this problem was the creation of an organisational subculture which could ensure a certain stylisation and regularisation of basic dissatisfaction and indignation. This subculture played a very important role in the socialist movement. There remained a tension, however, between the rational, well-thought-out, self-interest of the movement and the emotions from which it derived its right to exist. The socialist workers' movement totally failed to domesticate all the existing forms of primitive and spontaneous social protest within its own social base. By no means did it reach all the workers. Socialist parties proved to be viable because most of the people who belonged to them realised that violent resistance or revolution was impossible in normal circumstances, or in any case entailed serious risks and could have unpredictable results. Nevertheless, they had joined because they believed in the necessity for and the possibility of fundamental changes. This was also the criterion against which the policy of their own party, trade union or club and the behaviour of their leaders was tested. And the survival of a protest movement would to an important extent depend on this assessment. It could never give up its role of social opposition without losing a considerable number of its present or future supporters.

For most socialist parties in the first quarter of this century it would probably have been fatal if they had rejected as useless the revolutionary inheritance left them by the previous century. These old emotions were too powerful for that. Many socialists were sceptical and doubtful and there was no lack of criticism of the revolutionary utopia. But it was probably still simply a question of common sense for moderate party leaders like Adler, Bebel, Jaurès and Troelstra to turn against Bernstein in the interests of their party and for the preservation of their position. The maintenance of the revolution as a target, however, confronted the socialists not only with the problem of future feasibility, but also with the nature of the Western European revolutionary tradition itself. For this was, despite all the intensity of feeling, essentially extremely flimsy. Marx had certainly asserted that all history was class warfare and our part of the world had indeed experienced many revolts and revolutions. But these had been neither socialist nor proletarian and thus were fundamentally unsuited to being absorbed into the historical mythology of the labour movement. If this happened, nevertheless, other social and political groups would claim their share of the intellectual heritage. The ideological claims of the French socialists to the Great Revolution of 1789 were attacked in this way by the radical liberals. In Italy the same situation occurred with regard to the Risorgimento. The Dutch socialists had virtually never claimed responsibility for the sixteenth-century uprising against Spain, because this had already been completely taken over by the Protestant emancipation movement.

For the socialist labour movement despite all its world-wide pretensions there were in fact only two events which were actually relevant, and they were neither international nor even national, but purely local in character, and these were the occurrences in the city of Paris in the years 1848 and 1871. Neither the workers' uprising of 1848 nor the Commune had led to any positive result, and they had ended in a bloodbath and a victory for reaction. In the socialist imagination they had been elevated into great mythological dramas full of heroes, martyrs, villains and tyrants who continued to play an important role in ideas about revolution. But it remained a sad fact that the socialist parties only had two pitiful failures in the European past available from which to derive historical inspiration.

To keep revolutionary conviction up to standard, one had better forget the past and seek for models among countries and peoples on the periphery of, or outside, European civilisation. The Poles had already managed to fulfil this role for a long time, but after 1881 the honour of serving as an inviting prospect for the Western socialist movement fell to the Russian revolutionaries. Both these Russians and their homeland fulfilled at that time almost the same function for the consciousness of the 'left' as the freedom movements and the dictatorial regimes do today in the Third World. But Russia was only truly to become a kind of model country as a result of the revolution of 1905.

The most remarkable thing about that year is that almost everything happened then in Russia, except a revolution. The political banquets, the formation of political parties, trade unions and workers' councils, the many mass meetings, demonstrations, strikes, street fights, political assassinations, riots and armed uprisings all showed that very many of the tsar's subjects were involved in that year in chaotic guerrilla warfare between the people and the regime. But tsarism did not collapse. Nevertheless, afterwards people continued to describe the events of 1905 as a revolution. In Soviet historical writing it has become usual to conceive of 1905 as the 'dress rehearsal' for 1917. It is questionable whether this is such a fitting metaphor, since the 'scripts' for the two events were quite different. On the other hand it is meaningful to look on the reaction of Western socialism to 1905 as a 'dress rehearsal' for 1917. The European labour movement reacted in a similar way to the great news from Russia in both years. And this behaviour was explicable, even almost predictable. For on both occasions the Western European image of Russia and socialist attitudes to revolution provided the established patterns and templates for it. This had already been evident around 1881, when Western socialists had had to decide their point of view about terrorist populism in Russia. After this first rehearsal, history repeated itself in 1905 and 1917, to such an extent that even the historian as its passive spectator is impressed, because the main characters were forced to play their roles with ever-increasing depth and drama.

Both Russian and Western socialists were waiting for the Russian revolution in 1904. The war with Japan was progressing disastrously, and political and social opposition in Russia was becoming acute. As the new year came in the Dutch socialist daily *Het Volk* wrote: 'And Russia! All our thoughts are there these days.'[1] On 6 January, the Independent Labour Party's paper the *Labour Leader* maintained: 'The coming year is full of portent. At home it may bring us a General Election, abroad it may see a revolution in Russia, and the whole spirit of Far Eastern civilisation changed.'[2] *Vorwärts*, the SPD's paper, too, greeted 1905 as a 'Russian year'.[3] A few weeks later in St Petersburg, shots were fired by the army and the police at a procession of 150,000 workers, who wanted to hand a petition to the tsar with their grievances. Several hundred died. This was the sign for almost everyone inside and outside Russia that the revolution had begun.

Undoubtedly many in the West derived this certainty from the barbaric primitiveness and cruelty which came to the fore so clearly in the descriptions of Bloody Sunday in the newspapers. The scope of the demonstration was 'orientally' gigantic. The naivety of these workers, who carried icons and, under the leadership of a priest, gave evidence of their affection for the tsar, was touching. The tsar and his servants showed that tsarism had no knowledge of civilisation or humanity and evidently could not make any significant intelligent contribution towards the solution of Russia's most pressing problems. Bloody Sunday was thus an event which fitted in perfectly with left-wing European traditional ideas about Russia and reactions to it were of the same order. 'Streams of blood will flow', wrote *Het Volk*, 'but freedom will grow from the blood-soaked fields. O, for a long time nothing has happened as beautiful as this Russian people which is rising against its tyrants. The proletariat of the entire world greets this revolution with emotions of love and hope.'[4]

In Holland it went no further than words. In England, Sweden, Austria, Italy and France socialist parties and trade unions organised numerous meetings and street demonstrations to celebrate the beginning of the Russian revolution and to give vent to their anger about the 'slaughter' in St Petersburg. In Paris, Vienna, Turin and Rome this went as far as serious clashes with the police and sometimes arrests and bomb explosions. But it was not only the socialists who reacted emotionally. The echo of Bloody Sunday reverberated around the whole world. Even in South America, as the Russian government was informed, an anti-tsarist movement had come into being which convened a well-attended meeting in Montevideo. In Chicago the students began to whistle as soon as the name of the tsar was mentioned, while in Paris students sang The Internationale on the Boulevard Saint-Michel. In the United States, Buffalo Bill ostentatiously scrapped 'the Cossack Extravaganza' from his famous Wild West Show, churchgoers were appalled, while writers like Mark Twain and Jack London protested as indignantly as George Bernard Shaw and Anatole France were doing in Europe.[5]

Both in the New and the Old Worlds liberal newspapers expressed their sympathy for the Russian struggle for freedom and their disgust for the tsar and his ministers. Liberal politicians, too, spoke in the same spirit. Winston Churchill, who had just become a liberal though formerly a conservative, larded his electoral addresses with odes to the Russian fighters. 'I cannot regret – I say it advisedly – even the blood that has been spilled, because I believe that blood will be the seed of the harvest of freedom in the future.'[6] At the same time it became the custom among socialists and liberals to label the less pleasant aspects of

Western European state power as 'Russian'. Policemen were designated 'Cossacks', and measures that had the least whiff of censorship, 'petty Russian post office rules'.[7] Another curious phenomenon of socialist–liberal unanimity resulting from Bloody Sunday was the Société des Amis du Peuple Russe et des Peuples Annexés which was set up in Paris at the beginning of February. This was a club of intellectuals and politicians the most prominent members of which were Georges Clemenceau, Ferdinand Buisson, Anatole France, Charles Seignobos, Lucien Herr, Pierre and Marie Curie and Madame Zola. It was the first clear demonstration of sympathy for revolutionary Russia from the side of learning and art, which after the 1917 revolution was to be so characteristic of the fellow-travellers and the organisations of which they were members. The Société wished to inform the French public about the true nature of tsarism and the Russian revolutionary movement, and to this end organised lectures and distributed brochures, so that its activities gained full coverage in a number of French newspapers.[8]

In Switzerland even the conservative press followed the liberal lead, but in general the political right took a different line. In many parts of the world state leaders like the Turkish sultan, Franz Josef and Wilhelm II, or newspapers like the German *Kreuzzeitung* and *The Times of India*, were somewhat concerned about the maintenance of public order in their own countries after the Russian riots. Many government leaders were also afraid of the revolutionary spectre. As early as March 1904 Germany, Austria, Denmark, Sweden, Romania, Russia, Turkey and Bulgaria had held a secret meeting in St Petersburg about their joint fight against anarchism. The year 1904 was notable for its rather violent labour conflicts in France, England and Germany. The danger of the 'Russian disease' infecting the rest of Europe was not entirely hypothetical.[9]

Russian diplomats proved bewildered and indignant about the anti-tsarist demonstrations which confronted them in many places, and reproached the governments to which they were accredited for doing nothing about them. In Germany – and most probably also in other countries such as France – a long series of measures was in fact taken to prevent the disorders spreading. In the European capitals it was hoped that the tsar would restore order with a firm hand, and if he proved incapable of this, he would have to be helped in some way. In the nationalistic German press one could read that Europe ought perhaps to intervene forcefully 'for the safety of its own national life, and the political existence of its civilised peoples'. Russia was clearly excluded from civilisation here, and the feeling that disasters would occur when 'the Slav beast in human form' with its inborn Asiatic brutality was let loose on mankind was widespread in these circles. For the right wing it was a foregone conclusion that the Russian nation was not ready for Western freedom. For a number of French newspapers, which had obtained large sums from the Russian government in exchange for favourable reporting, the indignation of the civilised world about Bloody Sunday was indeed a problem. One solution to it was found by journalists like Drumont, who pointed to the Jews as the cause of all Russian difficulties. The year 1905 saw a revival of anti-Semitism in France and Germany.[10] Each event in Russia which caused a stir in the West acted as an extra stimulus in the political debate there and exacerbated existing ideological differences. More important was the fact that reaction to Bloody Sunday was so violent, and that for more than a year afterwards fuel continued to come from the tsarist empire to keep the European boiler at top pressure. Relationships within the socialist parties also came under greater strain. The Russian mirror had been held out to the Western social democrats for so long that they were beginning to wonder if their revolutionary appearance was indeed in harmony with their deepest being. European socialism functioned best when this insoluble problem was glossed over as much as possible.

Within the SPD it was already evident in January 1905 that the Russian development would hinder this well-tried tactic. *Vorwärts* wrote then: 'under the Russian ice palace the cracking ice-floes are breaking up'. The masses were awakened 'as if out of a prolonged enchantment, passionate, strange, with a mystical urge, into a movement, unknown in Russia, and impossible in civilised nations'. The workers' demonstration on Bloody Sunday offered 'an image of mysterious sinister power', and the 'storm tide of blood and horror' which had arisen in Russia was likewise labelled 'mysterious'. The situation was thus described as a sort of barbaric fairy-tale, with the adjectives for it that had become commonplace in Western journalism devoted to Russia.

This did not happen by chance. Of course *Vorwärts* was looking forward in advance to the fall of tsarism, which, once more completely in line with tradition, was called 'the bulwark of international reaction'. But first of all it had to be made clear to the German workers that there was a world of difference between the civilised activities of their powerful and orderly organisations and the savage spontaneity of the Russian proletariat.[11]

Rosa Luxemburg would of course have nothing to do with this sort of writing. 'And it is quite clear', she wrote in *Die Neue Zeit*, 'that the present-day Russian revolution can in no way be tackled with phrases like 'disintegrating ice-floes', 'endless steppes', 'dumb, weeping, weary souls' and such-like resounding rhetorical expressions in the minds of middle-class journalists whose entire knowledge of Russia is based on the latest theatrical performance of Gorki's *The Lower Depths* or on a couple of Tolstoy's novels and which leads off with similar well-meaning ignorance about the social problems of both hemispheres.'[12] How then should the Russian situation be assessed? Luxemburg linked it directly with Germany, where a large miners' strike had broken out in the Ruhr. The trade unions were forced against their will to recognise this and 250,000 workers went on strike from 17 January. Rosa did not hesitate to call this a general strike and it was indeed one of the largest in German history. In her view almost at the same time in both Russia and Germany 'two violent social struggles, two mass proletarian uprisings' had broken out, which had in one stroke destroyed all illusions about a peaceful, law-abiding, reformist development. Neither of these activities had been started at the instigation of socialist organisations, but they were the result of years of social democrat propaganda and agitation.

The fact that many inside and outside Russia were surprised by the events in St Petersburg was, in Luxemburg's view, simply due to continued underestimation of the importance of Russian social democracy.[13] Not only in Russia, but in the West as well, socialists had relied on the peasants, on student terrorists, on the liberals and the Japanese to bring about the fall of autocracy, and now it had been shown who was right. It was 'the Marxist spirit' which had produced the first pitched battle in the Russian capital, and 'with the necessity of a natural law' would 'sooner or later' achieve victory. 'Anyone who believes that the mill wheel drives the water', wrote Luxemburg a few weeks later in *Vorwärts*, 'may think that Father Gapon [the priest who led the workers on Bloody Sunday] is the originator and leader of the proletarian revolution.'[14]

Besides the opinions in *Vorwärts* and those of Rosa Luxemburg those of the reformists could also be distinguished. Their enthusiasm about Russian events was much more scant. In the General Commission of Trade Unions' paper the 'St Petersburg affair' was described as a 'product of a crazy fantasy'.[15] In the *Sozialistische Monatshefte* Richard Calwer observed, wrongly in fact, that Russian terrorist activities had formerly been universally condemned by European public opinion. After Bloody Sunday this opinion was reversed: 'one can acknowledge without hesitation that the Russian people, driven to despair, are in a position of self-defence which justifies every tactic. THE way of organic reform, which we in general have recognised as the best for Germany and the civilised nations, which leads forwards to a target, is impracticable for Russia.'[16] In the same paper Bernstein emphasised that the Russian revolution could have no socialist character and belonged to the type of bourgeois revolution which had taken place in a much earlier period in the West. The implication of this kind of view was that the Western working class had very little to do with the Russian revolution. Nor did the reformist press, in comparison with the other socialist papers, devote much attention to it.[17]

These various approaches to Bloody Sunday already show that the debate about the 1905 revolution would, in important respects, be a repetition of the debate in the SPD around 1881 on the significance of Russian terrorism. Then, the right wing of the party had dissociated itself from this. The greater part of the SPD, with Marx and Bernstein as spokesmen, had expressed themselves with especial enthusiasm about it, but considered the application of this violence to Germany inadmissible. The anarchists, and a few party members who tended towards anarchy such as Most and Hasselmann, wished to follow the Russian example. Rosa Luxemburg and her associates were now treading, unawares, in the footsteps of this latter group. But of course the main difference between this and the earlier period was that it was no longer the question of terrorism which kept opinions divided. In 1905 the proletarian mass action, in which the Russians seemed to be so outstanding, was to prove to be the great problem with which European social democracy felt it was faced.

Everyone seemed to be in agreement for the present – and in this respect Calwer had the right end of the stick – about terrorism. Within the European socialist parties there was no longer anyone to be found who wanted to use knives and bombs himself in the class war. But at the same time nobody was in principle opposed to the use of these measures elsewhere in the world. This in effect meant that the socialist revolutionaries could do no more harm, and that the Russian social democrats who did not wish to co-operate with these 'heroes' were regarded critically by many of their Western sympathisers. It is remarkable that it was the reformists of the *Sozialistische Monatshefte*, of all people, who expressed themselves in a most cutting way about 'the internal bickering' among the leaders of the RSDRP and their 'fratricidal war' against the PSR. According to the paper, the Russian social democrats had not achieved anything, while the socialist revolutionaries had saved 'the honour of Russian socialism'.[18] Many Western socialists had a busy time of it defending the terrorist deeds in Russia against the allegations of right-wing politicians and newspapers. In Germany this was already evident in February 1905, when *Vorwärts* somewhat exultantly greeted the murder of the grand duke Sergei Alexandrovich by the socialist revolutionary Kalyayev as a deed of justice. This led to a battle of words in parliament between Erzberger, a representative of the Catholic Centre Party, and the socialist Ledebour.[19]

Similar discussions were afterwards repeatedly to be held, not only in the German Reichstag, but also in the other European parliaments. Things were especially heated in the French Chamber of Representatives. In Jaurès's *l'Humanité*, Hyndman's *Justice*, Adler's *Arbeiterzeitung* and the Dutch *Het Volk* Kalyayev was written about in the same vein as in *Vorwärts*. Hyndman recounts in his memoirs that even *The Times* was able to summon up some understanding for the terrorist. On the other hand in Holland the liberal *Handelsblad* reproached the socialist *Het Volk* for glorifying political murders in Russia and, because of its habit of equating Dutch situations with those in Russia, inciting its fellow countrymen to terrorism. Part of the liberal press in Europe, however, could hardly be distinguished from the socialist press in its judgement of terrorism in Russia.[20] This is also true of the statements of the Western intellectuals who can be regarded as fellow-travellers *avant la lettre*. When the socialist Gustav Hervé introduced one of the leaders of the PSR's terrorist organisation to Anatole France as 'Boris Savinkov, assassin', he seemed delighted to meet him and asked: 'Whom did he murder?' Savinkov answered: 'Minister Pleve and grand duke Sergei.' 'Big game', was the writer's reaction.[21]

The discussion in 1881 also had a direct role to play in 1905. The socialist revolutionaries repeatedly referred to Marx's attitude at the time. Hyndman reproached the Western socialists with the fact that they had become far too tame in their assessment of revolutionary violence and likewise put forward Marx to them as an example. In February, *La Vie Socialiste*, the paper which embodied the struggle for unity among the French socialists, published Marx's letter to his daughter Jenny Longuet in which he expressed his great admiration for the murderers of Alexander II. *Vorwärts* took this letter over in March and quoted the passage from it which reflected Marx's contempt for the Russian opponents of terrorism, namely Akselrod, Plekhanov and Zasulich, 'who are up to their mischief in Geneva . . . whose influence on the battlefield in Russia is practically nil'.[22]

## FURTHER REACTIONS TO 1905

This thrust in the direction of the Russian social democrats was no coincidence. Since the 1904 congress in Amsterdam the demand for restoration of unity within the Russian revolutionary movement had never really ceased. The Bureau of the International, but especially Bebel, had made great efforts to promote this end energetically. This was a result of the appreciation which Western socialists felt for non-social-democratic groups such as the PSR and the Russian liberals, who around the New Year of 1905 had decided to co-operate with the Finnish and Polish revolutionaries. The Polish, Jewish and Russian social democrats had said at the congress in Amsterdam that they would not take part in this sort of discussion, since their conversational partners either did not accept the idea of the class war, or tended towards revolutionary adventurism. This was swallowed at the time, but six months later Jaurès, Bebel, Adler and Kautsky thought that the situation in Russia no longer justified such a rigid attitude. Since their attempt to establish unity had failed completely, Bebel, Adler and Kautsky were already convinced at the beginning of 1905 that the Russian revolution could not be led by the social democrats, who were hanging on to ideological and organisational problems and knew no better than to quarrel while their country went up in smoke. Although all these negotiations took place in private, a certain amount of information about them filtered out.[23] The popularity of the RSDRP sank to nothing in the process. The coverage of Bloody Sunday and Russian terrorism in *Vorwärts* and the cutting remarks about Russian social democracy were the result of this. Rosa Luxemburg's attempts to offer some counterbalance were rather forced. It was extremely far-fetched to suggest that Bloody Sunday was a result of social democratic propaganda, as she had written.[24]

Her critical remark about father Gapon went unheeded, although it was generally known in the West that his workers' organisation had initially been set up in close co-operation with the authorities and the police. After Bloody Sunday Gapon fled to the West, and despite his curious career as a workers' leader he was brought into socialist circles as a true Russian hero, in roughly the same way as the terrorist Hartman had been a quarter of a century before. Lenin and the socialist revolutionaries also showed great interest in Gapon, who believed that his popularity compelled him to play the role of instigator of unity. Through Rubanovich's mediation, the PSR's delegates on the board of the International acquired for Gapon the support of the Belgian Huysmans, who had just become secretary of the Bureau of the Socialist International. Huysmans's letter to the socialist parties about Gapon's initiative was published in all the socialist newspapers.[25] The PSR very emphatically declared itself ready for discussion and *La Tribune Russe* also laid the admonitions of Vaillant and Jaurès at the Russians' door. Jaurès thought that 'in the drama which is developing, one of the grandest and most terrible which humanity has ever seen, the Russian socialist parties cannot deploy all their forces unless they are united...'[26] Gapon then organised a conference in Switzerland to which he invited representatives of almost all the revolutionary organisations in the Russian empire. The Mensheviks refused to reply to the invitation. The Bolsheviks and the Bund left the conference soon after it began and the meeting itself did not achieve a single lasting result.

Of course this was not surprising. The aims of the revolutionaries were too widely separated. The Western socialists' demand for unity was not free from a certain naive arrogance. After all, they always differed passionately amongst themselves as soon as there was any question of fundamental issues. Only Kautsky had been annoyed by the rash action of Huysmans, who had not consulted the board of the International about the Gapon question.[27] He knew that non-committal calls to unity were pointless and tried to inform the German socialists, who seemed to understand nothing of the differences of opinion in the Russian camp. In an article in *Die Neue Zeit* he reproached *Vorwärts* for having acted in an unfriendly way towards the Russian social democrats. Kautsky's account of the problems within the RSDRP, however, was even less flattering. Since there was no reformism or revisionism within Russian social democracy, the differences between Bolsheviks and Mensheviks were, in matters of principle, less significant than those between the left and right wings of the SPD. The mutual enmity was therefore in Kautsky's view mainly to be attributed to personal mistrust and personal embitterment. He implied that all sorts of fruitless attempts had been made to eradicate this hatred and jealousy. The role of outsiders in the conflict had been played out and it was up to the Russians themselves to restore the desperately needed harmony.

After discussing the views of Marx and Engels on Russian terrorism he emphasised that after Marx's death times had changed in Russia, and that because of this all the most acute aspects of the old conflict between populists and Marxists had been smoothed away. Nevertheless, the differences between the parties remained so great that Kautsky had to agree with the social democrats, who did not want to join forces with the socialist revolutionaries. The PSR had no clear programme and was so loosely organised that members who in the West would have been counted as liberals or anarchists felt at home there. The socialist revolutionaries could easily take a tolerant attitude in this way, but *Vorwärts* had no reason to be so jubilant about this. After all, the union between the PSR and the Russian liberals had not achieved much either. For genuine concerted action during a revolution complete agreement about the tactics to be followed was essential, and in the present circumstances between the social democrats, socialist revolutionaries and liberals this was unthinkable. But Kautsky did not rule out some kind of co-operation between these parties on certain points.[28]

Although Kautsky did not reject terrorism in principle in this article, and thought that the PSR had a right to the sympathy and support of Western socialism, his article stimulated a fierce and lengthy reaction in *La Tribune Russe* from the socialist revolutionary Tarasov (pseudonym for Rusanov) who considered that Kautsky was trying to impart to his disciples 'a philistine fear of Russian terrorism'.[29] But the later numbers of *La Tribune Russe* proved that every undertaking in this direction was doomed to failure. The PSR's popularity in the West seemed unassailable. Time after time its newspaper reported proudly how socialists in many European countries were taking up the cudgels on behalf of party members wanted for robbery or murder, and were trying to prevent their deportation or persecution. At the same time prominent liberal or socialist lawyers developed splendid theories in which political offences were carefully distinguished from ordinary criminality. Western socialists were not only helpful in the distribution and transport of revolutionary literature. They also collected substantial sums, with which they knew the PSR, the RSDRP and other groups were also buying weapons. A number of socialists, among them the Dutch syndicalist Cornelissen, and Huysmans the secretary of the International, were actively involved in the purchase and transport of weapons. Representatives of many socialist parties would, at Gotz's funeral in Berlin in 1906, and that of Gershuni in Paris in 1908, pay their last tributes to these leaders of the PSR and organisers of terrorism. 'The men and women', as Friedrich Stampfer, then editor of *Vorwärts*, was later to write in his memoirs, 'who fought against that barbarian Colossus, were saints to us.' It went without saying that people did everything for them without being asked. It did not matter where the weapons which were hidden for them came from, who produced the writings that were printed and smuggled over the frontier for them, or what the origin of the roubles was that were exchanged for them.[30]

While revolutionary violence was exonerated from blame, the reaction of the Russian government, which from December 1905 onwards took a heavy-handed line with the rebels, was denounced by socialists at every opportunity as inhuman and barbarian. The number of executions of revolutionaries by government officials was, however, certainly no greater than the number of executions of government officials by revolutionaries.[31] It was curious that French socialists like Jaurès and Vaillant, who in the French House of Representatives repeatedly cried shame that their republic remained allied to an uncivilised, semi-Asiatic power, did not realise that the reaction of the tsar and his ministers to this serious rebellion was much more moderate and controlled than that of the founders of the Third Republic had been to something as relatively harmless as the Paris Commune. Western socialists were to some extent cured of this blindness to the similarities between Russia and Europe with regard to the use of political violence, when in 1909 it transpired that the leader of the PSR's terrorist organisation, Azeff, was an *agent provocateur*. This scandal made it clear that in Russia, too, the boundary between ordinary crime and noble revolutionary violence was vague, and it clearly damaged the prestige of the PSR in the West.

Not until after the October revolution in 1917 would it become evident what consequences this tolerant attitude of left-wing groups in the West towards Russian revolutionary violence would have. The Russian revolution of 1905 did not yet bring this to light, and the violence-euphoria remained mainly theoretical and non-committal. This came about, of course, because the uprising failed and its eventual results proved to be slight, certainly for Western Europe. The Western socialists had not yet reached the ordeal of having to suit the action to the word. Another reason was that developments in Russia in 1905 displayed such kaleidoscopically changing configurations that they refrained from forming clear, immediate opinions. This was distressing enough for the Russian revolutionaries, since the spasmodic jolts and judderings of the insurrection did not fit in with their much-discussed revolutionary plans; the Western socialists could often make neither head nor tail of things. All the European socialist newspapers devoted daily attention to Russia, but it was difficult to discover any consistency in the piecemeal news. *Het Volk*, which for two weeks after Bloody Sunday had provided Russian coverage under the headline 'The revolution in Russia', replaced this at the beginning of February with the insipid legend 'The movement in Russia' and maintained this until July. Afterwards the editorial board changed its mind and went back to the old title. It was also characteristic that some socialist newspapers like *l' Humanité* even after December refused to believe that the revolution had been put down, while 'bourgeois' papers gave a much more realistic assessment of the situation.[32]

In the second half of 1905 the Western socialist parties were overcome by the feverish feeling that developments in Russia might radically influence their situation in the short term. Not one of them knew in precisely what respect, and reactions were thus extremely uncertain, though this fact was camouflaged under a torrent of eloquence. The attitude of the Dutch SDAP was most enlightening in this connection. On 30 July the party executive inserted a full-page manifesto into *Het Volk* in which the Russian revolution was exalted into 'the most important event of our time'. But the only concrete suggestion put forward by the party executive was the collection of money for the Russian revolutionaries.[33] During the short-lived armed revolt in Moscow, Troelstra gave a Christmas address in Amsterdam in which he criticised the 'Russian' conditions in democratic countries and made a fierce attack on the bourgeois parliamentary system. 'We are waiting to see what the revolution will bring in Russia, but we are fighting for revolution in Holland. (Loud, prolonged applause).'[34]

In January 1906 it was clear even to the Dutch socialists that the revolution in Russia had failed for the time being. Nevertheless, H. Roland Holst announced the end of bourgeois, parliamentary supremacy, and the beginning of the transition from capitalism to socialism.[35] The party called on its members, in a headline over the whole front page of *Het Volk*, to take part in the world-wide commemoration of Bloody Sunday organised by the ISB, to which a hearing was given *en masse*.[36] At a crowded meeting in Amsterdam, H. Roland Holst claimed that the Russian revolution was not dead, but had only taken a pause for breath in order to regain its strength. Troelstra thought the Dutch workers ought to be ready to take over power in the state as soon as circumstances allowed.[37]

The Russian revolution thus certainly provided for some excitement in the party, which had lately, to many people, seemed so dull and lifeless. Not everyone valued this, however. In March 1906 the reformist wing, with J. H. Schaper as mouthpiece, raised a number of objections to the tenor of the party propaganda in the previous year. He spoke of a 'feverish, unnatural, bombastic enthusiasm'; about 'this playing with the word revolution, this verbal revolutionarism'. Schaper had suggested that at the next party congress the party executive should come up with a resolution mentioning 'unattainable expectations', that could only lead to 'great disappointment'. This proposal was thrown out by the executive. Troelstra answered that the socialist parties in other countries were likewise making a comeback under the influence of the events in Russia and were also seeking for different fighting methods from those of the parliamentarians. This observation was correct, and the central position which Troelstra occupied showed that in the SDAP, just as for instance in the SPD, a group was being defined between the left and the right which, as centrist, would make more and more of a name for itself in time to come.[38]

## THE DEBATE ABOUT THE GENERAL STRIKE IN HOLLAND AND GERMANY

The different groups in the Dutch party defined their positions more clearly under the influence of the Russian revolution; and in the other socialist parties such as the SPD this was equally the case. The debate concentrated on what Troelstra had called 'alternative fighting methods' and the Dutch discussions about them proved to be of international significance. In 1905 the enormous strike movement in Russia forced the autocracy to make great political concessions which were laid down in the October Manifesto, and of which the most important was the establishment of a people's representative body or Duma. This revived a very old discussion about the general strike as a practicable method of forcing through fundamental social reforms, avoiding wars, or making revolutions. Long ago, at the beginning of the French revolution, no less a person than Mirabeau had once aptly put the irresistible logic of this idea into words: 'Take care! do not irritate this multitude which produces everything and which, in order to be formidable has only to remain immobile!'[39] The British Chartists had been the first to try in vain to put this into practice, both the First and the Second Internationals had repeatedly argued about it, and general strikes had taken place in Belgium (1893 and 1902), Sweden (1902), Holland (1903) and Italy (1904).

International social democracy had particularly exerted itself to collect as many practical objections as possible against the idea of a general strike, which had once been summed up by the cynical German socialist Ignaz Auer under the motto: 'General strike is general nonsense.' There was a great deal of truth in this, for the strikes which had taken place in Western Europe had either failed or not been an unqualified success. Auer's argument was not entirely convincing, however, for the strikes had, in fact, actually broken out, supported by socialist parties or even called out on their own initiative. Moreover revolutionary syndicalism, which in those years was developing into the rightful successor to anarchy and a formidable competitor of the socialist labour movement, proclaimed the general strike as the only way to the great goal. With this ideology, which was often articulated with more subtle distinctions than the socialist opponents would believe, the syndicalists had gained the support of many workers in France. The French proletariat's manifest aversion to parliamentary politics, even when perpetrated by socialists, was also present in other countries in a latent form.

This was also true for Holland, where it has become usual to regard the disastrous failure of the great rail strike in 1903 as a turning-point in the history of socialism. The workers would have lost their illusions by 1903 and therefore the emergence and florescence of a modern, reformist trade union movement, which was averse to every revolutionary adventure, had become inevitable. This was unmistakably the case, but at the same time the left wing of the SDAP stressed its distinctive features by undisguised criticism of the attitude of the party leadership during the strike. One of the results of this was that the parliamentary reformist trend came under increasing fire from its own members and the concept of the general strike was officially adopted as part of the ideological arsenal of the party. This was remarkable, because the SDAP had been founded as a counter-reaction to the radicalism of the 'old movement' led by Domela Nieuwenhuis. One of the most prominent spokesmen of the

SDAP, the reformist W. H. Vliegen, had emphatically rejected the general strike in *Die Neue Zeit* in 1903.[40]

At the Amsterdam congress of the International the general strike was also on the agenda and the Dutch played the leading part in the preparation and consideration of this point. The SDAP's resolution was adopted almost word for word by the International. As almost always happens with decisions of this kind, it was a compromise which could satisfy neither supporters nor opponents. It gave no guidelines whatsoever to socialists and trade union leaders about how they should proceed if a substantial workers' conflict broke out anywhere for political reasons.[41] This meant that the discussion was not yet concluded and it went without saying that Kautsky asked Henriette Roland Holst, who had been the main reporter of this affair at the Dutch and the International congresses, to explain the whole question in a book. Roland Holst belonged to the small group of extremely civilised and even somewhat dignified intellectuals in Holland, mostly of not impecunious middle-class origins, who had been converted to Marxism. The Russian revolution of 1905 made a very great impression on these Dutch Marxists, who also enjoyed some recognition abroad and were mainly responsible for the 'bombastic enthusiasm' in the SPD which Schaper had complained so much about. To a large extent this was true of the poetess Roland Holst, who was not entirely free from the fanaticism of a true devotee. The presence of Russian delegates at the Amsterdam international congress had moved her deeply and the news of Bloody Sunday was received by her and her fellow party member, fellow Marxist and poet, Herman Gorter, 'with tears in their eyes'. In many articles written in 1905 she gave evidence of her enthusiasm for the wonderful Russian proletariat. Afterwards she was to give these exaggerated emotions about Russia free rein in *De Opstandelingen* (*The Rebels*), a lyrical tragedy in verse which she wrote between 1906 and 1908. While writing her book she frequently stayed at the Kautskys' in Berlin, where, in those days, the Russian revolution was the subject of conversation and where moreover she regularly met Russian revolutionaries for whom she cherished a deep admiration.[42]

Her *General Strike and Social Democracy* came out in Germany in the summer of 1905. A revised version, likewise in German, appeared six months later. It was a decent book, the only passion displayed in it being in the repudiation of syndicalism and the glorification of the Russian revolution.[43] All social democratic opponents had their say. They had partly explained their scruples about the strike in *Die Neue Zeit*, but did this more fully in the interesting enquiry which was held in 1904 by the syndicalist paper *Mouvement Socialiste*. Social democratic criticism of the strike was tackled by Holst in two ways. In the first place, she held to the view that the general strike did not, as the syndicalists claimed, replace parliamentary action, but should be seen as a complement to it. The socialists, who were completely wrapped up in 'parliamentary illusionism', as Holst put it, were not convinced by this argument. And even if they had been, they could still contend that a general strike was impossible in practice.[44] The Russian revolution furnished Holst with fitting ammunition to bombard this conservative position. There the proletariat was scarcely organised at all, and the strike actions were not only reasonably general, but also followed one another in waves. The different groups of workers, as it were, relieved one another and thus increased the staying power of the movement. Since the proletariat was supported by various other sections of the population, and the authorities could not fully deploy the army because of the aftermath of the war with Japan, the government had to bow to the opposition.

Roland Holst made no mention of the existence of differences in principle between the situation in Russia and that in the West. Opponents of her ideas there would naturally keep hammering away at her. What was more serious was that Holst was not aware of the fact that the revolutionaries in Russia felt the general strike to be of subordinate importance, and were already directing their attention towards an armed uprising which would make an end to the tsar's regime. This was later seen, especially by the Mensheviks, as the main cause for the failure of the revolution, which had offered a unique chance for the realisation of a genuine constitutional government in Russia. Holst did not deny that the struggle in Russia had shed a great deal of blood. 'A revolution without victims, especially one against Asiatic barbaric absolutism, is however impossible.' Her conclusion therefore read: 'The political mass strike ... is, as appears from Russian events, the best means of putting up a resistance against state power ... It is the only possible form of civil war, in which only "the uncovered breast and the unprotected heart" on the one side, are placed against soldiers equipped with the most refined resources of modern technology on the other, and nevertheless it is not the armed ruling power but the unarmed heroic courage of the masses which decides.'[45] This optimism was scarcely tempered by the tragic course of Russian events. Holst thought the brutal suppression of the armed uprising in Moscow was indeed 'devastating', but still 'nothing more than an episode in the Russian revolution'.[46]

Roland Holst left it in no doubt that the political general strike could be much more than an incidental means of pressure alongside parliamentary activities. The political strike should in Holst's view be accepted as a 'form of proletarian, that is to say, social, revolution'.[47] So the truth was out and, despite the vehement avowal to the contrary, the chief distinction in principle between the social democratic and the revolutionary syndicalist strike ideology was abandoned. The Russian general strike took on for Holst the function of an inspiring story which conjured up an image of the future of Europe. Here – at about the same time as Sorel was writing his book about it – a myth was being dreamed up which ought to inspire the movement to action.

With this she took up a far more radical standpoint than most other social democratic defenders of the general strike. Only Parvus[48] and Rudof Hilferding[49] had defended similar views. Their publications had only confirmed many German socialists in their fear of experiments with extra-parliamentary activities. To these party members belonged first of all the union leaders, who after the failure of the great miners' strike had conceived an aggressive aversion to meretricious men of letters who bore no responsibilities whatsoever. Their main support in the party was *Vorwärts*, in which, in the summer of 1905, Roland Holst's book was reviewed in a very negative way, since it met 'the anarchistic view of the general strike half-way'. Kautsky had opposed the rigid attitude of the trade unions both in *Die Neue Zeit* and in the introduction to his Dutch friend's book. Afterwards, in a vehement controversy with *Vorwärts*, he defended 'by far the most important socialist publication of this year'. The party newspaper did not flinch, and continued to consider the propaganda for the general strike as 'day-dreaming and play'. The editorial board of *Vorwärts* felt that talking so much about the revolution and threatening with it so frequently would be more likely to mobilise the reactionaries against social democracy than to harden one's own workers for the struggle.[50]

Kautsky claimed that he blushed with shame when he had to read this kind of prose 'in the year of the glorious Russian revolution' in the central organ of his party. He was convinced that a general strike could break out in Germany and that the SPD and the trade unions ought to prepare themselves for this by means of thorough discussion. This was indeed reasonable but a debate of this kind would unavoidably bring the possibility of an immediate social revolution to the attention of the German workers. However, Kautsky refused to accept this implication of the political general strike and categorically denied that he or Roland Holst were trying to incite the movement to revolution. The party theoretician thus disputed that theorising could also have practical consequences, while the people who were always commenting so condescendingly about romantic idealist Marxists were now afraid of exactly this.[51]

Thus it was no surprise that the most thorough rejection of Holst's book was expressed by the reformist Wolfgang Heine in the *Sozialistische Monatshefte*. In his view there was only a purely theoretical difference between the anarchistic idea of the general strike and that of Roland Holst. 'Therefore the whole distinction, so much emphasised, has as good as no meaning for the practical question that now confronts German social democracy.' Naturally he insisted that there was an enormous difference between Germany and Russia.

> In countries where the power or self-confidence of the rulers is so weak, and a revolutionary tradition so strong, that the government must yield to a general strike, it may be successful, but for Germany this does not follow. Mrs Roland-Holst's description accepts here too the most convenient possibility as a general norm ... In Germany today the political general strike will inevitably lead to resolute street fights between the people and the army. Practically no one disputes that, this way, the people will have to submit.[52]

Everyone understood that this skirmish would have to come to an end by decision of the party congress which would be held in Jena in September 1905. The party leadership had prepared itself thoroughly for this. The day before the congress opened, Bebel wrote to Adler: 'Naturally we are determined as far as possible to quench the fire in Jena. Hopefully we shall succeed. So there is no question of our permitting these pleasant disputations to continue any further.' Bebel's verdict over the international situation, which in his view was not only characterised by the Russian revolution but also by the 'absurd' foreign policy of the German government during the Morocco crisis, was extremely sombre. 'As far as final results are concerned, I have remained sceptical about the Russian revolution from the start. The proletariat is conducting itself magnificently, but what can it do against the prodigious mass of the peasants and the stupendous size and diversity of the social structure of the empire, with its mishmash of nationalities and races which far surpasses your own [Adler's Austrian] mishmash.'[53]

Bebel was well aware that the enthusiasm in the party for the Russian revolution and its aversion to parliamentarianism would create a frame of mind at the forthcoming congress which would have to be taken into consideration. The sarcastic and challenging remarks of Jaurès at the Amsterdam congress of the International about the virtual impotence of the SPD and the growing anti-democratic and anti-socialist tendencies in German government circles were now waiting for an answer. Bebel thought that the SPD could demonstrate its force and independence from Kaiser Wilhelm's state by showing its readiness, if necessary, for a general political strike. The party could do no more, and ought not to do less. The attitude of the *Vorwärts* editorial board was therefore to be condemned, while Heine's point of view was simply cowardly: 'We could not get on with such mucky-pants . . .' On the other hand, the time was not yet ripe for rash deeds or writings. The party was not strong enough for a real confrontation with the state. Bebel therefore shared Adler's objections to Kautsky and Holst. 'I am also of the opinion that K.K. [Kautsky] has blundered in the affair of the general strike, as too his comrade Roland Holst – in her by all accounts otherwise excellent essay – the horse has bolted.'[54]

The congress in Jena went exactly as Bebel wished. He himself lit a three-hour-long oratorical firework, in which he dealt out praise and criticism to left and right in the party, and heartened the congress-goers as much as possible.

The war in Russia affects our governments far more to the bone
than they think. (Quite rightly!) They are mortally afraid that
the fire might leap across; they ask themselves, if it is possible in
Russia, where no organisation exists and where the proletariat
is relatively small in number, what could happen in Germany,
where we have politically enlightened masses and an organised
proletariat, and where there are already not only battalions, but
entire regiments composed of social democrats in the army; and,
if the reserves and territorial army are mobilised, whole brigades
of social democrats will be drawn in (boisterous applause). Then
one asks oneself what will become of us? Well! They would be
dense if they didn't say that. That also belongs to the story of
the power of social democracy.

But the resolution he suggested only provided for 'the most
comprehensive deployment of the general strike' if an attempt
was made in Germany to attack universal suffrage or the right
of association.[55]

There was some resistance to this moderate proposal from
the side of the unions and from reformists like Heine and Robert
Schmidt; not from Bernstein, who believed much less than his
sympathisers from the *Sozialistische Monatshefte* did, that
prudence was the better part of socialist valour. Kautsky was
absent from the debate, so that the defence of the left wing was
left to Rosa Luxemburg. She limited herself to a vehement attack
on Heine and Schmidt. After their speeches she opined: 'one
must literally rack one's brains and ask: are we really living in
the year of the glorious Russian revolution or are we in the
period ten years before it?' There should not be too much
grumbling in the party about the shedding of blood. Revolutions
were always paid for in blood.

The whole difference is that up to now the blood of the people
has been shed for the ruling classes and now, when the possibility
of their blood being shed for their own class is under discussion,
cautious so-called social democrats come along and say no, this
blood is too precious for us ... Why didn't they learn something
from the Russian revolution! The masses, with almost no trace
of a trade union organisation, are being driven by the revolution
and now, step by step, they are establishing their organisations
through the struggle.

The reformist David answered her fiery words most directly:

Comrade Luxemburg has repeatedly referred to the revolution in Russia. (A shout: she should go there!) The revolution in Russia teaches us a great deal, but exactly the opposite of what Rosa Luxemburg is arguing; above all it teaches us that in no circumstances can one compare the revolution in Luxemburg (boisterous hilarity) – in Russia – with our German conditions. What may be right there can be totally wrong for us, and it is sheer madness to draw conclusions from Russian conditions about the tactics necessary for us! (Quite right!) But there is method in Comrade Luxemburg's madness.[56]

So, once more, everyone was riding the hobby horse of their image of Russia, but the only result was that Bebel's resolution was passed by 287 votes to 14. Emotions about the revolution in Russia were soothed by a fine declaration in which deep sympathy and admiration were expressed for the Russian workers and the social democrats who led them, and moreover the 'barbaric tantrums' of tsarism were denounced.[57] The attitude of the SPD to Russian events was thus in fact just as non-committal as that of Marx and Engels had been a quarter of a century before towards Russian terrorism. For Luxemburg and Holst – and to a lesser extent for Kautsky, whose point of view was nearer to Bebel's than either of them realised – there was little reason for rejoicing. Their disappointment is also evident in their correspondence at this time, but in the second edition of her book Roland Holst still spoke of the congress as the chief sign of 'a great turning-point' in the attitude of European social democracy to the political strike.[58]

Thus everyone made Bebel's victory his own. But in 1906 it was to become evident what the power relationships within German socialism actually were. However, the SPD's small shift to the left was also interpreted outside the party, in the press and in parliament as a political landslide. 'Blood will flow' had become the motto of the congress, according to the *Antisozial-demokratischer Korrespondenz*, and the *Kreuzzeitung* spoke of 'the bloody conclusion of the red week' in Jena. And although other newspapers did recognise the weaknesses of the movement and pointed out the irreconcilable differences of opinion between party and trade unions, nevertheless they longed for a counter-move from the authorities. The government did not need these incentives. It had careful research carried out into whether the speeches at the congress gave cause for criminal proceedings. Rosa Luxemburg was indeed sentenced to two months' imprisonment. Furthermore, the government gave careful consideration to measures against general strikes which varied from amendment of the law to military suppression.[59]

These steps were not entirely superfluous. The echo of the great October strike and the proclamation of the tsar's manifesto in Russia was most powerful in Austria and resulted in strikes and large-scale street demonstrations there on behalf of universal suffrage, led by the socialist party. But also in Saxony and Prussia a similar, equally spontaneous and clamorous movement for voting reforms, which only faded again around the summer of 1906, came into existence in those countries of the German empire. Debate within the SPD about the general strike was freshly nourished by this and spread insidiously like a sort of ever-recurring self-reproducing weed over the once so neatly raked ideological path of German social democracy. Practically the same participants, almost the same arguments. Bebel's resolution had thus brought no real peace to the party. Only the most prominent voice in the debate, that of the Polish siren of the general strike, was missing. Rosa Luxemburg had left for her fatherland at the end of December, to take part in the revolution. She did not come back to Germany until September 1906, a week before the beginning of the SPD congress in Mannheim, after a sojourn in a Polish prison and in Finland. Then she had with her a manuscript that she had been asked to write by the party organisation in Hamburg, one of the most fiercely burning hearths of seditious unrest, and this was immediately printed in a limited edition for the participants at the congress.

*General Strike, Party and Trade Unions* was written completely under the influence of the Russian revolution, in which the author had just been taking part. One of the most prominent Marxist intellectuals in the SPD, Franz Mehring, told the Dutchman Pannekoek what a splendid book he thought it was, and how much Roland Holst's work paled before it. Pannekoek agreed with him: 'after the cool, sober analysis of the old tactics, this was all of a sudden like a fiery furnace which threatened to spark off the solid German labour movement. It made the trade union leaders fiercer and more decisive in their resistance, but has inspired in numerous workers a more resolute enthusiasm to carry on resolutely along this road.' That such a remark could come from the mouth of a man who complains so much in his memoirs about the German workers' 'lack of independent daring, of autonomous spirit' probably has more than anything else to say about the attractiveness of Rosa's ideas for left-wing theoreticians.[60]

The brochure did not actually contain anything new, but it was certainly Luxemburg's most succinct formulation of her theory of spontaneity, an ode to the general strike and at the same time a Marxist canonisation of the Russian revolution. Even the comparison she made between Russia and Germany was not surprising to anyone who had followed her development to date. It had already become evident, during the debates about the Polish question and revisionism, that she was the only one among European Marxists who adamantly denied that the differences between nations could ever be an excuse for reformist or nationalistic deviations from Marxist orthodoxy. This dogmatic partiality made her into a consistent opponent of the prejudices on which the Western socialists' image of Russia had been based since the days of Marx and Engels. She also distanced herself as ostentatiously as possible from the idea, which was also alive among sympathisers like her friend Roland Holst, that the Russian workers were the 'noble savages' of twentieth-century socialism and therefore also capable of miracles. It had in fact been the German trade union leaders such as Bömelburg and reformists like Heine who concealed themselves behind the idea that in Russia 'everything' was 'different'.

According to Luxemburg, absolutism and capitalism had created very similar circumstances in Germany and Russia. The 'class instinct' of the Russian proletariat was, however, 'infinitely stronger' than that of the German. 'And this refers not to a particular virtue of the "young, fresh East" in comparison with the "decaying West", but is simply a result of direct revolutionary mass action.'[61] Luxemburg's good news for German socialism was that the Russian revolution was the link which bound the European bourgeois revolutions of the eighteenth and nineteenth centuries to the socialist ones of the near future. In Germany the dictatorship of the proletariat would be heralded by one of a series of massive strikes, which were to break out spontaneously. The general strike was for Luxemburg not only the mould into which the social revolution would be poured, it was above all a school which would provide the proletariat with the right mentality, the true insight and the necessary unity and organisation, in record time. The possible objection that this idea was beginning to smack rather strongly of anarchism and syndicalism was waived in advance. In Russia these currents had in fact no influence whatever. It was the social democrats who had led the proletariat there in 1905. Luxemburg did not wonder what parties or trade unions should actually be doing, since the general strike could do it all better and more quickly. On the contrary, she demanded a great deal from the existing organisations, who had to free themselves of their reformist routines in order to prepare themselves as thoroughly as possible for the last offensive between capitalism and absolutism.

She shared with Lenin, whom she had met in Finland and learnt to appreciate, a curious short-sightedness through which actual reality projected itself in the mind exclusively as the doorway to an extremely simple utopia. Her rhetorical talent enabled her, better than Lenin could, to convey this vision to large groups of people. She was a popular speaker and she always had an appreciative audience. Luxemburg therefore got the mistaken idea that there really were large groups of people behind her. But they quickly forgot the content of her beautiful lectures. The magical effect of the fanfare of trumpets by such heralds of socialism as Rosa was short-lived and could therefore be appraised by leaders like Bebel as useful but harmless. However, they themselves had other worries. For if they regarded Luxemburg's elimination of the differences between Russia and Germany as correct, then the fact that a revolution had been put down with violence in Russia was placed in the brightest possible light. Russia became a frightening example to the party leadership, not one that deserved to be followed.

In *Die Neue Zeit* it was argued by the hotheaded Stampfer that the general strike should now be called. Kautsky had opposed this idea as unrealistic, and was therefore accused by Stampfer of being a traitor to the Russian revolution. At the same time Kautsky was attacked by the trade unions because of his moderate defence of the Russian revolution and the extra-parliamentary activities in Germany as interdependent

phenomena. Moreover Kautsky remained an outspoken supporter of the supremacy of the party over the trade unions. The
unions had the feeling, however, that at the congress in Jena
they were being driven into a corner by the Marxist left wing
and by the party leadership. The wave of strikes in Germany
had proved to be a serious financial drain for them, and they
now presented the bill to the SPD. During secret discussions,
the results of which were in fact soon known all over Germany,
they refused to accept the responsibility for political demonstrations dressed up as strikes. These should be organised and paid
for by the party. Bebel and his followers had to accept this, since
many more workers were members of the trade unions than of
the SPD. But everyone knew that the party did not have sufficient
funds at its disposal to cover the cost of a large-scale strike. It
was a piece of luck that the German proletariat had shown no
readiness for a general political strike on behalf of a democratic
Germany.[62]

The cards had thus already been shuffled before the start of
the Mannheim congress, and the wearisome debates about the
strike and the relationship between the trade unions and the
party which characterised the meeting simply strengthened the
agreements made. The resolutions about the Russian revolution
and the political strike were so formulated that the party leadership could maintain that nothing essential had in fact changed
since Jena. The self-satisfaction of the trade union delegates at
the congress naturally aroused Rosa Luxemburg's anger, but
her tirades, the content of which could be predicted by every
participant at the congress, had no effect. When she reproached
the chairman of the General Commission of the Trade Unions,
Legien, for not having learnt anything from the Russian revolution, he answered coolly: 'Quite right!'[63] According to the
*Sozialistische Monatshefte* the congress was a great success. Unity
was restored between party and trade union and '*revolutionary
romanticism* within German social democracy may hopefully be
buried at last with Mannheim'.[64]

This seemed to be a realistic evaluation of the situation. Even
non-socialist newspapers reported with appreciation that the
party had regained or gained its common sense at the congress.
The victory of the trade unions over the SPD in 1906 is sometimes indicated by historians as the moment when the develop-

ment of the SPD from a revolutionary Marxist party into one which was only distinguishable from the other political groups of the period by the number of its disciplined followers and its bureaucratic leadership, became irrevocable. And indeed, before Mannheim, the Marxist left led by Kautsky and Luxemburg had been able to set its ideological stamp on the party. After Mannheim Kautsky was no longer the leader of the left, because he tried to remain faithful both to his party and his Marxism in the hope that the irreconcilable could still be reconciled. What could still be called left wing after Mannheim were small groups which were becoming more and more disappointed in the party in order afterwards to render homage to 'the masses' as a new idol. Obviously these people were Rosa Luxemburg's kindred spirits. But they did not regard themselves as the followers or adherents of this Polish outsider and did not organise themselves as a clear pressure group within the party.[65]

It is not, however, correct to regard the reduction of the left wing to a powerless splinter group as the only lasting result of the Russian revolution for the SPD. After all, the domination of revolutionary Marxism before Mannheim had to a large extent been only show, and after Mannheim it was unthinkable that the party would emerge from the political isolation in which it was imprisoned in Germany. The outside world continued to resist the red peril with horror and inflicted a crushing defeat on the SPD in a fiercely nationalistic and anti-socialistic campaign at the following election in 1907. The German socialists stuck to the opinion that isolation had made their party great, and that this could not be broken down by a revolutionary adventure or some kind of pact with other parties. Thus people accepted the status quo and awaited the future full of misplaced confidence. But the party had always done this. There was little reason, therefore, for the *Sozialistische Monatshefte* to put out the flags after Mannheim. The left-wing Marxists were and remained members of the party with a certain influence and the official revolutionary Marxist party ideology was not thrown overboard.

For as long as the German socialists knew no better than to wait for state power to fall into their hands, they had to pass the time by cherishing their illusions. In this the Russian revolution played a most essential role. It was a great feat to keep a socialist movement in existence and the leaders of German socialism had up till then proved themselves masters at this. They demonstrated their skill by the meticulousness with which they manipulated the beliefs of the grass-roots supporters into certain ideological myths. They did this not from the perfidious considerations of power of which the left-wing opposition sometimes accused them, but from sincere concern for the movement entrusted to them. Thus it is not of such great importance that the party rejected Rosa Luxemburg's point of view, which showed little evidence of realism. What is important is that the SPD was intensively occupied with the Russian revolution and the general strike for at least a year and a half. This was the only way in which the ever-present powerful emotional need for revolutionary mythology could be satisfied. The SPD could refresh its energy and recharge its empty batteries at the Russian power supply, so that the party could once more issue its usual, uniformly socialist low-voltage current.

The party leadership knew that the SPD needed this enthusiasm imported from Russia, but also knew how dangerous it was if large sections of its supporters actually allowed themselves to be tempted to carry out impetuous actions. In these years it successfully kept the situation in control. However, things began to go wrong with German socialism when the World War and the October revolution in Russia presented the party with much more difficult tasks, and it no longer had at its disposal leaders like Bebel, who were capable of combining an emotional appeal to socialist messianism with the practical, more sober demands of the policies of the day. The result was that unity in the party was lost. One section of its following broke adrift, at first on the waves of German nationalism and later, after the defeat, swept along by the storm which had blown up in Russia.

## DEVELOPMENTS IN OTHER COUNTRIES

In the years 1905–6 a great measure of circumspection and flexibility was also demanded of the leaders of other socialist parties. In Austria this was evident to a greater extent than in Germany, since Franz Josef's government had been compelled by the socialists to make important concessions in the matter of the franchise. Adler, who realised within what narrow limits he had to act, was therefore very apprehensive of the results of non-committal discussions, even if these were carried out not in Austria but in Germany. He had reacted to the Jena congress very trenchantly in the *Arbeiterzeitung*. Kautsky had been incensed about this and a temporary estrangement arose between the two men. On the eve of Mannheim, Adler warned Bebel once more not to associate the Austrian situation with the inevitable debate about the general strike. The Austrian socialists now had the task before them of consolidating in parliament the victory they had achieved by strikes and street demonstrations.

> In these circumstances public discussion of the methods of combat which we have used and which we – perhaps – will have to use again is totally uncalled for, indeed dangerous. We can neither hope that someone will cry out in Mannheim that 'Austrian social democracy has at last forced every party to the franchise' – which is the truth – nor is it desirable that people say that 'Austrian social democracy has only been able to win with the help of the Kaiser, the Russian revolution, the Hungarian troubles, etc. – alone, it would have been much too weak' – which is also true. You understand, I don't want our party to be either too much vaunted or too much belittled.

Adler described how his party had actually been ready in June 1906 to call out the general strike and had managed to convince both the government and the army of the seriousness of the situation. 'This realisation was sufficient for success and I heaved a sigh of relief ... We mustn't allow our power to be discussed now ...'[66]
In almost all European countries discussion about the general strike took place under the influence of the Russian revolution; though this happened least in England. But the electoral victories of the liberals at the beginning of 1906 and the appearance of the Labour Party in parliament were regarded by the defeated Conservative leader Balfour as 'the faint echo of the same movement which has produced massacres in St. Petersburg, riots in Vienna and Socialist processions in Berlin'.[67] Massive strikes of extremely militant British workers only broke out four years later. Nevertheless, in the reactions to this, by peaceful English standards, astonishingly aggressive dissatisfaction with capitalist

society which lasted until the First World War, reference was repeatedly made to Russia to explain both the behaviour of the workers and that of the government.[68]

The situation in Sweden was more comparable with that in Germany. The Norwegians' struggle for independence created great tensions which were only accentuated by a series of intense industrial disputes in Sweden itself. The socialist party supported the Norwegians unanimously, but the strikes caused conflicts between the left and right wings of the party and discord with the trade unions, who in principle were in favour of a general strike there.[69] In Italy no significant strikes took place in 1905–6, but involvement in Russian events was great and, as early as 1904, inspired the bizarre plan to support the Russian revolution with an armed detachment of Italians. In 1905 this Garibaldiesque idea was revived by the syndicalist Marangoni. Fierce debates were held about the appropriateness of this proposition, but of course nothing came of it.[70]

Nowhere in Europe was the echo of 1905 greater than in France. Many Frenchmen regarded the Russian disturbances and the resulting increased chance of German aggression, which was to manifest itself in the Moroccan crisis of 1905, as a direct threat to their national safety and economic interests. Because of this the socialists, syndicalists and left-wing intellectuals who took the side of revolutionary Russia adopted an anti-French position in the eyes of their opponents. The discord in the French nation, which had formerly seen the light of day in such dramatic fashion in the Dreyfus affair, was now once more apparent. But in 1905–6 the dividing lines were drawn quite differently.

The opposition's enthusiastic talk and writing about Russian events was less non-committal in France than in other countries. The labour disturbances in 1905 and the years which followed were generally local and spontaneous in character, but at the same time so unusually vehement that the French government was compelled to call in the army against the strikers. These clashes frequently ended in injury and sometimes death. Internal tensions, because of Russian events, were seen in such a revolutionary context that law and order seemed to be seriously threatened and some groups of French bourgeois panicked somewhat. In parliament both the internal situation and the attitude of the state towards autocratic Russia were the subject of lengthy and passionate debate. An unbridgeable gulf now opened up between the socialists and the radicals, who had formed a block in the preceding years during and after the Dreyfus affair. It was not the survival of the republic but the social question and foreign policy which now formed the breaking-point in French politics. This had important results for the development of French socialism which up till then had been very divided. After the socialist members of parliament under the leadership of Jaurès and Vaillant had freed themselves from their association with the French liberals, they could more easily hold out an olive branch to the representatives of other socialist groupings. The Russian revolution, which was continually applauded in every socialist newspaper and at every socialist meeting, thus simplified the difficult process of unification, and in 1905 the SFIO (Section Française d'Internationale Ouvrière) could be set up.

However, there continued to be considerable differences of opinion between French socialists, even with regard to their approach to Russia. Jaurès was chiefly orientated towards the socialist revolutionaries, and in his many statements about Russia was supported by Rubanovich with advice and assistance. Rubanovich also talked him out of his objections to the PSR's terrorism. For the Guesdists Plekhanov remained a distant, but much-quoted mentor in Russian affairs. Krichevsky, the former opponent of *Iskra*, had become one of the Russian guides of the syndicalists. In their view, the success of the Russian general strike had convincingly proved the superfluity of political parties.[71]

Elsewhere as well, for instance in Holland[72] or Italy, syndicalists and socialists disputed each other's right to incorporate the Russian revolution into their own movement. But in France the socialists were sharply divided in their reaction to syndicalism. The Guesdists continued to oppose the general strike implacably even after 1905, and thought the trade unions should be subordinate to the party. Jaurès and his associates, under the influence of Russian events, began to have a more positive approach to the general strike and syndicalism. This was to be of great importance, for it had been the French syndicalists who had continued to regard the strike as an effective weapon against the threat of war. In contrast to Guesde, Jaurès now also tended to see something in this idea, and risked a confrontation with Bebel about it at the congress of the International in Stuttgart in 1907. After October 1905 Jaurès had somewhat irritated his Eastern neighbours – for whom he otherwise showed more understanding than most of his fellow countrymen – with his exhortation to follow the Russian example by also putting a constitutional and democratic strait-jacket on princely absolutism in Germany and Austria. He continued to doubt the usefulness of a political general strike in the French republic with its universal suffrage.

However, in 1905 and the years afterwards, the syndicalist trade union, the CGT (Confédération Générale du Travail), was in a state of revolutionary euphoria. The syndicalists attempted several times to put the general strike into practice, or rather to view the explosions of labour unrest in the period 1905–12 as an expression of proletarian readiness for it. But the result of the extensive and sometimes bloody strikes was simply that the weakness of syndicalism and the labour movement and the strength of the French state were demonstrated. Because of this, in the syndicalist's world view, the idea of the general strike was shifted further and further into a future that lay as far away as the social revolution did for the socialist movement. The only positive outcome was that the syndicalists no longer rejected the French socialist politicians as arrogantly as before and little by little a basis for mutual co-operation was laid down.[73]

To what extent the radicalisation of the French workers and of French syndicalism was a direct result of the Russian revolution naturally remains an open question. But 1905 was an exciting story full of proletarian glory and martyrdom to add to socialist mythology. In the years 1905–6 it was presented to a wide and enthusiastic public on countless occasions by speakers and writers. But how the telling of it changed the minds of all those people, history does not relate. In this connection it is interesting to examine how Georges Sorel, who was the first to recognise the importance of a socialist mythology, reacted to the events in Russia. All the more so since his famous book *Réflections sur la violence*, in which he considered the general strike primarily as a myth, consisted of a series of articles which he had written in 1905 for the syndicalist paper *Mouvement Socialiste*.

Like many socialist thinkers before and after him he thought that the labour movement should itself be the womb from which a new society would be born. The impressions which existed there about the future were therefore of vital importance. He attached no value whatsoever to the futurological accuracy of these images. The idea of a general strike was an ideal myth because it could incite such a large group of people to zeal and bring them to decisive action. The rightness or wrongness of the many arguments put forward by the opposition, which thought that a general strike was doomed to failure, were therefore insignificant.[74]

Sorel, in contrast to Luxemburg or Roland Holst, had no need whatsoever of Russia. After all he did not need to show that the general strike was not a fantasy dreamed up by unworldly visionaries. However, it was curious that in his book he regarded the October strike in Russia as a political strike, which according to the syndicalist definition could not be in the workers' interest. The myth that Jaurès and other French socialists had woven around the Russian strikes was one which ought to be exploded. In Sorel's view the strike had been launched by Minister Witte in collaboration with the Russian revolutionary intelligentsia in order to scare the living daylights out of the tsar and force him to make concessions. The Russian workers had become the victims of plotting behind the scenes and skilful demagogy. The tragic outcome of Russian developments only proved that political strikes were doomed to end in chaos and repression. Sorel then preferred to leave admiration for this kind of activity to the 'boursicotiers qui lisent *l'Humanité*', Jaurès's paper.[75]

Sorel's thoughts about Russia in 1905 betray the intellectual provincial rather than the original thinker. Nor did this change in the case of the October revolution. The ex-conservative, ex-Marxist and ex-revisionist Sorel, after his love for syndicalism had cooled down and his consequent flirtation with the Action Française had ended, would succumb to the Russian myth of the soviet system as a genuine form of workers' self-government. In 1919 he added a chapter about Lenin to the fourth edition of his *Réflections*, which was as lyrical as it was naive. This intelligent opponent of Jacobin utopianism and Jacobin revolutionary violence was unaware of the grim reality which was concealed behind the Soviet fairy-tale.[76]

## THE 'BOURGEOIS REVOLUTION' UNDER FIRE

Though Sorel may thus have been the only socialist in Europe for whom the Russian strikes were nothing special, the attitude of the Russians themselves was actually much stranger. In 1904, in the paper *Mouvement Socialiste*, the French syndicalist Lagardelle had held an extensive enquiry amongst Western socialists into the general strike. In responding to this enquiry Plekhanov had argued that the general strike as a social revolution was a perfect utopia. The workers would have died of hunger long before they could dare to make an attempt to rob the bourgeoisie of its power. Thus it was not so odd that Lagardelle, when he published the results of his research in book form at the beginning of 1905, could still write about Russia: 'It is understandable that in Russia the idea of the general strike has not penetrated the working masses.'[77]

But even in the course of 1905 and afterwards the Russian socialists made no substantial contribution to the great debate about the proletarian mass actions that were continuing to sweep through the West. The Russian social democrat Lensky claimed in 1906:

> While social democratic thought in the West was already working out this question in detail, while in Germany two social democratic congresses and a trade union congress were engaged in evaluating it, and it was continually occupying the minds of the proletariat in France – the problem of the general strike lost all its significance for us. In the course of 1905 the Russian proletariat showed the entire world a whole series of hitherto unknown general strikes; for the first time in history the idea of the general strike was glorified on a gigantic scale – while our social democratic literature had not yet managed to utilise this new phenomenon; the study of these new, powerful, interesting and because of their magnitude, shocking, facts, has been left to the freer Europeans.[78]

The cause of this was not that the revolutionaries were too busy in 1905 to be able to concern themselves with theory in depth. The revolution had only stimulated the internal ideological warfare in which the Russian revolutionaries remained entangled. But since there was no public political life in Russia the general strike could not be for the Russians what it meant

for the Europeans: a theoretical alternative to uninspiring parliamentary policies, a rejuvenation for socialist organisations
which were beginning to show signs of bureaucratic fossilisation
and of acceptance of the political and social status quo. Most
Western socialists were convinced that armed insurrections to
overthrow the capitalist state were superfluous and at the same
time had no chance of success. The example of the Paris Commune was still exerting its deterrent effect. The general strike
was not an armed uprising. It was non-violent inaction, from
which as the Russian experience had taught, in contrast to the
minute socialist triumphs in parliament, immediate substantial
results might be expected. Strike tactics could thus be presented
as the way out of an impasse and that is the reason why the
debate about them was conducted so passionately.

In Russia this was less tempting. Since the failed Decembrist
revolt in 1825 the revolutionary movement had set itself the
objective of overthrowing tsarism by force of arms. As long as
the chance of a successful rebellion was extremely small, they
had to be content with the perpetration of propaganda among
the intelligentsia, the peasants and the workers. The founders
of Russian social democracy had even initially concentrated
chiefly on propaganda. But around the beginning of the present
century the idea of an armed uprising increasingly gained adherents in social democratic circles and an ever more powerful
advocate in Lenin. The socialist revolutionaries were of course
even more dedicated adherents of armed rebellion. It was thus
only to be expected that they were the only ones who cried out
against the bloodless resolution about the general strike during
the congress of the International in Amsterdam in 1905. In
their paper *La Tribune Russe*, this spineless outcome of the
congress was attributed to the influence of theoreticians like
Kautsky, who according to the socialist revolutionaries were
opponents in principle of any form of violent action by the
modern industrial proletariat.[79]

In September 1904 Plekhanov pointed this allegation out to
Kautsky in a letter. It was inadmissible that Kautsky's prestige
in Russia should be attacked in such a way. Plekhanov therefore
thought that Kautsky ought to write an open letter to *Iskra* in
order to defend himself against this slander.[80] Kautsky did not
follow Plekhanov's advice. Plekhanov did, however, publish a
reaction to the Amsterdam congress in *Iskra*, in which he argued

that the recognition of the general strike by the International did not rule out the possibility of an armed uprising. He was not an unqualified supporter of armed uprising, though. He would condemn the December 1905 uprising in Moscow as an irresponsible adventure and was derided by Lenin for this. But neither before 1905 nor after did Russian socialists of any persuasion see the general strike as their principal aim. The Western discussion was certainly followed. The writings of Lagardelle and Roland Holst were translated, even Sorel was read in Russia, but that was as far as things went.[81]

Only Parvus and Trotsky, shortly before Bloody Sunday, praised the political general strike as a truly revolutionary tactic for Russia. But they, too, quickly subordinated this idea to that of a people's revolt. The importance of the large-scale strikes in Russia was naturally denied by no one. But they were nevertheless seen by the revolutionaries as a kind of mobilisation of the troops which had been predestined to deal the last blow to tsarism, not as a measure that was powerful enough by itself to force the autocracy to its knees. This was certainly strange, for the government was able to suppress all the armed uprisings in 1905, while the October strike forced the tsar to make substantial political concessions. Even among the Mensheviks a certain optimism also prevailed about the chances of armed action being successful. In *Iskra* some revolutionary strategists based their case on the extensive specialist military literature about the Boer War, which according to some experts had proved how little suited a professional army was to guerrilla warfare. Mensheviks like Martov and Akselrod were fundamentally just as worried about the possibility of an armed uprising succeeding as about the chance that it would fail. For if the general strike, as Trotsky and Lenin claimed, were to result in an armed rebellion, this uprising would have to be followed by a *coup d'état*, and to this were attached consequences which the Mensheviks found difficult to digest.

The most prominent Menshevik ideologists' aversion to the conquest of the state has been interpreted by their opponents and by later historians mainly as a sign of dogmatic inflexibility, as the expression of a pedantic kind of Marxism, and as the main cause of this political movement's downfall. Revolutions – it was reasoned – are violent political upheavals and they are regarded as successful at the moment when the revolutionaries have become the new leaders. Revolutionaries who do not crave for power are doomed to failure and cannot be taken seriously as revolutionaries. The logic of this reasoning is difficult to deny. This is not to say that in the case of the Mensheviks it is historically correct. At the same time it is doubtful whether the Mensheviks should be castigated for their lack of consistency.

The Mensheviks' supposed tendency to abstain from force is mostly linked to the social democratic concept of the future Russian revolution. In this view Russia would still have to go through the revolutionary phase which Western Europe had already experienced in 1789–1848. Russia was thus waiting for a 'bourgeois revolution' and the aim of the RSDRP, according to their 1903 programme, was the replacement of autocracy by a democratic republic. Russian capitalism would then be freed from its feudal shackles and the bourgeoisie would take over the power of the state. In contrast to the Europe of a century before, Russia was, however, industrialised to some extent and had a proletariat, which according to the social democrats was predestined to give the impulse which would undermine the Romanovs' throne. The bourgeoisie was thus considered to be capable of taking over power, but not of conquering it in a revolution. On the other hand, the proletariat was certainly able to serve as the most prominent revolutionary actor, but would not yet be able to lead the state at the existing stage of Russia's socio-economic development.

In this Marxist model of the Russian revolution two extensive social groupings existed which were perpetually in a state of class war with each other and at the same time were totally dependent on each other. This meant that everything would go wrong if, in practice, one of the two partners refrained from complying with its prescribed role. For the historian as a 'prophet with hindsight' it is easy to predict that such theoretical hubris was heading for a fall and that the model would succumb to the fiery baptism of a real revolution. It is then only a small step to the assumption that only those revolutionaries who were prepared to move with the ideological times as soon as they had understood how the revolutionary tide was in fact flowing, would reach their goal. In 1905 both Trotsky and Lenin introduced modifications into the old model of the bourgeois revolution, while the Mensheviks seem to have retained it. Since it can rightly be maintained that in October 1917 Lenin and Trotsky made use of what they had learnt about the revolution in 1905, the downfall of Menshevism could be attributed in the same way to the lack of theoretical flexibility which they were already displaying in 1905.

Trotsky and Lenin both searched for a solution in a simplification of the complicated division of roles between the proletariat and the bourgeoisie. In their revolutionary strategy, the bourgeoisie was reduced not only in its role as a revolutionary class, but also in its role as leader, to being a mere cipher or spectator. The bourgeois revolution was thus filled, to as large an extent as possible, with proletarian and consequently also socialist elements. In this respect they did not stand alone, for the ideas of the socialist revolutionaries were similar, even if they put the accent rather more strongly on the possibilities of agrarian socialism. Thus socialism – if hesitantly and without committing themselves – was put on to the agenda of the revolution by all revolutionaries, who were trying with might and main to enforce an armed rebellion. In their theory the Russian revolution ought to fill the space between the bourgeois revolutions which had taken place in the West, and those which, according to the Marxist scenario, were yet to be put into effect. This was of paramount importance, not for the developments in 1905 itself, for they gave the lie to every theory, but because the intentions of the Russian revolutionaries were departing more and more emphatically from those of Western European socialism. Although in theory the Western world was on the eve of the collapse of capitalism, no concrete plans had been developed by the socialists for the introduction of socialism. Idealistic 'dare-devils' who wanted to suit the action to the word were always fiercely opposed since they endangered the vested interests of the workers and those of their organisations.

However, it was mostly accepted that the Russian workers and revolutionaries had nothing to lose apart from the fetters with which they had been chained by tsarist absolutism. It would be admirable if these brave fighters were to venture into the unknown territory of the social revolution, although at the same time everyone had to admit that the circumstances were considerably less favourable for it than in the West. In this way Russia was the subject of a great deal of writing and discussion in the West, but the great Russian debate about the nature of the revolution to a large extent passed most socialists by. In Russia itself, however, everything in the way of socialistica which appeared in the West was eagerly followed. The freedom of the press which had originated in 1905 was gratefully made use of in order to translate a great deal and print long runs of it. The Menshevik Dan could proudly write to Kautsky: 'Every social democratic worker in Russia knows your Ehrfurt programme . . .', because there were more than 200,000 copies sold in July 1905.[82]

The Russians still showed themselves to be pupils of Western socialism, while in Europe the Russian proclivity for theory was found rather embarrassing. This was not right, for in Russia in 1905 concepts were developed which were to have a great influence on revolutionary practice in 1917 and moreover had far-reaching consequences for the international labour movement. These Russian ideas, because of their utopian character, were urgently in need of correction. However, the Western socialists did not make use of their authority, partly out of ignorance of the Russian discussion, and partly because they thought that, in fact, different standards applied to Russia. The lack of serious, critical reactions to the revolutionary strategy of Trotsky, Lenin and the socialist revolutionaries was also one of the many circumstances the concurrence of which made the October revolution possible.

Trotsky went the furthest with the destruction of the bourgeois revolution. The proletariat should not hand over the power it had conquered to the bourgeoisie, but should form a government itself. In 1903, during the debate on the concept of the dictatorship of the proletariat, Trotsky had argued that this could only mean the rule of the majority of the nation.[83] But what he was suggesting in 1905 was despotism by a small minority, for that was what the Russian workers then were. The long and active Jacobin tradition of the Russian revolutionary movement was to find in him in 1905 its most intrepid representative and it was his vision which would prevail in October 1917. But then, as in 1905, Trotsky used international socialism as a cloak to conceal the readiness for brute force on a large scale. In 1905 and 1917, Trotsky was convinced that a proletarian government could not hold its own in Russia for long. The Russian revolution would be the flaming torch which would be thrown into the European capitalist powder keg. The social revolution which would then break out in the West would save the Russian proletariat and socialist Russia from ruin. In Trotsky's line of reasoning, Russia and Europe would be joined together by a 'permanent revolution'.

Of course this was no original concept. Since the days of Marx and Engels the Western socialists had also toyed with this idea. The great enthusiasm for the Russian revolution among Western socialists could only be explained by this line of reasoning. But neither in 1905, nor later in 1917, was it ever explicitly stated that Russia would take all the risks and the West none. In launching the West as a sort of *deus ex machina* in order to provide the Russian revolutionary drama with a happy ending Trotsky was leaning very heavily on the future, and eventually this was to turn out to be a complete miscalculation. The thought of a salutary Western intervention in the Russian revolution was also present for Lenin and the Mensheviks in 1905, and in and after 1917 this played a fatal role in their revolutionary schemes. Nevertheless, they had never been prepared to leave the fate of the revolution so completely in Western hands as was Trotsky.

In 1905, Lenin wanted to increase the Russian proletariat's extremely narrow base of power by an alliance with the rebellious peasants. On behalf of the majority of the population a revolutionary coalition government could then be formed to fight reaction whether in tsarist or in bourgeois form. In 1905 Lenin was still convinced that socialism could not be realised immediately in Russia. The struggle thus continued to be directed towards a democratic republic with a capitalist economy, but in which the bourgeoisie was ruled out as the ruling class. The bourgeois revolution would thus have to be carried out without, even against, the bourgeoisie. Lenin's formula of 'a democratic dictatorship of workers and peasants' remained exceedingly vague. It has not infrequently been remarked that Lenin's genius was proved by his open recognition of the overriding importance which the peasants possessed as an element of power in Russia, while in the original social democratic revolutionary plan no role of any significance had been assigned to this group. But the socialist revolutionaries and, as we have seen, many Western socialists including Kautsky, had never abandoned this idea. In fact, in 1905, everyone in Russia became convinced that there would be no future for the country unless an immediate solution was found to the pressing agrarian question. For Lenin's Menshevik critics, however, there was no question about which would prove to be the stronger partner in Lenin's confederacy. It was, of course, the peasants, who in their view ought not to be regarded as democrats or socialists.

Another problem was how a government could stem from this revolutionary alliance between two social classes. Even in the revolutionary year 1905 the relationship between the neo-populists and the peasants was extremely precarious. The same was true of the social democrats and the workers. It was more a case of the revolutionaries being driven on by the masses than their being able to profess to rule them. Moreover the PSR had never lost the former populist illusions about the peasants as born socialists. The outcome of the revolution ought, according to this party, to be a democratic republic in which agrarian socialism would be combined with urban industrial capitalism. How could such a coalition government be so united that they would be able with dictatorial force to rob not only tsarist reaction but also the liberal bourgeoisie of all influence on national policy? What would remain of the democracy for which both Lenin and the socialist revolutionaries claimed to be striving? For the most part Lenin's version of the concept of the bourgeois revolution raised questions which were not answered by the 1905 revolution. Even in 1917 Lenin found no real solution to the agrarian question. In the 1920s the Bolshevik party dictatorship proved even less to have an appropriate answer to this question at its disposal. This power structure simply smoothed the way for the 'final solution' which Stalin had up his sleeve.

Thus Lenin and Trotsky did not find any actual way out of the dilemma presented to the social democrats by the idea of the bourgeois revolution. Nor did the 1905 and 1917 revolutions prove in practice to be events for which theoreticians could delineate the right tactics in advance. But it was already clear in 1905 that Lenin's and Trotsky's ideas could have far-reaching consequences. However, it was then impossible to foresee how serious they would prove to be after 1917. No one had the least premonition of the orgy of violence which would be organised a quarter of a century later in order to obliterate from history the theoretical problems raised in 1905. The worst that the revolutionaries could fear around the turn of the century was a repetition of the Jacobin terror from the time of the French revolution.

Even most Western socialists thought that the use of violence, although not without risks, was sometimes justified by circumstances. In the exciting days which followed the publication of the October Manifesto by the tsar, there were many Mensheviks in Russia who were prepared to take these risks. Akselrod and Plekhanov, however, were not in favour of this, but they remained in the West, and it was thus simpler for them to maintain a certain detachment from the turbulent events in their fatherland. Their main partisan was Martov, who had every possible objection to the course formulated by Trotsky and Lenin. But even he wrote to Akselrod, shortly after his arrival in St Petersburg at the end of October:

> Social democracy is held in incredibly high regard. It is difficult to imagine anything like it ... The ideological influence is so colossal that, if this stormy development continues, a 'grab for power' sometimes almost begins to seem inevitable (this is not to say that there is something alluring about such a coup [d'état], I am also afraid that this will be a turning-point in the revolution, but no worse than the Jacobin dictatorship was).[84]

Martov's brother-in-law Dan, who was increasingly turning out to be the most prominent practical politician in the Menshevik camp, was for a time completely carried away by Trotsky's idea of a permanent revolution which gave such a tempting prospect to the situation which had arisen at the end of October and beginning of November. In the midst of the revolutionary disturbances he wrote short letters in inarticulate German to Victor Adler and Kautsky with such characteristic phrases as: 'Now we have all happily arrived in Petersburg and are eagerly breathing the all-conquering revolutionary air.' 'We live here as if intoxicated, the revolutionary air acts like wine.' 'At any rate there is a smell of powder and we are probably on the eve of bloody events.'[85]

These sanguine hopes were the result of observations which were evidently based on optical illusions. It seemed as if the government could not manage to take any action against the rebels, and as if the liberals, who at the beginning had been the driving force behind the rebel movement, had now left the political stage. The workers' mood, however, was changeable. Their struggle was certainly not exclusively directed towards the creation of a socialist or even a democratic Russia. They also demanded concrete improvements in their living conditions. The social democrats, who regarded themselves primarily as representatives of the working class, found themselves forced to support strike action for an eight-hour working day, though they knew that the anti-tsarist camp would be further weakened by this. Many employers who had been favourably disposed towards the political strikes in October responded to their employees' new activities with dismissal and locking out. As a result the workers were beginning to show ever clearer signs of exhaustion and apathy. The 'days of freedom' were evidently numbered. The counter-revolutionary offensive which the government had mounted in November was successful. The St Petersburg Soviet was arrested and this event did not provoke a mass uprising of the workers in the capital.

This did happen in December in Moscow, where the Bolsheviks had taken up a strong position. This undertaking was in no sense an attempt to bring about the fall of the regime and was actually already doomed to total failure beforehand. The Moscow Mensheviks believed that they ought not to shirk from a valiant culmination of the revolution and fought with the Bolsheviks and the socialist revolutionaries at the barricades. The result was a sad and not particularly heroic repetition of the bloody finale of the Paris Commune. However, the Moscow *semaine sanglante* differed from its Parisian predecessor in important respects. The behaviour of the government troops was certainly excessively violent, but much less bloodthirsty than in 1871. Only thirteen victims fell among the fighting rebels. The police and the army lost about a hundred dead; on the other hand, the fights and artillery bombardments accounted for more than a thousand deaths among totally innocent Muscovite citizens.[86] Plekhanov's reproach that arms should never have been resorted to was thus completely correct, but at the same time it became evident that the Mensheviks could hardly be blamed for dogmatic obstinacy in those months. They were, like every other group of revolutionaries, taken by surprise and swept along by events, and they had even foreseen this possibility in their theoretical speculations. Nevertheless, because of their interpretation of actual developments, their ideas about what ought to have happened and their critical reactions to ideological opponents, they were time and again led back to the original version of the 'bourgeois revolution' from the early years of Russian social democracy.

It was not illogical that the impressive activities of the liberal opposition in 1904 and early 1905 were seen by them as the beginning of the era of the Russian middle class. In this new period of the supremacy of the bourgeoisie, only a united and well-organised working class could offer resistance to capitalist exploitation. The leading Mensheviks therefore wanted to make use of the opportunities of the existing political and social unrest, not only to speed up the birth of a new society along a revolutionary route, but also to prepare the workers as well as possible for that future. Akselrod's plans for a 'workers' congress' and Martov's ideas concerning 'revolutionary self-government' were chiefly aimed at bringing to life the entire Russian proletariat as an independent social and political class. It was the Mensheviks working in Russia who actively tried to hold firmly to this course during the revolutionary storm, took advantage of the activities of the liberals and made use of the concessions allowed by the government in the course of 1905. The government's plans to enable workers to take part in a social advisory commission (the Shidlovsky commission) or in a national political assembly (the Bulygin Duma) were used by the Mensheviks as a pretext for proletarian organisation and as a basis for agitatory campaigns for further reform of state and society. In a similar manner strike committees were converted or extended into workers' clubs, insurance offices, proletarian militias, trade unions or workers' councils.

The Bolsheviks could not or would not be left behind in this and likewise founded trade unions, took positions in Soviets, and so on. But among their members there was much hesitation and distrust, for all these organisations which had sprung out of the ground like mushrooms in the autumn hardly, if at all, complied with their image of the proletariat as a disciplined party army which, at the signal of the Bolshevik general staff, could be brought into action for the last assault on autocracy. In practice, in 1905, the behaviour of Mensheviks and Bolsheviks differed so little from each other that even Lenin could no longer resist the universal loudly resounding call for unity. However, this had little effect on the significance of the lengthy, still unremitting debate about the nature and the aims of the 1905 revolution for the future of Russia and socialism. The participants each had some right on their side.

Lenin and Trotsky realised that revolutions could not be won without flagrant violence and demagogical manipulation of the masses, and tried to act accordingly. However, they looked forward to the post-revolutionary period with an extremely naive optimism. Despite his schoolmasterly emphasis on discipline and authoritarian leadership, in essence Lenin retained an extremely utopian view of the proletariat. His statement in *What Is To be Done* in 1902 about the workers who, left to themselves, would never progress beyond a small-minded trade union mentality, was amply compensated for by many other passages from his work in which the workers were held up in an almost lyrical manner as an example to the social democrats because of their revolutionary zeal, their decisiveness and their enthusiasm, which would make the conquest of socialism possible.

The ideas of the most prominent Mensheviks about the social class to which they had linked their lives were also a curious mixture of realism and castles in the air. Nor did they want to leave anything to chance or to the elemental force of the proletariat. They too tried to influence the workers and to use them for their own ends. But the fiery baptism of the revolution strengthened their conviction that Lenin's and Trotsky's *putsch* mentality was using ignorant workers for improper ends. If radicals of this sort could get their own way, the chance of a true liberation of the proletariat, of the elimination of despotism and oppression – that is to say, the chance of the glorification of the essence of socialism – would be even more slender. This point of view was in almost complete agreement with the attitude of most Western socialist leaders towards radicalism in their own circle. But it was much more difficult to keep this under control in the middle of a revolution in Russia or under tsarist repression, than under the more stable circumstances in the West where people also had their hands full. Circumspection in revolutionary tactics, which was being unremittingly preached in the Menshevik camp by figures such as Akselrod, was seldom actually perpetrated and was not particularly effective. But it is difficult to come to any other conclusion than that this Menshevik caution was justified by later developments.

What then was the Menshevik alternative to the radicalism of Lenin and Trotsky? The only remedy against the degeneration of the revolution and of their own movement continued to be, in Menshevik eyes, the creation of a self-confident, developed and organised working class – Akselrod's old prescription. Of course this, too, was a utopian train of thought, for there was no guarantee that if the social democrats were to succeed in promoting the emancipation of the workers in such a way, the implementation of socialism in its most perfect form would follow as a matter of course. But most Western socialists held views of this sort, and naturally the Mensheviks pointed out the flourishing Western socialist parties and trade unions as the embryo of a future desired by everyone. Since these organisations could only exist thanks to the more developed bourgeois democracy in the West, the desirability of such a development in Russia was merely underlined by it. Not only did Marxist historical necessity dictate the advent of a bourgeois system of law, but this was also necessary in order to safeguard the socialist future and to protect the movement against decay from within.

Not only Trotsky and Lenin, but also Akselrod and Martov, were searching, though in the midst of a revolution, for a practicable road to socialism. Later it would become evident that the projected routes would lead to something other than the object in view. In both cases the objectives were naive and the results regrettable. As long as the communist autocracy was manifestly present in the Soviet Union, the interest of Western and Soviet historians in the history of Bolshevism was perfectly self-evident. And even Western historians, however much their sympathy might go out to the socialist losers of the revolution in 1917, until recently found it difficult to look at the tragic fate of those revolutionaries within the framework of Russian history as anything but an interesting episode from the early history of the communist dictatorship.[87]

The Gorbachev era made a new political pluralism possible and even saw the renaissance of a social democratic movement. It also created opportunities for new approaches to Soviet history and the history of the Russian revolutionary movement. Soviet historians have started to look at the historical relations of their country with the West in a different perspective. It might therefore be more apt than ever to describe the development of Russian social democracy before 1917 as a chapter in the history of the international socialist movement. In that movement there had always been authoritarian and anti-authoritarian currents, which were often at loggerheads with one another, and sometimes even curiously mutually intertwined. In this respect the party feuds within the RSDRP were nothing special, though their consequences reached much further than was usual with socialist quarrels in the West. Differences of opinion within Russian social democracy were the cause of the split which occurred in the entire socialist movement after 1917, and even the global political dichotomy between capitalism and communism originated from it. Behind the debates between Bolsheviks and Mensheviks lay concealed a contrast between democracy and dictatorship of which the protagonists in the discussion were not always clearly aware before 1917, and which has to be revealed by a historian. The problem then arises that the development of modern democratic socialism is difficult to describe, while the genesis of totalitarian socialism can be sketched out with a few strokes of the pen. Its decisive moment was Lenin's and Trotsky's choice against what they called 'bourgeois democracy' in 1905. The consequences of this basic position were not to become visible until after the October revolution, but then they did so immediately. The attempts to make a democratic republic of Russia after the fall of the autocracy came to an abrupt end, and a dictatorial form of state capitalism was called into being. The fiction that this would be socialism could, from the very beginning, only be kept alive with deceit and terror, though this did not prevent the rulers and their followers in the East and the West from believing it.

The course of history in the other part of the socialist labour movement is more difficult to detail. Everyone knows that Western socialism withdrew further and further from the revolution, and moved in the direction of an acceptance of society as it was and as it was developing. But there was not much consistency in this process, and it is hardly possible to indicate its beginning or end. For example, it seemed as if socialism, in the struggle with anarchism and syndicalism, had definitively accepted parliament as the principal element for the carrying out of social reforms. But soon this decision was once more brought up for discussion in the debates around Millerand and Bernstein, and the Russian revolution of 1905 gave a number of Western socialists another opportunity to lay mines under the bridge which was in the process of linking their movement with the bourgeois state. Subsequently it was also impossible to identify the precise moment when socialists had accepted parliamentary democracy lock, stock and barrel. They in fact always continued to resist complete integration to some extent and moreover the state, the economy and social relationships had been altered fundamentally in character through their agency. Around 1900 the socialists were anything but democrats in the modern sense of the word, but themselves thought that they were better democrats than others were. Even Lenin and Trotsky condemned the bourgeois state not because it was undemocratic, but because they believed that socialism ought to embody a higher form of democracy. The totalitarian state which they later helped to set up, however, made many of their socialist opponents into full-blooded democrats in the long run.

Naturally there were individuals and groups everywhere in the socialist world who steeled themselves against authoritarian tendencies within their own movement. Before 1917, the doubtful honour fell to the Mensheviks of being the principal opponents of a kind of autocratic socialism, which afterwards was to subject a large part of the world to itself. After 1917, they conducted a struggle as honourable as it was hopeless, against the Bolshevik dictatorship. Even then many Western socialists were not as yet prepared to learn the lesson to be drawn from the collapse of moderate socialism in Russia. Before 1917 it was in fact not at all clear what could be learnt from the Russian experiences. Obviously the Russians themselves must take the blame for this. In 1905 the Mensheviks had been fervent supporters of the 'bourgeois revolution' but this did not of course make them into defenders of the bourgeois capitalist state. It was to be a long time before they regarded democracy as fundamentally more important than the revolution and some of them, like Dan, would refuse to take this view until their dying day. Nor did the Mensheviks differ in this respect from certain Western socialists. But this also meant that their attempts to gain

support from European socialism, in their struggle against Bolshevism and the communist dictatorship, were never rewarded
with much success. Relations between the Western and the
Russian socialists not only give us a good insight into the way
in which the Western European image of Russia influenced the
formation of opinions within an extremely large group of
people. They also form an interesting subject of study because
they show us the remarkable way in which the entire socialist
movement wrestled with the principles of dictatorship and
democracy and how tangled the evolution they experienced as
a result of this was.

# 5

─────────────────────────

# INTERMEZZO 1906-1918

The character of European history in the years 1906–18 was determined by increasing international tension, the First World War and the Russian revolution. Developments within the international socialist movement were to a large extent a reflection of this. Numerous publications have already dealt with the discussions about war and peace at the congresses of the Second International, the 'collapse' of this organisation in 1914, the politics of *Burgfrieden* (civil truce) and *union sacrée* and the increasing opposition to them. The period 1918–23 which followed then seemed a logical result of the preceding one. The five-year-long social and political unrest which took on a revolutionary character in both Eastern and Central Europe and resulted in the definitive split of the socialist movement, was defined as the inevitable aftermath of the First World War. However, if the relationship between Russia and Europe is chosen as the guiding principle in the treatment of both periods it becomes more difficult to regard 1918–23 as a consequence of the years 1906–18.

There are sufficient indications to enable one to accept that the reactions of the European public, including the socialists, to the October revolution and the early history of Soviet Russia were to a large extent prompted by the old stereotypes of fear, contempt and admiration for Russia. In other words, these reactions followed more or less the same pattern as those which succeeded Russian events around 1881 or in 1905. Since the periods before 1881, 1905 and 1918 have little in common, the interpretation of European reactions to the October revolution exclusively in terms of events in the period 1906–18 is hardly a foregone conclusion. This all the more since just at this time European public opinion appeared to be less preoccupied with the traditional image of Russia than in the period before or afterwards. Never had the West tended to such an extent to regard Russia as a more or less ordinary country.

The fear of Russia as a dangerous imperialistic power and a bulwark of reaction was diminished by her ignominious defeat at the hands of Japan. Fear of or delight in a destabilising Russian influence on social and political attitudes in the West was decreased by the failure of the insurrection in 1905 and the impotent and languorous existence of the revolutionary movement until 1917. The introduction of a constitution with popular representation, the swift progress of Russia's modernisation in the fields of technology, industrialisation, urbanisation, education and culture, the intensive contacts between Russians and non-Russians, the importance attached to the alliance of England and France with Russia, and the increased familiarity in the West with the tsarist empire, all ensured that the usual emotions aroused by Russia's being 'different' were toned down.

Naturally these feelings did not entirely disappear, not even during the war, whose levelling effect was far greater still. At first the Germans allowed themselves to be dominated by their time-honoured fear of the arrival of the Cossacks, but they soon scored their greatest successes on the Russian front. England, France and later America had to be taken more seriously as enemies than Russia. In the camp of the Entente, the feeling of solidarity and even affinity with the Russian ally who was so necessary in the struggle increased. Here it was the Germans, often depicted as Huns, who summoned up the old spectres about barbarians. The war dominated everyone's thoughts so much that, in the West, events in Russia in 1917 were judged exclusively on their possible consequences for the progress of the conflict between the European nations. Not until after the separate peace of Brest–Litovsk, and to an even greater extent after the armistice in November 1918, was there sufficient room for other considerations. Only afterwards did the old clichés work their way again into the forefront in order to define the image of the revolution.

When looked at in this way, Europe's reaction to the existence and growth of the communist dictatorship in Soviet Russia was thus not a result of the war, but separate from it. This is not to say that the events in the years 1906–18 had no influence upon those in the years 1918–23, but only that this influence on the Western image of Russia, and consequently also on Western opinion about Bolshevik Russia, is much less clearly apparent than is generally assumed. The image of Russia was used as soon as the need for forceful statements about that country was felt. Since there was less reason for this in the years 1906–18, this period will be treated as an intermezzo in the relations between socialist Europe and revolutionary Russia.

Since the relationship between both groups of socialists in the years after 1905 was dominated by the situation in Russia, it might have been illuminating to have started this chapter with a short, objective characterisation of the final period of the tsarist regime. However, this would create the problem that assessing it even in retrospect might still cause us the same troubles as it caused the people of the day who could not expect the outcome of events as known by us, but who speculated about it all the more enthusiastically. In no other European country was politics so dominated by one fundamental question, and the different political pressure groups made their future dependent on the answer which they thought they ought to provide to it. This question was whether the mitigation of the autocracy under pressure from the 1905 revolution would enable the regime to ensure its survival, to prevent another revolution and, eventually, to liberate the country from its political and economic backwardness. And, in essence, this is still the most important problem for the present-day historian of Russia in the period 1906–17.[1]

Of course there were many at that time, in both East and West, who believed neither that the tsarist regime was viable, nor that the revolution could be avoided. They were later able to point to 1917 as the definitive proof of their assumptions. Since then most historians have repeated the arguments of these opponents of tsarism. But it is fundamentally impossible to prove that the 1917 revolution was entirely, or even chiefly, the result of the *ancien régime*'s inability to adapt itself to the demands of the twentieth century. Here, too, the view of East and West and the war had a curious role to play. If one wants to believe that political conditions in Western Europe were normal, one tends to ascribe its temporary disruption in the period 1918–23 to the influence of the war. However, if one wants to believe that political conditions were abnormal in pre-revolutionary Russia, then the consequences of the war are brushed aside as being of no overriding significance. But both the participants in the Russian drama and later historians who tried to deny the inevitability of the revolution, naturally retained every right to nominate the First World War – an external factor – as the most important cause of the great revolution. After all this war had also been, in the conviction of many, disastrous for the German empire whose viability before 1914 – to say nothing of its *Kriegsfähigkeit* or military capability – was never doubted as much as was Russia's. There is thus little point in observing the formation of opinions about Russia in the period 1906–18 from a present-day historical point of view, since historical writing itself is determined to such a great extent by this earlier formation of opinion. Perhaps it would be more useful to choose one of these prejudices as a starting-point. One which gained great force both in Russia and elsewhere, and is still adhered to by some modern historians, was expressed by the famous German sociologist Max Weber in 1906 during the elections for the first Duma. He described Russia's new form of government as *Scheinkonstitutionalismus* or sham constitutionalism.[2]

The term *Scheinkonstitutionalismus* was a value judgement, not a realistic profile of the actual situation. Of course there were many more liberal constitutions than the Russian, but sham it certainly was not. However, many progressive people in the West were able to reconcile themselves with Weber's outlook. On the other hand, in moderately conservative circles there was much appreciation for the tsar's initiative, although in more right-wing milieux the opinion could still be heard that the Russians were not fit for any kind of Western political freedom whatsoever.[3] In Russia, where the political centre was narrow and the extremist wings extended over a great width, even more people could agree with Weber. The tsar and his fervent adherents thought that a constitution was not suitable for Russia and were thus inclined to see it as a bogus solution. These reactionary opponents of the constitution were, however, incapable of implementing a clear-cut alternative. Not only were they driven *nolens volens* to operate within the new form of government, but a great many of the tsar's conservative counsellors appear to have eventually accepted it. A right-wing authoritarian dictatorship could of course have set about tackling Russia's problems, and measured against later developments in the world its establishment would not have been an anachronism. However, that would have necessitated the tsar's delegating his power to a military junta or to ministers with more talent and character than he himself possessed. Nicholas II was not prepared to do this, which proved that he had understood little of the spirit of the times and still less of his own self.

In opposition to the tsar and his entourage were Weber's Russian political friends, the Constitutional Democrats, who considered the immediate implementation of a fully-fledged Western parliamentary system as a necessary condition for Russia's successful entry into the twentieth century. They were of course in complete agreement with the term *Scheinkonstitutionalismus*. Most of the liberals regarded the Duma as a national forum, in which the extension of the constitutional rights of the Russian people should be fought for and which should only secondarily be used as a place for normal, regular co-operation between the people's representatives and the government. Liberals sought for co-operation with the socialists especially in order to exert the greatest possible pressure on the government to bring about concessions.

In practice, however, the Cadets were also more and more constrained to take part in the political game of give and take, and to choose the 'sham constitution' and not their dreams about an ideal constitutional law as the starting-point of their political activities. The policy of hundred per cent opposition to tsarism was difficult to implement and also met with much resistance from within their own ranks.[4] Even the socialists had, in the long run, to take the existence of a written constitution and people's representation into account. This situation not only influenced their ideology, tactics and methods, but was also responsible for changes in the image of Russia as seen by Western socialists, which were not without repercussions on their Russian comrades. Initially, however, that is to say at the end of 1905 or beginning of 1906, many of these comrades were involved in a struggle for life and death with the tsarist regime. They were living under the illusion that the revolution would soon flare up again and their thoughts were fixated on armed uprising and terrorism. They considered the October Manifesto a pure deception of the people, and it was almost unanimously believed that the Duma elections should be boycotted. The socialists did not think of co-operating with the liberals; in their eyes the Cadets as opponents of armed rebellion had 'betrayed' the revolution.

Comment in the Western socialist press about events in Russia was also almost totally dominated by emotions of this kind.[5] But revolutionary unanimity in East and West was disturbed by Menshevik dissonance. Even before the October Manifesto the Menshevik leaders in exile had made dissenting noises by declaring themselves against a boycott of the elections for the so-called Bulygin-Duma during the summer. The Mensheviks saw this proposal for the creation of a national assembly with strictly advisory competence as nothing more than a manoeuvre to contain the revolution. But in the election campaign they discovered excellent opportunities to organise and mobilise the proletariat in the struggle for the expansion of political rights. Naturally they defended this tactic, which fitted in with their revolutionary strategy at the time, in their paper *Iskra*, and Martov wrote an article about it in *Die Neue Zeit* that was taken over by the socialist press in other Western countries.[6]    Nothing came of the Bulygin-Duma, since the tsar was soon compelled to make greater concessions. But the reactions of the Menshevik party leaders to the October Manifesto and the Duma once more retained the rejection of the boycott. Dan had defended this point of view in full in a letter to Kautsky. He argued that the elections could not actually be prevented by the social democrats. A boycott meant that all the available opportunities for agitation would be exploited only by the opponents of socialism. According to Dan, one did not need to wonder 'which was more revolutionary: revolutionary intervention in the elections, electoral agitation, the mobilisation of all the "disenfranchised" in the name of the Constituent Assembly and the general [that is to say, universal, secret, immediate and equal] franchise, a summons to seize the right which the state does not give out of free will, and the initiation of the building of a broader organisation in the form of agitation committees, clubs, etc., or passive abstention, which amounts to the famous *boycott*'.[7]

Here Dan was making an appeal to the tried and tested Western social democratic policy in which not only revolutionary tradition but also parliamentary debate and the struggle for the extension of the general franchise had their own place. But once more it proved difficult to convince the Western comrades that this policy was also applicable to Russia. The Mensheviks were justifiably worried that prominent socialists like Bebel, Kautsky or Adler under the influence of Luxemburg and other Eastern European radicals would lend moral support to the boycott. In fact it is evident from Luxemburg's correspondence with Jogiches that Kautsky refused to speak out against the boycott when a request to do so reached him from the German reformist side. Bebel, who was taken for a friend of the Russian liberals by a Russian newspaper, defended himself against this accusation by claiming in *Vorwärts* that it had never entered his head to wish that his Russian socialist friends should discontinue their revolutionary activities 'and that they should subject themselves to the parliamentary constitution of the Duma, as granted by the grace of the tsar, which is a monstrosity spawned by filth'.[8]

The leading Mensheviks thus had no Western support for their convictions and even among their fellow party members doubts about their propriety prevailed. The result was that both the RSDRP and the PSR refused to take part in the elections for the Duma, which now achieved a resounding victory for the liberals. The fact that the socialists had let their main chance slip by is proved by the Georgian social democrats and the group of neopopulist socialists, who had indeed put themselves forward as candidates, and were mostly elected. Thus the boycott was pointless and this was recognised afterwards by all the Mensheviks. The Bolsheviks on the other hand refused to accept the failure of the revolution. In preparation for the armed uprising they organised illegal armed partisan groups, who, in anticipation of the revolution, occupied themselves amongst other things with robbery. But these revolutionary 'expropriations' aroused great disgust in a number of Lenin's moderate followers. By the Mensheviks such actions were dismissed as downright criminal.

The Mensheviks succeeded in imposing their will on the party at the so-called Unity Congress of the RSDRP which was held in Stockholm in May 1906. The Bolsheviks and Mensheviks had decided, under pressure from the local divisions of the party, to lay aside their feuds and to confirm their unity at a congress, at which at the same time the Latvian and Polish social democrats and the Jewish Bund were allowed into the party. The Mensheviks were in a majority in Stockholm and thus it was decided to abandon the Duma boycott and condemn the 'expropriations' as prohibited. However, the Menshevik victory was less spectacular than the course of the congress seemed to guarantee. Lenin did not reconcile himself to its decisions. He surreptitiously kept his own organisation in existence, and the Bolshevik robberies, which supplied him with secret funds, simply carried on.[9]

Furthermore, abroad, Stockholm did not produce the dividend for which the Mensheviks had hoped. At last the unity which the Western comrades had been urging for so long was reached. Genuine support for the Russian social democrats' aspirations to follow the parliamentary path was only given by the reformist *Sozialistische Monatshefte*. Bernstein wrote an article there in which he emphasised that the differences between Europe and Russia should not be exaggerated. The Duma formed an important alternative to armed uprising and terrorism for the Russian socialists. This was their opportunity to rid themselves of the tradition of revolutionary violence, which undermined the morale of the movement and 'whose effect with time must be a lowering of the standard of culture to a still lower level than Russia now enjoys'. However sensible Bernstein's words may have been, revisionist agreement with their policy only made the Mensheviks more suspect in the eyes of the very members whom they were trying to convince of the rightness of their point of view, that is to say, the leadership and the press of the SPD.[10] *Vorwärts* continued to show a preference for the tactic of boycott. Kautsky, who was much influenced by Luxemburg, admitted in *Die Neue Zeit* that the boycott had become pointless, but he continued to arouse sympathy for it since the Duma deserved the name of people's representation even less than did the German and Austrian 'shadow parliaments'. In this matter Kautsky was far less the self-evident supporter of the Mensheviks than they had assumed in their correspondence with the German theoretician. In Stockholm the Bolsheviks, not entirely wide of the mark, claimed that Kautsky was in favour of the boycott, which was fiercely denied by Dan.

Initially, Kautsky's attitude proved typical of that of the international socialist community as a whole. Plekhanov, the representative of the RSDRP at the Second International, surprised Huysmans, the secretary of the ISB, in June 1906 with a letter in which he informed him that the Duma was involved in a severe conflict with the government. 'It will be of great significance for our movement if foreign parliaments give evidence of their sympathy to the Duma.' Plekhanov thought that the ISB ought to appeal to them to do so in a circular. He reported that the party had denounced the boycott 'as totally sterile' and ended with the sentence: 'At this moment the Duma is one of the levers of the Russian revolution if not the principal one.' Plekhanov's action was probably aimed not only at arousing Western support for Menshevik policies, but also at calling their opponents within the RSDRP to order, with the help of the International.[11]

Huysmans was clearly somewhat at a loss over this letter. The French socialist Vaillant first recommended him to ask the other Eastern European parties and groups for advice. Plekhanov protested against this. All these organisations – in so far as they were a part of the party – had to accept the decisions of the congress. He added the text of the Stockholm resolution about the Duma, which the Mensheviks had crammed with revolutionary fervour, to his correspondence with Huysmans. Plekhanov regretted the fact that the International gave the opponents of the Duma and of party unity within the RSDRP the opportunity to expand. The other Russian party that was represented in the Bureau of the International, the PSR, had not yet forsworn the boycott, but this could not prevent international social democracy from supporting the Russian social democrats in their struggle for political freedom. 'Do not forget that the socialist revolutionary party is in no way a workers' party.'[12]

Kautsky, who spoke on behalf of Rosa Luxemburg, let it be known that he, like Plekhanov, wanted to support the Duma's struggle against tsarism, but that he did not know if the Polish comrades had forsworn the boycott. He therefore did not wish to make any pronouncement about Plekhanov's proposal. Huysmans rejected Plekhanov's request about it as politely as possible. Rubanovich, the PSR representative, suggested asking the members of parliament of the affiliated parties to protest against 'the atrocities of tsarism'. This idea had already been brought up at the last sitting of the ISB by the English representatives, Hyndman and Keir Hardy. However, such actions had frequently been taken in 1905 and a repetition of them did not signify any recognition of the fact that with the Duma a new situation had come into being which had consequences for socialist tactics with regard to Russia.

Rubanovich, who certainly did not personally oppose parliamentary government and who was one of the critics of terrorism within the PSR (though as principal representative of his party abroad he could not admit it openly), did however keep the door open for such an admission and did so much more skilfully than Plekhanov. As we have seen, despite the boycott, a number of socialist revolutionary sympathisers were elected to the Duma. According to Rubanovich, these socialists, who called themselves *trudoviki* (the Labourites), instituted an investigation into the counter-revolutionary terrorism of the tsarist government. The International would be able to ask the *trudoviki* to send their findings to the ISB so that socialist members of parliament in the West could make use of them. 'By this action the prestige of the Labour Group of the Duma [i.e. the *trudoviki*] and through it that of the Duma itself will be conspicuously enhanced in the eyes of the entire world.'[13]

The success of this approach was demonstrated in July 1906 in London at the first sitting of the Interparliamentary Commission, a mouthpiece of the International that was set up at the Amsterdam congress under the leadership of Troelstra and Mannoury. At this gathering Anikin, one of the Duma *trudoviki*, was received tumultuously. 'The applause lasts several minutes. The ladies wave their handkerchiefs. The scene is deeply moving.' Anikin outlined a somber and bloody picture of tsarist repression. He reported that the Duma had collected detailed information about this, but said that in Russia there was no legal system which could call a halt to oppression and cruelty. 'It only remains to the proletariat to appeal to the civilised world. Faith in the tsar as harbinger of prosperity is in fact dead. The population only has confidence in the Duma and it is demanding the nomination of an assembly based on universal suffrage.' Of course the conference invited the socialist members of parliament all over the world, in a solemn resolution with a great accolade to the proletariat, the peasants and the Russian rev-

olutionaries within and outside the Duma, to grasp every opportunity to denounce the tsarist outrages and mobilise public
opinion against the Russian government's attempts to prevent
inevitable national bankruptcy by means of substantial loans
from the West. At the same time Troelstra suggested raising
this matter at the forthcoming 'bourgeois' Interparliamentary
Peace Conference, which was to take place a few days later in
London. All members of parliament, even the non-socialists,
should be called upon to support the Duma.[14]

Naturally the effect of this kind of exhortation by resolution
was not particularly great. If the socialists in the East and the
West had actually managed to co-ordinate their activities with
the liberals in their countries, then it might have been possible
to put pressure on the French and the English and through
them also on the Russian government. But since this did not
happen, the tsarist authorities did not need to take the anti-
Russian pinpricks in the West seriously. They obtained their
money and with it a free hand to disband the troublesome Duma.
It was certainly important that the Western socialists, who tended
to see only *Scheinkonstitutionalismus* in Russia, were, in practice,
accepting the new political order as a definite reality. Recognition
of the Duma as the Russian people's representation *in statu
nascendi* meant recognition of the possibility of legal protest in
Russia. Afterwards the tsar's empire could no longer be regarded
exclusively with horror and fear as a barbaric power. And this
meant that any form of revolutionary violence exerted by
Russian socialists could no longer automatically rely on deferen-
tial admiration. Some signs of this altered attitude were already
detectable. On 16 February 1906 the following appeared in *Het
Volk*: 'Nothing can be changed, the Russian revolutionaries'
attempt to bring about the fall of tsarism has failed ... The
terrorist deeds which occur should probably be regarded as the
deeds of revolutionaries who through disappointment have been
filled with utter despair. A socialist party cannot suppose that
the shooting of heads of police or a few government officials
can have any effect.'[15]   However, no consistency in the attitude
of the Western socialists was immediately perceptible. The situation in Russia, where revolutionaries and the government continued to compete with each other in violence, gave little occasion
for it. Not only the ISB but also the socialist press and the socialist

members of parliament continued to exhaust themselves in accusations against the tsar and hastened to defend the Russian socialists or anarchists who had fled to the West, and who, accused of robbery or murder, were threatened with extradition to Russia. Such illegal activities were still being directly supported. Huysmans, the secretary of the International, was, as he himself said, helpful to Stalin in 1907 in the provision of weapons, which were probably used at the now notorious bank robbery in Tiflis in the June of that year. But at the same time the fate of the Duma was receiving ample attention and, as we shall see later in this chapter, in the long term a marked repugnance for the violent, criminal and undemocratic practices of certain groups of Russian revolutionaries emerged in the socialist West.[16]

### THE ENQUIRY INTO THE RUSSIAN REVOLUTION

Parliamentarianism was not only a question of political practices. It had always been a matter for intense ideological discussion, and things were no different within Russian social democracy. At the Stockholm congress the theory of this question had been very thoroughly debated. In an impressive speech Akselrod had again emphasised that the Duma – despite its manifest shortcomings as a parliamentary institution – deserved to be taken seriously as an important step forward. The social democrats should conduct themselves with moderation and as true members of parliament. They ought not to alienate the liberals, so that in the event of a conflict between the Duma and the government, parliament would be able to count on as much support as possible from the people.[17] But a significant minority at the congress was not convinced by Akselrod, and the party controversy about parliamentarianism continued unabated after the congress. Plekhanov followed his partially successful campaign in the ISB with another which was intended to give the tried and tested concept of the bourgeois revolution more theoretical splendour in Russian eyes. Thanks mainly to Plekhanov's theoretical work, this idea had been the principal axiom of Russian Marxism since 1883. But through the agency of Lenin, Parvus and Trotsky many RSDRP members were no longer convinced of the infallible accuracy of this point of view. Plekhanov therefore wrote a letter to a number of prominent Western socialists in which he asked for the answer to three questions. These were concerned with the character of the 1905 revolution, co-operation of socialists with the liberals, and the attitude towards the Duma.

Plekhanov's questionnaire was answered by the Italians Turati and Ferri, the Frenchmen Lafargue, Vaillant and Milhaud (an associate of Jaurès), the Belgian Vandervelde and the British Marxist and editor of *Justice*, Quelch – in short, by a fairly representative selection of left and right within European socialism. Of course their answers were not identical, but more or less amounted to the same thing. They implied cautious support for the Menshevik point of view. Most Western socialists were modest and did not want to play the role of armchair critic. But they all thought that the Russian revolution could not be a socialist one, and only at best a bourgeois revolution with socialist elements. They all considered the Duma boycott a mistake, and co-operation with the bourgeois opposition in any form was essential. From this it is once more evident that during the six months which had gone by since the failure of the armed workers' uprising in Moscow in December 1905, European socialist opinion had moderated and adapted itself to the changed circumstances in Russia.[18]

There was, however, one important exception and that was Kautsky. Kautsky gave no straightforward answer to Plekhanov's questions but wrote a long essay on the 'Triebkräfte und Aussichten der russischen Revolution' ('Driving forces and prospects of the Russian revolution') which he published at the end of 1906 in *Die Neue Zeit*. In this article the problem of the character of the Russian revolution was mainly related to the agricultural question in Russia. Kautsky's interest in it dated from much earlier. In the 1890s he had successfully defended the idea that the SPD should preserve its 'class character' as the party of the industrial proletariat and resisted Bebel and others who wanted to meet the peasants half-way and to broaden the social base of German socialism. But he had never agreed with Plekhanov and other Russian social democrats who defended this point of view for Russia as well. In 1905 he devoted the introduction to the Russian translation of his book *Das Erfurter Programm* entirely to the problem of the Russian peasants. This book about the SPD programme which he had helped to develop in 1891, and which became the ideological basis for social democracy throughout the world, had contained no clearly agricultural paragraph.[19]

He saw the only solution for Russia in the radical abolition of large-scale landownership and in boosting agricultural productivity. A prerequisite for this was the revolution, through which the balance of property would be drastically altered. Moreover an end would come to the aggressive and imperialistic policy of tsarism. The money that was at first devoted to the military apparatus could then be freed for the improvement of agriculture and the training of peasants. About a million copies of Kautsky's book with this optimistic outlook were sold in Russia in 1905–6.[20] After the urban labour force had tasted defeat in December 1905, Kautsky continued to keep his hopes focused on the peasants. In a letter to Plekhanov in March 1906 he wrote:

> I am expecting a great deal from the next two months, because then it will become clear whether the peasants will begin the struggle for the land or not. If it does not come to such a fight, if the peasants calmly continue to accept the fact that the large landowners' land will be worked by them as non-owners even in the future, then there will be absolutely nothing to be expected from the agrarian movement and one will have to think up tactics which no longer depend on this kind of catastrophe [namely a mass peasant revolt] for the future. The urban workers alone will not be capable of bringing off an engagement of any significance in the immediate future.[21]

Although the peasant uprisings continued until the summer of 1906, it must have become clear to every open-minded observer in those months that the government, with the help of punitive expeditions, summary justice and the declaration of martial law in many provinces, had the countryside completely under control. A logical conclusion could then have been that the new tactics which Kautsky was discussing ought to consist of as much social democratic support as possible for the Duma, which had just become involved in a vehement conflict with the government about new agricultural legislation. Kautsky, however, did not come to this conclusion. In his answer to Plekhanov's circular he stuck to his former point of view. He considered the tsarist system incapable of solving the agrarian question. Nor were the liberals any more capable. Kautsky regarded them as large landowners in opposition to the regime, who perhaps had the best intentions towards the peasants, but who could never take the drastic measures necessary to combat agrarian misery because these measures went directly against their own interests.

It was for this reason that Kautsky emphatically warned against comparisons between the European 'bourgeois' revolutions, like the great French one in 1789, and the future Russian revolution. In the West at the time *das Kleinbürgertum* (the lower middle class or *petite bourgeoisie*) formed the most numerous and economically important class in the opposition against the *ancien régime*. This group had been the real mainspring of the revolution because it was in contact with the capitalist bourgeoisie and the pre-industrial proletariat. Kautsky's Russia, however, was fundamentally different. It 'lacks the strong backbone of a bourgeois democracy which, because of its community of economic interests, would be able to weld together the bourgeoisie and the proletariat for a joint struggle for the acquisition of political freedom'. Kautsky's conclusion runs: 'The age of bourgeois revolutions, namely revolutions whose driving force is formed by the bourgeoisie, has come to an end, even for Russia.'[22]

Since the industrial proletariat there was too weak to capture power alone, it needed allies. And the peasants were the only allies. Their rebellious activities formed the best safeguard for the development of the flagging agriculture and the people's victory over tsarism. Revolutionary alliances, in Kautsky's view, ought to be based on common economic interests and these existed only between the workers and the peasants. The peasants would be driven straight into the arms of the social democrats by the reactionary policies of the tsar and the conservative attitude of the liberals. The agreement between the two classes should therefore form 'the foundations of all the revolutionary tactics of social democratic Russia'. 'Without the peasants we cannot win so quickly.'[23]

Obviously Kautsky still considered the Russian revolution as not yet finished. What form victory would take, he left undecided. But social democracy must not hesitate to strive for it, 'for one cannot fight successfully if one renounces victory from the first'. The introduction of socialist production methods in

Russia – even if the socialists were temporarily to gain power – seemed unthinkable to him. The day of the 'dictatorship of the proletariat' had not yet dawned. 'We shall be confronted there with entirely new situations and problems which do not conform to any hitherto existing pattern.' The Russian revolution ought to be considered 'as a peculiar process that occurs on the borders between bourgeois and socialist society, promoting the dissolution of the one and preparing for the formation of the other, and in any event bringing the entire capitalist civilisation a decisive step forward along the course of its development'.[24]

Here Kautsky emphatically decided against the bourgeois revolution as it was couched in the party programme of Russian social democracy, and continually defended by the Mensheviks – if with a few changes of heart in 1905. His reaction, in which the reality of 1906 was to a large extent ignored, can only be explained if we accept that for the time being Kautsky found it impossible to free himself from the idea that the Russian revolution was the crowbar which would liberate the West from the capitalist prison. In Kautsky's mind, too, the traditional socialist image of Russia still produced this kind of wishful thinking. When the Russian socialists strayed from the narrow ultra-revolutionary path and, just as despondently as their Western counterparts, continued to blunder around the dim forest of piecemeal reforms, stumbling over all the obstacles furnished by parliaments and other legal institutions, then the radiant hopes for a radical liberation disappeared, perhaps for good, over the horizon.

Kautsky's Marxist analysis of Russian society with its emphasis on the absence of a bourgeoisie was rather traditional. At the same time it was a typically German socialist view. The bourgeoisie, which was much more ostentatiously present in Germany than in Russia, had, according to the socialists, neglected to perform the task allotted to it by history. It had not brought about the political liberation of Germany, nor had it built up a liberal movement that could have given shape to Germany's politics in the twentieth century. The SPD professed to have taken over this historic task from the liberals. In this way, German socialists could agree, more easily than for instance French socialists like Jaurès, with the absolute contempt for Russian liberalism displayed by radicals like Lenin, Trotsky or

Luxemburg. Kautsky thought that the SPD must indeed be a revolutionary party, though not one that made revolutions. That honour he preferred to leave to the Russians. The German situation was thus judged considerably more soberly than the Russian. A few years later, this was to lead to a major conflict with Rosa Luxemburg. Rosa in fact wished to make no distinction between Germany and Russia. Gradually, under the influence of this split, Kautsky's point of view about Russia changed completely.

In 1906, however, Kautsky's revolutionary simplicity in Russian affairs corresponded with the ideas of the left wing in the Russian revolutionary movement. Lenin, especially, had every reason to rejoice. The most prominent Western Marxist, who before the 1905 revolution would not give him any opportunity to defend Bolshevik opinions about party organisation in *Die Neue Zeit* against Luxemburg's attack, was now entirely on his side. Moreover, Kautsky also seemed to be an enthusiastic supporter of a revolutionary alliance between the workers and the peasants. Lenin published the Russian translation of Kautsky's article as a separate pamphlet and supplied it with a triumphant introduction.[25] He criticized Plekhanov, who had formulated his questions to the Western socialists in such a way that they already contained within themselves a distortion of reality and suggested the answer. It had been to Kautsky's immense credit that he rejected such a questionnaire as un-Marxist and emphasised that the Russian party could be victorious if it could summon up the necessary will-power. Kautsky's statements formed the 'most splendid acknowledgement of the revolutionary tactics of the revolutionary wing of Russian social democracy, namely the tactics of the Bolsheviks'.[26]

Plekhanov's defence against this was weak. His attack was firstly directed at Lenin, whom he wrongly reproached with having misunderstood Kautsky. Plekhanov was undoubtedly very disappointed with Kautsky's answer, but he refused to admit that there was any question of a fundamental difference of opinion. Kautsky, in Plekhanov's view, only overestimated the speed of Russian developments. The Russian social democrats certainly ought not to abandon their chance of victory, but the liberals were not yet reactionary *en masse*, while on the other hand the interests of the peasants and the workers were now diverging sharply. In view of the supposed character of the revolution, there was no question of the bourgeoisie being supported by social democracy. He had always let the slogan 'March separately and strike together' be valid for co-operation with the liberals.[27]

While Plekhanov, because of his exhibition of arrogant vanity as a theoretician and Jacobin temperament as a politician, was brought to a point where he presented his arguments as no less radical than anyone else's, Martov made a positive attempt at a fundamental refutation of Kautsky's ideas. Since history has devoted extremely thorough treatments to Trotsky's and Lenin's aberrations from the idea of the bourgeois revolution, Martov's justification of it deserves serious attention. According to Martov, Kautsky maintained that as soon as the agrarian question had been solved as a result of the establishment of modern capitalist landownership and the acceleration of agricultural productivity, the principal driving force behind the Russian revolution would be eliminated. After that capitalism could blossom freely. A development like this – as Martov alleged – could not be characterised within the Marxist tradition otherwise than as a bourgeois revolution. But Kautsky refused to do this, for in his view the bourgeoisie had no revolutionary role to play in it. At the same time he maintained that the revolution could not be socialistic, because the proletariat was incapable of taking power permanently or of introducing socialist production methods. He therefore considered this revolution as a separate phenomenon on the borderline between bourgeois and socialist society. But, as Martov established with irrefutable logic, such a phenomenon could, in Marxist eyes, be nothing other than a socialist revolution. Subsequently he categorically stated: 'A revolution in the twentieth century, a revolution which is enacted in the atmosphere of world-wide capitalism, is either bourgeois or socialist. It leads directly to the supremacy of capitalism or to its abolition. *Tertium non datur.*'[28]

One could of course call a revolution after the person who carried it out. In that case the Russian revolution was not bourgeois, but Martov thought it better to call it not a socialist, but a peasant-proletarian revolution. One should not, however, pay as much attention to the class which carried out the revolution as to its eventual result. The Russian Marxists had there-

fore always regarded it as bourgeois. But Kautsky could not
cope with this strange contrast between form and content. He
continued to wrestle with the special role which the Russian
proletariat could play at this juncture. Kautsky attached a special
meaning to the concepts of bourgeois and socialist, because he
hoped that the proletariat in Russia and Europe would be able
to carry out certain tasks. The Russian revolution was still seen
as a prerequisite for a socialist upheaval in the West. But this
was turning things upside down. The judgement of historical
reality ought not to be inferred from the task which is laid upon
a certain social group, rather this task should be inferred from
an analysis of reality.

Like Plekhanov, Martov opposed Kautsky's proposition that
the liberals had ended up in the conservative camp. For the
landowners in the propertied class perhaps this held good, but
certainly not for the Russians who held sway over the commer-
cial-industrial sector. For them there continued to be substantial
advantages in the abolition of the autocracy, even if they would
not join the fight for it at the barricades. This was also less
relevant, for Martov pointed out that according to Kautsky
himself the bourgeoisie had not to any great extent been the
driving force behind the French revolution. It was the *petite
bourgeoisie* which had taken up this position. According to
Kautsky this group had now become so reactionary that it could
no longer fulfil its role as a connecting link between the
bourgeoisie and the proletariat. Martov thought this untrue. It
was after all no longer exclusively the self-employed tradesmen
who filled this layer of society. Not only during the 1905 revolution but also during the elections for the Duma it had emerged
that the 'white-collared-proletariat' (*platnye intelligentnye rabot-
niki*) which had become numerous in Russia too, working for
the railways, banking, trade, industry, the machinery of government and the liberal professions, could be counted as opponents
of the *ancien régime*. It had been this group which had functioned
once more in Russia as the connecting link between the liberal
bourgeoisie and the workers. In the future the new urban middle
class would be very well able to unite with the up-and-coming
group of the small peasant landowners. Kautsky's assertion that
in Russia the strong backbone of bourgeois democracy was
lacking was mistaken, and in this way the problem of the

bourgeois revolution without a bourgeoisie was, as far as Martov was concerned, solved.

At the same time the need for a revolutionary alliance between the proletariat and the peasants declined. The disadvantages of a temporary dictatorship of workers and peasants in Russia were evident. The social democrats would sooner or later be confronted with the very divergent interests of the peasant landowners and the agrarian proletariat. Martov conceded that, given the peasants' underdeveloped political awareness, in principle it was quite possible for a socialist party to qualify as the head of the agrarian movement. For social democracy this meant that it had to give up its Marxist character and its independence as a modern workers' movement for the sake of a successful grab for power. As long as the 'dictatorship of the proletariat', which would have to effect the transition from capitalism to socialism, remained an impossibility, such a putsch-orientated course of action would mean that the party would be handed over to Blanquist and anarchistic elements.

> In contrast to Kautsky we think that Russian social democracy, as the party of the proletariat, would only be performing its task correctly if it refused 'from the very beginning' to strive towards the only victory which is possible under present circumstances. A victory which made the party into the representative of the masses would only mean that they would be drowned disastrously in a lower-middle-class ideology.[29]

For the present-day reader it is astounding that people like Kautsky, Lenin, Plekhanov and Martov saw fit to criticise or defend the policies of a party with such long, dogmatic speculations. But every political culture of every era has its own specific codes and frameworks for discussion and these Marxists' habits of communication were basically no more strange or laborious than those of our time. As has already been explained in the previous chapter, the problem is rather whether the importance of these speculations should be measured against their predictive power. It could after all be maintained that Kautsky had perhaps too simple an idea of Russian society in 1906, but that he, like Lenin, foresaw that only the 'will for power' and the winning over of the goodwill of the masses could lead to victory, as happened in October 1917. On the other hand, Kautsky would fully realise from 1918 onwards (and Lenin in 1922–3 to some extent) that this coup had not yielded the victory for which they had been striving before the revolution. Martov's belief in the inevitable decay of social democracy as a result of a premature seizure of power had more lasting worth.

Martov's criticism of Kautsky had another quality which made it stand out above the level of the usual Marxist scholastic polemic. It was the first time since 1905 that a Russian socialist had so emphatically turned against his Western sympathisers' image of Russia. This did not happen because Martov, Akselrod or Dan had become convinced that tsarism would disappear even without a revolution, and had thus become reformist adherents of parliamentarianism. Martov wanted to make it clear that social and political circumstances in Russia did not force the social democrats to an ultra-revolutionary course of action and at the same time offered the opportunity for a more Western development of the workers' movement. The differences between Russia and Europe were not so great that the Russian workers had to do the revolutionary dirty work as a matter of course, so that their Western comrades could complete the transition from capitalism to socialism without soiling their hands. The changed situation in Russia placed new arguments at the Mensheviks' disposal, so that they could once more emphasise that a policy which was exclusively directed towards the conquest of power, was not only catastrophic for the future but also unnecessary for the present.

It is, however, unlikely that Kautsky, who knew no Russian, could ever have become acquainted with Martov's article. It was written for a Russian public and was directed less against Kautsky than against Lenin. Martov ridiculed the most self-assured revolutionary of all the Russians for his secret need for confirmation and support from the side of authority. Contrary to Trotsky, Parvus and the theoretician of the PSR, Chernov, Lenin had always maintained that the coming revolution could not be a socialist one. This was why he was now delighted to be able to greet Kautsky as an associate, especially since the reactions of other Western Marxists like Lafargue had been so disappointing for the Bolsheviks. 'Kautsky gave comrade Lenin the tempting occasion to cut the umbilical cord which was still binding him to the intellectual traditions of Russian social democracy.' After Kautsky's discovery of the non-bourgeois revolution, which was also non-socialist, Lenin could dismiss Plekhanov's defence of the classical theory as un-Marxist metaphysics. An independent, class-conscious Russian proletariat had evidently become – so scoffed Martov – a completely unnecessary luxury.[30]

The debate about the character of the Russian revolution has been described here because it influenced relations between Western and Russian socialists through Kautsky's intervention and was to continue to do so in the years to come. For us it sheds some light on developments which were still hidden for their participants in the lap of the gods. These discussions did not have much relevance for the determination of the party policies of the time. The First Duma was disbanded in 1906 and all attempts at mobilising the population against this decision of the tsar failed dismally. One advantage for the Russian socialists was that the vehement conflicts between the government and the people's representation made the Duma acceptable in the West as the most important Russian centre of resistance against autocracy. This is evident from the point of view taken up by the International and the socialist press. Besides this it was of vital importance that the RSDRP was successful at the elections for the Second Duma and that the sixty-man social democratic parliamentary party, dominated by the Mensheviks, was brilliantly led by their Georgian fellow party member Irakli Tsereteli. For a short time the social democrats took over the leadership of the opposition to the government in parliament.[31]

## QUARRELS AND SCANDALS

While the Mensheviks were demonstrating that parliamentary politics in Russia could be meaningful, and were also trying, in their work for trade unions, insurance and strike funds and workers' clubs, to take advantage of the new legal possibilities, Lenin and his followers had not been inactive. Nothing came of the preparations for an armed revolt, but the revolutionary 'expropriations' did ensure that the 'Bolshevik centre', illegal according to party decisions, possessed reasonably generous financial means and could undertake all kinds of activities which the Menshevik Central Committee, though in a majority, had to refrain from doing for lack of funds. It is evident from the correspondence of the Mensheviks that they had lost all faith in party unity, for they were reasonably well informed about the Bolshevik machinations aimed at taking over power in the party. In the long run no effective resistance could any longer be made against Lenin's campaign for another party congress, and when the party met in London in 1907, the Bolsheviks turned out to have built up a small majority. But their numerical superiority was too slight for a real takeover, mainly because the Mensheviks were in most cases supported by the Bund. Thus Lenin was dependent on the Poles and the Latvians, who were not always in agreement with him.[32]

There was no longer any question of boycotting the Duma since Lenin himself had abandoned that viewpoint. Parliament, the congress decided, should only be used as a propaganda forum. Any kind of co-operation with the liberals was absolutely forbidden. The policy of the parliamentary party was attacked sharply because it was not revolutionary enough. On these points Lenin gained important support from the Poles, especially Rosa Luxemburg, who was attending the congress as the official representative of the SPD. She made three speeches, which were completely in line with Kautsky's contribution to the discussion about the Russian revolution. Luxemburg, too, attacked the classic ideology of Russian social democracy, as this was articulated by Plekhanov and Akselrod, on account of its rigid and metaphysical character. 'Into what sort of an anxiously clucking hen, searching for a pearl on the dunghill of bourgeois parliamentarianism, have you transformed this teaching [Marxism], which represents the great eagle's wings of the proletariat!'[33]

Although her sympathies clearly lay with the Bolsheviks, their ideas about armed rebellion were dismissed by Luxemburg as utopian. The resolution in which the tactic of 'expropriations' was once more condemned, was accepted, thanks to Polish support. On behalf of the German social democrats both factions in the RSDRP were once more urged to unity by Luxemburg, though what they should agree about remained vague. Besides, the self-assured but hardly revolutionary Germans could not easily agree with the extremely headstrong way in which Luxemburg depicted relations between the Russian and the German party. 'The German proletariat expects from you not only victory over absolutism, not only a new point of support for the liberation movement in Europe, but also an extension and broadening of the perspectives of proletarian tactics: it wishes to learn from you how to act in periods of open revolutionary struggle.'[34] It was pointed out to the Russians that they, as the vanguard of the international proletariat, had the duty to penetrate into the unknown territory between the bourgeois revolutions of the past and the socialist revolutions of the future. Luxemburg's visionary rhetoric, her 'volatile, airy-fairy Marxism' – as Plekhanov expressed it – had little in common with the grim reality of Russia. The Mensheviks felt insulted by her behaviour. Dan wrote an angry letter to Kautsky about it: 'It stands to reason that this tactless interference, in the name of the executive committee of the German party, in internal disputes in our party could not possibly be intended by the executive committee.' But Dan was barking up the wrong tree with Kautsky.[35]

The interminable discussions in London lasted for nearly two months and afterwards the RSDRP was more divided than ever. However, it was not this congress but the Russian government which decided the fate of the Russia labour movement. In June 1907, a few days after the end of the London meetings, prime minister Stolypin had the social democratic parliamentary party in the Duma arrested, allegedly because of an attempt at the revolutionary undermining of the army. Afterwards he abolished the Second Duma. The socialist members of parliament, on the basis of a trumped up charge, were sentenced a year later to forced labour and deportation to Siberia. Four of them died in prison, the remainder, Tsereteli among them, were not set free until after the February revolution in 1917. After Stolypin had disposed of the tiresome opposition in this way, the electoral law was changed to the conservatives' liking. In the Third and Fourth Dumas social democrats were again elected, but they were too few in number to be able to play an important role in national politics. The Mensheviks' interesting experiment with parliamentarianism in the Second Duma had not lasted more than three months.

Stolypin's attempts to create a strong, conservative Russia à la Prussia were unsuccessful. His policy was undermined by his reactionary opponents and in the long run he also lost the tsar's confidence. He was repeatedly the butt of left-wing terrorism and lost his life in a bomb attack in 1911. However, his period of government was a nadir in the history of the Russian revolutionary movement. The RSDRP, which in 1905 had estimated its membership at 250,000 and could rely on a multitude of sympathisers, in 1906 and 1907 had already seen the number of its adherents decrease greatly, but after Stolypin's 'coup d'état' it went downhill at an increased tempo. In 1910 the membership had shrunk to 10,000 according to Trotsky's assessment. The opportunities for legal party work had also sharply diminished after June 1907, and the underground party apparatus became larded with *agents provocateurs*. Arrests and banishments occurred as regularly as clockwork and before long most of the underground party committees existed in name only. The dwindling membership of the RSDRP and the other revolutionary parties and groups was, however, not primarily occasioned by the Ochrana, the Russian security police, but by a mass desertion of the intelligentsia, which lost its interest in socialism, Marxism and revolution and devoted itself to normal intellectual careers or became engrossed in religion, mysticism, faith healing, spiritualism or pornography. The RSDRP would never completely recover from this Russian *trahison des clercs*, not even in 1917. For the leaders of the party in exile, who were almost without exception professional revolutionaries, materialists and Victorians, this volte-face in the intellectual history of Russia was a great shock. Since the Russian workers seemed to have sunk into apathy, in fact they had nothing more to fight for and no one but each other to fight with. And this they did, as happens in every exile, with the result that the two rival factions in the party soon broke up into subfactions squabbling amongst themselves.[36]

The history of this melancholy series of events can be read elsewhere and it does not need to be repeated here in detail.[37] But the great discrepancy between the illusions about Russia which European socialism cherished in its less contemplative moments, and the sobering reality of those years did have repercussions on the relationship between East and West within the international labour movement. This took some time, though. The emigrants continued to clutch at every straw which could prove that the revolutionary crop in Russia had not been completely mown down by reaction. They had little need to complain to their Western comrades about their lack of success. For the time being, therefore, everything remained unchanged. At the arrest of the parliamentary party of the Duma there followed a small avalanche of the usual protest which the Bureau of the International unleashed over practically every injustice which arose in the world. The extradition of Russian revolutionaries was nevertheless still such an injustice. In February 1907, for instance, the PSR alerted the International because of the possible extradition by Sweden of Chernyak, a socialist revolutionary who had committed attempted murder in St Petersburg. The BSI sent out a circular about this to the affiliated parties, and because of this ample attention was devoted to the case in the socialist press. Socialists like Jaurès and Ferri, supported by left-wing literary men like Anatole France and the Danish critic Brandes, became involved in it. The most active was the Swedish party leader, Branting. The tenor of his articles in *Socialdemokraten*, in which he chiefly addressed himself to the attacks of the right-wing press, was that a civil war was raging in Russia and that the terrorist actions should not be judged as if they had taken place in 'a peaceful country under normal circumstances'. He also defended this point of view amid vehement uproar – 'I will not be silenced!' – in parliament. The result of the socialist campaign was that Sweden did not extradite Chernyak, but made him leave for Belgium. On his way there by sea the terrorist met his end in mysterious circumstances by suffocation. His funeral was attended by many socialists, including Huysmans.[38]

Thus it seemed as if the Western socialists' point of view with regard to Russian revolutionary violence had remained unchanged. In the PSR's voluminous report to the congress of the International at Stuttgart in August 1907, it was once more argued, and without the least embarrassment, that terrorism was still necessary, and full attention was devoted to its defence by the party delegates in the Duma. But something curious happened at the congress itself. During the sixth plenary sitting, on 24 August, chairman Paul Singer read out a declaration from the British, Austrian, French and Dutch delegations, in which they again expressed their sympathy with the participants in the Russian revolution. To this he added a document, signed by all the Russians at the congress, in which the activities of the tsarist police in the West were examined. In order to drive the Russian emigrants out of liberally governed countries, the Ochrana with the help of *agents provocateurs* organised

> incidents and so-called expropriations in countries where there was a right of asylum, with the obvious goal of discrediting the revolutionaries. It is for these reasons that the organisations which signed this document declared that every action of a similar nature – and especially the so-called expropriations – constituted a betrayal of the revolution, a cowardly deed directed against the emigrants because it enabled the government and their police to suspend the right of asylum.[39]

It had evidently become necessary for the Russians, in the presence of the international socialist community, to distance themselves somewhat from these practices. In the declaration only the provocations of the Ochrana – and these did indeed take place – were expressly mentioned, but all activities of this kind were implicitly condemned. This was in complete agreement with the resolution on this question which had been accepted at the last congress of the RSDRP. But Lenin with, amongst others, Litvinov who was also present in Stuttgart, simply carried on with them. In the PSR and the left wing of the nationalistic Polish party, the PPS, which was in competition with Rosa Luxemburg's party, the official party tactics were put into effect with the 'expropriations'. Both parties were acknowledged members of the International, and remained so. Azeff, the still undiscovered *agent provocateur*, who led these operations in the PSR, was also present at Stuttgart. But in Europe the heroic radiance of Russian revolutionary terrorism was beginning to wane. The PSR's attempts to restore its old splendour in *La Tribune Russe*, its widely read informative paper for the West, with accounts of the support which *Narodnaya Volya* had formerly received from Marx and other Western socialists, were less effective. The relief measures for Russians, who were regularly being made out to be thieves and murderers in the press and in the parliaments by the right wing in European politics, had disadvantageous aspects for the socialists who were helping them in the West. The image of its own respectable legality which Western socialism was so keen to present, was somewhat besmirched by this. After the failure of the Russian revolution the Western socialists found unfavourable consequences of this kind anything but pleasing.

It was also significant here that the congress of the International was held in Stuttgart. The German police and judiciary meticulously checked up on the activities of the Russians who remained in Germany. Especial attention was paid to noting if there were any contacts between the Russians suspected of revolutionary dealings and members of the SPD. Consequently it was in the interests of Western socialists, if illegal activities came to light in investigations of this kind, to deny their involvement. The same was true for the Russians. Neither the supporters nor the opponents of terrorism had any wish to hang up their party's dirty linen in the West.[40]

But in the months that followed a series of sensational incidents took place, which focused the attention of the public on the expropriations which were being carried out by the Bolshevik 'centre'. On 9 November 1907 Kamo was arrested in Berlin. He was the 'hero' of the Tiflis bank robbery, which had yielded at least 200,000 roubles for the Bolshevik party. Kamo was found in possession of a suitcase with a false bottom, which contained dynamite. As later emerged from an investigation carried out by the Menshevik Chicherin, the explosives were intended for blowing up the safe in the Mendelsohn bank in Berlin. Kamo, who successfully feigned insanity before the German police, was defended in court by the social democrat Oscar Cohn. After the Russian police had informed the German that Kamo was a probable member of the RSDRP, he was extradited to Russia. On 25 November the police made a raid on a house in the Pankstrasse in Berlin which had long been under police observation. No arrests could be made, but the house was shown to contain a Bolshevik store, in which revolutionary literature and cases of ammunition and pistols were found. Moreover 19,000 sheets of paper were discovered with a special watermark suitable for forging banknotes. Soon afterwards Bolsheviks were arrested in different European towns for trying to exchange the 500 rouble banknotes from the Tiflis bank robbery.[41]

Akselrod wrote to Martov about the events in the Pankstrasse that the Bolsheviks 'had all but fabricated forged money and betrayed both the Mensheviks and the executive committee of the SPD. If this is all true, then you may question whether it is possible to continue to be in the same party as them.' Plekhanov, too, found that 'this affair is so scandalous that it is time for us to break with the Bolsheviks'. The party leadership of the SPD indeed had reason to be incensed. It emerged from Chicherin's investigation that some of the watermarked paper which the Bolsheviks had managed to get hold of had been sent to Finland with help from *Vorwärts*. This newspaper's transport system and warehouses had for years been used by the Russian social democrats for the storing and despatch of revolutionary literature. This took place with the permission of the SPD, although it was certainly not without risk for the Germans. Now, without their knowledge, they had become accessories to attempted forgery. And this was just at the time when the papers were full of the Pankstrasse affair, and in the Reichstag strict measures were being demanded by right-wing delegates against these 'roving fellows and their accomplices'.[42]

However, the question was, what could be done about it? Dan wrote to Kautsky expressing the hope that the party would be cleansed of 'common bandits'. But Martov had already informed his friends that this would be no simple matter.

> I am afraid that the Berlin affair will have rather lamentable consequences for us. I can imagine how indignant the Germans are! But at the same time it is difficult to think of any way in which the Bolsheviks ought to pay the penalty for their mean tricks. Of course they take their measures and under cover of illegality and conspiracy they pass the whole matter off on to a couple of characters who turn out not to be party members.'

Lenin and his people did indeed use everything, even their ascendancy in the administrative organs of the RSDRP, to keep their practices secret. Poles like Luxemburg had always spoken out against the 'expropriations', but her party, which was also represented in the leadership of the RSDRP, had certainly accepted Bolshevik subsidies. Thus the Poles were also living in glass houses.[43]

Moreover the Bolsheviks could profit from the fact that their Menshevik fellow party members and the Western comrades were in an awkward predicament. They did not want to make a fuss, either. Chicherin was able to make use of the circumstance that no arrests were made in the Pankstrasse in order to explain in *Vorwärts* that the RSDRP had nothing to do with the matter. An article in Russian by an infuriated Martov about Bolshevik partisan activities was abridged and revised by his comrades because the facts stated in it could be misused by the police and in anti-socialist propaganda. Akselrod had toyed with the idea of disclosing the state of affairs in full to the Western socialists, 'but a certain feeling of party pride dissuaded me'. What the Mensheviks did decide was to enlighten the ISB, the party leadership of the SPD, Kautsky, Adler and other prominent socialists in a discreet manner, but it is extremely doubtful whether this was ever done. In any case it did not prevent left-wing circles in France from taking up arms for Litvinov, who was picked up in Paris with a suitcase full of 500 rouble notes from the Tiflis bank robbery. The result was that Aristide Briand, the French minister of justice, did not deport him because the Bolshevik had only committed a 'political' crime.[44]

It is clear from all this that the Western socialists' viewpoint about Russian terrorism was shifting, though as yet there was no question of a complete swing. The Mensheviks had to bear this in mind in their fight against Bolshevism. Moreover they realised that the people in the West with whom they were seeking the closest association, such as Kautsky, were nearer to the Bolsheviks than to them from an ideological point of view. But the most important reason which dissuaded the Mensheviks from breaking with Lenin and his followers was their startling discovery that Menshevism had almost completely ceased to exist as an organised force in Russia. The only remaining Menshevik bulwark was agrarian Georgia, which constituted a separate chapter in the history of democratic socialism. The comrades there, who did not belong to the intimate circle of Menshevik literary men, were against a split in the party. An all too public unmasking of Lenin and his confederates would be interpreted by the party as treason, even by those Bolsheviks who were against the 'expropriations' and in favour of reconciliation with the Mensheviks. Still less was this to produce any advantage for the Mensheviks. If they wanted to avoid political suicide, then the only other choice remaining to them was to try once more to de-Leninise Bolshevism with tactful tenacity and at the same time to earn more understanding for their ideological ideas in the West.[45]

The only weapon they could employ was the pen, and Dan immediately accepted the opportunity offered him by Kautsky early in 1908 during a personal meeting to explain his views on the revolutionary perspectives of Russia in *Die Neue Zeit*. The Mensheviks could certainly do with some publicity. Kautsky, who was as objective as possible about the age-old quarrels in the RSDRP, had a clear preference for contributions from authors who he assumed were outside or above this conflict. He therefore favoured Poles like Luxemburg or Marchlewski or Russians such as Trotsky, Parvus and Riazanov. These people's point of view was, however, just as subjective as that of Martov and Lenin, and the articles published in *Die Neue Zeit* were just as much a contribution to party dissension which was now being fought out mainly by literary means. As a summing-up of 1905 there appeared in Kautsky's paper only pieces by Trotsky and Parvus which exuded powerful revolutionary enthusiasm and optimism. Martov was only permitted to record the vicissitudes of the social democratic parliamentary party in the Duma. When in 1908 the fact could be commemorated that both *Die Neue Zeit* and Russian social democracy had been founded a quarter of a century before, the actual founders and old friends Akselrod, Plekhanov and Zasulich were not allowed a voice. This honour fell to Trotsky, who, as chairman of the St Petersburg Soviet during the 1905 revolution, enjoyed great prestige in the West and augmented this by posing as the only real promoter of unity within the RSDRP. Of course he did not make use of the occasion of this double jubilee to celebrate the concept of the 'bourgeois revolution' which, too, had now been in existence for a quarter of a century.[46]

Dan's article, which appeared in April 1908, was the last but one article by Mensheviks in *Die Neue Zeit*. Lenin never had a voice there, but it is questionable whether this injured him so long as Luxemburg and Kautsky himself defended positions there which to a large extent coincided with his own. Dan apologised to Kautsky about the length of his contribution, but he believed that this was necessary in order not to create misunderstandings with the Western comrades. He was expecting manifestly hostile reactions from fellow party members and these did not fail to occur.[47] The workers and the vast majority of the peasants – so reasoned Dan in *Die Neue Zeit* – had no reason whatsoever to be satisfied with the current situation, but this was in fact also true for the citizenry. It had left the revolution out of aversion to chaos and longing for order, but in the process had fallen out of the frying-pan into the fire. The government certainly tried to strike a bargain with the bourgeoisie, but it did not succeed since the character of tsarism had altered fundamentally. In fact it no longer formed an independent power. It was the nobility, a social group well past its prime, which enforced a reactionary dictatorship in Russia.[48] This situation could not be endlessly prolonged and according to Dan signs of growing political awareness, indicating the gradual formation of a new urban opposition, could be detected among the bourgeois intelligentsia. This group would not be capable of leading the revolution. The revolutionary *avant-garde* would, as predicted by the Russian social democrats since 1883 and proved in 1905, be formed by the proletariat. But the condition for the renewed existence of a revolutionary situation in Russia was the growth of a bourgeois opposition movement, while the peasants would continue to form the elemental force behind the revolution.

Dan's conclusion was right. In Russia, as in almost every other country, a revolutionary situation only came into being because different social and political groups took up a position against the *ancien régime*. The bourgeoisie was an indispensable ingredient in the revolutionary opposition both in 1905 and in 1917. The disastrous developments after 1917 were to show what would happen if state and society had to manage without the bourgeois elite. Thus the value of the concept of the bourgeois revolution was not insignificant. But its weakness was that it had nothing concrete to communicate about what should actually happen as soon as the desired revolutionary situation was a fact. How could the different groupings, which had voiced revolutionary or oppositional ideas with such divergent motives, give collective form to the revolution and its consolidation? This had to be paid for in 1905 and the same happened again in 1917.

The opponents of the Mensheviks appear to have given more thought to this problem. Three months later Kautsky published a reaction to Dan's article by the Pole Maletski, who was one of Luxemburg's political associates. Of course Maletski repeated the old arguments about the dogmatic character of the Menshevik strategy. But he also made a number of cogent remarks.

Dan had only been able to point out a few noisy congresses of independent professional workers in support of his position about the growth of a bourgeois opposition. Nevertheless, things were in a state of ferment in this circle and there had even been meetings between radical liberals and Mensheviks.[49] But Dan could not admit this in public. The Bolsheviks and the Poles, in that case, would have immediately give the Mensheviks a real roasting because they were actively promoting an alliance with the liberals. Maletski could thus simply continue to emphasise that the Russian bourgeoisie was incapable of forming a revolutionary element. Even if Dan had correctly gauged the mood of the Russian bourgeoisie, what would then guarantee, he wondered, that the 1905 situation would not be repeated? Then the bourgeoisie had changed from revolutionary to reactionary within a month, as soon as it had to face the anti-capitalist emotions and economic demands of the proletariat.[50] In Russia, Maletski concluded, only the proletariat supported by the rebellious peasants had stepped into the breach for bourgeois democracy. In other words, Lenin's (and Kautsky's) formula for the revolution still held good.

According to the Mensheviks this analysis of the revolution could only lead to a dictatorship of the intelligentsia over the workers and peasants and thus possibly also to a definitive elimination of bourgeois democracy. Dan therefore immediately asked Kautsky if he might make a counter-attack on Maletski: 'The point at issue is, as it were, the historical justification of Russian social democracy as a whole. For the ostensible new analysis and prognosis of Russian reality, now offered by Maletzky, Trotzky, Luxemburg, Parvus and the like, is essentially nothing else than the slightly modernised old analysis and prognosis of the Russian Bakunists and *narodniki* dressed up in Marxist phraseology.'[51] At the same time Dan pointed out to Kautsky that this utopian approach would also imply the boycott of the Duma, the mysticism of armed rebellion, 'expropriations' and other partisan activities, and moreover would result in the curious religiously tinged revision of Marxism, which intellectual Bolsheviks like Bogdanov and Lunacharsky had started. Like Akselrod, who had described the Bolsheviks in the same terms in his letters to Kautsky in the years before 1905, Dan far overshot the mark with this kind of outburst. Maletski's criticism of Dan was clear and intelligent, apparently did not contain a single Bakuninist barbarism and undoubtedly agreed with Kautsky's own views.

Soon after the publication of Dan's article, a study of the revolution year written by the Menshevik Cherevanin appeared from the German socialist publisher Dietz. Dietz provided Cherevanin's book with a foreword from which it was evident that he had published this Menshevik document 'not indeed without deliberation'. Henriette Roland Holst, who had written a foreword at the request of the translator, her Russian friend Levitin, was no less critical. The reader was thus doubly warned before he actually began to read. Moreover Trotsky and Luxemburg, in response to the publications of Dan and Cherevanin, had informed Kautsky that they would be glad to subject Menshevik views to a thorough criticism in *Die Neue Zeit*. Kautsky therefore asked Dan to wait for these reactions.[52]

Cherevanin's book was first and foremost a clear survey of the events of 1905. Next he severely criticised the behaviour of his fellow party members in the months of November and December. He pointed out that it was not only the workers who had brought the tsar to his knees, but that it had been the simultaneous actions of government officials, the professional classes, students, their teachers *and* workers which had enforced the October Manifesto. This did not end the fight for the winning of political rights, and the bourgeois intelligentsia carried on with it, as was evident from the congresses of the local administrations or *zemstva* and of the liberal party, and later in the Duma. However, their struggle was no longer supported by the socialists because the liberals were opposed to the overthrowing of the government by force of arms. They were therefore accused of treachery, and the socialists set up everything in an ultra-revolutionary direction, which, given the limited power of the proletariat, was doomed to failure. In this way the chance of giving Russia a real democratic-constitutional government had vanished into thin air. The workers saw even the limited improvement in their position which they had acquired during the revolution slip through their fingers.

The social democrats bore a heavy responsibility for this because of their ill-advised political course of action. 'This tactic was entirely wrong. It may be' – as Cherevanin admitted – 'that it was perhaps inevitable, perhaps every other tactic had become impossible at this time because of the totally antagonistic attitude of the government and because of the revolutionary disposition of the proletariat.'[53] This was honest, but with it Cherevanin undermined his entire argument. Thus he gave Roland Holst the chance to maintain in her introduction that she could see no possibility of a different tactic. If the influence of social democracy on the masses was as limited as Cherevanin argued, then he should not hold it responsible for the disastrous course of events. Naturally Trotsky rode roughshod over Cherevanin in *Die Neue Zeit*: 'But what shall we say of that 'realistic' tactic, whose only weakness is that it cannot be applied?' Rosa Luxemburg evidently had nothing to add to his arguments against the concept of the bourgeois revolution, and abandoned her contribution. But neither Dan nor Cherevanin were given the opportunity by Kautsky to publish a rejoinder.

Dan could comment with acerbity that 'we once again, as has often happened before, have our German comrades not with us but against us'. It was cold comfort that the French journal *Le Socialiste* also published Dan's article. The criticism of Maletski's and Trotsky's provided 'with the authoritative imprimatur of *Die Neue Zeit*' could produce its effects on socialism undisturbed in Russia and elsewhere. Trotsky did have the opportunity before long to explain his views in *Der Kampf*, the theoretical paper of the Austrian party. The extent to which the praise and blame he distributed to the Bolsheviks and Mensheviks there was accepted as the authoritative judgement about Russian social democracy is evident from the positive reactions to this article in other socialist periodicals such as the Dutch *De Nieuwe Tijd*.[54]

THE AZEFF AFFAIR AND THE KAUTSKY–LUXEMBURG
CONTROVERSY

Just as aspiring grand masters prepare themselves for the next match by analysing chess games which have already been played, so the Russian socialists continued to replay the revolution in numerous books and articles. The publications discussed here, which were intended for a Western public, formed only the foothills of a small paper mountain which was built up in Russia by the polemic concerning 1905. But the lesson which most of the participants had learnt, without much study, from the popular uprising and the situation which resulted from it in Russia, was that the revolution in Russia no longer had much future. Even among the socialists who did not desert their parties, the number who no longer believed in a revolutionary finale to the tsarist regime was growing. These people entertained an increasing aversion for the practice of that illegality which never in fact lent itself to being clearly separated from ordinary criminality, but which inevitably belonged to a genuine revolutionary party. Among the Mensheviks in Russia – with Potresov as principal spokesman – this mood was likewise clearly noticeable.

Their comrades in exile like Dan and Martov certainly held firmly to the revolutionary point of view, but by no means unconditionally. Like almost all Western socialist leaders they did not have limitless confidence in THE revolution and even less in THE proletariat or THE intelligentsia. Therefore it was not surprising that their viewpoint clashed with that of Lenin, Trotsky or Luxemburg, who radiated revolutionary self-confidence. This self-assurance also made the greatest impression on the Western socialists, who had added 1905 to 1848 and 1871 in the socialist pantheon of heroic failures. In order to avoid these in the future it seemed that more heroism, not less, was necessary. The Mensheviks' strategic circumspection, for which the interests of future socialism in the East and the West was being sacrificed to bourgeois democracy – which according to Roland Holst and many with her had already passed its zenith everywhere in the capitalist world – could in the eyes of few Western socialists pass for the highest political wisdom.

Doubt about the practicability of the Menshevik policy was to be confirmed by events in 1917. But soon afterwards the disastrous results which the policies of their opponents in the RSDRP would have for Russia and the rest of the world, became visible – at least for anyone who dared to face up to the truth. It could not, however, be inferred from the events of 1905 that a victory for Trotsky and Lenin would imply dictatorship, terrorism, civil war, famine and economic disruption. And so what the Mensheviks actually wanted to prevent with their circumspection remained totally obscure. Indeed they did not even know this exactly themselves. They could only indicate the dangers they foresaw with words like 'anarcho-Blanquism' and the like: slogans from a socialist past which seemed to have gone for good and which no longer inspired fear in anyone.

The Menshevik arguments did not possess sufficient conviction to destroy the illusions which resulted from the Western socialists' image of Russia. They were not capable of refuting the revolutionary ideology of Russian radicalism in the West. At the same time they felt that they were not free to disclose the real truth about the criminal practices of the Bolshevik 'centre' against which they were carrying on a fierce struggle in private. But at the end of 1908 and beginning of 1909 the revelation of the century within international socialism occurred, which proved to be strong medicine against the bad habit of Western socialists of applying double standards to things in the East and the West. Azeff, the head of the terrorist organisation of the PSR and the brain behind the assassination of Pleve and many other Russian dignitaries, was unmasked as an *agent provocateur*. This sensational news engaged Western and Russian public opinion for weeks.

The Socialist Revolutionary Party (PSR), which was even more internally divided than the RSDRP, did not recover from this blow before 1917. Many party members, amongst them Rubanovich, the PSR representative in the International, wanted to see terrorism as a socialist method of fighting abolished. But a majority of the party leadership headed by Victor Chernov, the party ideologist, continued to hold on to it. In practice the demoralised party could no longer summon up the necessary strength, and from henceforth the PSR led a sorry existence. The unmasking of Azeff meant not only the downfall of the PSR, but also the humiliation of tsarism as a corrupt power, which in the struggle against the revolution was evidently prepared to employ someone who took the lives of ministers and members of the tsar's family. Both Western and Russian socialists naturally took advantage of this. In the Duma the social democrats tried to make things as difficult as possible for Stolypin. The aftermath of the affair remained world news when, in the summer of 1909, it emerged from fresh disclosures by Burtsev that the tsarist police were also operating in the West and were harassing Russian citizens in Paris. Jaurès was assured by President Clemenceau in the French Chamber of Deputies that all

Russian police officials would be expelled from the country. The Azeff question thus gave the socialists the opportunity to plan a fresh campaign in the old style against tsarism, which the Bureau of the International did indeed organise, at Lenin's and Rubanovich's request, on the occasion of the tsar's proposed visit to Western Europe. In a declaration by the International Nicholas II was called more barbaric than Abdul-Hamid. There were 20,000 political prisoners in Russia and their government staged political murders purely in order to be able to punish the culprits.[55]

On the basis of this kind of argumentation it was not wholly illogical that the PSR refused to give up terrorism and that the French socialist fanatic Gustave Hervé supported it. But in general the socialists did not come to this conclusion. Rosa Luxemburg was the first 'to say a few serious words *pro doma sua*', in *Vorwärts*, to declare herself once more vehemently against revolutionary terrorism, and to commend the Russian social democrats' traditional aversion to it. The Russian expert on Marx Riazanov, who, like Trotsky, did not belong to either of the two factions in the RSDRP and about whose cutting judgement concerning the Russian disputes Kautsky was very sensitive, inveighed bitterly against the Western socialists in *Die Neue Zeit*. They had seriously complicated the struggle against terrorism in Russia. The socialist revolutionaries could repeatedly confront the workers with the fact that if their tactics could really be regarded as anarchistic, they would never be accepted by the International as a fully-fledged party. It was therefore time for the Western socialists, on the occasion of the Azeff affair, to reconsider their curious enthusiasm for Russian terrorism. Naturally Riazanov knew how much the socialist revolutionaries had exploited Marx's sympathy for the terrorists from *Narodnaya Volya* in order to make their tactics acceptable to the Western public. He now made a riposte with a number of quotations from Marx's *Nachlass*, newly published by Mehring, from which it ought to have been evident how well Marx had understood what the pernicious work of police spies consisted of.[56]

Riazanov had observed that it was chiefly the reformists and revisionists among Western socialists who had excelled themselves in eulogies for Russian terrorists. Broadly speaking this remark was not fair – one has only to think of the enthusiasm of the Dutch Marxist Roland Holst or a British Marxist like Hyndman for Russian political murders. On the other hand, Kautsky had been much more unfavourably disposed towards them and was commended for this by the Russian co-workers on his newspaper. In *Die Neue Zeit* Trotsky elaborated on the theme that terrorism and Marxist conviction were incompatible variables: 'The fact appears almost touching, that precisely those comrades in the West who in their homeland least of all resemble bloodthirsty assassins of ministers and annihilators of monarchs, were nevertheless of the opinion that in Russia a canister filled with dynamite remained always the best argument.' Trotsky, never afraid of any kind of intellectual acrobatics, afterwards lectured the reader about the deeper intellectual and psychological affinity between revolutionary adventure and political opportunism, between the secret parliamentary intrigue of reformist Millerandists and the conspiracies of terrorism. For both groups it was possible, after all, to achieve immediate practical results, in which they forgot the masses whom they professed to represent, and appealed directly to princes and ministers. The Russian social democrats, whatever mistakes they may have made, had never been guilty of either of these two forms of utopianism.[57]

Trotsky poured as much salt as possible into the wounds of the PSR, which had become the main competitor of Russian social democracy. He also made use of the sympathy which Kautsky showed for his ideological views in order to prove once more in the pages of *Die Neue Zeit* how absurd it actually was of the Mensheviks to accuse him, an avowed opponent of terrorism, of revolutionary adventurousness. Ten years later, his version of Marxism was to enable him to appear as the principal defender of terrorism. For Trotsky there was never any question of a moral aversion to violence. Even the critical Riazanov saw no reason later, during the communist terrorism, for giving up his party membership.

The admonitions which Trotsky, Riazanov and Luxemburg meant to aim at the Western socialists were somewhat superfluous, for people in Europe were perfectly capable of drawing their own conclusions from the Azeff affair. Thus *Het Volk* complained that 'a shroud of secrecy' hung over the Socialist Revolutionary Party. But, as the Dutch paper added somewhat hypocritically, 'we were anything but blind to the dangers and disadvantages of their tactics'. Next they sang the praises of *Golos Sotsialdemokrata*, Martov's and Dan's paper, in which the organisation of the workers, 'the peaceful, apparently insignificant work, which in fact gives the best and the safest results in the long run', was rated at its true value.[58]

Trotsky's remarks had chiefly been directed at the French socialists who had maintained the most cordial relations with the PSR. This was mainly thanks to Rubanovich, who had once been jokingly pointed out by Chernov as the party's minister of foreign affairs. Rubanovich was a French national, a professor at the Sorbonne, editor of *La Tribune Russe* and a close friend of Jaurès. He was even an opponent of terrorism, but as a loyal party member he had done his best to relieve Jaurès of his objections to this revolutionary violence. After the unmasking of Azeff, which occurred in Paris, Rubanovich advocated in *L'Humanité* the abolition of the Boevaya Organizatsiya, the extremely high-handed party organisation responsible for terrorism. Jaurès tried in his editorials to encourage the socialist revolutionaries and to sugar the pill principally by attacking tsarism. But he argued with clarity that terrorism was no longer fitting for the altered social and economic circumstances of 'the new Russia'. He paid homage to the Russian social democrats, 'who, with the inevitable hesitations and not without useless dogmatic rigidity, have prepared proletarian methods of action consistent with the state of modern Russia'. He made much of the possibilities in the constitutional field, 'the modest but fruitful victory of the revolution'. The Russian socialists had to make an effort to obtain these in full. That this was indeed the definitive opinion of the SFIO was evident from a 250-page book about the Azeff affair, which was published a year later by Karl Marx's grandson, Jean Longuet. Longuet quoted not only his grandfather, but also Martov, in order to show that the terrorist path had been a mistaken one. The Societé des Amis des Peuples Russes also felt obliged to publish a book about Azeff.[59]

Thus at last Russia appears to have after all become a fairly ordinary country for Western socialists, where a normal workers' movement had a right to exist. According to Trotsky it could now no longer be held against Russian social democracy that it 'looked at Russian life through German spectacles'. The saying

'What is healthy for the Germans is death to the Russians' no longer held water. Riazanov could now quietly publish an article in *Die Neue Zeit* in which he rejected Karl Marx's views on Russian history and Russia's pursuit of hegemony in Europe as the product of outdated prejudices, and replaced the master's words with sound, modern Marxist historical writing.[60]

Russian social democracy would gain little advantage from this altered view of the Western socialists. This was due less to the fact that naturally not all the illusions about Russia had disappeared in one fell swoop, than to the deplorable state of affairs within the RSDRP itself. Nevertheless, one thing after another changed there, too. Lenin was convinced that the Russian revolution could not be aroused artificially to new life and that a legal tactic would, even for Bolshevism, offer the best chances for its continued existence as an intellectual trend and organisation. It is no longer possible to determine to what extent the Azeff affair alongside the seemingly hopeless situation in Russia was responsible for this reversal. The immediate effect was that he isolated himself within his own circle. He broke with the supporters of a boycott of the Duma, and disbanded the Bolshevik 'centre', which resulted in organisers of 'expropriations', like Krasin, and unorthodox Marxists such as Bogdanov and Lunacharsky temporarily ceasing to be Bolsheviks. However, he likewise alienated from himself the Bolshevik supporters of party reconciliation. For Lenin continued to carry on a vehement campaign against the Mensheviks. The aversion felt by some of them for illegal practices gave him the pretext to accuse his opponents of the attempted 'liquidation' of the party.

However, no one in the RSDRP believed that the situation was ripe in Russia for a completely legal workers' movement. Lenin's fight against the *likvidatorstvo* was, especially in view of his own political reversal, at least as strange as the struggle of the former *Iskra* editorial board against so-called 'Economism' at the turn of the century. Even stranger was that before long he acquired the theoretical support of Plekhanov, who until then had shown himself to be a Menshevik to the bitter end, but now, after a petty quarrel with Potresov, even washed his hands of his lifelong friend Akselrod, and formed his own club. Although Plekhanov never became a Bolshevik, the loss of someone who was regarded in the West as one of the most important Marxist theorists was a painful blow for the Mensheviks. The centre of power now coming into being in the RSDRP nevertheless offered them the opportunity of driving Lenin into a corner and of making one last attempt at more or less restoring the unity of the party. This occurred at a party conference in Paris in 1910. At this meeting both *likvidatorstvo* and the 'expropriations' were condemned. The capital of around 200,000 roubles which the Bolsheviks had appropriated by, to put it mildly, improper methods from the inheritance of a wealthy party member, would be managed for the RSDRP by three trusted agents from the SPD, namely Kautsky, Mehring and Clara Zetkin. Furthermore, all the factions were once more abolished and the party organs and editorial boards of periodicals were re-established as far as possible on an equal footing. This compromise, reached through laborious negotiations, from which the participants had no great expectations beforehand, in fact achieved absolutely nothing. The Mensheviks in Russia were not prepared to co-operate with the Bolsheviks. Lenin had firmly decided to rectify his defeat in Paris, which had formed the absolute nadir in his career as party leader, and to dissociate himself as much as possible from the rest of the party. This meant that all the groups were quite soon living in the same dissension with one another as before, and each independently made claims on the party funds managed by the three Germans. Only now did Kautsky come into close contact with the Russian quarrels which had plagued him for so long, and his opinion of the Eastern comrades was not improved by it.

The details of these extremely complicated intrigues, which were spun out for years and drove not only Kautsky, but Mehring and Zetkin as well, to despair, need not concern us here.[61] But some background knowledge is necessary to be able to follow the course of the debate about Russia. The Mensheviks were to make one more attempt before 1914 at interesting Kautsky, and through him Western socialism, in the ideological basis of their policy. Until now they had failed in this because, as we have seen, Kautsky attached more weight to the opinions of Poles like Luxemburg and her colleagues who wrote in the German press, or to those of 'independent' Russian social democrats like Trotsky, Riazanov or Plekhanov. In 1909 Trotsky had published a substantial book about 1905 which certainly won considerable recognition in the West. Socialist critics readily gave preference to his representation of events over that of Cherevanin, and not only because Trotsky was undoubtedly a much better writer. The above-mentioned Poles and Russians wasted no opportunity in describing the current situation in the Russian party in such a way that there remained little left of Bolshevism or Menshevism. The old feuds between the two currents were presented as completely outdated. To some extent this was even true. Everyone within the RSDRP agreed that the situation in the party was deplorable and that every precedence should be given to the organisation of the proletariat in Russia. Everyone knew that only an extremely modest beginning had been made towards the execution of this task. It was no time for revolutionary heroism in either word or deed.[62]

The generally accepted policy within the RSDRP thus appeared to be pure unadulterated Menshevism. Riazanov, Trotsky and Plekhanov expressed themselves extremely critically about Bolshevism and Lenin both in private and in their letters to Kautsky, but they laid into the Mensheviks just as severely. Luxemburg had even spoken of Bolshevism as 'a Tartar-Mongolian barbarism' in a letter to Jogiches, but in the same letter she wrote that the Mensheviks were 'our most bitter enemies'.[63] In the final judgement of both Luxemburg and Trotsky their emotional objections to Menshevism always outweighed their intellectual criticism of Bolshevism.[64] Around 1910, however, Trotsky was a zealous advocate of the normalisation of the Western socialists' image of Russia so that they could be convinced of the usefulness of a 'normal' workers' movement in Russia. Rosa Luxemburg had fought against the prejudices about Russia all her life.

During the Stuttgart congress of the International in 1907 the general strike again came up for discussion as a means of preventing the outbreak of a European war. There, Luxemburg, together with Lenin and Martov, succeeded in giving more acerbity and substance to the anaemic and vague resolution on this subject. In defending this Russian amendment she reproached those present once again for not having learnt a lesson from the events of 1905, despite all the tributes to the martyrs of the revolution: 'if the blood-stained shades of the revolutionaries were present here they would say: "We do not need your homage, but learn from us"[65] In 1910 a situation arose in Germany which once more gave her the opportunity to proclaim this message. The Prussian government had submitted some extremely moderate proposals for reform of the suffrage in that country, but they encountered resistance from the Herrenhaus, or Prussian House of Lords. The SPD seized this opportunity to start a new campaign against the hated *Dreiklassenwahlrecht* or three-class franchise. The socialist demonstrations for universal suffrage assumed massive proportions and acquired a dynamism of their own. Moreover at the same time huge miners' and builders' strikes broke out. Both protest movements merged and, according to Luxemburg, this meant that there was a whiff of revolution in the air. The circumstances, in her view, were similar to those in the years 1905–6 when the masses in Germany had started to move under the influence of the Russian revolution. She thought that a general strike should be called. A German democratic republic ought to be the slogan of the action.

Although Luxemburg's oratorical talent again in these days guaranteed for her enthusiastic crowds, she had underestimated not only the balance of power in Germany but also the number of actual adherents of her views. The franchise movement ebbed away within a few months. Even the radicals in the SPD, with the exception of her friend Zetkin, left her in the lurch. Since Kautsky now deserted her openly, the friendship between the two Marxists, which had already cooled down somewhat, deteriorated into undisguised hostility in Luxemburg's case. Some people, such as Victor Adler who had already frequently felt the sharp side of Rosa's tongue and pen, experienced a certain malicious joy now that their friend Karl was also at loggerheads with 'that poisonous trollop'.[66] Nor was the conflict inopportune for the Russians. Everyone knew how Kautsky had let himself be guided by Luxemburg in Russian questions. This was the ideal opportunity for increasing their influence on the Germans. For the Russians quarrelling amongst themselves not only ideological interests were at stake, but material ones as well, since Kautsky was one of the three trustees of the Russian party funds.

Plekhanov wrote to Kautsky that in the polemic with Luxemburg he was on Kautsky's side 'even to the smallest detail'.[67] As far as Plekhanov was concerned this was certainly more or less true, but other critics of Luxemburg likewise gave evidence of their endorsement of Kautsky. Lenin, reported Trotsky, was on Kautsky's side. Neither among the Bolsheviks nor among the Mensheviks were there any members who were completely behind Luxemburg. But the Mensheviks, he cautioned, want to 'interpret' your point of view 'as a 'change' from tactical intransigence to Menshevism .... As far as my humble self is concerned, I fancy that the driving tactical impetus behind Lux[emburg] is noble impatience. That is a very fine quality, but it would be folly to elevate it to the leading principle of the party. That is nevertheless the ancient, authentically Russian method ...'[68] It was what is called a *gotspe* that Trotsky, who certainly did not possess his revolutionary soul in patience, should so depict the ideas of a Polish Jewess who had always done her very best to resist all attempts to label her as 'typically Russian' and whose opinion at the time was only partly, and at an extremely intellectual level, shared by a Dutch scholarly recluse like Pannekoek.

The debate about the general strike between Kautsky and Luxemburg was to a large extent a repetition of the discussion about the same question which had been rampant in the SPD in 1905–6. All that was new was that Kautsky had to some extent further moderated his views. In contrast to Luxemburg's description of the revolution as a series of tidal waves dramatically increasing in strength, which he called *Niederwerfungsstrategie* or overthrow strategy, he had formulated an *Ermattungsstrategie* or exhaustion strategy, which he thought more fitting to a modern labour movement, the SPD and Kaiser Wilhelm's Germany. With this concept he tried to fight not Luxemburg in the first place, but, in his view, the greater danger of reformism and revisionism. The growth of the party as a whole, of the parliamentary party and of the trade unions, and the few political successes which all this provided, did not guarantee a socialist victory. That would actually have to be fought for, but at the right moment. Kautsky did not still believe in Bernstein's thesis of the *Hineinwachsen* or gradual takeover of socialism. The Prussian state remained supreme. The SPD had to go all out to win over to the socialist ideal the German workers, whom, despite its impressive organisation, it had only been able to reach to a very limited extent. The capitalist bastion could not be prematurely taken by storm. It had to be besieged with stubborn persistence with as much proletarian power as possible, and forced to surrender from exhaustion under unremitting pressure.[69]

Naturally Luxemburg could not resist flaunting the Russian example once again,[70] but she also pointed to non-revolutionary Belgium where the socialists in 1886 had tried to win universal suffrage with a general strike.[71] Kautsky placed a stronger accent than he had done in the past on the differences between Russia and Prussia. The uncoordinated, amorphous and primitive strikes of the 1905 revolution were a product of Russia's backwardness.[72] He did not in principle rule out a general strike in Germany, but if the choice were 'shall we talk Russian or Belgian?' then he would choose the second. Kautsky wanted to commit his party to a middle course between revisionist reformism and revolutionary adventurousness. It went without saying that in his view this was the only genuinely Marxist course. With mock wit he pointed out that between Luxemburg and Baden, a hotbed of reformism, Trier was situated, Karl Marx's birthplace.[73]

Luxemburg found Kautsky's image of the Russian strikes 'a blooming phantasy'. As she had explained earlier in her *Massenstreik, Partei und Gewerkschaften* of 1906, she argued afresh that the Russian strikes were not wildly amorphous and so on, and that these actions, if temporarily, had brought about greater material progress than all the German trade unions together in the forty years of their existence. Kautsky's present position with regard to Russia, Luxemburg remarked, was clearly a backward step in comparison with points of view adopted earlier. Then he had criticised right-wing socialists who appealed to the differences between Russia and Germany in order not to need to be revolutionary. Earlier he had willingly quoted and explained Luxemburg's text about the general strike:

> Just as the English workers must get out of the habit of looking down on the German proletariat as a backward race, so must we in Germany get out of the habit of treating the Russians in the same way ... The English workers stand today much lower as a political factor than the workers in the most economically backward and politically least free of European states: Russia. It is

their lively revolutionary consciousness which gives them their great political strength; it was the renunciation of revolution, the concentration on the interests of the moment, the so-called *realpolitik*, which reduced the former to a nonentity in actual politics.[74]

## CENTRISM

In this way Luxemburg had nicely stalemated Kautsky. He probably agreed with the Eastern European correspondents of *Die Neue Zeit* that the prejudices about Russia and the exaggeration of the differences between East and West had aroused much unnecessary misunderstanding and incomprehension. But his acceptance of Luxemburg's view, that there were no differences worthy of mention between Russia and Prussia, would make the defence of his strategy of attrition unusually difficult. This was a fortunate moment for the Mensheviks. 'We have a chance to win the German's trust once more', Martov wrote to Akselrod in August 1910.[75] In fact a short time later an article of his was published in *Die Neue Zeit* under the title 'The Prussian question and the Russian experience' ('Die preussische Diskussion und die russische Erfahrung'). Martov wrote that the discussion between Pannekoek and Luxemburg on the one hand and Kautsky on the other had left intact the illusions that Western European socialists cherished about Russia's most recent past. Therefore this important trump card could still be played by Luxemburg, and on the other hand the only defence was to claim 'that Russian circumstances are totally special circumstances'. The answer to the question 'Shall we speak Russian or Belgian?' was then certainly given, but 'to tell the truth we are not entirely captivated with such a formulation of the question, such a setting up of the dilemma'.[76]

He gave a survey of the struggle which the Russian social democrats had had to wage from the beginning against prejudice about Russia in the Western socialist environment, and sighed: 'Whilst these fellows reject conspiracy, dynamite, putsch, and neglect of the class standpoint for their own political struggle, whilst they see no guarantee that the social backwardness of their own countries would facilitate an upheaval, they are ready to grant all these in the case of Russia: this will do admirably for Russia.' Since 1905 there had fortunately been changes here, and the Western socialists had become convinced that the ordinary norms and concepts of European social democracy could also be applied to the social development of modern Russia. It was nevertheless also evident that there was sufficient scope left over for illusions 'about the "peculiar" functions of the Russian proletariat ... which excavated a profound abyss between the method of class warfare in Russia and that in the West'.[77]

In the whole of Western Europe the strength of the proletariat was judged by the scope and force of its organisation and by its political maturity. But as far as Russia was concerned, attention was only paid to the subjective 'will to power' of part of the proletariat, or even only of its ideologists. Nowhere in Western Europe would the socialists have dreamt of rushing headlong into an alliance with the peasants. But it was indeed considered possible for the numerically weak Russian proletariat to unite themselves with a hundred million peasants who belonged to the poorest and least developed mass of people in Europe. In the West only the anarchists and syndicalists refrained from political action, but it was regarded as normal that the Russian socialists, even when the revolution was over, would continue to work for the overthrow of the state and the boycott of the Duma, to commit terrorist attacks or be guilty of 'expropriations', that is to say, partisan activities which had no longer taken place in the West in a socialist environment since 1848.

For the participants in the Russian revolution it was 'extraordinarily flattering' to be regarded as heroes and Titans in the West. But it was more in line with reality to see all these eulogies as the *privilegium odiosum* of the Russian socialists, who had shown themselves in reality, during the revolutionary baptism of fire, as 'human, all too human'. They had had to experience the fact that the Russian workers could not live on enthusiasm alone, any more than their Belgian and German opposite numbers could. They needed bread, and a shortage of it decreased rather than increased their belligerence. This should of course have been realised beforehand, but in Russia too the owls of Minerva only started to fly at dusk. Even for the most stubborn leaders of the most 'typically Russian' current within Russian social democracy, the revolutionary experience was now being handled in the right way. In 1909 Lenin had said: 'Up till now we have spoken "French" – according to Martov this meant 'Blanquistic' – it is high time that we learnt to speak German.' But a few months later Luxemburg had called on the Germans to 'speak Russian'.

Police terrorism in Russia fostered the need among the revolutionaries to reach continually for more efficacious methods. But the results of these were mostly disastrous to an ever-increasing degree. It was better to exploit a partial victory for the consolidation of one's own position and the expansion of one's own organisations. In other words, Martov was advocating Kautsky's *Ermattungsstrategie* for Russia as well. 'Russian social democracy spoke "Russian" all too eagerly even when the social circumstances of Russia had already developed so far that it could speak "European" . . .'[78]

Kautsky was extraordinarily taken with Martov's article and admitted to having learnt a great deal from it. 'Much that hitherto appeared to me in Comrade Luxemburg merely as an unduly abrupt sharpening of perfectly sound views caused by her temperament I now see in another light, as a deep-going separation not only of our temperaments but of our ideas.'[79] This was an important conclusion. Under the influence of the conflict with Luxemburg and the opinions about it of Russians like Martov, Kautsky's illusions about the Russian revolution were eventually to disappear completely. At the same time a close relationship emerged between Kautsky's way of thinking at that time, which has sometimes been described as *revolutionärer Attentismus* or a 'wait and see' attitude to revolution, and Menshevik ideology. Perhaps that is the reason why Luxemburg's and Lenin's extremely negative criticism of Kautsky has continued to define the man's image in the historical literature. Sometimes he is blamed for almost everything that went wrong in Germany. In this way the ideology was honoured too much and the man was wronged. Kautsky's works are seen too much as an attempt to reconcile the idea of the revolution with the reformist practices of the SPD. But Kautsky realised that ideological beliefs played scarcely any role among the party leaders.

He was concerned about the bureaucratisation and the organisational inflexibility of his party. He assumed that the Germany of Kaiser Wilhelm would come to grief in 'wars, crises and catastrophes' and he was by no means sure that the SPD would survive a similar period unscathed.[80]

The ideological debates described above were thus not only illustrative of the development of the socialist image of Russia. For the first time the vague contours of a new ideological school of thought, which Kautsky himself referred to as 'centrism', emerged in them. Since this intellectual current within international socialism will take up an increasingly important role in our account, it is necessary now to give it some further consideration. The historical view of socialism in the first quarter of this century has continued to be strongly determined by the contrasts between reformists and revolutionaries. The centrists hardly got any attention. There were many variations and nuances in the ideological world of socialism, but if one tries to sort them out, it is more logical to start not from a twofold but from a threefold division. To summarise briefly, these are as follows.

Trust in the proletariat as a class or in its organisations or in the peaceful possibilities for a gradual implementation of socialism could be so great that the revolution was dismissed as unnecessary or even harmful for the workers and their socialist future. Alongside this reformist or revisionist premise, filled with patient evolutionary optimism, there was an impatient utopian-revolutionary school of thought. In this the revolution was seen as inevitable, necessary and desirable. For the utopian revolutionaries the revolution was a *sine qua non* for a speedy realisation of socialism. Something like this was possible, according to these high-spirited socialists, because the proletariat was pre-eminently the revolutionary class. If the workers themselves considered this insufficient, then a revolutionary situation or an ideologist would have to make them see the error of their ways. The third school of thought, that of the centrists, was slightly less optimistic than the other two. Like the utopian revolutionaries, the centrists considered the revolution an inevitable matter. But this filled them with as much anxiety as joy. They saw the revolution primarily as a sort of elemental natural occurrence, as the blind result of social forces and developments, as something that lay 'beyond good and evil'. The revolution would not achieve socialism if it came too early, if the proletariat was not sufficiently prepared, or if it was badly led.

Of course it is possible to trace views of this kind back into the nineteenth century, in a certain sense even into all times. But after 1900 they gradually became crystallised in such a way that they formed a striking ideological trinity, which, taken as a whole, was a reaction to and a consequence of Marx's intellectual heritage. None of the three viewpoints stood alone, but each developed from the criticism of one of the others. However, centrism was neither recognised nor acknowledged as a separate ideological school of thought by either of the other trends. The revolutionaries soon descried in the centrists secret supporters of Bernstein, while the reformists continued to see them as by no means innocuous revolutionaries. Each school of thought represented the ideas of both the other trends as impracticable and thought that attempts to realise such ideas could be disastrous. In view of the unworkability of the socialist ideal, they were all three right.

The existence of this trichotomy of ideological trends was very much a product of its time and was in fact limited to the first quarter of the twentieth century. In the second quarter of this century the international labour movement abandoned Marxism. In Russia it became fossilised into a state ideology. Lenin's idea of a revolutionary advance guard had little to do with the bureaucratic Moloch which made the decisions in the Soviet Union. In the West Marxism was discarded by the parties. At the same time democratic socialism was not a realisation of Bernstein's ideas, because it was more the result of capitalism growing into socialism than the other way round. Marx remained a source of inspiration for extremely divergent intellectual groups, but no leaders of the European labour movement were to arise from them.

As an ideological orientation centrism, like the two other schools of thought, contained strong points as well as manifest weaknesses. The centrists took the revolution extremely seriously and because of this their criticism of the revolutionary utopias differed materially from that of the revisionists and reformists. Since revolutions did indeed break out in the first quarter of this century, not only in Russia but also in Central Europe and with an important scatter westwards and southwards, the centrist analysis of the symptoms of crisis in our society and of revolutionary ardour within the socialist movement was not devoid of realism. The politics of centrism were difficult to carry out in revolutionary times, but they certainly still betokened a remarkable attempt to apply the age-old virtue of *prudentia* to extreme situations.

The Menshevism articulated by Akselrod and Martov had from the very beginning been a kind of centrism in advance. There were many socialists among the socialist revolutionaries, the Bundists or the Latvian social democrats who cherished similar ideas, but they had not characterised themselves to any extent as socialist ideologists, and even less had they sought for support or recognition for their ideas in the arena of international socialism. Evidently, before 1910, only the Russian situation gave rise to definite forms of centrist thinking. In the years 1900–10 the revolution was not an urgent problem for Western Europeans while it certainly was for the Russians. Centrism only became a significant international phenomenon in the period of ideological confusion during the First World War and afterwards. It even found a temporary organisational home then in the so-called Vienna or Second-and-a-Half International. Like both the other ideological schools of thought, centrism remained, first and foremost, an intellectual orientation. It never became a separate, closed movement with a precisely spelt out doctrine, a fixed following and a few acknowledged leaders. The great significance of the Menshevik example during the whole development of centrism into an international movement can certainly be established with hindsight. For contemporaries themselves, however, things were different. The Mensheviks had never striven for leadership over their kindred spirits, their authority was never acknowledged, their influence seldom recognised.

This diversity could also be found in the other schools of thought. The reformist group around the *Sozialistische Monatshefte* formed a completely different company from, for example, Jaurès and his followers. In the extreme left-wing camp too, little unity was to be found, even amongst Lenin's adherents. Nevertheless, it could offer little resistance to the attraction which emanated from Russian communism after October 1917. But the differences amongst them continued to be of great importance even afterwards, and the Bolsheviks could only bring unity into the utopian revolutionary camp by, at the same time, extinguishing all life from it. Thus it is not surprising that the beginning of international Bolshevism or communism in the socialist world of before 1917 is difficult to locate, although historians have certainly searched for it diligently.

For centrism, or 'international Menshevism' as it was later named by communist ideologists, the same was true. The moment of its birth could be taken as the time of Kautsky's positive reaction to Martov's article, but that would be a very artificial reconstruction of historical reality. Although Kautsky realised that a world of difference yawned between his ideas and those of Lenin and Luxemburg he certainly did not plan to draw all the possible conclusions from this fact. Kautsky was indeed jokingly called the pope of the Second International, but he was not the generally accepted ideological leader of international socialism and nor did he pretend to be. He nevertheless derived his authority and status as a Marxist primarily from his role as an extremely influential arbiter and adviser for many parties and groups within the international socialist community. Only by maintaining a great distance from every kind of conflict was he able to retain his impartiality and gain enough space for the development of his own ideas. Since in this period he had been very much involved in Russian quarrels because he was one of the trustees of the Russian party funds, he could not afford to take sides for one or the other.

Martov's contribution to *Die Neue Zeit* had of course not only been a purely theoretical exercise but also a definite move on the chess board of party discord. Kautsky tended to see Russian ideological thought as exclusively derived from the conflicts within the RSDRP, which in his view were in their turn the result of personal animosities. Letters from Riazanov and Plekhanov, which likewise played down the importance of the ideological antitheses, fortified him in this opinion. To keep the balance he neutralised Martov's article with polemic contributions from the Poles Radek and Marchlewsky. The latter had written his piece in consultation with Luxemburg and Lenin. The content of both articles was almost predictable. Mensheviks like Martov were only men of letters in exile without contact with the workers in Russia. Their opinions had to be regarded as 'the very essence of opportunism'. Martov's route did not, like Kautsky's, go neatly between Baden and Luxemburg to Trier 'but far, far astray to the sandy Bernstein coast'. Nor did Riazanov enable Kautsky to see any great difference between Martov and the German reformists. Kautsky took remarks of this kind with a grain of salt. He still really thought that the ideological contrasts within the SPD were larger than those in the RSDRP. The differences between the German reformists and Luxemburg were in his view more fundamental than those between Martov and Lenin.[81]    Thus there was no question before 1914 of centrism being perceived by the ideologists themselves as a fully-fledged ideological trend. The misunderstandings between Kautsky and the Mensheviks did not disappear. On the contrary, the emotional and sometimes tearful tone of their letters and publications only increased the distance between them. A letter from Akselrod, full of complaints against the Bolsheviks and the reproach to his German friend that he could not put any trust at all in these people, was dismissed by Kautsky as 'hysterical caterwauling', and he left his wife to reply to it.[82] In 1911 the same boomerang effect was created by a long polemical pamphlet by Martov, which, in considerable anger and irritation about the most recent Bolshevik activities in the party struggle, divulged to the public all the scandals and secrets about the 'expropriations'. This was not only, as he himself admitted, three years too late, but also extraordinarily clumsy. Since Kautsky, Mehring and Zetkin administered Russian money, his pamphlet could easily create the impression that the SPD was involved in one way or another in questionable Russian affairs. Of course Lenin did not forget to inform Kautsky that the reactionary press in Russia was thankfully making use of Martov's pamphlet in order to discredit the RSDRP. To the Bolsheviks' delight, Kautsky and Zetkin, who had obtained the German translation of the pamphlet, were enraged about this publication, which in their view was making the split among the Russian party members quite unnecessarily irreconcilable. Martov had indeed thoroughly ruined the favourable impression he had managed to make on Kautsky a year before.[83]

However, Kautsky did not return to the point of view he had adopted towards the Russian revolution before the quarrel with Luxemburg. He no longer expressed his approval of the ideology of the left wing within the RSDRP. His relationship with Lenin, whom he presented as 'a curious mixture of brute and pettifogger', likewise deteriorated. A letter to Riazanov written at the beginning of 1914 shows the evolution of his ideas about Russia. Stolypin's agrarian reforms had, in Kautsky's view, resulted in the peasants gradually ceasing to be a revolutionary factor. The proletariat thus stood alone, for the liberal bourgeoisie could not be relied upon, either. 'From about 1900 to 1905 I counted on Russia to seize the initiative in the European revolution and only in such a context could the Russian revolution end with a victory of the proletariat. Today it seems to me that a revolution in Russia is only likely if it is introduced from the West . . .' Revolution was no longer in order in Russia. First priority would have to be given to the organisation of the proletariat. To this end every means whether legal or illegal would have to be employed. '. . . I have no more trust in the peasants' revolution. And still less in the bourgeois revolution. The general development of world capitalism has progressed too far for that . . .' The most striking thing about this letter is the almost total erosion of the traditional socialist image of Russia which is expressed in it. Even for the most authoritative Marxist in Europe Russia had ceased to be the country of revolutionary expectations.[84]

In this period the image of tsarism as a barbaric, Asiatic power was also rapidly wearing out. But for a number of socialists it was very difficult to renounce the tsarist bugbear that had always fulfilled such a special role in their thoughts about foreign countries. In the years before the war, Karl Liebknecht, as the worthy son of a Russophobic father, was one of the fiercest Western opponents of tsarism. Liebknecht, as a lawyer, had often done his best for Russian comrades who, in Germany, were threatened with deportation or imprisonment. In 1909 he had made every effort to get Kropotkin's pamphlet, *The Terror in Russia*, in which political oppression in Russia was denounced, translated into German and printed. At SPD meetings he regularly asked for attention to the question of the Russian political prisoners and he had planned to do the same at the International congress in Vienna which did not take place because of the outbreak of war.[85]

But Liebknecht thought that not only socialists but also bourgeois circles were insufficiently aware of how perfidious tsarism was. He therefore formed a commission with other German social democrats which was to set up an anti-tsarist campaign. Curiously enough the pretext for this was the amnesty which the tsar proclaimed on the occasion of the three hundred year jubilee of the Romanov dynasty. Political prisoners were excluded from this decree of reprieve, but exiles like Martov and Dan were allowed to return to Russia and they and many others made use of this right. The situation with regard to 'human rights' in Russia was much better in 1913 than it had been in 1906–9. However, the commission drew up a pamphlet entitled *Für die politischen Gefangenen Russlands* (*For the Russian Political Prisoners*). This text was based on information provided by Kropotkin and even on the totally outdated but famous book by George Kennan about the system of Siberian exile in the previous century. The outcry was thus more an expression of anti-tsarist rites which had remained alive in left-wing circles than a well-founded criticism of current political practices in Russia. Kropotkin emphatically dissociated himself from this document, called the references to Kennan 'archaic' and pointed out that the suicides and torture described in his book no longer occurred nowadays. In general the Russian emigrants took no part in this German initiative, which in their opinion would do more harm than good to the matter in hand. But the brochure was distributed in six European countries and about five hundred prominent figures in the world of scholarship, art and socialism declared their sympathy with it. Amongst these were Bebel, Bernstein, Gerard Hauptmann, Engelbert Humperdinck, Ferdinand Tönnies, Victor Adler, Arthur Schnitzler, Jaurès, Debussy, Emile Durkheim, Ramsay MacDonald, H. G. Wells, Troelstra and H. Roland Holst.[86]

The action thus had great repercussions, even though the protest was directed against circumstances in Russia which to some extent no longer existed. Liebknecht's attitude is curious, for this passionate anti-militarist by no means approached the situation in his own country uncritically. He was one of the first to see that the German government had taken advantage of the

German fear of Russia in August 1914 in order to obtain the
support of the nation – including socialists – for its war policy.
The idea that Germany was not carrying out a righteous defensive war against Russia, but was perpetrating an aggressive
annexationist policy in the East and the West, was, in the years
that followed, to form the basis of the increasing socialist resistance to the war towards which Liebknecht made the first moves.
The usual favourable and unfavourable representations of
Russia as a revolutionary example and as a reactionary world
conqueror, disappeared for the time being from the field of
view of very many German workers and socialists.[87]
   In other European countries a comparable situation originated during the war. The attempts by prominent German social
democrats to earn the understanding of socialists in the neutral
countries for the viewpoint of the SPD's parliamentary party in
the Reichstag towards the war by reference to the Russian threat,
met with little comprehension. The German violation of Belgian
neutrality aroused much more alarm. The French socialists'
usual complaints against the alliance with Russia could no longer
be heard. In England, where the Labour Party had also regularly
inveighed against the treaty with the tsar before 1914, the voice
of protest was not completely silenced in August. Ramsay Mac-
Donald, the leader of the Independent Labour Party, continued
to oppose the Russian alliance. But in the United Kingdom, too,
the German invasion of Belgium overshadowed the Russian
danger, and the vast majority of the British labour movement
sided with the government. The traditional image of Russia in
the Western socialist world was almost wiped out by the war.[88]

## THE FIRST WORLD WAR

As is explained at the beginning of this chapter, the war and
the year of the Russian revolution fall somewhat outside the
framework of an account of the influence of the Western image
of Russia on the relationship between Western and Russian
socialists. Nevertheless, so much happened in these years that a
survey of the principal developments is essential for a proper
understanding of what occurred afterwards. This also applies
to the period immediately before August 1914. The consequences, whether fatal or otherwise, of the First World War for the

subsequent course of Russian history are the subject of a debate which has been carried on for decades among historians. This has led to penetrating research and interesting interpretations, but never to generally accepted conclusions. The dramatic link between the flaring up of a world conflagration and a fundamental crisis in international socialism has been recorded in numerous other publications. Both historical traditions have had repercussions on research into the past of Russian social democracy and have led to two contrasting historical speculations. According to the Soviet historians supported by the American Haimson, the workers' disorders in St Petersburg in the early summer of 1914 already carried the distinct embryo of the later Bolshevik revolution within them. The outbreak of war finished off this revolutionary development for the time being. According to Schapiro, later supported in this by Elwood, in 1914 Lenin had been driven into a corner by many of his opponents in the party helped by the Bureau of the International. If the Bolshevik leader had not taken the demands to restore unity in the party seriously, a sharp denunciation, or even expulsion from the world-wide socialist community, would have been waiting for him in August 1914 at the congress of the Second International in Vienna. A Lenin totally isolated in this way could never have developed into a revolutionary leader of world stature. However, the congress in Vienna could not take place because of the outbreak of war.[89]

Both interpretations derive too much of their merit from the drama of August 1914 to be totally convincing. The war did not *always* form a total break with what had preceded it. Remarkable developments certainly occurred within the RSDRP in the last years before the war. Lenin and his close followers had founded a Central Committee of the party on their own initiative in 1912 and in the process had actually set themselves up as a separate political group. Through these and other schismatical activities by the Bolsheviks, Lenin's opponents were driven together. The anti-Leninist coalition, which consisted not only of the Mensheviks but also of a number of other groups within the RSDRP, exhibited little cohesion and therefore presented no real threat to Lenin. The Bolsheviks moreover profited from the Russian workers' change in mood. In the period 1912–14 there was a great deal of social unrest in Russia, and Bolshevik radicalism was better suited to the emotions which were then being released in working circles. That is why the leadership of the Russian trade unions, which during Stolypin's rule had been built up with great difficulty by Menshevik 'liquidators', fell into Bolshevik hands. The Mensheviks had to admit that they had underestimated Bolshevism. All hope of the realisation of their ideal – a labour movement of Western scope in Russia – had once more gone up in smoke.

On the other hand, the small, new Russian trade union movement was anything but under the direct control of the Bolshevik party. Lenin's categorical ideas about the subordinate relationship of the trade unions to the party were not popular in Russia. The Bolshevik trade union leaders were also bent on maintaining the independence of their organisations. Moreover the organised workers were mostly staunch supporters of the restoration of unity within the RSDRP and opposed to Bolshevik schisms. The outburst of violent dissatisfaction, especially among the youthful section of the metropolitan proletariat, in the early summer of 1914 was neither organised nor foreseen by the Bolsheviks. Nor were they then capable of keeping this rebellious movement in hand. The question of whether the workers in Russia at this time should be regarded as more primitive, more violent and more revolutionary than their Western equivalents remains difficult to judge.[90]

Given the unbalanced economic and political climate in Russia after 1905, workers' conflicts of a revolutionary nature were certainly a more serious matter than similar phenomena in England, France or Germany. After all, in the first quarter of the twentieth century in those countries too, large-scale unofficial strikes took place which deteriorated into bloody clashes with the army and the police and on which socialists and trade unions could exert hardly any moderating influence. The situation in the Russian capital can perhaps be compared with that in the Romagna in Italy, where during the so-called Red Week in June 1914 a large-scale agricultural strike took place which soon assumed the character of a rebellion. *La settimana rossa* has also often been seen as a harbinger of the post-war political disturbances. In Italy too socialism had a strongly radical wing, and large sections of the industrial and agrarian proletariat showed little enthusiasm at crucial times for a liberal democratic form of government and the moderation of the class war which went with it. In 1914, however, neither in Russia nor in Italy was the continuity of the existing political structure endangered by these local, isolated actions by the workers. The turbulent period 1914–22 was to result in a Fascist dictatorship in Italy. Historical developments there were thus to turn out completely differently from in Russia. Perhaps it is therefore prudent not to attach too much importance to the violent aspect of the workers' protest in St Petersburg in 1914.[91]

If one may speak of the instability of Russian circumstances in 1914 and thereafter, then these also resulted from the ever-changing moods of the Russian proletariat, which naturally never formed an undifferentiated mass, but was put together in an extremely complicated way. It was clear in August 1914 that the workers, too, were to some extent capable of the patriotic euphoria which had overcome the Russian urban population after the outbreak of war. The socialist parties and the trade union movement were then almost immediately disbanded by the government. The Bolshevik representatives in the Duma were arrested, but Mensheviks like Dan were also run in. However, the workers' protest died down. Not until 1915 did massive strikes break out again. But in the period immediately before the revolution it was the right-wing Mensheviks who succeeded in exercising a degree of leadership over the Russian proletariat. In the year of the revolution as well it was the Mensheviks and the socialist revolutionaries who at first dominated the Soviets, and that would have been impossible without a minimum of active support from the side of the workers. In the summer of 1917 they lost this preponderance and the Bolsheviks got their chance to conquer power. But in the years afterwards the popularity of the communists among the Russian proletariat fell sharply. Both in the first half of 1918 and after the end of the civil war in 1921–2, the Soviet regime was only able to prevent a political comeback by the Mensheviks and other moderate socialists by using dictatorial violence.

It is not very plausible that it was only the outbreak of the First World War which delayed the Bolsheviks' assumption of power by three years. For even if we assume the theoretical possibility that the Bolsheviks could have managed to maintain their authority over the Russian working class after 1914 as well, a Bolshevik coup at an earlier date does not become more likely. On the contrary, in the main the Bolsheviks had to thank the failure of the moderate socialists in the second half of 1917 for their success in that year. In theory history could have progressed totally differently if Lenin and his followers – and not the leaders of the Mensheviks and the socialist revolutionaries – had already had to face up to the consequences of their political ideas during the first phase of the revolution.

The intervention of the International on behalf of Lenin's opponents in the RSDRP was also less important and suffered less from the outbreak of the war than is usually assumed. In 1914 Lenin thought that the Bolsheviks had most of the Russian workers' organisations in their hands and that he could therefore set the warnings of the International aside. He knew in advance that he would not be able to convince the ISB he was right and he had no wish to be subjected to indignities himself. He therefore sent two of his subordinates to the session in Brussels, although he had himself been a member of the Bureau of the International for years and had had a reasonably good relationship with Huysmans. To a large extent Lenin was right. Although all the personalities within the party known to the West, such as Plekhanov, Akselrod, Martov, Luxemburg and Trotsky, now summoned him before the tribunal of the International, their action was more a sign of impotence than of strength. A short time beforehand the Mensheviks had toyed with the idea of calling Plekhanov to order with the help of the International because they were not in a position to defend themselves effectively against the attacks of the obstinate father of Russian Marxism.[92]

In a restrained resolution about the situation within the Russian party in July 1914, the ISB explained that the restoration of unity was both possible and necessary while avoiding a direct denunciation of Lenin's practices. But the decision gave Lenin's opponents the opportunity to approach the Russian workers with a request for support for the call to unity, and to point out to them that the Bolsheviks were sabotaging this effort of practically all the groups within the RSDRP. It is, however, unlikely that the congress of the International in Vienna would have excommunicated the Bolsheviks or have condemned them in particularly drastic terms. Most decisions of the Second International were, in fact, classic examples of caution and lack of clarity. The discussions during the congress would possibly have offered Lenin's opponents some propagandist advantage. But it is extremely doubtful if in the short term the Mensheviks or Trotsky and his followers would have been able because of it to reinforce their grip on the rebellious masses of workers in the capital.

Nevertheless, the action of the International in another respect is notable and was not without consequences. The historians who have concerned themselves with this question in detail mostly assumed that the Western socialists' support for Lenin's opponents went without saying. It seemed to them normal that their European comrades, who were little disposed to revolution, would side with the moderates within the Russian parties. In this book we have tried to demonstrate that this was by no means the case. In the period around 1905 as well, Western socialism had repeatedly pressed the Russians to unite. But at the time every attempt by the International to have a group of Russian radicals with a large following of rebellious Russian workers at their disposal branded as schismatics and troublemakers would have been completely hopeless, given the nature of Western enthusiasm for revolutionary Russia. Now there was little of this to be seen. Lenin and his faithful followers were not expelled or condemned, though they had become an exceptionally isolated group within the international socialist community. This was not immediately of great significance for the situation in Russia, but it was all the more so for the relationship between Western and Russian socialists in the period to come. It was not Lenin but the Mensheviks who were to profit most from the temporary absence of the traditional image of Russia amongst Western socialists during the war years. In this respect too, historical developments were not interrupted but continued by the First World War.

However, in August 1914 it seemed that not only Lenin but the whole of Russian socialism had alienated itself from the Western labour movement. While the war united the socialists in the West not only amongst themselves but also with the nation, the Russian situation was characterised by discord and confusion among its socialist members. In the West the socialist members of parliament sided with the governments' war policies. In France, England and Belgium they even joined the government. The socialist delegates in the Duma, however, refused to take part in the voting about the war budget. Only a few socialists, amongst them well-known figures like Plekhanov, Kropotkin and Rubanovich, identified themselves completely with the affairs of the Entente and declared themselves supporters of national defence. There were even Bolsheviks in exile who went to the Western front as volunteers. Parvus, in contrast, opted for the Central Powers and afterwards turned out to be a socialist war profiteer. The vast majority of Russian socialists sided with their Duma parliamentary parties, but the way they did it varied enormously. The right-wing Menshevik Potresov, for instance, continued to oppose tsarism and a Russian civil truce, but still believed that an Entente victory would be best for the socialist cause. The Russian socialists ought not to sabotage their country's war effort. On the left wing of this wide spectrum of opinions was the standpoint of Lenin. He took it for granted that a possible German victory as the outcome of the war would do the least harm and a socialist revolution the most good. He wished to change the war between nations into a civil war between the proletariat and the bourgeoisie. The Second International was bankrupt since a majority of it seemed to consist of adherents of the policy of civil truce, with which they had betrayed socialism and the proletariat. In the Third International which he now wanted to set up, there would be no room for these social chauvinists amongst whom he counted Potresov.

Between the 'defensist' Potresov and the 'defeatist' Lenin, there was a large group of social democrats who, like Lenin, approached the issue of the war not from a Russian but from an international point of view. However, for them a victory for one party or another was not the greatest problem, nor did they fervently hope for a revolutionary finale to the war. They wanted peace as soon as possible and in their view that could only be achieved if the belligerents were to leave the question of war debts out of consideration in the negotiations and were prepared for a restoration of the *status quo ante*. This peace 'without indemnity and annexations' could only be enforced by the international socialist movement. Before that, the International would have to be convened, and naturally that would only be possible when the current crisis within the European labour movement had been overcome and European international proletarian solidarity restored. Martov and Akselrod were the most distinguished *auctores intellectuales* behind these ideas. But to a lesser or greater extent these beliefs were also shared by many Russian social democrats not only from their own but also from the Bolshevik faction. Even independent figures like Trotsky were initially closer to this point of view than to Lenin's. This shift in relationships within the RSDRP naturally gave occasion for renewed attempts at the restoration of party unity. But once again these failed because of the distrust between Lenin and the Menshevik émigrés under Akselrod's leadership.[93]

The ideas of the moderate 'Internationalists' also found many adherents among the Polish socialists and the socialist revolutionaries. Even more significant was the fact that ideas like these were slowly but surely finding acceptance in the socialist parties both of the remaining countries waging war and of the neutral nations. The three ideological currents within international socialism described in this chapter each developed its own view of the war. The Austrian reformist Karl Renner has given the best theoretical defence of the supporters of *Burgfrieden* and *union sacrée* in his *Marxismus, Krieg und Internationale*. Lenin's writings in this period summarise most clearly the point of view of the very small utopian-revolutionary trend in East and West. Akselrod's pamphlet entitled *Die Krise und die Aufgaben der internationalen Sozialdemokratie* gave the most systematic exposé of the centrist point of view which gained an ever-increasing number of supporters during the war and captured the majority within the international socialist movement in 1917 and 1918.[94]

Akselrod's train of thought was, as so often before, primarily a reaction against Lenin, whose ideas he once more rejected as primitive and dangerous. The restoration and reinforcement of pre-war proletarian solidarity and of the International as an organisation could not be enforced by purely organisational measures such as the formation of a Third International. Nor was it relevant to call the adherents of *Burgfrieden* and *union sacrée* traitors. At the time they temporarily formed the majority within the principal socialist parties and the prospective renewed International would have had no right to exist without them. It was absolutely vital to recognise the power of nationalist ideology within the socialist movement and to search for the most effective means of overcoming it. At the time this was the amalgamation of the socialist opposition to the war in all countries into an international pressure group for a speedy and just peace.

Akselrod's evaluation of the situation was more reasonable and realistic than Lenin's. But his view of the future of the International and of the prospects of a socialist peace offensive remained wishful thinking. The national states, which had been steadily growing in power and influence for many centuries, had a stronger grip on their supporters than the new, weak, divided socialist movement had on its adherents. The states defended their prerogatives to wage war and conclude peace with great vigour and efficiency. So the Second International was incapable of preventing the outbreak of war, nor could it function properly in the years 1914–18. During this period and afterwards the socialists would not be in a position to enforce the peace they were hoping for. Nevertheless, it would be going too far to maintain that the socialists were merely chasing shadows not only before but also during and after the war.[95]

The image of the 'collapse' of the International which has been so often touted since 1914, has hampered a description of historical reality which tries to be detached and in perspective. Of course great despondency prevailed in the socialist camp about their own dissension and impotence. The Russian socialists especially, who as a group more or less continued to side against the war, got the impression that the Western comrades, who had been unable to offer any resistance to war psychosis, were suffering from mental derangement. But the question is whether the vehemence of these emotions was justified. After all, in all the debates about war and peace, the International had never forbidden socialists to defend their own fatherland, because, if the worst came to the worst, everyone knew that no one would listen to such a decision. The socialists knew in fact that the ISB was not much more than a post-box and that the international congresses made only elastic decisions.[96]

Thus there was not very much that could 'collapse' in 1914. The only thing that happened was that the ISB did not meet in its entirety for four years and that the planned Vienna congress did not take place. On the other hand, at no period in the history of the socialist movement was there so much international discussion as precisely during the war. The animosity between socialists on both sides of the front was mostly not so great that it rendered every contact impossible. Akselrod's plan was a curious mixture of naive idealism and realism. For what was astonishing about the socialist peace offensive was not that it eventually failed, but that despite the apparently hopeless situation in 1914 within the socialist movement, it got into its stride in such an impressive way in the years afterwards. The initiative for this came from three sides. The socialists from the northern neutral areas, Scandinavia and Holland, and from the southern neutrals, Italy and Switzerland, were both active, while the opposition movement within the socialist parties of the countries involved in the war formed an increasingly important element as time went on.[97]

In the beginning this opposition movement consisted almost solely of Russians. For the first time it proved to be a great advantage that many Russian socialists, among them the most important leaders, were in exile. Because of this it was possible not only to influence socialists in the neutral countries but also to encourage the opposition against the war in the belligerents. Lenin and Trotsky maintained contact with the small minority of more or less revolutionarily inclined Europeans and thus laid down the foundations for the Third International. Which is not to say that these two Russians were in complete agreement with each other at the time.[98] The Mensheviks were important for the mobilisation of the entire socialist resistance to the war and in this way unconsciously laid the foundations for the post-war centrist movement and the Vienna International. Thus it was in these years that the struggle between Menshevism and Bolshevism really began to assume international proportions.

The ideas of Akselrod, who remained in Switzerland, formed not the only, but certainly the principal, intellectual base for the so-called Zimmerwald movement. His conversations with the Italian Morgari, the Swiss Grimm and the Dutchman Troelstra were of importance in launching international socialist discussion about the war and in opening up the way to Zimmerwald. Martov performed a comparable role in Paris. For the most part he influenced the moderate leaders of the CGT like Merrheim, who also attended Zimmerwald. These contacts were also to prove significant after the war for the political direction which French syndicalism was to take. Participation at Zimmerwald (1915) and its sequel at Kiental (1916) was sharply determined by chance and the state of war. The variegated gathering of the Zimmerwald movement was only to a certain extent characteristic of the growing socialist opposition to the war as a whole. Therefore it was less relevant that the left-wing minority led by Lenin had evidently become larger in Kiental. This certainly did not yet mean that support in the West for the establishment of a Third International had actually become substantial. On the other hand, the centrist majority acquired ever-increasing influence, since the further the war progressed the more a gradual radicalisation of the entire socialist movement took place. The growing opposition within the French party in 1915 and 1916, the so-called *minoritaires*, the 'independents' within the SPD who were to form the USPD in 1917, and the British socialists of the Independent Labour Party were evidently adherents of ideas which had not infrequently been put forward earlier or more clearly by the Mensheviks.[99]

Zimmerwald also stimulated the activities of the northern neutral countries, which up till then had made fruitless attempts to initiate peace talks in co-operation with the Bureau of the International, which had moved from Brussels to The Hague. Their plans for an international socialist conference in Stockholm were spurred on in 1917 by the February revolution in Russia. The Provisional Government, which had taken over power from the tsar, wished to pursue the war in a forceful manner. However, the new administration was dependent to a considerable extent on the Soviets, the councils of workers' and soldiers' representatives which had been established with the help of the Mensheviks after the fall of the tsarist monarchy. During the first six months of its existence, the Soviet movement was dominated by Mensheviks and socialist revolutionaries, an overwhelming majority of whom were adherents of Zimmerwald. The socialist revolutionaries played a rather subordinate role in the formulation of the Soviets' policy. This was chiefly determined by the Mensheviks Tsereteli, Dan and Liber. They took it for granted that the 'deepening of the revolution', that is to say the safeguarding of the interests of the workers and the peasants, could not take place in the desired democratic manner in wartime. Peace was needed for that. It remained necessary to defend the revolution against German aggression but at the same time Russia ought to take the initiative in negotiations which would bring a speedy and just end to the war. Their view was that if the revolution did not end the war, the war would end the revolution. The clash between the Soviets and the Provisional Government about this question in April led to disturbances in the streets, stormy sittings in the Soviets, and a crisis in the cabinet. The moderate socialists subsequently decided to join the government. In this way they hoped to lend weight to the Russian struggle for peace. They believed their plan could succeed if the governments of the countries in the Entente could be put under pressure by an international socialist campaign. The leaders of the Soviets therefore decided to join forces with the Dutch-Scandinavian committee and to convene an international conference in Stockholm.

The situation which came into being in 1917 did not rule out the Mensheviks' idea in advance, but did make it dependent on a large number of factors over which they had little or no control. Russian events had aroused a great deal of enthusiasm in England and France. Everyone hoped that Russia would now again dedicate herself with united forces to the struggle against Germany, which up till now had gone badly for the Russians. The revolution had made Russia into a democratic country. The Entente's war effort could now be presented as a valiant and concerted struggle for the preservation of liberal democratic freedom. At the same time, however, this noble struggle was undermined by the Russian desire for peace. Consequently the widespread and increasing dissatisfaction of the populations of England and France and of the troops at the Western front was fuelled. In Germany and Austria it was hoped that the revolution would soon force Russia to concede. But the Central Powers, too, had to take into account an opposition which the Russian revolution saw as a sign that it was time to abolish the *Militär-monarchie* in their own country.

In all the countries at war, the maintenance of socialist support had become an important condition for the preservation of the national will to continue the struggle. In the three Entente countries, which had been dependent on one another for the success of their military operations, the government was formed by a coalition of which the socialists comprised a part. Socialist opinion could not therefore be completely ignored. England and France were little inclined to negotiate with the Central Powers or to a radical revision of the war objectives and the international treaties about them. But the Russian peace initiative could not be disposed of without much ado. Austria, who had really already lost the war with Russia, proved to be ready to negotiate at this time. England and France took no notice, but failed to inform the Russian government of this in time. The Western governments knew that a revolution in Germany, for which the soviet leaders were fervently hoping, would not be forthcoming for the moment. Rejection of the Russian peace plans could however lead to Russian negotiations with the Central Powers and result in a separate peace in the East. It could have been disastrous for the course of the war in France if Germany were to use its divisions on the Eastern front in order to force a breakthrough in the West. America had indeed joined the Entente in 1917 but was not capable of sending troops to Europe in time to turn back a German offensive.

The chance of Russia's concluding a separate peace with the Central Powers in 1917 was not particularly great. The Provisional Government managed to remain faithful to the alliance with the democratic West. The socialist leaders of the Soviets, too, were convinced that a German victory would constitute a deadly danger to their own revolution and to Western socialism. Even Lenin did not risk propagating the slogan of a separate peace in 1917. (The idea was so unpopular that in 1918 Lenin had to exert a great deal of pressure to convince his own party of the necessity of a peace treaty with the Central Powers.) This was greatly to the advantage of England and France, who were only prepared to consider peace under Russian pressure. Now Russian pressure could only be effective if Russia, in exchange for Western readiness for peace, demonstrated the will and the capability to continue the war for as long as necessary. The Western Powers would gladly make an indispensable contribution to this with supplies of arms. But a certain consolidation of Russian political conditions and a restoration of discipline in the army were still more important conditions, especially since a purely defensive strategy by the Russians was not considered sufficient to sustain both Eastern and Western fronts. A Russian offensive would be necessary in order to tie up the German divisions in the East. So the success of the Menshevik peace plan was dependent on the Western Powers' readiness for peace, the Western socialists, the Russian liberals and the Russian army's battle readiness. The Russian ruling coalition between the liberals and the socialist democrats would therefore have to be maintained whatever the cost. Thus the socialist politicians' freedom of movement was reduced to nil.

In short, the situation was more or less that the Western Powers wanted a Russian offensive while the Russian socialists wanted to hold a meeting in Stockholm. The Russian government's position continued to be rather obscure and the first reaction of England, France and Belgium was to send socialist supporters of their government to Russia for consultation with the Soviets. They were to convince their political friends in Russia that their country should pursue the war with every means. If the Russians could not be deflected from their peace plans, then there was still time to win in any case. It was with this aim in view that the socialist delegations led by the Belgian Vandervelde, the Englishman Henderson and the Frenchman Thomas departed for Russia. In the Russian capital they all fell somewhat under the spell of the revolution. They were aghast at the insensibility of the Petrograd Soviet to the Western point of view, but also impressed by the seriousness and intelligence with which socialists like Tsereteli put forward the Russian arguments. The self-assured revolutionary Messianism which the Russian comrades displayed did not suit most of their Western discussion partners and there continued to be differences of opinion. But the ultimate result of these negotiations and of a soviet delegation to Western Europe was that the Labour Party, the SFIO and the Italian socialists took up a position in support of Stockholm. The German USPD did so also, while even the SPD proved susceptible to Russian pressure. The Mensheviks thus succeeded in winning the socialists both in the neutral countries and in the countries at war over to their point of view. They had never had a greater influence on the Western labour movement.

Nevertheless, eventually everything went wrong, and first of all in Russia. After initial successes the Russian offensive failed completely in July. The unstable, complicated balance of political, military and social forces on which the Menshevik coalition policy rested was upset by this and the revolution slid backwards in the direction of utter chaos. The military setback, the fragmented power position of the Provisional Government and of the moderate leaders of the Soviets undermined Russia's position as an ally. In the West the governments were no longer prepared to listen to the Russian message of peace. The danger of the German U-boat attacks had remained limited and the United States would soon be reinforcing the Western front. With this the Western Entente countries became convinced that it ought to be possible to beat Germany even if they had to go without the Russian support which had been considered essential up till then. The battle weariness and dissatisfaction in their own countries were not sufficiently widespread to obstruct the continuation of the war. But the French government in particular was afraid of disturbances and demoralisation of the army if the international socialist peace talks took place. It therefore refused to issue passports to socialists wishing to travel to Stockholm. Its example was followed by other Entente countries. This led to the resignation of the socialists in the French and British governments and a very marked drop in the popularity of the *union sacrée*. But the socialists in the East and the West were now out of the game: they had to give up their struggle for a speedy and just peace. This fact was of crucial significance for the fate of democracy in Russia.[100]

### 1917

The defeat which the moderate socialists in Russia had to suffer in 1917 is chiefly attributed in historical tradition to their lack of decisiveness and organisational vigour, to a faulty assessment of the political possibilities at the time and to insufficient ideological flexibility. The success of the October revolution is not infrequently explained in the same way by attributing to the Bolsheviks the qualities which were so unfortunately lacking in their socialist competitors. For the most part there is not much difference of opinion about this between Western historians and their Soviet colleagues. It is curious that in Western accounts of 1917 little importance is attached to the ideological motives behind the Bolshevik coup. A mainly demagogical significance is attributed to the revolutionary rhetoric of the Bolsheviks. The simple and arresting slogans circulated by them were only intended to win the favour of the masses and in this they were extremely successful. It was evidently difficult to imagine that ideals which appear naive to us could be the principal motive behind successful political action. There is, however, little reason to assume that Trotsky did not take absolutely seriously his idea of permanent revolution – which Lenin seems to have first accepted in full in 1917. We also have to accept that Lenin truly believed in the idyllic views which he had incorporated in his *State and Revolution* written in 1917. There is no discrepancy between revolutionary utopianism and cynical power politics if its perpetrators are under the illusion that the possession of power is sufficient for the realisation of utopia. The entire history of Russian social democracy before 1917 makes it probable that the two antagonistic views about revolution and socialism which were elaborated by the Bolsheviks and the Mensheviks in unremitting polemics, also determined the activities of both groups in the year of the revolution.[101]     The Bolsheviks captured the Russian state and in the process acquired the opportunity of changing the face of the world, but not, as was to become apparent, of realising their ideals. The Mensheviks did not believe in the Leninist-Trotskyist utopia. They were not interested in power, but in influence. The fall of tsarism had, after all, immediately realised their principal aim. The last days of the *ancien régime* saw the growth in the Duma and elsewhere of a powerful opposition movement, which according to Marxist usage could be called 'bourgeois'. Rebellious workers and mutinous soldiers had set the ball rolling for the real political revolution. Afterwards these groups of people constituted themselves into a sort of revolutionary opposition in the Soviets, while the former bourgeois opposition had taken over the administration by means of the Provisional Government. The February revolution had thus turned out exactly according to the Menshevik script. Since both the extreme right wing and the extreme left wing had practically disappeared from the scene at that moment, there appeared to be a reasonable prospect of steering the revolution into the safe harbour of a capitalist republic and a parliamentary democracy.

As is argued in this chapter, the weakness of the Menshevik revolutionary concept lay in the vagueness with which the change from the old regime to the new was portrayed and in the denial of the insuperable problems which might thereby come into being. This meant that in 1917 the Mensheviks would find themselves faced with difficult dilemmas and painful decisions. The first problem to confront them was that the Provisional Government proved to have no power. The real power lay with the demonstrating crowds in the streets, over whom the Petrograd Soviet alone could exert any authority. The Soviet was dominated by the Mensheviks who were the only ones to have an acceptable answer to the situation at their disposal. From their midst was to emerge the man who combined the qualities of a practical politician and statesman with visionary and charismatic leadership and great oratorical talent: Irakli Tsereteli. He proposed supporting the government as long as it made every effort towards a speedy peace and the democratisation of the state. This policy met with wide approval in Petrograd and the national soviet movement. The not wholly imaginary danger of a counter-revolution and the restoration of the *ancien régime* also, according to the Mensheviks, prompted close co-operation with the government. Only in this way could the bourgeoisie be kept on democratic lines. On the other hand, an attempt by the Soviets to take over power would inevitably lead to civil war and this ought to be avoided at all costs.

In April, however, it emerged that putting pressure on the government was not sufficient and that only participation in it would succeed in achieving the desired results. It once more appeared that the only alternative was chaos and counter-revolution. The decision to participate in the coalition hit the Mensheviks extremely hard. A decision of this kind was difficult to reconcile with their traditional concept of the Russian revolution or with their equally beloved dogmas about pre-war, international socialism. They realised that by taking this step they were depriving themselves of their freedom of action and running a serious risk of coming into conflict with their proletarian supporters. After all, they would not only have to promote the interests of the peasants, workers, soldiers, Soviets or Russian socialist parties, but also take into account the non-socialist ministers, the other political parties, the military leaders and the employers in Russia. Besides, it was necessary to go some way towards their Western allies and the Western socialists. The Russian socialists did not believe that the state could be led in wartime without

K

the existing administrative, military, technological, economic and educational chief executives, the overwhelming majority of whom were non-socialist. Thus they did not even toy with the idea of introducing socialism, nor had they pressed for a socialist majority in the cabinet.

This change of course in Menshevik policy was evidence of daring, vision and love of democracy. Tsereteli, who was the principal brain behind the coalition, proved capable of convincing a majority in his own party, among the socialist revolutionaries and in the Soviets, of the necessity of this decisive step. The democratic government, of which the socialists were to form a part, possessed in fact absolutely no constitutional legitimacy. It derived its authority entirely from the revolution and not from a democratically elected majority in parliament. The government continued to be dependent on the benevolence of extremely divergent interest groups from which it demanded very great sacrifices. Looked at legally, it had no other means of enforcing these than its own powers of persuasion. On the other hand, its subjects were celebrating their newly acquired political freedom in a euphoric manner by presenting their many – and mostly not unjustified – grievances and demands during the truly innumerable meetings and demonstrations which were characteristic of the revolutionary year.

No one in Russia had any experience of democratic government and opinions varied widely about its value and content. Only the socialists and liberals who formed the coalition had from time immemorial entertained Western democratic aspirations and set them down in party programmes. But even the integrity of the democratic intentions of the adherents of these parties could be called in question. Not only in Russia but also in the West the democratic longings and socialist wishes which existed in the workers' movement seldom agreed with one another in a completely harmonious fashion. And certainly in the left wing of the Russian socialists there was little respect for 'bourgeois' democracy. As far as liberalism in the East and West was concerned it was true that in critical circumstances it could exhibit a clear preference for authoritarian rule. The extreme nationalist Russian liberals were definitely sensitive to the argumentation of right-wing groups, who maintained that in 1917 only a forceful government – that is, one which dared to use violence, thus if necessary a military dictatorship – could restore law and order and save Russia from certain ruin. In so far as there existed articulate support for democracy among the peasants, workers and soldiers, it was chiefly in terms of direct forms such as the soviet system, because this seemed to them to offer the best solution to the most pressing problems in their immediate environment. The socialist ministers derived their political influence entirely from these social groups. But the democratic government, which had the modesty to call itself 'provisional', could not possibly see the Soviets as anything but strictly temporary organisations, which would sooner or later have to make way for a parliament. Finally for the Western allies, Russian democracy was merely a nice incidental circumstance and they would only support it as long as it could fight against Germany.

It might be called a small miracle or a unique achievement that Russian democracy remained in existence in circumstances like this from February till October. Until the summer of 1917 'the revolutionary democracy', as the supporters of the coalition proudly styled themselves, succeeded in dominating the political scene and thus averting the danger of a left- or right-wing coup. Afterwards democratic rhetoric was no longer in a position to reconcile the existing differences of opinion. Political conditions became unstable and the once-so-optimistic revolutionary spirit of harmony was replaced by increasing mistrust and polarisation between left and right. Now that the government could boast so few concrete results, a section of the population withdrew from the revolution in disappointment and reacted passively to further developments. Another section began to take the law into its own hands: the soldiers deserted, the peasants divided up the land, the workers went on strike and wheeled their bosses out of the factories in wheelbarrows. The Provisional Government gradually lost all credit and support in these months. The coalition was continued in various forms but no longer enjoyed the trust of the parties which were part of it.

Both in military circles and among the Bolsheviks, plans were formulated for the taking over of power. But the idea of a left- or a right-wing *coup d'état* was not popular. In July a Bolshevik attempt, in August one by General Kornilov, failed. Eventually the Bolsheviks were able to win control because no one was ready to defend the old government any more. They now had command of a majority in the Soviets and in this way were able to present the new regime as the realisation of soviet-style democracy. The Bolshevik Central Committee had decided on the *coup d'état* at Lenin's insistence, but this was chiefly carried out by the Kronstadt seamen and a newcomer in the Bolshevik ranks, Trotsky. Lenin himself, the workers and the garrison soldiers of Petrograd scarcely took an active part in it. Prominent Bolshevik leaders such as Kamenev and Zinoviev were so hesitant about the lonely adventure Lenin wanted to start with the party that they expressed themselves openly against the undertaking. Other leaders, such as Stalin, had voiced no criticism, but they had borne scarcely any responsibility for the event which would be put on record as the October revolution.

The Bolshevik regime was able to maintain its position not so much by its own efforts as because disagreements among its opponents proved insurmountable. It was a few years before a terrorist-dictatorial apparatus was built up by which all opposition could be eliminated. The confusion in the non-Bolshevik section of Russian socialism at the time of the October putsch was a result of the failure of the democratic coalition. In the end Tsereteli and his supporters had brought about exactly the calamitous development of the revolution which they had hoped their action would avoid. On the other hand, the mutual disagreement among the Bolsheviks' socialist opponents was precisely a result of attempts to formulate alternatives to Tsereteli's course of action. Looking back at 1917, it is clear to us that the Provisional Government was overthrown because it could not achieve peace, did too little to alleviate the social and economic needs of large sections of the population, while above all it neglected to provide itself in time with the constitutional base which would have legalised more forceful action against its opponents.

The liberal coalition partner was to a large extent responsible for this state of affairs. The Cadets regarded themselves not as an ordinary political party like all the others, but as the thinking elite of the nation which ought to be above class or party interests. The main reason for their support of the revolution and their participation in the government was their vigorous desire to carry on with the war until victory. All other problems ought to be made subordinate to this. They therefore agreed with the socialist peace policy very reluctantly. Since they did not have a massive following among the peasants, soldiers or workers, the wishes of these subjects attracted their attention less than did foreign policy, defence or constitutional problems. But the elections for the Constituent Assembly were not held in time; partly because the liberals wanted to organise them in proper democratic fashion and prepare for them carefully, partly because they did not expect much help in the preservation of governmental authority from them and preferred not to convene parliament until after the war.

Consequently the logical alternative for Tsereteli's course of action was a rejection of the coalition. In fact this would have meant that the socialist opposition party, still via the Soviets, would have to increase their pressure on the government so that it submitted to their demands. If that proved impossible, a takeover of power and the creation of a completely socialist government would be inescapable. A socialist government which wanted to save democracy and avoid civil war could in fact do little else than hold elections as quickly as possible. A Constituent Assembly elected in this way would then have to decide on the definitive form of government and the legislation for a necessary and fundamental social and economic reform. But it was predictable that the election, the convening and the deliberations of this parliament would take a long time. There was a good chance that substantial sections of the population and extremist political groups would lose their patience in the meantime and would take what the Constituent Assembly would not give them in time. Chaos, civil war and counter-revolution would then be on the horizon.

The socialists could only avoid this undesirable situation by forming a government which would immediately meet, as far as was possible, the desires of their following for land, bread and peace. They ought in that case not to trouble themselves much with the fate of democracy and ought at the same time to accept the social and economic upheaval, which would be the result of the activities of such a government, without having any certainty that the possibility of a conquest from abroad, the collapse of the Russian empire or a civil war were ruled out. In other words, the socialist moderates would have to carry out

Lenin's and Trotsky's programmes in the hope that they could bring a somewhat more humane and democratic character to this instant-socialism than their socialist competitors. A rather unattractive alternative, but perhaps the only way of preserving something of the spirit of February 1917 and the Russian democratic socialist tradition.

It was Martov who was the principal propagandist for another Menshevik policy in 1917. In May he had gone back to Russia and came forward as an opponent of the coalition. He regarded Tsereteli's policy as an inadmissible violation of the idea of the bourgeois revolution which before 1917 he had vigorously defended against Kautsky, Lenin and Trotsky. Since he, next to Akselrod, was the most prominent Menshevik ideologist and equally beloved, he was a troublesome millstone around the necks of Tsereteli and his brother-in-law Dan. Martov's dogmatic attitude was also a result of his views about the war which he interpreted in the first place as an imperialistic conflict. Any complicity in this atrocious crime of the international bourgeoisie was in Martov's view fatal for the revolution. In peace talks with the Entente or with its socialist vassals he saw little benefit. If a Russian call for a cease-fire remained unanswered, then the revolution would have to be defended against German aggression without imperialist support.

Martov's assumption that the bourgeoisie could be compelled to govern Russia along the lines of the socialist opposition and to pursue a war without the vital Western arms supplies gave evidence of little realism. Nor did he meet with much support for it. The problem of challenging the Bolsheviks was another matter. Martov was one of the most vehement opponents of the use of violence against fellow socialists. Tsereteli, who in June had suggested to the Petrograd Soviet that the Bolshevik soldiers and workers should be disarmed, met with no understanding whatsoever. Later Tsereteli regarded this as one of the principal reasons for the downfall of Russian democracy. His socialist comrades, however, also realised that Bolshevik exploitation of the rebellious feelings of the masses could lead to catastrophe. But they wondered what right they had to oppress the Bolsheviks, who were supported by the same social groups as those on which their revolutionary legitimation was based. They were afraid of a boomerang effect if it turned out that the Soviets possessed too little power to carry out repressive measures of this kind. Still less did they allow the Bolsheviks the propagandist advantage linked to the role of revolutionary martyrdom.

Tsereteli, as minister, nevertheless ratified the arrest of several Bolshevik leaders and the disarming of several military units. But this did not lead to the permanent elimination of the Bolsheviks as a political factor. They certainly exploited this minimum repression for propaganda purposes, even in their relationships with foreign socialists. During the Kornilov rebellion, which as was feared could not be effectively resisted without the pro-Bolshevik section of the population in the capital, the government was compelled to revoke most of these measures. Of course the possibility of large-scale terrorism against the population was never contemplated by the Provisional Government. It did not have at its disposal a special police force and nor did it probably have sufficiently trustworthy troops to be able to undertake anything of the kind.

The proposal to form a socialist government which could be considered capable of attacking the fundamental problems of the revolution was Martov's answer to the crises in July and August. But even in September and October most Mensheviks and socialist revolutionaries continued to see this as a desperate move. They had little trust in their own strength and were afraid of ending up in total isolation. The liberals, who had compromised themselves in the Kornilov rebellion, were no longer acceptable as allies. The same was also true of the Bolsheviks who in fact could only with difficulty have been kept outside a socialist government. Moreover, what else could such a government do but accept a humiliating peace, sanction the spontaneous and often violent distribution of land which was worsening the agrarian situation and increasing Russia's food shortages, and give way to the utopian longings of the workers for soviet democracy and workers' self-rule? Immediately afterwards the apparently hopeless struggle against social and economic chaos and the counter-revolution loomed up.

Only the abominable situation which the revolution and they themselves had got into forced the Mensheviks to reconsider their point of view about taking power. But they did this without any zest or enthusiasm. It worked to Martov's disadvantage that he was a typical party leader and could only work outside that framework with difficulty. His strengths lay in the literary and intellectual fields. He functioned as the moral and social conscience of the party. But he lacked Lenin's concentration on organisation and discipline. Nor did he possess Tsereteli's natural charismatic leadership or Trotsky's demagogic talent, which could have provided him with great influence even outside the party. This was a pity, for not only among the Mensheviks and the Bundists, but also among the socialist revolutionaries and even the Bolsheviks, there had from the beginning been a clear nucleus of like-minded people, who, out of protest against Tsereteli's 'revolutionary defensism', continued to call themselves 'internationalists'.

Martov's policy could have had a chance of success if he had managed in time to unite these people into a separate group. Now his opposition to the coalition simply played into Lenin's hands, for Martov only managed to get a majority of the party behind him on the eve of the October revolution, and of course that was too late. How attractive his ideas were, however, emerged during the Second All-Russian Soviet Congress which met in October during the *coup d'état* and also legitimised it since the meeting was dominated by the Bolsheviks. In spite of this Martov's proposal of forming a socialist government, in which different parties would be represented, was accepted. Lenin and Trotsky did indeed later incorporate a number of left-wing socialists into the Council of People's Commissars, as the new government was called.

The moderate socialists displayed little energy in the crucial months before October and this had fatal consequences. However, this had little to do with lack of insight into reality or rigid ideological dogmatism. Their hesitation about resolutely altering their direction is perfectly understandable. They had the choice before them of either sticking to their old course in the hope that the mood of the population would change and the crisis would resolve itself, or of taking the scalpel to the revolutionary process and yielding to Jacobin impulses, which as revolutionaries they also possessed. To do this they would have to conquer their abhorrence of terrorism, violence and absolute power, and set aside their conviction that Russia was not ready for the socialism which they advocated.

The Mensheviks, like no other group in Russia, embodied the

internal contrast between democracy and dictatorship, between revolution and evolution, between utopia and reality, which were typical of centrist socialism. The fact that in 1917 the majority of the party first followed Tsereteli in order afterwards, when it was too late, to swing over to Martov, speaks volumes. During the period 1918–23, similar tensions existed within large sections of the socialist labour movement in Western Europe as well. But with the exception of Italy, where things also went wrong, the situation in Western Europe at that time was different. Circumstances in Russia in 1917 were not conducive to the establishment of a democracy, but formed an almost ideal breeding-ground for a dictatorship. A similarly dangerous situation occurred in the West in the thirties, when Western socialism, with far larger parties and trade unions and a much longer and more stable democratic tradition, still turned out to be unable to hold its own against dictatorship. This was true not only for the German socialists in 1933, but also afterwards for the Austrians and Spaniards who tried to make an armed stand against Fascism. Italian socialism had already succumbed at the beginning of the twenties. It continued to be evident that the democratic preferences of the socialists and their aversion to violence prevented them from spiking the guns of an opponent who was little troubled by such scruples. In the West this all happened not, as in Russia, in the middle of a revolution and during a world war. The Nazis and the Fascists were moreover more clearly recognisable as opponents than the Bolsheviks, who had originated in their own camp.

The weaknesses of moderate socialism in Russia proved to a large extent to be the weaknesses of democracy and socialism in general. The impressive burgeoning of democracy and socialism in Western Europe after the Second World War was only possible thanks to the victory of the allied armies in 1945. The period of Fascist sovereignty in Europe should not be interpreted as an incidental interruption of the natural development of socialism and democracy in this century. The Entente's victory in the First World War had indeed created better opportunities in the West, but had not in the peace of Versailles safeguarded these sufficiently against future dictatorial threats. But Russia met with a considerably less advantageous fate. The course of the First World War undid the modest beginnings there in the direction of a pluriform and democratic society. The result of the Second World War was that during the next four decades the communist regime in Russia was to remain a most stable dictatorship. It was evidently beyond the capacities of the relatively small group of newcomers in Russian politics to change the course of events in the few months in which the chance was offered to them in 1917. But their attempt to do so gives all the people with genuinely democratic intentions in the Soviet Union the encouraging idea that the political history of Russia before 1985 did not consist purely and solely of a depressing and unparalleled growth of despotic authority.[102]

# 6

SOCIALIST EUROPE AND THE OCTOBER
REVOLUTION 1918–1919

As we have already seen, after 1815, 1918 and 1945 the Europeans took up similar positions with regard to Russia. There is also a certain parallelism between the situations which came into being in Europe in those years, although most historians tend rather to emphasise the differences than to point out the similarities. In 1815, 1918 and 1945, however, it was important for contemporaries that Russia had functioned as an indispensable ally in a major war fought by a number of European states against another European country which had tried to acquire for itself a dominant position in Europe. Each time this danger was averted by the allied victory, and each time there followed a period in which Russia, although she had made great sacrifices in every one of these wars to save Europe, was seen as the principal threat to the restored European balance of power. In 1918 there was no great fear, as after 1815 and 1945, of military invasion, but rather for the overthrow of the European social structure from within. The reaction to this threat was almost always fierce, frequently extremely exaggerated and sometimes hysterical. This vehemence is understandable. The takeover of power by the Bolsheviks suddenly made it possible to link the old spectre of an aggressive, expansionary and barbaric Russia with the existing abhorrence of socialism. The clichés of anti-socialist propaganda, which in 1918 could also boast a fairly long historical tradition, could therefore be used. In this period, therefore, not only was there a kind of repetition of the worst forms of Russophobia from the first half of the nineteenth century, but the fear of a dissemination of the typically Russian, revolutionary virus – a fear which had first made itself felt around 1880 in the West and had once more become operative in 1905 – now manifested itself again, but on a far wider scale and much more frantic in character.

In the year which followed the October revolution the outcome of the war still loomed much more importantly on the horizon than the revolution. In the press of the Entente countries the Bolsheviks, because of their separate peace with Germany, were denounced as traitors to the common cause. The only suitable Western answer to the change of power in Russia was, in the view of many papers, non-recognition and armed intervention. There would also be a good deal of fantasising about the Jewish origins and German connections of the new rulers in the Kremlin.[1] After the armistice in November 1918 the accent was more strongly placed on the perfidious and subversive character of the Soviet regime and this continued for some time. Although more moderate and balanced judgements were not wholly absent, the following arbitrarily chosen quotation is characteristic: 'Russian communism distinguishes itself through the fact that it unleashes the worst instincts of mankind's predatory nature, which have been muffled through centuries of incomplete civilisation, into unbounded activity: the passion for snatching other people's property, destroying what has been built up, trampling every moral precept underfoot, and experiencing sadistic enjoyment in murder and torture.'[2] Bolshevism was presented in the Western press or by prominent politicians as 'Asiatic socialism', 'the Tartar-Asiatic form of Marxism', 'the madness of famished men', 'barbarism', 'the greatest danger of the civilised world', the 'absolute rule of delinquency', 'arbitrariness and violence', 'systematic murder and robbery', and naturally also as the 'instrument of power of international Jewry'. The Bolsheviks were 'mass murderers', a 'band of anthropoid apes'. They practised terrorism with electrically driven guillotines which could chop off 500 heads per hour. Equally fantastic were the stories of free love and the communal possession of women, as if those were the things communism was all about. Naturally the image of hordes from the East was far from absent.[3]

It was not by chance that it was primarily the right-wing press in Germany which depicted Bolshevism in such glaring colours. For a long time there had been an uninterruptedly

Russophobian, anti-socialist and anti-Semitist tradition in these circles. In countries with a far less powerful anti-Russian tradition in pre-war publicistics, there was also some mention of a kind of crusade against communism, and the reporting about Soviet Russia was just as inaccurate and tendentious. In the United States, for instance, where absolutely no danger from a communist revolution existed, reaction to the October revolution manifested itself in a hysterical manner in the so-called Red Scare and the infamous Palmer Raids, in which in 1920 more than 4,000 people suspected of left-wing sympathies were run in. In the same year Walter Lippmann and Charles Merz demonstrated in convincing fashion just how untrustworthy the reporting about Russia in the *New York Times* had been in the preceding years.[4]

Thus there was something strange about the fear of the Red Danger. In his *Politics and Diplomacy of Peacemaking 1918–1919* Arno Mayer has shown that the phantom of communism continued to occupy a prominent place at the negotiating table at Versailles. The American sociologist Thorstein Veblen was the first to notice at the time that the Russian issue 'was not written into the text of the Treaty [but] may rather be said to have been the parchment upon which the text has been written'.[5] The 'Big Four' spent a great deal of time in discussing the possibilities of eliminating Bolshevism by force of arms or by containing it by setting up a *cordon sanitaire (nomen est omen)* consisting of anti-communist states. Not only did they believe in this threat, but they even deliberately exaggerated it, for example in internal election campaigns. It was highly unlikely that the Russian communists, who were engaged in a large-scale civil war, would be capable of transporting the revolution at the tip of a bayonet into the heart of Europe. Food consignments to Germany and Austria were therefore regarded as better weapons against communism than bullets. At Versailles it was soon realised that opportunities for armed intervention in Russian internal affairs were very limited. Curiously enough there was some doubt as to whether anything of the sort was actually necessary. Few believed that the Soviet system would be able to maintain itself. The 'real, old' Russia, by whom they had been befriended and with whom they had been allied, would soon rise again. Not a day went by on which the speedy fall of the communist regime in Russia was not announced in one paper or another. The *New York Times*, for instance, foretold this ninety-one times between November 1917 and November 1919. What exactly were people afraid of?[6]

Bolshevism was compared at this time to a serious, contagious disease like the plague or syphilis. Statesmen and other manipulators of public opinion behaved as if they really wanted to inoculate the West against it. They used the unfavourable elements of the Western image of Russia mixed with a substantial dose of anti-socialism as a serum. Since neither rebellion nor dissatisfaction was leading to the establishment of a stable communist regime in any country except Russia, they were later able to claim that their patient had remained healthy. But the question is whether the patient would have become seriously ill without their preventive medicine. It is nevertheless important to realise that the anti-Bolshevik campaign started well in the United States and Europe. Once more it became evident how powerful the old stereotyped images could be in certain situations. It is only when we appreciate how slowly the formation of public opinion about Fascism was to get under way later, that it becomes clear how significant the existence of a centuries-old image of Russia had been. It was only during, and especially after, the Second World War that Fascism became a commonplace concept that automatically evoked rejection when it was bandied about. In 1918, however, there was a whole arsenal of tried and tested expressions and ideas about Russia and socialism in the store-cupboard for the adversaries of Bolshevism which could not only be used but also understood by everyone. The susceptibility of the public to this propaganda was substantial. This, however, does not tell us as much about the danger of communism as it does about our political culture.

As is well known, the result of vaccination is that the patient becomes infected to a slight degree with the sickness against which he is inoculated. Did the anti-Bolshevik campaign also have this effect on the European body politic? One would expect the opposition to the European status quo to adopt a completely different concept of Soviet Russia. This was all the more so because the new government in that far-off country pretended to be socialist and Marxist and claimed to have realised the dream of many in the West: a social revolution which had given power to the proletariat and which signified a deliverance from the desperation created by the war in most people's lives. Left-wing Europe was predestined in this way to becoming the natural ally of the new Soviet republic. This did not actually happen, at least not to the degree that might have been expected on the grounds of socialist reactions in the past to Russian revolutionary events. To a large extent this was because it was no longer open to the Western socialists to extol Russian radicalism in a way that did not commit them to anything. Gone were the days in which Marx or Kautsky and many other Western socialists could freely admire Russian revolutionaries, because this hardly affected their own doings. Now in 1918, it seemed, everywhere in Europe, that the socialist revolution could be a possible result of the war. Even if prominent socialists found that revolution in their country was not a real possibility, they would certainly have to convince their following of the rightness of their ideas in order to avoid undesirable situations. And where there was a chance that the socialists would soon set themselves up at the head of a victorious revolution as, for example, in Germany, Austria or Hungary, it was realised that ill-considered following of the Bolshevik example could lead to civil war, famine, dictatorship, terrorism or counter-revolution.[7]

The situation in the United States differed greatly from that in Europe. Thus it is not so strange that John Reed's fascinating coverage of the *Ten Days that Shook the World* provided the most successful literary expression of the myth of the October revolution. The Menshevik Voitinsky once sarcastically observed that the author knew too little of Russian circumstances to know whether he was attending a wedding or a funeral in October 1917. Lenin, on the other hand, immediately recognised the enormous propagandist significance of the book. Its influence on American labor was very limited, however. The overwhelming majority of organised American workers was attached to the non-socialist American Federation of Labor under the forceful leadership of Samuel Gompers, who was an outspoken communist-hater. The AFL joined fully in the crusade against Bolshevism.[8]

In 1917–18 the most enthusiastic reactions to the October revolution, sometimes confirmed by a call to revolution in their own country, came from small groups of socialists from the extreme left wing of the movement, mostly led by young intellectuals who had been totally unknown before 1914. From among them the Communist International, before it had been officially established, gained its first adherents. In the remaining socialists' judgement of the change of regime in Russia, concern for the future of Russia and Europe could often be discerned. Fear was mingled with hope when people wondered what the influence of Russian events could be on the progress of the war and the chances of far-reaching social and political reforms in Europe. Within the SPD, as happened earlier in 1905, the Russian situation was immediately rejected as an example for Germany. Nevertheless, the majority of German socialists initially abstained from a too negative judgement of the Bolsheviks, because they regarded them as the most radical peace party in Russia. Within the USPD things were of course no different, but among the Independents a debate almost immediately arose between the supporters and opponents of Bolshevism. In neutral Holland the SDAP for the most part devoted cautious, critical commentary to the October revolution, but opinion within the party was certainly not unanimous. By the left-wing Marxists, who had united into a separate party in Holland, the revolution in Russia was heartily applauded. However, in *De Tribune*, this group's mouthpiece, the editors Wijnkoop and Van Ravensteyn, who were both supporters of the Entente, rejected Lenin's peace policy. In France and England opinion about Bolshevism was initially entirely determined by attitudes to the war. The opponents of *union sacrée*, who were still in a minority in both countries, were mostly considerably more positive in their judgement than the supporters of this policy, but glorification or total rejection were rare.

After the peace of Brest–Litovsk in March 1918 there were Belgian, British and French socialists who thought that armed intervention in Russia ought not to be ruled out in advance if the struggle against Germany, which was entering a particularly critical phase in those months, made it necessary. Meanwhile, opinion about the Russian communists had become significantly less favourable because of the violent disintegration in January of the Russian Constituent Assembly chosen by free general elections. No one in the West could thereafter deny that the Bolsheviks were pursuing a dictatorship. But there were socialists like Mehring in Germany, Loriot in France and Van der Goes in Holland who had little difficulty with the abolition of democracy in Russia. A larger number considered it dubious, but nevertheless tried to show some understanding of the necessity for terrorism and absolute power in the special circumstances prevailing in Russia.[9]

In the course of 1918 and 1919 the socialists' point of view about communism would crystallise further and the mutual disagreements would intensify. The initial reaction of Western socialism to the October revolution, however, was generally rather vague and cautious, and that was not, in itself, ill-advised. Trustworthy accounts of the situation in Russia were scarce, and imprudent pronouncements could have unpredictable consequences. This was of course not pleasing for the Bolsheviks and their Russian socialist opponents. Both groups had the greatest interest in winning Western socialism over to their point of view and in mobilising its support in their mutual conflict. The situation after 1917 had become completely different from that in the period before 1914, when Russian revolutionaries had likewise repeatedly sought assent for their programme among the international socialist community, or had asked for arbitration in order to settle their quarrels. The Bolsheviks, who before the war had formed a small group with scarcely any influence in the West, now had at their disposal all the means the Russian state could extend to them for the airing of their opinions. They were no longer entirely dependent on party members fortuitously living abroad, or on a handful of Western sympathisers. They used their diplomatic posts abroad as centres of agitation and spent large sums on the spreading of their propaganda. Since the Russian communists were convinced that only a social revolution in the West could guarantee the continued existence of their regime in Russia, they were not particularly restrained in the use of the opportunities at their disposal.

The Mensheviks and socialist revolutionaries, on the other hand, suffered much under Bolshevik oppression. In the summer of 1918 they were excluded as counter-revolutionaries from membership of the Soviets. In this way, at the beginning of the civil war, they were completely outside the law and every legal possibility of political action was denied to them. The socialist parties were sharply divided, both internally and mutually, about how, in their view, the Bolsheviks should be combated. There were very divergent opinions about the nature of the Bolshevik regime, peace policies and the economic measures of the Soviet government, about the civil war and Western intervention. The Russian socialists were divided, disorganised and chronically short of money. They had no effective representation abroad and in this matter too were thwarted by the Bolsheviks. Thus the Soviet government refused to grant an exit visa to Russian socialists who wanted to attend the Interallied Socialist Conference which was held in London in February 1918.[10]

The anti-Bolshevism of the Russian socialists was very understandable but their point of view was, as they were soon painfully to discover, seldom wholly acceptable to Western socialists. For example, a number of articles in a series about Russia written by Boris Krichevsky were rejected by the editorial board of *L'Humanité*. The October revolution was described by this well-known opponent of Lenin from the days of *Iskra* as 'a plot in every sense of the word, well organised in broad daylight, in front of the very nose of a lamentably impotent government'.[11] *L'Humanité* remained until October 1918 in the hands of the *majoritaires*. They hoped to avoid an intensification of the differences of opinion in the party and censured such extreme statements about Bolshevism. This did not mean that from now on *L'Humanité* only sang Soviet Russia's praises: reports appeared in it about the Red Terror and even some cutting articles by Martov, the leader of the Mensheviks in Russia, and by Lozovsky, the communist trade union leader who, between 1917 and 1919, led a short-term but fierce opposition to the dictatorship of the Bolshevik Central Committee. In Germany Alexander Stein's articles caused protests. Stein was a Menshevik and follower of Martov who had lived in Germany since 1906 and had made continual efforts to provide the German socialists with information about Russia. In 1918 he was a prominent member of the USPD and a regular correspondent of the *Leipziger Volkszeitung*. His bitter complaints against the Bolshevik dictatorship led to excited discussions in the columns of that paper, so that the editorial board dissociated itself from Stein, and Franz Mehring attacked him severely.[12]

In 1918 there were two Russian socialists in the West who were very well known internationally. The first was Alexander

Kerensky, the former premier of the Provisional Government, who had fled from Russia in disguise in 1918 with the help of the Entente. The second was the already elderly Akselrod who, since the end of 1917, under pressure from the Menshevik party leadership had lived in the West, 'in order to promote the interests of the revolution in the International'. Since the new government in Russia was not recognised by the Entente, Kerensky tried to plead the cause of the deposed Provisional Government with Lloyd George and Clemenceau without actually achieving very much. Kerensky was an ardent supporter of allied intervention in order to restore democracy in Russia. He also sought support for this from the French and British socialists, who were very divided on this question but nevertheless received him with respect in London and Paris. The Bolsheviks had refused to take part in the Interallied Socialist Conference which was held in London in February 1918, and they were also absent from a similar meeting in September. However, Litvinov, the Bolsheviks' agent in England, did everything he could behind the scenes to prevent the Western socialists from approving intervention in Russia. In September Kerensky had the opportunity of making an ardent plea for intervention at the meeting of the Entente socialists in London. But he was only admitted to the conference as a guest and not as the official representative of his party, the PSR. This was illustrative of the discord which the Russian question had brought about in the Western socialist environment. Not until after the armistice in November 1918 would the English and French socialists openly declare themselves against intervention.[13]

After 1918 Kerensky no longer played a prominent role in the Western socialist milieu. He never appeared at the meetings of the International. Akselrod made more effort to influence the formation of socialist opinion in a systematic way. In 1918, in co-operation with the socialist revolutionaries Rusanov and Sukhomlin, he published several numbers of two journals entitled *Les Echos de Russie* and *Stimmen aus Rusland* which were specially intended to enlighten the socialist West about the situation in Russia. In the autumn of 1918 these publications had to be discontinued because of lack of money. Akselrod had appealed in the main to the socialist centre, with the intention of protecting his political friends from Zimmerwald days against conversion to communism. But although his reporting about

Russia was as accurate as possible, the tone adopted by these papers was almost as anti-Bolshevik as that in the bourgeois press. Akselrod and his correspondents therefore met with little success. They had to discover that dogmatic statements of an unfavourable nature about Soviet Russia, even if they were completely correct, were mostly counterproductive in a socialist environment. Akselrod received encouraging letters only from the Swiss socialist Hermann Greulich and from Kautsky and Bernstein; the rest of socialist Europe appeared to be deaf.[14]

But Akselrod continued his work indefatigably. In August 1918 he sent an open letter 'To the socialist parties of every country'. After their 'bloody' coup – he wrote – the Bolsheviks had systematically destroyed all democratic freedom, had wrecked the economy under the banner of 'socialism', and handed over the country to German imperialism at the peace of Brest–Litovsk. All socialist parties were 'mercilessly' persecuted by them. Their 'wild and unbridled' terrorism directed itself against the whole Russian nation. In Akselrod's view, however, an important section of Western socialists sanctioned the deeds of the Bolsheviks and rejected the complaints and protests of great masses of the people and of the socialist parties in Russia as counter-revolutionary.

He regarded the ubiquitously prevailing ignorance about the real situation in Russia as the principal cause of this 'disastrous error' of international socialism. Akselrod therefore suggested sending a commission of inquiry to Russia consisting of representatives of all the socialist parties. If it came to the conclusion that his point of view was correct, then the socialists ought to change their attitude towards Soviet Russia fundamentally by helping the democratic groups, which were now so weak, as much as possible in their life-and-death struggle against the dangers of the ultra-left and the ultra-right.[15] This idea of a moral socialist intervention in Russia instead of a military one by the Entente powers was heartily supported by the socialist revolutionaries Gavronsky, Sukhomlin and Rusanov. Akselrod's open letter was circulated on a fairly large scale. The plan was also submitted by telegram to the socialist conference at which Kerensky was speaking. Moreover Akselrod himself defended his proposal again in a series of personal letters to socialist leaders. In these he emphasised the fact that he was not demanding a condemnation of Bolshevism. At the same time he made it clear that he himself was an opponent of military intervention and that he considered an armed rebellion against the regime by Russian workers or socialists would be highly injudicious under present-day circumstances.

The results of all this effort remained extremely meagre. The Interallied Socialist Conference did not discuss his proposal. Only a Swedish socialist paper published Akselrod's letter in full. In the Bolshevik press the idea was ridiculed. In *Vorwärts*, the SPD's party newspaper, it was emphatically condemned. The paper firstly established that at this moment no International existed which could carry out the proposal.

> But should the International shortly acquire new vitality, as we hope it will, then its worst conceivable use would be to become a board for the arraignment of those of its members who have been the first to make the practical attempt really to transmit socialism to an entire people. The serious mistakes and errors of the Bolsheviks are frequently and severely criticised in this paper, but the less we agree with the Bolsheviks' methods, the more we esteem their courage and the pureness of their views.[16]

Even the right-wing socialists in Russia thus showed little understanding of Akselrod's ideas. Akselrod himself had occasioned this. He had given the impression that a socialist commission of inquiry in Russia could do nothing else than make his conclusions its own. It is extremely unlikely that a socialist investigation would have achieved this result. It is strange that Akselrod harboured such naive expectations. After all, he had spent a lifetime in the Western socialist milieu. He had been indignant at the illusions cherished by Marx and Engels about Russia, and had had a serious conflict with a good friend like Karl Kautsky about the evaluation of Bolshevism. Earlier, too, his powers of persuasion had not been adequate.

His rejection of the October revolution was so total that he lost the ability to move people, who were fascinated by Bolshevism because it appealed so strongly to socialist ideals, towards a greater detachment and a more critical position. Akselrod saw his plan for a moral intervention in Russia as a sort of last resort for saving the revolution. This became a kind of obsession with him, an *idée fixe* to which he held firmly with the obstinate stubbornness of an old man. But *Vorwärts* was right: in 1918 it was impossible to organise a visit to Russia for a delegation from the International. Akselrod could only see the lack of favourable reactions as a sign of 'the moral and political degeneration' of Western socialism – erroneously, for after the armistice there certainly proved to be serious interest in his proposal.

Over the years Akselrod's judgement about Bolshevism gradually had become more negative and oversimplified. The new regime in Russia was a *soldateska*, a 'Prätorianendiktatur', 'tsarist-Bonapartism' under the name of socialism, and so on. On the first day after the October revolution, thus, when nothing so very terrible had yet happened in Russia, in a speech to Swedish socialists he compared the Bolsheviks with Herostratus, the citizen of Ephesus who had set fire to the temple of Artemis in 356 B.C. because he wanted to be famous at all costs. 'The despotism of the commissars will certainly find its place in history, not however as a world-historical attempt of the proletariat to acquire power in the state, but as a gigantic Herostratian attempt to play a world-historical role under a Marxist banner and using the proletarian masses and the revolutionary army.'[17] These were statements which not only made little impression on the group he wanted to influence in the West, but also failed to convince a large section of his own fellow party members in Russia.

### KAUTSKY, LENIN, LUXEMBURG AND BAUER ON DICTATORSHIP AND DEMOCRACY

Akselrod, however, had made an important ally before the end of the war who wielded great influence over international socialist opinion, and who was to a substantial extent to determine the framework within which socialist discussion about communism would take place in the years to come, and that was Karl Kautsky. As a result of the war the serious differences of opinion which had broken up the close friendship between Akselrod, Kautsky and Bernstein had become blurred. In the post-war period they renewed their old friendship and came to regard one another, not without self-criticism, as the three wise, grey-haired patriarchs of European socialism who had certainly been honoured everywhere, but who were no longer listened to very attentively. Akselrod's ideas about the problem of war and socialism were almost identical to Kautsky's, and Bernstein had also become an opponent of the SPD's *Burgfriedenpolitik*. Kautsky was deeply convinced of the special role which the Russian socialists, and especially Akselrod and Martov, had played since August 1914. He would gladly have seen the two Mensheviks bring about a reconciliation between the German and the French socialists. Lenin, on the other hand, had in these years made Kautsky the foremost subject of his eternal tirades and torrents of abuse, because he regarded him as the most authoritative ideologist in the centrist stream of international socialism.

It is questionable whether this really was the case. Kautsky and Bernstein had both joined the USPD in 1917. The SPD leadership had reacted to this brusquely by depriving Kautsky of *Die Neue Zeit*, the paper which he had edited since 1883, and on which his fame as a Marxist theoretician was to a large extent based. But the USPD harboured very divergent groups which had only found one another through their aversion to the SPD leadership. Kautsky and Bernstein belonged to the extreme right wing within the USPD. Like Akselrod, Kautsky had also in those years shifted into a position which was clearly to the right of centre. Their old feud with Bernstein about revisionism therefore did not, in practice, have very much significance any more. But between them and the most prominent spokesmen of the Centre – Martov in Russia, Hilferding in Germany, Bauer in Austria, Longuet in France and MacDonald in England – there were considerable differences, even though these would not become clear to everyone until after the war.

Kautsky's ideas about Bolshevism had completely changed. There was nothing left of his former zeal for Russian radicalism. In September 1917 he admitted to Akselrod that Akselrod had always been right in his judgement of Bolshevism. Lenin's incessant polemical attacks on Kautsky may well have contributed to this change of view. Kautsky was sincerely grateful for the detailed information that Akselrod could provide to a German who could read no Russian. But the Bolshevik revolution raised totally different problems for him than it did for Akselrod. Kautsky's first concern was Germany, not Russia.[18] Already long before he had expressed the thought that a European war would result in revolution in Eastern and Central

Europe. He did not entirely regret this. Perhaps it was the only way in which countries like Russia, Germany and Austria would be able to free themselves from their *Militärmonarchie*. He conceived of these revolutions as shocking and sudden political events, by means of which a semi-feudal power structure would be replaced by a modern, democratic state. The social revolution was another matter. In Kautsky's opinion, that was not a revolution in the traditional sense of the word, but rather a gradual process.[19]

With this distinction between democratic and social revolution which showed much similarity to the thoughts of the Russian Marxists about the 'bourgeois' revolution, Kautsky expressed the hope that the proletariat would one day come to power in a peaceful manner as a democratic majority. But before 1914 he had already been doubtful if the bureaucratically fossilised SPD would ever be capable of leading a socialist transformation of society. In 1918 the situation was even more alarming. Of the impressive unity which the SPD had formed before the war little remained. The SPD and the USPD were almost like fire and water. Of the workers, who had witnessed four years of war, it could not be assumed as a matter of course that they would only use peaceful measures to obtain compliance with their demands, especially now that they knew only too well how to make use of weapons. The Russian example had demonstrated the decisive role a radical mass of soldiery could play in a revolution. Kautsky's nightmare was that, as a result of a military defeat, a chaotic situation would come about in Germany which would indeed drive the socialists into power, but give them no chance to build up socialism.

In this context the message that was broadcast to the world from the Kremlin could only have a catastrophic effect. Almost immediately after the Bolshevik coup Kautsky had contended in the German press that Russia was not ripe for a socialist revolution. The Russian working class was not yet capable of taking over the apparatus of government, let alone of introducing socialism into a predominantly agrarian country. An experiment with a proletarian dictatorship could only lead to chaos and victory for the counter-revolution. Kautsky, no less than Akselrod, believed that the Bolshevik regime could not endure for very long, but it would be able to do enormous damage in a short time in Russia and Europe. That was why Kautsky in the summer of 1918 wrote a long anti-Bolshevik tract entitled *Die Diktatur des Proletariats.* This was the first serious study in the West to be dedicated to communism.

Kautsky's booklet was written with the author's usual honesty and detachment. His somewhat pedantic need to reduce complicated up-to-the-minute reality to a clear abstract definition of the problem, mostly produced rather boring prose. But since the October revolution had caused a sort of avalanche of hasty judgements and confused emotions in the world of the written word, this was no great disadvantage. Alexander Stein, in December 1917, thus before the dissolution of the Constituent Assembly in Russia, had already asked the question which by 1918 was to be a problem for every socialist, and which Kautsky was to try to answer: democracy or dictatorship? According to Stein the Bolshevik policy had driven a wedge into the ranks of the Russian proletariat and increased the chance of civil war. The so-called 'dictatorship of the proletariat and the poor peasants' was nothing more than the dictatorship of one party. But Mehring and others had defended the right of a minority to use a dictatorship in order to carry out a social revolution. Kautsky tried to lift the level of this debate above that of a 'yes it is, no it isn't' discussion, since in his view the issue of democracy had become the most pressing problem of international socialism.[20]

In this he was right. At the beginning of the post-war period democracy would take definitive shape in a number of European countries through the introduction of universal suffrage. This happened under pressure from the revolutionary situation, not because all the representatives of the most important political movements had suddenly become passionate supporters of this new-style democracy. This was true also for the socialists. Trends and individuals who had continued the traditions of French Jacobinism had always been part of socialism, and therefore cannot be regarded as strictly democratic according to our modern criteria. As long as socialism remained an opposition movement, the differences in opinion which existed within the movement about democracy only occasionally emerged on the surface. The successful Bolshevik revolution first raised the pressing problem of whether socialist rulers were also bound in all circumstances by the rules of a democratic form of government. Kautsky had the honour of being the first Western socialist who surveyed and charted the democracy/dictatorship issue. This does not of course mean that this question, particularly when related to the Soviet Union, had then the same import as later in the days of the Cold War. Naturally, in 1918, Kautsky had not foreseen the development of the Bolshevik dictatorship in the direction of a totalitarian regime.

Above all, Kautsky wanted to challenge socialists like Mehring and Otto Bauer who were creating a rift between the concepts of socialism and democracy. They refused to see democracy as a necessary measure by which to achieve the socialist end: the nationalisation of the means of production. This after all gave them the opportunity to welcome whatever occurred in Russia as something socialist.[21] To Kautsky socialism meant an unambiguous choice for democracy. The class war as a mass phenomenon demanded, as it were, democratic attitudes. Under an absolute despotism the emancipation of the proletariat would be impossible.[22] A bureaucracy or a dictatorial minority could abolish private property by decree and place production under state control. But this sort of thing had nothing to do with socialism. Self-government could only be learnt in the school of democracy. It could not be carried out in a meaningful way if the majority of the nation did not want it or if a people was still insufficiently fitted for it. Naturally there was no exact method of determining the moment when the proletariat would be capable of 'transferring democracy from politics to the economy'.[23] Kautsky thought that the proletariat would best learn its own strength in the democratic arena. Democracy could not obscure class differences, nor could it make the workers averse to the social revolution, but it could protect them from disastrous, premature experiments. He moreover believed that the proletariat, in contrast to the bourgeoisie in the eighteenth and nineteenth centuries, simply because of its democratic achievements, would be capable of a revolution which could be fought out with economic, legislative and moral means and not with physical violence.

In theory there was little to be said against Kautsky's eulogy of democracy, but he had not yet set up alongside it an attractive programme of action for all German socialists in 1918. He did not answer the question of who should lead the proletariat if it proved to be vindictive and violent instead of democratic. Kautsky was well aware that many Spartacists and a considerable number of people within the USPD hoped to gain a majority by revolutionary activities amongst which the use of violence was not excluded. Their concept of 'majority' was actually much vaguer than Kautsky's. Democratic parliamentary elections played an insignificant or non-existent role in it. Decisive in their line of reasoning was the dogged resistance of the proper-tied class against which all peaceful action by the workers would break down. According to Kautsky the proletariat ought to defend democracy tooth and nail whenever it was threatened by a privileged minority. In this case he did not rule out armed violence by the proletariat. Socialists with more radical ideas than Kautsky, however, thought that the opposition of the bourgeoisie could only be broken by the immediate establish-ment of a proletarian dictatorship. Marx had given the theoreti-cal justification for this, the Paris Commune had first put this dictatorship into practice, and the Bolshevik regime in Russia was a living proof and magnificent example of it.

Kautsky defended himself against this kind of view by extract-ing all the teeth from Marx's dictatorship of the proletariat. He emphasised that this idea could scarcely be reckoned one of the central issues in Marx's teaching. Marx had once used this 'little word' in a letter of 1875 and described it vaguely as a necessary interval between the conquest of political power and the introduction of socialism. However, according to Kautsky, he had 'unfortunately omitted' to indicate further how he imagined this dictatorship. In this connection Kautsky pointed to Marx's famous speech in The Hague in 1871, in which the possibility of a gradual, peaceful and democratic route to socialism was expressly left open. Kautsky found further indications at the same time in *Der Bürgerkrieg in Frankreich* in which Marx had introduced the Paris Commune as 'the finally discovered political form under which the economic liberation of labour can come about'.[24]

The dictatorship of the proletariat ought then, according to Kautsky's interpretation of Marx, to be seen as a situation which comes about of necessity when the proletariat in a perfect democ-racy proves to be the strongest group in society. A situation therefore, a state of affairs, and certainly not a form of government. Just as the nobility or the bourgeoisie had formerly been, now the proletariat would also be the ruling class. A social class, that is to say, an amorphous mass, can indeed be in power, but it cannot govern. Only an organisation, a group, a faction or a party that acts on behalf of the ruling class, can govern. A social class can, however, be represented by several parties or organisations. Since it was not unusual for such groups to struggle against and succeed one another, in a democracy the government of the parties changed much more rapidly than the rule of classes. Democracy included, because of this, not only the rule of the majority, but equally the protection of the minority. Even majorities changed around, after all. The dictatorship of the proletariat conceived as a government could only be the inadmissible dictatorship of one organisation or party, that is to say, the dictatorship of one section of the proletariat over the other.[25]

Kautsky's discerning distinction between a democratic dictatorship of the proletariat and a dictatorial workers' government can undoubtedly by justified on the grounds of passages from the work of Marx and Engels. However, their writings were determined by different problems and different historical circumstances and therefore in scarcely any sense still offered a guideline for the future. They were democrats, but not like Kautsky who saw democracy on the basis of universal suffrage as an absolute good. Kautsky's attempt to incorporate the Commune, with Marx's help, into his democratic views was not therefore very convincing. The Parisians had seized power at the time not as a result of a victory, but as a reaction to a crushing defeat of left-wing France in a general election. For a socialist like Louis Blanc this had been a reason to condemn the Commune at the time, though for Marx it was not. The myth, created by Marx, about the Commune as a blood-soaked experiment in socialism and democracy was still very much alive. In Russia it was exploited as propaganda in order to gain Western support for the October revolution. In socialist circles the argument was also used that if the Commune had had the right to take armed action against Versailles, Lenin also had the right to do the same with regard to the Russian Constituent Assembly. A certain logic in this reasoning could not be denied.

Kautsky most emphatically refused to put the situation in France in 1871 on a par with Russia in 1918. He emphasised, in the very first sentences of his essay, that there was a fundamental difference between the Commune and the Bolshevik regime. The Commune had been the work of the entire Parisian proletariat. All the schools of thought within French socialism were represented in it. On the other hand, the Bolsheviks came to power as a result of their struggle against other socialist parties and they had afterwards excluded them from the national government and outlawed them. A position for or against Bolshevism was, in Kautsky's opinion, like a choice for or against dictatorship. In Russia the communists did not have the majority behind them and genuine socialism was thus impossible there.

Naturally Kautsky made another comparison. The parallel with the French revolution was obvious. What was interesting was that in 1918 Kautsky revised his views of 1907. Then he had urgently warned that comparisons between the Russian revolution of 1905 and the great French revolution were not valid. He thought at the time that the period of the 'bourgeois revolutions' was closed for Europe and also for Russia. Now he thought that Russia was indeed like France in 1793 and actually was only now approaching its bourgeois revolution. Kautsky observed that many socialists were still living so much under the spell of the French revolution that they confused civil war with social revolution and therefore considered that even atrocities and large-scale devastation were justified. Kautsky was right about this. In France socialists who defended Soviet Russia in this way in 1918 even gained the support of historical specialists in the field of the French revolution such as Aulard.

According to Kautsky a civil war precluded a social revolution, but it did produce people like Cromwell and Napoleon. The Bonapartism which was perfected by both Napoleons was capable of forming a dictatorial regime which was extremely stable. He considered a repetition of 1789 out of the question in Western Europe. The proletariat could carry out its social revolution peaceably there. But Russia could only be saved from a long-lasting civil war or a Bonapartist dictatorship by a return to democracy. From this point of view Kautsky subjected the Bolshevik regime to sharp criticism. Nothing had come of the Bolsheviks' assumption that their revolution would give impetus to a revolution in the West. Now they were faced with a series of impossible tasks which they were trying to carry out with violence and dictatorship. This statement by Kautsky in August 1918, coming on the eve of the German revolution, was extremely strange and Lenin and Trotsky would make merry about it. But in a deeper sense he was nevertheless right in his remark that, as in 1848 and 1905, Russia and Europe would undergo separate developments.

Kautsky was extremely unfavourably disposed towards the economic policy of the Russian government, which in his view had no chance of success. A dictatorship could destroy a great deal of capitalist property, change many capitalists into proletarians and deprive the bourgeoisie of its rights but import no socialist production methods. And as long as that was not successful, capitalism would be as inevitable as an ineradicable weed which repeatedly blooms up again. The Russian state was a peasant state. The peasants could accept democracy, but they would also tolerate a reactionary emperor or dictator who gave them possession of a piece of land. All the attainments of the revolution would in that case be lost and the workers would have to languish under a Bonapartist dictatorship, which had been prepared by Bolshevik policy.

Kautsky's critique of Russian communism contained few factual elements which had not already been more thoroughly aired by the Mensheviks and other Russian socialists. The idea that the peasants held the Russian revolution in a sort of stranglehold was also widespread outside Marxist circles. Even the Bolsheviks were deeply convinced of it and Stalin's horrifying collectivisation of agriculture would eventually be the means by which the 'socialist' state freed itself from this danger. Relatively new was Kautsky's speculation about a Bonapartist finale to the revolution. With this Kautsky was already outlining the framework within which political development in the Soviet Union would be analysed by some socialists and communists in the course of the twenties. Later, however, the danger of a Bonapartist degeneration was looked for not outside, but within the communist party.

Kautsky's 1918 pamphlet would play an important role in the discussions which were to be carried out in socialist circles about the problem of democracy and dictatorship. But his booklet was nevertheless chiefly used by reformist socialists to heap abuse on their more revolutionarily inclined comrades. His ideas were eagerly received by the SPD. Most of Kautsky's fellow party members within the USPD would have nothing to do with them, and that was the group he had been addressing himself to in the first place. Kautsky was also in the years to come to remain the most prominent critic of communism in the right wing of European socialism. His prestige as a theoretician suffered much under the reputation he acquired in those years as an anti-communist.

Not only Kautsky himself but also the Bolsheviks were responsible for this. They realised that Kautsky's opinion carried great weight with Western socialists and they felt obliged to react at length to much that he wrote in these years. But they were unaware that Kautsky's influence on the socialist centre could be practically disregarded. This was the group, however, to which communist propaganda had chiefly been addressed and this explains the violence of their reaction. Lenin must have been furious when he read *Die Diktatur des Proletariats*. The civil war had begun and the future of the Soviet republic was in great danger. Only a revolution in the West seemed capable of saving the country from a threatening doom. Lenin regarded Kautsky's writing as a stab in the back. The government leader therefore took the time to write a book entitled *The Proletarian Revolution and Kautsky the Renegade*. It was published a few months after the appearance of *Die Diktatur des Proletariats* and displayed every sign of an essay composed in great haste and anger. In about a hundred pages Lenin dealt with each paragraph of Kautsky's booklet in detail, but to a large extent by means of tirades and torrents of abuse and by repeating all the arguments he had already used against Kautsky and other socialists in earlier publications such as *State and Revolution*. What was new was that Lenin emphasised the great influence which, in his view, Mensheviks like Akselrod, Stein and Martov had exerted on Kautsky. They had supplied Kautsky with all the material for his criticism of Bolshevism, and his work was 'the libel of an embittered Menshevik'.[26]

Statements like this were understandable. Kautsky had finally after 1905 shown himself to be a supporter of Lenin's ideas about the Russian revolution. It looked as if the German Marxist had only become a true opponent of the Bolsheviks when they tried to put their words into action. Of course it was not difficult for Lenin to pick some sizeable holes in Kautsky's argument about the nature of dictatorship and proletariat. Naturally he could also add a number of quotations which seemed to serve his ends and from which it would be evident that Marx and Engels had carefully considered the 'dictatorship of the proletariat' a revolutionary instrument of power with which to oppose the bourgeoisie with violence. Here he was stronger than Kautsky who had tried to prove the squaring of the Marxist circle by identifying non-violent democracy with the proletarian class struggle and the revolution. 'We, revolutionary Marxists, have never made 'pure' democracy into an idol', wrote Lenin. A state or a governmental system ought not, in his view, to be judged by the extent to which democracy had been realised in it. In the first place a socialist should ask himself: democracy for whom, for which class?[27]

Even in the most democratic bourgeois state there was a glaring contrast, in Lenin's view, between 'formal equality' and 'the thousands of factual limitations and obstacles which turn the proletarians into wage slaves'. Soviet power, on the other hand, attracted the exploited masses into the government and was therefore 'millions' of times more democratic than the most democratic bourgeois republic. Kautsky's defence of the Constituent Assembly was a betrayal of the revolution in Lenin's opinion. Kautsky should have asked himself which class the Constituent Assembly was the mouthpiece of. For Lenin the answer to this question was clear: the bourgeoisie and the ruling classes of the *ancien régime*.[28] Lenin thought Kautsky's plea for the protection of the rights of the opposition laughable. A revolution simply precluded opposition. It was an idea that hailed entirely from the peaceful parliamentary struggle. The removal of the Mensheviks and socialist revolutionaries from the Soviets was, according to Lenin, completely justified by the support of these parties for the counter-revolution and the present civil war. The Bolsheviks had formed about two-thirds of the total number of representatives at the last Soviet congress. Thus in Lenin's view there was no occasion to believe in 'the laughable fairy-tale' of Kautsky and others, that the Bolshevik regime was an atrocious despotism which was only supported by a small minority of the population.[29]

From this reasoning it is clear to what extent Lenin treated the class war as an abstraction which had no clear relationship with reality. The Bolsheviks had disbanded the Constituent Assembly which had commanded a large socialist majority. They had manipulated the elections for the Soviets by excluding from participation the socialist parties, who were prepared to act as a sort of legal opposition under this system. In this way the Bolsheviks had been able to render useless all the instruments by which their real support from among the population could be measured. Nevertheless, for socialists like Kautsky, the most substantial problem was not whether the Bolsheviks had the majority of the Russian people behind them or not. Still less did they criticise the Bolsheviks for taking action against a counter-revolutionary movement or against armed intervention by the Entente. What Kautsky – following the Mensheviks and the socialist revolutionaries – flung in their faces was the fact that they had swallowed up the revolution, socialism and the proletariat. Because of this civil war was made inevitable, and what the Bolsheviks had labelled 'the class war' had degenerated into a relentless war between the Bolsheviks and all their opponents.

Lenin had reproached Kautsky for only listening to the Mensheviks. Kautsky had certainly been influenced by Akselrod, but his criticism of Bolshevism was not typically Menshevik. This was proved by Rosa Luxemburg. Since 1905 she had shown that she completely disagreed with Menshevik ideology, and since 1910 she had made even less attempt to disguise her contempt for Kautsky's views. Nevertheless, in the spring of 1918 she came to some conclusions about the October revolution which, in important respects, were in agreement with the judgements of the Russian socialists and with those of Kautsky. Among the Spartacists, who embodied the most radical resistance to the war within the USPD, there were certainly more critical opinions about Soviet Russia, but these were carefully kept behind closed doors. The main reason for this restraint was that left-wing criticism of Bolshevism, which could only survive with the support of the Western socialists, was grist to the mill of reaction. Even Rosa Luxemburg after much discussion let herself be convinced that this self-censorship was necessary. Nevertheless, she wanted to put her thoughts down on paper in full and in this way to exert a certain influence on the young radicals in her group. Thus one of them, Paul Levi, obtained a manuscript from her which, when he had been expelled from the communist party after a great deal of conflict, he published in 1922 under the title *Die russische Revolution. Eine kritische Würdigung.*[30]

Like Kautsky, Luxemburg covered themes in this essay which she had broached earlier. In this piece she also once more severely criticised the Mensheviks. In 1917, their mistake had been to hold fast to the fiction that the revolution could only be bourgeois in character. Since then they had refused to learn anything from further developments in Russia. This was also true of Kautsky. On the other hand, the Bolsheviks had understood perfectly well what was going on in 1917. Lenin's party had been the 'driving force' of the revolution. It had handed power over to the workers and peasants in the Soviets. This had been the only possible way of saving democracy in Russia. The German social democrats and Kautsky did not dare to do anything until they had a majority. Lenin had understood that they ought not to wait for this and that only revolutionary methods would provide them with a majority. By proclaiming the dictatorship of the proletariat the Bolsheviks had, for the first time, declared 'the final goal of socialism as an immediate programme of practical politics'. 'Their October uprising not only actually saved the Russian revolution but was also a vindication of international socialism.'[31]

After making it clear in this way whose side she was on, Luxemburg showed that she did not wish to glorify the October revolution. She absolutely did not believe that the Russians would be capable of carrying out a social revolution without the help of the West. Of course the Bolsheviks scarcely believed this either at the time, but Rosa Luxemburg was, like Kautsky, not particularly optimistic about the prospects of a social revolution in Europe. The German proletariat had certainly gone on strike for peace and bread, but up till then had shown little evidence of revolutionary inclination. As in 1905 Luxemburg compared Russian courage with German cowardice. The chance that the Russian revolution would finish the same way as the Paris Commune was exceptionally great. But it was as if she thought it more important that the Russian revolutionaries, after they had, to no avail, given the world a heroic example, should leave the stage with clean hands, than that they should defile the socialist conscience for ever by trying to keep themselves in existence with immoral or otherwise mistaken methods of exercising power.

Luxemburg had no good word for the agrarian policy of the Bolsheviks. By sanctioning the fragmentation of landed property, they had 'created a powerful new social stratum in the countryside that was hostile to socialism'. By propagating within the Russian empire the right of all peoples to create their own destiny, they had at the same time infinitely increased the opportunities for the counter-revolution and German imperialism. 'Terrorism and the suppression of democracy arose from this situation.' Luxemburg aimed the principal arrows of her criticism at this.[32] The abolition of democracy was a cure that was worse than the diseases of the bourgeois parliamentary system: 'for it blocked up the very life-giving spring out of which alone all the innate inadequacies of social institutions could be made good: the active, unrestrained, energetic political life of the broadest mass of the people'. This life was impossible without freedom of the press, without the completely unhindered basic rights of association and assembly. 'Freedom only for the supporters of the government, only for the members of a party – however numerous they may be – is no freedom.' Freedom, according to Luxemburg, was 'never anything but freedom to think otherwise'. If this was lacking then political life would die and 'would become a half-life in which bureaucracy remains the only active element'.[33]

It was wrong of Lenin and Trotsky, Luxemburg thought, to place dictatorship opposite democracy, precisely as Kautsky did, and moreover, only to think of 'bourgeois' democracy and dictatorship. The proletariat could not follow Kautsky's advice to abandon the social revolution because of their own immaturity or that of the circumstances and limit themselves to democracy, without betraying socialism. It should take the most radical measures and enforce dictatorship. 'Yes! Dictatorship! But this dictatorship consists in the art of *utilising* not *abolishing* democracy, in energetic, determined encroachments on the duly acquired rights and economic relationships of civil society, without which the socialist revolution cannot be realised. But this dictatorship must be the work of the *class*, and not of a small dominating minority in the name of the class.' The terrorism which the communists practised was to a large extent a product of circumstances. 'The danger arises when, making a virtue of necessity, they now theoretically decide on every aspect of the tactic forced on them by these awkward conditions and want to recommend it to the international proletariat as a model of socialist tactics for imitation.'[34]

And this was of course what the Bolsheviks were in a short time to do. The word 'recommend' gave a very euphemistic description of what was to happen later. In this piece also, Luxemburg was the rhetorical personification of a utopian, socialist ideal, which grimly tried to hold its own when confronted with reality, but did not succeed. In her views about the dictatorship of the proletariat she was closer to Kautsky than to Lenin. But her flamboyant prose attested to considerably less political expertise than the dry account of Kautsky, who had rightly observed that social classes could not govern. Luxemburg did not have sufficient information at her disposal in prison to make a balanced judgement about the October revolution. But she can indeed be blamed for the fact that she scarcely seemed to realise that the Bolsheviks, because of their dynamism which she so much admired, had also to a large extent created their own circumstances. These could not be permanently advanced as an excuse for Bolshevik misdeeds. Luxemburg herself had no other alternative to offer than her vitalistic mystique of the proletarian masses and revolutionary activities, which – although she did not mean this – in fact amounted to a passionate plea for 'mob rule' and 'popular instinct'. When this essay was published three years after Luxemburg's violent death in January 1919, there was some excitement among the members of the Comintern because the memory of her was surrounded by a halo of communist martyrdom. The pamphlet was to be reprinted repeatedly in many languages as the proof that a 'left-wing' rejection of the communist dictatorship could nevertheless be relevant. But since she failed to make her criticism public during her lifetime her point of view about the October revolution remained unclear and controversial. She offered no counterbalance to the adoration of Soviet Russia which was precisely the principal reason for most Spartacists to regard themselves as communists in 1919.[35]

There were other socialist leaders who also felt sympathy with

the Russian experiment and had a great deal of understanding
for such feelings amongst their adherents, though they nevertheless hoped to render these harmless by continuing to hammer
in the differences between Russia and Europe. The most striking
example of this kind of approach can be found in the extensive
works of the Austrian Marxist Otto Bauer. Next to Kautsky he
was to be generally known as the most prominent writer on
communism and Soviet Russia among Western socialists in the
period between the wars. As a brilliant theorist, statesman and
party leader Bauer is the most notable representative of Austro-
Marxism in this period which united so many resounding names.
Early on in the war Bauer, as an officer, was taken prisoner by
the Russians. During these three years of enforced idleness he
learned Russian well. In 1917 Victor Adler and the Swedish
socialist Branting drew the attention of the socialist leaders of
the Petrograd Soviet to Bauer's lot. He was discharged from
prison by the Provisional Government. Afterwards he remained
for several weeks in the Russian capital, where he stayed with
Dan's family. So he was in a position to witness the Russian
revolution from nearby. In September he returned to Vienna.
In a letter to Akselrod he thanked his Russian comrades for
their hospitality. He went on to write: 'People here are so
incompletely informed and have the strangest ideas about events
in Russia . . . Perhaps I shall decide to write a pamphlet about
Russia.'[36]

In fact he did this under the pen name Heinrich Weber. The
booklet, entitled *Die russische Revolution und das europäische Proletariat,* appeared before the Bolshevik coup had taken place
and presented a clear survey of events in Russia until the beginning of October. It was only in his final conclusions about the
future of the revolution that Menshevik influence filtered
through: 'Even if the Russian revolution overcomes all the
dangers that threaten it the result cannot be otherwise than a
bourgeois democratic republic.'[37] Bauer, thus, had no different
ideas about the nature of the Russian revolution and the significance of the Russian peasants than the Mensheviks or
Kautsky. But in letters he showed himself to be an opponent of
Tsereteli's and Dan's policy in 1917. Immediately after his return
he wrote to Kautsky about them: 'They have reasoned more or
less as follows. If the nation demands more than a bourgeois

revolution can guarantee, a Cavaignac will come and suppress it. In order to prevent him coming, we will provide a Cavaignac ourselves. Thus we will save the revolution and achieve as much as possible for the proletariat.' Cavaignac had been the general who put down the rebellion of the Parisian workers in 1848 and Bauer was referring to the repressive measures which the Provisional Government had taken against the Bolsheviks after their failed putsch in July 1917. In his view, the result of this policy had been that the Mensheviks had lost the support of the workers. But Bauer had no good word to say about the behaviour of the Bolsheviks. They were perpetrating a kind of revolutionary adventurism based on an exaggerated representation of the ability of the proletariat and on a belief in pure violence. 'The superstition of the omnipotence of the guillotine has reappeared in Petersburg as the superstition of the omnipotence of the machine gun. Between these two extremes the Menshevik-Internationalists under Martov's leadership have kept to the correct middle path. Right lies here too with the *Marxist centre*.'[38]

After October 1917 Bauer introduced a number of modifications into his judgement about the revolution and the Bolsheviks. In a letter written in January 1918 he did not breathe a word about democracy which, in his opinion of a few months earlier, ought to be preserved in order to save the revolution. Now he had great expectations from the dictatorship. 'Of utmost importance is the dictatorship of the proletariat which will probably be only transitory in nature but will nevertheless face each government of the future with a number of accomplished facts.' Bauer thought that the Mensheviks no longer had the right to protest against the suppression of newspapers and similar measures, for when Tsereteli was minister, he had done the same to the Bolsheviks. The Bolsheviks deserved the sympathy and support of the Western socialists as long as they were the representatives of the Russian workers. Bauer had no doubt that this was what they actually were. The workers in Germany ought to have the great importance of 'the social side' of Russian events, their significance 'as a class war', pointed out to them. 'My sympathies were never with the Bolsheviks but always with Martov's group', wrote Bauer. But he considered criticism of the October revolution 'to be inexpedient because we cannot revolutionise the mind of the German workers by making the revolution seem rotten to them'.[39]

Bauer fairly soon came back to this view. The Austrian socialists' enthusiasm for the Soviets was, on closer inspection, a touch too exuberant for his taste.[40] At the beginning of 1918 the Danube monarchy had in fact already lost the war and the chance that the empire would survive this defeat was small. There was a good chance that the socialists would be able or would be forced to take over power in Vienna. But if, in that situation, 'the dictatorship of the proletariat' and the 'Austrian soviet-style republic' were proclaimed by the Viennese workers in imitation of the Russians, then civil war with the Catholic and conservative section of the population of German Austria would be virtually inevitable. Bauer, who enjoyed great popularity among the Viennese workers, had no wish to start the history of socialist Austria with a blood bath, by means of which the newly acquired independence of the country would again be lost. It was thus vitally important in his view to temper the zeal for Bolshevik Russia and direct it into the proper channels.[41]

As early as February 1918 Bauer wrote an article for *Der Kampf* entitled 'We and the Bolsheviks' in which he explained his point of view much more cautiously and moderately than in the letter to Kautsky. He carefully avoided using the term 'dictatorship of the proletariat' in it. Once more Martov and his followers were held up as paragons of revolutionary propriety as opposed to the Bolsheviks, but now because they had resisted dictatorship, terrorism and the breaking up of the Constituent Assembly.[42] In contrast to Akselrod, Kautsky, Luxemburg *and* Martov, Bauer made a sharp – and not particularly justified – distinction between Western and Central Europe, which were advanced in his view, and backward Russia. In this way he created an opportunity for European socialists to admire the Russians without being obliged to follow them as well. What was good for the uncivilised Russians was not after all necessarily also good for the civilised Austrians. Bauer's attitude towards revolutionary Russia was thus to a large extent identical to the point of view that Marx and Engels had adopted around 1880 and Kautsky and others around 1905.

Bauer thought that the situation in Russia could not be compared, for example, with that in Germany. The German proletariat, he claimed, formed the majority of the population and thus had the opportunity to win power democratically. Russia was more like France in 1848 or 1871. It is inconceivable that someone of this intellectual stature, so informed about German circumstances, did not know perfectly well that the industrial proletariat in Germany was in a minority and moreover was only to a very small extent socialist or organised. At the same time one might well wonder – if there is any point in comparisons like this – whether circumstances in the still sparsely industrialised Austria of 1918, where the proletariat was chiefly concentrated in Vienna, were not also like those in France and Paris around 1870 or for the same reasons like those in Russia and Petrograd in 1918. The differences cannot possibly have been fundamental in nature. But of course Bauer had a special purpose with his parallel between France and Russia.

When the proletarian minority in France tried to grasp power, he wrote, it encountered the resistance of a democratic parliament which was ruled by a bourgeoisie supported by the peasantry. Because of this the French workers at the time had also proposed a federation of free communes and rejected a centralised democratic republic. The Bolsheviks had also done this and the Soviet system was the Russian counterpart of the French communal federation. Both formed, according to Bauer, the 'necessary national ideal' of a revolutionary proletariat that was in a minority. The theory and practice of Bolshevism were, in Bauer's view, nothing more than an adaptation of socialism to the economic and social circumstances of underdeveloped and backward Russia. Here Bauer, without using the term 'dictatorship of the proletariat', had nevertheless put Bolshevism on a par with the Paris Commune. As we have seen, Kautsky had done his very best to show that the Commune and Soviet Russia had nothing to do with each other. This was to prevent Western workers and socialists from following the Bolshevik example. Bauer tried to achieve the same end by declaring the Commune and the Soviet state to be products of intellectual backwardness.[43]

In the France of 1871 and the Russia of 1917 where capitalistic industry was still in its infancy, the overthrow of capitalism could not, in Bauer's view, form the substance of a national revolution. This certainty enabled him to adopt a sort of neutral benevolence with regard to Bolshevism. The human suffering which could result from an experimentation with socialism, which was doomed to failure, had no role to play in his cool analysis.

Because Martov had shown that the aims of Bolshevik policy were illusory, he supported him. But Martov, Akselrod, Kautsky and Luxemburg had also condemned dictatorship and terrorism on moral grounds. The ease with which Bauer had utopian and undemocratic forms of socialism inevitably stemming from the backwardness of Russia, implied that in his opinion there was scarcely any task set aside for democratic socialists in Russia. This was an aspect of Bauer's approach which was to increase in importance in later years, when it would become evident that the regime in Russia was consolidating itself. By assigning to the Bolsheviks a fundamentally subordinate position in the evolution of the socialist workers' movement, Bauer hoped to curb Western enthusiasm for the October revolution. This was indeed successful in his own party, but for European centrism in its totality, of which he was the most prominent ideologist, such reasoning produced little result.

## THE SECOND INTERNATIONAL IN BERNE AND LUCERNE

The curious love–hate relationship between socialism and communism remained fairly stable in the period between the wars. Despite all the mutual animosity, the idea that communists and socialists had much in common never disappeared completely. The changing feelings and thoughts that the one held about the other were more determined by altering circumstances than by continually renewed attempts to take an original and fundamental stand. The socialists continued to differ in opinion amongst themselves as far as this subject was concerned. The discord was particularly great in the period described in this chapter. The differences between ideologists of Western socialism like Akselrod, Kautsky, Luxemburg, Bauer and Martov were less significant than those between the socialist politicians. The position with regard to the Bolsheviks was after all not primarily a matter for peaceful reflection, but a very urgent practical question. This certainly did not improve the quality of the debate about it. We must, however, try to follow these confusing discussions somewhat, for only thus can we determine the extent of the Russian problem for Western socialism of that time.

The year 1918 ended with the armistice, the collapse of Kaiser

Wilhelm's empire and the disintegration of that of the Habsburgs. In Germany, during the revolution, workers' councils had been formed and the national administration had been handed over to a coalition of the SPD and the USPD. In German Austria, the socialists, led by Renner, Bauer and Friedrich Adler, took power. In Hungary and Czechoslovakia the socialists also gained greatly in influence. Everywhere in Central Europe communistically inclined groups or parties were formed, which were preparing to take over the state and hoped for support for this from Soviet Russia. In January 1919 at a communist uprising in Berlin which was suppressed by the military, Liebknecht and Luxemburg were murdered in cowardly fashion. Events of this kind very much aggravated the contrasts between communists and socialists. In Western European countries too, where the mentality of the population was supposed to be stable and conservative, there was great political tension. In Holland the leader of the hardly-radical SDAP, Troelstra, made an attempt at a revolution in November 1918, which, in burlesque fashion, had already failed before it had begun, but nevertheless influenced relationships within the party and the country for a long time. In Switzerland, strikes and demonstrations of a revolutionary character took place in the same month. Everywhere in Europe the socialist labour movement had suddenly become a political factor of the utmost importance, while other political and social groups, full of anxiety and awe, were taking it into account.

In countries where nothing special had happened before January 1919, a sort of calm before the storm prevailed. In the course of that year, even in England, renowned for its phlegm, a stiff revolutionary breeze was to spring up. This wind blew even harder in France. In 1919 Italy began its *biennio rosso*, two years of revolutionary disturbances with fatal consequences. In Hungary a communist soviet-style dictatorship was set up in 1919. In Russia the civil war was in full swing and no one could predict its outcome. No prophetic gift was necessary to grasp that at any moment unforeseen things could happen which could once more turn the already extremely unbalanced relationships in Europe topsy-turvy. It was in this tense situation at the beginning of 1919 that peace talks started in Paris and that the socialists held their first large international conference for a long time, in the Swiss capital. The eyes of the world were of course mostly fixed on Paris. The meeting in Berne was not, however, in all respects subordinate in significance. The socialists knew that collectively they formed the largest political group in Europe. There were many million people who expected that they would make a greater contribution to the peace, freedom, welfare and social security of the world than the statesmen in Paris.

At the Interallied Socialist Conference in September 1918 in London it had been agreed that as soon as possible after the war international socialist consideration should be given to the peace which would have to be concluded in Europe. After the failure of the socialist peace initiative in Stockholm in 1917, a great deal of sympathy for the peace programme set out by the American president Woodrow Wilson in his famous Fourteen Points developed among the socialist parties. Wilson himself was well aware of this. He even sent a representative to Berne. But it was difficult for him to commit himself closely to the opposition against the governments with which he had to deliberate. The radicalism which was surfacing within Western socialism also made him very cautious. The socialists wanted to hold their conference in Paris. Clemenceau, who did not support Wilson, had no desire to have a kind of socialist competition for official negotiations in the French capital, and the socialists were thus obliged to choose another meeting-place.[44]

This was not, however, their main problem. The hostility between the French and Belgian parties on the one hand and the German SPD on the other was still very great. An equally serious problem was the conflict about the civil truce during the war, which up till then had chiefly been fought out within the parties. The opponents of co-operation with or participation in the 'bourgeois' governments had become very numerous in 1917 and 1918. In France, in 1918, they had gained a majority in the SFIO. This disruptive factor could also reach European dimensions during an international conference and once more nullify the unity of Western socialism. No less dangerous of course were the recently developed differences of opinion about Bolshevism. At the socialist conference it would become evident that this question was 'the most thorny on the agenda'.[45] It was thus hardly surprising that a number of prominent socialists saw little benefit in an international discussion which would perhaps yield more rumpus than unity.

Nevertheless it was held, because the British made a special effort. It was realised on all sides that however much German socialism had dominated the International before the war, it had lost its prestige because of its attitude in 1914, its internal dissension during the war and the military defeat of Germany. The leading role of the Germans was taken over after the war by the British. Even though there were substantial differences of opinion within the British party about the policy pursued during the war, the contrasts between figures like Henderson and MacDonald were much less sharply defined than those between the *majoritaires* and the *minoritaires* in France and the leaders of the SPD and the USPD in Germany. Because of this the Labour Party was capable of speaking with a powerful voice and exerting great influence on the behaviour of the parties in other countries. The British socialists, who were rowing against the chauvinistic tide prevailing in their own country by carrying out a campaign for a conciliatory peace with Germany, attached great significance to a socialist counterweight to Versailles, especially after they had lost the British elections in December 1918. It was largely thanks to them that, on 3–10 February 1919, 103 delegates from 26 countries assembled in Berne for the International Labour and Socialist Conference.[46]

Nevertheless, this result was less impressive than it appeared at first sight. Only a part of the world proletariat was represented in Berne. The American Federation of Labour had failed to appear and was also absent from the almost simultaneous international trade union conference. Gompers and his followers were convinced that 'approximately one third of the membership of the Conference are recognised by the Bolsheviks' chief in Russia as Bolsheviks in good standing'.[47] This was utter nonsense. The problem was simply that the Bolsheviks had not come to Berne, because they had no desire 'to resuscitate the corpse of the Second International'.[48] The other communist parties and groups also stayed away *en masse*. Numerically they did not represent very much, but important socialist parties like the Italian and the Swiss were likewise absent, since they were more in favour of the idea of a new, Third or Communist International than of a restoration of the Second which had failed so dismally during the war. The Swiss had even refused to have anything to do with the organisation of the conference. The Belgians did not appear either, because they would not sit at the same table as the German majority socialists of the SPD. Only the Belgian Huysmans functioned as secretary of this meeting as he had done of old. The meeting in Berne also differed sharply for another reason from the congresses of the pre-war International: a whole series of well-known personalities such as Bebel, Jaurès, Keir Hardy, Plekhanov, Victor Adler and Rosa Luxemburg, who had added weight and colour to the International with their distinction and eloquence, were dead. Furthermore, a number of prominent socialists were prevented from attending by pressing state business, something that did not occur before the war. Bauer, who had become foreign minister, was absent, and SPD politicians such as Ebert and Scheidemann had also made their excuses.

There was a great deal of discussion in Berne. The protocol of the conference filled 400 closely printed pages. In general the results of these talks were encouraging. Right-wing socialists like Renaudel and Thomas naturally became involved in long controversies about the war with Germans like Wels and Müller. Equally inevitable was the fact that Wels justified the attitude of the SPD in 1914 in one long sentence with a reference to Russia. 'We German social democrats lived from the day on which social democracy began its organised existence, and we fought our battles, under the nightmare of tsarist Russia, which Marx and Engels described as a danger for Europe, a Russia which threatened the democratic development of the whole of the European West and represented a danger for civilised mankind as a whole.'[49] At the same time he reproached Thomas and the other Entente socialists for putting Russia under so much pressure to keep her in the war that she had succumbed to revolution. 'In this way Bolshevism was born and became possible in Russia, comrade Thomas!'[50] Nevertheless, neither the question of the war, nor the problem of the peace could keep the socialists divided any longer and good compromises were achieved. Still Berne was not a real success. The socialists, despite their concerted and extremely reasonable view of post-war Europe, did not succeed in making their mark on the Treaty of Versailles. Moreover it proved impossible in Berne to maintain the so much longed for socialist unity as soon as the question of communism and in connection with it the future of the International was brought up.

In the last months of 1918 Akselrod and his friends from the PSR had continued their attempts to win over the British and French socialists to their point of view. The Russians had pleaded at various meetings for the presence of a Russian delegation, consisting of members of the banished Constituent Assembly, at the peace talks in Paris. They also wanted the Russian participants at the Berne conference to be chosen in Russia and supplied with exit visas by the Bolsheviks. The plan for a visit of the International to Soviet Russia was likewise considered once more. They did not get much reaction to their proposals, which, to be honest, were not particularly realistic.[51] In Berne the Mensheviks were represented by Shchupak and Binshtok (Bienstock), who had just come from Russia, and Akselrod. For the socialist revolutionaries Gavronsky was present with Rubanovich, who before the war had been a member of the Bureau of the International. Furthermore there were socialists from the Jewish Bund, the Ukraine, Armenia, Georgia, Lithuania and Estonia present at Berne. Akselrod, who from disappointment about the Western socialists' attitude to the Russian question, had toyed with the idea of not going to Berne, noticed to his amazement that his idea concerning a socialist inquiry into Soviet Russia hardly met with any resistance. Both the left and right wings of the socialists present agreed that the International should visit Russia. But about Bolshevism they were very divided.[52]

In his opening speech the chairman of the conference, the Swedish party leader Hjalmar Branting who was a keen anti-communist, had already remarked that among the socialists there were schools of thought which wished to establish 'the rule of a terrorist minority' under the slogan of the dictatorship of the proletariat.[53] The next speaker Albert Thomas also declared that 'the future of socialism in the world is threatened with the greatest danger by the new trends called bolshevik'.[54] Thomas therefore wanted the conference to discuss in detail the function of democracy in the establishment of socialism. His fellow party member Mistral immediately opposed this. The socialists should not pronounce judgements on 'the methods, the procedures which certain revolutionary elements believed they had to use'.[55] This view was supported by the Dutchman Troelstra, the Frenchman Longuet and the Austrian Friedrich Adler.[56]

But these were only warning shots. The real discussion about this problem of democracy and dictatorship took place in a specially appointed committee, which met for a whole night to no avail. Adler even threatened to leave the conference with thirty-three delegates if it condemned the Bolsheviks. The deliberations were then carried on by a subcommittee which, after many hours of meeting, produced no less than five different draft resolutions. Thereupon it was left to Branting to work out a compromise.[57] In the text which he eventually presented to the plenary meeting he warned again against 'a dictatorship which is itself supported by only a part of the proletariat. That can only lead to the decimation of the proletariat in a civil war. The end would be the dictatorship of reaction.' The Russian delegates' proposal to send a commission of inquiry to Russia was adopted. In anticipation of its results the question of Bolshevism was placed on the agenda of the next congress.[58]

Branting admitted frankly that he had not succeeded in reconciling the existing differences of opinion with this proposal. He found, however, that the question was too important 'to be treated with soothing statements. We need a frank clear statement, if we are still democrats, if we are against all oppression, whether by majorities or minorities.'[59] Branting's opinion was shared by many. They regarded, as Otto Wels expressed it, 'parliamentarianism as the immutable foundation of all socialist policy'. Ramsay MacDonald, however, thought that this idea had formerly caught on generally, but he doubted if this was still the case. A condemnation of Bolshevism was premature. 'Bolshevism in theory is still working itself out. Who among us can define Bolshevism?' The Bolsheviks themselves would also have to be heard for that. For a discussion about this matter the Italians and the Swiss ought not to be absent.[60]

Frenchmen like Loriot, Mistral and Longuet agreed with MacDonald. Branting's categorical statements about democracy ought to be removed from the draft resolution. They were 'of the kind to put a weapon into the hands of Clemenceau and Lloyd George to fight the government of the Soviets'.[61] This heated debate, which lasted until Sunday evening, was now adjourned until the following day. The Russian delegates had indeed made a contribution to the committee meetings, but had not yet had a chance to say anything about this matter, which was of vital importance to them, at the plenary meetings. When the conference was reopened on Monday 10 February, however, a number of participants had already gone home. Loriot, who could not be stopped and who spoke first, concentrated especially on the Russians and attacked them fiercely. The socialist commission of enquiry ought in his opinion to investigate whether the dictatorship in Soviet Russia was not a necessary reaction to the circumstances which were created by 'the counter-revolutionary propaganda of certain socialists'.[62]

After this French outburst of enthusiasm for the October revolution, Akselrod took the floor. He was 'greeted with approbation'. However, he did not let this unsettle him and reproached his audience for hushing up the business on hand by means of an improvised discussion about the fundamental problem of democracy and dictatorship. The Russians at the conference did not ask for an immediate condemnation of Bolshevism. They simply demanded an objective investigation. But they refused to abdicate their right to make their appearance before the forum of the International as the prosecutors of Bolshevism. But on this point Akselrod had little new to offer the meeting. He once more pointed out the 'deeply tragic, lamentable, humiliating and disastrous fact' for social democracy that it was not the socialist but the bourgeois press which had, generally speaking, reported on Russian events in a trustworthy manner. Then he read out several documents from Russia in which the oppression of socialists and workers was denounced. These had already been published, however, in 1918 in *Stimmen aus Russland*, a paper which Akselrod co-edited. It was not friendly, but understandable that the Viennese *Arbeiterzeitung* in its account of the conference wrote that Akselrod had explained his plan for socialist intervention in the Russian revolution 'between impetuous, rather well-known complaints against the Bolsheviks'.[63]

After Akselrod Friedrich Adler spoke. He was the hero of the conference. In October 1916 Adler, by way of a desperate protest against the war, had shot the Austrian prime minister. He was afterwards condemned to death, then pardoned, and had remained in prison until the end of 1918. After his release he filled a leading role in the Austrian revolution. Adler was to be a key figure in the international movement in the years to come and to make special efforts for the restoration of unity. This was also his principal argument against the 'denouncement' of Bolshevism, even in Branting's disguised form, and he therefore also dissociated himself from the previous speaker. 'Comrade Akselrod has said that it would break his heart – I am a very old friend of Comrade Akselrod and do not doubt a single word – if he did not dare to enlarge on what was on his mind to the International here. Comrade Akselrod has however produced nothing for us except to read out about Russian events from a newspaper which is some months old and which we, who are passionately interested, have also read.'[64]

Adler expressly wished to keep the door of the International open for the Bolsheviks. He pointed out that before October 1917 the Mensheviks and the socialist revolutionaries had imprisoned the Bolsheviks. 'Yes Comrade Akselrod, you said it was fine when the others were imprisoned, and only bad when it is oneself that is imprisoned.' To Akselrod's interruption that it then concerned only a few people and now involved thousands, Adler answered: 'Comrade Akselrod confirms that this is not only a question of quality, but one of quantity.' This was not crass cynicism on Adler's part. In October 1918 he had approached Lenin with the request that the socialists be freed from Russian prisons. 'He was not capable of writing anything more sensible to us' had been Lenin's reaction. But in the same speech in which he made this remark, the Soviet leader announced that the opposition of 'petty-bourgeois democracy', that is of the PSR and the RSDRP, would again be legalised. The Mensheviks and the socialist revolutionaries were indeed readmitted to the Soviets a short time afterwards. The repression was once more resumed in 1919, and it was not clear to what extent the Bolsheviks were sensitive to foreign socialist pressure. But the conviction that an absolute condemnation of Bolshevism would rob Western socialism of every opportunity of exerting a moderating influence on the dictatorship in Russia may have played a part in Adler's reaction to Akselrod.[65]

Afterwards Adler submitted a resolution which was countersigned by the French majority and the Norwegians and which was intended to counterbalance Branting's statement about democracy. In this document the socialists, who during the war had disregarded every appeal for proletarian unity, were reproached for now being in such a hurry to condemn Bolshevism. The socialist movement could not rely on reports in the press to make a fair judgement of the situation in that country without becoming victims of 'the arts of calumny'. Nor could they base their case on the reports of their Russian comrades present at the conference 'who represent only a minority of the Russian proletariat. Without calling their good faith into question, we must insist that the International holds fast to the old principle, that both sides must be heard before a decision is made.'[66] After Adler a whole succession of speakers took the floor, including Rubanovich, Kautsky, Bernstein, Gavronsky, Binshtok, Troelstra and Henderson, without anything much new being added to the very lively, but not particularly enlightening, discussion. They did not reach a vote about either of the resolutions: for the sake of unity the taking of decisions was renounced, though a sort of opinion poll was held. From this it transpired that a majority, namely eighteen delegations, including the German, the British, the Swedish, the Danish and the Russian, would support Branting's proposal. Only the Spanish, Dutch and Irish delegates were for Adler, while the French and Austrian delegates remained divided on this matter.

Nevertheless, there was little reason for satisfaction among the Russians. The preference which most of the socialists had shown for democracy did not yet mean that they were also prepared to support the struggle of the democratic socialists in Russia through thick and thin. They had mostly declared their adherence to Branting's resolution out of some, or even great concern about the continued existence of a democratic outlook in the West. Russia was of secondary importance for them. It was misleading that the USPD delegates, including Kautsky and Eisner, had been in favour of Branting's resolution, for their point of view did not reflect the prevailing opinion in their party. Even less was it clearly evident from the opinion poll that the French and Austrian opponents of Branting were speaking on behalf of the majority of their party. Within the Independent Labour Party, represented by MacDonald, there was more enthusiasm for Soviet Russia and less objection to the Bolshevik dictatorship than was evident in Berne. The opposite was only true for the Dutch delegation, consisting of Troelstra and Wibaut, who had spoken out in favour of Adler. Their opinion was certainly not representative of the SDAP as a whole.[67]

It was depressing for Russians like Akselrod or Gavronsky, who had both been very actively involved in Zimmerwald, that the socialists against whom they had struggled then and to whom they still had many objections now, were at present on their side, whereas their sympathisers from the war years, such as Adler, had turned against them. Nevertheless, it was not the intention of most of the centrists in Berne, apart from a proto-communist like Loriot, to challenge the democratic socialists in Russia. In their attitude they were fundamentally actuated by the same motives as were Branting's associates. They, too, wanted the radicalisation of their own parties, if not contained, at any rate steered in the right direction. They thought, however, that criticism of Bolshevism would be counterproductive. But what the leaders of the centre, such as Adler and Longuet, did not realise at this moment was that because their attitude at the time was little based on principle, they would later be unable to call a halt to the enthusiasm for communism within their own group, even when this actually began to assume dangerous proportions and threatened the survival of their party.

In the period following the Berne conference the cause of the Russian socialists did not prosper. The efforts of the socialists for a balanced peace in Europe led to nothing. Socialist delegates were indeed received politely by Lloyd George and Clemenceau, but had no detectable influence on the negotiations or the text of the treaty. This development was closely watched especially by the moderate socialists. A failed peace or a German refusal to sign the treaty might lead to the Bolshevisation of Europe. In Great Britain widespread strikes had broken out. Glasgow, the centre of the turmoil, gave the appearance of a town in civil war; public order could only be maintained there with the help of heavily armed soldiers. Henderson feared that the Labour Party might 'split into a constitutional and a machine-gun-wielding wing'.[68] In Paris, in May, bloody riots broke out after massive demonstrations which the CGT and SFIO had incited. A month later 200,000 metal workers came out on strike.[69] The moderate socialists could not give up in despair, because their competitors were making formidable efforts. In March the founding congress of the Third or Communist International was held in Moscow. This was chiefly the work of the Russian communist party supported by a handful of foreign sympathisers living in Russia. But the Italian party, which had a great number of adherents at its disposal – the PSI had become the largest party in the Italian parliament in 1919 – immediately joined the Comintern. The Swiss rapidly followed the Italians. A delegation from the re-established Second International in Berne under the leadership of MacDonald and Longuet tried in vain to reach agreement with the Italians. The split in the International had become a fact.

Naturally Western socialists like MacDonald did not at once give up hope that the rift could be patched up again. The Italians had let it be known that they had left the Second International because it had failed in wartime. They did not agree with everything that took place in Soviet Russia. But this state was threatened by the combined forces of European capitalism on account of its proletarian character. International socialism was therefore obliged to assist the Russians. The Italians' point of view was shared by the Swiss and the Norwegians and sympathy for it existed in practically every socialist party. MacDonald was convinced that socialist action for the benefit of Soviet Russia ought to have absolute priority in the whole of Europe if they wanted to prevent the collapse of the Second International. 'A mere anti-Bolshevist attitude is [likely] to be fatal, because that would have no response from the rank and file who do not concern themselves with niceties of method but who value something being done.' Troelstra also added to this opinion: 'The Russian and German revolutions will find their own way to practical socialism and we ought not to barricade this way by making of the Second International an anti-Bolshevist organ.'[70]

The Italians' wish to hold a short general strike in the whole of Europe, in demonstration against Western intervention in Russia, was not, however, fulfilled. But the Italians did go on strike and in France, England and Germany more modest actions took place and these were to be repeated in a more forceful manner in the course of 1919 and 1920. The climate of opinion for a critical approach to the Soviet dictatorship within the European workers' movement deteriorated unremittingly.

Moreover the implementation of the decision of the Berne conference to send a commission of inquiry to Russia encountered considerable difficulties. The Permanent Commission, which had been set up as an interim administration for the Second International, appointed, during its first meeting on 10 February, a delegation from eight countries, namely Tomaso (Argentina), Kautsky or Hilferding (Germany), Adler or Bauer (Austria), Longuet or Faure (France), MacDonald (England), an as yet unknown Italian, and the British Roden Buxton as secretary. Both Lloyd George and Clemenceau were informed of the decision of the International to pay a visit to Russia. But the Allied Council decided not to issue exit visas to the French, British and Italian members of the delegation, and all attempts to rescind this decision failed. The administration of the Second International decided to form a delegation of socialists from the 'neutral countries', that is to say from Holland, Sweden, Denmark and Finland, unless the passport problem was solved.[71]

Binshtok, the Menshevik, who attended the meeting of the Permanent Commission of the International in Amsterdam in April, suggested to Huysmans that the French and British delegates should empower the 'neutral' socialists to act in their names. The Germans and Austrians would, in his opinion, form part of the delegation in any case. 'Huysmans showed himself to be highly indignant [*podnyal skandal*]' and declared that he would be the first to protest against such a 'biased' structure of the delegation.[72] The Western socialists' curious idea of a visit by the International to Soviet Russia was also expressed at a number of meetings between Binshtok and future delegation members. In The Hague he had a long talk with Troelstra. 'He agreed with me about everything and even said that he had already thought of it all before. But afterwards he suddenly asked whether the Bolsheviks could not, by means of an agreement, be prevailed upon to relinquish their power. Nor could he fully understand what political significance the commission of inquiry could have, and was doubtful about the possibility of being able to do anything in practice.'[73]

MacDonald's attitude was simply shocking: 'I gave him a complete explanation of our ideas about the situation in Russia, intervention, the role of the Bolsheviks in Europe, the provision of food for Russia, and so forth. I even pointed to Dan's arrest.

But that evidently made little impression on him. He said that the Bolsheviks would have no success with the English workers. It was impossible in his view to interest the English workers in Russian events.' MacDonald told Binshtok: 'The English workers would be prepared to destroy the whole of England and the whole world besides for the sake of sixpence more per hour, but they would not lift a finger for anything which did not directly concern their stomachs.' He added that 'there are no powers in Russia apart from Lenin and Kolchak, and one must choose between them'.[74] This proved how much the intensification of the civil war had influenced the attitudes of Western socialists. Binshtok noticed this in Sweden also. The socialists there, he wrote to Akselrod, are 'hypnotised by Kolchak's victory; they attribute a tremendous importance to it and are awaiting the course of events'. Binshtok's attempts to persuade the Swedish party to take the initiative of a journey to Russia together with the socialist parties from other 'neutral' countries, were likewise unsuccessful.[75]

In August the Russian question came up once more at the meeting of the Second International in Lucerne. Once more attempts were made to reconcile the differences of opinion by means of a joint protest against the intervention in Russia. But they got no further in the democracy–dictatorship question and these passionate debates yielded little new. The importance of a socialist delegation to Russia was still felt by all those present in Lucerne. But the views of Western socialists about this no longer had much to do with Akselrod's original idea about moral intervention in the Russian revolution. Henderson, the chairman of the conference, wanted to 'get in touch with all classes of socialists and with the Revolutionary Government generally, and endeavour to promote better relations . . .'[76] The representatives of the French majority spoke in more vehement terms. 'If we are forced to choose between Noske and Lenin, then we are for Lenin!', Frossard exclaimed.[77] This was also the opinion of the USPD, which had only let Crispien and Hilferding go to Lucerne to put forward a 'revolutionary point of view' there. Kautsky, who had been severely attacked within the party for his statements in Berne, could not be used for this purpose. Crispien announced that 'the dictatorship of the proletariat is necessary in all capitalist states'.[78] Only the Belgians, who had meanwhile joined the Second International, gave, from the mouth of de Brouckère, an impassioned apologia for democracy.[79]

There were six Russians present in Lucerne, including Akselrod and Shchupak. They also had the support of a Georgian delegation to which Tsereteli belonged. Tsereteli, whose career as a Russian statesman had been cut short by the October revolution, was the representative of socialist Georgia at the Paris peace talks in 1919. Georgia, which had always been a bulwark of Menshevism, had declared its independence in May 1918. The social democrats had gained an overwhelming majority at general elections in that country. The Georgian Bolsheviks, to which Stalin had originally belonged, were merely a socialist splinter group. Tsereteli had little success in Paris. In the international socialist milieu, where, as the most prominent Russian leader of the February revolution, he enjoyed great notoriety, he gained more support. In Lucerne Georgian independence was expressly recognised. In the years to come the permanently threatened existence of Georgia, which was overrun by the Red Army in 1921, alongside the question of the socialist political prisoners in Russia, was an almost continual subject for discussion at socialist international meetings.[80]

Tsereteli shared Akselrod's opinion about the October revolution. Thus the debate which had taken place between Akselrod and Adler in Berne could be repeated in Lucerne between Tsereteli and Hilferding. According to *Vorwärts* 'the still passionate Akselrod had burst into tears, when Tsereteli – almost without gestures, merely by changing emphasis but with glowing eyes – spoke about the dreadful misery of the "*raskii* [*sic*!] *proletariat*" under the bloodthirsty Soviet dictatorship'.[81] In fact Tsereteli's speech was short and businesslike, but it contained nothing new. He only explained why, in his view, the sympathy of the socialist West for communist Russia was based on a misconception. Hilferding on the other hand regarded this enthusiasm as perfectly legitimate. This did not mean that the Bolsheviks' actions should also be imitated in the West, for it was certainly possible to criticise their methods. But there were no grounds for condemning Bolshevism. Finally the conference gave Tsereteli and Hilferding the task of working out a compromise. The results were two resolutions which were both accepted, of which the first, a protest against intervention, was the more important.

In the second resolution, in which Tsereteli's hand can be recognised, the conference renewed the decision to send a delegation to Russia for an investigation 'into the differences between the socialist parties, the source of the oppression, and also into the reasons for the conflicts between the Soviet government and the governments of the bordering countries'. The Russian government was invited to lend its assistance to the work of the delegation, which promised to behave 'in an impartial and friendly manner towards the Russian working class'. This text seemed to go some way towards meeting the wishes of the Russian socialists. Nevertheless, the chosen wording must have been a setback for them, in comparison with the original proposal which had been tabled. In that the Soviet government had been asked if it would guarantee the commission of inquiry complete freedom of investigation, and if it was prepared to restore the political rights of the other socialist parties after the end of the civil war. There was, however, a certain amount of resistance to this wording.[82] Above all the debates in Lucerne showed the divisions of European socialism.[83] It is thus hardly surprising that the plan to send a delegation to Russia was never implemented. The Second International soon proved to be no longer capable of putting together a delegation representative of European socialism, for it had failed to convince a number of important socialist parties of its right to exist. According to Huysmans, the secretary of the Second International, it was agreed in Lucerne that if the necessary passports were not successfully obtained, the Swedes would go to Russia on behalf of the International. But this, too, came to nothing.[84]

After Lucerne the Russian socialists living in the West could only observe bewildered how the centrist section of the European workers' movement was becoming more radical. 'The whole struggle is directed towards the defence of Bolshevik barbarity', wrote the appalled Tsereteli to Akselrod about the French socialists' election campaign in 1919.[85] Akselrod became convinced that at that moment they ought to take 'the real, actual impossibility of making an inroad into the social consciousness' of the French socialists into account. At the end of 1919 he even feared that a French edition of his collected speeches, letters and articles would be counterproductive.[86] In Germany the situation was not much better for them. The Menshevik Alexander Stein was apparently in a better position there to influence opinion within the USPD. He was one of the editors of *Freiheit*, the most distinguished party paper. Although leaders like Crispien and Hilferding had spoken without equivocation in Lucerne, they nevertheless had very little desire for the Bolshevisation of the USPD. But Binshtok, after a long talk with Hilferding, formed the impression that Hilferding could only maintain his position as general editor of the party paper *Freiheit* by publicly omitting any criticism of the Bolshevik regime. Another leader of the USPD, Hugo Haase, had not wanted to meet Binshtok 'for fear of learning the horrible truth'. Nevertheless, Stein was becoming increasingly important for the right wing of the Independents as adviser on Russian affairs. His series of articles about the problem of the International was even printed as a separate pamphlet in 1919. According to Stein it was not a matter of a choice between the Second and the Third Internationals. Neither Berne nor Moscow could be seen as actual representatives of the international proletariat. The USPD ought, in his view, to apply its influence to arriving at the formation of a real International. This ought to be based on a kind of ideological synthesis of the best elements from the Second and Third Internationals. For Akselrod and Tsereteli, who remained faithful to the Second International, Stein's point of view was unacceptable, but it approached the outlook of most of the Mensheviks in Russia with whom Stein was in contact.[87]

Stein, however, was absolutely incapable of offering any counterbalance to the attraction which communist Russia was exerting on most of the supporters of the USPD, whose membership was growing at enormous speed during this period and which threatened to outstrip the SPD. At its conference in Leipzig in November 1919, the party decided to leave the Second International and to seek a rapprochement with the parties which had done the same. In February 1920 the French socialist party definitively broke off relations with Berne. In April the Independent Labour Party and the Austrian party followed with the same decision. The socialist centre had no joint plan of action, no concerted and clear point of view about Russian communism, but seemed to be irresistibly attracted by Moscow.

Among the intellectuals and workers who had flocked into membership of the centrist parties the longing for fundamental changes was intense. To a large extent they belonged to a group of people who, for the first time in history, imagined themselves to be a separate generation, a generation which was created and marked by the war and had a great preference for rapid, radical solutions to pressing topical issues.[88] But the year 1919 had not brought the social revolution within reach in the West. Both in the leadership and in the grass-roots support of the centrist movement there was considerable uncertainty about the future. Western parliamentary democracy was regarded as too sluggish an instrument for social reforms. On the other hand, only a few people believed that any results could be achieved in the present situation in the West, by the dictatorial and violent methods of the Russians. Above all the centrists realised that they had far too little power and strength at their disposal to be able to disrupt capitalistic society. Thus they needed help. The centrists did not expect much from the socialists, who were in a majority in the Second International and who both during and after the war had seemed to be striving for a reconciliation between capital and labour. Moscow was the only alternative which presented itself. Their enthusiasm for Russian communism was first of all a consequence of their own impotence. Zeal for the great, mysterious experiment in that far-off country was actually the only way the centrists could show their revolutionary convictions. Especially when the Bolsheviks seemed to be winning the civil war and there still had not been a single revolutionary breakthrough in the West, the tendency to conceal their own failures in this way became irresistible. They therefore cut themselves off more and more from information which interfered with the idealisation of the Soviet regime. They let themselves be guided in the main by their own frustrations and the old traditions of socialist imagery about Russia.

All the well-known Russian socialists in the West like Kerensky, Rubanovich, Tsereteli and Akselrod had joined the right wing of European socialism. They had no authority over the centre. This meant that the Bolsheviks, virtually undisturbed, could continue their attempts to capture this bastion which was extremely important for their strategy. After all, the centre afforded access to large revolutionarily inclined masses of workers in Europe. There was little to be done against this, unless socialist opposition in Russia was itself capable of creating obstacles, for the Italians, the British, the Germans and the French were to size up the situation in Moscow in 1920. Akselrod's proposal to the Western socialists that they should themselves investigate Russia was thus eventually carried out. And although this happened in a way which was especially distressing for Akselrod, it nevertheless offered the Russian socialists new, though modest, opportunities for influencing the formation of opinion in socialist Europe.

# 7

# SOCIAL DEMOCRACY IN SOVIET RUSSIA AND THE CONTINUATION OF THE DEBATE ABOUT COMMUNISM IN 1919–1920

The Bolshevik coup and the establishment of a communist dictatorship placed all the remaining political groups in Russia in a predicament which was much more awkward and hopeless than they initially realised. Even the Bolsheviks themselves were far from sure that they could maintain their position. This would, in their view, to a large extent depend on the course of the war in the West. Only a European social revolution could save Russia. History was, however, to turn out differently from what any of the parties involved foresaw. The ease with which power could be taken over in the capital, and successively also in large sections of the Russian empire, was at once amazingly favourable for the Bolsheviks and ominous for their opponents. There was little real enthusiasm for the coup in the country. The railway workers' union, in which the Mensheviks and the socialist revolutionaries were strongly represented, and which controlled the vital communication network of railways and telegraph lines, threatened a general strike if discussions about the formation of a socialist government were not immediately begun. Lenin and Trotsky had to give way to this pressure, but they broke off the negotiations as soon as it became clear that they need no longer fear any significant military opposition in the country.

Nevertheless, Lenin could only face his party's substantial opposition to the resolution to establish a dictatorship when the Germans agreed to an armistice in November. The new regime, now that it could rely on the passive support of the soldiers, could make a beginning on the consolidation of its power. A number of prominent Bolsheviks who had resigned important posts in protest against the breaking-off of the coalition negotiations and other measures such as the muzzling of the liberal and socialist press, now decided once more to participate in the administration of the party and the country. The railway union was dealt with in a manner which was soon to become classical. The union was disbanded with violence and the Bolsheviks set up a new one in which there was no place for members of other parties. The same thing happened wherever possible with other recalcitrant trade unions or Soviets. For this oppression the government had created a special instrument, the Cheka, the communist security police led by the Polish communist Dzerzhinsky, who was totally dedicated to Lenin. In spite of all this the position of the new regime remained unstable. It had no control whatsoever over large parts of the country and many sections of Russian society. Moreover revulsion in its own circles for far too repressive measures was still considerable.

The elections for the Constituent Assembly could in any case proceed undisturbed. The Bolsheviks obtained a quarter of the votes, while the socialist revolutionaries gained an absolute majority. That was unacceptable to Lenin and his political associates. After meeting for one day, in January 1918, this parliament, the first and last to be elected in Russia in a Western democratic manner with universal suffrage, was prorogued. With this the era of 'bourgeois' democracy was over. There was no question of forceful resistance to the disbanding of the Constituent Assembly. The Bolsheviks were able to profit enormously from the hesitant attitude of their socialist opponents.[1] The socialists all began to realise that the Bolsheviks might well remain in the saddle for longer than they had initially thought.[2]

After October 1917 the Mensheviks had stuck firmly to the principle that armed rebellions against the regime were absolutely forbidden. The social democrats, as they now called themselves after the Bolsheviks had chosen the name communists, were in a disastrous situation. At the elections for the Constituent Assembly, the RSDRP had gained a resounding victory only in Georgia. In the rest of the country, especially among the workers in the large cities, the Mensheviks had virtually lost all their adherents. The RSDRP, which had been one of the most influential political trends in Russia at the beginning of 1917, was one year later reduced to a political splinter group. Nevertheless, the Mensheviks were more inclined to be pessimistic about the future of their country in 1918 than about that of their party. Living conditions worsened rapidly. Dissatisfaction with the communist administration increased daily. As early as the spring of 1918, the Bolsheviks' adherents seemed to be melting away. The Mensheviks noticed that the workers were coming back to them. Even before the World War had ended in a completely different manner from that feared by very many Russians, including those within the communist party, the civil war broke out, and it was not until the course of 1921 that the situation in Russia became somewhat more orderly. In 1918 Menshevik hopes for a political 'comeback' were not wholly unjustified given the appalling situation in the country, the disagreements in the Bolshevik camp and the tense relationship between the communists and a considerable section of the Russian workers.

The Mensheviks hoped that the new rulers, whom they knew better than anyone, would increasingly realise that the way to utopia could not be paved with terrorism. They had acquaintances and relatives who were members of the other party and were thus well informed about the serious differences of opinion which constantly threatened to split the communist party. It was by no means certain beforehand that these disputes were merely playing into the hands of a further strengthening of communist dictatorship. The Mensheviks managed to persuade themselves that these undercurrents and counterflows within Bolshevism would secure more control on developments in the near future, and attuned their policies to this. Of course the Mensheviks had not suddenly forgotten that the principal characteristics of Lenin's Bolshevism had been formed through fanaticism and boundless trust in violence. In the opinion of Akselrod and Potresov Bolshevism ought to be regarded and treated as counter-revolutionary despotism. But Martov, who in this was followed by a majority of his fellow party members, believed that this pessimistic view would condemn the Mensheviks to complete political passivity. For if Bolshevism was indeed something which had to be eliminated with violence, then neither the Mensheviks nor the other socialist parties could carry out this task. They would in that case have to unite with foreign powers, which in Martov's view were imperialistic, or with internal groups which were more or less reactionary. If the Russian social democrats wanted to continue to regard themselves as good revolutionaries and socialists then they could not steer this course.

Nor did they need to, for according to Martov, it was nearer the truth to regard the Bolsheviks not as counter-revolutionaries but as comrades who had gone astray. Despite everything they were still Marxists who – though in a barbaric manner – were trying to achieve a socialist utopia. For this reason they still enjoyed the support and sympathy of a section of the Russian proletariat. The takeover of power by the Bolsheviks had been possible because of the mistakes the Mensheviks had made in 1917. The communist dictatorship was an abnormal and unhealthy phase in the Russian revolution which should be rapidly brought to an end, but not by a fratricidal war or a partial or complete restoration of the *ancien régime*. Both in the Russian proletariat and in the communist party there were forces present which, though now weak, could soon, helped by the pressure of circumstances, bring about a change of policy. Even Lenin was known not only for his autocratic tendencies, but also for his tactical versatility. It would not be the first time that this man, if driven by necessity, would make a political swing of 180 degrees.

The Russian social democrats could themselves make a significant contribution to the desired developments. They could try to win back its supporters among the Russian proletariat. The RSDRP could also utilise the remaining constitutional possibilities of the Soviet system. The Mensheviks could participate in the Soviets and make efforts for free elections and the restoration of their power. If the workers and ruling Bolsheviks were to see the need for it then a modicum of democracy could exist again in Russia. This could afterwards serve as a starting-point for further normalisation of political relationships. By presenting themselves as a sort of legal socialist opposition the Mensheviks could also command the respect of the Western socialists. This was of the utmost importance since the Bolsheviks, like the Mensheviks, were convinced that Western socialism would decide about the future of Soviet Russia. The Mensheviks would have to ensure that the healing process of the sickly revolution was hastened under the salutary influence of the European labour movement so that Russia could free herself from the grip of the present Asiatic barbarism as soon as possible.[3]

In evaluating Menshevik views about Bolshevism, these should be seen in the light of the development which Western ideas about Russian communism and the Soviet Union underwent after 1917. Akselrod's and Martov's points of view then prove to have been the prototypes of two different approaches which to a large extent determined the Western attitude towards the Soviet Union. Martov's ideas and plans proved to be impossible to implement. The history of Soviet Russia in the twenties and thirties seemed to conform to Akselrod's diagnosis of the sickly and immoral characteristics of Russian communism. Historians and political scientists later trod in the footsteps of Akselrod and his kindred spirits and described the origin of Stalinist totalitarianism as a gradual, but in itself completely logical and inevitable, process. The mechanism of the communist dictatorship was perfected by Stalin. But it was set in motion by the October revolution. The ideological mainspring behind it was formed by Lenin's ideas which he had already partly set down in his pamphlet *What Is To Be Done* in 1902. The emergence and downfall of Hitler's Germany moreover prompted these scholars to the thought that a totalitarian state, once it has reached full maturity can no longer be changed from within, since the whole populace has been terrorised. Stalin's terrorist machinery, too, was a sort of infernal *perpetuum mobile* that could only be reduced to a standstill by an external cause, namely superior military power from abroad.

This appeared to be a premature conclusion. Stalin's successors have themselves partly dismantled the machinery of Stalinist power. The question whether the Soviet Union after 1953 was still a totalitarian state was no longer answered with a positive 'yes' by most Western experts. For the Western approach to Russian communism, the 'de-Stalinisation' under Khrushchev the partial 're-Stalinisation' under Brezhnev had significant consequences. The history of Soviet Russia could no longer be seen as an inevitable, linear process. There arose great interest in the 'might have beens' and the fluctuations in modern Russian history. At the same time more and more prominent politicians became convinced that a completely unfavourable attitude towards the Soviet Union reduced the possibilities of the West exerting a moderating influence on the leadership of that state. The development that took place after Gorbachev's coming to power confirmed the opinion of a number of scholars that communism would be able to launch fundamental reforms. The years 1989–91 finally vindicated Martov's idea that the communists could be forced by circumstances to a voluntary liquidation of their dictatorship and a resignation from power.

Because of this similarity with Western conceptions of the communist system, especially in the period after Stalin, we cannot brush aside the ideas of Martov and his associates as totally naive. The Menshevik policy was without doubt the result of wishful thinking. But at the same time it reflected the potential opportunities inherent in the Russian society of the time and in the development of the communist regime. There is, however, another reason why it is interesting to study the fate of Russian social democracy after 1917. There is also another analogy between the period which followed the October revolution and the Brezhnev era. The game of cat and mouse between the Bolshevik dictatorship and the Menshevik opposition can well be compared with the conflict which occurred between the regime and the dissidents' movement in the sixties and seventies. In both periods the citizens of the Soviet state were uncertain whether the minimal political freedom which prevailed could have been liberalised. Like the later dissidents, the Mensheviks limited themselves to legal forms of protest against political oppression and sought support for their endeavour in the West. In both cases the unequal struggle was to the definite advantage of the government. Both the dissidents and the Mensheviks had to discontinue their activities. If they were not prepared to do this, they were forced to emigrate, were exiled within Russia, or ended up in a camp or a prison.

But neither development, however disastrous it eventually was for the opponents, progressed smoothly, for both were full of curious twists and turns. Because of the actions of the dissident movement we have come to learn a great deal about the caprices and ambivalence of the post-Stalinist dictatorship. Something of the kind is also true for the actions of the Mensheviks half a century earlier. The aversion to Lenin's dictatorship was much more general and more varied in nature than the protests at the time of Khrushchev and Brezhnev. There were more different groups of the population involved, and the opposition ranged from the passive to the extremely violent. In fact, the Mensheviks then formed the only group which sounded out with extreme care the boundaries within which opposition was possible without immediately provoking terrorist counter-action from the government. In this way the vicissitudes of Russian social democracy afford us a special measure of insight into the way in which the communist dictatorship developed in its early stages.

In 1918 the social democrats were able to make use of the dissatisfaction of the workers, and began to call meetings in the factories of Petrograd and later also in Moscow and other centres of industry in Central Russia. The Bolsheviks did not immediately take action against them. Menshevik newspapers were frequently banned, but they could mostly reappear shortly afterwards under another name, while the content remained just as critical. Those trade unions which were still under social democratic influence were likewise for the time being left undisturbed by the government. At the First All-Russian Trade Union Congress, in January 1918, Martov acted as spokesman for the opposition.[4] More important was the development which took place in the provinces. In numerous towns the Mensheviks and the socialist revolutionaries recaptured the majority in the Soviets which they had lost to the Bolsheviks in the autumn of 1917. Without exception the local communists responded to this challenge with violence. Soviets were disbanded with the help of the Cheka. The Menshevik press was banned, the offices of the socialist parties were closed down. The authorities tried to suffocate the workers' protest against these measures by proclaiming a state of siege, firing at street demonstrations and rounding up workers and socialists. A few months after the declaration of the Soviet state, it was already clear that the communists could only maintain their position by terrorism. Free elections for the Soviets would in many cases have yielded a majority for the other socialist parties. Despite all the draconian measures in 1918, there was no end to the violent workers' disturbances in the provinces which mainly found expression in wild-cat strikes.[5]

One national forum that the Mensheviks could use for their political activity was the Central Executive Committee of the

All-Russian Soviet Congress. This filled a sort of parliamentary function and the socialists could let their voices be heard there. For, while they had to suffer from the arbitrariness and misuse of power of the communists in the provinces, in the first half of 1918 there was an almost Western touch of tolerance of the opposition at this highest level. The most prominent social democratic spokesmen, Martov, Dan and also Abramovich, a former Bundist who was to become one of the most important Menshevik leaders during this period, made fierce attacks on government policy. But the chairman of the Central Executive Committee, Sverdlov, who was regarded as Lenin's right-hand man at this time, gave them every opportunity. The opposition was not only tolerated to a certain extent, but also taken extremely seriously. As it had done before and during 1917, the Bolshevik press devoted a great deal of attention to the refutation of the Mensheviks' practical arguments and their ideological points of view.[6]

This situation, which in comparison with what occurred later could almost be called idyllic, continued to exist in the first half of 1918. The reversal which took place afterwards had a number of causes. The movement of workers' representatives began to take on a role which was more prominent, and thus more threatening to the regime. The Left S.R.s – a group that had split off from the Party of Socialist Revolutionaries and until the conclusion of the separate peace with Germany had taken part in the Soviet government – also gained more and more support in the Soviets. The Bolsheviks thus had to bear in mind the possibility that they might suffer a defeat in June 1918 at the elections for the Fifth Soviet Congress. Moreover the civil war had broken out in the meantime. An emergency situation had now come into existence for the communists in which there was no room, in their opinion, for constitutional frills such as a socialist opposition. On 14 June 1918, on the eve of the elections for the Fifth Soviet Congress, the Mensheviks and the socialist revolutionaries were banned from the Soviets and outlawed. All their publications were prohibited. At the beginning of the summer of 1918 the workers' representatives movement had expanded enormously and it commanded tens of thousands of workers. On 20 July the building in Moscow where a conference was being held by this movement was surrounded by troops.

The participants were arrested and imprisoned for a short time. The Mensheviks would never again be offered the chance of capturing 'the masses'. The 'Red Terror' which was now being officially propagated was not the only obstacle to this. During the civil war, conditions in the towns had become so bad that most of the workers had to seek refuge in the countryside because of lack of food. The Russian proletariat virtually disappeared. Consequently the social base on which the Soviet dictatorship was nominally founded, crumbled away. But the Mensheviks were likewise robbed of the chief basis of their opposition to the regime.[7]

The Bolshevik government justified its oppression of the socialists with the allegation that they were counter-revolutionaries who had associated themselves with the reactionaries in a civil war against communism. There was little truth in this accusation. By no means all the groups which rebelled against the regime could justifiably be called counter-revolutionary or reactionary. The PSR had sincerely tried to unite all the democratic forces into one, armed, anti-Bolshevik movement. Given the outcome of the elections for the Constituent Assembly, this was a far from illegitimate struggle by the party. Nevertheless, it failed completely, chiefly because of the dictatorial behaviour of Admiral Kolchak. Afterwards in fact the socialist revolutionaries gave up armed resistance.[8] Among the Mensheviks, too, there were votes in favour of taking up arms. But the majority in the party considered such activities a disastrous matter in present circumstances, and in this, given the failure of the PSR's policy, they were not entirely wrong. Party members who, despite this party decision, nevertheless participated in rebellions against the regime were expelled without mercy. The civil war had disastrous results for the RSDRP as an organisation. It was no longer possible to maintain regular contact with the local departments; the party funds were used up; many members left the party because they regarded the continuation of social democratic opposition to be totally pointless. The Red Terror made little distinction between the widely divergent opponents of the regime.[9] Social democrats were also shot and many ended up in prison for longer or shorter periods. The Menshevik leaders remained out of range for the time being. Martov was once arrested in 1918, but only detained for a couple of days.

The Mensheviks' success among the workers in early 1918 should not be overestimated. The modest achievements of the social democrats were to a considerable extent the result of the hesitations and internal disagreements of the ruling party.[10] The socialist opposition also maintained a certain degree of latitude because the Bolsheviks realised that not only would violations of the Soviet constitution provoke resistance within their own party and prompt their adherents among the peasants and workers to armed revolt, but also that measures of this kind would make a bad impression abroad. Six months later, at the end of 1918, with the civil war in full swing, the importance of Western proletarian support for the survival of the Soviet state was evident to all the socialists and communists in Russia. The revolution in Germany and Austria in November was greeted with jubilation by both groups and expectations about the speedy socialist revolution in the West were very sanguine. We must therefore assume that there is a direct connection between these events and the decision of the communist government to readmit the Mensheviks into the Soviets in December, and a few months later also the socialist revolutionaries. It had meanwhile become clear to the rulers that these parties were not actually prepared to support the Whites in the civil war. But communist policy towards the socialist opposition remained extremely capricious. Early in 1919, especially after the failure of the Spartacus uprising in Berlin, it became evident that the revolution in the West was not progressing in a manner that the Bolsheviks considered desirable. Since they blamed the European socialists, who were then meeting in Berne, for this, they initiated an anti-socialist offensive which had a negative influence on their policy with regard to the Russian socialist parties. It also resulted in the immediate setting up of the Comintern, a pet idea of Lenin since 1914. On the other hand, with regard to the future of the Third International it was unwise to provide their socialist adversaries inside and outside Russia with too much ammunition. Their accounts of an essentially anti-socialist and anti-proletarian dictatorship in Russia could after all also have an unfavourable effect on the large mass of workers in the West.[11]

Moreover at the beginning of 1919 a radio message was received in Russia from the American president Woodrow Wilson, inviting all those involved in the Russian civil war, on behalf of the Big Four, to peace talks. Chicherin, the people's commissar for foreign affairs, informed the Paris peace conference that his government would agree to this proposal on certain conditions. At the same time he wrote that the Russian democratic socialists acknowledged the Soviet government as a lawful administration. The communists evidently thought it important to pose, before the statesmen in Paris, as a legitimate, constitutional and respected state power. This was difficult to reconcile with terrorism against the socialists. But when, a month later, it became evident that nothing would come of the peace talks, this terrorism could not simply be resumed. President Wilson sent William C. Bullitt as a special envoy to Russia in March, and the Bolsheviks attached great importance to his diplomatic mission. Bullitt had talks with prominent Mensheviks and socialist revolutionaries in Moscow and they assured him that their parties, too, were vehemently against allied intervention.[12]

It was, however, extremely annoying for the communists that the Russian socialists were not prepared to prostrate themselves to the regime. For the most part they made use of the scanty opportunities for legal opposition to provide unvarnished criticism and they attracted a great deal of attention in this way. On 22 January 1919 the Central Committee of the RSDRP began to publish *Vsegda Vperëd* (*Ever Forwards*). After its fourth number this paper appeared as a daily and it reached a circulation of 100,000 copies. The popularity of the paper was annoying for the Bolsheviks. In practically every edition of *Pravda* the communists felt obliged to reply to the Menshevik press. At the same time they tried to prevent the spread of the newspaper by limiting the allocation of paper.[13] The situation became even more complicated for the Bolsheviks when the international socialist conference in Berne adopted Akselrod's proposal to send a commission of inquiry to Russia. On 15 February *Pravda* reported this decision of the re-established Second International in a short notice. Four days later the Bolsheviks were officially informed of this by the German minister of foreign affairs, Brockdorff-Rantzau. In a telegram to the Soviet government he let them know that this commission of the International was requesting, through him, permission to enter Russian territory. Chicherin replied on the same day: 'Although we do not regard the Berne conference as socialist and do not think that the working class is represented in any way by it, we permit the commission you mention to visit Russia, and we guarantee it the possibility of a full investigation, just as we would not withhold this right from any bourgeois commission which wants to keep itself informed, even if it is directly or incidentally linked to bourgeois governments engaged in military action against the Soviet Republic.'[14]

The supercilious and detached tone of this telegram was not in harmony with the actual reaction in Moscow to the proposed visit of the Second International. The British journalist Arthur Ransome, who was staying there at the time, recounted that 'on February 20th everybody who came to see me was talking about it, and from that date the question as to the reception of the delegates was the most urgently debated of all political subjects'. Many of them thought that Chicherin's reaction was wrong. It was dangerous to allow these socialists into Russia without reason.[15] According to Ransome, Litvinov, the second man at the people's commissariat for foreign affairs, made himself into the spokesman of this group. 'Litvinov said he considered the sending of the Commission from Berne the most dangerous weapon yet conceived by their opponents.' He clarified his words by saying: 'These idiots here [i.e. Litvinov's fellow party members like Lenin and Chicherin] think the delegation is coming to seek a ground for peace. It is nothing of the sort. It is bound to condemn us and the Bourgeois Governments will know how to profit by the criticism, however mild, that is signed by men who still retain authority as socialists.'[16]

It is clear from these reactions how poorly informed the Bolsheviks in fact were. They evidently did not know that the socialists had achieved nothing in Paris and that their visit to Russia was thus impossible to link with the attempts to end the civil war. When the question came up for consideration at the Council of People's Commissars on 22 February, Kamenev drew the government's attention to the fact that the coming of the Berne 'representatives of Western European bourgeoisie' indicated a change in the attitude of Western Europe with regard to Russia. Of course the Soviet government could not receive these gentlemen officially, but the confederation of journalists would be able to act as hosts. They ought to be shown that despite the miserable situation of the Russian people, 'something new is still being built up in our country'.[17] Kamenev suggested inviting the commission to a series of meetings at which German and Russian communists would subject the Bern International to 'scathing criticism'. A few days later the Moscow party committee under Kamenev's leadership passed a resolution on the reception of the commission. In this it was noted about the centrists, who, as the communists knew, would form the majority of the delegation: 'While the centre in every country struggles against the dictatorship of the proletariat, it supports the watchword of "democracy", that is, the cloak for bourgeois sovereignty, and it tries to identify the proletariat with the Scheidemanns, the executioners of the working class.' The Bolsheviks, by their statements, created the impression that they were rather worried about the Western socialists' visit. Perhaps even the precipitous setting up of the Comintern was to some extent an answer to this decision by the Berne conference.[18]

The Mensheviks, on the other hand, realised very well that the communist rulers could be embarrassed by the presence of a socialist commission of inquiry. They decided to exploit every opportunity to focus the attention of the Western delegation on the socialist opposition in Russia. They formed a special reception committee and prepared a series of informal talks to inform the workers in the capital about the coming of the commission and to ask them to send their representatives to a large-scale meeting in honour of the delegates. In this way the social democrats would be able to give evidence of their not inconsiderable influence on the Moscow proletariat, even though it was reduced in number because of wartime circumstances. In a resolution of the Moscow committee of the RSDRP a violent protest was made against the slander which was poured forth by the Bolshevik press about the Berne commission, and the workers were asked to prepare a dignified reception for the Western socialists.[19]

As was explained in the preceding chapter, nothing came of the Second International's plans to send a commission to Russia. It was not until the middle of 1920 that official representatives of the Western socialist parties were able to pay a visit to Russia. In this way it was out of the question for Western socialism to exert a moderating influence on the treatment of the socialist opposition in Russia in 1919. Terrorism against it was quickly resumed. At the end of February *Vsegda Vperëd*, the popular Menshevik daily paper, was banned at the suggestion of no less a person than Lenin. The socialist revolutionaries were allowed to have their *Delo Naroda (The People's Cause)* published in March, but after that, this too came to an end. On 20 March almost all the Central Committee and the Moscow committee of the RSDRP were arrested. In the provinces similar actions followed against the Mensheviks. The socialist revolutionaries suffered less here. After the renewed legalisation of the PSR they had left their underground party organisation intact and could not be so easily rounded up as the social democrats, who conducted all their activities in public.

In any case most of the Mensheviks were set free after a day. Some measures, such as the sealing up of the social democrats' building in Moscow and the imprisonment of Dan, were abrogated after bitter Menshevik protest. But the publication of social democratic periodicals and papers was made virtually impossible. On the eve of the elections for the Soviets the Menshevik candidates were mostly arrested and held prisoner until the elections were over. For this reason, Martov was subjected to house arrest for five days in June 1919. Nevertheless, at the Seventh Soviet Congress in December 1919, Martov and Dan were given the opportunity to make long speeches in which they expounded the most burning questions of internal and foreign policy, much to the interest of their audience. Moreover, the two Mensheviks were both approached at about the same time with a request as to whether they would not be prepared to occupy a high administrative post within the government. Naturally they refused to consider this. During this period rumour was rife that an agreement would be reached between the social democrats and the communists and that they would form a coalition government. According to Martov ridiculous communications of this kind were launched by the 'Asiatic' diplomat Litvinov in order to impress the West, especially the European socialists.[20]    The Mensheviks thought that in the first place the capriciousness of the communist oppression was a result of fear. In their view the communist dictators, despite their military successes in the civil war and their progressively gigantic set of instruments of oppression, were in such an isolated position that they were terrified whenever the truth was told in a paltry Menshevik newspaper. The Bolsheviks were still afraid that the social democrats could convert their popularity into political power if they were allowed to take part freely in the elections for the Soviets. At the same time the rulers flinched from wholly eliminating the opposition because they feared the repercussions which this could have at home and abroad. But this was not the whole story. In the course of 1919, the Mensheviks' party ideology experienced an interesting evolution. The left-wing majority of the RSDRP was now prepared, under certain conditions – which the Bolsheviks however were unwilling to accept – to acknowledge the October revolution and communism. Such a position no longer completely ruled out, in principle, an agreement and prospective co-operation between Menshevism and Bolshevism. The attitude of the social democrats could in any case no longer be described as diametrically opposed to the regime. Since they also let this be outwardly evident, the Bolsheviks' attitude towards the social democratic opposition was probably in some measure influenced by it.

### FURTHER REFLECTIONS ON THE SOVIET REGIME

The development of Menshevik thought is not only important for a better understanding of the socialist opposition in Soviet Russia and the communist reactions to it. The Russian social democrats also made a fundamental contribution to Marxist theorising about Bolshevism. For this reason their ideology ought not to be considered exclusively in its Russian context. Menshevik reflections about the October revolution can only rightly be understood by comparing them with the attempts of Western socialists to reach a more definitive evaluation of the communist regime. That is why this European development must be discussed first. The thoughts of the Western Marxists were dominated by one elemental fact which thereafter determined the attitude of European socialism towards Soviet Russia: in Western Europe no social revolution took place. This meant that in the West people again began to see Russia as a special country. The 'building up' of a socialist society which seemed to be taking place there and the heroic struggle which was being carried out for its defence against internal and foreign enemies gave 'the country of the Soviets' an almost supernatural radiance.

For very many people, Russia was a country about which one knew practically nothing, but hoped for everything. The glorification of Russia thus became a political factor of great importance. For about a quarter of the European labour movement the Soviet state became at this time the only guide to a socialist future. These advocates of communism had nothing good to say for capitalist society, and thought that the socialist leaders in their own party or union were lacking in revolutionary zeal and decisiveness. They scarcely criticised what happened in Russia. They wanted to follow the Russian example. With Russian support the social revolution could certainly be victorious in the West. For this reason they also wanted their party to associate itself with the Moscow-based Communist International.

The remaining three-quarters of the European labour movement, which continued to call itself socialist, was internally divided about the evaluation of European capitalism and Russian communism. In these circles criticism and appreciation of both types of society existed in very varying degrees. In general no one believed that Russian communism could flourish in the West. An important school was more inclined to resign itself to the Western status quo than to oppose it with all its power. These reformist-inclined socialists also went the furthest in their rejection of the communist dictatorship and in combating its Western adherents. But in this a certain sympathy and not infrequently also admiration for certain aspects of Soviet society was not ruled out.

The socialist image of Soviet Russia in the interwar period thus remained, in many respects, related to the socialist image of Russia in the period before 1910. After all, then too it was emphasised in every possible way that the Russian situation was different and ought not to be judged by the same standards as Western circumstances. An important difference was that it was certainly no longer possible to make a sharp distinction between the unfavourable clichés which had once been used to characterise tsarism and the favourable commonplaces which had earlier been customarily used to typify the Russian revolutionary movement. These two images had now converged since the revolutionaries had taken over power. Russian communism, like tsarism before it, could be decried as a terrible despotism, but also glorified as a marvellous socialist experiment. Which side of this image was emphasised the most depended very much on circumstances, which differed sharply as to time, country, party and even to individual. But despite the changing accentuation of its darker and lighter sides, the usual characterisation of Soviet Russia in the period after 1920, in both socialist and communist circles, was extremely conventional and was to remain so for a long time. Seldom was anything said or written about Soviet Russia which rose above the squabbling of the parties. It was chiefly centrist ideologists and leaders who, in their struggle against the Soviet myth, sometimes brought to light things about communism which were worthy of earnest consideration.

The most prominent figures among them were once again Kautsky and Bauer, who wrote serious studies in these years also, in order, each in his own way, to offer resistance to the radicalisation and the glorification of Soviet Russia in their own movement. Since there was no one among the Western sympathisers of communism with sufficient authority to be able to combat them – Gramsci was still unknown in socialist Europe – it was once more the prominent leaders of the Russian communist party, namely Trotsky and Radek, who made the counter-attack. Kautsky once more set the ball rolling. He evidently did not want to reply to Lenin's personal and poisonous attack on his first book in a similar way. His next treatise against Bolshevism, which appeared in June 1919, was once more a scholarly attempt to demonstrate that the use of unlimited violence against political opponents was not legitimised by socialist traditions. *Terrorism and Communism*, some 150 pages long, had as its subtitle *A contribution to the natural history of the revolution*, and was a much more historical disquisition than *The Dictatorship of the Proletariat*. But it too turned into an exhaustive condemnation of the politics of the Russian rulers and compelled Trotsky to write a comprehensive refutation.

Kautsky justified his work in the introduction by referring not only to the Russian, but also to the German chaos. Before the war many socialists had thought that the time for revolutions in Europe, including Germany and Austria, was over for good. 'Now we have the revolution, and it assumes forms of savagery which even the most whimsical of the revolutionary romantics among us had never expected.'[21] Socialists entrusted with military power persecuted other socialists with the same savagery as once the Versailles troops had meted out to the Communards. Noske had energetically followed Trotsky's example. Mindless glorification of the revolution was therefore fundamentally wrong. According to Kautsky, one of the most widespread misconceptions was the idea that terrorism was an essential element of revolution. As proof, references were always made to the great French revolution because it counted as the revolution *par excellence*. For Kautsky this was again occasion for a, this time, very detailed historical analysis, in which the parallels with Bolshevik Russia were there for the taking.

To understand fully the regime of Robespierre and terrorism, one should first, according to Kautsky, make a study of the Parisian masses in the French revolution. He explained in detail that the Parisian *petite bourgeoisie* had been the driving force behind the revolutionary events. As long as the masses believed that the revolution could free them from all their misery, they did not recoil from deeds of barbaric violence in order to enforce their will. In spite of all this they were evidently incapable of fundamentally changing their social position. It was not therefore surprising that in the years 1793–4 the mood of the masses swung round from enthusiasm to apathy. Then the revolution was past its peak. Robespierre next made a desperate attempt to keep the revolution going in a social vacuum and in so doing could only rely on the intensified terrorism of bureaucratic machinery.[22] This fact was barely acknowledged by later revolutionaries. Since the horrors of terrorism were pointed out by many in order to be able to condemn the revolution, the nineteenth-century revolutionaries frequently considered it their duty to glorify terrorism.[23]

It goes without saying that Kautsky here once again held up the Commune as a shining example to the Bolshevik regime, which for him represented a regression to the violent revolutionary and thus bourgeois practices of the eighteenth century. But for the rest he tried, in a long chapter, to expose the imperfections of the Commune and to compare them, as Bauer had done before him, with the shortcomings of the Bolshevik regime. This was a form of criticism which he had scrupulously avoided in his previous pamphlet. Probably Kautsky was trying here to react to socialists who thought that the Commune had failed because of a too-humane attitude towards its enemies and who wanted to prevent a repetition of this. He therefore argued now that the Utopian ideas of most Communards had not been amenable to implementation. In Moscow and Budapest too, Kautsky added bitterly, people nowadays were again thinking about possessing the philosopher's stone.[24] Marx had written about the Parisian workers in 1871: 'The working class expected no miracles from the Commune. It could not establish ready-made utopias by decree of the people . . . It can only release those elements of a new society which have already developed in the womb of the collapsing bourgeois society.'

This quotation, in Kautsky's view, revealed the core of Marx's teaching and also provided the axiom on which a criticism of Bolshevism could be based. Communism was utopian and propagated revolutionary policy as the art of the impossible. An attempt to realise socialism by means of a dictatorship in a backward country was in Kautsky's view a dangerous absurdity.[25] The moderate attitude of the Parisian workers at the time of the Commune had, according to Kautsky, been no coincidence. In a separate chapter he devoted many pages to acknowledging his distaste for violence and his belief in a humane proletariat and he defended this with a series of biological, sociological and historical arguments. Since Marxism ruled the socialist movement, it had not experienced a single defeat before the World War 'and the idea of carrying on by means of a reign of terror had completely disappeared from their ranks'.[26]

Before the World War no defeats! What had changed then? In Kautsky's view the war had changed the mentality of the workers and once more plunged them, as the economically weakest members of society, into the deepest misery. The rank and file of the skilled workers, who had formed the backbone of the socialist movement, were severely depleted by the war. They had had to give up their places to new groups of unskilled workers, and impoverished *petits bourgeois*. These masses had not passed through the school of pre-war socialism. They did not try to implement a realistic programme but impossible slogans. Once more it was the war which had offered these workers in the backward areas of Europe the chance of grasping power.[27] It was the task of a Marxist party to resist the instincts of the primitive masses. It could not decide on total socialisation of the means of production in a country with an underdeveloped form of capitalism like Russia. Marx had dared to call the German workers backward, because they applauded a 'charlatan saviour' like Lassalle, 'who promised to help them with a leap into the Promised Land'.[28]

Finally Kautsky subjected the concrete measures of the Bolsheviks to an investigation in which he drew most of his data from official communist sources. After he had passed dictatorship, censorship, terrorism, bureaucracy and economic chaos in review, he could not conclude otherwise than that there might well be a couple of honest, idealistic Bolsheviks around, but only 'in the midst of a growing mud-flood of uncertainty, corruption and despair which reaches ever higher and finally threatens to drown them'.[29] Russian communism had 'in fact in every respect become barrack-room socialism'.[30] It was wronging Asia, which had brought forth Confucius and Buddha, to call Bolshevism 'Asiatic'. 'One should rather call it Tartar socialism.'[31] Kautsky did not predict a long life for this regime. 'The final result is predictable. It does not exactly need to be a 9 Thermidor, but I fear it will not be very different from that.'[32] Kautsky was convinced that the 'World revolution' on which the communists were depending would never break out. He did not underestimate the sympathies for Bolshevism in the German and French labour movements, but he refused to believe that communism had any real chance of success in the West.

Kautsky's analysis of the situation was closely related to that of right-wing Mensheviks like Potresov, Akselrod and Tsereteli. Martov's objection to their total rejection of Bolshevism had always been that the socialists in Russia were thereby condemned to doing nothing. After all, they could not unite themselves with armed counter-revolution. The same objection could be brought against Kautsky. He advised the socialists to retire into their studies, as Marx had done into the British Museum, as soon as a revolution did not go according to plan. This advice was not particularly practical. Marx had hardly any adherents in about 1850. The leaders of European socialism could not run away from their responsibilities, for they had millions of followers. They would lose a significant number of them to communism. In fact Kautsky was now – and he would do the same in about 1933 – skirting the problem that circumstances could crop up in which democracy could no longer be saved, and socialists, too, would have to choose between their own downfall or a coup by which the civil rights of political adversaries would be drastically restricted. This had in fact been the major lesson of 1917 for socialism.

Kautsky's anti-communism was unacceptable to the USPD, but very useful to the SPD. This party's press devoted only laudatory words to his pamphlets, and his arguments against the Bolshevik danger were to constitute a permanent part of the party ideology. Kautsky had unintentionally contributed in this way to the fossilisation of the image of Soviet Russia and helped to make the gulf between communism and socialism unbridgeable in Germany. This would have fatal consequences in 1933.[33] Kautsky himself must have experienced this renewed solidarity between the party and its former teacher with mixed feelings. The editorship of *Die Neue Zeit* was never offered to him again and his pamphlets were sometimes very strangely used. When, in 1919, the International Socialist Conference of Lucerne decided, at the suggestion of the Dutchman Troelstra, to establish a commission to develop a political system which could be the answer to the burning questions of the time, the SPD's only contribution to this concerted work was the sending of a complimentary copy of one of Kautsky's anti-communist pamphlets to Troelstra.[34] But Kautsky had included no detailed plan for a socialist state constitution in it. It had been his intention, by means of his criticism of the regime in Russia, to give a sort of ethical code of behaviour to the socialists in the West, and in 1919 the SPD had not adhered to this in any way.

With his book *Terrorism and Communism* Kautsky had thrown down the gauntlet to the Bolsheviks for the second time and this time it was not Lenin but Trotsky who took up the challenge. During the course of 1919 and in the first months of 1920 the People's Commissar for War dictated a book in the armour-plated train which he used to travel to and from the front during the civil war, a book which he challengingly also entitled *Terrorism and Communism*. Trotsky partly followed the same arguments as Lenin in his opposition to Kautsky, but Lenin's choleric outbursts of anger were replaced by Trotsky with ice-cold sarcasm. His book was ably written and gave evidence not only of the intellectual originality but also of the arrogant self-assurance

of the author. Now that the Red Army had almost totally eliminated the enemy, Trotsky could boast about the impressive
successes which could be achieved by a revolutionary dictatorship. Trotsky did not deny that Russia was impoverished,
exhausted and half-starved. But Kautsky was completely wrong
if he blamed the Bolsheviks or the Russian proletariat for this.
Bolshevism was not a kind of warmed-up Proudhonism, the
proletariat was not backward and lawless. The successes of the
civil war had adequately refuted these monstrous allegations of
Kautsky. The desperate straits which the country was in were
the result of a grand, all-embracing revolution. The French
revolution had also led to economic disruption, and the suffering
of the masses was for a long time increased instead of relieved.
Russia was experiencing the stormy transition from capitalism
to socialism and the old democracies of Western Europe were
on the threshold of the same events. The hope that 'a normal,
peaceful, truly Kautskyesque maturation' could really be
achieved was in Trotsky's view a childish illusion.

Amazingly enough Trotsky, like Kautsky, clarified his argument with a digression about the *petite bourgeoisie* (*meshchanstvo*),
the middle class, that is to say, the group between the capitalist
bourgeoisie and the proletariat. Evidently it was also important
to Trotsky to indicate a social group against which the good
qualities of the proletariat would stand out clearly. The words
'petty bourgeois' were more than a favourite term of abuse which
some socialists used to describe certain comrades or ideas which
they did not like. A great deal of discussion took place in Marxist
circles about the function of the middle class in the development
of modern society. Bernstein and others had pointed out that,
contrary to expectations, this social stratum was unlikely to
disappear. The numerical strength of the middle class in the
Western world was undoubtedly still very substantial, Trotsky
admitted, but its share in the process of production had dropped
sharply. Nineteenth-century bourgeois democracy had always
flourished best in countries where this group was in fact widespread and powerful, and thus capable of fulfilling a mediatory
function between capital and labour. This was no longer the
case. The desperation and total dependence on the capitalist
elite of the middle groups and the parties formed by them –
amongst which to some extent Trotsky also counted the reformist socialist parties – was in his view undeniable.

In the long run this proved fatal for democracy. The World War had made this clear to anyone who was willing to look and listen. The capitalist clique had brought mankind to the edge of the abyss. All the imperialist illusions had gone up in smoke. The representatives of the middle class in the parliaments had chosen the side of imperialism during the war. Even the socialist members of parliament had betrayed and sold their grass-roots support. The workers were turning further away from their former leaders every day and preparing themselves for the definitive encounter with their oppressors. There was no way back. Of course there were people like Kautsky who dared not look harsh reality in the face and therefore attributed an everlasting and absolute value to democracy. According to Trotsky this view was in conflict with socialist tradition. Socialist parties had seen democracy and parliament simply as matters which could be instrumental for their objectives for a certain period. Many socialists, for example Marx's son-in-law Lafargue, had already long before shown that the more universal the suffrage became, the more the real power became the monopoly of an ever-decreasing number of individuals. This was where the secret of the so-called government of the majority lay.[36]

Trotsky's scepticism about the survival of democracy and his belief in an impending world revolution were probably sincere. Much less honestly, Trotsky conjured with the facts in defending Bolshevik policy or in describing political opponents. The deeds of the Russian communists – and also Trotsky's plans for a total military absorption of the Russian proletariat into industrial armies – were defended against critics like Kautsky or a Menshevik like Abramovich by an appeal to the class character of the Soviet dictatorship. He depicted the Mensheviks as counterrevolutionaries who had supported intervention and the White armies. The disintegration of the Constituent Assembly was justified by Trotsky with the lie that this had mainly been a military necessity.[37]

In his apologia for Bolshevik terrorism, Trotsky deployed all his polemical talent. He gave a brief description of Kautsky's views and then announced that he regarded theorising about terrorism pointless. After all, the 'living history of mankind' gave the answers to every question.[38] The religious wars, the 'Great Rebellion', the French revolution, the American civil war and the Commune were next passed in review. Here Trotsky quoted exclusively bourgeois or socialist authors of irreproachable fame and of course demonstrated that terrorism had been an obvious and necessary element in all these events. The cardinal problem in every war, civil war or revolution was, in his view, the fact that the will of the enemy ought to be entirely broken. This could only happen through the resolute use of violence. The situation in which Soviet Russia had found herself from the outset was in essence the same as that of revolutionary France at the beginning of the Jacobin terror. The country was under attack from all sides by foreign troops, while internally it had to contend with domestic uprisings and colossal economic problems. Had the Soviet government done anything different from the Jacobin government during the French revolution? Robespierre's government had – as Plekhanov had once written – summoned up 'the gigantic courage' to 'take all the measures which were necessary for the safety of the country, however arbitrary and harsh they in fact were'.[39]

In Trotsky's argument also the Commune formed the *pièce de résistance*. He showed that even the Communards had exercised violence, although it was, in the opinion of the Russian People's Commissar for War, on too small a scale and lacking in efficiency. Trotsky ascribed this to the disastrous indecision and lack of vigour of the leaders of the Paris uprising. The result had been that the Commune was struck down with a great deal of violent bloodshed. In support he quoted from the book of an eyewitness of the Commune, the Russian socialist theorist Lavrov, who was certainly not famous as a proponent of revolutionary terrorism: 'Precisely those people to whom human life and human blood is precious must try to organise the possibility of a rapid and decisive victory and afterwards to act with the greatest possible speed and energy to crush the enemy. For only in this way can inevitable sacrifice and loss of blood be reduced to a minimum.'[40]

This quotation was Trotsky's reproach to socialists like Longuet, Martov, Bauer, Adler and Hilferding. These representatives of 'international Kautskyanism' were, by their cowardice, hypocrisy and predilection for conciliatory compromise, preventing an important section of the European working class from unanimously uniting itself to the communist camp. History, and above all the year 1914, had shown that 'a resolute push from left or right is sufficient to make the proletariat gravitate to one side or the other for a certain period'. Thus a great responsibility rested on the centrists. They formed 'the principal element on which the unstable equilibrium of capitalist society' was resting.[41] Trotsky's criticism of the centrists was not deserved, but it certainly found its mark. As in 1914, so in 1919, it was not the leaders who led the way for the masses, but rather the other way around. Circumstances in Europe did not lend themselves to a large-scale social revolution and most workers were not prepared to stake their lives on a revolutionary adventure. Only a substantial minority of European workers and socialists continued to be inclined towards rebellion. For most of the leaders of the centrist parties also the idea of a reconciliation with capitalism was intolerable. They certainly wanted a revolution, but they preferred to wait for a decent one. This made them extremely sensitive and vulnerable to the kind of criticism which Trotsky had expressed against them.

They had no wish, however, to follow the Bolshevik example in Europe. Fifteen years later Trotsky himself was to prove that they were right. After he had been banned from the Soviet Union, he published in 1935 an English edition of his book against Kautsky. In this he took nothing back, but he did add an introduction in which he made remarks with a Kautskyesque flavour about the situation in Russia. Like Kautsky in 1918 and 1919 he spoke of the impotence and ineptitude of the Russian workers in comparison with the corrupt and bureaucratic party organisation, and of the disastrous elimination of the Soviets as vehicles of self-rule and opposition to the government. In his book he had fiercely defended the militarisation of the workers as an inevitable step in the direction of socialism. Now he postulated the impossibility of solving the problem of a socialist economy by order of the powers that be, and he spoke of the necessity for 'free, creative initiatives by the organised producers and consumers'. This was exactly what Kautsky and other socialist critics of communism had maintained in the years 1918–19.[42]

As is already evident from the foregoing, the criticism levelled by most of the centrists at communism – in contrast to what Trotsky wrote – was not completely identical with Kautsky's. In

Kautsky's own party, the USPD, people were chiefly at variance with him and for this reason he was to resign his membership in 1919. Bernstein had already done this at the beginning of the year. The most important ideologist of the centre, Otto Bauer, likewise disagreed with Kautsky on a number of points. This was again to become evident from Bauer's book, entitled *Bolshevism or Social Democracy?*, which appeared in 1920 at about the same time as Trotsky's attack on Kautsky. In a letter to Kautsky he tried to explain why the Austrian socialist press was scrupulously avoiding any clearly hostile criticism of Bolshevism and might at times exercise some caution over the publication of an article by Kautsky. The workers clung to the hope that Russia would disrupt the capitalist world. Every direct attack on Moscow therefore came up against vociferous protest, and might even have led to a split in the party.[43]

Bauer, as party leader, naturally had to take these sentiments into account. His journalistic work, which was characterised by cool detachment and gave the impression of strict Marxist objectivity, was basically determined by undisclosed political considerations. In the years between the wars his party continually found itself in a most difficult position. Before the rise of Fascism, small Austria was a Catholic peasants' country with one enormous 'red' city, Vienna. Almost nowhere in Europe were the contrasts between town and country sharper than in this republic. Bauer's attempt, as minister of foreign affairs in 1919, to bring about an *Anschluss*, or union, with Germany – after all, socialism was much more powerful there – failed because of intervention by the Entente. In the same year the Austrian government, supported by the social democrats, managed to frustrate a *coup d'état* by a handful of communists. But this provisional government of socialists and Catholic nationalists was already falling apart at the beginning of 1920. The social democrats lost the elections in that year and afterwards remained in the opposition. This was the situation when Bauer's book about communism appeared.[44]

One ought to try to make clear to the Austrian workers, Bauer wrote to Kautsky, that Bolshevik methods were determined 'by specific Russian relationships' and 'are not applicable to our situation'.[45] This observation and the contrast between town and country formed the two main themes in Bauer's book on to which he tacked all kinds of Marxist variations. In a detailed exposition he described how Russia had been through an agrarian revolution in 1917. The peasants had divided the land between them and at the same time dealt the death blow to the *ancien régime* and made possible the proletarian revolution in the cities. The Bolsheviks had only been able to hold their own in the civil war because of the support of the peasants, who feared that the counter-revolution would once more rob them of their land. All attempts by the Soviet government to introduce socialism in the countryside had, however, been prevented by the unwillingness and backwardness of the peasant masses. Since the peasants had withdrawn from the revolution and from world history in order to concentrate exclusively on the promotion of their own interests, political power could remain in the hands of the town, of the proletariat.[46]

Bauer then discussed the socialist experiments in the cities. The Russian workers, characterised by Bauer with the adjectives unskilled, disorganised, spontaneous, wild, juvenile and under-developed, had supported the Bolshevik coup *en masse* and Soviet power formed at the start a true dictatorship of the proletariat. The bourgeoisie had been effectively dispossessed, but the experiment with workers' self-government in industry had degenerated into absolute anarchy. The Bolsheviks had had to restore order and discipline with a heavy hand. This develop-ment was represented by Bauer as something inevitable.

> Only the Russian peasants' lack of culture [*Kulturlosigkeit*] explains why tsarist despotism had to be replaced, not by the democratic self-government of the Russian people, but by the dictatorship of the proletariat which forms a small minority of the Russian people. Only the cultural underdevelopment of the Russian worker explains why the dictatorship of the proletariat had to be changed from the rule of the masses themselves into the despotism of a small progressive minority of the proletariat ... Despotic socialism is the product of Russian lack of culture.[47]

The Russian revolution was a bourgeois one, and comparable with the French revolution of 1789, when town and country both had been revolutionary. At the same time, however, what Marx and Engels had hoped for in vain in 1848 was now actually happening in Russia. Not the *petite bourgeoisie* as in the French revolution, but the urban proletariat, had taken the lead. The

Soviet republic could not, however, remain stuck at the stage reached by the French revolution. The contrasts between town and country, workers and peasants which were now still latent, would harden and become more profound there, too. Russia would be forced to make some kind of compromise with her capitalist neighbours.

In other words, the communists could only maintain their power by keeping the peasants satisfied with the products of foreign industry. The Bolsheviks could only pay for these goods with the surplus of the agrarian sector and thus had to force the peasants to produce more. According to Bauer, experience had taught the Soviet government that with the peasant nothing could be achieved by violence. They would therefore have to provide for better material, social and educational facilities in the country. Contact with urban culture would, however, awaken the peasants out of their political slumber. Eventually even this overwhelming majority of the population would demand their rights as citizens and bring the Bolshevik dictatorship to an end.[48] They would then probably help the bourgeoisie, or a dictator who put himself forward as the saviour of bourgeois order, to power.[49] In fact, as Bauer argued, the dictatorship in Russia rested 'not so much on the open subjection of the bourgeoisie as on the veiled removal of the peasants' rights' which had become a possible consequence of it.[50] If, in the future, Russian society were to show permanent socialist traits, then these could only be the consequence of a Russian socialism which had evolved from despotic to democratic.

Bauer's attitude ruled out criticism of the Bolsheviks since he wished to consider their actions exclusively as the result of an inevitable historical development. From this it becomes evident that Bauer's ideas had also changed under the influence of the stabilisation of the regime in Russia and the great problems with which Western socialism had been faced after the war. In 1917 and 1918 he had introduced the left-wing Mensheviks as the only people who had any true insight into the Russian situation. The aims of the Bolsheviks were then, in his view, just as illusory as those of the French socialists in 1848 and 1871. Two years later he thought it was no longer necessary to hold up Martov as an example to Lenin. The revolution had sidetracked the Russian social democrats for an indefinite time and therefore they could no longer play a role in Bauer's argument. Besides, he now considered it more correct to see Russian events as a kind of repetition of the great French revolution of 1789 and not of the failed, short-lived uprisings of 1848 and 1871.

A detailed analysis of the situation in Western Europe formed the vital counterpart to Bauer's considerations about the Russian revolution. If the rise of despotic socialism in Russia had been historically inevitable, then the absence of a socialist and democratic revolution in the West must logically point to its provisional impossibility. The Bolsheviks had 'received' their revolution and not 'made' it. Thus imitation of the communist example could not, according to Bauer, have the desired revolutionary results. In his arguments the European middle class also played an important role. Like Trotsky he assumed that this group was closely linked to the capitalist summit of the social pyramid. According to Trotsky the proletarian revolution could easily push aside the middle class. Its political power was merely show, since it was no longer founded on an economic base. Bauer denied this. The very development of banking and credit systems (*Finanzkapital*) had 'democratised' the possession of capital. The violent and sudden liquidation of private enterprise in Russia had mainly hit the foreign capital owner, since industry there was to a large extent a non-Russian phenomenon. In Europe a similar measure would not only have dispossessed the capitalists, but at the same time have uprooted the livelihood of very great numbers of intellectuals, civil servants, farmers, shopkeepers and other representatives of the middle class, who held key positions in economic life.

Together these groups would form a tremendous millstone around the necks of the European proletariat as soon as it tried to raise itself up for its last fight with capitalism. Even in Russia, where the intelligentsia had been so susceptible to socialism, the October revolution had aroused embittered resistance among these very people. In Western and Central Europe the intellectuals were the principal bearers of nationalist and imperialist ideas. Without them no government could rule, no factory produce goods. Their opposition could be one of the most prominent bulwarks against a proletarian revolution. The same was true for the peasants. Intensive contact with urban culture, the establishment of farmer's credit banks, the intensivisation and rationalisation of agriculture and the rise of world trade prices for grain had converted the peasants into a politically conscious and pro-capitalist class. Urbanised Western society was completely dependent on this group for its supplies of food. The peasants were capable of starving out and destroying a proletarian revolution and were probably also ready to do this.[51]

A Soviet-style dictatorship was only capable of a sudden, violent and total expropriation and in the West this would lead to a complete and irreparable disruption of the economic mechanism.[52] The Russian worker put up with the fact that the Soviet authorities conscripted him into a workers' army and then commandeered him wherever he was needed. The Western workers would not have tolerated this. They wished to take part in decisions about matters which affected their interests directly. In contrast to the Russian proletariat it was not exclusively indignation about economic inequality which convinced them of the rightness of the collectivist system. They were equally drawn to socialism by the arbitrariness of their employers and by the tinkering of a state bureaucracy which was becoming more and more powerful. Socialism meant for them not only equality, but also freedom. Ideas about an industrial democracy, such as those of Guild Socialism in England, were more suited to the Western workers who were simply more self-confident, more educated and better organised than their Russian comrades.

Bauer recognised that the World War had shaped the subjective, psychological conditions for the revolution in the West as well. A substantial section of the industrial and agricultural workers had revolutionary inclinations and were full of impatience. However, in Bauer's line of reasoning, they ought to wait until their time actually came. Of course the possibility could not be excluded that the workers might be forced, by developments in the class war, to make a premature grab for power, for example, to avoid a counter-revolutionary despotism. A proletarian government would in fact be driven in circumstances of this kind to the quickest possible restoration of democratic relations, since it would otherwise be unable to carry out its social revolution.[53]

Trotsky, throwing vitriol at all Austro-Marxists, had said of Bauer that he was a learned, but at the same time irritating and prosaic, pedant. Bauer had 'no political will' and when he occasionally 'demonstrated something like temperament' this was exclusively 'in the collection of arguments, facts and quotations *against* revolutionary action'. Bauer's latest book gave Trotsky no reason whatsoever to change his damning judgement.[54] Kautsky praised the book because of 'the masterly way in which the research methods of historical materialism' were employed in it. Nevertheless, he wrote in his review:

> One thing, however, remains at issue after this piece by Bauer: whether Bolshevism represents the form which every revolutionary movement in an economically backward country ought to take. I cannot agree with this view. For me Bolshevism seems to be not only a product of the special economic situation in an agrarian state, where a militant, industrial proletariat is active together with the revolutionary mass of peasantry, but to a greater extent a product of the special circumstances which came into being in Russia after the World War.[55]

Kautsky was stating here precisely where he disagreed with Bauer. Consciously or unconsciously Bauer had embroidered and accentuated the contrast between underdeveloped Russia and the progressive West. This gave the Austrian party leader two great advantages. It relieved him of the duty of criticising the Bolshevik regime openly on moral grounds and at the same time provided him with an acceptable explanation for the still poignant difference in revolutionary zeal between East and West. Kautsky, who had formerly also held ideas of this kind, now hoped to judge Bolshevism like any other Western phenomenon. Because of his pamphlets, a condemnation of communism just on the grounds of simple ideological and moral principles had been generally accepted by a significant section of the socialist world. Bauer was thus partly responsible for the positive and Kautsky for the negative elements which were to determine socialist views about Russian communism.

Bauer had forced reality into too simple a framework by presenting the Bolsheviks' coup in October 1917 as a product of Russian backwardness. The October revolution can with justification also be seen as the result of a unique coincidence. Kautsky was right about this and no one realised it better than Lenin, who, in 1917, had continually urged his fellow party members to grasp power and not to let the opportune moment slip by. Bauer handled the differences between East and West in an irresponsible manner. Thus he claimed that every social revolution in Austria, given that country's dependence on food imports from foreign powers, could be nipped in the bud. For Russia this problem did not exist since the overwhelming majority of the population lived in the country. The Russian cities, however, became quite depopulated by lack of food during the civil war. A good year after the appearance of Bauer's book, a famine occurred as a result of the Bolshevik agricultural policy, which claimed millions of victims in the countryside. Bauer's theories had at the same time to make it acceptable that the primitive, uncultured and disorganised Russian workers could easily let themselves be assembled into disciplined workers' armies, while naturally the Austrian workers would not submit to anything like that. The Bolsheviks did not, however, carry out Trotsky's plans, for they feared widespread resistance from the workers. Their position of power was not yet sufficiently strong for the realisation of ideas of this kind. Bauer may well have wondered whether the Western workers would have been able to resist despotic arbitrariness, if they, like their Russian fellow workers, had been deprived of independent organisations and if the almighty state had been able to decide if they deserved to starve to death or not.

In Kautsky's view the Bolsheviks were responsible for their deeds and this gave the Western socialists the right to praise or condemn them. On the other hand, it had then to be recognised that the Russian communists might have wondered whether Western socialism had indeed made proper use of the opportunities offered by the post-war situation for a social revolution. European criticism of Russia justified Russian criticism of Europe. Kautsky had provoked it with his anti-Bolshevik writings and a significant section of his public had proved sensitive to communist arguments. Bauer had tried to find a way in which to prevent this situation, since both forms of criticism were unwelcome to him for political reasons.

How fruitless his attempt was became evident from the special pamphlet which Karl Radek, the Polish communist journalist and influential adviser of the Comintern on European affairs, devoted to Bauer's book. Radek was prepared for and capable

of attacking or defending every point of view whenever convenient for his patrons, and his pen could be both witty and
vitriolic. Like Trotsky, he had written a pamphlet against
Kautsky.[56] His anti-Bauer piece, entitled *The Problems of the World
Revolution in the Light of Menshevism*, was nothing more than
fluently written propaganda, but it nevertheless contained some
telling remarks. In his book Bauer had clearly dissociated himself
from his Russian social democrat friends, but this of course did
not make any difference to Radek. For the Russian communists
centrism was identical with 'international Menshevism'. The
right-wing Mensheviks, Radek wrote, regarded the events of
October 1917 as a crime and their left-wing comrades saw it as
a political adventure. 'The Mensheviks could make Karl Kautsky
dance to their tune so well that the former theorist of the Second
International ... refused to recognise the Russian revolution.'
This sort of attack, however, had been counterproductive. The
Mensheviks were forced by circumstances to accept Soviet power
and they had even exhorted their 'fellow believers' to defend
it. Nor did 'international Menshevism' have the strength to
defend Kautsky's point of view any longer. It had to seek for
new ways in which Bolshevism could be combated and its own
cowardly reformism defended. Bauer's book could act as a model
for this means of attack. His attempt to give Menshevik tactics
a fresh base by recognising Bolshevism as an element of progress
exclusively in Russia and emphatically not in the rest of Europe,
naturally had to come to grief no less than Kautsky's.[57]

Radek admitted that winning over the proletariat had nowhere been simpler than in Russia. It went without saying that
he also tried to knock down every obstacle to a social revolution
in the West indicated by Bauer. Radek pointed to the increased
power of the proletariat, the radicalisation of agricultural workers and to the many impoverished and *déclassé* intellectuals who
had chosen the side of the revolution. The Western proletariat
would not die of hunger if it decided to liquidate capitalism. As
an ally of Soviet Russia it would have at its disposal the granaries
of the Balkans, the Ukraine and Siberia. According to Radek,
the European proletariat was ready for revolution. The conceptual world of Guild Socialism which Bauer was advertising, was
alien to the workers. Even in England this was only reflected in
the mentality of intellectuals like G. D. H. Cole or Sidney Webb.

Bauer's book was nothing more than a complete capitulation to the capitalist bourgeoisie.

Radek did not clothe his assertions with any factual material. Undoubtedly Bauer went to work much more seriously. But this did not make his argumentation better in every respect. His ideas about the progressive role of violence and terrorism in an underdeveloped society stemmed from misplaced feelings of superiority which many Western socialists continued to entertain about Russia. Their identification of culture with democracy and of dictatorship with cultural backwardness is no longer acceptable to the modern reader. We know that history is capable of interchanging both pairs of ideas. In Europe not all roads lead to democracy. The Fascist revolution was partly to accomplish what Bauer thought the proletarian revolution was incapable of. The fragile, extremely complicated economic mechanism of continental Europe was rebuilt during the Second World War by the German occupation into an effectively working war machinery which could only be deranged by substantial military pressure from outside. It is true that national socialism left capitalist ownership undisturbed, but the Europe ruled by Hitler had much in common with Stalin's Russia. The differences between Russia and Europe proved to be much smaller than Bauer wished to believe. In 1934 this would become evident in an extremely painful manner for the Austrian party which he was leading. The overestimation of the strength of Western democracy from which both Bauer's and Kautsky's work suffered was to have fatal consequences for Western socialism.

## MARTOV AS THE IDEOLOGIST OF CENTRISM

Bauer's attempt to keep enthusiasm for Bolshevism in the socialist milieu within certain bounds was only successful in Austria. The influence of his writings was extremely slight in 1920 on the USPD and the other centrist parties, who felt themselves under pressure from their left-wing supporters to negotiate with Moscow about the restructuring of the International. Only the Mensheviks in Russia could now risk another attempt to cure Western socialism of the illusions which Russian revolutionary radicalism had once more aroused. If Russian social democracy's past seemed to indicate anything, then it was that this had continued to be one of the principal and virtually impossible tasks of Menshevism. More was at stake now than ever before and circumstances were also much more adverse than in any previous period. Nor would the Mensheviks now be in a position to change the course of the history of the international labour movement. But they were certainly not entirely without influence and this was mainly because – as Radek had rightly remarked – they had taken up an extremely individual position in the struggle between communism and socialism.

Menshevik ideology became more radical under the influence of the civil war, War Communism, the democratic revolutions in Central Europe and the almost total isolation of Russia in 1919. The idea of the Russian revolution as a bourgeois revolution, which Martov had once defended as an infallible dogma against Lenin, Trotsky, Chernov and Kautsky, was increasingly abandoned. Martov and his followers became convinced that not only Russia but the whole world was ending up in a transitional stage between capitalism and socialism. The October revolution ought consequently to be seen as an inevitable and necessary first step in this direction. In the eyes of a group of prominent party members this was an inadmissible capitulation to Bolshevism. The majority of the party dismissed this imputation. There was no question of a less critical approach to current Bolshevik policy. Nothing but sarcastic comments were made about the socialist pretensions of the dictatorship. According to the RSDRP, the so-called War Communism could only lead to economic chaos. In 1919, within the party, a series of proposals was indeed developed which would prove to have a very close affinity with the measures which were to be introduced by the regime in 1921 under the appellation New Economic Policy.[58]

Nevertheless, it was, according to the left-wing Mensheviks, of historical significance for the development of Russian and of European socialism that the land had been divided among the peasants, industry had been nationalised and the decisive battle between proletarian revolution and capitalist counter-revolution had been fought in Russia. Martov and his followers remained indefatigable opponents of communist terrorism, but when the civil war went through a particularly critical period in 1919, they appealed to their fellow party members to volunteer for the Red

Army because the revolution had to be defended. They were against party dictatorship, but saw less and less advantage in attempts to restore bourgeois democracy in Russia. During this transitional period there ought, in their view, to be a workers' government, a democratic coalition of socialist parties and groups. This was true not only for Russia, where at that moment the chances of this kind of national government were very slender, but also for the rest of Europe for which the Mensheviks as well as the Bolsheviks had high expectations. The Russian social democrats continued to be advocates of a powerful new International, in which all socialists would be reunited. However, they were just as critical of the Second International re-established in Berne as of the Third, set up in Moscow, and they had no wish to form an active part of either of them. In May 1919 the Central Committee of the RSDRP stated:

> A section of the [world] proletariat has been seized by an anarchic-Bolshevik sentiment. It is trying to overthrow the economic and political supremacy of the bourgeoisie and to introduce a socialist system by means of a minority dictatorship which is terrorising the majority of the populace. Another section of the proletariat has been led astray by the practices of the *union sacrée* with the capitalist classes during the war, and is trying to recover from the devastations of the World War and to restore national productivity by frenetically carrying on its co-operation with the bourgeoisie. It does not recoil from violently opposing, together with the capitalists, the workers who embraced immediate revolution in principle.[59]

This reference to the behaviour of the SPD towards the Spartacus League was revealing. The Mensheviks believed in the socialist world revolution so fervently that they left no room for the bourgeoisie in their politics and scarcely any for the reformist socialists. On the other hand, they still hoped that a certain degree of agreement would prove possible with the communists if they saw the error of their ways. The reformists had disqualified themselves from being socialists to such an extent, Martov wrote to Akselrod, that any attempt on their part to interfere in Russian internal affairs had no chance at all.

> Every condemnation of Bolshevik methods and the formulation of a point of view about the issue of the dictatorship is already robbed of all political or moral significance beforehand, if it

proves to be a compromise with Vandervelde, Gompers, Thomas or Scheidemann ... The policy of these socialists has already become sufficiently clear through their ideas about democracy. They understand this word to mean the forms (and only the forms) of parliamentarianism, which mask the present-day military police dictatorship of the plutocracy.[60]

Martov continued to hope that the socialist centre would indeed be able to have a corrective effect on the Russian revolution. But developments in the West did not augur well for this. It was shocking, he thought, that even the USPD, which was regarded by the Mensheviks as the backbone of a future International, was preparing to eat humble pie. It was imperative that the socialist parties of the centre should join forces more and give evidence of their own identity in a joint programme. Only then could they negotiate with Moscow from a position of authority about the conditions which would have to be laid down for collective action by communists and centrists. After the collapse of the First International socialism had gone through a period of reorientation before a new International could be set up. Martov now considered something of the sort vital once more 'for the conquest of intellectual chaos and the crystallisation of a political ideology'. At the same time he wrote to Kautsky: 'Above all it is necessary to form an intellectual meeting place, to have an international mouthpiece in which all the problems of our revolutionary period can be illuminated from an international point of view. A new *Neue Zeit* is imperative ...' Only thus, in Martov's view, could a powerful counterweight be offered to the intrusion of Bolshevik theory and practice.[61]

The new Menshevik ideology was in many respects a typical product of the exciting but at the same time disastrous times which the Russians were going through, cut off from the rest of the world. When regular contacts with the West again became possible, the Russian social democrats were gradually forced to recognise that they had greatly overestimated the chances of revolutionary developments in the West. Nevertheless, it was remarkable that the Mensheviks had not only understood two years before the Bolsheviks that Russia could not escape from economic reforms in the spirit of the NEP, but were also the first to point out the way which international centrism was to take, though not until 1921. Then the parties and groups which had remained faithful to centrism in Vienna set up a Working Union with the long-term purpose of forming an International, which would not fall into the extremes of communism or reformism and would be able to reunite all the workers and socialists. Menshevism, as it was expressed mainly by Martov in 1920–1, therefore remained an interesting approach to the problems with which socialists were faced in those years.

Martov never provided a comprehensive and systematic exposé of his ideas at that time, as Kautsky and Bauer had done. He did write a number of articles in Russia which, during his lifetime, partly appeared in a German translation and after his death were published by Dan in French with the title *Le Bolchevisme mondial*.[62] This title shows the extent to which Martov differed in opinion from Akselrod, Kautsky and above all Bauer. Bolshevism was not, in his view, a degenerate form of typical Russian radicalism. It was an international phenomenon, a product of the World War and the disorganisation which followed from it. It was moreover something for which the socialists themselves, not excluding the Mensheviks, bore a certain responsibility. Martov was no less opposed to the Bolshevik cult of violence and terrorism than Kautsky or Akselrod. His blazing protest against the degradation of human life in Bolshevik Russia entitled *Down with the Death Penalty!* was among the best he ever wrote. The barbaric traits of a regime which called itself socialist not only aroused his indignation, but also, as he wrote to a friend, made 'you feel, as it were, guilty in the presence of every civilised bourgeois'.[63] These feelings of guilt and shame were totally alien to Akselrod. He considered himself in no way responsible for the events in Russia after 1917, although he did think that the politics of Mensheviks like Tsereteli in the year of the revolution had facilitated the Bolshevik coup. Tsereteli himself dismissed this accusation. He was not in the least ashamed of his policy, though of course he recognised that it had failed. 'But', he wrote to Akselrod, 'the more I think about it, the more convinced I become that within the objective and subjective parameters of the revolution there was no political strategy to be devised which could have guarded Russia against Bolshevism.'[64]

This view was not shared by Martov. He had always dissociated himself completely from Tsereteli's coalition policy in 1917. But

N

he also realised that he himself was, at the time, even less able to offer a workable and popular alternative to Bolshevik demagogy. In his view, all the moderate socialists in Russia had failed. They had not managed to solve the fundamental problems of the revolution in time and had left it to the Bolsheviks to cut through a series of Gordian knots. The Western socialists ought also, in Martov's view, to be reproached for the same sort of thing. Initially they had considered it impossible, Martov wrote in his *Bolchevisme mondial*, for communism to gain any grip on the labour movement in their civilised and thoroughly industrialised countries. It was therefore glorified by them and defended against all attack from the bourgeois side. 'And when "world-wide Bolshevism" had become an unmistakable element in the revolutionary process, the European Marxists proved to be as badly prepared as the Russian, if not worse, for understanding the scope of this event and discovering the causes which ensured its continued existence.'[65]

Many socialists had identified Bolshevism with the trench mentality of the military hordes, which found expression in a primitive collectivism, an abhorrence of laborious democratic procedures and a predilection for speedy, violent solutions. Others observed that many workers also wanted immediate, tangible and complete social change. They, like the soldiers, believed that all social and political difficulties could be cleared up by the use of violence. A number of socialist authors, including Kautsky, had tried to explain these character traits by pointing out the changes in the composition and mentality of the proletariat as a result of the war. Martov did not deny all this. Such developments had undoubtedly simplified the advance of Bolshevism but they still did not form an adequate explanation. He pointed out that in many countries the workers felt a deep-rooted distrust for the organisations which had led the socialist movement before August 1914. Wild-cat strikes were the order of the day. Spontaneous forms of organisation, such as workers' councils and factory committees, sprang up like mushrooms all over Europe. They filled the vacuum created by the collapse of the International and the permanent crisis in the European labour movement.[66] Like Lenin and Trotsky, Martov was inclined to attribute the 1914 fiasco to the leaders. He was insufficiently aware of the fact that the workers' masses which had then pressed on socialism a nationalist course and were now preventing it from making a revolution, still comprised the majority of the European proletariat.

He showed more realism in his critical analysis of Bolshevik ideology. The Bolshevik-oriented revolutionary movement in Europe had accepted the workers' council as the only organisation capable of freeing the proletariat. Martov therefore gave due attention to 'the mysticism of Sovietism'.[67] The adherents of the Soviet movement saw the councils as the great and inevitable step in the direction of the total dismantling of the state and the abolition of all social oppression. 'A mystery', Martov wrote, 'which escapes the intellectual faculties of revolutionary believers just as obstinately as the mystery of the Immaculate Conception has always escaped the rational understanding of Christian believers.'[68]

The Soviets were propagated as a replacement to bourgeois democracy. In theory democracy was not abolished by them but temporarily limited to the workers and the poor peasants. In contrast to Kautsky and Akselrod, Martov saw nothing fundamentally reprehensible in this. The essence of democracy did not consist, in his view, of a strictly numerical universal suffrage. The classical democracy of Ancient Athens had excluded the slaves from voting rights, American democracy had not recognised the Negroes as fully-fledged citizens, and even women, soldiers and young people had had no part in the pre-war democracy of some European countries. But it was pointless to dismiss these forms of government as undemocratic. All citizens who kept servants and all members of the professions were robbed of their voting rights in Russia. This was a damaging and regrettable limitation of the people's will, but the Soviet constitution was not thereby undemocratic. A regime could not be called undemocratic unless the free relationships between the citizens, who acted as the privileged guardians of national sovereignty, were encroached upon in an unacceptable manner. This was precisely what the Bolsheviks had done by their manipulation of the elections and the authority of the workers' councils. The Soviet system, by its abolition of all forms of *internal* democracy, had degenerated into the dictatorship of a minority. Martov's criticism therefore applied not so much to the theoretical ideas about democracy of the supporters of the Soviet system, as to their ideas about the functioning of a proletarian dictatorship.[69]

Martov recalled how a fervent adherent of this mystical sovietism, Ernst Daümig, had been annoyed by the behaviour of the First Congress of councils in Germany in December 1918. 'No revolutionary parliament in history has ever displayed such a cowardly attitude, has ever shown itself so commonplace and narrow-minded', Daümig exclaimed. In short, scoffed Martov, the key to the solution of all the problems of the social revolution was: 'either "All power to the Soviets", or "all strength to the cowardly", as a means of raising oneself manfully above the simple formula of universal suffrage. What a bizarre paradox!' Slogans like 'All power to the Soviets!' became understandable when their propagandists admitted in moments of candour – and Martov gave a few examples of this – that the only purpose of the Soviets was to put real power into the hands of the communists.[70]

This strange ambivalence in the thinking of the Soviet adepts seems to have further strengthened their pretensions. When the Soviets had degenerated into cogs in the bureaucratic machinery of the dictatorship, the evangelists of the new doctrine no longer needed to convince the majority of the population of the correctness of their views. Furthermore, Sovietism, in this dictatorial packaging, lent itself admirably for export to all corners of the globe. It offered people the opportunity to remain fervent opponents of bourgeois parliamentarianism, and at the same time to smuggle in again at the back door those elements of the bourgeois state, such as bureaucracy, the police and the army, to which parliament had always formed an essential counterweight. Just as the theory of Sovietism was linked to the ideology of the Paris Commune, so did its practice seem to run parallel to the traditions of the French revolution. In the years 1792–4 the Jacobins, organised into clubs comparable with the communist party cells, exercised their dictatorship over the people by means of a large number of organisations like the communes, sections, revolutionary committees, and so forth, which were like the Soviets and the factory committees of today.

Nevertheless, the Bolsheviks regarded themselves first and foremost as the faithful servants of the working class. In this respect they behaved no differently from many of their illustrious predecessors such as Buonaroti, Weitling, Cabet, Blanqui and Barbès in the nineteenth century, or from their contemporaries, the leaders of French syndicalism like Emile Pouget. The idea that only the dictatorship of an active vanguard could protect the proletariat against the reactionary narrow-mindedness which it was carrying around in its own membership was, according to Martov, deeply anchored in socialism. Marx had long ago impressed upon these benevolent dictators that the educators ought also to be educated and that they should never consider themselves as superhuman or above society. The social circumstances under which the workers had to live could only change through the class war, and by fighting out this war the workers would also be changed from slaves into free men. But the road to be travelled in this way was extremely long and difficult. Because of this there was a powerful temptation to choose a shorter line of march: that of dictatorship, terrorism and bureaucracy. But, Martov argued, not a single man was ever freed by this apparently effective triad.[71]

Martov therefore considered it of the greatest importance to investigate how Lenin, basing himself on statements by Marx and Engels, had arrived at this theoretical justification of the dictatorship. In the *Communist Manifesto* it was after all bluntly stated that the 'elevation of the proletariat into a ruling class' could be equated with the 'conquest of democracy'. After 1914 Lenin gradually came to the conclusion that this formulation was too vague and abstract. A further elaboration of it was not given, in his view, until *The Eighteenth Brumaire* and especially *The Civil War in France*. In addition he was able to make use of the undoubtedly very critical sounds which Marx and Engels had made about the bourgeois state and bourgeois democracy. Marx had repeatedly claimed that the complete dismantlement of the militaristic and bureaucratic machinery of the bourgeois state was an absolute condition for the success of a people's revolution on the continent of Europe. Of course Lenin did not refrain from pointing out to his readers that the Bolsheviks had destroyed the bourgeois state and by the establishment of the Soviet state had shown themselves to be the only true *exécuteurs testamentaires* of Marx and Engels.[72]

There was, however, an important obstacle which stood in the way of reasonably conclusive proof of this. In 1871 Marx had designated England as a capitalist country, in which democracy as such had remained free from bureaucratic and military excrescences, so that it could be taken over by the revolutionary proletariat in its existing form. Kautsky had used this statement in order to incorporate Marx into his democratic views. Lenin's answer, however, had been that since the days of Marx and Engels, imperialism had also got England into its grip. The present-day British state no longer stood out in favourable comparison with the continental ones. A peaceful, evolutionary development towards socialism was consequently no longer possible. Martov did not dispute this. But according to him it was not of essential significance that the exception, which Marx had made for England, was still only a theoretical possibility now. The critical attitude of Marx and Engels with regard to the sovereignty of the bourgeoisie had not made them into supporters of the elimination of the democratic state as such. They only wanted to purify it radically from the bureaucratic and military influences with which it was overrun, and which were characteristic of the Bonapartist system of government they hated. This was also the basis for their enthusiasm for the Commune. In 1891, Engels had yet again said in all clarity, that the Commune had shown how the democratic republic could be used as 'the specific form of the dictatorship of the proletariat'. Engels could never have been thinking of a form of government in using the term 'dictatorship'. He was simply referring to the social structure of state power. In essence Marx and Engels had adhered to the wording of the *Communist Manifesto*: the proletariat could only achieve power by conquering democracy.[73]

Thus Martov had come, along another route, to the same conclusion as Kautsky, without fully sharing his views about democracy. Just because of this subtle difference in approach Martov's criticism of Lenin was interesting and important. Many radical socialists dismissed Kautsky's thesis that the proletariat ought to take over the bourgeois state simply because it recognised universal suffrage and was thus truly democratic. They were too firmly convinced of the class character of bourgeois public institutions and of the rottenness of parliamentary democracy to be able to accept it. Martov tried, with Marx in his hand, to show that this need not be so and at the same time showed that Marxists ought not to let themselves be led astray into a total rejection of the democratic state. Whoever did that, like Lenin, was going against the essential intentions of Marx and Engels and would eventually, in practice, be doing the exact opposite of what they had in mind. Bolshevik Russia had deteriorated into a classic example of a bureaucratic and military dictatorship, in other words, a proletarian state completely subjected to those very elements which Marx and Engels had detested.

In Martov's view Lenin's way of thinking was very similar to that of the utopian socialists of the first half of the nineteenth century. They had believed that the workers actually already had at their disposal the structure of future socialism. Then, the trade unions or the communes were regarded as the embodiment of this ideal. Now, this was the case with the Soviets. Martov acknowledged, however, that Marx in *The Civil War in France* had made the cryptic remark that the Commune was 'the ultimately discovered form' in which economic emancipation of the workers could take place. Kautsky had also drawn this expression without any difficulty into the sphere of his political ideas. In 1917 Lenin based a whole new theory on it which was diametrically opposed to Kautsky's. But Martov's reasoning was completely destroyed if this well-known utterance of Marx meant that he had rejected his own thesis concerning the necessary conquest of the state by the proletariat.

Like all Marxists, Martov also had a tendency to assume that the ideas of Marx and Engels which did not tally with his own were only small, insignificant deviations from the clear pattern which he believed to be present in their work. There are, however, several conflicting patterns to be found in the thought of Marx. His sympathy for the ideas of the Russian populists, with which, in fact, Lenin and Martov were not sufficiently familiar, points towards the possibility of a kind of federalistic socialism. After 1914 Lenin was to base himself more and more on this undercurrent in Marx's thinking. The question, purely academic for us, of whether Martov or Lenin had the most right to appeal to Marx is therefore scarcely worth answering, but in 1920 it was of the greatest significance to Marxists. Martov referred Lenin with pleasure to the biography of Marx, completed in 1918 by Franz Mehring, who as a Spartacist and Marxist historian was held in very great esteem by the communists.

Mehring had written that Marx's statements about the Commune 'are actually somewhat contradictory to the opinions which Marx and Engels have professed for a quarter of a century and proclaimed in the *Communist Manifesto*'. This, of course, was also Martov's opinion, but proof that this was only a matter of a passing aberration by Marx was not provided here.[74]

For Martov there were important grounds for dissociating himself from the attitudes to Bolshevism of Kautsky, Akselrod and Bauer, which were more consistent in themselves. Kautsky's and Akselrod's total condemnation of Bolshevism took too little account for his taste of the great degree of affinity which, despite everything, still continued to exist between communism and socialism. At the same time the development of communism into a more moderate, humanitarian and democratic movement was implicitly excluded by them. According to Martov something of this sort should not be seen as impossible in advance. He moreover thought that an attitude of this kind would have unfavourable repercussions on socialism itself. It would lead unintentionally but inevitably to a weakening of the internationalist, revolutionary and Marxist traits of the movement. For other reasons he had great objections to Otto Bauer's attitude. He had concentrated far too much on the supposed socialist character and Russian background of Bolshevism and had therefore refused to draw general conclusions from the criminal, terrorist practices of the regime. Martov considered that a tacit approval of these because they were limited only to Russia was just as disastrous for the future development of socialism, which ought to be not only humane but also international.

Martov's attempt at combining together the elements he considered valuable from the opinions of others, of necessity had something forced and unstable about it. On the other hand, Martov's very strength lay in his critical and original handling of other people's views. In his analysis of mysticism about the Soviets and the relationship between democracy and dictatorship he penetrated, more deeply than Kautsky and Bauer, into the heart of the problems which faced the Russian and Western socialists as a result of the October revolution. It was partly thanks to this quality in Martov's versatile intellect that a small group of Mensheviks were able, within the limited space left them by a despotic power apparatus, to make themselves felt –

as Lenin himself also admitted – as the only ideological opponents of the regime in Russia to be taken seriously. At the same time Martov's arguments enabled Western socialists like Hilferding, Longuet, Adler and Bauer to take a more discerning and defensible attitude towards Bolshevism.

## LABOUR IN RUSSIA

The disastrous situation in which the RSDRP found itself and the illusions which the Mensheviks cherished about the socialist future of Europe made the task which they had set themselves, to cure international socialism of its 'deviations', extremely troublesome. Bolshevik terrorism and the Western military blockade effectively prevented propaganda for their point of view. Even regular correspondence with Western socialists was impossible, for these letters were intercepted by the regime. For any exchange of ideas, the Russian socialists were dependent on travellers to and from Russia who took post with them in secret. Moreover the Mensheviks realised that Akselrod could no longer be regarded as spokesman for the majority of the party in the West. They were well aware of his point of view from the accounts of Binshtok, who, with Akselrod, had represented the party at the Lucerne conference and had returned to Russia in the late summer of 1919. Akselrod totally rejected the decision of the RSDRP to leave the Second International. During a conference in Moscow in April 1920 the party decided to send a special representative abroad. This was embarrassing, for the decision repudiated the spiritual father of Menshevism's activities in the West. Akselrod had already concluded from the letters he was getting from Russia that he could no longer represent the party and he resigned his mandate. However, he was less isolated in the party then he thought. There were prominent fellow party members in Russia who agreed with him to a great extent, but until his death in 1928 he never again filled any official post whatsoever within the RSDRP.[75]

The Mensheviks did not immediately get round to sending a delegation to the West. They first devoted all their attention to the possibilities offered to them in Russia for influencing foreign socialists. In 1920 it again became possible to visit Russia for the first time in several years, and the Western labour movement made use of this to send a large number of delegations there. But a joint action by Western socialist parties in the form of an international commission to research into the current situation in Russia had become out of the question by 1920. The socialists who visited Russia in that year were representatives of national parties. The delegations arrived one after another, without having consulted each other beforehand, and with different directives from their parties. The Bolsheviks were thus not confronted with a unified Western socialist bloc and this gave them ample opportunity to use propaganda and bring pressure to bear on a highly heterogeneous and therefore pretty defenceless group of Europeans. For the Mensheviks this made the situation even more difficult than it already was.

The first important group to come to Russia was the British. On 9 December 1919 the Trades Union Congress had decided to send a delegation to the Soviet republic 'for an unbiased and independent investigation into the political, industrial and economic circumstances' of that country.[76] The TUC afterwards asked the Labour Party to participate in the project and it agreed to do so. The British socialists clearly saw the delegation as an alternative to the failed attempts of the Second International to send a commission of inquiry to Russia. The Permanent Committee of this organisation discussed the British decision at a meeting in Rotterdam on 23 March 1920 and put forward the suggestion that the delegation should be supplemented with socialists from other countries. In this way the decision of the conferences of Berne and Lucerne, though in an altered form, could nevertheless still be implemented. Lack of time, passport difficulties and fundamental differences of opinion about the Russian issue between the British and other socialists prevented the implementation of this idea. The British government had changed its policy towards Russia at the beginning of 1920 and the British socialists had no problem in getting exit visas. The delegation left Britain on 27 April.[77] Great importance was attached to the arrival of the British by all the communists and socialists in Russia. Before 1914 the British labour movement had never been very susceptible to Marxist or revolutionary influences and thus in Russian eyes was less respectable than German socialism, for example. But the Russians did realise that much had been changed by the World War. The Entente's

victory had given the proletariat in England and the United
States a dominant position within the international labour movement, all the more so because the attention of the French and
the German movements was almost totally occupied by internal
problems. The Russians had waited in vain for a social revolution
to break out in England. But they still believed that the British
verdict on the Bolshevik regime would be of fundamental significance for the future. The Bolsheviks considered that the
Labour Party, even though it had never planned to join the
Comintern, was nevertheless of great importance to them at that
moment. Anglo-Russian negotiations were now actually under
way about a definitive ending of the blockade and intervention,
which would hopefully be followed by a trade agreement and
diplomatic recognition.[78]

The composition of the delegation offered the communists a
good opportunity for winning over the British. The initiative
for the journey had been taken by left-wing elements in the
British labour movement. The delegation was not led by a
reformist like Henderson, but by Robert Williams who had
sympathies with Bolshevism. The same could be said of the
members of the delegation who had been sent by the trade
unions such as Ben Turner and A. A. Purcell. Clifford Allen
and Richard Wallhead were also in the British party on behalf
of the Independent Labour Party, which had severed its links
with the Second International a few weeks beforehand. They
had been instructed to seek contact with the Comintern. The
British were therefore entertained by the Bolsheviks on a most
lavish scale. The Red Army held a parade in their honour. There
were festive receptions given by various government and party
organisations, alternated with excursions on the Volga and to
the front. The delegation drove through the poverty-stricken
Moscow of 1920 in gleaming limousines. They were accommo-
dated in luxury and entertained at banquets which, according
to a Menshevik observer, evoked the atmosphere of 'a long-
forgotten bourgeois paradise'.[79]

The comfort with which the British were surrounded served
at the same time to isolate them from the Russian populace,
which was in a pathetic situation at the height of 'wartime
communism'. Akselrod had already pointed out to the Western
socialists in 1918 and 1919 that the Bolsheviks would strain every

nerve to show their socialist guests a Potemkinesque decor instead of harsh Russian reality. He had insisted that the socialist delegation demand complete freedom of movement and that they provide themselves with trustworthy and independent guides and interpreters. The British delegation was, however, incapable of making use of the freedom guaranteed to them by their hosts. Only one of the two secretaries, Charles Roden Buxton, spoke some Russian. Tom Shaw knew French and German. The rest were completely dependent on the guides and interpreters allotted to them. These watched over them like Cerberus and were probably members of the Cheka. It seemed to the Mensheviks as if the delegation was surrounded by an impenetrable wall. Letters to the British were either not delivered or destroyed, as happened to a letter from the Menshevik party organisation in Petrograd. Chekists were posted at the entrance to the hotel in Moscow where the delegation was staying, with instructions to interrogate anyone who wished to contact the delegation. No one was allowed in without a special pass issued by the authorities.[80]

But at the same time the Bolsheviks were burning to convince their guests that they also had their 'most loyal opposition' in the Menshevik party. The RSDRP had just somewhat strengthened its position again at the beginning of 1920. 'Recently', wrote Martov to Alexander Stein, 'despite the fact that the regime is maintaining lawlessness, we have been successful in a series of elections (in Moscow we have gained 40 people [elected to the Soviet], in Charkov more than 100, in Bryansk, Tula, Vitebsk and Smolensk a few dozen). These numbers are always drowned in the communist majority thanks to their system of "rotten boroughs", but the mentality of the regime is such that even this small breakthrough of an opposition group puts the ruling party in a panic. As a result of it fresh oppression has begun in Kiev, where it was feared that the elections would provide us with even greater victories [than elsewhere].'[81] Since the social democrats evidently had a greater following among the population than the Soviets proved to have from the rigged elections, the authorities were, on the other hand, certainly very pleased with the political support the Mensheviks had given them when the Poles attacked Russia at the end of April 1920. The RSDRP had ostentatiously mobilised its members for the military defence of the revolutionary fatherland.

Therefore it was not wholly incomprehensible that the Menshevik group in the Moscow Soviet was invited to attend a solemn reception for the British delegation at the Bolshoi Theatre on 18 May 1920. The gathering was organised by the Bolshevik trade union federation, the All-Russian Executive Committee of the Soviets and a whole series of metropolitan organisations. Besides communist leaders like Tomsky, Bukharin and Kamenev, Martov's associate Abramovich was to act as spokesman on behalf of the Central Committees of the RSDRP and the Bund. A public appearance of the opposition at meetings of such magnitude had become a relative rarity. Martov had shortly beforehand warned the regime that it ought not to make use of the Polish war to transport the revolution at bayonet point into Europe. He knew that Lenin and his followers were toying with ideas of this kind. Bolshevik agitation in the West was an extremely sensitive issue in the negotiations with the British government. The communists were therefore waiting with a certain trepidation to see what subjects would be raised by the social democrats in the presence of such important guests. Abramovich had a reputation as an excellent speaker. The Menshevik Aronson, who belonged to the right wing of the party and did not therefore agree with Abramovich's, Dan's and Martov's course of action, wrote later that he would never forget 'the immensely moving impression' that this 'self-restrained and dry' speech made on the meeting.[82]

Abramovich was delighted that the British were trying to solve 'the riddle of the Sphinx-like Russian revolution' from their own observations. 'After all many problems with which the Russian working class is now wrestling ... could perhaps in a not too distant future be of current significance for England and even for the whole of Europe.' Therefore the speaker considered it of importance that the British delegation should take note of the differences of opinion which existed between his party and the communists.[83] According to Abramovich socialism was no longer 'a pious doctrinaires' dream'. It had changed into 'a practical slogan of realistic politics, the battle-cry of the million-headed masses in their daily struggle'. The Mensheviks were, like the communists, firmly convinced of the advent of the world revolution and the dictatorship of the proletariat. But they did not believe that these developments could be forced or hastened by violence. Abramovich thought that a theoretical discussion about the problem of whether parliaments or workers' councils offered the best guarantees for optimal democracy was rather meaningless. The experience of the Russian revolution had taught him that the existence of a constitution, ideal on paper, could not prevent the Soviets from being completely subjected to the power of one party.

In this connection he pointed out the position of his own party, which had not been able to greet the British delegation at the station, which could no longer distribute a newspaper or journal, which in most places no longer had a local committee, simply because all this was forbidden. 'Here at this meeting you see our small group of a few dozen people, although – and we hope to convince you of this – a considerable section of the workers are behind us, both here and in the provinces.' The speaker hoped to find another time and place at which to acquaint the Labour delegation further with Menshevik ideas about the current situation in Russia. As Abramovich was finishing his speech an incident took place about this very point. He wished to add a few words to it, but the chairman Tomsky tried to prevent this and gave the translator no opportunity to translate it. The British were of course interested in this incident and understood from the tumult in the hall that Abramovich had wanted to invite them to a meeting on behalf of the typographers' union, the only trade union which was still under Menshevik leadership. Tomsky was subsequently forced to make it clear that all the organisations which wanted to come into contact with the Labour delegation would have the opportunity to do so. In this way a considerable breach was made in the isolation of the British party.

Some of the Labour delegates were in fact determined to take a look behind the communist façade. Roden Buxton had obtained Dan's address from Akselrod and thus tried to make contact with the Menshevik party leadership. Although the programme that the Bolsheviks had made for their guests hardly left them any time for their own initiatives, some of the delegates nevertheless demanded the freedom of movement promised by the communists. These Englishmen went out on their own, making grateful use of guides and interpreters who were placed at their disposal by the Mensheviks. Martov, Dan and Abramovich were able to make an unimpeded visit to the delegation at their hotel and they invited them, on behalf of the Central Committee, to pay a return visit.[84]

A number of Englishmen therefore paid two visits to the Menshevik headquarters in Moscow, which, according to Aronson, after all the official pomp and circumstance, must have struck them as particularly shabby. 'A tumbledown entrance, a staircase which had not been swept for a long time, our meagre "buffet" where fish and millet porridge figured as delicacies, a number of bare wooden benches in a large room, the walls only decorated with banners and two or three portraits: Plekhanov, Tsereteli, and a table without a tablecloth, around which we ranged ourselves for the conversation.'[85] At the request of the foreign socialists, the Mensheviks had prepared a number of detailed reports about the economic and political situation in Russia. These were now elucidated by the economic specialists in the party, Cherevanin and Groman, and the political leaders Martov and Dan. The British proved receptive to Menshevik criticism of communist power. 'The utopian-paternalistic character of the present-day socialist state was perfectly clear to them', wrote Martov to Akselrod, 'and the link between the oppression of freedom and independence and internal rottenness, corruption and administrative inefficiency now possessed no more secrets for them.'

'More difficult were the economic problems, although they did their best to become familiar with them. But the agrarian structure of Russia and social attitudes here are completely unknown to them.'[86] The British had seen with their own eyes the scale of the economic chaos, and understood perfectly well that the Mensheviks, in spite of their socialist convictions, were supporters of a large-scale de-nationalisation of industry. 'Can nothing then remain in the hands of the state?', they nevertheless asked. But they nodded affirmatively when Martov with great pessimism proclaimed that the Bolsheviks, with their obtuse policies, had reduced the entire economy to chaos. Naturally the Mensheviks were extremely anxious to know what the prospects for a social revolution in England were. The British put a damper on them by all, from the 'left-wing' Ben Turner to the 'right-wing' Tom Shaw, declaring categorically that in their country any other route to socialism except the parliamentary democratic one was totally out of the question. Even on the question of the International, agreement between the delegation and the Mensheviks proved impossible. Shaw said that the British socialists could not understand why all parties, from communist to reformist, could not feel at home in the Second International.[87]

'The Bolsheviks had shown the British a great deal', wrote Dan, 'but one thing they could not show them: a free workers' meeting. And for a very simple reason. The mood of the Moscow workers was then absolutely not of such a nature that the Bolsheviks could be proud of it. But what the Bolsheviks did not do, we did . . .'[88] The typographers' union convened a meeting attended by 4,000 or 5,000 workers in the large hall of the academy of music in the centre of Moscow. This striking social democratic demonstration, not a stone's throw from the Kremlin, was attended by a number of members of the Labour delegation. Speeches were made by Kefali (Kammermacher) on behalf of the typographers and by Dan on behalf of the Central Committee of the RSDRP. The speakers' unvarnished criticism of the regime obviously had the endorsement of the public, with the exception, of course, of the small contingent of Bolsheviks in the hall. The sudden appearance of the leader of the PSR, Victor Chernov, who was wanted by the communists, caused a sensation. The Cheka was immediately warned by a Bolshevik present, but Chernov managed to escape after his speech thanks to a perfectly organised retreat. This was an impressive demonstration of the opposition in the capital. But it was also the last meeting of its kind which the Bolsheviks were to tolerate.[89]

Among the many Soviet institutions which the Labour delegation visited was the Cheka. Ksenofontov, the deputy head of the security police, received the British on 27 May. He told them amongst other things the absurd story that the personnel of the Cheka consisted of 4,500 people, whereas its strength was then probably already almost 100,000 men. The Mensheviks had pointed out to their British guests during their visit that repression of the socialists would probably be tightened up as a result of their contacts with the delegation. The British therefore asked Ksenofontov whether this would really happen. He answered with a solemn denial and informed them that the people referred to by the British could only be arrested 'for crimes against which the Cheka has been fighting ever since its establishment', that is to say, counter-revolutionary activities and speculation. Martov informed Akselrod that the British had fully understood the sinister meaning of this answer. According to Ksenofontov the Cheka had proof at its disposal that the Mensheviks and the socialist revolutionaries were jointly responsible for the actions of Denikin, Kolchak and Iudenich. Martov handed over to the British socialists a copy of an official protest by the RSDRP against these insinuations. In this it was explained that any social democrat who was linked in any way whatsoever to a counter-revolutionary organisation automatically lost his membership. This decision of the RSDRP was repeatedly published in the Soviet press and Ksenofontov's claim was a cynical lie.[90]

While the Labour delegation was making a boat trip on the Volga, the communists telegraphed to England that the British delegates had attended a public meeting at which Victor Chernov had been able to make a speech in complete freedom. At the same time Martov wrote to Akselrod:

> The Bolsheviks took a different attitude to the English when they noticed that they did not want to be kept in ignorance, and went to look for information among the opposition. They began to treat them as opportunists in the presence of the workers. And against us, who are regarded as the most important culprits in what has happened, a campaign has started which even exceeds that which occurred in 1918 and 1919 in its savagery and bloodthirsty shamelessness. Consequently there is no doubt whatever that today or tomorrow a new wave of repression will inundate us, whether in the form of exclusion from the Moscow Soviet (in the provinces we have already been eliminated in Odessa, Gomel and Nikolaev) and the abolition of the typographers' union and the closing of two of our clubs, or in the form of mass arrests; possibly both these things will happen ... It is possible that before they [the British] leave no arrests will have as yet taken place, although the tenor of the papers is such that it reeks not of arrests but rather of executions ... Two weeks ago the same press was rejoicing in every possible way that we had signed a truce because of the war with Poland ...[91]

Martov was right. The campaign of slander in the Bolshevik papers was continued. Dan, who was serving as a military doctor in the Red Army, was removed from Moscow in the second week of June and sent to Yekaterinburg in the Urals.

Abramovich was forced to withdraw from the Moscow Soviet, under pressure from his own voters who were threatened by the communist authorities with decreases in their grocery rations. And in the night of 17 to 18 June 1920 eleven members of the board of the typographers' union and twenty-nine elected representatives and members of factory committees were removed from their beds and arrested. Among the arrests were a number of Menshevik members of the Moscow Soviet. Some of the typographers tried to enforce the release of their democratically chosen leaders by means of a strike, but harsh measures were taken against them. In a persuasive appeal to the British delegation Kefali wrote: 'The masters of the situation are using methods of waging war of which the bourgeoisie in every country of the world can only dream, but which they can never use. The withholding of food, in these circumstances, is the most frightful measure which can be used against starving people. This is being done.'[92]

The Mensheviks had tried with every means at their disposal to reach the European proletariat via the British delegation. To this end they had risked their position as opposition party, and brought about the abolition of the last free trade union in Russia. Had it been worth while? Martov expressed himself, 'given the composition of the delegation', as not dissatisfied. In his view the opinion of the British visitors about Soviet Russia had changed radically. But in fact, the result was not so encouraging. A minority of the British group, including Williams and Purcell, had avoided contact with the opposition. It was largely thanks to the intolerant attitude of the Bolsheviks that most of the members of the Independent Labour Party no longer considered joining the Comintern after the return of their deputation. The remaining delegates, of whom most were far further from Bolshevism from a political point of view than the left-wing majority of the RSDRP, had made grateful use of the services of the opposition. But in no way were they converted to the Menshevik view about the socialist problems of the day inside and outside Russia. Thus Wallhead did inform the Independent Labour Party in his report of 'interesting meetings' with the Menshevik leaders in Moscow. But he nevertheless accepted the Bolshevik explanations concerning the necessity of repressing the opposition.[93]

Undoubtedly some of the British delegates returned to England completely disillusioned with the Bolshevik experiment, but this was not the case for the deputation as a whole. Probably because its members were not in agreement amongst themselves, they refrained, in the report which was brought out about their journey, from direct critical commentary on terrorism and adopted the tone of objective observers. 'Whether Russia ... could be governed in another way – or in particular whether it is to be expected that the normal process of democracy could function well there – is a question to which we can give no adequate reply ... The Russian revolution has not had a fair chance ... The circumstances were such that they made a revolution in social attitudes extraordinarily difficult, no matter who tried to do it and what measures were taken.' The way in which they answered the question of who was to blame for this situation was characteristic: 'We cannot forget that the responsibility for these events which are the result of foreign interference, lies not with the revolutionaries in Russia but with the capitalist governments of other countries, including our own.'[94]

These were not the specific statements for which the Mensheviks had been waiting. Martov overestimated the Menshevik influence on the delegation when he wrote: 'For the first time here we are seeing people who can look at the problem of [Western, socialist] support for the Russian revolution against imperialism independently from the judgement of Bolshevik methods and principles.'[95] Kefali's appeal to the British labour movement to exert its influence on behalf of the oppressed typographers in Russia, was not followed by any effective action from the Labour Party or the British trade unions. This was no coincidence. The British socialists were averse to dictatorial social experiments in their own country. At the same time they were anxious not to disrupt the improvement of the relations between Great Britain and Soviet Russia by showing too much sympathy for the Menshevik cause.

The delegation therefore, without any comment, included a substantial quantity of material about the socialist opposition as appendices to their report. Most of these documents related to Russian social democracy, such as an account of the meeting of the typographers' union and a report by Kefali about the persecution and abolition of his organisation by the Bolsheviks. Some important passages from the party programme which the RSDRP had drawn up in 1920 were also reproduced. Even these met with criticism. According to the *Labour Leader*, the ILP's paper, L. Haden Guest, the editor of the report, had not been objective, 'so that full weight is given to Menshevik manifestos against the Soviet Government'. In November 1920 some Russian social democrats living in London tried, by means of an open letter, to interest the Labour Party in the oppression of socialists in Russia. This in fact led to a correspondence in the British socialist press between Henderson, secretary of the Labour Party, and Krasin, the authorised agent of the Soviet government at the Anglo-Russian negotiations. Things were not, however, made too difficult for Krasin, who dismissed this interference in the internal affairs of his country. The British socialists were evidently unwilling to put any extra obstacles in the way of the lingering and laborious discussion about the trade agreement. But three members of the British delegation did publish critical books about their experiences.[96] Ethel Snowden in *Through Bolshevik Russia* spoke with great appreciation and sympathy about the opposition and had hardly a good word for Bolshevism. But her impressions were highly emotional and not very accurate. The only good work about Russia that the journey produced was Bertrand Russell's book. He was not an official member of the delegation, however, and his shrewd repudiation of Russian communism was not directly based on Menshevik information.[97]

The result of the British visit was thus not very satisfactory either for the opposition or for the Russian rulers.[98] The publications of the delegation simply confirmed that the majority of the British labour movement persevered in its categorical rejection of Bolshevism for internal use. The Mensheviks would later learn once more that the British socialists were not prepared for forceful intervention on behalf of the Russian socialist opposition, and that, for a significant section of the trade unions, enthusiasm for communist Russia was increasing rather than decreasing. The Russians could indeed expect – and that was the only positive thing – that the socialists in England would demand an end to intervention and the blockade with even more emphasis, and would work diligently for diplomatic recognition of the Soviet republic. But there were no differences of opinion about the importance of this between Mensheviks and Bolsheviks.

## THE SECOND COMINTERN CONGRESS

The next round in the fight between the socialist opposition and the communist regime, with Western socialism at stake, was less spectacular but no less important. The Second Congress of the Communist International met in the summer of 1920. In April 1919 the Comintern had been established by the Russian communists with the co-operation of a handful of dedicated foreigners who were also present in Moscow, but not one of them represented a single important Western socialist party. Expectations about a socialist revolution near at hand were nevertheless extremely high. After a year this enthusiasm was somewhat tempered, but the number of groups and parties that sent a delegation to Russia in 1920 was much greater and formed a fairly accurate reflection of Western revolutionary socialism. As already mentioned, the Bolsheviks were more inclined to ascribe the failure of the attempted revolutions in the West to 'treachery' by the leaders than to lack of revolutionary zeal among the working masses themselves. As a result of this the accent was placed, by the Russian leadership of the Third International, more and more on discipline, organisation and the following of orders from Moscow. At the same time the Bolsheviks tried to gain a real grip on the Western workers' movement via the centre parties, which had sought a rapprochement with Moscow.

The communist tactic was to bend the hesitant leaders of the centre to their will by alternately intimidating and humouring them. As much capital as possible was made of the Bolsheviks' great prestige as leaders of the first successful 'socialist' revolution in the world. Moscow did not succeed in actually convincing the Western centrists that the Bolshevik doctrines were right or in making them believe that 'Russian' methods were applicable in the West. A considerable number of foreign communists also refused to accept this. Most of the centrists who appeared at the Second Congress had travelled to Russia under pressure from the revolutionary and pro-communist left wing of their party. The illusions of these socialists and workers about Soviet Russia were sometimes completely shared by them, sometimes partly or not at all. Because they continued to have to bear in mind the possibility of a split in their own party and the loss of their supporters, a section of the travellers to Russia were prepared to put up with very harsh requirements for joining the Comintern, and later to defend fiercely this total capitulation to communism before their own party.[99]

The most striking success for the Bolsheviks was the behaviour of the two delegates from the SFIO, Cachin and Frossard. The prominent Bolshevik L. M. Karakhan informed a friendly socialist in confidence: 'We are very pleased about Cachin and Frossard, especially the former, who is a splendid fellow. They were both a little ashamed of their "patriotic" past and are now doing everything to make up for it. Otherwise they are afraid of causing a scandal: their exile [from Russia] or our refusal to listen to them. One has to adopt this kind of attitude towards the French, then they become as malleable as wax.' Because they were afraid of bringing the Bolsheviks' anger upon themselves and endangering their unstable negotiating position, the French delegates made no contact with the opposition. Cachin even handed over to the communist authorities a letter for Martov which he had received in France.[100] The Mensheviks were not particularly surprised by the behaviour of this French socialist, for in 1917, during his visit to Russia, he also had swung to the other extreme, and from being a passionate supporter of *union sacrée* had become a vehement champion of the Stockholm peace conference. Martov, who had lived in France for years and was well informed about the relationships within French socialism, remarked in a letter to Kautsky about both the Frenchmen in Moscow: 'These peoples only want to be "salonfähig" [presentable] for the Bolsheviks, but Lenin and Co. know perfectly well that these politicians are "ultra-révolutionnaires, par l'opportunisme même" [ultra-revolutionaries only through opportunism], because they do not want to be rejected by the [working] masses.'[101]

Martov tried to fight the danger of a Bolshevisation of the French workers' movement by means of a letter to the syndicalist leader, Merrheim, with whom Martov had maintained a close relationship during the war and whose point of view with regard to the international socialist problems of the time he had shared completely. He warned the Frenchman of the attempts which would be made by the Bolsheviks to split the international trade union movement and bend it to their will.

> Do you not believe that if one is not in a position to criticise actual Bolshevism like that ruling in Russia, one cannot defend oneself effectively against the penetration of Bolshevism into the European movements either? Up till now one has consoled oneself with the sophism: let us make the social revolution as well as we can, without having Bolshevik methods imposed on us, for Bolshevism may well be very suitable for the Russian bears, but that does not apply here. Unfortunately, the Russian bears are not satisfied with the paradise they have established for themselves, they want to saddle everyone else with it.

Martov therefore asked the CGT to send a strong delegation to Moscow composed of people with a spotless socialist war record. The Bolsheviks ought not to have the opportunity – an opportunity which was offered them in the case of Cachin and Frossard – of driving the French socialists into a corner on the grounds of their former commitment to the policy of *union sacrée*. However, no delegation from the CGT went to Moscow. French syndicalism was then, contrary to Martov's fears, less sensitive to communist influences than the SFIO. Moreover Merrheim published Martov's letter in the syndicalist paper *L'Information Ouvrière et Sociale*.[102]

Not all the socialists in Moscow reacted like the two Frenchmen. A number of foreigners, often more revolutionarily inclined than the centrists of the SFIO, broke through the Bolshevik cordon and visited the Menshevik club in the Russian capital. Felix Platten, the Swiss socialist who had prevented his party from attending the Berne conference at the beginning of 1919 out of sympathy with the communists, expressed his disappointment about 'Bolshevism at work' to Martov. So did two young English syndicalists, representatives of the shop stewards' movement which had been described by the leaders of the Comintern as 'the true representatives of the proletarian masses in England' and proposed as the revolutionary antithesis of the British Labour delegation. They could see through the 'paradisiacal' façade put up by the Bolsheviks of a regime which in reality had nothing to do with their ideas about proletarian self-government. The Dutch communist David Wijnkoop and his Scandinavian comrades Friis and Grimlund made enquiries of the opposition. The most important contacts, however, were those between the Mensheviks and parts of the delegations of the Italian socialist party and of the USPD.[103]

The Italians were received by the Russian communists with even more respect than the English had been a month earlier. There was a reason for this, for the Italian party, the PSI, had joined the Comintern immediately after it was set up. The PSI was the only large Western socialist party within the communist camp and the Italian delegates were the 'spoilt children' of the Second Congress. But the Italian party leader Serrati made no attempt to disguise the fact that he disagreed with the Bolsheviks on almost every point. He did not believe there was anything to be gained by exporting Bolshevik ideas and methods and he had no wish to place the unity of his party in the balance by breaking with the reformists.[104] The Mensheviks sent the Italian delegation, the most distinguished members of which they knew from the conferences at Zimmerwald and Kiental, a cordial letter welcoming them to Russia. They expressed the hope that the Italians would come to know 'the real economic and political situation in Russia' and 'the true character of the ideas and trends within the different parties of the Russian proletariat' during their stay. Only in this way would they be able to cultivate understanding in the Western proletariat 'for the most essential problems of the social revolution'. The socialists would 'only after an impartial study of the revolutionary movement in every country be in a position to establish a new, decisive International on the ruins of the old one'. Not until then would it be possible for the socialists to join forces 'on a basis of sharing the same goals and the same methods'.[105]

The practical sense of this somewhat utopian train of thought was well understood by Serrati. He made contact with the Central Committee of the RSDRP and asked for a detailed report of the persecution of the socialist opposition under communist rule. Thus this member of the Presidium of the Comintern did what, according to the Mensheviks, every right-minded member of a foreign communist or socialist delegation in Russia ought to have done. Naturally they gladly complied with Serrati's request. 'The facts and names which we have mentioned in this memorandum', wrote the party leadership, 'have been verified and we take full responsibility for them ... We declare every communist party or group a moral accomplice to the policy of persecution of socialist ideas by means of imprisonment, censorship of the press or bloody violence, unless it exerts its influence at the Third International in order to call a halt to this infamous policy directed against a considerable section of the Russian proletariat.'[106]

Of course the Mensheviks knew that this curious version of Akselrod's idea of a socialist intervention in the development of the Russian revolution had no chance of success. But they hoped to achieve a concrete goal with this appeal to the consciences of the foreign delegates at the communist congress. Martov and Abramovich had been appointed by the Central Committee as the future representatives of the party abroad. The RSDRP had deliberately requested an exit visa for them during the conference. If they were refused they had the possibility of an appeal to the foreign communists in Moscow. But the Mensheviks continued to be pessimistic in mood: 'Lenin and his people would rather give passports for foreign travel to twenty tsarist generals or ex-ministers than to one of us', wrote Martov to Kautsky.[107] Little is known about the discussions between the Mensheviks and the Italian delegates Bombacci and Serrati. When Serrati, who remained an adherent of the Comintern until his death in 1923, returned to Italy, he showed his disappointment with the Russian communists in an almost Menshevik manner. In his view the Bolsheviks formed 'an unimportant minority which rules over a tremendously passive majority'. He spoke of their 'miraculous' belief that a small elite of dedicated and well-organised revolutionaries could take the place of the absent objective circumstances necessary for a social revolution. 'I have never felt so strange at an International congress', he said in Moscow to Crispien, a member of the four-man delegation from the USPD, which had arrived in Moscow in the middle of July.[108]

Martov had recommended to Kautsky that the USPD send a delegation which did not consist only of politicians, but which also included economists, trade union leaders and more people of this sort. 'The discussions with the Italians and the English have firmly convinced me that only through the beginning of intellectual traffic with Soviet Russia can the emancipation of the European workers' movement from "Bolshevik supremacy" take place, even if this happens very slowly.'[109] The delegation which was sent to Russia reflected the great dissension which reigned in this party. The delegates Daümig and Stoecker belonged to the left wing, which wanted to join the Comintern at once, while the other two members of the deputation, Dittmann and Crispien, faithful to the assignment they had received from their party, wished to attach certain conditions to this. In Moscow Dittmann and Crispien accused the Russian communists of making a series of slanderous attacks on leading figures in their party. They dismissed as ludicrous the Bolshevik requirement that people like Ströbel, Kautsky and Hilferding should be expelled. They parried these attempts to enforce a kind of purification on the USPD by demanding complete internal autonomy for every party within the Comintern. Neither Dittmann and Crispien nor Serrati had anything against engaging in a debate with Trotsky or Lenin, who were venerated as demi-gods at the congress, if they thought it necessary. But like the Italian leader they felt like fish out of water. They decided to consult the opposition in the hope of obtaining 'trustworthy and detailed information'.[110]

But Daümig and Stoecker were not keen on this. Under pressure from both their fellow party members, they were prepared if need be to meet Martov and other Mensheviks for a private conversation. They did not want an official meeting between the delegation and the Central Committee of the RSDRP, because they thought this would be disloyal to their Bolshevik hosts. However, the Mensheviks informed Dittmann, who conveyed this proposal to them, that they were grateful for the honour, but would refrain from a discussion with the German delegation as a whole. Instead they submitted a formal protest to the party leadership of the USPD. In this letter the Central Committee expressed its indignation at the behaviour of the delegation, which in its opinion was contrary to the decisions of the USPD congress the previous year in Leipzig. There the German party had, after all, decided to contact all the parties which had left the Second International. The RSDRP pointed out to the German party leadership that it had already dissociated itself from the Berne organisation in May 1919. Since Zimmerwald days the Mensheviks had been closely linked to the German 'independents' and had frequently defended them against slanderous criticism from the Russian and German communists. While representatives of the *communist* parties of Italy, Holland, Switzerland, Norway, Sweden and England had certainly found their way to the opposition, the USPD delegation seemed to be animated by a sort of 'neophyte zeal' which made this impossible. The RSDRP consequently asked the board of the USPD if it was prepared to maintain normal relations and to give information about its viewpoint in one of its party organs.[111]

Dittmann told the Mensheviks that he regarded their harsh reaction as a 'well-deserved box on the ears' and was delighted that they were fully prepared to have detailed discussions with him and Crispien.[112] Crispien later wrote about these meetings:

> When we first visited the accommodation of the Menshevik Committee, we were struck by the gigantic contrast which existed between the outward appearance of the residence of the ruling party and the headquarters of the 'legal opposition' . . . But in what a comradely environment we felt ourselves to be in the midst of these people . . . With the sharp lancet of Marxist analysis Martov and his friends stripped Bolshevism in a merciless manner of all its brilliant tinsel and revealed its actual substance: the perniciousness of the policy of wartime communism, which was then experiencing its greatest florescence, the utopian and illusory character of the so-called 'dictatorship of the proletariat' and of the 'Soviet system', which in fact formed simply a poorly masked tyranny of one party or [rather] of one party clique. Then for the first time we understood in all clarity what we had beforehand only vaguely suspected.[113]

The Mensheviks, however, pointed out to the Germans that their demand for autonomy of the national parties within the Comintern also meant that the European socialists were releasing the Bolsheviks from any international control over Russian internal policy. They would also be sanctioning the continued existence of a terrorist dictatorship. Complete freedom of action would enable the Kremlin unremittingly to confront the international proletariat via the Comintern with disagreeable surprises. The Bolsheviks' performance in the Polish war spoke volumes. 'Dittmann admitted', wrote Martov to Akselrod, 'that the Europeans had been placed [by the Bolsheviks] in the uncomfortable and unbefitting situation of "second-rate citizens", from which they and their friends could see no exit. Therefore for the time being there is not much else for us to do except support them in their "circumspection", so that no new opportunities are offered to the Bolsheviks . . .' However, Dittmann did express to Martov the expectation that it might be possible for the USPD to rectify the Leipzig decisions because of their experiences with the Russian communists. Crispien too thought that association with the Comintern as the Bolsheviks wanted it was 'unthinkable'.[114]

The decision about this would of course be taken in Germany. The Italian and French parties were now also faced with this decision. The Mensheviks were reasonably optimistic about the future. The Third International was in their view doomed to failure. Martov wrote about this to Kautsky: 'the Third International has already reached the stage in its development in which its overruling spirit of sectarian uniformity and "iron discipline" of which Lenin is so fond, and which is inherent in Bolshevism, has come into irreconcilable conflict with the medley of revolutionary processes occurring in the modern labour movement.' Martov believed that not only in the Italian but also in the left wing of the Scandinavian labour movement, under the appearance of a romantic communism, a deeply rooted 'developmental process of socialist consciousness was occurring' and that in other words these parties could be won back to the position of the socialist centre.

He did not therefore foresee great triumphs for the Comintern in the near future. But one should be on the alert for 'fortuitous communist successes' which could be prevented with some effort on the socialist side. Not only did the Third International function as the 'great disorganisation factory for the general class movement', but Bolshevik policy also contained great dangers. The Comintern ought to keep a 'permanent revolution' alive. Russia would therefore have to remain the focus of European revolution, in a continual state of war against all the capitalist states. But actual practice forced the Soviet state to peace and to a compromise with capitalism, because – as many Bolsheviks themselves recognised – without its help the Russian economy could not be saved. The communist rulers' policy had therefore acquired an equivocal character with dangerous extremist aspects. Martov once more pointed out in this connection the failed attempt of the Bolsheviks to make use of the Polish war to expand the communist revolution by directing the Red Army into the West. At the same time the regime was carrying out, partly in secret, partly in public, an imperialistic and annexationist policy in Siberia and the Caucasus. The Bolsheviks had even greeted the formation of the reactionary Kapp government with joy, for a German regime which was nationalistic, anti-Polish and anti-Entente suited them down to the ground.[115]

There was a great deal of truth in what Martov wrote. The Western communist movement would be characterised by violent internal disagreements and conflicts. The exodus of one generation after another of supporters disappointed in communism and in Soviet Russia began in 1920 and continued until very recently when the communist party of the Soviet Union itself became defunct. In France and Germany communist influence on workers and other voters fluctuated sharply in the period between the wars. The cause of this lay to a large extent in the capricious policy of the communist dictatorship in Russia. But neither Martov nor Western centrists like Dittmann were much of a judge of the frustrations which the absence of a socialist revolution was then already causing in a considerable section of the European labour movement. These people had no more patience. Admiration for the Bolshevik revolution as a compensation for their own impotence had become so embedded in many workers and socialists in 1920 that no modification of their pro-communist attitude could be brought about. They had temporarily cut themselves off from rational arguments and unpleasant facts which damaged their new idol.

Thus to some extent the Bolsheviks had free play in the West. It seemed as if they even realised this fully when the Council of People's Commissars gave permission to Martov and Abramovich to leave for the West. The RSDRP had earlier informed the government that they wanted some representation abroad, since Akselrod had resigned his mandate. In their letter the Mensheviks expressed the hope that 'the Soviet power considers itself sufficiently strong not to have to fear our pernicious influence on our Western associates'. Copies of this letter in French and German translations were distributed among the foreigners attending the Second Comintern Congress. 'Probably this resulted in the government's decision to consent', wrote Martov to Akselrod.[116]

There is, however, also evidence that the Bolsheviks were less sure of their ground. According to tradition, Bukharin, on leaving the meeting of the Politbureau at which this matter was discussed, said to a friend: 'The majority was against; the Mensheviks will throw a spanner in the works of the Comintern, but we can accomplish nothing against Ilich [Lenin], who is in love with Martov and will help him to go abroad whatever it costs.'[117] It was generally known that Lenin had retained a soft spot for his former friend, while Martov had long since written Lenin off. Martov's great fear was that his departure from Russia – although he did not think of staying away for longer than six to eight months – would mean that the Bolsheviks could now proceed to the complete elimination of his party. It is possible that another consideration had played a part with the Bolsheviks. Litvinov explained to David Dalin, a Menshevik who applied for an exit visa a few months later and likewise had to wait for a government decision, 'Lenin thinks that you can do a great deal of damage here. It is better for you to be abroad. There at least you can make an effort for the recognition of Soviet authority.'[118] Undoubtedly the Mensheviks would argue strongly in its favour, but, for Martov, this was not the reason for going. He believed that his stay in the West, where the socialist centre was faced with the cardinal decision of whether or not to side with communism, could be very useful. His first destination was Germany. Dittmann had strongly urged Martov to attend the discussions in the USPD and to try to influence them.

# 8

1920–1921: DIVISION IN THE WEST,
UPRISING AND FAMINE IN RUSSIA

At approximately the same time as the Moscow congress, the Second International met once more in the summer of 1920 at Geneva. This congress was chiefly a concern of the Labour Party and the SPD, seconded by the socialist parties of smaller countries like Sweden, Denmark, Holland and Belgium. Only splinter groups of the socialist movement in Italy, Switzerland and France took part in the deliberations. The centrists of course were absent, with the exception of the ILP which was represented via the Labour Party. Russia was scarcely represented in Geneva. The PSR, which had also left the Second International, had sent an observer, while Akselrod attended the congress as a guest. Tsereteli and Voitinsky formed part of the Georgian delegation. The Second International in Geneva was certainly no longer a reflection of international labour as a whole, but it nevertheless still represented the majority of the movement as regards the membership and the electoral status of the affiliated parties. The absent communists and centrist socialists regarded the congress as nothing more than a meeting of the right-wing, nationalist-democratic and parliamentary-reformist sections of socialism.[1] This was a one-sided view, for the congress still avoided harsh criticism of communism, although many speakers once more expressed their aversion to dictatorship and their loyalty to parliamentary democracy. The attitude of the Englishman Tom Shaw, who as a member of the Labour delegation to Russia could speak with the most authority about the Soviet republic, was an example of this. In his view Bolshevism was a crime. The workers in Russia were deprived of all their freedoms and rights. Nevertheless he impressed on the delegates that the Second

International, although it ought to dissociate itself from communism, should not adopt a hostile attitude with regard to Soviet Russia.[2]

Not only Shaw but also many other socialists spoke with considerably more subtlety at Geneva about the current problems of socialism than was claimed in communist or centrist circles. They were well aware that the congress formed a kind of rump-international and they still hoped, in co-operation with those who had not appeared at the congress, to restore the proletarian unity of before 1914. In the resolution about the League of Nations the meeting pleaded for the admission of all peoples. It even regarded the admission of an undemocratically ruled state such as Soviet Russia as desirable.[3] The congress was in favour of a 'complete nationalisation of all means of production' and spoke of 'the continuing disintegration of the capitalist system' and of 'the urgent task' of the working class to take over power. But it rejected violent methods and any form of terrorism and regarded the perfection of democracy as the historic assignment of socialism.[4]

This recognised that parliamentary democracy was not the only true democracy. A number of speakers felt that the prestige of parliament had dropped sharply in recent times and pointed out the importance of extra-parliamentary actions and organisations. The Dutchman Troelstra, who presented a detailed proposal on this question to the congress, claimed that democracy without socialism would no longer satisfy the workers. Limited social reforms were therefore no longer sufficient. The world would have to be completely reorganised and this, in his view, could not be realised within a bourgeois democratic framework.[5] Troelstra's attitude and that of a number of others in Geneva made it clear that the Second International, even after the resignation of the centrists, was more than an informal co-operation between parties which no longer had anything in common with the traditions of pre-war socialism. At the same time an important section of the centre, which was trying so ostentatiously to preserve the revolutionary, international and Marxist legacy of social democracy, began, in the late summer and autumn of 1920, to come nearer to the point of view of the Second International about communism. Naturally the cause of this should be sought in the Comintern. The twenty-one harsh conditions of entry laid down by the Second Congress, and the experiences gained at the same time about the mentality and conduct of prominent Bolsheviks, cooled down the initial enthusiasm of many leaders of the centre party for the communist issue.

Eva Broido, a member of the Menshevik party leadership, noticed this volte-face in the centrists' attitude immediately. At the beginning of her stay in the West, in April–May 1920, she had tried in vain to have a series of articles about the situation in Russia published in the Viennese *Arbeiterzeitung* and the USPD's paper, *Freiheit*. In private conversation the Austrian and German centrists were full of interest for her opinions, but they were unwilling to publish them. In the course of the summer this gradually changed. From her letters to Akselrod it became evident that the socialist delegations returning from Russia, who often broke their journey in Berlin, played an important role here. At the end of July Ethel Snowden brought out an account of her experiences and contacts with the opposition in Russia. In the middle of August part of the Italian delegation passed through Berlin, and even these socialists, who reported their talks with Martov, could muster up very little enthusiasm for Bolshevism.[6]

At the same time the divergence of opinions within the USPD began to be more clearly apparent. 'A split will probably occur among the "independents". The delegation has not yet returned but as soon as it does, they say, party disputes will break out', Broido informed Akselrod.[7] Dittmann and Crispien did indeed launch an attack immediately after their return. Their critical articles about the Comintern and Bolshevism were naturally answered by Daümig and Stoecker and thus a passionate debate arose in the party which was to continue until the party congress in Halle in October.[8] At the USPD national conference at the beginning of September Dittmann made use of a statement by the RSDRP about the Russian and international situation as ammunition in the fight about the Comintern. Dittmann observed that the Mensheviks did not cling frantically to formal democracy in all circumstances. It was therefore slanderous to put them on a par with 'the German Scheidemann party' as was done by the Russian communists.[9] The Menshevik declaration was published in the USPD paper *Der Sozialist*. The *Arbeiterzeitung* now also proved ready to print a long letter from Abramovich to Adler in which an account was given of the persecution of socialists in Russia. The dictatorship had established itself as a permanent system in Russia. This was not a coincidence, but a phenomenon which was closely connected to Bolshevik ideology, that 'peculiar mixture of botched-up Dühringian-Blanquist theories and the real Russian traditions of the Narodniki, once so harshly opposed by the Marxists – and by Lenin'.[10] It was evident from the publication of such harsh Menshevik criticism that 'the inviolability of Bolshevism' about which Eva Broido had complained so bitterly to Akselrod, now no longer existed for the right wing of the socialist centre. But the USPD, the SFIO and the Italian party, which had increased strongly since the war, had filled their ranks with a great mass of new adherents who had not been educated in the pre-war traditions of Western socialism. These newcomers were mostly still prepared to throw in their lot with the Russian communists. A split of the centre had thus become inevitable. This was the state of affairs in European socialism when the RSDRP sent its representatives abroad.

Martov arrived in Germany in October 1920 just before the beginning of the USPD congress in Halle. He gained 'a rather depressing impression' of the situation in the USPD. He wrote to Akselrod:

> The leaders of the party are bewildered by the rapid collapse of the splendid organisational edifice. Their confusion is clearly evident from the completely non-German nonchalance with which the congress is being prepared. The *Vorstand*, without any consideration, has agreed to the left-wing proposal to hold the congress in Halle, where the local party organisation is fanatically Bolshevik, so that the congress will take place in a poisoned atmosphere from the outset. No one has bothered about inviting parties from abroad to the congress. Longuet proposed coming of his own accord, but no one thought of the Austrians, the only people who could have acted here with any authority. I sent a telegram to Fritz (Adler) on my own initiative, informing him that his presence or that of Bauer is imperative here.

But the Austrians did not come although, besides the French delegation, only a Swiss deputation was present at the congress.[11]

The 'extraordinary party gathering' in Halle, which was held in October 1920, was indeed a surprising event in many respects. The split in the party had already been firmly established beforehand. The left-wing majority and the right-wing minority sat divided from one another on either side of the central aisle of the hall which was decorated with Bolshevik slogans and Soviet emblems. Despite all the long speeches by party leaders and prominent guests there were only three delegates who were to change their opinions with regard to the split. But all the arguments for and against the Comintern were repeated once more and interspersed with frequent exclamations and interruptions from a noisy public.[12] At the presentation of the foreign guests to the meeting, Martov was characterized by Dittmann as 'the representative of the Marxist party, which has gone the same way ever since the first day of the establishment of the USPD'. The president of the Comintern Zinoviev, however, was introduced as a Bolshevik who had played a very dubious role in the negotiations with the USPD delegation in Moscow. It had been agreed that the foreign guests would not have more than half an hour in which to speak. Nevertheless, Zinoviev made a speech which lasted for four-and-a-half hours. His behaviour was, according to Martov, 'a pearl of demagogic art, which could confuse many a scatter-brain'. He made a profound impression on the meeting.[13]

'The party congress today', Zinoviev said, 'reminds me and other Russian comrades very forcibly of the congresses we Bolsheviks held together with the Mensheviks before our organisational separation. Many similar arguments, the same atmosphere ... Menshevism is an international phenomenon, just like Bolshevism ... Now you must choose in all clarity either for Bolshevism or for Menshevism.'[14] Furthermore Zinoviev equated Menshevism with reformism and basically reproached the right wing of the USPD for not having wanted a revolution, although, whatever that side might argue, the economic conditions for socialism were present in Germany. 'We, [however] are not divided because you cannot accept 21, but [only] 18 proposals; if a rift occurs, then it will happen because you do not agree [with us] about the issue of the world revolution, democracy, the dictatorship of the proletariat.'[15] In spite of everything a section of the right wing would, according to Zinoviev, join the communists; because that had also happened with the Mensheviks. Naturally Zinoviev could not get round the issue of terrorism. He told his audience that the Bolsheviks had only exercised violence when it was necessary and had done away with it after the victory over Denikin. Zinoviev defended the oppression of 'so-called socialists' in Russia but spoke only of Chernov and the PSR. He was not being very particular about the truth when he reported that the socialist revolutionaries had supported Western intervention, and in passing he laid the responsibility for the attack on Lenin by Fania Kaplan at the door of their party, whereupon Martov justifiably protested from the hall. But in this connection it was curious that Zinoviev made absolutely no mention of Menshevik policy towards the Bolshevik regime.[16] A few days later Martov wrote to Akselrod that Zinoviev's 'friendliness' had helped him greatly. 'In one way or another he made a mistake in his calculations.' By presenting the Mensheviks as honest opponents who, however, had not yet found true understanding of the revolution, 'after my appearance it was no longer possible for him to brand the facts I had revealed as lies or slander'.[17]

Hilferding, who had consulted Alexander Stein about the passages concerning Russia in his speech, spoke after Zinoviev.[18] He not only rejected the image of Menshevism formulated by Zinoviev, but also the communist assumption that in Germany there was a contrast like that between Menshevism and Bolshevism. Germany's problem was that it was in a revolutionary situation, while a large number of workers were not interested in a revolution.[19] According to Hilferding the USPD, in contrast to the communists, was reasonably successful in diminishing the German workers' reluctance for revolution. But this task was by no means complete. The socialists had no wish for 'cut-throat competition in radicalism' which would lead to a fragmentation of power. The independent and autonomous labour movement in the West should not become an instrument of Bolshevik power politics. 'We proclaim ourselves against the arbitrary nullification of elections for the soviets or the workers' councils, which produce a Menshevik majority or a considerable Menshevik minority. We are against trade unions with a Menshevik governing body being robbed of their leadership by arrests and a new governing body being appointed from above. We are against such methods and that is what we mean when we speak of terrorism.'[20] Clearly this was a different Hilferding speaking from the one who had defended Bolshevism against Tsereteli's attack in Lucerne a year before. That a sharp-witted man like Hilferding really believed so firmly in the future social revolution in Germany is not easy to imagine. Among the right-wing socialists there was more scepticism and doubt than they could show to this public which was expecting worship of the revolution at every party meeting.

Martov, who was suffering from throat cancer, was no longer capable of making a long speech. His text, on which he had worked until the last moment, was therefore read out by Alexander Stein. However, there had been no time to rewrite or type out the text, and 'as a result of my infernal handwriting and incomplete explanation Stein got stuck in some passages'.[21] Of course Martov also dismissed Zinoviev's view that the differences between the communist and the left-wing socialist parties could be reduced to the conflict between revolutionary socialism and reformism. It was understandable that the communists considered the centre parties, the Marxist supporters of the social revolution, as their principal opponents. The twenty-one admission requirements were completely justified from a Bolshevik point of view. There could after all be no question of equal rights for the powerful Soviet state and the weak foreign communist parties and sects which together formed the Comintern. But now that large Western parties, accustomed to independence and self-government, were seeking admission, there was a danger that the Third International would change into a sort of socialist parliament. It was to be expected that the Russian communists would take measures against this.[22]

The Second Congress of the Comintern in the summer of 1920 had, according to Martov, occupied itself minutely with the internal politics of Western parties. It had wondered whether the Austrian communists would be allowed to take part in parliamentary elections, whether the English communists could be members of the Labour Party and which of the leaders of the Western labour movement would be acceptable or ought to be excommunicated in advance. Meanwhile Russia was involved in a fight to the finish with the Entente. But the proposal to transport the revolution to the Rhine via Poland with the help of the Red Army, risking the possibility that Germany would once more become involved in a war with the Entente, was not submitted to the congress. Nor was this the case with Soviet

Russia's unwarrantable policy in Asia, with which the Bolsheviks were trying to arouse the colonial peoples and use the influence of the Russian revolution in the interests of the Russian state. And it goes without saying that the Bolsheviks' internal policies remained completely out of range. The argument that all criticism of Bolshevism was grist to the mill of international reaction had done a great deal of harm both to the Russian and the international revolution. 'The Russian revolution is sick and can only be restored to health by the influence of the international proletariat.'[23]

This, continued Martov via Stein, was clearly evident from the terrorism which had become the basis of the Bolsheviks' internal policy. Zinoviev's statements about this merely proved that he was nothing more than 'a petty bourgeois gone rabid'.[24] People like Trotsky and Zinoviev were responsible for the fact that the bestiality generated by the war was again being aroused in the masses. 'We, Russian social democrats', concluded Martov, 'resolutely protest against the attempt to recognise terror as necessary for "backward and uncivilised" Russia while rejecting it in Europe.'[25] At these statements about terrorism tumult repeatedly broke out in the hall and there was danger of fighting. Martov later wrote: 'Shouts of: Bloodhound! Hangman! Noske! Butcher! and the like resounded throughout the hall, the left-wing was clearly dismayed and did not produce sufficient noise to drown the minority.'[26] According to the records of the congress Stein concluded Martov's address amidst 'lively hand clapping on the right – cries of bravo – counter cries on the left. Whistles – long drawn out constantly renewed approval – the chairman's bell – excited shouting from the left.'[27]

Martov's presence in Halle had made a great impression. After the split, when the right wing of the party congress had left and was continuing the meeting separately in a large hall in the Halle zoo, Hilferding compared Martov to his oppressor Zinoviev who had a corpulent, flabby appearance: 'And our hearts trembled when we saw Comrade Martov, this representative of the Russian proletariat, flesh of our flesh and blood of our blood, one of the oppressed, one of the socialists in Russia against whom Bolshevism directs its terrorism. No more powerful protest against terrorist methods could be raised than the pallid, emaciated visage of Comrade Martov suddenly appearing on the tribune.'[28] The right-wing independents immediately decided to publish Martov's speech as a separate pamphlet in an issue of 100,000 copies.[29] Zinoviev, who in the account of his German experiences devoted pages to Martov's performance, indignantly mentioned that the 'anti-Bolshevik league', under the influence of Martov's lies, had covered the posters announcing his appearance in Berlin with stickers bearing the text: 'Zinoviev, butcher of the Mensheviks. German workers, come forward *en masse* to salute the murderer of your proletarian Russian brothers.'[30]

According to Zinoviev, Martov 'never stopped moaning, crying and snivelling about the fact that the workers in this century are so immature, so uneducated and so primitive that they believe in a kind of miracle: in the possibility of a speedy realisation of socialism.'[31] Zinoviev wrote an article in the same vein in the German communist party's paper. Martov replied to him in *Freiheit* that the naive, mystical belief of the oblivious masses in Germany obliged the leaders of the labour movement to use the greatest possible honesty towards the people who followed them. The success of Bolshevism was to a large extent due to deception.[32] Most of the leaders of the right wing of the centre pursued reasoning of this kind in their rejection of Bolshevism. 'What do the communists live on?', Hilferding wondered. In his view they lived on the degradation of mankind, the result of the mass murders during the war. 'And we, comrades, we live on the fact that, for us, historical evolution means that capitalism produces its own grave-diggers.'[33] Statements of this kind made the weaknesses of centrist ideology painfully obvious. In practice socialists like Hilferding left the rebellious masses, which were relying on their leadership, out in the cold. Their revolutionary idealism eventually came close to a 'Kautskyesque' postponement of the great day of revolutionary action until an indefinite future. The communists and the reformist socialists were thus to a large extent right in their caustic criticism of centrism. They were indeed displaying much more political realism.

## THE FOUNDATION OF THE VIENNA INTERNATIONAL

After his appearance in Halle Martov was assailed with requests for interviews and articles for the international socialist press.

But he realised that his sudden fame in the West was linked in a tragic manner to the defeat suffered by the right wing of the USPD. The right-wing Independents, he wrote to Akselrod, would now be in a Menshevik position for a certain time, 'an *avant-garde* without masses'. It was difficult to foresee whether, in these circumstances, they would be able to summon up enough 'inner perseverance and civil courage', though they were strengthened by their conviction that they were defending European socialism against the attacks of the 'uncivilised'.[34] Martov cherished few illusions about the European centrists. Some of them had, in his view, evolved in the direction of communism out of conviction or with an eye to their careers; another section 'was simply following the crowd'.[35] It did not escape him that Longuet, the Frenchman, a socialist for whom Martov had a certain respect and who had spoken after him in Halle, had carefully refrained from any criticism of the communist regime in Russia. He had in this way offered Zinoviev the opportunity to claim that Longuet had reacted to the 'baseness' which Martov had held against Bolshevism in Halle.[36]

Thus a great deal would have to happen before centrism was completely cured of its Bolshevik sympathies. Still Martov was not pessimistic. 'All relations between Bolshevism and the "centre" have been broken off and that is only the first step. I arrived at exactly the right moment, after the "21 points" our time will come', he wrote to Akselrod.[37] 'In the development of this sick European revolution the moment has now come when the socialists and the workers are open (or rather, are forced to be open) to the whole truth about Russia, which they did not want to discover for themselves.'[38] He believed that the conditions had then been created for the realisation of the plan which the Menshevik Central Committee had launched six months previously: a conference of Marxist parties or sections of them, which would be equally objective about communism and reformism. Thus a beginning could be made with the troublesome and protracted work which would now have to be undertaken in order to restore unity in the international labour movement.

In his talks with Hilferding and others Martov tried to move the centrists to convene such a conference as quickly as possible. It was only necessary to exert a little pressure on them. The British ILP, the Austrian party and the USPD had decided in December to go to a meeting in Berne organised by the Swiss socialists. Martov was of course pleased about this, but he remained on his guard. Even after the split in the party the right wing of the USPD continued to be in favour of a unification with the Third International, although the Germans had no wish to agree to a Russian ultimatum.[39] Martov wrote to Akselrod that he would refuse to take part in the proposed conference unless the RSDRP received an official invitation to it from the Swiss. He would not come if they invited him only *à titre personnel* so as not to annoy the Bolsheviks.[40] Martov received the invitation he wanted, but he could not much admire the formulation of the aims of the conference set out in it. The Swiss spoke of a meeting 'of all parties which had resigned from the Second International and cherished the wish, jointly with the Third International, to lay the foundations for a socialist international'. He therefore feared that he 'would have to make a great deal of fuss' in Berne and still would not be able to achieve very much.[41]   Martov was only allowed to stay in Switzerland for the duration of the conference. Like the other foreign socialists he had to promise solemnly to refrain from any political activities and he was thoroughly searched at the frontier.[42] The conference, which was held from 5 to 7 December in the Volkshaus in Berne, was attended by representatives of the SFIO, the ILP, the USPD (that is to say the right wing of the party which had retained this name after the split) and by the Austrian, German-Czech and Swiss social democrats. The American socialists under the leadership of Morris Hillquit sent an observer to the conference. The PSR and the 'left-wing' social revolutionaries that had split from the PSR did not appear. Probably they had not obtained a visa. The ILP's position was equivocal, for this party was a subdivision of the Labour Party, which had remained faithful to the Second International. And one of its most prominent members, Ramsay MacDonald, was even secretary of this organisation. He did not go to Berne after the Swiss socialist Grimm had protested against his attending the conference. The French socialist Renaudel stayed away for the same reason.[43]

Martov thought Grimm was 'tactless'. People who might perhaps be able to make a useful contribution to the deliberations should not be excluded beforehand. But he was not dissatisfied with the results of the debate. 'There were practically no disagreements or discussions ... Towards us – towards the party and me personally – everyone behaved in the best possible way, there was no sign of fear ... that people might fraternise with the counter-revolutionary Mensheviks.'[44] The extent of Martov's influence on the meeting in Berne became evident from the statement drawn up by Adler and Grimm which was accepted by the conference. This document showed a striking similarity to the series of resolutions which had been published by the RSDRP since May 1919 about international socialist problems. The socialists in Berne distanced themselves clearly from the ideology and practice of Bolshevism. At the same time it also became evident that in 1920 the centrists were still seeking refuge in a dream world. These party leaders really thought, or wanted to make the rest of the world believe, that the decisive fight between the proletariat and the bourgeoisie had broken out. They based their criticism of the Second and Third Internationals on this. One organisation was rejected because it was not revolutionarily inclined, the other because it thrust the methods which the Bolsheviks had used in Russia upon the workers' parties of other countries like a template. In Berne everyone agreed that the situation varied too much from one country to another for it to be possible to lay down the law for the proletariat. Of course they also thought that the Russian Soviet republic as 'the advanced post of the social revolution' should be defended against Western imperialism.[45]

In Martov's view Berne was a step in the right direction, but he continued to watch the doings of the centrists like a lynx. He was annoyed at Longuet's translation of the Berne manifesto because Russia was described in it in French as the '*avant-garde* of the social revolution'. Clearly there was a difference in emphasis here, wrote Martov to Shchupak. The German text established a fact; the French version elevated it with the honorary title of 'vanguard'.[46] Shchupak, less susceptible than Martov to the refinements of Marxist scholasticism, told him that he thought both wordings were too flattering for the Bolsheviks. In two letters Martov returned to the question.[47]

> You do not want to recognise that social reaction is ruling the whole world and that in only one country, Russia, is an anti-bourgeois government in power ... Whatever happens in the future, the situation now is exactly like that during the Paris Commune. And if, in 1871, Marx was firmly convinced that nothing [good] would come of the Commune (as was in fact the

case), he nevertheless spoke about the Commune as the forward-going banner of the socialist revolution ... One needs a clear answer to the question of what happened in the October days [of 1917] in Russia: a revolution, as we think, or a counter-revolution, as Chernov claims?[48]

The recognition that Bolshevism had carried out a revolution was, in Martov's view, no apology for Bolshevism.

Shchupak was not the only one who had difficulty following Martov's subtleties. Many Mensheviks in Russia, as well as Aksel-rod and Tsereteli in Western Europe, were nearer to Chernov's opinions. Martov had searched out Akselrod in Switzerland and the two men had renewed their former friendship. But their differences of opinion remained and Akselrod had no intention of glossing them over. In a long letter composed with much care – which he, with his typical hesitation about the right wording, did not send until later – he reproached Martov with the fact that his assessment of the October revolution was basically identical with Otto Bauer's. Akselrod thought Bauer's views pernicious in every respect, for he had tried to explain away the Bolshevik regime by comparing it with the French revolution and the Paris Commune. In this way he had strengthened the disastrous illusion of splendid proletarian and communist salvation spread by the Bolsheviks among the ranks of the European proletariat, and made resistance to it on principle impossible. Of course there were superficial similarities between the events of 1793, 1871 and the coup of 1917. It had been Kautsky's great merit that he had demonstrated very thoroughly that these comparisons did not hold water.

However fatal Bauer's view might be, Akselrod thought, at least he was consistent and that could not be said of Martov's point of view. It was paradoxical to combat the Bolsheviks and at the same time to claim that, despite everything, they were the ones who were carrying out 'the historic tasks' of the revolution. If these Asiatic anarcho-Blanquists were really twentieth-century Jacobins, then all resistance against them was a counter-revolutionary act. In that event it would be the revolutionary duty of the Mensheviks to join the communist party. The present-day struggle of the Mensheviks for the democratisation of the Soviets under a regime which also silenced peaceful and legal opposition to violent methods, was wrong in principle and doomed to failure in practice. Naturally it remained totally reprehensible to try to overthrow the Bolshevik dictatorship arm in arm with Kolchak and Denikin. But the fundamental right of the people to rebel against their new oppressors ought to be clearly and publicly recognised. The very last thing the Mensheviks ought to let themselves be enticed into was a half-hearted and totally pointless form of opposition.[49]

If such fundamental differences continued to exist among the Mensheviks, then of course the centrists could hardly be reproached for not having even noticed the fragile balance in Martov's arguments. Besides, among them there were people who were totally unable to agree with the Berne statement. Ramsay MacDonald, the secretary of the Second International, who because of his attitude during and after the war clearly belonged to the centre, expressed his disappointment about this document in a letter to Martov and Adler. In his view there was nothing in it which could not have been said by the Second International, with the exception of the exaggerated and unjustifiable criticism of that organisation. He denied a number of people and parties, who had attended the conference, the right of playing the inquisitor, since their attitude during the war had not been spotless either.

> I personally have no wish to enter into disputes with old friends, especially when our differences of opinion only consist of words, and because I believe that these are intended rather to sort out certain of your own emotions than actually to justify anything essential. The way you use, for example, the expression 'the dictatorship of the proletariat' in your manifesto, amuses me. It is presented as the fanfare of trumpets of the revolution, then afterwards you explain this concept so that nothing remains of it but the most obvious actions of a democratic majority under certain circumstances which, as you yourselves say, might well, but also might not, take place.[50]

Adler reacted to this letter with an article in *Der Kampf*, but in it the position of the centre was explained in a somewhat propagandist manner, and Adler did not even trouble to explain in which respects their view about dictatorship was more than pure verbalism.[51] Martov, on the other hand, wrote MacDonald a friendly eight-page letter. He understood that MacDonald had lost patience with the continental centrists because 'yielding to the mood of the masses, they hesitated to take decisive steps in order not to be accused of falling out with Moscow'. The Mensheviks had also been enraged about this, but that was no reason for them to return to the Second International. This organisation caused 'more and more thousands and thousands' of workers to seek salvation in Moscow. 'I am very glad that our interpretation of the relationship between dictatorship and democracy had amused you. In these sombre times it is always agreeable to arouse a comrade to laughter.' But the bourgeoisie would lose its inclination to laugh 'when we use dictatorship in our – anti-Bolshevik – sense of the word'. In Germany the SPD had left the privileges of the ruling Prussian military clique untouched after November 1918. After Luxemburg and Liebknecht had been assassinated by soldiers, the German socialist government had handed over the trial of the suspects to the same clique. It was understandable that 'the bourgeoisie had been thoroughly amused by so "democratic" a policy of the proletariat'. A proletarian dictatorship had the task of preventing things of this kind and was thus no empty concept.[52]

Martov already knew beforehand that he would not convince MacDonald, and that was not his first concern. He believed rather that a candid and personal exchange of ideas was important to clear up misunderstandings. Both he and Abramovich displayed great activity in the first months of their stay outside Russia. They tried, by means of publications in the press and by visits to sister parties, to give the RSDRP as loud a voice as possible in the debate about the future of socialism. Martov's attention was chiefly directed towards Tours, where the French socialists were to hold a congress at the end of December. Longuet had told Martov in Berne that he and his supporters did not yet know whether they would leave the SFIO after it joined the Comintern, something which had already been fixed in advance. They hoped to be able to stay in the party without breaking their links with the future organisation of the centrists. 'I do not think that Zinoviev will allow them that right', Martov had observed, and he had been right.[53] Martov repeatedly tried to obtain a visa for France, but did not succeed. And actually he did not regret this much. It was clear beforehand that the atmosphere at the congress 'would be very disagreeable and little suited to the influencing of those who should and could be influenced'.[54] Not only French socialists, but also Shchupak, who lived in France, had warned him that he would have found himself in an extremely precarious position in Tours.[55]

Martov's appearance in Halle had not, however, gone unremarked in France and it went without saying that his attitude was a subject of debate at the congress. Cachin, in his major speech, recognised that the internal struggle in Russia had been accompanied by extreme violence. Martov was, in his view, 'one of the most remarkable spirits of international socialism. He has an upright and pure conscience.' But Martov should realise that he would have to offer every help to the revolution, given the dangers which were threatening it. Interruptions from the delegates followed these words. 'He has offered it!' shouted one. 'In order to criticise the Russian revolution!' chipped in someone else. 'No', continued Cachin, 'he has borne arms too often for the counter-revolution.'[56] Cachin defended himself against the accusation that he and Frossard had avoided all contact with the opposition in Russia. They had indeed held a respectable conversation with old, well-known Mensheviks like Khinchuk (a right-wing Menshevik who had left the party in 1920 and was working for the Soviet government). He had told the two Frenchmen that the Mensheviks had no positive alternatives whatsoever to offer. And since Russian reaction in its old form had completely disappeared, all the dissatisfaction was crystallising around the doctrine and the personalities of Menshevism.

Martov would of course have liked to add something to this. The Mensheviks, for instance, had proof at their disposal that the Russian workers had been threatened in advance with withdrawal of provisions if they did not behave reasonably when they met the foreign delegates after the Second Comintern Congress.[57] But Tours was not the appropriate place in which to criticise Russian communism. In December 1920 three-quarters of the French socialist party was ready to join Moscow as the Parti Communiste Français. The remainder of the SFIO, with Renaudel and Thomas, Faure and Longuet, Bracke and Blum, formed anything but a united group. One could, in Martov's words, only hope for the future. Turati and other Italian socialists had invited Martov to attend their congress in Leghorn which was to be held in January 1921. But even for this journey he could not obtain a visa. No majority for the

Comintern could be found in the Italian party, which was much more inclined towards revolution than the French, and it fell apart in Leghorn. This meant the end of Italian socialism as a significant political force, with all the disastrous consequences thereof. The party splits seriously weakened the socialist centre which united into a separate organisation at this period.[58]

The parties which met in Vienna in February 1921 to establish the International Working Union of Socialist Parties were, taken together, about as strong as the Comintern. But the 'bankrupt' Second International, with its membership of about seven-and-a-half million, was five times the size of the Vienna International. The new organisation, which was immediately dubbed the Second-and-a-Half International by its opponents, was formed of the Austrians and the Swiss party, the right wings of the USPD and the SFIO, and a series of parties and groups from the Baltic states and Eastern Europe. It was curious that the Scandinavian socialists and the followers of Serrati, whom Martov had assumed would evolve in the direction of the centre, did not attend the conference. Akselrod, who was invited by Martov to take a seat in the Menshevik delegation, had declined this honour and did not go to Vienna. Kautsky on the other hand attended the meeting as a guest and Troelstra was present as a journalist. Troelstra himself was keen on an association with Vienna, but once more the majority of Dutch socialists had no desire to follow their leader. According to Eva Broido the Georgian Mensheviks and the Russian PSR were also on the point of joining Vienna. The PSR did in fact apply, but its membership was never realised. The Georgians remained faithful to the Second International.[59]

Undoubtedly many centrists held unjustified expectations about the attraction which the Vienna Union would be able to exert on the whole labour movement, at the expense of both the Second and Third Internationals. Socialists like Troelstra, MacDonald and Kautsky were rather an illustration of the fact that the difference between the 'reformists' of Geneva and the 'revolutionaries' of Vienna was not very clear in practice. After all, even a number of socialists of a 'right-wing' nature, for example the Frenchman Renaudel, found their niche within the Vienna organisation. At the opening of the meeting Adler had insinuated that the socialists present would be mockingly called 'the centre' by the others. 'And I believe that we really are the centre. We are the centre in the sense that we are just as far from naive impatience as we are from sceptical disbelief.'[60] The Menshevik David Dalin who attended Vienna wrote to Akselrod about the conference: 'Good, honest socialists, but with no backbone. In every way Second and a half; that is to say, take the Second, take the Third, add them up and divide by two. Then you sometimes get strange results, but it is not easy to organise the masses around a sort of arithmetical mean.'[61]

The formation of the International Working Union of Socialist Parties betokened the realisation of a plan which the Mensheviks had launched almost two years beforehand. Otto Bauer, Friedrich Adler and Rudolf Hilferding later recognised and praised the fundamental significance of Martov's ideas for what was accomplished in Vienna.[62] The general statement about imperialism and the methods of the class war which was accepted by the conference did indeed reflect the views of the left-wing majority of the RSDRP.[63] But the Menshevik delegation did not play much of a role during the public debates of the conference and Martov, Abramovich, Broido and Dalin eventually left the Austrian capital in an embittered mood. Martov found it wrong in principle that this conference too had fallen into the bad habit of so many earlier international socialist gatherings of hiding the discussion of thorny questions away in committee meetings and afterwards glossing them over with vague resolutions.[64] In his fanatical pursuit of clarity and publicity he proved himself a not very pragmatic, not to say foolish, politician. But afterwards many agreed with Martov that the rigidity with which unity had been maintained at the conference had extremely disastrous consequences for the treatment of the Georgian question.

Georgia had cut itself off from Russia and declared itself an independent republic in May 1918. Social democratic Georgia was unique in the entire world. The Georgian Mensheviks, who had broken away from the RSDRP at the beginning of 1918 – for which the Russian social democrats did not thank them – were all-powerful there. At democratic elections they had managed to unite 70 per cent of the vote on their side, while the Bolsheviks gained only 2.5 per cent. But the socialist government of this small country had to contend with tremendous political problems, and the continued existence of Georgian independence was entirely dependent on foreign support. Chkheidze and Tsereteli were therefore sent to Europe to plead the cause of the Georgians at the peace conference in Paris and before the forum of international socialism. This resulted in the Entente's recognising Georgia *de facto* in January 1920 and in a delegation from the Second International, which included amongst others Kautsky, MacDonald, Renaudel, Huysmans and Vandervelde, honouring the country with a visit. But this of course did not ensure the future existence of Georgia.[65]

On Thursday 24 February 1921 President Zhordaniya, the trade unions and the social democratic party leadership of Georgia sent telegrams to the socialist conference in Vienna, in which mention was made of a Bolshevik invasion of Georgia. The Mensheviks, immediately after this news was made known, submitted resolutions requesting the meeting's opinion about the communist attack.[66] Much against Martov's wishes, the newly elected executive committee referred consideration of this problem to a specially appointed committee, without public discussion beforehand at the plenary meeting. At the request of Abramovich, who together with Dalin had a seat on the committee, Bronsky, the representative of the Soviet republic in Vienna, was asked to throw some light on the situation in Georgia for the members of the committee. Bronsky appeared and showed his amazement at the news, which he refused to believe. He promised to take further steps to obtain trustworthy information, but he was not seen again.[67] In the meantime the papers were full of news about Georgia, which after a few weeks of fierce fighting was taken over by the Red Army and afterwards incorporated into Soviet Russia. It was clear that communist Russia had unexpectedly invaded a small, neighbouring socialist country, with which it had signed a non-aggression treaty, and which was not in a position to defend itself against this superior military power.

The participants at the conference were not unprejudiced observers, and opinions within the committee differed widely. The Mensheviks, as spokesmen for a minority in the committee, demanded that the conference protest vehemently against the Bolshevik outrage. The majority, represented by its most active member, the German Henke, declared that insufficient information was available to determine precisely what was happening in Georgia. After all the Bolshevik side had informed them that local uprisings had broken out in Georgia and the Russian government was simply arbitrating between these and the Georgian government.[68] 'In the committee', Martov later wrote to Akselrod, 'Abramovich fought until his strength broke down. I once broke in and caused a complete outcry in connection with the hesitations of Henke and someone else. For three hours they prevented any agreement being reached over a concerted text. We then suggested again: let us go to the plenary meeting with two draft resolutions (there would have been a majority for the more acerbic text there). But once again, whatever it cost, public debates were to be avoided.'[69]

The final draft resolution, which was approved by the committee, satisfied no one. In the text the statements by the Georgian social democrats and the Russian communists were compared. The conference declared it was not in a position to pronounce a verdict about Bolshevik policy on the grounds of the same argument which Adler had used two years earlier in Berne: we are not sure. 'If it were however true', continued the resolution, 'that great Russia, ruled by a communist party, is waging war, even indirectly, on tiny Georgia, then the whole European proletariat ought resolutely to protest against this.' The resolution then stressed that it was the duty of all proletarians to defend the Russian revolution against reaction. But this 'would be particularly complicated if the Soviet government, even for other considerations, were to pursue a policy of intervention against Georgia'. The conference therefore 'expected' that the conflict between Georgia and Russia would be settled in a peaceful manner and that Russia would not encroach on the autonomy and independence of Georgia.[70]

This cowardly resolution was a slap in the face for Georgian social democracy and a very great disappointment to the Menshevik delegation. 'Even worse', Martov wrote, 'was the fact that it was put to the vote in the following form: The conference takes due note of this resolution and gives the Executive Committee authority to take further steps.' The resolution was thus downgraded from an appeal to world opinion into a communication from the meeting to the governing body of the Viennese Working Union of Socialists. 'The Germans insisted on this at the last minute, because of a kind of absurd 'caution', that is to say, for fear that the Bolsheviks would accuse them of having urged the Entente to use Georgia as an excuse for a fresh intervention.'[71] The Mensheviks were furious about these steps and voted against the resolution, in which they were supported by the Frenchmen Renaudel and Bracke and the left-wing socialist revolutionary Grigorovich. 'We were left with such a bitter taste in our mouths after all this', wrote Broido, 'that not one of us wanted to stay in Vienna a day longer, as we had earlier planned. Adler saw us off at the station, and in fact he personally was the least to blame of all. He had been continually terrorised by the Swiss, or rather by two of them, and one or two of the Germans.'[72] Hilferding had also apologised to the Mensheviks for the behaviour of a section of the German delegation. A furious Martov had rubbed his nose in the fact that this was, in no small measure, the result of the attitude which Hilferding himself had originally adopted towards Bolshevism.

It is extremely doubtful whether the Western socialists 'could have easily saved' Georgia if they had pursued a concerted campaign, as Tsereteli thought.[73] Like those of the other Mensheviks, his expectations concerning the influence and power of a united European labour movement were much too high. This does not alter the fact that it was precisely in clear and tangible political issues of this kind that Western socialism could have achieved something. After all, neither Lenin nor Trotsky were very favourably disposed towards the aggressive annexationism which the people's commissar for nationalities, Stalin, had demonstrated in the 'solution' of the Georgian problem, although they did not vaunt this opinion publicly. Later, when the 'Viennese' socialists realised in full the fate that had befallen Georgia, they were prepared to express their disapproval openly. But by then it was too late to change anything in the actual situation.[74]

### KRONSTADT

The members of the small foreign delegation of the RSDRP continued their activities indefatigably. The hopeless situation in which their party was situated in Russia left them no other choice. But it had of course become clear in Vienna that the Western socialists could not for the time being be completely cured of the reverence they felt for Soviet Russia. Like Tsereteli and Akselrod in 1918–19, Martov and Abramovich in 1920–1 discovered how difficult it was to make the Western socialists change their essential ideas about Soviet Russia. Since many Russian social democrats even before 1917 had lived for a long time in this milieu, they did not need to spend very long guessing the causes of this. They were familiar with the cult of the social revolution which the mostly so moderate Western socialists had kept alive. They had also previously come into conflict with the long tradition of admiration for Russian radicalism. Moreover they realised that many of their European comrades were tormented by the feeling that they themselves had failed in their duty as revolutionaries.

For a number of Western socialists the simple truth continued to hold good that whoever imagined he was a revolutionary in his heart had to opt for the Bolsheviks, and whoever was against the Bolsheviks could not also be a revolutionary. Criticism of communism à la Kautsky was totally unacceptable to them, while Martov's attitude was too subtle for them to understand. But they did think that the Russian communists ought to be given the chance to carry out their socialist experiment. That is why they attached an enormous significance to the defence of Russia against Western imperialist influences. They continued to do this even when it became extremely unlikely that capitalism could do much more damage in Russia. The Bolsheviks, despite the outrages they were perpetrating in Russia and despite the anti-socialist campaign they were leading in both East and West, had a huge reservoir of socialist goodwill on their side and, of course, they used it shamelessly. The most divergent circumstances determined how long these sympathisers of communism and Soviet Russia continued to cut themselves off from trustworthy information about its unfavourable aspects.

Almost immediately after the end of the Vienna conference, at the beginning of March 1921, the Western socialists were confronted with the seamen's uprising at the naval base of Kronstadt, an island in the Gulf of Finland near Petrograd. This bloody tragedy changed little of the attitude which the Vienna and the Second International had taken towards Soviet Russia. But the brutal repression of this spontaneous rebellion, which was clearly left-wing socialist in character, did indeed suddenly open the eyes of a number of Western communists and anarchists. They realised with a shock that the Bolsheviks had betrayed the ideals of their own revolution, and afterwards they could no longer muster up any sympathy for Russian communism.[75] Kronstadt was certainly not the first case in which justifiable resistance by the workers, peasants or soldiers was broken down with violence by the communist regime. On the contrary, the massive peasants' rebellion in the province of Tambov, for example, which lasted from August 1920 until the summer of 1921, was at least as significant as Kronstadt.[76] After Kronstadt a whole series of events, such as Stalin's victory over Trotsky, the liquidation of the Kulaks, the great purges, the Nazi–Soviet pact, the de-Stalinisation campaign, the Hungarian uprising and the Prague Spring, once more afforded a turning-point in the lives of ever more groups of people who up till then had felt themselves committed to the ups and downs of the Soviet Union in one way or another. They too changed their minds after their turn had come to meet 'their Kronstadt'. Until 1985 the history of Soviet Russia formed a whole textbook of lessons which had never been properly learnt by everyone in the West, and to which again and again new and instructive chapters were added. But Kronstadt acquired a great symbolic significance because it gained the reputation – wrongly – of being the first event which had such a sobering effect. Because the myth of Kronstadt as the 'Third' – and thus authentic – Russian revolution' acquired such a substantial position in anti-communist literature with a left-wing socialist slant, it is important to verify how the organised international socialist movement actually reacted to Kronstadt in 1921.

At the beginning of 1921 news about Soviet Russia still consisted mainly of a stream of often fantastic rumours. Socialist papers like *Vorwärts, Le Populaire, Die Arbeiterzeitung, Freiheit* and *Het Volk* reported only some of them summarily and without comment. The socialist reader was therefore well informed about the crisis situation which continued to exist in Russia after the end of the civil war. His paper repeatedly reported economic malaise, strikes and rebellious movements. But he remained in the dark about the veracity and significance of these facts. This was also true of the first reports about Kronstadt. Many liberal and conservative newspapers were ready with sensational news about the uprising, which they treated with great sympathy: the fall of the Soviet government was at hand; Lenin and Trotsky had fled to the Crimea; Trotsky had been proclaimed dictator; French warships were steaming towards Kronstadt and had disembarked troops in Reval; fifty communist commissars had also fled to this place with their bags full of gold, platinum and jewellery, etc., etc.[77] The Soviet authorities, with the entire international communist press at their heels, initially dismissed all these reports about rebellious movements as slander. A few days later it was officially admitted that an uprising had broken out in Kronstadt which was led by former tsarist generals, French secret agents and reactionary émigrés supported by socialist revolutionaries and Mensheviks.[78]

The socialist press was, in fact, at a loss over the news about Kronstadt. The aforementioned papers confined themselves to a concise account of the conflicting reports about Russian developments and in the beginning scarcely even gave a very detached commentary on them. *Het Volk*, the Dutch SDAP's daily paper, thought that the Soviet government had gone 'a bit too far' in its categorical denial of all the riots. *The Daily Herald*, the paper of the British labour movement's left wing, was prepared fully to endorse the Soviet view.[79] According to the mouthpiece of the French socialist party *Le Populaire* the rebellion had not been instigated by reactionaries, but ought to be seen as a 'spontaneous manifestation of the suffering masses'. *Vorwärts*, the SPD's paper, devoted unusually little attention to Kronstadt, but did give the warning that the 'black jackals' of reaction might make improper use of the situation.[80] Only André Pierre of *Le Populaire* expressed his sympathy for Kronstadt in general terms: 'Whoever the oppressors may be, we are for the oppressed who are trying to throw off the yoke of slavery.'[81]

But it did not occur to the socialists to declare their actual solidarity with the Kronstadt seamen, or at least to assure them of their full moral support. Neither the Second nor the Vienna International made any attempt to prevent a cruel repression of the uprising by insisting on negotiations or clement treatment of the imprisoned rebels. Something of the sort would certainly have been possible, and could perhaps have had a certain moderating effect, for the Bolsheviks were in an awkward position and had realised that they needed Western economic support. But Western socialist organisations were generally in no position and ill prepared to get mixed up in the extraordinarily complicated internal Russian affairs. They had to be continually helped and urged to do this, and this was the principal task of the Foreign Delegation of the RSDRP. But Martov, Abramovich and Dalin had not proposed anything to their Western comrades. This is remarkable because they did write detailed analyses of the uprising for *Die Arbeiterzeitung* and *Freiheit,* the standard of which stood out far above the average socialist editorial comment. From the fact that these articles were quoted in full or in part by other socialist papers, it is evident that substantial value was attached to their opinion.

It was also very difficult for the Mensheviks in Berlin to make out what was happening in Kronstadt. They had received no letters from Russia for some weeks and, like everyone else in Western Europe, had to go by the stream of rumours and Bolshevik communiqués. In the past the Mensheviks had had little appreciation for the primitive, anarchistically biased socialism of the seamen, who had helped the Bolsheviks to power. But now the inhabitants of Kronstadt were concentrating on the dictatorship of the communist commissars. The rebels' programme showed a remarkable similarity to a political pamphlet which the Mensheviks had stuck by the thousand all over the walls of Petrograd at the end of February 1921, in which the freedom of the spoken and written word, freedom of association and assembly, and above all, free elections for the Soviets, were demanded.[82] How ill-informed Martov was about all this became evident when, a few days after the outbreak of the uprising, he wrote to Akselrod that he did to some extent believe the report that a former tsarist general, Kozlovsky, was leading it. What was manifesting itself for the first time at the naval base was the Bonapartism which, as the Mensheviks had predicted, would be the eventual result of the Bolshevik dictatorship. Lenin would certainly subjugate Kronstadt, and the internally divided Bolshevik party would, under the threat of this danger, close its ranks again. But this kind of counter-revolution was much more dangerous in the long run for the communists than the armies of Vrangel or Denikin, for it emanated from their own circle.[83]

Abramovich wrote an article in the same vein for *Freiheit,* which was taken over by *Le Populaire, Die Arbeiterzeitung* and *Het Volk.*[84] The unfair suggestion that Kronstadt could be little more than a military plot doomed to failure, which was a harbinger of the inevitable Thermidor or Bonapartist finale to the Russian revolution, thus did not remain without influence on Western socialist opinion. This prejudice was not entirely the consequence of lack of knowledge or of the Menshevik rejection of armed uprising against the Bolshevik regime. It even contained a small kernel of truth. The Foreign Delegation of the RSDRP followed the activities of the other Russian parties with much suspicion. Among the Russian political émigrés many hoped to profit from the extremely unstable and confused situation which was characteristic of Russia in the last weeks of wartime communism. Moreover Kronstadt was not in every respect – as later myths would have it – a proletarian and socialist uprising of the first water. Kozlovsky was certainly not the leader of the rebels, but he and other prominent officers did indeed play a certain role as military advisers. Nor were extreme right-wing Russian emigrants and their representatives in Russia involved in the leadership or the preparation of Kronstadt. But they had followed developments on the island for months and were certainly planning to make use of any possible armed uprising. In March they developed a feverish – if totally fruitless – diligence to help the rebels.

The Bolsheviks, who were to some extent aware of the activities of the émigrés, exaggerated these facts out of all proportion in their propaganda offensive, which was supposed to justify to the outside world their military action against the rebels. Their allegation that socialist revolutionaries and Mensheviks had played a leading role in the uprising was also a deliberate lie with a whiff of the truth in it. In the fifteen-man-strong Revolutionary Committee which had taken over power at the naval base, there were Mensheviks and socialist revolutionaries. But they were not acting on the instructions of their parties. The members of the PSR among the émigrés were delighted about Kronstadt. They immediately began to collect money to help the rebels, though they did not ask the Western socialists for support in this.[85] A group of Russian social democrats, who had left the RSDRP because of its left-wing direction after the October revolution, spread leaflets in Petrograd at the time of Kronstadt which called for a general strike and an armed uprising against the Bolshevik dictatorship.[86] But of active participation in Kronstadt itself by prominent social democrats or socialist revolutionaries there was nothing to be seen, even though on most issues the seamen's revolutionary programme seemed to have been inspired by the demands of the socialist opposition.

The RSDRP took no part in the military protest at Kronstadt. It had not even been actively involved in the workers' resistance against the Bolsheviks, which had found expression in the early months of 1921 in wild-cat strikes in Petrograd, Moscow and other industrial centres. This was not so much the result of the organisational weakness of the persecuted and terrorised party, but rather of the political line to which it had rigidly adhered until then. In their frenetic endeavour to remain a legal opposition party and to work only within the framework of the existing Soviet structure, the Mensheviks were outspoken opponents of spontaneous proletarian actions which could only lead to violent confrontations with the regime and would be disastrous for the workers. An armed uprising was absolutely taboo. Nevertheless, Kronstadt led to vehement discussions and to refinement of the party point of view. The few members of the central and Moscow committees of the party who were not in prison in March did not agree amongst themselves about Kronstadt. Two meetings had held protracted debates on this question. Two members of the governing body of the party realised that this uprising had broken out in an initially pro-Bolshevik milieu and thus could not be condemned as counter-revolutionary. Nonetheless, the Central Committee eventually dissociated itself in forceful terms from the rebel seamen in a short resolution.[87] The Petrograd party committee, which was nearer to the revolutionary hotbed, assessed the situation more flexibly. It knew that the rebel seamen – like the workers on strike – had demanded free elections for the Soviets in the whole of Russia. This was exactly what the Mensheviks had been proposing for years. The aim of Menshevik politics had up till then been to force the Bolsheviks into a different political course by means of continual confrontation with the wishes and desires of the workers. This policy now seemed to have a spectacular chance of success. In a proclamation on 7 March 1921 the committee therefore made an urgent appeal to the Kronstadt seamen, the soldiers of the Red Army and the Petrograd workers to end armed conflict. They ought immediately to demand negotiations from the government and choose representatives for these.[88] There was no reaction to this proclamation. These Mensheviks will not have been unduly optimistic about their initiative. But they cherished the illusion that the crisis of War Communism, which had compelled the government to economic concessions, could also lead to political reform. And of course there were not only political but also humanitarian reasons to press for a peaceful settlement.

Not until after the uprising had been quelled did the foreign delegation of the RSDRP receive letters from Russia in which they were informed of the party's point of view with regard to Kronstadt. Martov's, Abramovich's and Dalin's verdict about Russian developments had meanwhile become more favourable. They had rapidly been convinced that this was a question of a spontaneous uprising closely linked to the workers' protest and not to the agents of reactionary émigrés.[89] Still the Mensheviks in Berlin remained very much on the alert. Even the initiatives of socialists like Victor Chernov were regarded by them with the gravest suspicion. 'It is our duty', Martov said in his newly established paper *Socialistichesky Vestnik* (*The Socialist Messenger*), 'to alert the international proletariat to the new danger of intervention and to exhort them to fight this danger with all their might.' He hoped that the insurgents would be prudent enough to repel all help from the suspect side, but he was not very confident of this.[90]

Dalin's analysis of Kronstadt written for the *Arbeiterzeitung* also proved that the spectre of counter-revolution had driven away all thought of any overt display of solidarity with the seamen of Kronstadt by the Berlin Mensheviks.[91] The Bolsheviks were of course held fully responsible by the Berlin Mensheviks for the disastrous situation in Russia. Martov pointed out that the proclamation of the NEP, a series of measures which the Mensheviks had been urging for a long time, was not enough. Economic liberalisation would remain meaningless if at the same time an end did not come to dictatorship and political terrorism. Martov therefore believed that Lenin would certainly be forced to take this next logical step. The Russian revolution could only be saved if – as Kronstadt had demanded – honest elections were held for the Soviets, and the Bolsheviks, as a result of these, were also prepared to share their power with others.[92] This rosy Menshevik image of the future, however, contained

no answer whatever to the obvious question of whether international socialism ought not to try to prevent the suppression
of the uprising, which would in all probability be extremely
cruel.

Not until after Kronstadt had fallen did Martov write down
a few afterthoughts in which he conveyed some real sympathy
for the rebels. He informed the Central Committee of his party
that he did not agree with their rejection of Kronstadt and could
reconcile himself fully with the proclamation of the Petrograd
Mensheviks. The text of this was published in *Vestnik* in its
entirety. The fundamental significance of Kronstadt was,
according to Martov, the fact that the initiative for the armed
uprising had originated from a group on which Bolshevism had
formerly depended for support. He had little respect for the
rebel seamen's attempts to elevate their uprising to the status
of a 'third' Russian revolution. Nevertheless, Kronstadt showed
that not every armed uprising against the communist dictatorship needed to end up as a reactionary adventure. Kronstadt
had shown that in principle it was possible to form a broadly
proletarian movement which could fight effectively for the
democratisation of the political structure created by the revolution. This was exactly what the Mensheviks had predicted, but
it had occurred earlier than they expected.[93]

This triumphant conclusion gave little evidence of modesty.
Kronstadt had forced the Mensheviks to recognise that their
rejection of all kinds of armed resistance to the Bolshevik regime
was far too inflexible. Now the uprising had been put down and
had proved to be immune to reactionary temptations Martov
could calmly claim that the regime 'has probably destroyed the
most trustworthy military power on which the revolution could
have depended in the critical moment of counter-revolutionary
danger'.[94] He did not, however, draw the necessary conclusion
that his party had made a serious error of judgement in not
supporting Kronstadt and the wild-cat strikes in Petrograd more
actively. The Mensheviks had been highly indignant when the
socialists at the Vienna International had refused to condemn
the Bolshevik invasion of Georgia with the excuse that they were
not sufficiently well informed about the facts and therefore were
afraid of playing into the hands of reactionary forces. They had
therefore only reacted when it was already too late. It seems

highly likely that the Mensheviks behaved in a similar way with regard to Kronstadt without being conscious of the contradictions in their behaviour. Now it was partly their fault that the Western socialists and workers scarcely reacted to the suppression of socialist workers and sailors in Russia.

### THE FAMINE

The New Economic Policy proclaimed in March could not prevent Russia from being hit by a severe famine, in which between 3 and 6 million people lost their lives. In the last years the food situation had constantly been acute. In the early spring of 1921 the Mensheviks in Moscow had already observed the first signs of the approaching disaster. But it was not until June, when the magnitude of the catastrophe had become a public secret, that the government broke its cautious silence. *Pravda* admitted that 25 million people were suffering from hunger. But by then the true number was already considerably higher. In 1919 and 1920 the attempts of the American Relief Administration and the Red Cross to relieve the food situation in Russia came up against the protests of White Russian émigrés and the unwillingness of the Entente to help communism. The Bolsheviks were also against it since they were afraid of an expansion of Western intervention under the pretext of humanitarian assistance. The famine of 1921 formed again a direct threat to their power, but without outside help it could not be effectively combated. The Soviet government tried to find a solution to this dilemma in various ways.[95]

In July both the patriarch of the Russian orthodox church and the famous writer Maxim Gorky, with the assent of the Soviet government, appealed to the West to help Russia. At the beginning of August, Chicherin, the People's Commissar for Foreign Affairs, asked the governments of Western Europe and America to lend all possible assistance in their countries to relief measures. At the same time Lenin appealed to the international proletariat to stand by his country. The American Relief Administration under the chairmanship of Herbert Hoover and the International Red Cross with Fridtjof Nansen as High Commissioner, now had the opportunity of offering support on a lavish scale. The socialist parties and the trade unions in Western

Europe, at the Mensheviks' instigation, also made substantial donations for the alleviation of Russian need. The very scanty financial prospects of the Western labour movement did not admit any initiatives comparable in scope with the actions organised by the ARA or the Red Cross, but it nevertheless showed itself clearly willing to step into the breach for Russia.

For the Mensheviks the famine was of course both a humanitarian and a political problem. They knew that the Bolsheviks could not handle it alone and this opened up favourable prospects for the RSDRP. In these months the party had just been suffering from a new wave of terrorism which surpassed all previous ones in its severity. Nevertheless, the Mensheviks used the famine only with great restraint as a political lever. They did not ask their Western comrades to make their support of Western relief measures dependent on the immediate release of socialists imprisoned in Russia. That was remarkable, for Hoover had made the help of the ARA conditional on the release of all American citizens imprisoned in Russia, and the Bolsheviks had acceded to this requirement. Still the Mensheviks' attitude showed a healthy realism. Only a few socialists in the West thought that such far-reaching political conditions should be attached to the relief measures. Moreover the Bolsheviks could find sufficient reason in them for totally rejecting socialist help, which was in fact not vitally important to them. But an unselfish action for starving Russia could well be a useful weapon against the anti-socialist campaign being carried out by communists inside and outside Russia. However, it was virtually inevitable that the issue of the *quid pro quo* and that of co-operation with the communists would lastingly influence the attitudes of the Mensheviks and of the Western socialists to the relief measures.[96]

In any case the Mensheviks in Moscow were hoping to convince the outside world that the famine was not, as the Bolsheviks claimed, exclusively the result of the extraordinary drought. The well-known economist and statistician V. G. Groman, at the party's request, wrote an analysis of the causes of the disaster. He explained that the famine was primarily the aftermath of War Communism. Bolshevik terrorism, the suppression of every private initiative and the absence of agricultural experts had resulted in the area of farmland being too much reduced. The NEP had taken effect too late to prevent the catastrophe. The

Central Committee added that the bureaucratic dictatorship was incapable of fighting the famine, and obstructed the vitally necessary help from non-communist organisations. This statement was duplicated in a primitive manner and sent, as the point of view of the legal opposition, to the Soviet newspapers, which of course did not print it, and to Martov in Berlin, who only received the information months later. Various earlier attempts to make contact with the foreign delegation failed, while in the meantime the famine assumed even larger proportions. As a last resort the Central Committee decided to ask the People's Commissariat for Foreign Affairs to send a telegram to Martov on their behalf, in which they appealed to the European proletariat for large-scale relief measures. The Mensheviks were counting on the Bolsheviks not daring to refuse a request of this kind. The telegram was indeed sent on 5 August but it was to be weeks before any reply was received from Berlin.[97]

Meanwhile the Bolsheviks had made an attempt to involve non-communists, not only abroad but even in Russia itself, in the struggle against famine. An All-Russian Committee for the Relief of Famine Victims was set up under the chairmanship of Kamenev. Besides other prominent figures from an almost forgotten past, such as the well-known doctor and liberal politician, Kishkin, former members of the RSDRP had seats on this committee. These were S. N. Prokopovich, who, against the wishes of his party, had formed part of the last cabinet of the Provisional Government as minister of food; his wife, the noted publicist Ekaterina Kuskova, and the leader of the expelled right wing of the party, A. N. Potresov, who had been imprisoned for six months in 1919. An eye-catching amount of publicity was given to the setting up of this committee. Martov observed that the Bolsheviks had evidently looked for it among moderately right-wing and at present non-political figures. The government certainly had no desire to co-operate with the still active political trends in Russia. For most of the non-communists on the committee this was no drawback, but for Potresov it was a reason for his immediate resignation.[98]

The RSDRP refused to recognise a so-called autonomous committee which was in fact a puppet of the government. The party remained an advocate of relief organisations which would actually be independent of the government. These were even set up in some places in Russia, such as Vologda. Conflict with the local government then proved inevitable. In the West the socialist press also quoted communist reporting concerning the general and independent character of the All-Russian Committee. For this reason the Mensheviks in Russia were worried about it. Dvinov wrote to Martov that the committee was mockingly called Prokukish after the names of the principal members, Prokopovich, Kuskova and Kishkin: a nickname with, for Russians, an indecent subsidiary meaning. The committee was intended to be a splendid façade for extracting support from the West. However, according to Dvinov, there was concern among the Bolsheviks about the possible political consequences of this manoeuvre. The so-called 'workers' opposition' in the communist party had stirred up a scandal by calling the establishment of the committee the beginning of 'a coalition with the bourgeoisie'. In another letter from Moscow a Menshevik even stated that 'the first steps have been taken on the long and thorny path towards the handing over of power . . . and the idea of the dictatorship of the RCP has received a dreadful blow from which it will not be able to recover'.[99]

A couple of years later Dvinov was to define this forlorn optimism as 'absurd dreams'. But the situation in 1921 was actually extremely confused and the Mensheviks had contacts with a number of Bolsheviks who were also convinced that the establishment of this committee was the beginning of the end. This was also seen in the same way in the West. On 24 June the *New York Tribune* reported the creation of the committee on its front page with the headline: 'Bolsheviki in panic, Call on Opposition to save Russia'. Meanwhile the Soviet government had also become concerned about the possible political consequences of co-operation between the committee and the foreign relief workers. Lenin suggested it should be disbanded and this proposition was adopted by the Politbureau. When on 27 August the first representative of the ARA arrived in Moscow and was to meet with Prokukish, the Cheka intervened by arresting all the non-communist members of the committee, with the exception of the celebrated revolutionary Vera Figner. In practice these people had been less accommodating than was desirable for the government. Prokopovich and Kuskova were even condemned to death without a trial, falsely accused of conspiring against the state. Gorky, Hoover and Nansen protested strongly against this, whereupon Lenin pardoned them.[100]

The Mensheviks in Berlin did not need to be spurred on by their comrades in order to take action. They were very active in encouraging the Western socialists to organise the most generous possible relief. As soon as the first reports about the famine reached the West they made a pressing appeal to the Vienna International and the International Federation of Trade Unions in Amsterdam. Friedrich Adler, as secretary, wrote a letter on this to all the parties affiliated to Vienna. In total accord with Menshevik wishes, he attached no political conditions whatsoever to the relief. But he did very clearly dissociate himself from the Bolshevik regime, which he blamed for 'fatal errors' and 'appalling blunders'. It however remained a 'socialist duty' to help the Russian workers. Adler's own party reacted in an exemplary way. The Austrian workers were in extremely dire straits themselves. At least a year beforehand the IFTU had organised relief for them. Now, in a short time it raised 11 million crowns, which, despite inflation, was still a substantial sum. The other 'Viennese' parties, such as the USPD, also collected considerable amounts.[101]

The Mensheviks hoped to be able to steer the relief in certain directions, but in this they were not completely successful. They were advocates of a European socialist committee for the coordination of workers' relief in Europe, on which the communists would also have a seat. This fitted in perfectly with the tactics of the RSDRP. The party was striving, in Russia as well, for forms of proletarian cooperation which would not be overruled by the communists. The Vienna International was certainly keen on the idea, but little came of it because animosity between Western socialists and communists was too heated. At the same time the foreign delegation of the RSDRP tried to establish a similar committee in Germany. The USPD reacted enthusiastically and even the German communists did not immediately dismiss it. But the SPD and the German Federation of Trade Unions united to it were opposed to the idea. One of their most prominent officials, Adolph Braun, declared to Dalin: 'We want neither Bolshevik nor Menshevik politics in this affair.'[102] They wished the relief to be regarded as purely humanitarian and therefore preferred a general national committee, to which the 'bourgeois' parties and groups could also belong. Naturally the Mensheviks deplored this, though they regarded the tremendous effort which the Western European bourgeoisie (together with liberal Russian émigrés) was making on behalf of starving Russia as extremely important. It discredited, as Martov expressed it, 'the zoological version of the class war' which was honoured by the communists, and could perhaps have a moderating influence on the terrorism which was being practised against every 'bourgeois' in Russia.[103]

Not only in the SPD, but also in other parties of the Second International, there was serious opposition to co-operating with the communists. In the Dutch SDAP there was substantial resistance to helping the Bolshevik regime, which had defiled the idea of socialism in a dreadful manner and 'driven out the best of our comrades, thrown them into prison and put them to death'. Abramovich, too, had pointed out that the Bolsheviks would have to give extremely firm guarantees for the freedom of movement of the relief authorities in Russia. The Central Committee of the RSDRP went one step further by requesting the Vienna International to send the money collected to the Mensheviks in Moscow and not to the Kremlin.[104] This did not happen because all the socialist relief measures were eventually co-ordinated by the International Federation of Trade Unions. The Mensheviks' proposal to hold a trade union conference in Berlin on this question was agreed to. Besides trade union leaders, representatives of Russian and Georgian social democracy were also invited to this conference, and they reported on the situation in their countries and made certain suggestions. In Berlin it was concluded that the IFTU with its more than 22 million affiliated members, among which were workers of all persuasions, was the most appropriate organisation in which to combine all the moneys collected by Western workers into one massive demonstration of proletarian solidarity with starving Russia. In principle this meant that the Mensheviks had achieved their goal: especially because the Second and Vienna Internationals were gladly leaving the leadership of this action to the IFTU and even the SPD and the German trade unions were abandoning their resistance to one-sided proletarian action. But at the beginning, the trade union leaders were somewhat hesitant about Abramovich's proposal to transport all the collected goods to Russia via a 'proletarian' consignment independent of governments, and to distribute it there. They feared that this could lead to all possible complications and they preferred to co-operate with the International Red Cross.[105]

Nevertheless, it was probably the attitude of the communists which persuaded the IFTU to accept this Menshevik idea. A communist Auslandkomitee für Russlandhilfe (Committee Abroad for Relief to Russia) had been set up under the leadership of the young and resourceful organiser Willy Münzenberg. He had tried to gain admission to the Berlin conference on the basis of a mandate issued by Kamenev. The governing body of the IFTU was only prepared to receive him after the conference was over. It pointed out to Münzenberg that the IFTU also had supporters of the Third International among its membership and was thus in the best possible position to co-ordinate proletarian relief measures outside Russia. But Münzenberg had no intention of allowing his activities to be made subordinate to those of the IFTU. This was noticed by the USPD, which was still negotiating with the German communists about a joint campaign in Germany. The communists suggested bringing this under Münzenberg's committee which would be supervised by trusted members of the SPD, USPD and the communist party. However, the USPD insisted that the communists should cease their separate collections and leave the management to the German Federation of Trade Unions and the IFTU.

This difference of opinion could not be bridged over, and Münzenberg's attempts to interest the Second and Vienna Internationals in his plans failed completely. According to the Comintern this 'inconsistent attitude' of the Western socialists was a result of their dependence on the counter-revolutionary governments in Europe. Of course this was not the case. The attitude of the 'capitalist' states towards the Russian famine did not excel in its generosity. Nansen's attempts to interest the League of Nations in helping Russia failed. The governments of the Entente countries were only willing to extend credit if the Bolsheviks were prepared to settle all their previous debts. The Western socialists were incensed by this reactionary policy of the Great Powers; it simply spurred them on to make the greatest possible sacrifices for Soviet Russia. This, however, did not prevent Münzenberg from subjecting the IFTU to formidable competition, so that there was no question of united proletarian action. According to Münzenberg, his International Workers' Aid set up in September 1921, one of the first of the communist umbrella organisations which were to continue to flourish for many years in Europe, had collected 200 million German marks in 1922: a sum which almost matched that raised by the IFTU.[106]

In October 1921 the IFTU opened negotiations with representatives of the Soviet government in Berlin. Since these did not lead to a satisfactory result, O'Grady of the British National Federation of General Workers left for Moscow. He concluded an agreement with the Russian government in which the IFTU undertook to feed 40,000 children from the Chuvash district. Although the IFTU fulfilled this obligation with great dedication until 1923, and sent many shiploads of food, medicine and clothing to Russia, the governing body was not at all happy with the arrangement. The area chosen was purely agrarian and no worker or worker's child could profit from the efforts of the IFTU. It was crystal-clear that the Bolsheviks were frittering away the help of the Amsterdam International and preventing any contact between Western trade union leaders and Russian workers. The delegation from Amsterdam was not officially received in Moscow. The request by delegates Stroht and Vollmerhaus to be allowed to visit a metal works led to panic reactions in the highest Bolshevik spheres. (According to the Mensheviks this was hardly surprising. The metal workers were in a state of ferment. Even the governing body of their union was part of the 'workers' opposition' within the RCP.) The delegation was given much less competence in Russia than the 'capitalist' ARA of the outspoken anti-communist Hoover. The only mark of appreciation that the IFTU ever received from the Bolshevik side for their efforts was the promise that the Amsterdam International would no longer be referred to in the Soviet press with the offensive adjective 'yellow'. This was a promise which was not kept.[107]

Perhaps all this was instructive, but nevertheless in later years it would become evident that even this kind of direct experience with the Bolshevik dictatorship was not enough. Part of the European trade union movement – especially the British TUC

– remained extremely susceptible to the favourable image of Soviet Russia which the communist propaganda machine continued to exude. The first activities of the foreign delegation of the RSDRP were thus by no means an unqualified success. The split in the European labour movement was an irrefutable fact and the influence even of Martov and his followers on the socialist centre proved to be very relative. The position of their party in Russia remained just as precarious as before. The famine in Russia was the most recent and most disastrous result of the economic policy of the foregoing years. The Bolsheviks had meanwhile changed course with their New Economic Policy. The 'new course' which the communist party was going to sail meant a gradual return to capitalism. In this way it was recognised that the experiment with communism in Russia had failed, partly because the socialist revolution in the West was so long in coming. In Europe, too, the left wing of the socialist labour movement increasingly realised in the course of 1921 that the hour of socialism had not yet come. Both in Russia and in the West capitalism proved to be a more vital economic system than had been thought immediately after the war. Because of this, in 1921 a new situation had come into being in East and West which, for the last time, afforded some hope to the Mensheviks that they could breathe new life into Russian social democracy.

# 9

1921–1923: THE ECLIPSE OF THE
SOCIALIST CENTRE IN THE WEST AND
THE DECLINE OF DEMOCRATIC
SOCIALISM IN SOVIET RUSSIA

Lenin had proclaimed that the New Economic Policy was seriously intended and would last for a long time. According to the Mensheviks the communist party had finally taken the path which the socialist opposition had long ago indicated as the only possible way. Some measures seemed to have been literally taken over from Menshevik proposals and programmes. The Mensheviks regarded the NEP as the inevitable return to more harmonious and natural relationships in society. There was no place there, in their view, for anything as abnormal as the terrorist dictatorship of the Politbureau of the communist party. The political superstructure of society could not continue to exist in permanent discord with its economic base. In other words economic freedom was pointless without political freedom. The Bolsheviks would have to dismantle their dictatorship in order to prevent their being swept away in the long run by the social forces which would be released as a result of the NEP. As was usually the case with Menshevik ideas, this thought contained a general truth. We know that economic reforms in communist countries have usually failed, because more freedom in the economy also assumes more freedom in politics. It is interesting to note that when a communist leader like Gorbachev at last tried to introduce political as well as economic reforms, he inevitably undermined the communist monopoly of power.

The formula that the Mensheviks gave for the influence of the economy on politics was not therefore wrong. But as Marxists they were inclined to think that this process was not reversible. However, for seven decades after 1921 the Bolsheviks proved that politics can also dominate the economy. The NEP was in fact little else than a series of concessions intended to safeguard the position of the communist regime. At the time, however, it was far from certain that it would succeed. The years 1921–7 formed a period in which a number of political and economic alternatives to the communist party's official course of action were not only conceivable, but even seemed to be realisable in practical terms. It was a time when a struggle for power was taking place in the communist party which, as far as ideology was concerned, was being fought out in vehement discussions about the long-term future of the Soviet state.[1]

It was therefore understandable that in 1921 the Mensheviks believed that the political prospects of their party need not be poor. They had always tried, within the Bolshevik-dominated Soviets, to be the mouthpiece for proletarian resistance to Bolshevik dictatorship. The situation at the end of 1920 and the beginning of 1921 in Russia seemed to offer fresh opportunities for success in this policy. The communists had forfeited a great deal of their credit among the workers, and had free elections taken place the Mensheviks would probably, as in 1918, have gained substantial victories. The dictatorship prevented this but nevertheless Russian social democracy seemed to be recovering. The RSDRP was attracting new, chiefly young and enthusiastic supporters, was once more gaining direct contact with the proletariat in the main industrial centres, and was exerting some influence on the still substantial group of delegates in the Soviets without a party affiliation. Wherever small groups of Mensheviks took action they set off political fireworks which often could not be completely extinguished by the Bolsheviks. In 1918 and 1919 many social democrats were weighed down by the thought that in 1917 they had lost their grip on the political situation through their own failure, and that history had therefore made the Bolsheviks into its *modus operandi*. After the proclamation of the NEP a cheerful, almost triumphant mood came into existence for a short time among the social democrats. The Mensheviks had the feeling that, from a moral and ideological point of view, they were in a much stronger position than the communist rulers. The strong internal tension within the communist party and the enormous dissatisfaction at all levels of the population strengthened their conviction that, not only in the economic field but also from a political point of view, they would win their case. However, they very soon found that, precisely on this point, Lenin's NEP did not answer their expectations.

This was also the main reason why, within the RSDRP, a heated discussion flared up about the political conclusions to be drawn from the new situation. Was it still possible to hold on to the revolutionarily slanted programme which had been formulated by the party in April 1920 and in which it was assumed that the world was situated in the transitional stage between capitalism and socialism? What possibilities were there now for democratic developments in Russia? Would the 'Bonapartist' tendencies in the communist party shortly gain the upper hand? Was it meaningful for the Mensheviks to remain as the legal opposition of a regime which showed no sign of bringing terrorism against the socialists to an end? Or would it be better not to let the party appear in public any more and thus save its strength for a better future? Or ought one perhaps to consider an underground and thus illegal continuation of the struggle against Bolshevism? What could be done by the capitalist and socialist West to hasten the normalisation of political relations in Russia? Was it possible to restore unity within international socialism, while there could be no possibility of co-operation between communists and socialists in Russia? Ought a more conciliatory attitude to be adopted towards the right-wing trends within their own party, within the PSR, or towards the reformist majority in the Western labour movement now that the chance of eliminating capitalism had become so much smaller? Ought not all democratic forces in and out of Russia really fight for a wide anti-Bolshevik front?

For the Russian social democrats who took an extreme left- or right-wing stand, answering these questions was simple. For Potresov, Liber and Portugeis, who were no longer members of the RSDRP, Bolshevism was something completely reprehensible. According to them it was pointless to rely on an evolution within the communist party. Left-wing social democrats or opportunistically thinking Mensheviks not infrequently also left the RSDRP because, along a completely different route, they had come to the conclusion that the legal opposition had become completely meaningless. Prominent party members like Troyanovsky, Ermansky, Martynov and Maisky went over to the Bolsheviks or were on the point of doing so. The Mensheviks who remained faithful to the party were very divided amongst themselves. The frank but confusing discussions between the more left-wing and the more right-wing persuasions did not achieve much. In 1921–2 the Mensheviks were swinging back and forth between hope and despair. But if they were unwilling to submit a definitive defeat of democratic socialism in Russia, there was little else they could do but try once again to induce the party ruling in the name of the proletariat, under pressure from the workers, to make political concessions and reforms.

Thus the RSDRP continued, as far as possible, to hold on to its policy of legal opposition to the Bolshevik regime and to strive towards a restoration of unity within international socialism. Nevertheless, in practice the party moved somewhat to the right, for it could no longer adhere so rigidly to the left-wing 1920 course of action. There was less talk of a socialist coalition government to replace the Bolshevik dictatorship, and more emphasis was given to the necessity of political rights for all social groups, thus also for the bourgeoisie and not only for the workers and the peasants. Martov and his disciples had great difficulty in giving up their revolutionary philosophy, but of course they realised that circumstances in Russia and Europe offered little prospect of a rapid breakthrough to socialism.[2]

Martov took the criticism levelled at him by the right wing seriously, especially when this came from men of integrity like Akselrod. His friend and mentor had, as we saw in the last chapter, put his objections down in writing in September 1920, but only sent the letter to Berlin at the end of March 1921. In his eighteen-page reply, Martov tried to dispel Akselrod's concern, and to defend his politics. He thought that the principal difference of opinion between himself and Akselrod did not relate to their assessment of Bolshevism. In the first place it was their appreciation of reformist socialism which differed widely. Akselrod was very critical of the right wing of the international workers' movement, but was prepared to recognise it as socialist and above all saw it as the principal counterweight to communism. Martov still wanted to have as little as possible to do with this group of people because of their attitude during the war.

He admitted that in doing this he was compelled to put up willingly with the unpleasant characteristics of some centrists. But he pointed out that, in comparison with one year earlier, there was some progress to be found. The recognition by ideologists like Bauer that a development was taking place in Russia which could not be compared to the Paris Commune of 1871 but was more akin to the French revolution of 1789, signified a clear erosion of the myth which had initially done the rounds about Bolshevism. Actually this was a step forward. Even half truths about Russia and Bolshevism were something to be pleased about in present circumstances. On the other hand, it remained a fact that the apologetic attitude which people like Bauer had taken towards Bolshevism had until now prevented them from taking the next step. Instead of enquiring about the rationale of a twentieth-century Jacobinism, they had been satisfied with the conclusion that something of the sort would indeed do duty as progress in a country like Russia.

The Mensheviks had been wrestling with this problem since 1903, and Akselrod in particular had pointed out the possibility at the time that Leninism would sweep along the masses into a bourgeois revolution and thus fulfil the same role as the Jacobins had done more than a century before. 'It was these ideas of yours, Pavel Borisovich, by which we were allowing ourselves to be led, when we saw how popular Bolshevism, in the fullest sense of the word, was becoming and how it was taking on the typical traits of the Jacobin *sans-culottes* under an international communist cloak.'[3] According to Martov the Bolshevik coup had been undemocratic, but not thereby inconsistent with the interests of the peasants, workers and soldiers. The October revolution had refloated the stranded Russian revolution and cleared the way for radical social reforms carried out by the people.

He thought that this possibility had not arisen in the French revolution. The Bolshevik revolution was thus indeed Jacobin but, luckily for it, its power was free from the limitations which had been so disastrous for its eighteenth-century predecessors. The Bolsheviks had, however, done nothing with the splendid opportunities that history had offered them. They had taken a different route. Their utopianism and their slavish imitation of the French Jacobins' terrorist methods had nullified the unique situation which they had themselves created through their coup. This was the main reason for the Menshevik opposition to their regime. 'The fundamental contrast, of which you write, between our judgement of October and our politics, does not therefore exist. Precisely because we see the Bolsheviks as the most radical executors of the historical process which led to the destruction of the old Russia, we are in conflict with them, for they are carrying out their "Jacobin" mission badly, and their subjective attempts to establish communism must inevitably lead to the demoralisation and weakening of the proletariat.'[4] Martov expected the urban and agrarian strata of the population, which had gone through a Bolshevik phase and had thus shown themselves very active in this eighteenth-century-style revolution, to distance themselves further and further in future from the Bolsheviks.

In Martov's view Akselrod had not taken sufficiently into account the fact that the Bolsheviks had long been supported by a substantial section of the wage labourers in town and country. Parliamentary democracy and other subtle alternatives which had been offered by the remaining socialist parties did not appeal to these workers. They were filled with true Bolshevik fanaticism. Thus an attempted overthrow of the Bolshevik regime would be faced not only with a small minority of corrupted communists, but also with large groups of 'real' workers. Considerations of this kind had brought the Mensheviks to cease demanding the restoration of the Constituent Assembly expelled by the Bolsheviks as soon as the reactionary generals came out with the same slogan. The struggle for the democratisation of the Soviets had been the only means of forging unity between the educated, skilled workers, who had long ago broken away from Bolshevism, and 'the darker levels' of the proletariat, who had only just begun to adopt a critical attitude towards the regime. Only thus would the Russian social democrats be able to confront the communists with a united front, formed of the majority of Russian workers. Of course Martov and his sympathisers were still far from reaching this goal. But the uprising in Kronstadt, once the staunchest bastion of Bolshevism, had nevertheless proved the correctness of these tactics.

Although the Mensheviks took pride in the fact that two years earlier they had already made proposals which amounted to a new economic policy, they were actually, like everyone else, bewildered by the political somersault which the communist regime had undertaken. This is evident from the remaining letters from Martov to Akselrod in the course of 1921. He had already been searching for some time in the most recent Russian past for indications of a Thermidor-like reaction, and the NEP, this 'bourgeoisification' of Bolshevik politics, taking place in his view at lightening speed, was grist to his mill. What was indeed special about the situation was that a kind of economic Thermidor preceded the fall of the Bolshevik regime, which in Martov's view was inevitable. But the Russian communists 'could make the task of their successors somewhat easier because they will be doing the dirty work themselves by returning the factories to their former owners, giving out concessions, recognising state debts, and so forth. If they do all this, then they themselves have to face the principal reproach which could be brought against a future socialist or democratic government: the reproach that it delivered up the proletariat to capitalism. That would be a true historical Nemesis!'[5]

In another letter Martov claimed that Lenin was antagonising the majority of his own party members because of the oversimplified way in which he was defending capitalism. 'One can therefore categorically predict that nothing will come of the "new policy" (the communists will sabotage it) unless Lenin decides, with the assent of a minority in the party which is a bit more sensible, to carry out a bonapartist revolution, that is to say, instead of a party dictatorship, to establish a personal [dictatorship] with the support of the non-Bolshevik section of the bureaucracy, the merchants and speculators, the military, and so forth.'[6] Two weeks later he let Akselrod know of the news he had received from his comrades in Russia about the spreading process of disintegration in the communist party, and the satisfaction with the regime which was increasing among the peasants as a result of the most recent agrarian measures. If Lenin had had a more egocentric personality, then immediately after 1917 he would have advertised himself as 'protector of the muzhik'. Now, too, the countryside was ready for the creation of a sort of Napoleonic legend about Lenin. 'This is the moment of the ninth Thermidor, when Robespierre tried to free himself from his small Committee of Public Safety. That was Robespierre's undoing. Let us see if Lenin can avoid this finale . . . .'[7]

Martov's statements were not unique, but typical of the tidal wave of speculations which had been unleashed by this new development in Soviet Russia, not only in the socialist or communist world but also elsewhere. Kautsky too, who in 1921 was defending himself against the polemical attack which Trotsky had made on him a year before, described in a new piece of writing entitled *From Democracy to the Slavery of the State*, 'the threatening breakdown' of the communist dictatorship. 'Bolshevism has passed its peak and has started on a decline whose pace is naturally becoming faster and faster.'[8] Kautsky also maintained that a 'new edition of the 9th Thermidor' was possible and he thought it probable that Russia would succumb to total anarchy after the fall of the Bolshevik regime.[9] Martov was 'not a little disappointed' about Kautsky's latest attack on Bolshevism.[10] Kautsky had indeed once more put his ideas about democracy and dictatorship on paper and his polemic with Trotsky was not particularly exciting. Nevertheless, the Mensheviks in Berlin translated this piece of Kautsky's and distributed it in Russia. Of course the appearance of this booklet in Soviet Russia, given the existing political situation there, had a completely different impact than in the West.

In the introduction written to the Russian edition, Abramovich touched on the fact that the Mensheviks had differed in opinion from Kautsky in the past and that he could sometimes be 'circumlocutory' in a 'really schoolmasterly fashion'. But this had little effect on his substantial merits. Kautsky's quarrel with the Bolsheviks was, according to Abramovich, 'the case between Marxism and its idealistic falsification'. Lenin, Trotsky, Radek, Zinoviev and Bukharin, in order to write books and articles against the 'senile', 'deranged renegade', 'robbed of all influence', had had to tear themselves away from the most pressing affairs of state in the most turbulent and darkest period of the Russian revolution.

> In this period Kautsky was the only foreign theorist of revolutionary Marxism who had the courage of his convictions to come out in public with a clear and explicit criticism of Bolshevism from a Marxist point of view. While Rosa Luxemburg, and after her death her closest friends Levi, Zetkin and others, considered it possible and useful to keep their differences of opinion with the Bolsheviks about the revolutionary method hidden from the proletariat, while people like Adler, Bauer, Hilferding and Longuet, partly for political reasons, and partly from a misconceived need for international solidarity, for a long time refrained from public criticism of Bolshevism and condemnation of its methods, Kautsky risked his position in the party and imperilled what was

left of his former popularity by rushing into the fight with youthful fervour.[11]

The new situation in the Soviet state had temporarily wiped out the serious differences in the interpretations of the Russian revolution by democratically inclined Marxists. It was evident from the Russian edition of Kautsky's pamphlet that the Mensheviks were broadly speaking in agreement with him. This was also true of Otto Bauer who likewise had a pamphlet published about the NEP under the title *The New Course in Russia*. The satisfactory development which Martov thought he could descry in centrist thinking had indeed gone ahead. Bauer, too, appreciated the daring way the Bolsheviks had broken 'with their economic illusions'. 'But this courageous deed would remain fruitless unless a new course in politics followed the new course in the economy in due time.'[12] The Russian revolution had finally been nothing more than a bourgeois revolution which, like all the bourgeois upheavals in the past, had been through a radical phase in which the revolution was 'carried significantly beyond its aim'.[13] It was in the interests of the Russian and the European proletariat that the inevitable fall of the communist dictatorship should take place in a gradual and peaceful manner. The solidarity of socialist Europe with Soviet Russia ought therefore not only to be demonstrated by protecting it as much as possible against counter-revolutionary threats or against famine. The Western socialists also had the duty, with all the intellectual weapons at their disposal, 'to support those forces within the Russian revolution which are urging the Soviet government towards that voluntary liquidation of the dictatorship which alone can avert its violent collapse'. Thus, without mentioning the Mensheviks, Bauer indicated that their policy was the only right one and deserved full support.[14]

### 'AFTER WARS AND REVOLUTIONS'

Thus in 1921 all the prominent Marxist socialists agreed with one another about Russia. Their unanimity was to endure until the moment when it became definitively clear that in the twenties a development had taken place in Russia which actually did not fit in with their analyses and about which analogies with European revolutions in the past were almost meaningless. But for the time being they could enjoy their intellectual triumph.

Their predictions had come true: harsh reality had prevailed over the utopian idea in Russia, too. The possibility that their interpretation of this reality was only very incompletely correct did not even occur to them. Towards the communists they not infrequently adopted the attitude of people who had been in the right from the very beginning. And given their own hesitations and changes of course, and the revolutionary illusions they had themselves cherished, this was not particularly honest or sensible. Nor was this triumphant *Rechthaberei* lacking in the Mensheviks, though the hopeless position of their party in Russian did temper it somewhat. They knew that being right would not give them much practical advantage at present, while the time of being proved right might perhaps never arrive. For them, in contrast to Western socialists like Kautsky and Bauer, the NEP was an occasion for a critical reassessment of their own ideas. The most thorough attempt at this was undertaken in 1921 by David Dalin. He wrote a book of nearly 300 pages which was published in Berlin under the title *Posle Voin i Revolyutsii* (*After Wars and Revolutions*).

Dalin, who had studied economics at Heidelberg, had been a faithful follower of Martov in 1917 and the years that followed. Because of his fluency in German, he had been an indispensable member of the Foreign Delegation of the RSDRP, especially during the earliest period of his political emigration. In 1920–1, as in the case of a number of Mensheviks, his political ideas moved to the right. Dalin began, Martov noticed, to be closer to Akselrod than to him. In 1921 his differences of opinion with Martov were fought out in *Socialistichesky Vestnik* (*The Socialist Messenger*), the paper the Mensheviks published in Berlin and smuggled into Russia. *Posle Voin i Revolyutsii* was the first detailed study by Dalin, who particularly after the Second World War was to make his name as a Russian expert with a number of books in the United States. This work was a sort of *tour d'horizon*. All the important problems of Russian communism and Western socialism were discussed in it and not in a purely speculative manner, but on the basis of a wide, primarily economic knowledge of the subject.

After the gun-smoke of the wars and revolutions had lifted, Dalin, like all Marxist socialists, maintained that nothing but a bourgeois revolution had taken place in Russia. In February

1917 only the monarchy, the beautiful cupola of the *ancien régime*, had been pulled down. The walls and foundations were not demolished until the October revolution. That had been the real function of the Bolshevik rule. All this had nothing to do with socialism. History had only performed a grandiose masquerade and scoffed at human intentions. The bourgeois revolution had been perpetrated by the deadly enemies of the bourgeoisie. The communists, as opponents of any kind of ownership, had fought a battle of life and death with the defenders of all forms of property. But the only result was that feudal ownership, that is, large-scale landownership, disappeared for ever.

Nevertheless, the social consequences of the revolution were far-reaching. The nobility, which had ruled since Catherine the Great, had completely lost its economic and political authority. The pre-revolutionary bourgeoisie had likewise disappeared from society. The intelligentsia, which had lost its belief in the revolution and also in itself, no longer formed a separate, important group in society. Like the Western intellectuals, the Russian intelligentsia had become peaceful, bourgeois and moderate, and was prepared to accept any regime which could deliver it from its material misery. For the proletariat the revolution was likewise a great disappointment. The attempt at workers' self-government failed completely and consequently the factory workers became apathetic and apolitical.

The peasants on the other hand had gained in self-respect. They had proved to be the strongest force in the revolution and effectively prevented not only the restoration of the *ancien régime* but also the introduction of a socialist economy. The once so backward Russian peasants were beginning to show an increasing similarity to the industrious and thrifty French *paysans*. The NEP offered them their best chance of a prosperous development, but a clash with the present communist regime could not in the long run be avoided. In the meantime another bourgeoisie had also come into being in Russia. The Cheka's crusade against speculation had hit the former middle class hard, but at the same time created a new class of philanderers and profiteers. Life was simply stronger than belief. In the West there was also a considerable group of *nouveaux riches* after the war. The Russian profiteers, however, formed a totally new and independent group whose existence was now legalized by the NEP.

Dalin regarded this 'bourgeoisification' of the social classes in Russia as highly significant. The tenor of the *ancien régime* had been anti-bourgeois. Tsarist Russia had experienced no separate petty bourgeois culture (*meshchansky byt*). Soviet Russia was now in the grip of a cultural process that was to last for years and certainly signified progress. The country was displaying the image of a bourgeois society which acquired its rights the moment the bourgeois revolution was completed. This did not automatically mean that Russia would also be suitable for a democracy. Dissatisfaction with the Bolshevik dictatorship was general. But the longing for a strong authority which would bring stability, order and prosperity was much greater than the demand for a democratic government. The remaining political parties were no longer in a position to spur on the people to mass action by which the dictatorship could be overthrown. The embryo of the new Russia must be found within the extremely heterogeneous communist party which was showing distinct signs of disintegration. The party and state bureaucracy with its 2 million civil servants had developed into a real Leviathan. The administration of the dictatorship was becoming more and more bourgeois. At the same time it assumed the attitude of an elite raised above all classes whose virtue it was to be cynical and realistic. These *apparatchiki* knew that they needed not so much the enthusiasm of their dwindling proletarian and communist supporters, as the assistance of all Russians and of foreign capital, in order to put the NEP into operation. But no one would invest money or work in the Russian economy as long as the regime failed to inspire any confidence and could guarantee no stability. The NEP could certainly gain limited successes, but constituted no solution to Russia's gigantic problems.

An easy transition from dictatorship to democracy was unlikely, given the longing for strong authority and the role that the army and the peasants were to play in the liquidation of the Bolshevik regime. It might be that a new political figure could suddenly arise from one of the rival cliques within the communist party; someone who up till now had not let himself be heard much and had only played a background role. 'A man who is committed to the revolution, an enemy of restoration, a fierce defender of the interests of the peasants', probably 'a Bolshevik without prejudices, sufficiently courageous, energetic and

insolent to subdue ruthlessly all the remains of Bolshevism . . .
who can keep the workers under his thumb with the lash
and with demagogy, who sees political freedom from the moral
point of view of a Hottentot and who jealously guards the sacred
right of property'. For the ignorant masses the economic revival
of Russia would only be the proof that the policy of this new
dictator was right and it would enable him to clear all opposition
out of the way and to develop into an unrestricted ruler with
the aura of the true 'leader of the people [*narodnyi vozhd*]'.[15]

Dalin thought that everyone in Russia should make an effort
for democracy. But he did not indicate how the RSDRP ought
to do this under present circumstances. There was, in fact, no
room in his analysis for an independent role for his party in the
near future. Nor did he devote a single word to the perspectives
of the Menshevik politics of the day. His comrades in Russia did
not thank him for that. His ideas about the future of Western
Europe likewise deprived the Menshevik orientation on the
socialism of the centre of any significance, and this had already
brought him into conflict with Martov. Since 1850 capitalism
had experienced a splendid florescence and although many
imaginary funerals of capitalism had taken place since then in
socialist theory, this florescence had still not come to an end.
Dalin wondered, departing from the classic passage in the foreword of Marx's *Critique of Political Economy*, what superior technology was actually appropriate to socialism if the windmill
applied to feudalism and the steam engine to capitalism. Some
writers – and here Dalin was of course referring to Lenin – had
claimed that the century of electrification would also be the
century of socialism. In Dalin's view this was totally wrong.
Capitalism had demonstrated everywhere that it was in a position
to make use of electricity on a grand scale. Dalin therefore
considered it better to leave Marx's criteria for the determination
of the period of social revolution for what they were. In the
increasing number of businesses in the West which were
exploited in a non-capitalist way – here he was thinking chiefly
of the so-called service industries in the hands of the
authorities – he even saw an indication that socialism still
possessed the future. But that future was far distant even in
Europe. There was no socialist majority in any part of the world
whatsoever and that meant that there were only a few people

who believed that capitalism was incapable of further development. In the West there was no other immediate task for socialism than the strengthening of democracy. Otherwise there was
not much for them do to.

Dalin was not the only socialist with ideas like this, but they
had seldom since the October revolution been expressed in such
detail or so clearly. Martov contended against him that Europe
was in a period of transition. Capitalism was still functioning
but it could not solve the enormous problems of the post-war
economy. The crisis created by the war still persisted. Martov
also thought that the present weakness of the Western proletariat
would prove to be only temporary in nature.[16] The analyses
which the democratic socialists made at the beginning of the
NEP period had little value as predictions. Capitalism did not
prevail in Russia and the communist dictatorship managed to
maintain itself. Economic recovery took place, especially in
agriculture, more rapidly and completely than Menshevik and
other critics thought possible. Afterwards everything which tended towards capitalism was swept away by Stalin in a second
revolution which far surpassed the years of War Communism
in scope, depth and the number of victims it took. Nevertheless,
the horrifying way in which this man made an end to the NEP
with collectivisation and five year plans and the enormous risks
he took in doing this, were a sign that the Bolsheviks were very
apprehensive of a revival of capitalism in Russia and extremely
afraid of the political power which an economically independent
peasantry could acquire for itself in Russia. Although capitalism
in Russia was then being exterminated root and branch, later
in the thirties it turned out that what was being outlined as
'socialist' meant in many respects a return to 'bourgeois' values
and norms in social life and culture. Even for the analysis of
the Soviet Union under Khrushchev, Brezhnev and Gorbachev
the Menshevik concept of the 'belated bourgeois revolution' has
remained in many respects a better instrument than the idea
that a socialist revolution had taken place.[17]

## POLITICAL PRISONERS

The NEP did not bring political freedom. The course of the
history of Soviet Russia in the twenties was first and foremost
determined by the decision of the communist party leadership

to maintain its position of power at the cost of everything else. Terrorism remained necessary and the security police indispensable. Many thousand people were killed in 1917–22. The somewhat gentle treatment of the social democrats contrasted sharply with this, for Europe, unprecedented policy of brutality. Evidently orders had been given to treat the socialists as special prisoners. It is unlikely that a specific policy was being carried out in the capricious actions of the Cheka. Lenin had publicly declared at the proclamation of the NEP: 'We shall carefully keep the Mensheviks and the socialist revolutionaries in prison.' But even from this pronouncement one can infer that the regime was not in a position to defeat the socialists in the political arena, and given the crisis situation in the country ravaged by famine, cholera and economic chaos, dared go no further than physically isolating the opposition.[18]

The strange relationship between the regime and the RSDRP was determined by multifarious factors. One of these was that the Mensheviks were still trying to be a legal opposition, and thus scarcely made use of conspiratorial techniques, as in tsarist times, to keep out of the clutches of the security police. Dzerzhinsky, the head of the Cheka, once said mockingly of them: 'You can arrest the Mensheviks by telephone, [you ring them up] and they come to you'.[19] The special branch of the security police which was concerned with the suppression of the socialists was actually also interested in maintaining the RSDRP in existence. Otherwise these Chekists would lose their jobs and the many privileges attached to them. Or, as the Menshevik Binshtok remarked at any of the many interrogations: 'If we were not here, then nor would you be.'[20] The Mensheviks not infrequently remained linked to some Bolsheviks by friendship or family relationships. This, too, was one of the reasons for the capricious and inconsistent character of the reign of terror against the RSDRP.

A few rather absurd events can be accounted for by the confusion and insecurity which had also seized some prominent Bolsheviks as a result of the new political developments. Thus the Marxist historian Rozhkov, who was no longer politically active and was later to join the communist party, was arrested together with Dan and other Mensheviks in 1921 and almost shot on a charge of Menshevik complicity at Kronstadt. When he was set free a few months later he was asked in all seriousness by the head of the Cheka in Petrograd what he thought of the NEP and of a compromise and a sharing of power between communists and socialists. In other ways too, the Mensheviks were sounded out about possible co-operation, and curiously enough at about the same time, reports in the West about negotiations concerning a coalition government in Soviet Russia appeared in respectable newspapers like *The Times* and the *Nieuwe Rotterdamsche Courant.* The Mensheviks moreover had the impression that the Politbureau was willing to limit terrorism with an eye to Western public opinion. Martov had indications at his disposal that not only the British but also the German government, during negotiations about the trade treaties in 1921 which were vital for the Soviet republic, had insisted on the moderation of repression. The Foreign Delegation of the RSDRP had worked extremely hard among the German socialists for a trade agreement with Russia, but in the process would not have failed to point out to them the hopeless position of the Russian socialists. At any rate Lenin complained that the Mensheviks in Berlin had sabotaged the conclusion of a treaty.[21]

From this it is evident that it was not so simple to isolate the RSDRP and that a handful of talented opponents could be particularly irksome for the regime. What was extraordinarily annoying for the Bolshevik rulers was that at the beginning of 1921 the Mensheviks in Berlin had succeeded in publishing a paper of which dozens, and sometimes hundreds of copies were smuggled into Russia and there served as a replacement for the social democratic press which had been forbidden and rendered impossible. *Socialistichesky Vestnik* (*The Socialist Messenger*) appeared twice a month and contained, besides political analyses of a high order, a gold mine of information about developments in Russia and the international labour movement. The paper formed a vehicle for the RSDRP, which was disorganised and split by terrorism, and every copy in Russia was literally read to shreds. Not infrequently the paper reached the imprisoned Mensheviks and was a source of great joy to them. Even Bolsheviks asked for numbers of *Vestnik,* because they considered their own party's reporting to be untrustworthy. The communist leaders, who naturally also read the paper, made every possible effort to prevent its circulation, but in this they were not successful.[22]

However optimistic the Mensheviks may have been, and by however many hesitations the Bolsheviks may have been overcome, relations between the regime and its legal opposition worsened rapidly in 1921 and the pressure of terrorism increased significantly. In December 1920 the RSDRP was still officially invited to participate with a delegation at the Eighth All-Russian Soviet Congress. Even Fyodor Dan, who had been banned to Smolensk, obtained permission from the authorities to come to Moscow for it. The interested communist public's reaction to Dan's extremely critical speech obliged the chairman of the congress to quadruple the length of his allotted speaking time, which had been limited to the minimum.[23] But during the workers' riots in February 1921 the security police made raids in numerous towns in which Mensheviks were also picked up in large numbers. Most of the members of the party's Central Committee were now under lock and key. The few party activists still at liberty in Moscow nevertheless decided to participate in the elections for the local Soviet in April 1921. The communists attached great significance to these elections because results in the capital were seen as a political gauge for the whole country. They took advantage of their exclusive rights of agitation and propaganda to the full and thwarted the Mensheviks wherever they could. Nevertheless, the social democrats' extremely modest performance was successful with the Moscow workers and in this way a couple of their people were elected into the Soviet. This convinced them that in free elections they would have gained a resounding victory.[24]

The party had even put forward some of its imprisoned leaders as candidates at these elections. At this, these demanded their immediate release. They sent a copy of their protest to Friedrich Adler, the secretary of the Vienna International. Zelinsky, the secretary of the Moscow committee of the communist party, subsequently announced with some honesty that Mensheviks were being held prisoner simply with an eye to the elections, but that they would be set free after these were over. Litovinov, the secretary of the executive committee of the All-Russian Soviet Congress, who was then in Germany, also explained that the imprisoned Mensheviks would soon be discharged because nothing had actually been found during searches of their houses. Martov's ironical reaction was that Litovinov must be told that the Chekists had evidently found the Menshevik economic programme. Lenin had stolen it and afterwards made use of it as his New Economic Policy.[25]

The imprisoned Menshevik leaders were not released. Far from it. *Pravda* complained that the socialist leaders imprisoned in the Butyrsky prison in Moscow were being treated as if they were staying in a sanatorium. The Cheka decided to make an example of them. During the night of 25 April the Mensheviks, socialist revolutionaries and anarchists in the Butyrsky prison were dragged out of their cells, maltreated and distributed among other prisons in and outside Moscow. In May a new wave of arrests swept the country. The prison regime was tightened up. Typhoid and cholera took their toll. Two young socialist revolutionaries ostentatiously committed suicide by burning themselves in desperation. Other prisoners started going on hunger strikes in protest. 'Let them die', Dzerzhinsky's deputy Unshlikht is said to have remarked, but in some cases the demands of the hunger strikers were nevertheless granted.[26]

The RSDRP protested strongly against the actions of the Cheka in the Butyrsky prison, which for the first time created the impression that the regime was out for the physical extermination of the opposition. The Menshevik protest encountered so much response among students in Moscow that on 8 June the People's Commissar of Education, Lunacharsky, closed the Moscow institutions for higher education. Nineteen student leaders were arrested. The Mensheviks also found a hearing among moderate Bolsheviks like Riazanov. The small but extremely active Menshevik group in the Moscow Soviet insisted that an investigation be made into the events in the Butyrsky prison.[27]

Martov and Abramovich, in response to these events, made an appeal to all socialist parties and trade unions in the West and asked for a financial contribution for the 2,000 Menshevik prisoners and their families.[28] This request produced a heart-warming response for the Mensheviks. It was published in practically all the important newspapers in Europe and provided with sympathetic commentary. Some comments were written by socialist journalists, who, up till then, had scarcely been willing to express their criticism of Bolshevism. The governing body of the UPSD sent a special circular to its local organisations, which were asked to make collections. The Bureau of the Vienna

International sent out a severe condemnation of Bolshevik terrorism and demanded full political freedom for all socialists in Russia.[29]

But not much money was collected. Nothing happened within the socialist movement which could be compared in any way with the action to fight famine in Russia. The attitude of the International Federation of Trade Unions, which did not react at all to the Foreign Delegation's appeal, was disappointing. When Abramovich enquired the reason, Edo Fimmen, the Dutch secretary of the IFTU, answered that the Federation simply could not meddle in politics because of its general and international character. Abramovich said that he did not understand this since the Federation had after all proclaimed an economic boycott against the Horthy dictatorship in Hungary. But according to Fimmen that was completely different. In Hungary the workers were fighting against a reactionary ruling class. In Russia, on the other hand, the struggle between Mensheviks and Bolsheviks was being carried out within the framework of one class, the working class, and the IFTU could not interfere in that. The real reason was that Fimmen, who was in favour of co-operation with the communist trade unions, did not want to anger the Bolsheviks.[30]

Russia's rulers did indeed react with extreme irritation and rudeness to the indignation about terrorism aroused by the Mensheviks in Western circles. During the sitting of the Moscow Soviet on 30 June 1921 the commission of inquiry gave an account of the events in the Butyrsky prison. It informed the meeting that the imprisoned socialists had not been thrashed, but on the contrary it was they who had used violence against properly acting agents of the Cheka. The opposition scarcely had the opportunity to defend itself against these ridiculous lies. The regime evidently attached considerable importance to this affair, because questions were also asked at the Third Comintern Congress, which was then meeting in Moscow, about the treatment of political prisoners. A number of congress delegates attended the meeting of the Soviet and probably because of this Bukharin gave another special address about this issue.[31]

Bukharin was one of the most prominent communist leaders. It was claimed that he was the 'darling' of the party because of his warm and spontaneous good nature. According to him, the social democrats' attempt to create a scandal at the time of the Comintern congress had failed completely because of the excellent work of the commission of inquiry. There were party members, chiefly young girls, who wept and wailed in sentimental fashion about the harsh treatment meted out to the opposition. But revolutionary violence had to be used against class enemies. It would not be the end of the world if a Menshevik lost a few hairs from his wise head. In the revolution the one who smashed in the other man's skull was the winner. During and after Bukharin's performance, speech was made impossible for the Mensheviks by a group of armed Chekists pressing in on them who shouted in chorus: 'Give them what for!', 'Shoot them!' The chairman, Kamenev, concluded the meeting by demanding harsh measures against any Mensheviks who made further contributions to the *Vestnik*.[32]

All this could rightly be regarded as a foretaste of what was to come. A number of Mensheviks were convinced that the attitude of those in power was forcing the party to give up its legal opposition and go completely underground into illegality. But the majority – including the imprisoned members of the Central Committee – were absolutely unwilling to do this. The party had always resolutely refused to rebel against the regime. By going underground the Mensheviks would indicate that they were no longer striving for a democratic evolution of the regime, but preparing a revolutionary fight against communism. This would play directly into the hands of the Bolsheviks, for the Cheka would then have a legitimate excuse for completely eliminating the party. The struggle for more political freedom could not be waged in illegality. Even if the party were to have to suffer many more setbacks, in the long run the period of the NEP would nevertheless offer good opportunities to a legal, proletarian opposition.

Opponents of illegality were right in so far as terrorism continued to fluctuate. Even in the second half of 1921 many social democrats were released again from prison, while at the same time others were picked up. But the general amnesty which was proclaimed on the occasion of the fourth anniversary of the October revolution applied only to soldiers who had fought in the White armies, participants in the Kronstadt and workers' uprisings, yes, even to ordinary criminals, but emphatically not to the Mensheviks and socialist revolutionaries. About two hundred social democrats remained imprisoned uninterruptedly, including the most prominent leaders of the Central Committee. The RSDRP regarded this as a sign that they were considered by the regime as its only important opponent. In fact Lenin declared that Menshevism was 'the most dangerous enemy'. His remarks about 'secret Menshevism' within his own party and the necessity for purges confirmed the Mensheviks in their conviction that there were groups in the communist party who were resisting the determination of Lenin and the Cheka leaders to liquidate the opposition completely.[33]

Meanwhile the question of the political prisoners continued to occupy the Western labour movement. This was the case, for instance, at the congress of the International Typographers' Union in Vienna in September 1921, to which the Soviet trade union sought admission. The congress demanded the liberation of the imprisoned social democrat typographers' leaders in Russia, who had been of such service to the international union. The meeting was not satisfied with the answer given by the Soviet representative and decided against the admission of his union.[34] During the last months of 1921 the comparison between socialist prisoners in Russia and communist prisoners elsewhere in Europe became an ever-recurring theme in the tense relations between socialists and communists.[35] In November the German communists who had been imprisoned because of their participation in the failed *putsch* of March 1921 began a hunger strike in Berlin's Lichtenburg prison. Their party started a vigorous campaign for amnesty, to which the socialists were accused of contributing too little. Even the Russian *Pravda* was dominated by the German hunger strike for days and filled its columns with horror stories about the enormities being perpetrated against the imprisoned German communists. In *Vestnik* the hunger strike in the Lichtenburg prison was compared to the hunger strike being held in the Orel prison at the same time by the Mensheviks. The paper observed bitterly that a campaign for amnesty such as that being carried out at the time in Germany was totally out of the question in Russia.[36]

The imprisoned Mensheviks let it be known that their comrades from the UPSD ought to support the communists provided they did not forget the political prisoners in Russia. The German party did indeed do this and its mouthpiece *Freiheit* criticised the hypocritical attitude of the German communists towards terrorism in Russia. That this point of view was not always to the advantage of the communists became evident in the Reichstag, where the SPD minister of justice, Radbruch, skilfully reduced the communist parliamentary party to silence by postulating that the German government behaved no differently with regard to those who endangered the safety of the state than the Russian government. Ledebour, the representative of the USPD, greatly to the delight of the Mensheviks, violently protested against this argumentation by a socialist minister, because in this way the Bolsheviks' terrorist policy was being sanctioned. Similar discussions between the SPD, the USPD and the communists also occurred in the Prussian Landtag.[37]

Meanwhile the regime in Russia continued its war of nerves against the socialist opposition. At the end of 1921 several social democrats were again released, but in some prisons the situation had become wretched. The hunger strike in Orel ended in defeat. The party leadership therefore forbade hunger strikes and enjoined the prisoners not to allow themselves to be provoked by the Cheka. The security police had now brought the imprisoned members of the Central Committees of the RSDRP and the PSR back together into the Butyrsky prison. Even from there a few Mensheviks were freed, and those who remained successfully engaged in a fight for more bearable conditions. That is why I. I. Rubin, a member of the Central Committee, was still able after his liberation to write rather cheerfully to Martov about the prison comrades, including Martov's brother Ezhov and his brother-in-law Dan. About B. I. Nikolaevsky, who was not only a member of the party leadership, but also an avid collector of socialist archivalia, he wrote:

> Boris Ivanovich has an enormous table on which books and materials concerning the history of the revolutionary movement are carefully displayed; he is organising a 'society' for studying the history of the revolutionary movement: the socialist revolutionaries are giving lectures about Siberia, Vasilev about the Don area. Prokopovich (who was also here recently) related his memoirs about the Provisional Government, and so on. After another year we shall be able to read the works of the Butyrsky Academy.[38]

But the days of this 'prisoners' paradise' were numbered. Together with several Mensheviks in provincial prisons, ten social democrats in the Butyrsky prison were condemned to exile in Turkestan without any form of trial. The prisoners did not accept this and protested strongly against the reintroduction of administrative banishment, one of the *ancien régime's* most detested instruments of suppression. Endless negotiations with the authorities followed. Shortly before the new year the Mensheviks were visited by Unshlikht, the deputy head of the Cheka. He told them that most of their wishes had been met.[39]

However, nothing happened. At the beginning of January 1922 the Cheka informed them that immediate banishment had nevertheless been decided upon and, as it turned out, to the most horribly remote corners of European and Asiatic Russia at that. The forty-five Mensheviks condemned to exile therefore decided on 4 January to go on a hunger strike which they would prepare for in detail and sustain until the bitter end. The Mensheviks who had not been condemned to exile as well as the socialist revolutionaries and anarchists in the Butyrsky prison were also willing to join the hunger strike out of solidarity. But the Menshevik strike committee would not give permission for this. The social democrats still seemed to be receiving some sort of preferential treatment. The Bolsheviks gave the impression that they were prepared to break any kind of resistance by socialist revolutionaries or anarchists with violence, while their attitude towards the Mensheviks was determined by a hesitant Politbureau. The strike committee was afraid it would not be able to lead the campaign firmly if the members of other parties took part.[40]

The free Mensheviks, who were of course very anxious about their comrades' decision, did everything possible to back up the campaign. They distributed 2,000 copies of a leaflet about the hunger strike some of which were stuck up in conspicuous places in Moscow, including the wall of the Butyrsky prison. This caused some concern among the Moscow workers and it was soon evident that excitement also reigned in the most elevated circles of the communist party about the behaviour of the Menshevik prisoners. Kamenev, a member of the Politbureau, said to the Menshevik Yugov: 'We shall be obliged to arrest you all.' But this did not happen. The major problem for the party members still in freedom was how to inform the Foreign Delegation in Berlin as soon as possible. Lev Lande, a member of the youth organisation of the party, had the bright idea of sending his father in Berlin the following telegram: 'Inform Uncle, Gurvich and Lipkin with families literally starving. Long journey awaits them. Immediate reaction necessary.' 'Uncle' meant Binshtok. In this way the Mensheviks in Berlin understood what was happening to Gurvich and Lipkin who were far better known under their pseudonyms Dan and Cherevanin. However, they wrongly supposed from the word 'family' that all 250 political prisoners in the Butyrsky prison, thus the socialist revolutionaries and anarchists as well, were participating in the hunger strike.[41]

The Foreign Delegation immediately approached the Vienna International and the International Federation of Trade Unions with a letter to all the socialist parties. Now that the civil war was over and recognition of the Soviet republic was being considered by the European governments, the Mensheviks wrote, the Western socialists need not fear that they would bring harm to the Russian revolution by protesting against Bolshevik terrorism. They therefore asked for a powerful reaction. The French socialist party wrote a letter about this to Krasin, the representative of the Soviet government in London, and requested him to use his influence on behalf of the socialists on hunger strike in Moscow. Many socialist newspapers also devoted substantial attention to the hunger strike. The communist press launched a counter-attack. *Die Rote Fahne*, the German communist party's paper, represented the banishment of the Mensheviks as a philanthropic action. In Turkestan and other regions to which they were exiled, after all, famine was not reigning as it was in Moscow.[42]

Such communist arguments did not make much impression and the Mensheviks were afforded every opportunity to carry out a campaign among the socialists and workers in Germany. At the USPD congress in Leipzig in January 1922 Abramovich's speech was followed most attentively. The congress declared itself in solidarity with the RSDRP in a 'fiery protest'. The Bolshevik terror was impeding the struggle in the West against the 'class justice' of capitalism. The party leadership had the task of doing everything possible for the liberation of the imprisoned socialists in Russia and Georgia. At an international meeting in the jam-packed building of the Leipzig Fair, Abramovich spoke to an audience of at least 20,000 about the situation of the Russian socialists. He also appeared at a similar meeting in Berlin a few days later. In Berlin factories protest motions with reference to the hunger strike in the Butyrsky prison were accepted by the workers. Perhaps more significant was the fact that important socialist newspapers, like the SPD's *Vorwärts* and the Austrian *Arbeiterzeitung*, pointed out that the united front of socialists and communists, proposed shortly beforehand by the communists, was unacceptable throughout the world as long as there were socialists in prison in Russia.[43]

These developments in the West did not remain without effect in Moscow. A mealy-mouthed Unshlikht visited the Mensheviks in the Butyrsky prison on 7 January and made some concessions. But these did not go far enough for the prisoners, who continued their hunger strike. The Cheka therefore released a number of them and on 10 January Unshlikht made new proposals. The places of exile were now more reasonable. Whoever wanted to go abroad could now do so at the expense of the state and the exiles had seven days in which to arrange their private affairs. The strike leaders in the prison received information from the outside world that the Politbureau was divided and had decided on this extreme concession much against Trotsky's wishes. The Mensheviks therefore accepted this compromise and ended the hunger strike. The very same day Dan was taken home in Unshlikht's car.[44]

Dan informed the party that he was planning to go abroad since the Bolsheviks had now prevented him for two years from being politically active. The Central Committee therefore made him a member of the Foreign Delegation. The decision by a number of others to emigrate also was not so well received. This was regarded as a kind of desertion. Eventually everyone who wanted to leave Russia obtained permission to do so. But this was a difficult decision. The party was slowly but surely being driven underground and was now also losing some of its most able members. But surprisingly enough they did not despair. Everyone was still hoping that economic developments in Russia would compel the regime to make concessions. The successful pressure which the socialist movement in the West had managed to exert on the communist government during the hunger strike also seemed to be highly significant. If the communists really wanted a united front with the socialists then the Bolshevik authorities could be even more effectively pressurised in the future to end terrorism against the Russian socialists.[45] Characteristic of the mood of many Mensheviks was the letter written to Akselrod by Nikolaevsky on his arrival in the West:

> after eight or ten months comrades leave the prison with a more ardent desire to work and to fight. Not infrequently people who for years have dedicated themselves exclusively to their private affairs, are now taking up party work. And most valuable of all, the young are now coming to strengthen the party. Real beardless social democrat recruits ... I do not want to exaggerate the significance of these phenomena .... But relatively speaking they are important because from them it becomes clear that we are past the worst. And that after all is better than nothing, isn't it, Pavel Borisovich?[46]

### THE UNITED FRONT

The most idealistic and fundamental supporters of a united front were of course the founders of the Vienna International, for they had intended their organisation exclusively as an instrument for restoring proletarian unity in the world. But it was clearly evident from the fact that they thought it necessary to have a separate organisation for this, that they regarded the establishment of a new, comprehensive and powerful International as a lengthy process. In 1921 some new parties did join the Vienna International, for instance the Independent Labour Party, the Spanish socialist party and some parties from the Balkans and the Baltic States. But alongside the Comintern and the Second International, Vienna was not nearly strong enough to bring about proletarian unity under its own power. Within the international labour movement itself, however, the pressure for unity was substantial. Post-war revolutionary tensions seemed at the time to be followed by a renewed consolidation of bourgeois society, although the capitalist economy had to contend with serious problems. According to this socialist analysis of the world situation at the time, the workers would become the victims of recent developments if their national and international organisations remained divided and impotent.

The initiative for restoration of unity did not, however, come from the Vienna International, but from the Labour Party. This party was a member of the Second International, although one of its subdivisions, the ILP, belonged to the Vienna International. Even the powerful British labour movement had encountered the consequences of the ebb of the revolutionary tide in Europe and the beginnings of post-war depression. In June 1921, at its congress in Brighton, the Labour Party decided to make every effort to lay the foundations for a new International. A meeting between the governing bodies of the Second and the Vienna Internationals would have to be the point of departure for this. The Second International took over the idea. There, too, an amalgamation with Vienna was regarded as the best guarantee for the restoration of unity. But Friedrich Adler and his followers reacted unfavourably to this. They had no objection to meetings with representatives of the Second International, but made it quite clear at these than an international conference without the communists would not be acceptable to them.[47]

Martov, as one of the most prominent intellectual fathers of Vienna, was in total agreement with this point of view. The chances that the much larger Second International would simply swallow up Vienna were too great. Vienna's socialist principles would then be robbed of their corporate basis and many radically inclined workers would be driven into the arms of the communists. A solution to the present economic malaise and glaring class differences could not, as many parties in the Second International thought, be found in a short-sighted nationalist policy.[48] Martov's attention was chiefly concentrated on Germany, where not only the SPD, but also the USPD and the communist party enjoyed massive support from the workers. In both socialist parties people in favour of unity could be found, but a majority of the USPD was for the time being unenthusiastic. Therefore Martov was given the opportunity, in their newspaper *Freiheit*, of delivering an attack on *Vorwärts*, the SPD paper. Martov found it incomprehensible that a party which was extolling its aggressive nationalist politics during the war was at the same time organising huge demonstrations with the USPD under the motto 'No more war!' *Vorwärts* replied with an article entitled 'Singular interference', in which Martov was held personally responsible for 'the tragic fate' which had befallen the Russian proletariat. 'The German workers, however, know what situation the Russian proletariat has ended up in as a result of the hairsplitting of its cigarette-smoking, tea-drinking leaders, and they do not appreciate their advice, doctrines or pronouncements.'[49]

Martov received polite, but also cutting criticism from Kautsky, who was a staunch supporter of a merger between the USPD and the SPD. He blamed Martov for approaching the situation within a too rigidly dogmatic framework. When the proletariat was too weak to take over power it would not infrequently be obliged to co-operate with a section of the bourgeoisie in order to defend its interests. It was unfair to reproach the SPD unilaterally for this, especially because its left wing, which was close to the USPD, currently constituted the leadership of the party. Since the USPD had been liberated from its communist hypnosis, there were good opportunities for fruitful co-operation. In other parties, such as the French, which belonged to the Vienna International, or the Dutch, Swedish and British, which had remained faithful to the Second, socialists of reformist and revolutionary inclinations had co-operated for a long time. The picture was thus less black and white than Martov had painted it.

Moreover Kautsky opposed Martov's theory that the workers, as a result of an alliance between the right wing and the centre, would defect to the left – to the communists. The communist alternative had proved its inferiority in Germany and was no longer attractive to the workers. A restoration of unity among the German socialists was therefore possible, and given the seriousness of the economic situation was also a pressing need. In fact this was also true for other countries. Martov was not convinced by Kautsky. The experience of the war years and also that of the recent period was that in the long run reformist socialists identified themselves with the interests of the state and the ruling classes. After that they were no longer in a position to leap into the breach for the needs of the proletariat. There was thus no question of working with them, and luckily the USPD had thought the same at its last congress in Leipzig.[50] Martov's emotional rejection of reformist socialism was shared by many in the Vienna International. The first steps in the direction of the communists had already been taken by the centrists at the end of 1921. For although, according to socialists like Martov and Adler, the time was not yet ripe for the restoration of socialist unity, nevertheless the pressure on the leadership of the Vienna International to try to reach concrete cooperation on a number of grounds increased substantially. In December 1921 the executive committees of both the other organisations were therefore invited to collaborate in a major international conference at which the economic situation in Europe and 'the defensive struggle of the proletariat against reaction' would be discussed.[51]

The Third International appeared to be ready for discussion with the socialists whom it had hitherto always denounced. This was the result of a change of course which the all-powerful Russian leadership had imposed upon the Comintern after the total failure of the contrived revolutionary action in Germany in March 1921. The launching of a world revolution was no longer seen as the principal task of communism. In March 1922 the Comintern promoted the struggle for a united proletarian front to its official policy. But it remained extremely doubtful whether the communists really meant this seriously. They continued to treat the Western socialists in a very unsympathetic manner.[52] The impression was thereby created that the slogan of a united front was nothing more than a tactical manoeuvre. There was perhaps yet another motive. The projected international socialist conference was regarded by socialists and communists as a necessary counterpart of the intensive European diplomatic deliberations in this period. Soviet Russia, which was to attend the conference at Genoa, as a weak country badly needed support. The Western socialists were not unwilling to give it. But it was well known that the decision to allow the interests of Russia's national politics to prevail over the cause of world communism aroused a great deal of indignation among the French and Italian communists. Shortly beforehand they had broken off from the former socialist parties at Moscow's orders and they had no wish suddenly to have to co-operate with them again. Thus real enthusiasm for the idea of the united front was also lacking among the Western communists.[53]

While the Second International for its part was perfectly prepared to start negotiations, it remained very distrustful of the communists. At the very least, they would have to abandon attempts at forming cells within, or splitting off from, existing socialist organisations. Moreover the Second International

R

hoped, at the very beginning of the negotiations, to raise the questions of the communist occupation of Georgia and the liberation of the political prisoners in Soviet Russia. This thwarted the cautious diplomacy of Friedrich Adler, who had also pointed out to the representative of the Comintern, Karl Radek, that the laying down of harsh preliminary conditions greatly increased the chance of failure for the undertaking.[54] The demands the Second International were making on the Comintern and the launching of a united front policy by the communists presented the Mensheviks with a knotty problem. They continued to hope that a comprehensive, powerful International could be a really effective instrument for curbing Bolshevik oppression. The Second International now stepped into the breach for the political prisoners in Russia. Its support was of the greatest importance, but according to Martov and his sympathisers, was not entirely unimpeachable. After all, it was out of the question for the communists to comply with such far-reaching demands from people to whom the Mensheviks and the remaining centrists also had serious objections. Moreover the reformists had up till now not troubled themselves too much about the fate of the socialists in Russia. Were not their demands to the Comintern chiefly an attempt to obstruct all co-operation with the communists? The Foreign Delegation of the RSDRP therefore backed up Friedrich Adler. In no way did they wish to be partly responsible for the failure of the first attempt at restoration of the unity which had been damaged by the 'collapse' of the International in 1914, the more so because the communists had not immediately refused to co-operate in this.

On the other hand, the aplomb with which the Bolsheviks dared to propagate the united front, while they kept the socialist parties in Russia gagged, gave evidence of a cynicism which could not be left unanswered. Martov's greatest problem here was that he himself had been the most prominent defender of proletarian unity in Russia since 1917, while political developments made its realisation less and less probable.[55] The socialist revolutionaries were ambivalent towards the Vienna International and did not believe in the united front. This was also true of the Georgians who had remained in the Second International. It was Tsereteli's doing that the Georgian question was put forward as a condition for the negotiations with the Comintern. S. U. Portugeis appeared as the most important representative in the West of the right-wing Mensheviks who had left the party. He prepared the publication of a paper which was ostentatiously to bear the name *Zarya* (*Dawn*), *organ of the Russian social democratic section of the Second International.* It was of course intended as a counterpart of Martov's left-wing *Vestnik*, and the relationship between Portugeis and the Foreign Delegation of the RSDRP was particularly bad. Portugeis did not succeed in recruiting Akselrod as a correspondent for *Zarya*; Kautsky, too, refused, although both of them more or less shared Portugeis's political views.

At Tsereteli's insistence Axelrod agreed, however, that his critical letter to Martov which had been printed in *Vestnik* should also be published in the French journal *La Vie Socialiste*.[56] Nor did Akselrod intend to remain silent with regard to the united front, and he gave his opinion in an interview with the French socialist party newspaper *Le Populaire*. According to Akselrod an association between the Second and the Vienna Internationals was certainly possible. Even with the Western European communist parties, which despite their demagogical, utopian politics were nevertheless real workers' parties, a *modus vivendi* would have to be found. But with Russian Bolshevism this was out of the question. Bolshevism was, after all, not a workers' party, but a 'governmental organisation' carrying out criminal, dictatorial, anti-socialist and anti-proletarian policies.[57] Akselrod's rejection of the united front was a powerful negative reaction to the information which had reached him via the French socialist Renaudel about the point of view of his friends in Berlin. The Foreign Delegation of the RSDRP had indeed informed the Vienna International that they did not want to make demands in advance 'on the parties belonging to the Third International about halting terrorism against the socialists in Russia and about the oppression of national groups'. Dan tried to explain to Akselrod by letter that only in this way could the premature failure of the negotiations be prevented. Of course the Mensheviks had no intention of keeping quiet about the persecution of socialists in Russia. But they had tried to find a form for their protest which would damage only the Bolsheviks and not the international proletariat. The Foreign Delegation had made it clear to the Bureau of the Vienna International that this question 'could not be entirely avoided' at the conference of the three Internationals. The Vienna parties ought to explain that there could be no question of a united front as long as socialist parties were being oppressed in Russia.

In the same vein Martov wrote to the party management in Moscow – that the proceedings of the conference should not be disrupted by a confrontation 'between us and our executioners'.[58] For Akselrod this kind of viewpoint remained unacceptable, and Martov's associates in Russia wanted the Menshevik delegation at the conference to hand over a separate memorandum, from which it would above all emerge how far the Bolshevik dictatorship had degenerated into outright oppression of the Russian proletariat. The party management did thus want to provoke some kind of incident, which was exactly what Martov was trying to avoid. Moreover it decided to send a special representative from its midst to the international discussions in Berlin as a living symbol of the party's struggle for legal existence. The Bolsheviks, who would have to provide exit visas for the Menshevik delegates, would thus at the same time be obliged to show how much they valued the united front. The party accordingly appointed as its representative Martov's brother Ezhov, who had been released from the Butyrsky prison before the hunger strike because of sickness but was now again under threat of banishment.

The RSDRP evidently hoped to be able to correct its Foreign Delegation's possibly too tolerant attitude at the Berlin conference. The communists, who were still carefully checking all foreign mail, had intercepted a telegram from Martov and thus came to know of the plan to send Ezhov as a delegate. Dignitaries such as Kamenev and Zinoviev evidently had no initial objections to granting a visa. But Ezhov was never to reach the West. After the end of the Berlin conference Martov learned that his brother had been picked up by the GPU and exiled to Vyatka. When Ezhov went on hunger strike in prison out of protest, he was sent to his place of exile by agents of the security police without money or luggage. But even before the beginning of the discussion between the three Internationals, Bolshevik terrorism intervened harshly in the subtle Menshevik strategy. In no way had the Bolsheviks let it seem that the motto of the united front would have the least influence on the situation in Russia. On the contrary, in the first months of 1922 numerous Mensheviks were arrested and exiled. The GPU had tracked down in particular the members of the small but extremely active youth society of the RSDRP, who were now for the most part behind bars. At the same time the police made a first systematic attempt to discover the whereabouts of all the Mensheviks in the capital. From this it is evident that the regime was now seriously trying to make every Menshevik activity impossible so that the party was gradually obliged to prepare itself for a totally illegal existence.[59]

The fact that the GPU was acting under instructions from the party top brass was evident from the statements of Lenin at the Eleventh Party Congress in March 1922, which left no room for doubt. The Menshevik Dvinov wrote to Berlin about it:

> Lenin's speech yesterday was in general without content and consisted of only one point: the Mensheviks must now not only be shut up but also shot. He is seriously ill. Some communist sources report that the doctors have diagnosed an undoubtedly psychological disorder as a result of overfatigue. He sometimes speaks gibberish, loses the thread of his argument, and so on. Serious consternation reigns among the Bolsheviks.[60]

At this congress in fact Lenin also used extremely threatening language against the opponents in his own party. Probably his speech impediments and pathological irritability were caused not so much by overfatigue as by a cerebral haemorrhage, undiagnosed by the doctors. In May and December he again suffered strokes and had to give up work completely. But even apart from Lenin, omens for the Russian socialists were serious enough. The political trial of forty-seven prominent members of the PSR, some of whom had already been in prison for three years, was under way, and it became increasingly probable that death sentences would be pronounced in it. The Bolsheviks had evidently overcome all their hesitation about repression of the socialist opposition. After the socialist revolutionaries in all probability the Mensheviks' turn would come for the final settlement.[61]

In the first months of 1922 the Foreign Delegation of the RSDRP had also done a great deal to keep the Western socialists and especially the Vienna International informed about the increasing repression in Russia. But at the same time they continued to work diligently for a socialist protest against the persecution of communists in some European countries such as Poland, where socialists had seats in the government. Feelings of righteousness and indignation had a role to play here, but also the conviction that terrorism against the communists in Europe would be used by the Bolsheviks as a justification for their terrorism against socialists in Russia. The same was true of the RSDRP's struggle for the diplomatic recognition of Soviet Russia by the Western Powers. Normalisation of the relations of Soviet Russia with the surrounding capitalist states could contribute to a normalisation of political relationships in Russia. Most other groups among Russian exiles were against a recognition of communist Russia and Martov had accordingly devoted various articles to this theme.

The Mensheviks in Berlin thought it very important that the international socialist movement should be put in a state of alarm about the trial of the socialist revolutionaries. The Foreign Delegation of the PSR under the leadership of Victor Chernov had been working diligently for this since the beginning of March 1922. One handicap for the socialist revolutionaries was that they had left the Second International in March 1920 but, as a result of all kinds of bickering, had not yet been admitted to the Vienna International. Thus they had become homeless within the international socialist community and certainly needed Menshevik support. Partly thanks to the Mensheviks in Berlin the PSR's campaign was a great success. Expressions of sympathy came in from every side. But, according to the socialist revolutionaries, some protests were not forceful enough. They were most indignant about the reaction of Friedrich Adler, who petitioned the Russian government by letter to spare the lives of the prisoners, even if they had perhaps been guilty of armed counter-revolutionary actions. Martov's *Vestnik* agreed with their criticism. The effect of the socialist protest against the political trial should not be weakened by socialists who found it necessary to dissociate themselves from the accused.[62]

But a number of Mensheviks in Moscow were of the opinion that the Foreign Delegation was already showing too much solidarity with the socialist revolutionaries. In their view the PSR had prejudiced the interests of the working class by its 'adven-turist' anti-Bolshevik politics after the October revolution, and it could no longer be regarded as a socialist party. Everything must, in their view, be done to ensure a fair trial for the accused, except making oneself jointly responsible for the political past of the PSR by withholding incriminating facts. The Central Committee of the RSDRP was so divided about this affair that it could not formulate an acceptable resolution until after many sittings. The text of this was never published and eventually it was captured by the Cheka at the arrest of a large number of Moscow party activists in July 1922.[63] The Mensheviks in Berlin did not take much notice of the criticism which was levelled at them in letters from Moscow and kept as firmly as possible to the tactics they had outlined before the conference of the three Internationals. This was evident at a meeting of the Foreign Delegations of the RSDRP and the PSR in Berlin at the end of March. The discussion was attended by Tsereteli, who wrote to Akselrod that Martov and Dan were still fostering 'a superstitious veneration' for the 'achievements of the revolution' which were being kept alive by the communist regime, even though at the same time they expressed themselves outspokenly in these dis-cussions about the 'criminal' nature of Bolshevik politics.[64]

During the meeting with the PSR Tsereteli proposed that the gravity of both the Russian and the Georgian issues ought to be made clear to the executive committees of the three Interna-tionals in the strongest terms. In his view socialist opinion in Europe was expecting every opportunity to be grasped to reach a real solution to these issues. But Martov thought that Tsereteli ought not to overestimate the striving for unity within the European labour movement. Most parties, because of their national interests, were only slightly interested in the united front. They hoped, for instance, that the Comintern would cease activities which could endanger the unity of their trade unions. The Second International made harsh demands on the Comintern because there was little enthusiasm for co-operation and not so much out of moral indignation about the persecution of socialists. The failure of the conference could only have an adverse effect on the situation in Russia. The necessary caution would have to be exercised. Only the trial against the socialist revolutionaries should be discussed, and a guarantee should be obtained that no death sentence would be passed. This would be a moral victory in itself. Dan added that the plenary meeting of the conference was not a suitable occasion for the airing of this point. The Comintern would reply to all the requirements concerning the trial with counter-requirements about the liberation of communist prisoners in the West. Guarantees for the preservation of the lives of the socialist revolutionaries could probably more easily be obtained in a personal conversation with the leader of the communist delegation, Radek.[65]

But the PSR leaders Chernov and Zenzinov were not keen on this. They agreed much more with Tsereteli. 'The whole account' should be presented to the Bolsheviks at once, at the beginning of the discussion. An impossible situation would arise if it were to turn out that 'the Russian question' was closer to the hearts of the Second International than to the Russians themselves. Once more it was evident that the Russian socialists were divided into two groups. There were Mensheviks such as Akselrod, who – like most socialist revolutionaries – did not expect anything from a united front because the Bolsheviks would still cheat. There were left-wing socialist revolutionaries who, with Martov, were convinced that the Bolsheviks would never accept orders from the reformist socialist leaders who were in a majority. They hoped that communism, under the pressure of extremely difficult circumstances, would prove to be sensitive to the international proletariat's longing for unity and for this reason take some of the criticism of the political situation in Russia seriously. Proponents of both the 'hard' and the 'soft' approach to Bolshevism were under an illusion. Western socialism was not in a position, nor prepared, to interfere actively in Russia's internal affairs, and at the time Russian communism was already evolving in the direction of a totalitarian regime. But neither group had much choice. In 1922 there was no conceivable third approach which offered better chances of saving the socialist movement in Russia from ruin.

THE BERLIN CONFERENCE

After this meeting the Mensheviks and socialist revolutionaries each went their own way. The PSR sent the three Internationals a detailed memorandum in which Bolshevik policy since 1917 was denounced. The socialist revolutionaries demanded that the Bolsheviks should end not only the repression of socialists but also the preparations for a trial against their party. They were not against an investigation into the past of the PSR if it were carried out by a mixed international commission of socialists and communists who would at the same time go into the activities of the Bolsheviks. On the eve of the conference of the three Internationals, the Second International invited a number of PSR leaders to a discussion. It was decided that the Second International would adhere to the demands from the Comintern it had formulated earlier. The PSR's suggestion concerning an international inquiry into its past was accepted. If the Comintern refused to go into this, an attempt would be made to send the Belgian Vandervelde to Moscow as defender of the accused. In short they were still toying with the idea of a kind of socialist intervention in Russia. Akselrod's idea still seemed to be productive. The Vienna International, on the other hand, decided to send the Mensheviks' proposal to the conference only in order to explain in general terms that a united front would not be possible until the proletarian parties ceased trying to settle their mutual differences of opinion with terrorist measures. Here reference was made not only to Bolshevik politics in Russia and Georgia. The persecution of communists and left-wing socialists and the violation of the people's right to autonomy by governments in which socialists held seats were also expressly mentioned. At the same time, following Martov's suggestion, it was stated that if the imprisoned leaders of the PSR were put to death there could be no question in the near future of a communal congress of both Internationals.[66]

On 2 April 1922 communists and socialists gathered for the first time in the assembly room of the SPD parliamentary party in the Reichstag building for a meeting at the highest level. In order to avoid too many problems about the proportional representation of the Internationals, it was agreed that each organisation besides a very limited number of official representatives would also be allowed to bring some guests and journalists. Thus Martov was a delegate, Abramovich a guest, while Dan attended the conference as a journalist. This proves how much importance the Vienna International attached to the RSDRP's opinion. Only the Italian party under Serrati's leadership was allowed into the deliberations separately in spite of the fact that it was not attached to any International. Martov, referring to this Italian precedent, had advised the PSR likewise to obtain formal admission. But the Comintern had pronounced its veto against this and only Victor Chernov was allowed to attend the meetings as a journalist. Tsereteli also nominally represented only the Georgian press.

'No one present', Adler remarked in his opening speech, 'was filled with exaggeratedly optimistic feelings.'[67] The conference could only be a small step in the direction of the restoration of unity, given the considerable differences between the three organisations. And these were almost immediately expressed in the speeches which Clara Zetkin, Vandervelde and Faure delivered on behalf of the Third, the Second and the Vienna Internationals. As was to be expected, Vandervelde's address consisted of a series of severe reproaches and demands to the Comintern, which were, however, formulated by the Belgian extremely courteously. Zetkin kept more to generalities, while Faure limited himself to an elaboration of the declaration drawn up by the Mensheviks. The reaction of the leader of the communist delegation accordingly determined the further course of the negotiations.

Radek's speech was a masterpiece of mock indignation, whole and half lies and excellently placed serious arguments. He held the representatives of the Second International responsible, among other things, for the deaths of Liebknecht, Luxemburg and 15,000 German workers in 1919. What right had these socialists, Radek asked, to be indignant about the as-yet-undecided punishments against socialist revolutionaries who were accused of the attempted murder of the leaders of the Russian revolution? Why were they so concerned about the fact that the communist Mdivani was now ruling over Georgia instead of Mensheviks like Zhordania and Chkheidze, and that the strategically important town of Baku was no longer in the hands of British imperialists? If the socialists of the Second International wanted to exchange the Russian terrorists they had canonised for communist prisoners in Germany this could be discussed. But ultimatums would not be accepted, and if that was a reason for letting the conference fail it was clear who would have to bear the responsibility for it.[68]

This reply to the Second International by the Comintern caused a kind of stalemate. The conference was adjourned for a day and the Vienna International used this break to attempt to convince the Second International of the need to moderate its demands on the Comintern. The Mensheviks played an important role in this. 'MacDonald, Huysmans, Wels and Vandervelde displayed clear incomprehension for what they saw as the inscrutable behaviour of the Menshevik delegates', Abramovich wrote later. While these Western socialists stood up for the socialist victims of Bolshevik terrorism as forcefully as possible, these victims themselves went to a great deal of trouble to talk them out of their efforts. Dan tried to explain that there were many people in Russia who had pinned their hopes on this discussion and it would be extremely unpleasant to have to tell them that it had been broken off because of the socialists' demanding attitude. Abramovich added that the failure of the conference would in all probability be followed by a new wave of terrorism against the socialist revolutionaries and social democrats. Accordingly it would be better to keep the thorny problems which had been raised by the Second International in reserve for the beginning of the great socialist conference of all the socialist parties. If the communists walked out of that, this could only be a humiliating defeat for them. The remaining centrist leaders used similar arguments. On further consideration, the leaders of the Second International were not very keen to be saddled with the responsibility for the talks ending in a fiasco.[69]

The result of this discussion behind the scenes was a second round of plenary talks, which seemed in many respects to be a repetition of the first, though the atmosphere was somewhat more reconciliatory. MacDonald spoke on behalf of the Second International and as a person he was undoubtedly more acceptable to the centrists and communists than Vandervelde. He remarked that extremely contradictory statements had been made by the communist leaders about the united front. Was it then unreasonable that the Second International should ask for some clarification from Radek about the real intentions of the Comintern? He could imagine that Radek might consider that the plan to leave the judgement of the political past of the socialist revolutionaries to a kind of international court of justice was an insult to Soviet jurisdiction. Nevertheless, the socialists ought to be assured that the trial would be fair, and in that way would have some control over it. Otherwise it would be impossible for them to co-operate with the Bolsheviks with a clear conscience. The defence of the socialists would have to be guaranteed. Vandervelde was prepared to undertake this. Radek's proposal for a kind of exchange of prisoners was a demagogical stunt. The Second International had no say about the communist prisoners in Germany and trading in persons like this was in any case a reprehensible business.[70]

Otto Bauer, the spokesman for the Vienna International, supported the demands of the Second International with regard to the socialist revolutionaries and Georgia in a long speech. But he once more strongly emphasised that the moral reserve which the London organisation fostered towards the communists could also be partly applied to itself. Even governments to which some of its parties had belonged had used political violence, taken political prisoners and infringed the people's right of self-determination.[71] It goes without saying that the next speaker, Radek, harped on this same theme. He wondered why the Second International was so worried about the 'so-called' cell building or formation of cells. Why should communists not be allowed to fight for their point of view within the European trade unions? Before the October revolution neither MacDonald nor any other Western socialist had pleaded for the independence of the Ukraine or Georgia. Now suddenly they did. The same was true of the Menshevik leaders of Georgia. They had only been able to maintain the fiction of Georgia's independence by subjecting themselves first to German and afterwards to British imperialism. Now it had turned out that not only British imperialists but also Russian workers needed the oil wells of Baku. If Abramovich does not know any better than to cry 'Oil communism', then he must clarify how he can introduce socialism by using nothing but the volcano of his indignation and his wild enthusiasm as energy sources.[72]

It was regrettable that Tsereteli did not ask to speak on this occasion. He was probably unwilling to bore the meeting with a lengthy explanation of the extremely complex politics of the socialist government of Georgia. He limited himself to a short written account which was later added to the protocol of the conference. In this he pointed out that the Bolsheviks, through

Radek, had admitted for the first time that they had occupied Georgia in order to provide themselves with oil. The Soviet government had, however, known perfectly well that independent Georgia was prepared to sign a treaty that would satisfy the economic interests of Russia in full. Thus there was no justification whatever for this imperialistic outrage against a socialist country.[73]

Radek, besides all his caustic cynicism, also made some important concessions in his speech. The communists had no objection to an international commission to investigate the Georgian issue. The imprisoned socialist revolutionaries would be in a position to choose whoever they wanted to defend them. But Radek did make skilful use of the confusion which had been created about the nature of the trial against these people. The Bolsheviks had always claimed that normal legal procedures would be followed, but had, at the same time, made many threatening statements about the crimes of the leaders of the PSR. The Western socialists were demanding a fair trial, but by their involvement were merely emphasising its political character.

What had Vandervelde actually come to do in Moscow, Radek wondered. Did he want to defend the socialist revolutionaries because, as a former member of the Allied Council which had undertaken the armed intervention in Russia during the civil war, he felt jointly responsible for their deeds? The Bolsheviks ought then to arrange for a prosecutor who would scrutinise the political past both of the defence and of the accused. When Martov indignantly cried out at this: 'All this is called a trial!', Radek immediately answered: 'Then I ask what sort of trial this "control of international socialism" is? What is it, please?' But Martov, not to be caught out so easily, replied: 'Make the documents accessible!' Radek promised that the Western socialists would be allowed to inspect all the documents about the case and would have the opportunity to make a stenographical report of the trial. These were not unimportant concessions, but a guarantee that the lives of the socialist revolutionaries would be spared was not obtained, and that for socialists like Martov remained the principal task of the conference.[74]

Separate talks now again took place, which were supposed to result in a combined closing statement from the three Internationals. The Vienna International again acted as arbitrator between the two other organisations. It was extremely difficult to find a compromise acceptable to everyone and the closing statement could not be submitted to the plenary meeting until near midnight on the following day. The Mensheviks had done their utmost to achieve this result. Abramovich made another attempt to convince the representatives of the Second International that it was pointless to adhere to their demands. In particular he tried to get them to share in the high expectations which the Foreign Delegation of the RSDRP still cherished about future developments in Soviet Russia and which were closely linked to its view about the united front. The Second International eventually decided not to ask the Comintern for immediate compliance with its demands, but to lay these before the so-called Committee of Nine. This committee, consisting of three representatives from each International, had formed the presidium of the conference and after its conclusion was entrusted with the organisation of the congress of all socialist and communist parties.[75]

Dan had a conversation with Radek. Little is known about its content. Radek revealed that Dan, after his arrest in Petrograd in March 1921, had almost been shot on Zinoviev's orders but was saved at the last moment because the Central Committee of the communist party had expressly opposed the execution of Menshevik leaders.[76] Given the nature of the conversation it is highly likely that Dan also brought up the question of the death penalty against the socialist revolutionaries. After all, before the conference he had already claimed that nothing could be achieved except by a personal talk with Radek. During the plenary meetings this point had only been raised by Faure. The Second International which had appointed itself as the great protector of the PSR had, curiously enough, devoted no attention whatever to this aspect of the trial. Perhaps Dan convinced Radek of the necessity of making this extremely significant concession. In any case Radek surprised his delegation members with the text of a statement in which the assurance was suddenly given that no death penalties would be imposed. Bukharin, supported by the French communist Rosmer, pointed out to Radek that only the Soviet government could decide about this and that this affair lay outside the competency of the Comintern.

At this Radek furiously burst out: 'If you have any criticism about what I have done, you should formulate an answer yourself!' The delegation nevertheless accepted his text on the subject with a small, but essential alteration. Death sentences might possibly be allowed to be pronounced, but should not be carried out.[77]

However, this correction was not incorporated into the closing statement of the conference. This document, thanks to the concessions made both by the Comintern and by the Second International, gave evidence in an impressive manner of the will to achieve unity. The Committee of Nine was given the task of maintaining further contact between the three organisations and the parties affiliated to them. The statement further mentioned what had been agreed concerning Georgia and the socialist revolutionaries. At the same time the readiness of all the people involved to call a general conference of all socialist parties as quickly as possible was confirmed.[78] Nevertheless, the effect of this concerted statement was to a large extent undone by a number of separate statements, amongst them Tsereteli's, which were added to the protocol. The Vienna International let it be known that it would willingly have seen all the proletarian parties committed to working hard for the immediate freeing of all political prisoners. The Second International had likewise shown itself in favour of this, but the Comintern had refused to support this effort. The centrists observed very bitterly on this point that the communists evidently considered it so important to keep the socialists in Russia in prison that they were prepared to give up the struggle for the liberation of communist prisoners in the capitalist states for this. The Comintern, on the other hand, maintained in its piece that the Second International had refused to put the revision of the Treaty of Versailles on the agenda of the next conference. For the sake of unity the Moscow organisation had temporarily waived their demand to initiate investigations into the assassination of Rosa Luxemburg and the role of the social democrats in the persecution of communists in Europe. The SPD in a statement by Otto Wels accepted responsibility for the liquidation of the Spartacists 'with pride before the German people, the international working class, and history'. The Berlin conference of the Three Internationals in

April 1922 had therefore not actually brought the united front any nearer.[79]

THE END OF LEGAL OPPOSITION IN RUSSIA

In the weeks that followed the conference, all hope of possible co-operation with the communists which had been raised by Radek's concessions were dashed. The Second International was conspicuously slow in appointing representatives for the 'Committee of Nine'. Because of this it became no longer possible for the international socialist congress to meet at the same time as the diplomatic discussions in Genoa. The Soviet delegation did not succeed in securing the economic support so keenly desired. But the Genoa conference nevertheless meant *de facto* recognition of Soviet Russia. Moreover the sensational treaty of friendship concluded with Germany at Rapallo made Russia much less dependent on Western socialist support and reduced the already extremely limited readiness of the Bolsheviks to take seriously the criticism which was levelled against their regime from that side.[80] Lenin had immediately put a damper on the centrists' sanguine expectations by declaring in *Pravda* that the representatives of the Comintern in Berlin ought not to have complied with the demands concerning the treatment of the socialist revolutionaries. Radek and Bukharin had made a serious mistake, but now the Comintern had better stand by the agreement made. How this was interpreted by the Russian communists became evident during the 1 May demonstration in Moscow. At it not only was the death penalty demanded for the socialist revolutionaries awaiting trial, but banners were also carried around with the text 'Death to the bourgeoisie and to the social democrats'. This was a far cry from the demonstration for the united front of socialists and communists which the participants at the Berlin conference had promised to organise in every country.[81]

It was moreover characteristic that the SPD also refused to take part in such meetings in Germany.[82] The leaders of the Vienna International very quickly discovered that the Second International's already tepid enthusiasm for the united front had now completely vanished and that the Kremlin, after Genoa, regarded it as little more than a propaganda slogan intended exclusively for foreign use. The Mensheviks in Moscow were not very enthusiastic about the outcome of the Berlin conference. Even the most left-wing member of their Central Committee, Pleskov, wrote to the Foreign Delegation that he wondered whether it had not adopted a too indulgent attitude. 'Our position is unbearable. The insolence and cynicism of the Bolsheviks have become unbounded. Arrests and exiles take place continuously.'[83] Dvinov too wrote in this spirit. 'Our little group is dwindling daily and we are all known by name to the Cheka.' What else could they in fact do except, at their wits' end, 'seize the red banner and take to the streets'? The best the Mensheviks could still do, on the inevitable failure of the further negotiations between the three Internationals, was to prevent the communists from being in a position to blame the Second International outright for this.[84]

With this aim in view the Central Committee sent a letter to the Committee of Nine. In this, in a very sober and business-like manner, an account was given of the terrorism perpetrated against the RSDRP in the first three weeks after the Berlin conference. In numerous Russian towns a total of about 160 arrests were made. The Mensheviks asked for special attention for the lengthy hunger strike of the imprisoned members of the youth league, the treatment of Ezhov and the death of Astrov, a well-known social democrat much loved by the workers, who had died of typhoid *en route* to his place of exile.[85] Unmentioned remained the fact that the Bolsheviks, by deliberately giving incorrect information about the railway station in Moscow where his mortal remains were to be brought, had tried to prevent Astrov's funeral from growing into a mass political demonstration. At about the same time the Foreign Delegation, in a circular letter to all the socialist parties, made it clear how the idea of the united front was being disseminated by the communists in Russia.[86]

Adler reacted at the beginning of May with a long letter to the members of the Committee of Nine in which he summed up all the difficulties he had encountered in his attempts to convene them. The persecution of socialists in Russia, he wrote, did not contribute to the creation of the right psychological climate for the meeting of an international workers' congress. A good week later he turned specifically to the communist delegation in the committee and once more observed with much bitterness that the oppression of socialists in Russia had been resumed in all its intensity after the Berlin conference. The attitude of the Russian parties affiliated to the Vienna International, the Mensheviks and the left-wing socialist revolutionaries, both before and during the conference, had been 'truly exemplary'. In order not to make the negotiations more difficult they had seen to it that demands were not made concerning the terrorism of which they themselves were victims. Accordingly he asked the communist members of the Committee to direct their influence towards the Soviet government so that there would be an end to this scandalous behaviour of a state which professed to represent the proletariat. The Vienna International was prepared to do everything to make an international congress possible. But it could not allow the Russian socialists to be asked to make 'inhuman sacrifices' for it. Adler achieved no result whatever with this. Probably interventions of this kind only increased Bolshevik aversion to international discussion, because each time they offered the socialists an excellent opportunity to interfere in Russian internal politics.[87]

After much bickering the Committee of Nine eventually met in Berlin on 23 May 1922.[88] The talks took place in a tense atmosphere. Radek prevented an orderly beginning to the negotiations with a shrill protest against the limitations of personal freedom of movement imposed on him by the socialist minister of internal affairs in Prussia. Wels replied by asking if Martov could by any chance go to Russia without restraint. Then Clara Zetkin began to complain about the opening of letters to the communist delegates by the German authorities. It became evident how seriously this was meant when Radek, during his speech, brazenly quoted in detail from a letter from Abramovich to the Mensheviks in Moscow, which had been intercepted by the Russian censorship. The first speaker, MacDonald, enumerated a long list of outrages which demonstrated that the communists had not taken the agreements reached in Berlin at all seriously. Lenin had said that a judge who pronounced anything other than the death sentence was a traitor. Meanwhile the terrorism against all socialists in Russia had simply been continued. The Red Army had quelled a socialist uprising in Georgia. Radek replied, as was to be expected, with reproaches directed at the Second International. He entirely agreed with Abramovich, who had informed his comrades in Moscow that the Second International would not regret a failure of the united front. Nevertheless, the Comintern was still prepared to guarantee both the right of the socialist revolutionaries to a Western socialist counsel for their defence and the public nature of the trial, even if the Second International were to sabotage the convening of an international congress.

Adler observed that the Third and the Second Internationals were firmly united in the determination not to co-operate with one another. An international congress in the near future was ruled out by this. Radek then declared that the communist delegation was withdrawing from the Committee of Nine. It had been empowered to do this by the Comintern in the event of a decision to convene a world-wide congress not being immediately taken by this meeting. Of course this meant that the united front had been torpedoed and that the communists would try to hold the socialists responsible for this. Indeed Radek later stated in the communist press that the Second International had demanded the impossible: the communists would have had to refrain from any criticism of the leaders of the socialist parties and trade unions and the Soviet government would have had to allow the Mensheviks and the socialist revolutionaries to organise uprisings unpunished.[89]

Of course the failure of the united front was a blow for the Vienna International, but it kept a stiff upper lip. In an appeal to 'the workers of all countries' it criticised both partners in this fruitless discussion, but continued to see these disagreements as transitory in nature. At a time when capitalist states the world over were threatening the rights of workers, all their organisations must in the long run realise that their common duties were more important than their mutual differences. The Vienna International would therefore continue in its efforts to restore unity. The self-confidence shown in this proclamation was not in fact all that great. An increasing number of leaders of the centre parties doubted if a united front really would be an attainable or desirable affair, even in the distant future. Blum, Bracke and Renaudel, who were now more in charge of the

French party than the left-wing Longuet, were supporters, even in public, of a merger with the Second International.[90]

The RSDRP too was dominated by doubts and differences of opinion. Dalin was the only one among the emigrants who drew far-reaching conclusions from the situation which was now arising. The Vienna International's united front politics had, in his view, 'a minor shortcoming': they were not realisable. It would be better simply to forget the illusions and the battle-cries of the turbulent period of the World War and the years afterwards. The centrists ought no longer to be led by their anachronistic objections to the parties of the Second International. The socialists affiliated to London had made efforts towards a diplomatic rapprochement between the West and Soviet Russia. They had also made great efforts against France's imperialistic policy towards the Weimar Republic. On the other hand, support for the Comintern had dropped sharply in Europe now that the adherents of the French and German parties in a short time had considerably decreased. On estimate they now united no more than 10 per cent of the European proletariat, the Vienna International about 20 and the Second International almost 70 per cent. It was more sensible to join battle against the onrushing forces of reaction with nine-tenths of the workers than to wait for the possibility of complete unity which might perhaps never occur.[91]

Martov expressed his disappointment about the failure of the united front in emotional terms from which it became evident that he could no longer visualise any real solution. As long as the communists dared to appear at meetings with 'the blood of Russian socialists' on their hands and 'the keys of prisons crammed with workers in their pockets' unity would be impossible. He did not agree with socialists like Kautsky, Dalin and many others who regarded the Western communist parties as a *quantité négligeable*. Their leaders' radicalism most predated the October revolution and they had at their disposal a proletarian following, which though perhaps not large, was certainly solid. The European communists were now faced with the important choice of whether to expose themselves to political isolation under Moscow's stringent leadership, or to dissociate themselves publicly from Bolshevik terrorism against the Russian socialists. And this was necessary if they wished to preserve their own dignity and independence.[92]

Martov thus already in 1922 saw clear possibilities for a kind of Eurocommunism *avant la lettre*. For this reason he continued to hold firm to the perspective of the united front in Europe. Against his better judgement he even maintained that in Russia, too, a breakthrough to the united front was still the only way out of the dead end which the revolution had got into. The trial of the socialist revolutionaries was a test case for this. Accordingly Martov made a persuasive appeal to the opposition within the Russian communist party to convince the rulers in the Kremlin that this trial was not only criminal, but would also be the decisive and fatal step in the wrong direction. This analysis left the Western socialists and the Mensheviks painfully few opportunities for making a contribution to the solution of the major issues which kept the communists and socialists divided. Dvinov had written to Martov that the only way to protect the party from total destruction was to go underground into illegality. Martov's last articles, in which he seemed to expect something exclusively from communist initiatives, understandably therefore once more created confusion amongst his fellow party members. Ought they now to expect salvation from a group within a party which Martov, after Akselrod, had been the first to characterise as an anti-socialist state organisation, and thus obviously no longer regarded as a workers' party? How could one form a united front with that?[93]

F. A. Cherevanin, a member of the Central Committee of the Mensheviks, wrote a long letter from prison about this issue to his friends in Berlin. He thought that retaining the policy of the united front put the party in a 'lamentable and humiliating' position. A party which was destroyed, crushed and completely cut off from the proletariat, was proposing a united front with a party which was ruling the country with violence. 'History has never before produced such a strange spectacle.' And why should the Bolsheviks want to enter into a united front with them? 'To give the people and the proletariat back their freedom and independence? To give us the opportunity to become an element of power again, after they have successfully eliminated us?' Or because, as the Mensheviks had so often claimed, the unfavourable economic situation forced them to allow more political freedom? The economist Cherevanin pointed out that the NEP had done exactly the opposite of what the Mensheviks had expected. Restoration of political freedom was ruled out.

However, the economy of the country was reviving.[94] This exchange of ideas did not, for the time being, lead to a clear change of course. The hopeless situation of the party ensured that every discussion about a vital section of Menshevik politics raised the fundamental question of whether it was still at all meaningful to continue with party work. There was a great deal of talk about an essential tactical and ideological reorientation in order to preserve at least a rudiment of the party in Russia for a better future. But no one was convinced that the future of the party would be assured if it merely went underground with a new party programme. Any other possibility would be better.[95]

Furthermore, the party was so completely dependent on developments in and out of Russia of which the significance and direction were still so difficult to discern that no one was inclined to take the drastic measures which in fact meant recognition of a definitive defeat. The proceedings against the socialist revolutionaries and the rapidly worsening situation in Germany accordingly held their interest. The Mensheviks were closely involved in the trial. The communists had launched a propaganda and agitation campaign around this affair which in its thoroughness and scope was unprecedented in Russian history. In this avalanche of meetings, demonstrations, resolutions and newspaper articles, which went on for weeks, the Mensheviks were continually put on a par with the socialist revolutionaries. Furthermore, the Russian socialist opposition was seen as a continuation of the Vienna and the Second Internationals, which in their turn were once more represented as tools of the capitalist bourgeoisie.

This central theme of the campaign of slander was a deliberate reply, partly devised by Lenin in person, to the activities of the Russian socialists in and outside Russia, and to the storm of protest against the trial which had been incited by them in the West. The Bolshevik leaders were all too conscious of the far-reaching political possibilities which the NEP was offering the opposition to their regime, unless this opposition was kept well under control by terrorism. They had now evidently decided to eliminate this danger as completely as possible and to engage in a 'merciless fight' against Western and Russian socialism. The RSDRP was in absolutely no position to fight back. The Mensheviks nevertheless still tried, by distributing clandestinely printed pamphlets, to explain to the workers what a united front – still the Comintern's official ambition – would have to consist of in Russia. They also appealed to them to fight for the liberation of political prisoners. Activities of this kind, however, no longer produced any noticeable effect, merely increasing the Mensheviks' feelings of impotence.[96]

After the failure of the negotiations about the united front it was by no means certain that the Bolsheviks would adhere to the concessions made by Radek at the Berlin conference. The foreign socialist counsels for the defence, Rosenfeld and Theodor Liebknecht on behalf of the Vienna International, and Wauters and Vandervelde on behalf of the Second, were admitted into Russia in June. But during their journey through Russia and on their arrival in Moscow, they became the target of a series of humiliating and intimidating demonstrations. Their protests against these 'spontaneous' outbursts of indignation by workers and peasants had no effect. The Mensheviks in Moscow wrote to the Western counsels for the defence expressing their indignation at this scandalous treatment. But at the same time they could not fail to express their own ambivalent attitude to the PSR, and they sought no further contact with Rosenfeld and his associates in order to outline a common course of action with regard to the trial.

In April the Menshevik Central Committee had requested the Foreign Delegation, via Pleskov, also to send a counsel for the defence to the trial. Martov had toyed with the idea of returning to Moscow, but probably his state of health no longer permitted it. The Central Committee afterwards changed its mind and no longer thought it in the interests of the socialist revolutionaries and the Mensheviks to depute counsels for the defence to the trial. It was after all inevitable that during the court case the RSDRP would point out the serious differences between the two parties in their approach to the Bolshevik regime, especially now that they were continually being represented in the propaganda campaign as one, great, counter-revolutionary block. But the right wing of the party argued that, precisely because of the Bolshevik slander, social democracy was in fact also being brought before the court. By means of this trial the Bolshevik dictatorship was giving it an excellent opportunity to defend itself in public. The Menshevik party was obliged to make use of this since it would probably never get a similar chance again.

This point of view was supported by the PSR leaders in the dock. They invited the right-wing Menshevik Dubois and his sympathiser Liber to take part in their defence. Liber, who had been one of the kingpins of the RSDRP in 1917, had afterwards left the party in protest against Martov's course of action. The Central Committee feared that Dubois and Liber would not interpret the party's point of view correctly and forbade even Dubois, who had remained a member of the party, to appear as counsel for the defence at the trial. Not until the party was officially invited by the PSR to contribute to the defence did the Central Committee comply with this request by sending three of its members. But the tribunal refused to admit Ber, Vainshtein and Rubin to the trial as counsels for the defence. A protest against this, in which it was of course mentioned that the tribunal was violating the agreements of the Berlin conference by doing this, was of no avail.[97]

It was even more difficult for the Mensheviks to react to the mass demonstration of workers on 20 June 1922, which formed the climax of the Bolshevik propaganda offensive. Two hundred thousand workers marched across Red Square and, with banners and chanting, demanded the death penalty for the socialist revolutionaries. They also demanded the heads of the Russian social democrats. A few demonstrators had the inconceivable courage to march in the demonstration with the text 'Down with the death penalty!' They were arrested shortly afterwards. By way of increasing the effect of the propaganda the tribunal allowed a delegation from the demonstrators into the court so that the 'will of the Moscow proletariat' would also be represented there. The Mensheviks had closely followed the preparations for this event. They reported in detail in *Vestnik* how the Bolsheviks, with all the means of intimidation and manipulation at their disposal, had used their influence in factory after factory in the capital, to be able to show the world that the Russian workers were demanding the heaviest penalty for the leaders of the PSR.[98]

After all that had happened it was nevertheless a severe shock for the Mensheviks that the regime had so effectively mobilised the partly apathetic, partly unwilling, Moscow workers against the socialist opposition by threatening them with unemployment and starvation. The spectacle on 20 June, when the proletariat, under fluttering red flags, requested the death of socialist leaders, had for them all the characteristics of an absurd drama, of something totally unreal. It was understandable that Dvinov saw the demonstration as a turning-point not only in the state of affairs surrounding the trial, but also in the progress of the Russian revolution. This was a shrewd observation. Political scientists were much later to regard the mass mobilisation of the population as one of the most notable methods with which a totalitarian system legitimises its existence. Not only the demonstration, but the lawsuit itself, which was the first major show trial in communist Russia, seen with hindsight were among the first clear signs that a system of this kind was coming into being there.[99]

The Mensheviks' main problem was what they could do against this. Dvinov had suggested taking to the streets with all the Moscow party activists (200 to 300 people) on the same day as the demonstration, and holding a counter-demonstration. An action of this kind would undoubtedly have led to mass arrests and probably also to a violent clash with the police in which victims would fall. But perhaps this was the decisive and last moment in which to fight for socialist thought in Russia. By such a desperate act the Menshevik party would in any case be able to counteract the effect the communists had in mind. The majority in the Central Committee was, however, unwilling to go further than the distribution of a special pamphlet. In this the workers were asked to stay at home. But the hope of being able to prolong the legal existence of the party was illusory. A fortnight later the security police arrested fifty Mensheviks in Moscow. The rest of the party disappeared underground: a situation for which the Mensheviks had actually been unwilling to prepare themselves. They had no money, false papers or places of hiding. They had left it to the regime to solve the problem of legal or illegal resistance for them. This had now been done.[100]

The foreign counsels for the defence at the trial of the socialist revolutionaries had already realised before the great demonstration that it would be impossible for them to carry out their task properly. The tribunal refused to admit either most of the witnesses *à décharge* or the defence counsels requested by the defendants. The court allowed no perusal of the stenographic record of the trial and the foreign defence was not allowed to have its own stenographic account made. Of course Vandervelde brought up the fact that this was in flagrant conflict with the

Berlin agreement. However, the chairman of the court, Piatakov, asserted that the proceedings were not bound by that in any way. The tribunal was independent of the Comintern. Later Bukharin explained on behalf of the Comintern that the Berlin agreement no longer existed. The Second International had refused to take part in a general socialist congress and thereby torpedoed the discussion and the agreement already achieved between the three Internationals. Both the socialist revolutionaries and Vandervelde, Wauters, Liebknecht and Rosenfeld then understood that the further presence of foreign defence counsels in Moscow had become meaningless. In prison they bade one another a moving farewell by singing The Internationale hand in hand. 'I shall never forget that moment', Vandervelde wrote in his book about the trial.[101]

The departure of the representatives of both socialist Internationals from Russia was followed by vigorous action by these organisations to increase the pressure of Western socialist opinion on Moscow. The Foreign Delegations of the RSDRP and the PSR had already sent a joint letter to all socialist parties with this aim in view. The socialist press showed itself to be highly indignant about the proceedings at the trial. Henderson and MacDonald sent a telegram to Moscow in which they once more called upon the Comintern to keep to the Berlin agreement and to spare the lives of the socialist revolutionaries. Even the centrists had to admit that any possibility of restoring international proletarian unity had been 'buried for a long time'. Among the communists in Europe there were people who expressed their objections in private to the practices of the Soviet judiciary and the methods which the Bolsheviks were using in the struggle against their political opponents. But the Western communist press responded to the socialist actions with a counter-offensive which was not surpassed by *Pravda* in the militancy of its language. Some distinguished writers sympathetic to Soviet Russia were also involved in this debate. Martov asked Maxim Gorky together with Anatole France to exert their influence to prevent a judicial murder.[102]

This attempt was not very successful either. On 7 August 1922 twelve socialist revolutionaries were condemned to death. The remaining defendants received heavy prison sentences. Only a few of the accused, who before and during the trial had done the regime a favour by fabricating charges and giving false evidence against their former party companions, were rewarded for their trouble with light sentences. However, the carrying out of the death sentences was deferred by the Presidium of the All Russian Soviet Congress on condition that the PSR refrained from all further armed resistance to the Soviet state. In this way the prisoners condemned to death remained hostages of the communist dictatorship for the rest of their lives. The trial and the campaign associated with it had, to a large extent, answered their appointed purpose. The socialist opposition, as a living political force, was publicly dishonoured and liquidated. Every Soviet citizen now knew what would await him if he got mixed up in one way or another with the socialist revolutionaries or the Mensheviks.

Martov's hope that the trial would mobilise all the opposition groups in the communist movement against the Politbureau and would detach the Western communist parties from Moscow proved totally groundless. The effect was rather exactly the opposite. The gulf between socialists and communists became virtually unbridgeable. Communists who were ill at ease about what had happened could only still exert some influence if they outwardly defended the Bolshevik dictatorship through thick and thin. Their political room for manoeuvre had thus become extremely small. Nevertheless, it was probably partly thanks to communists like these, of whom Bukharin was perhaps the most important, that the lives of the PSR leaders were temporarily spared. The principal factor in this was undoubtedly the pressure of Western socialist opinion. In 1936 when Bukharin, on behalf of the Soviet government, was negotiating the purchase of the SPD's archives – which included the Marx–Engels papers – and had long talks with the curator of these documents, the Menshevik Nikolaevsky, he observed: 'Yes, one has to admit that, at the beginning of the twenties, you socialists were in a position to mobilise the whole of Europe, and consequently to prevent the execution of the sentence against the socialist revolutionaries.'[103] It thus became clear that Akselrod's idea in 1922 of a socialist moral intervention in Russian affairs was not entirely impracticable.

The attitude of the principal defendants during the trial must also have given the Bolsheviks the impression that they had not achieved an unqualified political success. The leaders of the PSR, who realised that they were literally defending the socialist cause with their lives, refuted the accusations brought against them with great courage and resolution. The court did not succeed in proving that the PSR was responsible for the attacks on Lenin and other Bolshevik leaders, or that the party had collaborated with Denikin. Thus the Bolsheviks could not dispose of their political adversaries and get off scot-free themselves. Probably this was the main reason why preparations for a similar trial against the Mensheviks were suspended. The RSDRP was virtually totally eliminated anyway. It would have been necessary to invent even worse lies to accuse a party, which had in principle rejected the use of violence against the regime, of crimes against the state.[104] Nor would the tumult among Western socialists over the outrages of the communist government have been in the least calmed down by a trial of the Mensheviks. And this was clearly not in the Bolsheviks' interests either. Not until after 1928 was the technique of the political trial again regularly used, and the security police then thoroughly saw to it that the accused fulfilled their roles during the sittings in an appropriate manner. Nevertheless, in 1931 a court case against a number of Mensheviks did not go entirely according to the GPU's script, mainly because the Foreign Delegation of the RSDRP managed to bring the Western socialist movement once again into a state of alarm.[105]

## TOWARDS A NEW SOCIALIST INTERNATIONAL

Although the Western socialists were rightly dismayed about Russian events, their attention during the trial was diverted by the crisis situation arising in Germany at the same time which caused them far more anxiety. The assassination of Walther Rathenau in June 1922 had gravely endangered the extremely precarious balance on which the Weimar Republic was based in both its domestic and its foreign politics. The German socialists thought that the survival of the Republic was gravely threatened by monarchistic and reactionary forces. In their opinion the danger of a civil war followed by Entente intervention was by no means hypothetical. Moreover the value of the German mark was plummeting. This had disastrous consequences for all Ger-

man citizens, not least for the workers among them. The USPD
and the SPD were driven together by these circumstances, the
parliamentary parties in the Reichstag merged, and the USPD
showed itself prepared to accept government responsibility for
the defence of the Republic. But attempts by the socialists to
reach agreement with the communists failed. The forceful call
for unity among the workers' adherents of the SPD and USPD
now became irresistible. Within a few weeks the leadership of
both parties decided on a complete merger which was officially
confirmed in September 1922 at the Nuremberg congress.[106]

The German crisis and the rapprochement between the SPD
and the USPD naturally also influenced relationships within the
international labour movement. The International Federation
of Trade Unions invited the Second and the Vienna Internationals for deliberations. There was no question of the communists also being involved in these. This came up against formal
objections from Adler, but the centrists did not shirk this discussion. It seemed easier to talk to each other if the communists
were not there.[107] The developments in Germany, which they were
experiencing from so close at hand, affected the Mensheviks in
Berlin as harsh blows by which the last supports were being
swept away from under their policies of the previous years. Ever
since the October revolution their hopes had been centred on
the purifying action that a European socialist revolution could
exercise on the Russian situation. Now they were watching the
sad finale of the German revolution and the political eclipse of
the USPD, a party from which they had expected so much.

'All this is tragic, tragic', wrote one of the Mensheviks to Berlin
in response to the many letters and articles from the Foreign
Delegation about the German crisis. He could scarcely imagine
that the USPD would inevitably have to be absorbed into the
party of Scheidemann and Noske. Were there then no alternatives? New elections, for example? Abramovich wrote a long
letter back because 'you have not completely understood what
is happening in Germany'. He described the mood in the country
in detail. 'The atmosphere of a pogrom dominates the streets,
the markets and the shops of Berlin. All foreigners, and
especially Jews, are looked at as if they were wolves, and there
is no reticence about making "remarks".' The socialists and the
workers were, according to Abramovich, the only Weimar sup-

porters, but formed a minority of the population. The proletariat was deeply disappointed in the SPD's reformist course of action, which had been able to do nothing about the deterioration in their economic situation. But the USPD could now no longer offer them a revolutionary prospect.[108]

In September the Vienna International recognised that the socialist unification in Germany was a powerful incentive for the achievement of unity at international level. The crimes committed in 1919 still hung over co-operation between German socialists like a black shadow, but no longer formed an insurmountable obstacle to it. Perhaps, despite the deep wounds which Bolshevism had inflicted on Russian socialism, it might be possible to co-operate with the communists again in the future. Now, however, this was out of the question. Only a minority objected to this point of view and thought that Vienna ought to preserve its total independence. Most of the leadership considered that the situation in Europe made a combination of socialist forces necessary. To this end a congress capable of setting up a permanent centre of action should be convened as soon as possible. Vienna, however, should remain faithful to its struggle for a genuinely all-embracing International. The door to the communists ought to remain open. This ambiguous attitude could not conceal the fact that work was under way on a treaty between the centrists and the parties of the Second International. Now there simply was no other alternative.[109]

Martov recognised this in one of the last articles he wrote before his death. And he reconciled himself, though with great reluctance, to the facts. Developments were indeed taking place in the direction indicated by his critics Kautsky and Dalin: an association of socialists *against* communists. But it was not true, as Kautsky had maintained, that the Mensheviks had previously wanted to postpone the restoration of unity until the day 'when the Moscow wolves are changed into vegetarians'. The merging of the Vienna International with the Second could not mean anything other than compliance with reformism, which had once, for the centrists, been the principal cause for breaking away. It was therefore nothing less than a total defeat. The reactionary changes within socialism during the war – Martov continued – had alienated an important section of the workers from the movement. In Zimmerwald the revolutionary Marxists had for the first time tried to change the course of events. The rebellious masses, however, had not followed them, but the communists. In Berne and Vienna the centrists had made another attempt and this, too, had failed. The masses in Europe, disappointed in communism, returned to a large extent to reformism. Reformism had given birth to communism and afterwards communism had strengthened reformism. The centrists had not succeeded in breaking out of this vicious circle.[110]

In general not only most of the centrists but also the Mensheviks accepted this view, which was published both in *Vestnik* and in *Der Kampf*, as a correct analysis. Only for the Second International and the Comintern was the merger cause for any joy. In his address to the Fourth Comintern Congress in November Zinoviev triumphantly emphasised that Martov regarded the development as a defeat for Vienna. But even if the centrists were unenthusiastic, Mussolini's coup in October had rubbed their noses in the fact that a lasting division of the proletariat could have disastrous consequences. At the beginning of December the executive committee of the Vienna Working Union of Socialist Parties, despite the passionate resistance of a small minority, decided to throw in their lot with London. The proposal made by Abramovich, who replaced the mortally ill Martov, to form a permanent commission with representatives of the Second International to discuss all the issues, was accepted.[111]

The next opportunity for making contact with the Second International was the peace congress in The Hague which was organised by the International Federation of Trade Unions. This promised to be one of the largest peace demonstrations of the century at which not only the trade unions of the IFTU, but also all the socialist parties, non-socialist pacifist groups and even communist trade unions from Russia would be represented. The gathering of more than 600 delegates from twenty-four countries on behalf of 40 million people was an impressive demonstration of 'the war against war' in which the IFTU had engaged. The foreign delegation of the RSDRP sent Abramovich to The Hague, 'although the high rate of exchange and the devilishly high prices in Holland mean a severe assault on our already pretty depleted funds', Dan wrote to Moscow.[112]

The many speeches at the conference in The Hague, which was held on 10–15 December, naturally gave evidence of the general aversion to war. But concrete political steps to ensure peace in Europe were not taken. The effect of this demonstration of proletarian unity was cancelled out by the oratorical battles between the communists and socialists. But these did supply the only lively moments among all the serious and moralising speeches. The Dutch government had refused six members of the communist delegation admission into the country. For this reason the congress was attended only by Radek, Lozovsky, Rothstein and Aleksandra Kollontay, who was described in the *Nieuwe Rotterdamsche Courant* as an 'opulent and lascivious lady'. This paper reported that the Russian communists and their Dutch comrades were hanging about in the coffee room more than in the assembly hall. 'The less interest they evidently had in the congress, the more the congress had for them, and when one of them was to speak the audience streamed in from all sides and crowded round the press table. The same interest was shown for the Homerical spectacle of their demolition.'[113]

The communist delegates reproached the organisers of the congress for having invited bourgeois pacifists, but not the Comintern, the Profintern or the proletarian parties from Asia. As opposed to this in-crowd of European bourgeoisie and reformist socialism which naturally could not lead a genuine struggle for peace, they put forward the politics of the united front. This met with no response from the congress. The communist speakers were showered with sarcasm. The English chairman Thomas tried in vain to contain the debate between communists and socialists by pointing out that the congress had not been convened for this. It was curious that the British trade union leaders did not criticise Soviet Russia in their addresses. The enthusiasm for the 'Russian experiment' had not yet subsided in their organisations. Among most of the continental trade unions and socialist parties the developments in Russia itself had contributed to the growth of a militant anti-Bolshevism. This was clearly evident from the way in which the Dutch socialist daily *Het Volk* described Abramovich's address: 'A slender figure with an emaciated face and glowing eyes then stepped up before the congress: Abramovich, one of the leaders of the Russian Social Democratic Workers' party. And he settled scores with the rulers of the Soviet Republic in a way they will not easily forget.'[114] It is evident from the minutes of the congress that

Abramovich's appearance met with a tremendous response, though he produced no new points of view. Even the *Nieuwe Rotterdamsche Courant*, which reported the whole congress in a rather ironic manner, had respect for 'the calm little man called Abramovich. The great ovation went to him for he was the living symbol of oppressed innocence . . . .'

Nevertheless, the foreign delegation of the RSDRP may have wondered whether this was the reaction which it had tried to provoke. The Mensheviks had to take into account the fact that most of the socialists in the new International would be inclined to listen to them as long as they, in their struggle against communism, needed expert information about the Soviet Union. This did not imply that the Russian socialists would obtain the help they so badly needed from them.[115] Moreover the leadership of the RSDRP had serious objections to the nature of the anti-communism of many socialist parties which ruled out a dialogue between communists and socialists. This had been the main reason for their affiliation to Vienna. After all the centrists were in favour of talks with communists. But in that case another danger threatened, as the Mensheviks had discovered. A more lenient evaluation of communism could easily lead to an almost uncritical acceptance of the Bolshevik dictatorship. If, as the Mensheviks were hoping, the relationship between the socialist and communist parties improved in years to come, then the new International might well also begin to show the same inclination to talk away the evil in Russia. The Mensheviks thus had every reason to watch further developments within the Western labour movement like a lynx. But, come what might, they realised they should try to use the new International as their forum whatever the circumstances. They ought to overcome their reluctance for a merger between London and Vienna. Their hundreds of comrades in Russian imprisonment or exile could not do without the support of Western socialism. A too-critical attitude of their foreign delegation with regard to the new International would avail them nothing.

It was therefore of considerable importance for the Mensheviks that their small impotent party should be regarded by the socialists at the peace conference in The Hague as the moral victor in the struggle with the dictatorship in Russia. Abramovich later wrote that the prestige of the RSDRP was considerably increased by the congress and that this guaranteed it a significant place in the new International. This was already evident in The Hague when a mixed commission of ten people from both socialist Internationals was set up in order to prepare for the congress at which their amalgamation would take place. Neither the Georgian socialists, nor the socialist revolutionaries or other socialist groups from Eastern Europe, who on the whole were hearty supporters of the merger, were represented in this. The RSDRP, which until then had been unable to muster up much enthusiasm for co-operation with London, did, however, obtain a seat, which was occupied by Abramovich.[116] Moreover Abramovich was designated as one of the most important rapporteurs for the congress. At the very least, all this expressed goodwill. The Mensheviks also had to acknowledge that all the socialist parties were protesting against the occupation of the Ruhr by French and Belgian troops and for that reason were co-operating intensively with one another. They noted that the Belgian Vandervelde was the first to call upon his party to resist. European socialism was thus still in a position to allow international solidarity to prevail over national interests, even though its result was nothing more than a powerless protest. Communist proposals for a general strike in Europe were rejected as irresponsible demagogy.[117]

For the Mensheviks it was most important that the 'committee of ten' adopted a strongly worded resolution on terrorism against socialists in Russia. No one had any illusions about the immediate consequences of such a statement. But it nevertheless gave the Mensheviks the feeling that the new International, too, would give them some backing in their grievous struggle. It strengthened their conviction that even in Russia not everything was lost. In various towns small groups of social democrats continued to be active underground. New life was breathed into these pathetic remains of the party by the Bureau of the Central Committee in Moscow, which was now under the inspired leadership of Georgy Dmitrievich Kuchin. In the party he was known by the pseudonym Oransky and had been exiled to Turkestan in 1922. Like a number of others he managed to escape and returned to the capital. Kuchin was the only man of any stature whom the party still had at its disposal in Russia. The remaining leaders had emigrated, were in prison, had been exiled or had left the party. Kuchin built up an underground party organisation. Now that the former ideological distinctions between left and right had virtually lost their meaning, Kuchin succeeded in getting the two groups to co-operate again. Party conferences were held in Moscow at which delegates from different parts of Russia met. Members of the party administration visited local organisations. It was still possible to maintain regular contact with the foreign delegation. Not only *Vestnik*, but even papers and pamphlets illegally printed in Russia itself were distributed. Although the great mass of workers remained apathetic and inaccessible, a small number of them still dared to show an interest in Menshevik propaganda.[118]

The Mensheviks in Russia hoped they could widen their activities in the future. The great measure of labour unrest at this time reinforced this expectation. In Kuchin's letters to Berlin he was full of enthusiasm for the 'fresh spirit' in the party and gave heroic examples of courage, dedication, self-sacrifice and comradeship among the frequently very young social democrats he was leading. But the same considerations which gave the Mensheviks hope prompted the regime to continue to round up an outlawed party which at present no longer constituted any direct threat. On 13 March 1923, the day on which both Bolsheviks and Mensheviks commemorated the fact that, twenty-five years before, Russian social democracy had held its first party congress, the GPU made a large-scale raid on the party organisation in Moscow. The Mensheviks discovered beforehand that the time and place of their celebratory meeting had been betrayed. But they were no longer able to warn everyone in time. The police had cordoned off the entire area, and were checking the papers of all the passers-by. A series of arrests throughout the country destroyed the network of underground connections and contacts. Kuchin started to reconstruct it with a few people. But for a long time they felt completely cut off from the remaining party members in Russia and this undermined their nerve.[119]

'In these hard times', Kuchin wrote later, 'we received the news of Martov's death.'[120] All the Mensheviks were very dismayed at the loss of such a beloved party leader, who, because of his extraordinary talents as a tribune and herald of democratic socialism, they considered indispensable and irreplaceable. In

Russia, too, they had known for a considerable time that Martov was seriously ill and was being nursed in a sanatorium. They had collected money for his treatment, although they themselves could scarcely make ends meet and the underground party was having to work almost entirely without financial means. It is notable that Zinoviev, at Lenin's express request, brought up the question of financial support for Martov in the Politbureau. 'They say that Martov is also dying', a sick and sad Lenin told his wife.[121] Rykov, a relative of the Menshevik Nikolaevsky and Lenin's successor as chairman of the Council of People's Commissars, was present as a private individual at Martov's cremation in Berlin on 10 April 1923.

This ceremony was attended by about a thousand people including many prominent socialists, but also a fairly large number of communists. Socialists from the entire world sent tokens of condolence to the Foreign Delegation. Kautsky, Hilferding, Crispien, Adler, Bauer, Bracke and Longuet wrote articles in which they gave him the honour due to him as a fighter against Bolshevism and as a champion of international socialism. Hilferding commemorated the USPD congress in Halle where Martov had occupied 'the most important position' in the 'battle between Bolshevism and European socialism' which took place there. Crispien praised his role as one of the principal founders of the Vienna International. Bauer expressed great admiration for Martov's work in the preceding period, when, a couple of years later, he described how difficult the centrists had found it at first to condemn communism.

> And if we eventually succeed in selecting a position which combines a historical understanding of the forces by which communism was animated, with a criticism of its illusions and errors, then, in the first place this is thanks to Martov's brilliant analysis. He was the first to teach European social democracy that Bolshevism should be criticised not from a bourgeois or counter-revolutionary point of view, but from a proletarian and revolutionary viewpoint.[122]

In April 1923, a quarter of a century after its foundation, what was there left of the RSDRP? The party had lost its most talented leader and had been virtually eliminated in Russia. What was the point of going any further? The Menshevik Vainshtein, who had escaped from his Siberian exile in February

1923 and died in Germany shortly after Martov, had commented on his arrival in Berlin: 'Who knows if this has not all been trouble in vain. Perhaps we are going to live another life, drink Tokay and kiss beautiful women...'[123] But this wry self-mockery did not go down well with his comrades. For them the commemorative speech made by Dan, Martov's successor as party leader, was a guideline for the future. 'We should be completely neglecting the last wishes of our teacher, friend and leader if we regarded his death as a reason for despondency. We must continue to the end his struggle for the liberation of the proletariat and the whole of mankind.'[124] It was indeed their dedication to this impossible task which enabled a group of emigrants as destitute as they were talented, to continue to exert a considerable influence on European socialism for a long time to come.

## THE HAMBURG CONGRESS

This was first of all to become evident in Hamburg during the foundation congress of the Labour and Socialist International held in May 1923. The company which met on Whit Monday in the festively decorated main hall of the trade union building in Hamburg to ratify the amalgamation of the Vienna and the Second Internationals, consisted of 120 delegates from 30 countries. They represented 41 parties which together numbered 6 million members and at least 25 million voters. All the movements and virtually all the important leaders of European socialism were present. The statutes adopted by the congress made the Labour and Socialist International into an organisation which, in many respect, was like the Second International. They left undisturbed the autonomy of the affiliated parties in the area of internal politics. Fundamental discussions about socialists joining bourgeois governments would not take place in the LSI. Foreign policy, however, was a different matter. 'The Labour and Socialist International is a living reality only in so far as its decisions on all international questions are binding on all its parts. Thus every decision of the international organisation means a conscious diminution of the autonomy of the parties in the different countries.' At least on paper this was an attempt to avoid the situation which had occurred in August 1914.[125]

The congress concerned itself with the international situation in detail, for this appeared to all those present to be particularly serious. The French occupation of the Ruhr since January 1923 had much increased the political and social tension in Germany, already in existence there. Inflation began to assume catastrophic proportions. In May 1923, 47,000 marks were paid for one American dollar. A few months later the money in Germany became completely worthless. In Italy and Hungary, Fascism and dictatorship had prevailed. In Germany itself the swastika had raised its head while the communists were again rapidly gaining in popularity. The most important point for discussion at the congress was, then, 'the international struggle against international reaction'. According to the socialists this 'offensive of the bourgeoisie' should be brought to a halt by the united proletariat of Europe. Unfortunately the communists were not prepared to make their own interests subservient to those of the whole labour movement. All attempts to reach agreement with them on this were rejected, while the problem of unity only became more serious 'through the barbaric and unceasing persecution of the Russian socialists'.[126]

Otto Bauer devoted a long speech to the international situation. Although democracy and socialism were being threatened everywhere in Europe, Russia, according to him, was the most important danger zone. Despite the continuation of terrorism in Russia itself, despite communist tactics of infiltration and subversion within the international labour movement, and despite the aggressive Soviet imperialism in Georgia and Armenia, the socialists had to continue to defend Russia against the anti-communist crusade of the Western powers. The European socialists' concern was mainly aroused by the diplomatic conflict which had recently broken out between Russia and England. The conservative British minister of foreign affairs, Lord Curzon, had sent the Soviet Union a strongly worded letter at the beginning of May, with a catalogue of complaints which mostly concerned the behaviour of the Russian communists in Asia. Curzon announced that in the absence of a satisfactory reply the 1921 trade agreement with Russia would be revoked by England. Because of the appearance of a British gunboat in the northern Baltic, the visit of top French and British military personnel to Warsaw and Prague and the assassination of the

Soviet diplomat Vorovsky in Switzerland, there was some anxiety in Moscow about a renewed armed intervention. Moreover this feeling, based on very few concrete facts, was also shared by the socialists present in Hamburg.[127]

The British socialists fought Curzon's ultimatum both in and out of parliament. For this reason MacDonald, as leader of the opposition, could not be spared in England and was not present in Hamburg. But Henderson brought the question up directly at the beginning of the congress and, as chairman of the meeting, protested against the British policy. Abramovich, who was acting as vice-chairman, heartily concurred with him. But not all the British were convinced by his attitude on this that the presence of Russian socialists at the congress was desirable or useful. Beatrice Webb, the representative of the Fabian Society, protested in a committee meeting against the important position that Abramovich was occupying. She felt that there was no place for such anti-Bolshevik groups as the PSR and the RSDRP within the new International. The Mensheviks were moreover aware that similar ideas existed among the Italian, Swiss and American socialists. The organisers of the congress had apparently decided, as had invariably happened at the meetings of the Second and Vienna Internationals, not to bring up the most important question which had to be resolved in Hamburg – the attitude of the LSI towards communist Russia – as a separate point. The Russian issue was now concealed in the agenda under the heading 'The international conflict against international reaction', where of course it did not belong at all.[128]

This put Abramovich, who had been appointed as a speaker on this matter by the congress organisers, in a difficult position. In the draft resolution which the Foreign Delegation of the RSDRP, after much discussion with their fellow party members in Berlin and in Russia, presented to the congress, a long passage was of course devoted to the duty of the LSI to defend the Russian revolution against Western imperialist aggression with every available means. But the congress was also asked to support the demands of the Russian socialists to the Bolsheviks.[129] According to the RSDRP the congress ought to state, in all clarity and publicity, that the communist experiment in Russia had ended in disaster. Russia was ruled by a corrupt bureaucracy supported by all-powerful military and police machinery. The resolution demanded that the Russian communists should stop their oppression of socialists, workers and the inhabitants of Georgia, free all political prisoners, abolish their dictatorship, and grant the Russian people political rights and democratic self-government. The Western socialists ought to give as much moral and material support as possible to the victims of political terrorism in Russia. The Mensheviks already knew, of course, that many socialists at the congress would be unwilling to insist on the Bolsheviks' liquidating their own dictatorship in this way. It was not to be expected that the Curzon ultimatum would be followed by an ultimatum from the LSI. Since the International had no real power, this did not seem very meaningful. Nor did the Russian socialists believe that making harsh demands would lead to substantial positive results. But in the past the Kremlin had proved not entirely insensitive to Western socialist pressure. At the same time they had all too often discovered that some of their Western comrades were inclined to gloss over the negative side of the Soviet regime when it suited them. Therefore, in their view, it was very important for the LSI to take a stand on principle.[130]

   The opportunistic attitude of the British socialists caused them the most trouble in Hamburg. The Labour Party had expressly refused to accept the religious persecution in Russia (which had been denounced by conservative politicians in England) as an argument for their country to adopt a more anti-Russian policy. The extent of these Englishmen's concern that the Russian socialists would say something in Hamburg that might undermine the LSI's opposition to Curzon's memorandum, was made evident by the way in which Wallhead, the representative of the Independent Labour Party who chaired the congress during the third sitting, introduced Abramovich. So much was at stake in the Anglo-Russian conflict, he said, that the speakers ought not to forget that the walls of the hall had ears. The reactionary camp listened attentively. Therefore nothing should be said which could harm the socialist movement. Portugeis, who was not accepted as an official Russian delegate and attended the congress as a journalist, regarded the concern about the threatening danger of war as 'pure lies and fabrications' (*blef*) which were intended to prevent criticism of the Soviet Union.

This was greatly exaggerated, but the behaviour of the British did mean a limitation of the influence of the Russian socialists at the congress.

This was evident from Abramovich's speech. He gave only a very general account of the NEP and the political and economic prospects in Russia that contained nothing which had not been described earlier and in more detail by Bauer or Kautsky. The fate of the political prisoners was only outlined in passing. Nevertheless the next speaker, the Italian Modigliani, found it necessary to dissociate himself from Abramovich. Although there were valid reasons for strongly disapproving of the Russian governmental system, the congress ought not, in his view, to limit itself to purely negative criticism. Bolshevism had after all caused a complete reversal in political and social attitudes in Russia by bringing about the downfall of tsarism. Against Modigliani's historical oversimplifications the interruptions of the Russians in the hall were not very helpful.[131] In exactly the same tradition which the socialists had developed at all the earlier international gatherings for dealing with thorny problems, the decisive debate about Soviet Russia took place in a closed committee meeting of which, as had also become the custom, no report was made or kept. The only result was that the RSDRP's draft resolution was toned down by the committee. The negative characterisation and the cutting condemnation of the Bolshevik regime were scrapped from the text. The demands concerning the cessation of terrorism and the restoration of democratic political relations were, however, retained. Moreover international socialism committed itself to 'every possible moral and material support' for the Russian socialists. In this form the resolution was accepted by the congress by 196 votes to 2.

In this way the LSI had committed itself to a clear point of view towards Soviet Russia and communism. This was of considerable importance to the Russian socialists. The Russian socialist parties in Russia at the time consisted chiefly of political prisoners, so it is certainly curious that the PSR and the RSDRP were accepted by the LSI as completely fully-fledged members. The extent of the weight that was attached to their contribution is above all evident from the election of Abramovich into the nine-man Bureau of the LSI which formed the executive board of the International. Some damage was done to this Menshevik success by the attitude of the British, who without question formed the most important group in the organisation. The English delegation, as well as the Swiss, had abstained from voting on the Russian resolution. Brailsford, who reported the deliberations of the committee to the congress, even had the nerve to claim once more that the excesses of the Russian revolution were a consequence of the Russian policies of the European states. 'Alongside all the justifiable democratic critic-ism of Russia we should never forget that those chiefly respon-sible for the victims in the Russian prisons, for the people who have been executed or exiled, are the capitalist governments in the West.' Even this statement met, according to the congress report, with 'hearty applause' from the hall.[132]

The immediate occasion for this remarkable behaviour by the British was removed when the Kremlin decided to adopt a conciliatory attitude in the conflict with England. The economic situation of the Soviet Union left the Politbureau little choice. The fear of a repetition of civil war and intervention in Russia, which had overcome communists and socialists alike, proved to be groundless. Things were not completely back to normal, but nevertheless a certain degree of stabilisation did take place in the relations between Russia and Europe. Within the Soviet Union itself developments also changed course in the middle twenties, and were less stormy than Russian and European socialists had predicted. The power of the Russian communist party was unassailable and fundamental political changes did not occur. The NEP provided for real economic recovery, especially in agriculture. The necessity for economic reforms on a grand scale was for a number of years not so strongly felt. After the crisis in the Ruhr there was also a temporary halt in the great tension and unrest which had been characteristic of Germany since its defeat in the World War. The communist uprising carried out at Moscow's instigation in the autumn of 1923 failed dismally. Both as regards their internal situation and in their relations with the rest of the world, in 1923 more normal times were dawning for Germans and Russians.

# CONCLUSION

The peace and quiet in Germany and Russia was deceptive and
Europe was granted only a short pause for breath. Nevertheless,
around 1923 an era was brought to an end. In the years 1917–23
the traditions of rebellion and resistance, which had come into
being in 1789, made themselves felt in our part of the world on
a grand scale for the last time. Only in Russia did the revolution
continue and the result was not only that the Western labour
movement split apart, but also that Europe became divided into
two camps. Eventually the contrast between communism on the
one hand and socialism and capitalism on the other caused a
dichotomy the like of which had not been seen since the sixteenth-century Reformation. The confused quarrel between
Martov and Lenin at the Second Party Congress in 1903 was
thus followed by an unexpected development which was by no
means concluded in 1923. Nevertheless, Martov's death in 1923
and that of Lenin in January 1924 certainly marked the end of
an era. The Russian communist party, which had experienced
a considerable transformation in the years 1917–23, was only
afterwards to undergo a complete metamorphosis. Stalin's
bureaucratic Moloch no longer in any way resembled the revolutionary vanguard which Lenin had drawn up on paper in
1902. In 1923 democratic socialism was as good as dead in Russia.
In the West it would continue to exist, though its significance
would be greatly altered. The centrist socialism which had tried
to maintain the norms and values of pre war socialism had
likewise lost its rationale in 1923, and was merely to continue
to exist for a while longer as a not particularly influential left
wing of the socialist workers' movement. Russian Bolshevism on

515

the other hand had acquired a power over part of the Western working class which no one before 1914 would have thought possible. But the socialist revolution had virtually disappeared from the European proletariat's field of vision, while the heritage of ideas passed down from the previous century under the names of socialism and Marxism had been robbed of much of their importance in this way. The Hamburg congress confirmed this development. The LSI and the Comintern were very different from the First and Second Internationals, not so much in form as in content.

Not every kind of historical continuity was cancelled out by the sharp twists and turns in the history of socialism, communism, Europe and Russia. But after 1923 relations between socialist Europe and revolutionary Russia could no longer be maintained in the same way as they had been in the previous three-quarters-of-a-century. Accordingly it is meaningful to bring the narrative of this period which began in about 1848 to an end in 1923, although the Mensheviks also continued to play a not unimportant role afterwards in the LSI, and 'the Russian question' remained a serious problem for Western socialists. In this book we have seen how, from Herzen to Martov, three generations of Russian revolutionaries tried to break through the prejudices about Russia of their kindred spirits in the West. The message of these *zapadniki* (Westerners) was that Russia, despite various differences, of course belonged to Europe. They also thought that the socialist ideal could and should be realised in their own country, without the ethical norms, which in their view were inherent in this ideal, being harmed. These norms, they were convinced, were not characteristic of the West, but of mankind in general. They did not succeed in convincing their contemporaries that this point of view was right.

Their failure made it difficult to write their history. Historical writing has always shown a certain preference for individuals, groups, ideas and events which have left an enduring mark on historical reality, and thus on the present-day situation. Boris Sapir, the historian and archivist of the Russian revolution and Menshevism who was in no way embittered by this, once observed to me: 'There is no greater success than success.' A historical account of the 'losers' of the Russian revolution quickly turns out to be either an investigation into the causes of their failure or an apologia for their misfortune. I have tried to avoid both approaches because the success of Bolshevism faces us with exactly the same problems as the defeat of their opponents. The Bolsheviks' success was very relative when measured against their own aims. It was no more than logical that groups originated within the communist party which tried to take over the critical function of the socialist opposition as soon as this had been eliminated as a political factor. In this context Lenin spoke threateningly of 'clandestine Menshevism'. But at the end of his life he himself realised that a bureaucratic monster had been created in the communist regime. Stalin described communist resistance against his struggle for absolute power as 'a Menshevik deviation from Leninism' and after he had liquidated the old Bolshevik guard it was no longer clear exactly who the 'losers' of the Russian revolution had been. When after 1985 the total failure of Stalinism was being acknowledged, these former Bolshevik leaders could be rehabilitated. The complete collapse of the communist system as a result of Gorbachev's frantic efforts to reform his party and his state, the rise of political pluralism and the re-emergence of a social democratic movement again give the history of the Mensheviks and the socialist revolutionaries a topical significance.

It therefore contributes little to our understanding of the Russian revolution if the downfall of moderate socialism is treated as an isolated fact. Menshevism and Bolshevism were like a pair of Siamese twins who could live neither together nor apart. The dividing line between the two groups has always remained vague. Many Russian social democrats belonged first to the one and then to the other movement. The impatient revolutionary radicalism of the Bolsheviks had a long history behind it, not only in Russia but also in Europe. Socialism was, not only for them, but also for practically all its followers, something which could be realised in the foreseeable future. No socialist in the East or the West had ever claimed that this ought to take place, everywhere and in all circumstances, solely along a legal and gradual route. It therefore almost went without saying that a group of socialists would one day try to achieve this splendid objective by unscrupulous methods. With this, of course, no claim is being made that the Bolsheviks should be relieved of their responsibility for one of the greatest political disasters in history. But as soon as the question of guilt is raised, the complicity of the other socialists ought also to be investigated.

The preference of certain revolutionaries for violence and dictatorship has, from the outset, met with determined opposition not only within Western socialism. The Mensheviks, and to a lesser extent the socialist revolutionaries, were the intellectual heirs of an important Russian movement which had its origins deep in the nineteenth century. Backwardness and autocracy did not prevent the development of moderate socialism in Russia, but they did delay it. We can therefore have nothing but respect for the Russians who dedicated themselves to it in such difficult circumstances. But at the same time it must be made clear that this fight could not be effectively carried out by people who continued to believe, even unconditionally, in the possibility of a complete social revolution. Their ambiguous attitude created too little ideological clarity and led to extremely sordid quarrels which weakened their position. This wreaked its revenge in the revolutionary year. The socialist revolutionaries and the Mensheviks were then willing to participate in government provided they thought they had a mandate from their supporters. But they were not deriving their influence from a normal state system but from a chaotic revolution. In these circumstances they were unwilling to attract any dictatorial power to themselves, to impose any radical reforms or to use any appreciable violence against their political opponents. Thus they were doing what would be praiseworthy in any politician, but this was fatal for them and also made possible the very things they had been hoping to frustrate.

The *parti pris* and the continual differences of opinion amongst these Russians had also been a serious obstacle to a better understanding of their subtle point of view in the West. Moreover the European socialists, because of their faith in the victory of socialism and their traditional prejudicies about Russia, were scarcely susceptible to it. Before 1917 they had seldom criticised and frequently encouraged Russian radicalism, and they therefore also bore a certain responsibility for what occurred in Russia. Of course they shrugged this off by claiming that events in Russia simply proved the innate unsuitability of that part of Europe for democracy. But shortly afterwards it became evident that this argument did not hold water. In many countries of 'civilised' Europe the longing for a revolutionary upheaval assisted by violence and terrorism was strong enough to dig the grave of democracy and help right-wing totalitarian regimes to power. In Russia the Mensheviks and socialist revolutionaries resisted the communist dictatorship, but many of their former fellow party members collaborated with the Soviet regime. The situation in the West was no different in principle. Western socialism had fought against Fascism and national socialism and had lost this battle. Nevertheless, the step to collaboration proved to present no serious problem for many Western socialists and syndicalists. There was little difference between the extreme forms of left-wing and right-wing activism and there were even similarities between the subculture and ideology of the two movements.

The differences between Russia and Europe were thus not too great and there were clear links between developments in East and West. For this reason too, the downfall of the socialist revolutionaries and Mensheviks in Russia cannot be interpreted as an isolated phenomenon. Their lives were so bound up with European socialism that their shortcomings cannot be explained away as typically Russian inadequacies. The history of the Russian revolutionary movement is part of the European, of our history. The Russian revolution revealed the unrealisability of the pre-eminently European socialist ideal of the nineteenth century. The history not only of Russian but also of European socialism is, in many respects, the story of failure. These were failures which are extremely instructive for the further development of our thinking about state and society. For this reason it is important to study the events in Russia and the West in connection with one another.

This historical approach, because of recent developments in East – West relations, takes on a topical significance. It is to be expected that Western Europe will become far more intensively involved in the problems of its Eastern counterpart than has been the case in the last forty years. This also makes the 'Russian question' within international socialism a subject deserving of the comprehensive consideration it has received in this book. It also goes without saying that in it a great deal of attention has been devoted to the most Western-minded Russian socialists. The very vicissitudes of these people show us how closely united

Russia and the West were with one another and how artificial the later separation between a communist and a capitalist Europe has been. The special position held by these Russians in the history of the development of European socialism ensured that they continued to be not only the instigators but also the subject of an international exchange of thought in which fundamental issues were raised.

Between 1848 and 1923 the 'Russian question' assumed all kinds of shapes. The socialists who were preoccupied with this issue originated from different countries and adopted various ideological points of view. But at the same time it was evident that their opinions about widely different events and developments which could be associated with Russia were influenced to a considerable degree by the traditions of the Western image of Russia. An assessment of the relationship between Russia and Europe which was open-minded and as realistic as possible was substantially complicated by this. Since socialism formed a European movement and comparable debates about Russia also took place in other political movements, it is possible in this respect to speak of a European political culture in which the cliché-ridden ideas and attitudes handed down from the past played a considerable and not infrequently dubious role. After 1923, too, the 'Russian question' continued to be an important problem both inside and outside the socialist movement. In the period between 1923 and 1985 the debate about Russia certainly altered in content, but scarcely at all in nature.

It is not so simple to give an answer to the obvious question of whether the political culture mentioned above will still profoundly influence future European relationships with Russia. Some people might argue that this will not be the case because such revolutionary changes have taken place. This book demonstrates, however, that changed reality does not automatically lead to the modification of our practice of looking at this reality in a certain way. In the past substantial changes, such as the revolution of 1917, caused no fundamental alteration in the ideas or attitudes with which Europeans had always approached events in Russia. On the other hand, present developments are in many ways linked with the past. Between 1917 and 1991 Russian history seems to have come full circle. Russia and the other nations of the former Soviet Union are again trying to introduce Western politics and capitalism. As a result they are faced with a great number of problems which remind us strongly of the last decade of the tsarist regime. It has also been shown in this study that during this most European period of Russian history, Western prejudices about Russia gradually lost much of their emotional flavour.

This could happen again if Russia's second experiment with a market economy and political pluralism, which now is going through such a critical phase, nevertheless succeeds. Unfortunately, we cannot exclude the possibility that economic backwardness and its traditional Russian companion, authoritarian rule, will again determine the fate of the country in the future. In that case we cannot expect that the grip which the past always had on our ideas of Russia will become looser. At the same time we are well aware that our image of Russia was not only a product of Russian developments but also originated in Western consciousness and Western needs. This circumstance might also induce future historians to write another book about Russia and Europe and the power of tradition and custom over our thoughts.

# NOTES

## INTRODUCTION

1 Duby, 'Histoire', 951.
2 For 'mental maps' see: Downs, *Maps in mind* and Gould, *Mental maps*. For an application of this concept see: Pellenberg, *Bedrijfsrelokatie*.
3 'What actually has been achieved can be represented by a small number of tiny dots and a large number of question marks on a world map.' Duyker, *National character*, 91. For the term 'macro-ethnocentrism' see: Preiswerk, *Ethnocentrism*, 15. See also: Lammig, *Osteuropabild*, 1–2. Hollander, *Volk*. Dröge, *Publizistik*, 150–62 and 214–19. Dellek, *Theory*, 175–207. LeVine, *Ethnocentrism*, 205–23. Sola Pool, 'Effects'. Lambert, *Children's views*. Buchanan, *How nations*.
4 Lovejoy, *Chain*, 23.
5 Caute, *Fellow-travellers*. Hollander, *Political pilgrims*.
6 Poliakov, *Mythe*. Cohn, *Pursuit*. Cohn, *Warrant*.

## 1 THE WESTERN EUROPEAN IMAGE OF RUSSIA

1 See for example: Baudet, *Paradijs*.
2 For an exception to this, see: Bitterli, *Die Wilden*.
3 Vliet, *Strabo*, 203, 220.
4 See for example: *Grecs et barbares*. Jüthner, *Hellenen*. Dörrie, 'Wertung'. Momigliano, *Wisdom*.
5 For the use of the words *Scythia* and *Scyths* instead of *Russia* and *Russians* after 1600 see: Matthes, *Russland*, 40–1, 47, 68, 301–2. Locher, *Geschiedenis*, 230. Anderson, *Britain*, 17. Rauch, *Studien*, 6. Groh, *Russland*, 37. Mohrenschildt, *Russia*, 142. Stammler, 'Wandlungen', 275. Brandes, *Impressions*, 10, 139–40, 236. Muchnic, 'Dostoevsky', 15. Cross, *Russia*, 39. Cadot, *Image*, 148, 168–70. Krautheim, *Meinung*, 294–5.
6 For examples see: Mohrenschildt, *Russia*, 113. Venturi, *Roots*, 478. Malia, *Herzen*, 357. See also: Hoffman, 'Scythianism'.
7 Balsdon, *Romans*. Christ, 'Römer'. Riese, *Idealisierung*.
8 Groh, *Russland*, 215. See also: Rauch, *Studien*, 158–200.
9 For instance: Jüthner, *Hellenen*, 17–18.

10 Groh, *Russland.* Stammler, 'Wandlungen', 280.
11 Lechner, 'Byzanz'. Leib, *Rome.*
12 Lozinsky, 'Russie'. Cross, 'Contacts'. Dvornik, 'Kiev state'. In France between 1300 and 1500 almost nothing was known about Russia. See: Langlois, *La vie. Livre de la description. Oeuvres de Lannoy.*
13 Southern, *Western views,* 2–3.
14 Graus, 'Slavs'. Dittrich, *Verleden,* 124ff. Krabbo, 'Schilderung'. Bosau, *Slawenchronik,* 11, 37, 41.
15 Bezzola, *Mongolen,* 72–3, 81–104, 124–49.
16 Vryonis, *Byzantium.* Ebels, *Byzantium,* 45, 264–5.
17 Daniel, *Islam,* 271ff.
18 For a bibliography see: Adelung, *Übersicht.* For anthologies see: Berry, *Kingdom.* Cross, *Russia.* See also: Locher, *Geschiedenis.* Anderson, *Britain.* Haney, 'Reflections'. Naarden, 'Nederlanders'.
19 Ključevskij, *Skazanija,* 9–10.
20 See for instance: Seredonin, *Sočinenie.* Man'kov, *Izvestija.* See also: Cross, *Russia,* 36–7. Parker, *Geography.*
21 Matthes, *Russland,* 430ff.
22 Naarden, 'Nederlanders', 17–19.
23 *Voyages,* 251. Baron, *Travels,* 151, 176. See also: Szamuely, *Tradition,* 8. Naarden, 'End of despotism'.
24 Locher, *Geschiedenis,* 233–4. Massa, *History,* 143. Naarden, 'Verbael', 135–6.
25 Herberstein, *Reise,* 80.
26 Kossmann, *Theorie,* 15, 22–3, 90. Ruffmann, *Russlandbild,* 161–4. Doerries, *Eindringen,* 89–97. For Russian criticism see: Seredonin, *Sočinenie,* 217–26.
27 Wittram, *Peter I,* I, 36–7.
28 Altmeyer, *Histoire,* 375 note 3.
29 Platzhoff, 'Auftauchen'. Kirchner, 'Bedeutung'. Adelung, *Übersicht,* 205–8.
30 Doerries, *Eindringen.* Rauch, *Studien,* 1–95. Stökl, 'Russland'.
31 Ruffmann, *Russlandbild,* 142. Cross, *Russia,* 39. Anderson, *Britain,* 18, 45, 80. See also: Edwardes, *Passage,* 25.
32 Billington, *Icon,* 171–3 and 692–4. Čiževskij, 'Zwei Ketzer'. Winter, *Halle.*
33 Anderson, *Britain,* 50.
34 Groh, *Russland,* 32–43.
35 Guerrier, *Leibniz,* II, 227.
36 Hazard, *Crise,* 78–9, 222–45, 376–82.
37 Hazard, *Pensée,* 14–16. Mohrenschildt, *Russia,* 44–5 and 238–9. Lortholary, *Philosophes,* 33–8. Anderson, *Britain,* 80–1.
38 Anderson, *Britain,* 79.
39 Doerries, *Eindringen,* 52–64.
40 Anderson, *Britain,* 80–197. Gerhard, *England.* Gleason, *Russophobia.* Martin, *Palmerston.* Krautheim, *Meinung.*
41 Lortholary, *Philosophes,* 135–46.
42 ibid., 63.
43 ibid., 95.

44  ibid., 109.
45  ibid., 112.
46  ibid., 131.
47  Koppelmann, *Nation*, 24.
48  Talmon, *Origins*, 10.
49  Schapiro, *Totalitarianism*, 74–5 and 93–4.
50  Lortholary, *Philosophes*, 88–91, 199–205 and 231–3.
51  Mohrenschildt, *Russia*, 142. Lortholary, *Philosophes*, 53.
52  Lortholary, *Philosophes*, 244.
53  McNally, 'Russlandbild'. Anderson, *Britain*, 216–32. Corbet, *Opinion*, 93–107. Cadot, *Image*, 9–10, 175–6. Groh, *Russland*, 61–2, 95, 101–7.
54  Benz, *Baader*. Benz, *Ostkirche*, 125ff. Jahn, *Russophilie*. Groh, *Russland*, 65–80, 113, 124, 141ff. Tschiževskij, *Europa*, 17–27, 94–105, 140–88. Goehrke, *Theorien*, 14–27. Starr, 'Introduction'.
55  Venturi, *Roots*, 22–4. Malia, *Herzen*, 310–1, 473 notes 27 and 28. Starr, 'Introduction', xxx–xxxiv. Družinin, 'Haxthausen'.
56  Groh, *Russland*, 124ff.
57  See also: Börne, 'Briefe'. These letters do not reveal that Börne counted on the tsar for the establishment of political and social equality in Europe as Cadot asserts: Cadot, *Image*, 248, 263.
58  Thul, 'Russland'. Oberländer, 'Wirkungsgeschichte'. Groh, *Russland*, 91. Dittrich, 'Testament'.
59  Cited by: Groh, *Russland*, 198. See also: Benz, *Baader*. For Russophobia in this period see: Gleason, *Russophobia*. Groh, *Russland*, 157ff. Laqueur, *Russia*, 13–38. Stammler, 'Wandlungen', 277–80. McNally, 'Russlandbild', 120ff. Corbet, *Opinion*, 33–91. Hammen, 'Europe'.
60  Cited by Groh, *Russland*, 215. See also: ibid., 148–56, 166–80, 199–202, 263–74. Rauch, *Studien*, 158–200. Gertler, 'Russlandpublizistik', 135–40.
61  Custine, *Lettres*. Szamuely, *Tradition*, 3–9. Jahn, *Russophilie*, 79. See also: Groh, *Russland*, 184–9. Marx, *Kommune*, 288–92. Schelting, *Russland*, 69ff. Hopper, 'Custine'. Lednicki, *Russia*, 21–104. Birke, *Frankreich*, 53ff. McNally, 'Russlandbild', 139ff. See also: Wieczynski, 'Khomyakovs Foreigners'.
62  *Journey*, i–viii.
63  Kennan, *Marquis*, 124ff.
64  Gleason, *Russophobia*, 164–204. Martin, *Palmerston*, 47–52, 130ff. Groh, *Russland*, 182–3, 192–4, 234–7.
65  McNally, 'Russlandbild', 131ff. Naarden, 'Nederlanders', 19ff.
66  Hollander, 'Amerika'. Barraclough, 'Europa'.
67  Honour, *Chinoiserie*. Reichwein, *China*. Gollwitzer, *Gefahr*. See also: Winter, *Chinezen*.
68  Laqueur, *Russia*, 26ff. Benz, *Ostkirche*, 218–29. Kahle, *Begegnung*, 180–1. Stökl, 'Scherr'. Gertler, 'Russlandpublizistik'. Ropponen, *Gefahr*. Lammig, *Osteuropabild*. Hecker, *Tat*. Fischer, *Krieg*, 77–84. Epstein, 'Komplex'. Haar, *Menace*, 1–58. Gollwitzer, *Europabild*, 374ff. A typical book written in this period is: Hehn, *Moribus*.
69  Corbet, *Opinion*. Butenschön, *Zarenhymne*.
70  Ropponen, *Kraft*. Hauser, *Deutschland*, 191–263.

71 Randall, 'Introduction', vii–viii. Brewster, *Passage*, 163. Ropponen, *Kraft*, 57ff. Brandes, *Impressions*, 16–29.
72 *Battle*, 131.
73 Brewster, *Passage*, 153–72. Hemmings, *Novel*. Romein, *Dostojewsky*. Muchnic, 'Dostoevsky'. For a Dutch example see: Wijk, 'Volkskarakter'.
74 Kaufman, *Nietzsche*, 340–1. Stammler, 'Wandlungen', 290. Salomé, *Lebensrückblick*, 117–23. *Rilke*, 30–46.
75 Stammler, 'Wandlungen', 204. See also: Mihailovich, 'Hesse'.
76 Mann, 'Anthologie', 235–6, 243.
77 Schwierkott, 'Dostojewski', 198. See also: Benz, *Ostkirche*, 297–9.
78 Tschižewskij, *Europa*, 529. Masaryk, *Bolchevisme*, 20. Masaryk, *Weltrevolution*, 145.
79 Cited by Muchnic, 'Dostoevsky', 138.
80 Brachfeld, *Gide*, 86ff. Muchnic, 'Dostoevsky', 148, 178. Caute, *Fellow-travellers*, 119.
81 Cited by Stammler, 'Wandlungen', 281.
82 Baak, *Verhouding*. *Vrij Nederland*, 21 XII 1946, 29. Muchnic, 'Dostoevsky', 138.

## 2 RUSSIAN AND EUROPEAN SOCIALISTS

1 Kohn, 'Dostoyevsky'. Schelting, *Russland*, 13–74 and 261–313. Rauch, 'Streiflichter'. Walicki, *Slavophyle controversy*, 83–118.
2 Gercen, *Byloe*, IV–V, 530.
3 MEW [Marx-Engels, *Werke*], XXXII, 566–7.
4 Cadot, *Image*, 21–91. Gercen, *Byloe*, VI–VIII, 24ff.
5 Malia, *Herzen*, 310–1, 473 note 27. Carr, *Bakunin*, 186.
6 Mervaud, 'Herzen', 122. This kind of Russian self-mockery remains. In 1884 Lavrov wrote to Engels: 'I never realised that you have such a good command of our barbarian language.' See: *Marks*, 505.
7 Michelet, *Légendes*. Herzen, *Shore*. Corbet, *Opinion*, 275–7.
8 Nettlau, *Vorfrühling*, 208–12. Gercen, *Byloe*, VI–VIII, 50–4. Coeurderoy, *Hurrah*, 475–81.
9 Carr, *Exiles*, 326–7. *Autour d'A. Herzen*, 325–9.
10 Gercen, *Byloe*, VI–VIII, 136. Cadot, *Image*, 520–1.
11 Groh, *Russland*, 248–50. Marx had the same opinions, see: MEW, V, 202.
12 Cited by Groh, *Russland*, 251–2.
13 Hess, *Briefwechsel*, 244–5, 256, 261. Groh, *Russland*, 253–7.
14 Gercen, *Byloe*, VI–VIII, 44, 138–47. MEW, XXIX, 6.
15 Marx, *Menace*. Marx, *Russie*. *Marx vs. Russia*. See also: Rjasanoff, 'Marx über den Ursprung'. Martin, *Palmerston*. Webster, *Policy*, II, 780ff. Krause, *Marx*. Rubel, 'Ecrits'. Szamuely, *Tradition*, 369–86.
16 It is pointless to make certain authors responsible for the ideas of Marx and Engels about Russia. See: Marx, *Kommune*, 288–92. Krause, *Marx*, 51–3. See also: Gercen, *Byloe*, VI–VIII, 145–6. MEW, XXVIII, 34–435.
17 Brupbacher, *Marx*. Rjasanoff, 'Marx als Verleumder'. Rjasanoff, 'Marx und seine russ. Bekannten'. 'Introduction' of Part I(2), II and IV of: Lehning, *Archives*.
18 MEW, XXVIII, 39–40.

19 MEW, XXVII, 266–7. Cf: Herod, *Nation.* Rosdolsky, *Engels.*
20 Krause, *Marx,* 93. MEW, XII, 673–82.
21 MEW, XXX, 324–8.
22 Krause, *Marx,* 53–4.
23 Amman, *Revolution,* 205–48. Dommanget, *Blanqui,* 157–86. Corbet, *Opinion,* 160–8.
24 MEW, XXX, 334. Marx, *Manuskripte,* 32ff. Lassalle, *Reden,* 492, 504. Kautsky, *Sozialisten,* 131–2.
25 *Address,* 12. Freymond, *Internationale,* I, 9. Rjasanoff, 'Politik', 360–1. *Council Minutes* 1864–66, 64, 74–5, 134–6, 287.
26 *Council Minutes* 1864–66, 117, 245–9. Lehning, *Archives,* II, 230–6. Rjasanoff, 'Politik', 362–3.
27 MEW, XXXI, 169. Woodcock, *Proudhon,* 239. Marx, *Menace,* 95–103. Mayer, *Engels,* II, 126–8. Freymond, *Internationale,* I, 78–9, 107. Rjasanoff, 'Politik', 364–9.
28 *Council Minutes* 1866-68, 130, 277–8.
29 MEW, XXXII, 443–4, 659.
30 MEW, XXXII, 234, 262, 273, 351, 354, 380, 421–3, 489. For opinions after 1871 see for instance: Loopuit, *Anarchisme,* 56ff.
31 Marx/Bakounine, I, 85–6. Silberner, *Hess,* 600–2. MEW, XXXII, 489. Freymond, *Internationale,* II, 139–44.
32 MEW, XXXII, 466. *Marks,* 168–70. See also: Koz'min, *Sekcija* and McClellan, *Exiles.*
33 *Council Minutes* 1868–70, 219–20.
34 Marx/Bakounine, I, 124ff. Lehning, *Archives,* I(2), 103–30 and II, 123ff, 147ff.
35 MEW, XVII, 268–70 and XXXIII, 5, 40 and XXXIV, 105. See also: Lehning, *Archives,* I(2), xv–xvi.
36 Venturi, *Roots,* 354–88. Camus, *Homme,* 202. Confino, *Violence,* 14.
37 Lehning, *Archives,* IV, lxix–lxxv and 103–33. Confino, *Violence,* 106–49.
38 Freymond, *Internationale,* II, 222, 425–55.
39 MEW, XVII, 269; XXXIII, 140; XXXIV, 48–9, 105, 464.
40 MEW, XXXIII, 487.
41 *Marks,* 335. McClellan, *Exiles,* 240. Sapir, *Lavrov,* I, l–li, 17, 78. MEW, XXXVI, 72. *Sovremenniki,* 103.
42 Pomper, *Lavrov,* 94–110, 155–61. Sapir, *Vpered,* I, 96–104. Sapir, 'Lavrov', 441–5. Weeks, *Bolshevik,* 50–4, 113–16.
43 Sapir, *Vpered,* I, 99–100.
44 MEW, XVIII, 541–2. *Marks,* 45–72, 313. *Sovremenniki,* 153.
45 Marx, *Kommune,* 192.
46 See: MEW, XXXIV, 374ff. *Marks,* 376–82. See also: Wolfe, *Marxism,* 151–64. Getzler, 'Revolutionaries'.
47 Cited by Schwarz, 'Populism', 43.
48 *Marks,* 278. For this correspondence see *Marks* and *Neudrucke.* See also: Goehrke, *Theorien.*
49 Marx, *Kapital,* I, 8–10.
50 Cited by Danielson: *Marks,* 619. See also: *Sovremenniki,* 78, 192–3. Walicki, *Controversy over capitalism,* 161–8. Kindersley, *Revisionists,* 9ff.

51 MEW, XXXIV, 296ff.
52 Sapir, *Lavrov*, I, liii–liv and 449–50.
53 Eckert, *Liebknecht*, 242–9. Kautsky, *Sozialisten*, 231–2. Carlson, *Anarchism*, 105. Kautsky, *Erinnerungen*, 358.
54 *Marks*, 351–2. MEW, XXXIV, 359ff. See also: Billington, *Mikhailovsky*, 65–70. Reuel', *Kapitala*, 86–118. Resis, 'Kapital'. Kindersley, *Revisionists*, 10–13. Walicki, *Controversy over capitalism*, 145–7.
55 Marx, *Kapital*, 762–3. See also: Marx, *Kommune*, 333–4.
56 Marx, *Kommune*, 50–3. Text also in: Marx, *Studienausgabe*, III, 191–4.
57 Geierhos, *Zasulič*, 68 note 65.
58 *Sovremenniki*, 52.
59 Marx, *Kommune*, 52.
60 MEW, XXXIV, 218ff and XXXVI, 46, 56. *Marks*, 159, 339, 377–9, 423–5, 437, 455, 489, 491–2, 494–5, 504, 510, 516–18. *Sovremenniki*, 183, 206. Lafargue, 'Erinnerungen', 560ff. See also: Walicki, *Controversy over capitalism*, 121–2. Kindersley, *Revisionists*, 17–18. Mendel, *Dilemmas*, 44–5.
61 MEW, XIX, 242–3. Marx, *Studienausgabe*, III, 194–5. Marx, *Kommune*, 54ff. See also: Geierhos, *Zasulič*, 62–3, 185–6. Kropotkin, *Memoirs*, 269–70.
62 Marx, *Kapital*, 35 note 30. MEW, XXXII, 197 and XXXIII, 577. Krader, *Notebooks*, 3, 5–6, 14, 28–9, 31, 49–50, 61, 86–9, 115. Krause, *Marx*, 98–100. Harris, *Rise*, 246ff. *Sovremenniki*, 66–9.
63 MEW, XIX, 384–406. Marx, *Studienausgabe*, III, 195–213. Marx, *Kommune*, 54ff.
64 *Marks*, 427–8. *Sovremenniki*, 86, 120–6. Geierhos, *Zasulič*, 129–44.
65 *Sovremenniki*, 42.
66 *Marx-Engels Gesamtausgabe*, III, Band IV, 377. MEW, XXXIII, 53. See also: Wolfe, *Marxism*, 165–210.
67 *Sovremenniki*, 74.
68 ibid., 83.
69 ibid., 180.
70 MEW, XXXV, 179ff.
71 Billington, *Mikhailovsky*, 101–20. Pomper, *Lavrov*, 206–11. Sapir, *Lavrov*, I, xlii–xliii and II, 65–6. *Sovremenniki*, 185, 311 note 187. See also: Footman, *Prelude*, 94–109. Venturi, *Roots*, 558ff.
72 MEW, XXXIV, 477.
73 Carlson, *Anarchism*, 205–47. Lidtke, *Party*, 115–16. Maitron, *Mouvement*, 206–12.
74 Kautsky, *Frühzeit*, 32.
75 Nettlau, *Anarchisten*, 202–31. Rubanovič, *Pressa*. For the Netherlands see: Mey, *Rusland*. See also: Trockij, *Sudy*, 315ff.
76 Cited by: Geierhos, '*Sozialdemokrat*', 226. See also: Lidtke, *Party*, 117–21.
77 MEW, XXXIV, 529–30. Geierhos, '*Sozialdemokrat*', 223–4. Geierhos, *Zasulič*, 133–5. *Sovremenniki*, 165–6, 310 note 180.
78 Cited by Geierhos, *Zasulič*, 222. See also: Geierhos, '*Sozialdemokrat*', 234–5. Hirsch, *Bernsteins Briefwechsel*, 22–37, 106. Bernstein, *Lehrjahre*, 123. Lidtke, *Party*, 127, 131–4, 221–2, 259.

79 Frankel, 'Voluntarism'. See also: Haimson, *Marxists*. Baron, *Plekhanov*. Ascher, *Axelrod*. Geierhos, *Zasulič*.
80 *Sovremenniki*, 116.
81 ibid., 90.
82 ibid., 195–6.
83 *Marks*, 457–8. See also: Baron, *Plekhanov*, 75–6. Kindersley, *Revisionists*, 238–9.
84 Marx, *Kommune*, 69–71, 335–6. Marx, *Manifest*, 18–20, 98–9 notes 12 and 13, 101 note 23.
85 *Marks*, 462–3, 489–90, 497–500, 508–9. *Sovremenniki*, 200–2. See also: Szamuely, *Tradition*, 390–1.
86 *Marks*, 512–15. Marx, *Kommune*, 228–31. Hirsch, *Bernsteins Briefwechsel*, 437–8.
87 MEW, XXI, 189–90.
88 *Marks*, 515–16.
89 Cited by Baron, *Plekhanov*, 122; and by Ascher, *Axelrod*, 98.
90 *Marks*, 599. See also: ibid., 533–5, 593–600.
91 *Marks*, 646. See also: ibid., 601–4, 610–15, 627–30, 644–6.
92 ibid., 559–660, 655–6.
93 MEW, XXXVII, 451.
94 MEW, XXII, 13–48. *Sovremenniki*, 99–112.
95 *Marks*, 695–6, 726–7.
96 ibid., 691–5, 699–701, 721–2, 724–6.
97 ibid., 722–4.
98 Marx, *Kommune*, 210–22.
99 Szamuely, *Tradition*, 379. See also: *Neudrucke*, i–xxxiv.

3 RUSSIAN AND WESTERN SOCIAL DEMOCRACY 1890–1905

1 Schapiro, *Party*, 11.
2 Thalheim, 'Entwicklung', 94–5.
3 Droz, *Geschichte*, VI, 67. Huggett, *Land question*, 119ff. Hussain, *Marxism*. Troelstra, *Gedenkschriften*, II, 246–51.
4 Lipset, 'Proletariat'. Laslett, *Failure*. Sombart, *Warum* or Sombart, *Why*. Moore, *Socialists*.
5 Moore, *Injustice*, 173–84.
6 Kautsky wrote in 1904: 'it is remarkable that only the Dutch and the Austrians are capable of achieving something as Marxists'. Adler, *Briefwechsel*, 439.
7 MEW, XXXVII, 225. Geierhos, *Zasulič*, 274.
8 *Protokoll Paris 1889*, 62–3.
9 *Protokoll Paris 1889*, 2, 4, 31–6, 91–6, 131. Lavroff, 'Socialisme'. *Marks*, 561 and 769. Ascher, *Axelrod*, 110. Polevoj, *Zaroždenie*, 251. Rusanov, *Emigracii*, 193.
10 Bonjean, 'Nihilisme'. Hyndman, *Record*, 68–70, 87, 259–260.
11 Stepnjak, 'Terrorismus'. Plechanow, 'Zustände'. Plechanow, 'Uspenskij'. Kritschewsky, 'Bewegung'. A [Axelrod], 'Erwachen'. Adler, *Briefwechsel*, 49, 91, 99, 117. *Bebels Briefwechsel*, 78.
12 Adler, *Briefwechsel*, 105.

13 Larsson, *Theories*, 140ff.
14 Adler, *Briefwechsel*, 105–6 note 13.
15 A [Axelrod], 'Erwachen'. Ascher, *Axelrod*, 110–11. *Protokoll Zürich* 1893, 61. Cf: Geyer, *Lenin*, 50.
16 *Congrès Bruxelles* 1891, 110–14. *Perepiska*, I, 74–7, 79–82. Rusanov, *Emigracii*, 194–5. *Protokoll Zürich* 1893, 6, 14–15. *Marks*, 681. Ascher, *Axelrod*, 111–16.
17 *Marks*, 683. *Perepiska*, I, 143 note 4.
18 *Protokoll Zürich* 1893, 20–1.
19 ibid., 21–33. See also: Corbet, *Opinion*, 401, 425–7, 439.
20 *Perepiska*, I, 86–7, 94–5, 98 note 8, 110. Geierhos, *Zasulič*, 38, 279. Baron, *Plekhanov*, 162.
21 *Protokoll Zürich* 1893, 44.
22 *Perepiska*, I, 102–3, 230–7.
23 Axelrod, 'Kräfte'.
24 *Perepiska*, I, 146–51. For Dutch reporting on the strike see: T [P. L. Tak], 'Voorteekenen', *De Kroniek*, II, 1896, no. 83.
25 *Perepiska*, I, 152–60. *Report Russian Social-Democrats*. Nicoll, 'Participation', 53–63.
26 Kautsky, 'Finis'. Nettl, *Luxemburg*, 101–11. Luxemburg, *Briefe*, 65. Adler, *Briefwechsel*, 207.
27 Luxemburg, *Briefe*, 81–2. *Perepiska*, I, 165–71, 173–4.
28 Axelrod, 'Rede'. *Perepiska*, I, 175–7. Geyer, *Lenin*, 129–30 note 18.
29 Luxemburg, *Briefe*, 97. *Perepiska*, II, 5–7.
30 Axelrod, 'Berechtigung', 100.
31 *Perepiska*, I, 205, 207.
32 Axelrod, 'Berechtigung', 146–7.
33 ibid., 106–7. Ascher, *Axelrod*, 132ff. Geyer, *Lenin*, 111ff.
34 Ascher, *Axelrod*, 134–5.
35 Axelrod, 'Berechtigung', 143.
36 *Perepiska*, I, 184–91.
37 Axelrod, 'Berechtigung', 143.
38 For the text see for instance: Elwood, *Resolutions*, 34–6.
39 *Soc. dem. dviženie v Rossii*, 36.
40 Pipes, *Struve*, I, 121–279.
41 Frankel, 'Economism'. Wildman, *Making*.
42 Lidtke, 'Revisionismus'. Luxemburg, *Werke*, I, 471–82.
43 Henderson, *Life*, II, 668.
44 Adler, *Briefwechsel*, 255–63, 272–8, 354–8. Steenson, *Kautsky*, 116–31.
45 Adler, *Briefwechsel*, 289, 258–63.
46 ibid., 273.
47 *Kongress Amsterdam* 1904, 40.
48 Droz, *Geschichte*, IV, 107ff.
49 Kautsky, *Sozialisten*, 315. *Bebels Briefwechsel*, 437–41, 446–50. Carroll, *Germany*, 317.
50 *Perepiska*, I, 189, 192–7.
51 Adler, *Briefwechsel*, 265–8.
52 ibid., 301, 305, 355. *Perepiska*, II, 72.

53 *Perepiska*, II, 60. Adler, *Briefwechsel*, 309. Schitlowsky, 'Polemik', 279. See also: Weill, *Marxistes*, 103–22. Nettl, *Luxemburg*, 149–247. Zeman, *Merchant*, 38–49. *Bebels Briefwechsel*, xxxiii, 139.

54 *Perepiska*, II, 69, 74. Adler, *Briefwechsel*, 268, 292.

55 *Soc. dem. dviženie v Rossii*, 49.

56 Bernstein, *Voraussetzungen*, 168ff.

57 Adler, *Briefwechsel*, 330.

58 See: Geyer, *Lenin*, 124–68. Ascher, *Axelrod*, 140–67. Baron, *Plekhanov*, 186–207.

59 Bernstein, *Voraussetzungen*, 169–70. *Perepiska*, II, 72–3.

60 *Perepiska*, II, 87–8, 116–17, 135–6. *Soc. dem. dviženie v Rossii*, 72–3, 360 notes 255 and 256.

61 *Compte rendu Paris* 1900, 181. *Soc. dem. dviženie v Rossii*, 75.

62 *Kongress Paris* 1900, 17, 18, 24.

63 See: Brachmann, *Sozialdemokraten*, 1–52.

64 *Soc. dem. dviženie v Rossii*, 75, 82, 362 note 275, 363 notes 312 and 314. Adler, *Briefwechsel*, 333–7. Troelstra, *Gedenkschriften*, II, 80, 223–4. Ascher, *Axelrod*, 173.

65 *Soc. dem. dviženie v Rossii*, 80. Lenin, *Werke*, XXXIV, 42. *Pis'ma*, 20–1.

66 *Soc. dem. dviženie v Rossii*, 79–80. *Pis'ma*, 19–21. Martov, *Geschichte*, 60–1. Burch, 'Unrest', 368ff., 430ff.

67 Kautsky–Aksel'rod, 25 V 1901 (Axelrod Archive, IISG). Ferry–Serwy, 6 IV 1901 and Turati–Serwy, 6-12 IV 1901 (Huysmans Archive, Antwerp). Haupt, *Bureau*, 27–9. Geyer, *Lenin*, 223 note 7. Heering, 'Turati', 115.

68 Kautsky, 'Bewegung'.

69 Weill, *Marxistes*, 141–57. Luxemburg, *Briefe*, 198–207.

70 *Pis'ma*, 39–40. *Soc. dem. dviženie v Rossii*, 82, 364 note 318. Sapir, *Dan letters*, 49. Luxemburg, *Lettres*, II, 86. Weill, *Marxistes*, 150.

71 Weill, *Marxistes*, 155. *Soc. dem. dviženie v Rossii*, 98. *Pis'ma*, 74–8. Luxemburg, *Werke*, I(2), 281.

72 Geyer, 'Parteispaltung', 196–7.

73 Luxemburg, *Werke*, I/2, 275–80.

74 Elwood, *Resolutions*, 51–2. Pearce, 1903. *Second Congress*, 20–1, 186, 466–70. Frankel, *Akimov*, 163–4. Lenin, *Werke*, V, 431–5.

75 *Soc. dem. dviženie v Rossii*, 100.

76 Zassulitch, 'Strömung', 329.

77 ibid. See also: *Pis'ma*, 58–74. *Soc. dem. dviženie v Rossii*, 89–98. *Perepiska*, II, 273–82. Dan, *Proischoždenie*, 266ff. Ascher, *Axelrod*, 173–83.

78 Rusanov, *Emigracii*, 264–5.

79 For descriptions of the congress see: Wolfe, *Three*, 263–83. Schapiro, *Party*, 48–54. For a translation of the minutes see: Pearce, *1903. Second Congress.*

80 Frankel, *Akimov.*

81 Aksel'rod, 'Ob'edinenie'. For a translation see: Ascher, *Mensheviks*, 48–52. For a detailed discussion see: Ascher, *Axelrod*, 196–202.

82 Kautsky, 'Wahlkreis', 39. Lenin, *Werke*, V, 477–8 and VII, 401–57. Cf: Reisberg, *Lenins Beziehungen*, 41–59. Wollschläger, 'Lenins Verhältnis', 31–66.

83 Adler, *Briefwechsel*, 381. In 1909 Kautsky is even gloomier: ibid., 500–2. See also: Steenson, *Kautsky*, 127–31. Salvadori, *Kautsky*, 84–90.

84 Geyer, 'Parteispaltung'. Ascher, 'Axelrod and Kautsky'. Weill, *Marxistes*, 123–40. Zeman, *Merchant*, 60–4.

85 Kautsky, 'Allerhand', 623–4.

86 Haupt, *Bureau*, 100.

87 *Leben für den Sozialismus*, 89.

88 *Soc. dem. dviženie v Rossii*, 124–5. See also: ibid., 108–22.

89 Geyer, 'Parteispaltung', 211.

90 Luxemburg, 'Organisationsfragen', 484–5, 492.

91 ibid., 532.

92 ibid., 485.

93 See: Nettl, *Luxemburg*, 253–88. Strobel, *Partei*, 151–203.

94 Manacorda, *Rivoluzione*, 193. Manakorda, 'Otkliki', 105–7. Baynac, *Socialistes révolutionnaires*, 348–9. Hildermeier, *Partei*, 360, 407. Rusanov, *Emigracii*, 251. *La Tribune Russe* (1904, no. 4) 51 and (Nov.–Dec. 1906, nos. 119–22) 1–11.

95 Haupt, *Bureau*, 72–3, 78.

96 Ferri–Serwy, 30 VI 1903 (Huysmans Archive, Antwerp). Haupt, *Bureau*, 81–2. *Congrès Amsterdam* 1904, 100. Manacorda, *Rivoluzione*, 194–8. Manakorda, 'Otkliki', 108–11. Lowe, *Policy*, 100–1.

97 Haupt, *Bureau*, 75–6.

98 *La Tribune Russe* (1904, nos. 12–13) 168.

99 Rusanov, *Emigracii*, 210, 213–6, 271–2. *Het Volk*, 17 VIII 1904 and 18 VIII 1904.

100 Brachmann, *Sozialdemokraten*, 40, 51.

101 *Soc. dem. dviženie v Rossii*, 116.

102 Eisner, *Geheimbund*. Weill, *Marxistes*, 216ff. Nettl, *Luxemburg*, 197. Trotnow, *Liebknecht*, 56–67.

103 Kautsky–Aksel'rod, 10 VI 1904 (Axelrod Archive, IISG). Garvi, *Vospominanija*, 397. Baynac, *Socialistes révolutionnaires*, 85–93. Pipes, *Struve*, I, 357–8.

104 *Soc. dem. dviženie v Rossii*, 131, 133. Martov, *Geschichte*, 95. Weill, *Marxistes*, 158–81.

105 Luxemburg, *Briefe*, 220–2. *La Tribune Russe* (1904) 242, 267–8, 283.

106 *La Tribune Russe* (1904) 127, 223.

107 Haupt, *Bureau*, 80.

108 ibid., 105–6, 108. *Sozialistische Monatshefte* (1904, 1) 232. *Die Neue Zeit*, XXII (1903–4, 1) 649–52. Hyndman, *Reminiscences*, 31–2. *Revue Socialiste* (1904, no. 231) 305–17 and (1904, no. 234) 679–95. *La Tribune Russe* (1904) 83. Manacorda, *Rivoluzione*, 198–204.

109 Martov, *Geschichte*, 92–5. Futrell, *Underground*, 66ff. *Het Volk*, 2 IV 1904 and 17 IV 1904. Haupt, *Bureau*, 107–8. *Kongress Amsterdam* 1904, 8.

110 De Leon, *Flashlights*, 19–20.

111 *Arbeiterpartei Russlands. Bericht* 1904.

112 *Het Volk*, 2 VI 1904. *Die Neue Zeit*, XXII (1904, 1) 740–2.

113 Lenin, *Werke*, VII, 542. Lydin, *Material. Raskol na II s' ezde. Istorii sozdanija.* Martov, *Geschichte*, 97. Plechanov, *Sočinenija*, XVI, 319–22.

114 *Tätigkeit Arbeiterbundes* 1904, 13–15.
115 *Russia. Report Russ. Soc. Rev. Party* 1904, 12. *Rapport Parti Soc. Rév.* 1904, 10, 16.
116 Haupt, *Bureau*, 106–7. Tobias, *Bund*, 278–80.
117 Ljadov, *Iz žizni.*
118 *Het Volk*, 17 VIII 1904. *Congrès Amsterdam* 1904, 146.
119 *Congrès Amsterdam* 1904, 138. *La Tribune Russe* (1904) 247–8.
120 Haupt, *Bureau*, 127.
121 *Congrès Amsterdam* 1904, 111, 182–3.
122 *Kongress Amsterdam* 1904, 32. *Het Volk*, 18 VIII 1904 and 19 VIII 1904. *Protokoll Parteitages Bremen* 1904, 311.

### 4 1905: A FAILED REVOLUTION IN RUSSIA

1 'Bij het nieuwe jaar', *Het Volk*, 3 I 1905.
2 Cited by Adams, 'Reactions', 174.
3 Reichard, 'Working class', 138.
4 'Revolutie', *Het Volk*, 27 I 1905.
5 *Perepiska*, II, 207. 'Otraženie', 41. Thomson, *Crusade*, 30–1. Domnič, 'Načalo', 88.
6 Cited by Adams, 'Reactions', 177. See also: Holt, 'Liberals', 212–17.
7 Lauridzen, 'Revolution', 59–60. Holt, *Liberals*, 28. *Het Volk*, 9 X 1905.
8 Northcutt, 'Evaluations', 88ff.
9 Kappeler, 'Öffentlichkeit', 401. Spector, *Revolution*, 61–2, 94. Mnuchina, 'Pod'em', 348. 'Vil'gel'm II'. Stern, *Revolution*, 2/III, 59. Stern, *Auswirkungen*, 2/I, 19–21. Mühlpfordt, 'Weltwirkung'.
10 'Otraženie', 35. Stern, *Auswirkungen*, 2/I. Stern, *Revolution*, 2/III, 83. Lauridzen, 'Revolution', 37, 39, 41. Northcutt, 'Evaluations', 69–70, 76, 81–2.
11 Stern, *Revolution*, 2/III, 17, 26, 28.
12 Luxemburg, 'Die Revolution', 573.
13 ibid., 573, 576.
14 Luxemburg, *Werke*, I/2, 505.
15 Stern, *Revolution*, 2/III, 148.
16 Calwer, 'Russland', 113.
17 Bernstein, 'Revolutionen'. See also: Meyer, 'Revolution'.
18 Gumplowicz, 'Kaisertum', 231.
19 *La Tribune Russe* (1905, no. 31) 452.
20 Stainbrook, 'La presse', 50–8. *La Tribune Russe* (1905, no. 28) 376. Geyer, 'Parteispaltung', 428–9. *Het Volk*, 21 I 1905, 21 II 1905, 20, 21 and 25 I 1906. Hyndman, *Reminiscences*, 384.
21 Northcutt, 'Evaluations', 91.
22 *Vorwärts*, 30 III 1905. Also in: *Het Volk*, 9 IV 1905. Cf.: Geyer, 'Parteispaltung', 437.
23 Ascher, *Axelrod*, 223–9. Geyer, 'Parteispaltung', 418–44.
24 Luxemburg, *Werke*, I/2, 515–22. *Het Volk*, 19 II 1905. See also: *Het Volk*, 18, 19 and 20 I 1906.
25 Stern, *Revolution*, 2/III, 33–7, 167–18. Wolfe, *Three*, 342–4. Lenin, *Werke*, VIII, 413–8. Haupt, *Bureau*, 133–4. *Het Volk*, 26 II 1905.

26 *La Tribune Russe* (1905, no. 28) 386 and (1905, no. 29) 432–3.

27 Stern, *Revolution*, 2/III, 169–70.

28 Kautsky, 'Differenzen'.

29 *La Tribune Russe* (1905, no. 31) 442–6.

30 Stern, *Auswirkungen*, 2/I, 235, 294-295 and 2/II 43–59, 68–9. Brachmann, *Sozialdemokraten*, 65–6. Fischer, *Sozialdemokratie*, 122–4. 'De revolution-aire babbelaar', *Het Volk*, 25 I 1906. Brautigam, *Havens*, 107–12. Stampfer, *Erfahrungen*, 104. *La Tribune Russe. Serv. de rens. rap.*, 30 IX 1906. *La Tribune Russe* (1908, no. 8) 1–15 and (1908, nos. 9–10) Supplément.

31 Vaillant mentioned on 24 June 1908 in the Chambre des Députés figures from Russian sources on the number of people sentenced to death: in 1906 – 1,292, in 1907 – 1,692, in 1908 – 901. Of these sentences 44% were executed, which means that 1,700 people were killed. The remaining condemned were pardoned. The number of victims of revolutionary terror in 1905–7, however, is estimated at more than 4,000. See: *La Tribune Russe* (1908, no. 7) 3–8. See also: Kropotkin, *Terror*, 33-39. Avrich, *Anarchists*, 64. Riasanovsky, *History*, 458. Riha, 'Developments', 103.

32 Stainbrook, 'La presse', 168–75.

33 For the amounts of money collected by the Dutch and other parties, see: Haupt, *Bureau*, 365–8. See also: *Perepiska*, II, 210. The distribution of these sums among the Russian parties was the cause of fierce quarrels.

34 *Het Volk*, 31 X 1905, 8–9 XI 1905, 28 XII 1905, 6–7 I 1906.

35 *Het Volk*, 21 I 1906.

36 *Het Volk*, 21 I 1906. Haupt, *Bureau*, 181–91, 343.

37 *Het Volk*, 24 I 1906.

38 *Het Volk*, 3, 13 and 22 III 1906.

39 Cited by Julliard, *Pelloutier*, 64.

40 Rüter, *Spoorwegstaking*, 543ff.

41 Vliegen, *Kracht*, II, 39–40, 49–50.

42 Roland Holst, *Vuur*, 116–27, 149–50. Roland Holst, *Geschiedenis*, 198ff.

43 Pannekoek, *Herinneringen*, 126–7, 137.

44 Roland Holst, *Werkstaking*, 6, 136.

45 ibid., 164–5.

46 ibid., xii.

47 ibid., 174–5.

48 Parvus 'Staatsstreich'. See also: Grunenberg, *Massenstreikdebatte*, 46–95. Zeman, *Merchant*, 35.

49 Hilferding, 'Parlementarismus'.

50 *Vorwärts*, 25 VI 1905. *Die Neue Zeit*, XXIII (1905, 2) 309–16, 494, 684, 781. See also: Stern, *Revolution*, 2/III, 296–334.

51 *Die Neue Zeit*, XXIII (1905, 2) 492–9, 681–93, 776–85. Stern, *Revolution*, 2/IV, 613–21. Steenson, *Kautsky*, 138–51.

52 *Sozialistische Monatshefte* (1905, 2) 754ff. Stern, *Revolution*, 2/IV, 626, 63–4.

53 Adler, *Briefwechsel*, 468.

54 ibid.

55 *Protokoll Jena* 1905, 298.

56 ibid., 320–1, 328.

57 ibid., 141–2.
58 Roland Holst, *Luxemburg*, 308–9. Roland Holst, *Werkstaking*, 195.
59 Stern, *Revolution*, 2/IV, 683–91, 697. Stern, *Auswirkungen*, 2/II, 137–255.
60 Pannekoek, *Herinneringen*, 127, 177.
61 Luxemburg, *Werke*, II, 144.
62 Stern, *Revolution*, 2/VI, 1676–740.
63 Luxemburg, *Werke*, II, 172. See also: *Protokoll Mannheim* 1906, 261.
64 Elm, 'Gewerkschaftsdebatte', 830.
65 Stern, *Revolution*, 2/VI, 1800–8. See for instance: Schorske, *German social democracy*, 49–53.
66 *Arbeiterzeitung*, 12 X 1905. Luxemburg, *Briefe*, 236–7. Adler, *Briefwechsel*, 471–2.
67 Cited by Adams, 'Reactions', 173.
68 Adams, 'Reactions', 182. Kendall, *Movement*, 79–80. *Revoljucija* 1905–7, II, 178–9.
69 *Revoljucija* 1905–7, II 181–205. Futtrell, *Underground*, 35–8.
70 Manacorda, *Rivoluzione*, 193–288.
71 See: Northcutt, 'Evaluations'. Lauridzen, 'Revolution'. Stainbrook, 'La presse'.
72 See Gorter's debate with the *Volksdagblad*: *Het Volk*, 10, 15 XII 1905 and 16, 18 I 1906 and 2, 20 II 1906.
73 Wiardi Beckman, *Syndicalisme*
74 Charzat, *Sorel*. Barth, *Masse und Mythos*. Horowitz, *Radicalism*.
75 Sorel, *Réflexions* (1908), 133.
76 Sorel, *Réflexions* (1972), 375–89.
77 Lagardelle, *Grève*, 384–6.
78 Lenskij, 'Voprosu', 150. Lensky's thesis is unintentionally confirmed by: Ivanova, *Lenin*.
79 Fischer, 'Lenin', 388–9. Fischer, *Sozialdemokratie*, 16–22. *La Tribune Russe* (1904, nos. 18–19) 247–8.
80 *Nasledie*, 175–8.
81 Plechanov, *Sočinenija*, XVI, 347–52. Roland Gol'st, *Stačka*. Lagardell', *Stačka*. Lenskij, 'Voprosu', 152–3.
82 Sapir, *Dan letters*, 147, 152. See also: Weber, 'Zur Lage', 346 note 90a.
83 Pearce, 1903. *Second Congress*, 170–1.
84 *Pis'ma*, 146.
85 Sapir, *Dan letters*, 165–7.
86 Engelstein, 'Moscow', 445.
87 For more details see: Fischer, *Sozialdemokratie*. Larsson, *Theories*. Mehringer, *Revolution*. Ascher, *Mensheviks*, 53–70. Carr, *History*, 38ff. Getzler, 'Revolutionaries'. Schwarz, *Revolution* 1905, 1–28, 246ff. Keep, *Rise*, 183–264. Dan, *Proischoždenie*, 375ff. See also: Ascher, *The revolution*. McDaniel, *Autocracy*. Suhr, *1905*.

### 5 INTERMEZZO 1906–1918

1 See: Mendel, 'On interpreting'. Naarden, 'Revolutie'.
2 Weber, 'Russlands Übergang'. Weber, 'Zur Lage'. For Weber's very traditional and German ideas about Russia, see: Baumgarten, *Weber*,

662–5. See also: Schultz, 'Verfassungsrecht'. Szeftel, *Russian constitution*, 339ff.

3  Stern, *Revolution*, 2/IV, 769–837. Stainbrook, 'La presse', 125–9.

4  Mackenzie Wallace, *Russia*, 51. Riha, *European*, 140-1. Pipes, *Struve*, II, 14.

5  See: *Het Volk*, 2 XI 1905 and 7 XII 1905. See also note 3.

6  Martoff, 'Die erste Epoche'. Martoff, 'De eerste periode'.

7  Sapir, *Dan letters*, 160.

8  *Pis'ma*, 132, 136. Luxemburg, *Briefe*, 236. Stern, *Revolution*, 2/IV, 539–41. *La Tribune Russe*, Serv. de rens. rapide, 24 X 1905.

9  See: Schapiro, *Party*, 72ff.

10  Bernstein, 'Fragen', 217.

11  Stern, *Revolution*, 2/VI, 1617–9. Kautsky, 'Duma', 241ff. Sapir, *Dan letters*, 169–76. Haupt, *Bureau*, 210.

12  Haupt, *Bureau*, 214.

13  ibid., 212–13.

14  ibid., 222.

15  *Het Volk*, 16 II 1906.

16  Haupt, *Correspondance*, 10. Haupt, *Bureau*, 231. See also: Wolfe, *Three*, 439ff.

17  Ascher, *Axelrod*, 244ff.

18  'Mnenie'.

19  The German text of this introduction, in: *Die Neue Zeit*, XXIII (1905, 1) 670–7. See also: Adler, *Briefwechsel*, 105. Steenson, *Kautsky*, 104–11. Hussain, *Marxism*, 102–32.

20  Lewitin, 'Das Jahr 1907', 167. Cf.: Sapir, *Dan letters*, 152.

21  *Nasledie*, 179–80.

22  Kautsky, 'Triebkräfte', 330–1.

23  ibid., 332.

24  ibid., 331–2.

25  Lenin, 'Predislovie', 1.

26  ibid., 4.

27  Plechanov, *Sočinenija*, 295–302.

28  Martov, 'Kautskij', 11.

29  ibid., 18.

30  ibid., 23.

31  Haupt, *Bureau*, 232–9. Stern, *Revolution*, 2/VI, 1624ff. Roobol, *Tsereteli*, 32–65.

32  *Perepiska*, II, 228–9, 241. Schapiro, *Party*, 86ff.

33  Luxemburg, *Werke*, II, 224.

34  ibid., 213.

35  Sapir, *Dan letters*, 178–9.

36  Elwood, *Social democracy*, 25ff.

37  Schapiro, *Party*, 97–101.

38  *Ternii bez roz*, 105–17. Haupt, *Bureau*, 261, 267–8. *La Tribune Russe* (1907, nos. 2, 3 and 4).

39  *Bericht Stuttgart 1907*, 5, 13, 19–20, 69–70, 74–7. *Congrès Stuttgart 1907*, 401.

40  Deutsch, *Lockspitzel*, 17. *La Tribune Russe* (1908, nos. 2–3) 31–2. *Kongress* *Stuttgart* 1907, 31–2. Trotzki, *Mein Leben*, 193.
41  Brachmann, *Sozialdemokraten*, 72ff. Wolfe, *Three*, 418–49.
42  *Pis'ma*, 175. *Soc. dem. dviženie v Rossii*, 175. Stern, *Auswirkungen*, 2/I, 295.
43  Sapir, *Dan letters*, 189. *Pis'ma*, 176. Schapiro, *Party*, 108–9.
44  Brachmann, *Sozialdemokraten*, 76. *Perepiska*, II, 257. Krupskaya, *Memories*, 152. Wolfe, *Three*, 444.
45  Sapir, *Dan letters*, 179–86. See also: Ascher, *Mensheviks*, 38–41.
46  Sapir, *Dan letters*, 188–9. Parvus, 'Lage'. Trotzki, 'Arbeiterdeputiertenrat'. Trotzki, 'Duma'. Trotzki, 'Marxismus'. Martoff, 'Staatsstreich'.
47  Sapir, *Dan letters*, 188.
48  Dan, 'Bedingungen', 56.
49  *Pis'ma*, 185–6 note 1. Sapir, *Dan letters*, 203.
50  Maletzki, 'Liberalismus', 556.
51  Sapir, *Dan letters*, 207.
52  Tscherewanin, *Proletariat*, vii, ix–xvi. Sapir, *Dan letters*, 211–12.
53  Tscherewanin, *Proletariat*, 92.
54  ibid., xv. Trotzki, 'Proletariat', 791. Sapir, *Dan letters*, 211, 214. *Der Kampf* (Sept.–Oct. 1908) 25–33. *De Nieuwe Tijd*, XIII (1908) 821–8.
55  Hildermeier, *Partei*, 309–402. Nikolajewsky, *Asew. La Tribune Russe* (1909, nos. 7 and 8). Haupt, *Correspondance*, 68–9. *Bureau Soc. Int. Aux comités. Bericht Kopenhagen* 1910, 13ff.
56  Deutsch, *Lockspitzel*, 36. Luxemburg, *Werke*, II, 264–8. N.R. [N. Rjasanoff], 'Der Fall Asew'.
57  Trotzki, 'Die verdorbene Suppe'. See also: *Die Neue Zeit*, XXVII (1909, 2) 184–7.
58  *Het Volk*, 23 I 1909 and 25 II 1909.
59  *L'Humanité*, 23 I 1909, 4 and 9 II 1909. Longuet, *Terroristes et policiers*. Bernstein, *L'affaire Azeff*.
60  Trotzki, 'Proletariat', 782. Rjasanoff, 'Marx über den Ursprung'.
61  See: Geyer, *Kautsky's Dossier*.
62  Trotzki, *Russland. Die Neue Zeit*, XXVIII (1910) 934–42. *Der Kampf* (1911, no. 4) 503–11. *De Nieuwe Tijd*, XV (1910) 503–14. Geyer, *Kautsky's Dossier*, Docs. 19, 21, 25 and 27.
63  Luxemburg, *Briefe*, 265–6.
64  Deutscher, *Prophet*, 183. Nettl, *Luxemburg*, 359.
65  *Kongress Stuttgart* 1907, 97.
66  Adler, *Briefwechsel*, 510.
67  *Nasledie*, 186–7.
68  Cited by Nettl, *Luxemburg*, 416–17.
69  Kautsky, 'Strategie'.
70  Luxemburg, *Werke*, II, 295, 325–6, 335–40, 353, 387–402.
71  Luxemburg, 'Ermattung', 263ff.
72  Kautsky, 'Was nun?', 35.
73  Kautsky, 'Zwischen Baden'.
74  Luxemburg, 'Die Theorie', 570–1, 573.
75  *Pis'ma*, 262.
76  Martoff, 'Diskussion', 907.

77 ibid., 908.
78 ibid., 919.
79 *Pis'ma*, 203.
80 Steenson, *Kautsky*, 257 note 2, 275 note 18. Kautsky Jr, 'Vorwort', xli–xlvi.
81 Radek, 'Erklärung', 27. Karski [Marschlevski], 'Missverständnis', 101, 103. Geyer, *Kautsky's Dossier*, 78ff.
82 Geyer, *Kautsky's Dossier*, 101ff. Ascher, *Axelrod*, 276.
83 Martov, *Spasiteli*. Getzler, *Martov*, 133–4.
84 Geyer, *Kautsky's Dossier*, Doc. 74. Laschitza, *Deutsche Linke*, 100.
85 Trotnow, *Liebknecht*, 62ff, 137ff.
86 Trotnow, 'Liebknecht'.
87 Trotnow, *Liebknecht*, 183ff.
88 Grass, *Friedensaktivität*, 50ff. Marquand, *MacDonald*, 164ff.
89 See: Haupt, *Socialism and the Great War*. Haimson, 'Problem of stability'. Mendel, 'Peasant and worker'. Schapiro, *Party*, 141–2. Elwood, 'Lenin'. Geyer, *Kautsky's Dossier*, 228ff. Gankin, *Bolsheviks*, 88–133. Haupt, 'Lénine', 389ff.
90 Swain, *Social democracy*.
91 Seton-Watson, *Italy*, 393–5. See also: Mitchell, *Labor movement* and Haimson, *Strikes*.
92 *Soc. dem. dviženie v Rossii*, 228.
93 See: Schapiro, *Party*, 143ff. Dvinov, *Pervaja mirovaja vojna*. Shaw, 'Nashe Slovo Group'. Wolfe, *Ideology*, 104–18.
94 Grass, *Friedensaktivität*, 69–70.
95 Ascher, *Axelrod*, 304ff. Grass, *Friedensaktivität*, 71–3.
96 See also: Drachkovitch, *Les socialismes*.
97 See: Fainsod, *International socialism*. Blänsdorf, *Zweite Internationale*. Kirby, *War*.
98 See: Seen, *Revolution*. Deutscher, *Prophet*, 211ff.
99 Kautsky, *Sozialisten*, 540ff. Blänsdorf, *Zweite Internationale*, 73–84, 204ff. Shaw, 'Nashe Slovo Group', 174ff. Lademacher, *Zimmerwalder Bewegung*.
100 See: Wade, *Search*. Stillig, *Februarrevolution*. Warth, *The Allies*. Slice, *International labor*. Kettle, *Allies*.
101 'The theory most widely accepted in America today is that the Bolsheviks won because they were the only well-organized, disciplined and intelligently led political group on the scene': Adams, *Revolution*, ix.
102 For the Mensheviks in 1917 see: Galili, *Menshevik leaders*. See also: Ferro, *Révolution de 1917. La chute*. Keep, *Revolution*. Cereteli, *Vospominanija*. Roobol, *Tsereteli*. Lande, 'Mensheviks'. Radkey, *Agrarian foes*. Rosenberg, *Liberals*. Rabinowitch, *Prelude*. Rabinowitch, *Bolsheviks come to power*. Koenker, *Moscow workers*. Schapiro, *1917*. Smith, *Red Petrograd*.

## 6 SOCIALIST EUROPE AND THE OCTOBER REVOLUTION
### 1918–1919

1 Peake, 'Impact', 146ff. Graubard, *Labour*, 45. Carroll, *Communism*, 1–20. Cohn, *Warrant*, 126–68. See also: Toynbee, 'Looking back'.
2 Cited by Döser, *Russland*, 43.

T

3 For quotations see: Döser, *Russland*, 99, 140, 43, 44, 103, 110. Mayer, *Politics*, 234, 260, 314, 334. See also: Foner, *Revolution*, 28ff.

4 Döser, *Russland*, 55ff. Haar, 'Menace'. Dupeux, *Stratégie*. Laqueur, *Russia*, 50ff. Murray, *Red-scare*, 210ff. Lasch, *Liberals*, 112.

5 Mayer, *Politics*, 29.

6 Foner, *Revolution*, 41.

7 See: Ferro, *L'Occident*. McInnes, 'The labour movement'.

8 Wolfe, 'Introduction'. Bezemer, *Revolutie*, 190ff. Rosenstone, *Revolutionary*, 278ff.

9 Fay, *Révolution*. Lindemann, *Red years*, 53ff. Drachkovitch, *Internationals*, 161ff. Lazitch, *Lenin*, 209, 467. Stoelinga, *Revolutie*, 100, 128, 153. Brinkman, *S.D.A.P.*, 3–11. Peake, 'Impact', 149–50, 166ff. Graubard, *Labour*, 46ff. Lösche, *Bolschewismus*, 100ff.

10 See: Schapiro, *Origin*, 147–209.

11 Jelen, *Aveuglement*, 23, 30, 33.

12 Lösche, *Bolchewismus*, 50, 56, 90, 122–3.

13 Kerensky, *Memoirs*, 489ff. Peake, 'Impact', 195–7. Wohl, *Communism*, 106. Graubard, *Labour*, 60ff. Fainsod, *Socialism*, 181, 188. Ritter, *Internationale*, 136, 154–5, 158–65. Jelen, *Aveuglement*, 37–8.

14 Ascher, *Axelrod*, 331ff.

15 Axelrod, Gavronsky, Roussanof, Soukhomline, 'An die sozialistischen Parteien aller Länder' (Kautsky Archive, IISG). Axelrod, *Revolution*, 159–68. See also: *Partis socialistes*. Ritter, *Internationale*, 138.

16 Ritter, *Internationale*, 138–9, 142–3, 155, 524.

17 Axelrod, *Revolution*, xxxvi, 158. See also: Aksel'rod, *Kto*.

18 Ascher, 'Axelrod', 106ff.

19 Steenson, *Kautsky*, 200ff. Kautsky, J. H., 'Introduction'.

20 Lösche, *Bolschewismus*, 122.

21 ibid., 123ff.

22 Kautsky, *Diktatur*, 4ff. For other editions see: Kautsky, *Dictatorship* and Lübbe, *Kautsky*.

23 Kautsky, *Diktatur*, 12.

24 ibid., 60, 20.

25 ibid., 21.

26 Lenin, *Keuze*, 149–51, 154–5, 157–9, 174–5.

27 ibid., 188–9.

28 ibid., 137, 139.

29 ibid., 190–1.

30 Liebknecht, *Aufzeichnungen*, 34. Lösche, *Bolschewismus*, 107–9. Trotnow, *Liebknecht*, 274ff. Nettl, *Luxemburg*, 656ff.

31 Luxemburg, *Revolution*, 50–5.

32 ibid., 59, 65.

33 ibid., 69, 73, 75.

34 ibid., 78–9.

35 Nettl, *Luxemburg*, 672ff.

36 Bourdet, *Bauer*. Leichter, *Bauer*. Amato, 'Bauer'. Croan, 'Prospects'. Bauer, *Werkausgabe*, I, 10. Sapir, *Dan letters*, xlvviii, l. Bauer–Aksel'rod, 28 IX 1917 (Axelrod Archive, IISG).

37 Weber, *Revolution*, 26.

38 Bauer, *Werkausgabe*, IX, 1039.

39 ibid., IX, 1041–4.

40 ibid., VIII, 931.

41 Bauer, 'Evropa'.

42 Bauer, 'Bolschewiki', 147.

43 ibid., 144–6.

44 Ritter, *Internationale*, 3ff. Braunthal, *Geschichte*, 167–8.

45 *Arbeiterzeitung*, 9 II 1919.

46 Ritter, *Internationale*, 18ff, 38ff. Graubard, *Labour*, 64ff. See also: Renaudel, *Internationale*. Braunthal, *Geschichte*, 168–74.

47 Ritter, *Internationale*, 828.

48 ibid., 67. See also: *Theses*, 25. Lazitch, *Lenin*, 52.

49 Ritter, *Internationale*, 212.

50 ibid., 218.

51 ibid., 54.

52 ibid., 787.

53 ibid., 199.

54 ibid., 208.

55 ibid., 209.

56 ibid., 270, 274, 285.

57 ibid., 500ff. Renaudel, *Internationale*, 125.

58 Ritter, *Internationale*, 507, 508.

59 ibid., 500–1.

60 ibid., 508, 510.

61 ibid., 518.

62 ibid., 523.

63 ibid., 524ff. *Arbeiterzeitung*, 11 II 1919. See: Axelrod, *Revolution*, 168–76. See also: P. Axelrod, *Zur Begründung der Anfrage der russ. Delegation auf der internat. soz. Konferenz in Bern* (Kautsky Archive, IISG). And: *Instruktion der ausserordentlichen Versammlung der Delegierten der Petersburger Fabriken und der nach Moskou entsandete Arbeiterdelegation* (Kautsky Archive, IISG).

64 Ritter, *Internationale*, 530.

65 ibid., 531. Lenin, *Sobranie*, XXXVII, 210, 220.

66 Ritter, *Internationale*, 533.

67 ibid., 534–68.

68 ibid., 853.

69 Braunthal, *Geschichte*, 201. Wohl, *Communism*, 117–22, 136–8.

70 Ritter, *Internationale*, 866–9.

71 ibid., 73, 595–6. *Labour Party. Report* (1919), 17–8, 26. See also: Axelrod, *Revolution*, 177–9.

72 Binštok–Aksel'rod, 3 V 1919 (Nic. Coll. Hoover Inst.).

73 Binštok–Aksel'rod, 8 V 1919 (Nic. Coll. Hoover Inst.).

74 See note 72.

75 Binštok–Aksel'rod, 27 V 1919 (Nic. Coll. Hoover Inst.).

76 Ritter, *Internationale*, 83, 611–12.

77 ibid., 626. *Vorwärts*, 8 VIII 1919.

78 Ritter, *Internationale*, 86, 623.
79 ibid., 627. See also: Hueting, *Troelstra*, 87–9. Hulst, *Vaandel*, 75–6.
80 Roobol, *Tsereteli*, 198ff.
81 *Vorwärts*, 11 VIII 1919. See also: *L'Humanité*, 6 VIII 1919.
82 Ritter, *Internationale*, 652–3, 666–7. *L'Humanité*, 9 VIII 1919 and 11 VIII 1919.
83 Ritter, *Internationale*, 655ff.
84 *Labour Party. Report* (1920), 81.
85 Cereteli–Aksel'rod, 2 XI 1919 (Axelrod Archive, IISG).
86 Aksel'rod–Ščupak, 25 X 1919 (Nic. Coll. Hoover Inst.).
87 Binštok–Aksel'rod, 20 V 1919 (Nic. Coll. Hoover Inst.). Stein, *Problem*. See also: Martov–Stein, 26 VI 1919 (Nic. Coll. Hoover Inst.).
88 Wohl, *Generation*.

7 SOCIAL DEMOCRACY IN SOVIET RUSSIA AND THE CONTINUATION OF THE DEBATE ABOUT COMMUNISM IN 1919–1920

1 *Novyj Luč*, 5 I 1918.
2 For descriptions of the situation after October 1917 see: Radkey, *Sickle*. Schapiro, *Origin*, 69ff. Rosenberg, *Liberals*, 263ff. Keep, *Revolution*, 249ff. Abramovitch, *Revolution*, 74ff. Burbank, 'Martov and Chernov'.
3 For the RSDRP after October 1917 see: Nikolaevskij, *Men'ševiki*. Haimson, *Mensheviks*, 43ff. Getzler, *Martov*, 168ff. Ascher, *Mensheviks*, 105ff.
4 Haimson, *Mensheviks*, 115–17. Aronson, *Dviženie*. Brügmann, *Gewerkschaften*, 113–22, 164, 201, 234–6, 267. Smith, *Red Petrograd*, 218. Getzler, *Martov*, 174.
5 Brovkin, 'Mensheviks' comeback'.
6 Haimson, *Mensheviks*, 136. Getzler, *Martov*, 179–80.
7 Brovkin, 'Mensheviks under attack'. Aronson, *Dviženie*. Haimson, *Mensheviks*, 150–1, 156ff. Abramovitch, *Revolution*, 156–67. Schapiro, *Origin*, 190–2. Getzler, *Martov*, 181–2.
8 Jansen, *Show trial*, 1–21.
9 Leggett, *Cheka*, 318–24, 359–60, 463–8.
10 See: Daniels, *Conscience*, 70ff. Lenin, *Studienausgabe*, II, 266.
11 Haimson, *Mensheviks*, 191ff. Ascher, 'Russian Marxism', 403ff.
12 Fischer, *Soviets*, 114–21.
13 Haimson, *Mensheviks*, 196ff.
14 *Pravda*, 20 II 1919.
15 Ransome, *Russia*, 156. *Pravda*, 6 II 1919. See also: *Theses*, 14, 22ff.
16 Ransome, *Russia*, 158–9.
17 *Petrogradskaja Pravda*, 23 II 1919 and 28 II 1919. See also: Ritter, *Internationale*, 71–3.
18 *Pravda*, 28 II 1919.
19 *Vsegda Vperëd*, 25 II 1919. *Rabočij Internacional*, 11 II 1919. Both papers in: Nicolaevsky Collection of Extracts from Mensheviks' Newspapers, Hoover Inst.

20 Haimson, *Mensheviks*, 196ff.
21 Kautsky, *Terrorismus*, 9.
22 ibid., 10–34.
23 ibid., 39–40.
24 ibid., 59–61.
25 ibid., 66.
26 ibid., 97, 100.
27 ibid., 102.
28 ibid., 106–7.
29 ibid., 132.
30 ibid., 137.
31 ibid., 152.
32 ibid., 146.
33 Cf: Lösche, *Bolschewismus*, 121, 124–5, 173, 250, 257, 284.
34 Troelstra, *Gedenkschriften*, IV, 320. Hueting, *Troelstra*, 125.
35 Trotsky, *Terrorism*, 7–8.
36 ibid., 28–42.
37 ibid., 43.
38 ibid., 48.
39 ibid., 50.
40 ibid., 74.
41 ibid., 10, 18.
42 ibid., xxxvii–xlvii.
43 Bauer, *Werkausgabe*, IX, 1069.
44 Braunthal, *Geschichte*, 154ff.
45 Bauer, *Werkausgabe*, IX, 1069.
46 Bauer, *Bolschewismus*, 7ff.
47 ibid., 53, 63–4.
48 ibid., 64ff.
49 ibid., 71, 69, 63.
50 ibid., 50.
51 ibid., 72ff.
52 ibid., 81ff.
53 ibid., 109ff.
54 Trotsky, *Terrorism*, 178. Trotzki, *Grundfragen*, 428–35.
55 Kautsky, 'Schrift', 261–2.
56 Radek, *Dictatorship*.
57 Radek, *Questions*, 3–4. Text resolutions of the RSDRP in: *Sbornik resoljucij*. See also: Ascher, *Mensheviks*, 111–17.
58 Haimson, *Mensheviks*, 180–2, 193–6, 210–7.
59 *Sbornik resoljucij*, 17–18.
60 Martov–Aksel'rod, 23 I 1920 (Nic. Coll. Hoover Inst.).
61 Martov–Kautsky, 23 I 1920 (Nic. Coll. Hoover Inst.).
62 For Martov's writings in this period see: Bourguina, *Social democracy*, 243–50.
63 *Martov*, 49.
64 Cereteli–Aksel'rod, 1 IX 1919 (Axelrod Archive, IISG).

65 Martov, *Bolchevisme*, 31.
66 ibid., 31–47.
67 ibid., 45–6.
68 ibid., 64.
69 ibid., 79ff.
70 ibid., 88–91.
71 ibid., 74–6, 92–105.
72 ibid., 107ff.
73 ibid., 112–24.
74 ibid., 124–71.
75 *Sbornik resoljucij*, 24–5. Ascher, *Axelrod*, 358ff. Haimson, *Mensheviks*, 228ff.
76 *Labour Delegation Report*, 5.
77 *Labour Party. Report* (1920), 4, 51.
78 Coates, *History*, 1–25. *Labour Delegation Report*, 63. Graubard, *Labour*, 83ff.
79 Aronson, 'Angličane', 331–2. Dan, *Dva goda*, 7. Graubard, *Labour*, 211ff.
80 Axelrod, *Revolution*, 181. Abramovič, 'Men'ševiki', 15–16.
81 Martov–Stein, 26 III 1920 (Nic. Coll. Hoover Inst.).
82 Goldschmidt, *Moskou* 1920, 51–3. Aronson, 'Angličane', 334. See also: *Pravda*, 19 V 1920.
83 Text speech Abramovič in: *Social-demokratija*, 54–7.
84 Dan, *Dva goda*, 9.
85 Aronson, 'Angličane', 335.
86 Martov–Aksel'rod, 30 V 1920 (Nic. Coll. Hoover Inst.).
87 Aronson, 'Angličane', 336.
88 Dan, *Dva goda*, 11.
89 *Labour Delegation Report*, 63–5. Aronson, 'Angličane', 337–9.
90 Legett, *Cheka*, 232–3. *Labour Delegation Report*, 55–7.
91 Martov–Aksel'rod, 30 V 1920 (Nic. Coll. Hoover Inst.).
92 *Labour Delegation Report*, 72. *An appeal of the Moscow Printers' Union to the international proletariat* (Rus/SOK/112, Labour Party Archive, London). *Protest of prisoners confined in the Taganskaia Prison in Moscow* (Portugeis Archive, IISG). See also: Haimson, *Mensheviks*, 227–8.
93 Graubard, *Labour*, 196, 197, 200.
94 *Labour Delegation Report*, 72. See also: Carroll, *Communism*, 170–4.
95 Martov–Aksel'rod, 30 V 1920 (Nic. Coll. Hoover Inst.).
96 Letters of Russian social democrats in London to Foreign Delegation RSDRP, 12 XII 1920 and 30 I 1921 (Portugeis Archive, IISG). (These Mensheviks were not acknowledged by Martov as party members. Such conflicts weakened the protests of the Russian socialists in the West.) See also: 'Labour Party and Krassin. "Broken Faith" charge answered', *Daily Herald*, 29 I 1921. 'Sčastlivoe stečenie obstojatel'stv' and 'Soveckaja vlast' i rabočie', *Socialističeskij Vestnik*, 16 II 1921.
97 Snowden wrote in her book that the Mensheviks occupied a quarter of the seats in the Soviet of Moscow and referred to 'the great Menshevik Tchernoff': Snowden, *Russia*, 142, 160. Russell, *Bolshevism*. Guest, *Struggle*. See also: Carroll, *Communism*, 16–18. Graubard, *Labour*, 217ff.
98 Lenin's judgement in: Eudin, *Soviet Russia*, 53–4.

99 For the Second Congress of the Comintern see: Lazitch, *Lenin*, 271ff. Braunthal, *Geschichte*, 186ff. Lindemann, *Red years*, 148ff. *Theses*, 61ff.
100 Sokolov, *Voyage*, 16–17.
101 Martov–Kautsky, 27 VI 1920 (Nic. Coll. Hoover Inst.).
102 Martov–Merrheim, 26 V 1920 (Nic. Coll. Hoover Inst.). See also Nic. Coll. for the French translation of this letter in *L'Information Ouvrière et Sociale*. The letter was also published in Russian: 'Bol'ševizm i sindikaty' (Pis'mo Martova Mergejmu. Moskva, 26 V 1920), *Volja Rossii*, 23 IX 1920.
103 *An den Vorstand der Unabhängigen Sozialdemokratischen Partei Deutschlands* (Nic. Coll. Hoover Inst.). See also: Martov–Kautsky, 27 VI 1920 (Nic. Coll. Hoover Inst.).
104 Lindemann, *Red years*, 162ff.
105 *A la délégation des camarades italiens*, 14 VI 1920 (Nic. Coll. Hoover Inst.).
106 *Les socialistes et le mouvement ouvrier sous la terreur bolchevik*, Moscow, July 1920 (Nic. Coll. Hoover Inst.).
107 Martov–Kautsky, 27 VI 1920 (Nic. Coll. Hoover Inst.).
108 Lindemann, 'Impressions', 44. See also: 'Ital'janskij kommunist o politike III Internacional ( Iz pis'ma Serrati k Leninu)', *Socialističeskij Vestnik*, 1 II 1921. Gruber, *Communism*, 247–9.
109 Martov–Kautsky, 27 VI 1920 (Nic. Coll. Hoover Inst.).
110 Lindemann, *Red years*, 196ff, 211ff. Krispin, 'Pamjati'.
111 *An den Vorstand der Unabhängigen Sozialdemokratischen Partei Deutschlands* (Nic. Coll. Hoover Inst.).
112 Martov–Aksel'rod, 4 VIII 1920 (Nic. Coll. Hoover Inst.).
113 Krispin, 'Pamjati'.
114 See note 112.
115 See note 109.
116 Martov–Aksel'rod, 27 VIII 1920 (Nic. Coll. Hoover Inst.).
117 Nikolaevskij, 'Stranicy'.
118 *Martov*, 105.

8 1920–1921: DIVISION IN THE WEST, UPRISING AND FAMINE IN RUSSIA

1 See: Braunthal, *Geschichte*, 178–9. *Report Conf. Labour Party*, 228–9.
2 *Arbeiterzeitung*, 1 VIII 1920. *Het Volk*, 9 VIII 1920 and 10 VIII 1920.
3 *Het Volk*, 5 VIII 1920.
4 ibid.
5 Hueting, *Troelstra*, 136ff. Troelstra, *Gedenkschriften*, IV, 312ff. Wibaut, *Levensbouw*, 395ff.
6 Brojdo–Aksel'rod, 29 V 1920, 16 VI 1920 and 23 VI 1920 (Axelrod Archive, IISG).
7 Brojdo–Aksel'rod, 15 VIII 1920 (Axelrod Archive, IISG).
8 Brojdo–Aksel'rod, 30 VIII 1920 (Axelrod Archive, IISG).
9 *Freiheit*, 4 IX 1920. Cf. Lindemann, *Red years*, 225–8.
10 *Arbeiterzeitung*, 6 IX 1920. See also: Brojdo–Aksel'rod, 15 IX 1920 (Axelrod Archive IISG).

11 Martov–Aksel'rod, 10 X 1920 (Axelrod Archive, IISG).
12 Wheeler, 'Party', 750–1. Wheeler, *USPD*, 259ff. Lazitch, *Lenin*, 425ff. Lindemann, *Red years*, 250ff.
13 Martov–Aksel'rod, 17 X 1920 (Axelrod Archive, IISG). *Protokoll Parteitages Halle*, 68, 127–8.
14 *Protokoll Parteitages Halle*, 145.
15 ibid., 156.
16 ibid., 166–8.
17 Martov–Aksel'rod, 17 X 1920 (Axelrod Archive, IISG).
18 Lösche, *Bolschewismus*, 267 note 60.
19 *Protokoll Parteitages Halle*, 179ff.
20 ibid., 184, 193, 196.
21 See note 17.
22 *Protokoll Parteitages Halle*, 208ff.
23 ibid., 214.
24 ibid., 215.
25 ibid., 217.
26 See note 17.
27 *Protokoll Parteitages Halle*, 218.
28 ibid., 230.
29 This did not happen. Martov's speech was published as a special Russian pamphlet: Martov, *Bol'ševizm*.
30 Zinov'ev, *Dvenadcat' dnej*, 76–7. See also: Zinoviev, *Douze jours*.
31 ibid., 54–5.
32 Martov, 'Antwort'.
33 *Freiheit*, 18 X 1920.
34 See note 17.
35 ibid.
36 *Protokoll Parteitages Halle*, 230. Zinov'ev, *Dvenadcat' dnej*, 52. See also: Geyer, *Illusion*, 219.
37 Martov–Aksel'rod, 15 X 1920 (Axelrod Archive, IISG).
38 See note 17.
39 *Freiheit*, 30 X 1920.
40 Martov–Aksel'rod, 28 X 1920 (Axelrod Archive, IISG).
41 Martov–Aksel'rod, 12 XI 1920 (Axelrod Archive, IISG).
42 Martov–Ščupak, 14 XII 1920 (Nic. Coll. Hoover Inst.).
43 Donneur, *Histoire*, 56–7.
44 See note 42.
45 *Protokoll Konferenz Wien*, 5.
46 See note 42.
47 Martov–Ščupak, 15 XII 1920 (Nic. Coll. Hoover Inst.). See also note 48.
48 Martov–Ščupak, 20 XII 1920 (Nic. Coll. Hoover Inst.).
49 The original letter has not been preserved. Fragments were published in: 'Tov. P. B. Aksel'rod o bol'ševizme'. Axelrod, *Observations.* Ascher, *Mensheviks*, 130–6. Cf: Ascher, *Axelrod*, 369ff.
50 MacDonald–Martov, 20 XII 1920 (Nic. Coll. Hoover Inst.).
51 Adler, 'Was'.
52 Martov–MacDonald, 4 I 1921 (Labour Party Archive, London).

53 Martov–Ščupak, 14 XII 1920 (Nic. Coll. Hoover Inst.).
54 Martov–Aksel'rod, 20 XII 1920 (Axelrod Archive, IISG).
55 Martov–Ščupak, 20 XII 1920 (Nic. Coll. Hoover Inst.).
56 Kriegel, *Congrès Tours*, 63–4.
57 ibid., 66. See also: 'Vnimaniju Marselja Kašena', *Socialističeskij Vestnik*, 1 II 1921.
58 Wohl, *Communism*, 197ff. Lindemann, *Red years*, 260–86.
59 Donneur, *Histoire*, 135–8. See also: Martov–Aksel'rod, 7 III 1921 and Brojdo–Aksel'rod, 9 III 1921 (Axelrod Archive, IISG).
60 *Protokoll Konferenz Wien*, 11.
61 Dalin–Aksel'rod, 1 III 1921 (Axelrod Archive, IISG).
62 See: *Socialističeskij Vestnik*, 24 IV 1923 and 4 IV 1925.
63 Cf: Donneur, *Histoire*, 129–34. Cole, *History*, IV, Part I, 339–42.
64 Martov, 'Konferencii'.
65 Woytinsky, *Démocratie*, 113. Roobol, *Tsereteli*, 183ff. *L'Internationale*.
66 *Protokoll Konferenz Wien*, 55.
67 Abramovič, 'Men'ševiki', 33–4.
68 ibid., 34–5.
69 Martov–Aksel'rod, 7 III 1921 (Axelrod Archive, IISG).
70 *Protokoll Konferenz Wien*, 115–16.
71 See note 69.
72 Brojdo–Aksel'rod, 9 III 1921 (Axelrod Archive, IISG).
73 Cereteli–Aksel'rod, 27 VI 1921 (Axelrod Archive, IISG).
74 Roobol, *Tsereteli*, 217. See also: *L'Internationale*.
75 See: Berkman, *Tragedy*. Kool, *Arbeiterdemokratie*, 291. Avrich, *Kronstadt*, 3–6. Avrich, *Anarchists*, 228ff. See also: Getzler, *Kronstadt*.
76 See: Radkey, *Unknown civil war*.
77 Carroll, *Communism*, 232–3.
78 Avrich, *Kronstadt*, 88–9, 95–6. Kool, *Arbeiterdemokratie*, 283–4.
79 *Het Volk*, 8 III 1921. Carroll, *Communism*, 234. Avrich, *Kronstadt*, 109, 118–19.
80 *Le Populaire*, 7 III 1921. *Het Volk*, 9 III 1921 and 12 III 1921. *Vorwärts*, 13 III 1921.
81 *Le Populaire*, 15 III 1921.
82 Dan, *Dva goda*, 114.
83 See note 69.
84 Abramovitsj, 'Krise'. See also: *Arbeiterzeitung*, 12 III 1921. *Le Populaire*, 12 III 1921. *Het Volk*, 10 III 1921.
85 Avrich, *Kronstadt*, 80–130. Getzler, *Kronstadt*, 223–5.
86 See: *Ko vsem graždanam, rabočim, krasnoarmejcam, matrosam. Ko vsem Tovarišči!. Tovarišči rabočie, vse čestnye graždane, vse vooruzennye* (Portugeis Archive, IISG).
87 *Rezoljucija C.K. o Kronštadte*, 7 III 1921 (Nic. Coll. Hoover Inst.). See also: Haimson, *Mensheviks*, 243–5. Dvinov, *Ot legal'nosti*, 30–1.
88 *K rabočim, matrosam, krasnoarmejcam i kursantam Petrograda*, 7 III 1921 (Nic. Coll. Hoover Inst.).
89 'Groznoe predostereženie', *Socialističeskij Vestnik*, 18 III 1921.
90 'Trogatel'no', *Socialističeskij Vestnik*, 18 III 1921.

91 Dalin, 'Aufstand'.
92 'Lenin otstupaet', *Socialističeskij Vestnik*, 18 III 1921.
93 Martov, 'Aufstand'.
94 Martov, 'Kronštadt'. See also: Martov–Aksel'rod, 24 III 1921 (Axelrod Archive, IISG).
95 Eudin, *Soviet Russia*, 28ff. Abramovitch, *Revolution*, 203ff. Weissman, *Hoover*, 3ff, 30ff.
96 Dalin, 'Golod'. *Het Volk*, 2 VIII 1921. *Freiheit*, 12 VIII 1921.
97 Dvinov, *Ot legal'nosti*, 58–9. See also: 'Na bor'bu s golodom (Vozzvanie C.K. R.S.D.R.P.)', *Socialističeskij Vestnik*, 1 IX 1921. Martov–Aksel'rod, 7 VIII 1921 (Axelrod Archive, IISG).
98 Weissman, *Hoover*, 12ff. Wolfe, *Bridge*, 107ff. Kuskova, 'Mesjac'.
99 Dvinov, *Ot legal'nosti*, 59–60. Letter Dvinov to Foreign Delegation RSDRP, 5 VIII 1921 (Nic. Coll. Hoover Inst.). 'Po Rossii', *Socialističeskij Vestnik* (1 IX 1921) 13. See also: *Freiheit*, 4 VIII 1921.
100 Weissman, *Hoover*, 16, 74ff. Wolfe, *Bridge*, 113ff.
101 For the text of this call see: *Socialističeskij Vestnik*, 5 VIII 1921, 7. See also: 'Pis'mo k tovariščam' (Letter Foreign Delegation RSDRP to CC RSDRP, 25 VIII 1921), *Socialističeskij Vestnik*, 1 IX 1921, 5–6. Cf: Donneur, *Histoire*, 154. For Adler's call see: *Socialističeskij Vestnik*, 1 IX 1921 or *Freiheit*, 4 VIII 1921.
102 Martov–Aksel'rod, 7 VIII 1921 (Axelrod Archive, IISG).
103 Martov–Aksel'rod, 15 VIII 1921 (Axelrod Archive, IISG).
104 *Het Volk*, 1, 2, 3, 11, 19, 21, 24 and 26 VIII 1921. Dvinov, *Ot legal'nosti*, 60.
105 *Socialističeskij Vestnik*, 1 IX 1921. Braunthal, *Geschichte*, 215. Wohl, *Communism*, 241–2. *Resolution* (Conference Berlin August 1921) (IFTU Archive, IISG). *To all affiliated Trade Union Centers* (Letter Bureau IFTU, 15 VIII 1921) (IFTU Archive, IISG).
106 *Het Volk*, 24 VIII 1921. *Freiheit*, 16 VIII 1921 and 17 VIII 1921. Weissman, *Hoover*, 167ff. Eudin, *Soviet Russia*, 29–30.
107 *Socialističeskij Vestnik*, 23 II 1922, 6 III 1922, 21 III 1922 and 3 IV 1922. 'Tätigkeitsbericht Int. Gewerkschaftb. 1919/1921', 55–8. 'Bericht Gewerkschafskongress Rom 1922', 25–6. *Tätigkeitsbericht Int. Gewerkschaftsb.* 1922/1923, 78–81. See also: Abramovitch, *Revolution*, 209 note 35. Dvinov, *Ot legal'nosti*, 90–1.

9 1921–1923: THE ECLIPSE OF THE SOCIALIST CENTRE IN THE WEST AND THE DECLINE OF DEMOCRATIC SOCIALISM IN SOVIET RUSSIA

1 See: Erlich, *Debate*. Lewin, *Undercurrents*. Cohen, *Bukharin*.
2 Haimson, *Mensheviks*, 243ff. Dvinov, *Ot legal'nosti*, 9–10, 23ff, 52ff. Schapiro, *Origin*, 198ff. Brovkin, 'Mensheviks and NEP'. Aronson, *K istorii*. See also: Kučin, 'Partii'.
3 Martov–Aksel'rod, 5 IV 1921 (Axelrod Archive, IISG).
4 ibid. See also: Martov, 'Po povodu'.

5 Martov–Aksel'rod, 13 V 1921 (Axelrod Archive, IISG).
6 Martov–Aksel'rod, 8 VI 1921 (Axelrod Archive, IISG).
7 Martov–Aksel'rod, 24 VI 1921 (Axelrod Archive, IISG).
8 Kautsky, *Demokratie*, 77.
9 ibid., 80–1.
10 Martov–Aksel'rod, 14 IX 1921 (Axelrod Archive, IISG). Martov–Aksel'rod, 31 VII 1921 (Nic. Coll. Hoover Inst.).
11 Abramovič, 'Predislovie', iv–v.
12 Bauer, *Kurs*, 6.
13 ibid., 29.
14 ibid., 36.
15 Dalin, *Posle vojn*, 61.
16 Dalin, 'Proč' illjuzii'. Martov, 'Illjuzii'. See also: Letter Kučin (?) to Mensheviks in Berlin, 3 IX 1922 (Nic. Coll. Hoover Inst.). Dalin–Aksel'rod, 6 VI 1921 (Axelrod Archive, IISG).
17 Cf.: Haimson, *Mensheviks*, 364.
18 Dvinov, *Ot legal'nosti*, 25.
19 ibid.
20 Legett, *Cheka*, 318–24, 359–60, 463–8. Daniels, *Conscience*, 137ff. Service, *Party*, 158ff. Haimson, *Mensheviks*, 210, 236, 260, 299. Dvinov, *Ot legal'nosti*, 10, 24–5, 31, 52–3, 70–1, 106–7. Schapiro, *Origin*, 204. Martov, *Geschichte*, 319. Dan, *Dva goda*, 150ff.
21 Dan, *Dva goda*, 179–80. Martov–Aksel'rod, 24 VI 1921 (Axelrod Archive, IISG). Dvinov, *Ot legal'nosti*, 61.
22 Dvinov, *Ot legal'nosti*, 25, 33–9, 74–5.
23 Dan, *Dva goda*, 87ff. 'Vos'moj s'ezd sovetov', *Socialističeskij Vestnik*, 16 II 1921, 7–12.
24 Dvinov, *Ot legal'nosti*, 29, 42ff. Haimson, *Mensheviks*, 262–3. Brovkin, 'Mensheviks and NEP', 350–5.
25 Dvinov, *Ot legal'nosti*, 45. Martov–Aksel'rod, 24 III 1921 (Axelrod Archive, IISG). See also: *Socialističeskij Vestnik*, 5 VI 1921, 5.
26 Dvinov, *Ot legal'nosti*, 45ff. *Appeal to the Workmen and Socialist Parties of the World* (Portugeis Archive, IISG). 'Pobeda na Butyrskom fronte', *Socialističeskij Vestnik*, 5 VI 1921, 1–2.
27 Dvinov, *Ot legal'nosti*, 46, 51, 54.
28 'Ko vsem socialističeskim partijam i professional'nym organizacijam', *Socialističeskij Vestnik*, 5 VI 1921, 9–10.
29 'Presledovanie socialistov v Rossii i zapadno-evropejskij proletariat', *Socialističeskij Vestnik*, 8 VII 1921, 8–10. Martov–Aksel'rod, 13 V 1921 (Axelrod Archive, IISG). Martov–Ščupak, 8 VI 1921 (Nic. Coll. Hoover Inst.).
30 Abramovič–Mensheviks in Moscow, no date (Nic. Coll. Hoover Inst.). Martov–Ščupak, 2 XI 1921 (Nic. Coll. Hoover Inst.).
31 Dvinov, *Ot legal'nosti*, 57–8. 'Pobeda na Butyrskom fronte', *Socialističeskij Vestnik*, 5 VI 1921, 1–2.
32 'Novaja sociologija' and 'Moskovskij sovet ob izbienijach arestovannych', *Socialističeskij Vestnik*, 1 XI 1921, 8–9 and 10–1.
33 Dvinov, *Ot legal'nosti*, 62ff. 'Amnistija', *Socialističeskij Vestnik*, 18 XI 1921.

34 *Socialističeskij Vestnik*, 1 IX 1921.
35 ibid., 18 XI 1921.
36 Braunthal, *Geschichte*, 244ff. 'Dve golodovki', *Socialističeskij Vestnik*, 2 XII 1921, 1-3.
37 Dvinov, *Ot legal'nosti*, 75. *Freiheit*, 20 XI 1921 and 22 XI 1921.
38 Dvinov, *Ot legal'nosti*, 76. Letter I. I. Rubin to Mensheviks in Berlin, 25 XI 1921 (Nic. Coll. Hoover Inst.). Dan, *Dva goda*, 208-30.
39 Dan, *Dva goda*, 231-7.
40 ibid., 231-41.
41 Dvinov, *Ot legal'nosti*, 82-3. Text Lande telegram: Letter B. M. Sapir to author, 21 II 1986.
42 'Butyrskaja golodovka', 'Otkliki meždunarodnogo proletariata' and 'Reč' tov. R. Abramoviča', *Socialističeskij Vestnik*, 19 I 1922, 3-9. 'Eine politische Demonstration', *Rote Fahne*, 7 I 1922. 'Was geht in Lichtenburg vor', *Rote Fahne*, 9 I 1922. 'Entrüstete Heuchler. Neue antibolschewistenhetze', *Rote Fahne*, 10 I 1922. 'Eine Hilferuf aus Russland', *Freiheit*, 7 I 1922. 'Die moskauer Tragödie', *Freiheit*, 8 I 1922.
43 'Eröffnung des Parteitages in Leipzig. Der erste Tag', 'Die russischen Kerker raus', 'Die moskauer Tragödie', 'Protest der Arbeiter', *Freiheit*, 9 I 1922. 'Otkliki meždunarodnogo proletariata', *Socialističeskij Vestnik*, 19 I 1922.
44 Dan, *Dva goda*, 241-52. Dvinov, *Ot legal'nosti*, 83-4.
45 Dvinov, *Ot legal'nosti*, 84.
46 Nikolaevskij-Aksel'rod, 1 III 1922 (Axelrod Archive, IISG). See also: Dan-Aksel'rod, 16 II 1922 (Nic. Coll. Hoover Inst.).
47 Donneur, *Histoire*, 139ff. Braunthal, *Geschichte*, 258-9.
48 Martov, 'Vosstanovlenie'.
49 *Freiheit*, 16 VIII 1921 and 18 VIII 1921.
50 'K voprocu o vosstanovlenii Internacionala', *Socialističeskij Vestnik*, 1 XI 1921, 3-6.
51 Donneur, *Histoire*, 162ff.
52 Lazitch, *Lenin*, 528ff.
53 Gruber, *Communism*, 314ff. Fischer, *Soviets*, 230ff. Eudin, *Soviet Russia*, 97ff.
54 Donneur, *Histoire*, 172ff.
55 Haimson, *Mensheviks*, 269ff. Aronson, *K istorii*, 115-16. Roobol, *Tsereteli*, 218. Jansen, *Show trial*, 29ff.
56 Axelrod, *Observations*.
57 'Le camarade Axelrod nous en expose les tragiques conséquences', *Le Populaire*, 7 XI 1921. 'P. B. Aksel'rod ob edinom fronte', *Socialističeskij Vestnik*, 3 IV 1922, 5.
58 Dan-Aksel'rod, 8 III 1922 (Nic. Coll. Hoover Inst.). See also: Letter Martov to Mensheviks in Moscow, no date (1922) (Nic. Coll. Hoover Inst.).
59 Letter CC RSDRP in Moscow to ZD RSDRP in Berlin, 9 III 1922 (Nic. Coll. Hoover Inst.). Dvinov, *Ot legal'nosti*, 101ff, 108.
60 Dvinov-ZD RSDRP, date illegible (1922) (Nic. Coll. Hoover Inst.). Dvinov, *Ot legal'nosti*, 107. Ulam, *Bolsheviks*, 543-4, 549. Fischer, *Life*, 597ff. Jansen, *Show trial*, 22ff. See also: Martov-Ščupak, 25 VIII 1922 (Nic.

Coll. Hoover Inst.). 'Sobirajut materialy', *Socialističeskij Vestnik*, 16 VIII 1922, 7.

61 See: *Socialističeskij Vestnik*, 1 II 1921 and 5 IV 1921. Dvinov, *Ot legal' nosti*, 96. Haimson, *Mensheviks*, 286.

62 Jansen, *Show trial*, 30–3.

63 Dvinov, *Ot legal' nosti*, 114–15.

64 Cereteli–Aksel'rod, 17 III 1922 (Axelrod Archive, IISG).

65 *Soveščanie predstavitelej Zagr. Del. S.D. sovmestno s predstaviteljami Zagr. Del P.S.R., sostojavšeesja 27 marta 1922 g.* (Nic. Coll. Hoover Inst.).

66 *Mémorandum.* Jansen, *Show trial*, 36–7. Donneur, *Histoire*, 187ff.

67 *Protokoll der intern. Konferenz*, 4.

68 ibid., 17–20.

69 Abramovič, 'Men'ševiki', 53–6. Donneur, *Histoire*, 203ff.

70 *Protokoll der intern. Konferenz*, 21–6.

71 ibid., 31–6.

72 ibid., 37–9.

73 ibid., 52. Roobol, *Tsereteli*, 219.

74 *Protokoll der intern. Konferenz*, 42–3.

75 Abramovič, 'Men'ševiki', 53–6. Donneur, *Histoire*, 203ff.

76 Dan, *Dva goda*, 136–7.

77 Rosmer, *Moscou*, 76. Jansen, *Show trial*, 38–40.

78 *Protokoll der intern. Konferenz*, 47.

79 ibid., 50–2.

80 Donneur, *Histoire*, 223, 225ff. Braunthal, *Geschichte*, 267–71. Laqueur, *Russia*, 129–31. Fischer, *Soviets*, 236–53. Abramovitch, *Revolution*, 248ff. Eudin, *Soviet Russia*, 167ff.

81 Dvinov–ZD RSDRP, 2 V 1922 (Nic. Coll. Hoover Inst.). Dvinov, *Ot legal' nosti*, 115–16.

82 Donneur, *Histoire*, 234.

83 Pleskov–ZD RSDRP, 22 IV 1922 (Nic. Coll. Hoover Inst.).

84 Dvinov–ZD RSDRP, 2 V 1922 (Nic. Coll. Hoover Inst.).

85 *Obraščenie C.K. R.S.D.R.P. v Kommissiju Devjati*, no date (Nic. Coll. Hoover Inst.). See also: *Une déclaration*, signed by R. Abramovitch, Th. Dan and L. Martoff, no date (Nic. Coll. Hoover Inst.).

86 Dvinov, *Ot legal' nosti*, 116–17.

87 Donneur, *Histoire*, 238–9.

88 'An die Mitglieder des Neunerorganisationskomitees' signed by F. Adler, 4 V 1922 (LSI Archive, IISG).

89 Donneur, *Histoire*, 245–56.

90 ibid., 260ff.

91 Dalin, 'Meždu Londonom'.

92 Martov, 'Problema'.

93 Dvinov, *Ot legal' nosti*, 93ff.

94 Čerevanin–ZD RSDRP, no date ( probably July 1922) (Nic. Coll. Hoover Inst.). See also: Čerevanin–ZD RSDRP, no date (probably Oct./Nov. 1922) (Nic. Coll. Hoover Inst.).

95 Dvinov, *Ot legal' nosti*, 127ff, 140ff.

96 Jansen, *Show trial*, 141ff. Dvinov, *Ot legal' nosti*, 115–16.

97 Jansen, *Show trial*, 55ff. Dvinov, *Ot legal'nosti*, 131ff.
98 Jansen, *Show trial*, 66ff, 147ff. Dvinov, *Ot legal'nosti*, 136. See also: Dvinov–ZD RSDRP, 28 VI 1922 (Nic. Coll. Hoover Inst.). 'K demonstracii 20-go ijunja', *Socialističeskij Vestnik*, 2 VIII 1922, 7–8.
99 Dvinov, *Ot legal'nosti*, 136. Schapiro, *Totalitarianism*, 38ff.
100 Dvinov, *Ot legal'nosti*, 137–46.
101 Jansen, *Show trial*, 64–6. Vandervelde, *Le procès*, 96.
102 Jansen, *Show trial*, 161ff. Donneur, *Histoire*, 274ff.
103 Nicolaevsky, *Power*, 10–11.
104 See Martov–Ščupak, 25 VIII 1922 (Nic. Coll. Hoover Inst.).
105 Haimson, *Mensheviks*, 394ff. Abramovitch, *Revolution*, 382ff.
106 Mann, *Geschichte*, 24ff. Eyck, *Geschichte*, I, 220–304.
107 Donneur, *Histoire*, 284ff. Abramovič, 'Men'ševiki', 65ff. *Socialističeskij Vestnik*, 21 IX 1922.
108 Letters without signatures from Menshevik circles in Moscow to Foreign Delegation RSDRP, 20 VIII 1922 and 27 VIII 1922 (Nic. Coll. Hoover Inst.). Letter Abramovič to Mensheviks in Moscow, no date (autumn 1922) (Nic. Coll. Hoover Inst.). See also: *Socialističeskij Vestnik*, 4 X 1922 and 19 X 1922 about the German crisis and the USPD.
109 Donneur, *Histoire*, 297ff.
110 Martov, 'Problema'. Martov, 'Problem'.
111 Donneur, *Histoire*, 307ff. Abramovič, 'Men'ševiki', 68ff.
112 Dan–Mensheviks in Moscow, 5 XII 1922 (Nic. Coll. Hoover Inst.).
113 'Het congres voor den Vrede. Een indruk', *Nieuwe Rotterdamsche Courant*, 15 XII 1922. See also: 'Uroki Gaagi' and 'Gaagskij kongress', *Socialističeskij Vestnik*, 1 I 1923, 4–5 and 17–18.
114 *Bericht Friedenskongress*, 92ff. *Het Volk*, 15 XII 1922.
115 See note 113. See also: *Het Nieuws van den Dag*, 14 XII 1922. *Bericht Friedenskongress*, 134ff. 'De toekomst van Sovjet Rusland. Een rede van Abramowitsch', *Het Volk*, 16 XII 1922.
116 Abramovič, 'Men'ševiki', 72.
117 Donneur, *Histoire*, 310–14, 323ff.
118 ibid., 341–2. Kučin, 'Zapiski', 167–71. Letters from Kučin to Foreign Delegation RSDRP, 21 XI 1922 and 27 XII 1922 (Nic. Coll. Hoover Inst.).
119 Kučin, 'Zapiski', 179.
120 ibid., 180.
121 Krupskaya, *Memories*, 93.
122 *Socialističeskij Vestnik*, 24 IV 1923.
123 *Martov*, 118.
124 'U groba', *Socialističeskij Vestnik* (Ekstrennyj Vypusk [special edition]), 10 IV 1923, 3–4.
125 Braunthal, *Geschichte*, 284–5. *Protokoll Kongress Hamburg*, 97.
126 *Protokoll Kongress Hamburg*, 4.
127 ibid., 21–30. Fischer, *Soviets*, 320–31. Eudin, *Soviet Russia*, 184–9. Coates, *History*, 102ff.
128 *Protokoll Kongress Hamburg*, 19–21. Abramovitch, *Revolution*, 272. Abramovič, 'Men'ševiki', 78, 85.

129 Portugeis–Ingerman, 17 IV 1923 (Nic. Coll. Hoover Inst.). Aksel'rod–
Portugeis, 21 IV 1923 (Axelrod Archive, IISG). Portugeis–Kautsky, 20
IV 1923 (Kautsky Archive, IISG). Baikaloff–Shaw, 3 VII 1923, and *An
appeal to the Hamburg Congress* (LSI Archive, IISG). Bureau des Zentral-
komitees der Sozialdemokratischen Arbeiterpartei Russlands, *An den
Internationalen Sozialistischen Kongress in Hamburg* (Dan Archive, IISG).
*K Gamburgskomu kongressu. Proekt nakaza pravych*, signed by Aronson,
Binštok, Kefali and Dubois (Nic. Coll. Hoover Inst.).
130 Text draft resolution: *Kongress konstatiruet* (Dan Archive, IISG).
131 Portugeis–Ingerman, 30 V 1923 (Nic. Coll. Hoover Inst.). *Protokoll Kongress Hamburg*, 30–40.
132 *Protokoll Kongress Hamburg*, 80, 107. See also: 'Gamburgskij kongress',
*Socialističeskij Vestnik*, 12 VI 1923, 1–4.

# BIBLIOGRAPHY

## ARCHIVES

Nicolaevsky Collection. Hoover Institution for War, Peace and Revolution. Stanford, Calif.
Axelrod Archive. IISG. Amsterdam.
Dan Archive. IISG. Amsterdam.
Portugeis Archive. IISG. Amsterdam.
Kautsky Archive. IISG. Amsterdam.
LSI Archive. IISG. Amsterdam.
IFTU Archive. IISG. Amsterdam.
Labour Party Archive. London.
Huysmans Archive. Antwerp.

## NEWSPAPERS AND JOURNALS

*Arbeiterzeitung*
*Freiheit*
*Iskra*
*De Kroniek*
*Nieuwe Rotterdamsche Courant*
*Het Nieuws van den Dag*
*Novyj Luč*
*Petrogradskaja Pravda*
*Pravda*
*Revue Socialiste*
*Socialističeskij Vestnik*
*La Tribune Russe*
*Het Volk*
*Vorwärts*

*Vsegda Vperëd*
*Daily Herald*
*L'Humanité*
*Der Kampf*
*Die Neue Zeit*
*De Nieuwe Tijd*
*NRC-Handelsblad*
*Le Populaire*
*Rabočij Internacional*
*Rote Fahne*
*Sozialistische Monatshefte*
*Volja Rossii*
*De Volkskrant*
*Vrij Nederland*

552

BOOKS AND ARTICLES

Abramovič, R. 'Predislovie' in: K. Kautsky, *Ot demokratii k gosudarstvennomu rabstvu*. Berlin, 1922.

Abramovič, R. R. 'Men'ševiki i socialističeskij Internacional 1918–1940'. Typescript in Hoover Institution, Stanford, Calif. *The Soviet revolution 1917–1939*. New York, 1962.

Abramovitsj, R. 'Die Krise in Russland'. *Freiheit*, 8 III 1921.

Adams, A. E., ed. *The Russian revolution and Bolshevik victory. Why and how?* Problems in European Civilisation. Boston, Mass., 1960.

Adams, W. S. 'British reactions to the 1905 revolution'. *Marxist Quarterly* (1955, no. 2) 173–86.

*Address and provisional rules of the Working Men's International Association*. London, 1864. Reprint: Bonn, 1977.

Adelung, F. von. *Kritisch-literarische Übersicht der Reisenden in Russland bis 1700, deren Berichte bekannt sind*. St Petersburg, 1846. Reprint: Amsterdam, 1960.

*Victor Adler. Briefwechsel mit August Bebel und Karl Kautsky*. Vienna, 1954.

Adler, F. 'Was trennt uns von der Zweite Internationale'. *Der Kampf*, XIV (Feb.– March 1921) 41–4.

Aksel'rod, P. B. 'Ob'edinenie rossijskoj social'demokratii i ee zadači'. *Iskra*, no. 55, 15 XII 1903 and no. 57, 15 I 1904.

*Kto izmenil socializmu? (Bol'ševizm i social'naja demokratija v Rossii)*. New York, 1919.

'Tov. P. B. Aksel'rod o bol'ševizme i bor'be s nim (Iz pis'ma k JU. O. Martovu, 6 sent. 1920 g.)'. *Socialističeskij Vestnik*, 20 IV 1921 and 4 V 1921.

Altmeyer, J. J. *Histoire des relations commerciales et diplomatiques des Pays Bas avec le Nord de l'Europe pendant le XVIe siècle*. Brussels, 1840.

Amann, P. H. *Revolution and mass democracy. The Paris club movement in 1848*. Princeton, N.J., 1975.

Amato, S. 'Otto Bauer and Austro-Marxism: a conference report'. *Telos. A quarterly journal of radical thought* XII, no. 2 (1979) 144–50.

Anderson, M. S. *Britain's discovery of Russia 1553–1815*. London, 1958.

*Die sozialdemokratische Arbeiterpartei Russlands. Bericht der Delegation der sozialdemokratischen Arbeiterpartei Russlands an den internationalen sozialistischen Kongress in Amsterdam 1904*. n.p., n.d.

Aronson, G. 'Angličane v Moskve'. *Novyj žurnal*, X (1945) 330.

*Dviženie upolnomčennych ot rabočich i fabrik v 1918 g*. New York, 1960.

*K istorii pravogo tečenija sredi men'ševikov*. Inter-university project on the history of the Menshevik movement. Paper no. 4. New York, 1960.

Ascher, A. 'Russian Marxism and the German revolution, 1917–1920'. *Archiv für Sozialgeschichte*, VI/VII (Hanover, 1966–7) 391–439.

'Axelrod and Kautsky'. *Slavic Review*, XXVI (1967) 94–112.

*Pavel Axelrod and the development of Menshevism*. Cambridge, Mass., 1972.

Ascher, A., ed. *The Mensheviks in the Russian revolution*. London, 1976.

Ascher, A. 'German socialists and the Russian revolution of 1905' in: E. Mendelsohn and M. Slitz, eds., *Imperial Russia 1700–1917*. De Kalb, Ill., 1988.

*The revolution of 1905: Russia in disarray*. Stanford, Calif., 1988.

*Autour d'Alexandre Herzen. Documents inédits*. Geneva, 1973.

Avrich, P. *The Russian anarchists*. Princeton, N.J., 1967.

*Kronstadt 1921*. Princeton, N.J., 1970.

A [Axelrod, P.]. 'Das politische Erwachen der russischen Arbeiter und ihre Maifeier von 1891'. *Die Neue Zeit*, X (1891–2, 2) 36–45 and 78–84.

Axelrod, P. 'Die revolutionären Kräfte Russlands einst und jetzt'. *Die Neue Zeit*, XIII (1894–5, 2) 261–72.

'Eine nur theilweise auf dem internationalen Arbeiterschutzkongress gehaltene Rede'. *Die Neue Zeit*, XVI (1897–8, 1) 45–50.

'Die historische Berechtigung der russischen Sozialdemokratie'. *Die Neue Zeit*, XVI (1897–8, 2) 100–11 and 140–9.

Axelrod, P. B. *Observations sur la tactique des socialistes dans la lutte contre le bolchévisme (Extraits d'une lettre à Martov)*. Paris, 1921.

Axelrod, P. *Die russische Revolution und die sozialistische Internationale*. Jena, 1932.

Baak, J. C. *De verhouding van den Russischen tot den West-Europeeschen mensch*. Amsterdam, 1945.

Balsdon, J. P. V. D. *Romans and aliens*. London, 1979.

Baron, S. H. *Plekhanov, the father of Russian Marxism*. Stanford, Calif., 1963.

Baron, S. H., ed. *The travels of Olearius in seventeenth-century Russia*. Stanford, Calif., 1967.

Barraclough, G. 'Europa, Amerika und Russland in Vorstellung und Denken des 19. Jahrhunderts'. *Historische Zeitschrift* (1966) 281–315.

*Into battle. Speeches by the Rt. Hon. Winston S. Churchill*. London, 1941.

Barth, H. *Masse und Mythos. Die ideologische Krise an der Wende zum 20. Jahrh. und die Theorie der Gewalt: Georges Sorel*. Hamburg, 1959.

Baudet, H. *Paradijs op aarde. Gedachten over de verhouding van de europese tot de buiteneuropese mens*. Assen, 1959.

Bauer, O. 'Die Bolscheviki und wir'. *Der Kampf*, XI (March 1918, no. 2) 137–50.

*Bolschevismus oder Sozialdemokratie?* Vienna, 1921.

*Der 'neue Kurs' in Sowjetrussland.* Vienna, 1921.

'Evropa i men'ševizm'. *Socialističeskij Vestnik, 4 IV 1925.*

*Werkausgabe.* 9 vols. Vienna, 1975–80.

Baumgarten, E. *Max Weber. Werk und Person.* Tübingen, 1964.

Baynac, J. *Les socialistes révolutionnaires.* Paris, 1979.

*August Bebels Briefwechsel mit Karl Kautsky.* Assen, 1971.

Benz, E. *Die Ostkirche im Lichte der protestantischen Geschichtsschreibung von der Reformation bis zur Gegenwart.* Freiburg, 1952.

*Franz von Baader und Kotzebue. Das Russlandbild der Restaurationszeit.* Wiesbaden, 1957.

*Bericht der Russischen Sozial-Revolutionären Partei an den Internationalen Sozialistenkongress zu Stuttgart.* n.p., 1907.

*Bericht der Russischen Sozial-Revolutionären Partei an den Internationalen Sozialistenkongress zu Kopenhagen.* n.p., 1910.

*Bericht über den internationalen Friedenskongress abgehalten im Haag (Holland) vom 10.–15. Dezember 1922 unter den Auspizien des Internationalen Gewerkschaftsbundes.* Amsterdam, n.d.

'Bericht über den internationalen Gewerkschaftskongress abgehalten in Rom vom 20.–26. April 1922 im Teatro Argentina'. *Die internationale Gewerkschaftsbewegung. Organ des Internationalen Gewerkschaftbundes,* Supp. X, 1923.

Berkman, A. *The Russian tragedy.* Sanday, Orkney, 1976.

Bernstein, E. *Die Voraussetzungen des Sozialismus und die Aufgaben der Sozialdemokratie.* Stuttgart, 1899.

'Revolutionen und Russland'. *Sozialistische Monatshefte,* IX (1905, 1) 289–95.

'Fragen der Taktik in Russland'. *Sozialistische Monatshefte,* X (1906, 1) 208–17.

*Sozialdemokratische Lehrjahre.* Berlin, 1928. Reprint: Berlin, 1978.

Bernstein, L. *L'affaire Azeff. Histoire et documents.* Publications de la Société des amis du peuple russe, no.16. Paris, 1909.

Berry, L. E. and Crumney, R. O., eds. *Rude and barbarous kingdom. Russia in the accounts of sixteenth-century English voyagers.* Madison, Wis., 1968.

Bezemer, J. W. *De Russische revolutie in Westerse ogen. Stemmen van ooggetuigen. Maart 1917–Maart 1918.* Amsterdam, 1956.

Bezzola, G. A. *Die Mongolen in abendländischer Sicht (1220–1270). Ein Beitrag zur Frage der Völkerbegegnungen.* Berne, 1974.

Billington, J. H. *Mikhailovsky and Russian populism.* Oxford, 1958.

*The icon and the axe. An interpretive history of Russian culture.* London, 1966.

Birke, E. *Frankreich und Ostmitteleuropa im 19. Jahrhundert.* Beiträge zur Politik und Geistesgeschichte. Cologne, 1960.

Bitterli, U. *Die 'Wilden' und die 'Zivilisierten'. Grundzüge einer Geistes-und Kulturgeschichte der europäisch-überseeischen Begegnung.* Munich, 1976.

Blänsdorf, A. *Die Zweite Internationale und der Krieg. Die Diskussion über die internationale Zusammenarbeit der sozialistischen Parteien 1914–1917.* Stuttgart, 1979.

Blumenberg, W., ed. *August Bebels Briefwechsel mit Friedrich Engels.* The Hague, 1965.

Boas, G. *Essays on primitivism and related ideas in the middle ages.* Baltimore, Md, 1948.

Bonjean, J. 'Nihilisme russe et anarchisme occidental'. *Revue Socialiste,* XV (1892, 1) 728–32.

Börne, L. 'Briefe aus Paris' in: L. Börne, *Sämtliche Schriften,* III. Darmstadt, 1964.

Bosau, Helmold von. *Slawenchronik.* Ausgewählte Quellen zur deutschen Geschichte des Mittelalters. Freiherr vom Stein Gedächtnis-Ausgabe vol. XIX. Berlin, 1963.

Bourdet, Y., ed. *Otto Bauer et la révolution. Textes choisis.* Paris, 1968.

Bourguina, A. *Russian social democracy. The Menshevik movement. A bibliography.* Stanford, Calif., 1968.

Brachfeld, G. I. *André Gide and the communist temptation.* Paris, 1959.

Brachmann, B. *Russische Sozialdemokraten in Berlin 1895–1914.* Berlin, 1962.

Brandes, G. *Impressions of Russia.* New York, 1966.

Braunthal, J. *Geschichte der Internationale,* II. Hanover, 1963.

Brautigam, J. *Langs de havens en op de schepen.* Amsterdam, 1956.

Brewster, D. *East–West passage. A study in literary relationships.* London, 1954.

Brinkman, M. *De S.D.A.P. en Sowjet-Rusland. Reacties in de sociaal-democratische pers op het bolsjewisme aan de macht: 1917–1921.* Utrechtse Historische Cahiers, 1980, no. 2.

Brovkin, V. 'The Mensheviks and NEP society in Russia'. *Russian History/Histoire Russe,* IX, nos. 2–3 (1982) 347–77.

'The Mensheviks' political comeback: the elections to the Provincial cities in spring 1918'. *Russian Review,* XIII (1983) 1–50.

'The Mensheviks under attack. The transformation of Soviet politics, June–September 1918'. *Jahrbücher für Geschichte Osteuropas,* n.s. XXXII (1984) 378–91.

Brügmann, U. *Die russischen Gewerkschaften in Revolution und Bürgerkrieg.* Frankfurt on Main, 1972.

Brupbacher, F. *Marx und Bakunin. Ein Beitrag zur Geschichte der Internationalen Arbeiterassoziation.* Berlin, 1976.

Buchanan, W. and Cantril, H. *How nations see each other.* Westport, Conn., 1953, 1973.

Burbank, J. 'Martov and Chernov: theory and practice of the socialist opposition.' *American Historical Association. Ninety-Eighth Annual Meeting*, San Francisco, Dec. 1983.

Burch, R. J. 'Social unrest in imperial Russia: the student movement at Moscow university, 1887–1905'. Unpublished Ph.D diss., University of Washington, 1972.

*Bureau Socialiste International. Aux comités centraux des partis affiliés.* 'Cher Citoyen, dans quelques jours, Nicolas II, tzar de Russie . . .'. Brussels, 1909.

Butenschön, M. *Zarenhymne und Marseillaise. Zur Geschichte der Russland-Ideologie in Frankreich (1870/71–1893/94)*. Stuttgart, 1978.

Cadot, M. *L'image de la Russie dans la vie intellectuelle française (1839–1856)*. Paris, 1967.

Calwer, R. 'Russland'. *Sozialistische Monatshefte*, IX (1905, no. 2) 111ff.

Camus, A. *L'homme révolté*. Paris, 1951.

Carlson, A. R. *Anarchism in Germany*, I: *The early movement*. Metuchen, N.J., 1972.

Carr, E. H. *Michael Bakunin*, New York, 1961.

*A history of Soviet Russia. The Bolshevik revolution*, I. Harmondsworth, 1964.

*Romantic exiles. A nineteenth-century portrait gallery*. London, 1968.

Carroll, E. M. *Soviet communism and Western opinion 1919–1921*. Chapel Hill, N.C., 1965.

*Germany and the great powers 1866–1914. A study in public opinion and foreign policy*. Hamden, Conn., 1966.

Caute, D. *The fellow-travellers. A postscript to the Enlightenment*. London, 1977.

Cereteli, I. *Vospominanija o fevral'skoj revoljucii*. Paris, 1976.

Charzat, M. *Georges Sorel et la révolution au XXe siècle*. Paris, 1963.

Christ, K. 'Römer und Barbaren in der hohen Kaiserzeit'. *Speculum*, X (1959) 273–88.

Čiževskij, D. 'Zwei Ketzer in Moskou' in: *Aus zwei Welten. Beiträge zur Geschichte der slawisch-westlichen literarischen Beziehungen*. The Hague, 1956.

Coates, W. P. and Coates, Z. K. *A history of Anglo-Soviet relations*. London, 1944.

Coeurderoy, E. *Hurrah!!! ou la révolution par les cosaques*. Paris, 1977.

Cohen, S. F. *Bukharin and the Bolshevik revolution 1888–1938*. New York, 1973.

Cohn, N. *Warrant for genocide. The myth of the Jewish world-conspiracy and the Protocols of the Elders of Zion*. London, 1967.

*The pursuit of the millennium. Revolutionary millenarians and mythical anarchists of the Middle Ages*. London, 1970.

Cole, G. D. H. *A history of socialist thought*. 5 vols. London, 1953–60.

*Compte rendu sténographique non officiel de la version française du cinquième congrès socialiste international tenu à Paris du 23 au 27 septembre 1900.* Paris, 1901.

Confino, M. *Violence dans la violence. Le débat Bakounine–Nečaev.* Paris, 1973.

*Congrès international ouvrier socialiste tenu à Brussels du 16 au 23 août 1891. Rapport publié par le Secrétariat Belge.* Brussels, 1893.

*Sixième congrès socialiste international tenu à Amsterdam du 14 au 20 août 1904. Compte-rendu analytique publié par le Secrétariat Socialiste International.* Brussels, 1904.

*Septième congrès socialiste international tenu à Stuttgart du 18 au 24 août 1907.* Brussels, 1908.

Corbet, C. *L'opinion française face à l'inconnue russe (1799–1894). A l'ère des nationalismes.* Paris, 1967.

*The General Council of the First International. Minutes.* Moscow, n.d.

Croan, M. 'Prospects for the Soviet dictatorship: Otto Bauer' in: L. Labedz, ed., *Revisionism. Essays on the history of Marxist ideas.* London, 1962.

Cross, A., ed. *Russia under Western eyes 1517–1825.* London, 1971.

Cross, S. H. 'Mediaeval Russian contacts with the West'. *Speculum,* X (1935) 137–44.

Custine, A. de. *Lettres de Russie. La Russie en 1839.* Paris, 1975.

Dalin, D. 'Der Aufstand in Kronstadt'. *Arbeiterzeitung,* 17 III 1921.

'Proč' illjuzii'. *Socialističeskij Vestnik,* 20 V 1921, 6–9.

'Golod'. *Socialističeskij Vestnik,* 5 VIII 1921, 3–6.

'Meždu Londonom i Moskvoj'. *Socialističeskij Vestnik,* 19 VI 1922, 7–9.

*Posle vojn i revoljucij.* Berlin, 1922.

Dan, F. *Dva goda skitanij.* Berlin, 1922.

*Proischoždenie bol'ševizma.* New York, 1946.

Dan, T. 'Die Bedingungen des erneuten Aufschwungs der russischen Revolution'. *Die Neue Zeit,* XXVI (1907–8, 2) 4–10, 49–58.

Daniel, N. *The Islam and the West. The making of an image.* Edinburgh, 1960.

Daniels, R. V. *The conscience of the revolution. Communist opposition in Soviet Russia.* Cambridge, Mass., 1965.

De Leon, D. *Flashlights of the Amsterdam international congress 1904.* New York, n.d.

Dellek, R. and Warren, A. *Theory of literature.* New York, 1956.

Deutsch, L. *Der Lockspitzel Asew und die terroristische Taktik.* Frankfurt on Main, 1909.

Deutscher, I. *The prophet armed. Trotsky: 1879–1927.* New York, n.d.

Dittrich, Z. R. *Het verleden van Oost-Europa. Maatschappelijke en culturele dynamiek tot het einde der Middeleeuwen.* Zeist, 1963.

'Het testament van Peter de Grote' in: Z. R. Dittrich, B. Naarden and H. Renner, eds., *Knoeien met het verleden*. Baarn, 1985.

Doerries, H. *Russlands Eindringen in Europa in der Epoche Peter des Grossen*. Königsberg, 1939.

Dommanget, M. *Auguste Blanqui et la révolution de 1848*. Paris, 1972.

Domnič, M. J. 'Načalo revoljucii 1905 g. i dviženie solidarnosti vo Francii'. *Voprocy Istorii* (1955, no. 1) 87–94.

Donneur, A. *Histoire de l'Union des partis socialistes pour l'action internationale (1920–1923)*. Sudbury, Ontario, 1967.

Downs, R. M. and Stea, D. *Maps in mind. Reflections on cognitive mapping*. New York, 1977.

Dörrie, H. 'Die Wertung der Barbaren im Urteil der Griechen. Knechtsnaturen? Oder Berater und Künder heilbringender Weisheit?' in: *Antike und Universalgeschichte. Festschrift Hans Erich Stier zum 70. Geburtstag*. Münster, 1972.

Döser, U. *Das bolschewistische Russland in der deutschen Rechtspresse 1918–1925. Eine Studie zum politischen Kampf in der Weimarer Republik*. Berlin, 1961.

Drachkovitch, M. *Les socialismes français et allemand et le problème de la guerre 1870–1914*. Geneva, 1953.

Drachkovitch, M. M., ed. *The revolutionary Internationals 1864–1943*. Stanford, Calif., 1968.

Dröge, F. W. *Publizistik und Vorurteil*. Münster, 1967.

Droz, J., ed. *Geschichte des Sozialismus*. 12 vols. Frankfurt on Main, 1975.

Družinin, N. M. 'A. v. Haxthausen und die russischen revolutionären Demokraten' in: *Ost und West in der Geschichte des Denkens und der kulturellen Beziehungen. Festschrift für E. Winter*. Berlin (DDR), 1966.

Duby, G. 'Histoire des mentalités' in: *Encyclopédie de la Pléiade. L'histoire et ses méthodes*. Paris, 1961.

Dupeux, L. 'Stratégie communiste et dynamique conservatrice. Essai sur les différents sens de l'expression "national-bolchevisme" en Allemagne sous la république de Weimar (1919–1923)'. Unpublished thesis, University of Lille, 1976.

Duyker, H. C. J. and Frijda, N. H. *National character and national stereotypes. A trend report prepared for the International Union of Scientific Psychology*. Amsterdam, 1960.

Dvinov, B. L. *Pervaja mirovaja vojna i rossijskaja social-demokratija*. New York, 1962.

Dvinov, B. *Ot legal'nosti k podpol'ju (1921–1922) (From legality to the underground (1921–1922))*. Stanford, Calif., 1968.

Dvornik, F. 'The Kiev state and its relations with Western Europe'. *Transactions Royal Historical Society*, 4th series, XXIX (1947) 27–46.

Ebels-Hoving, B. *Byzantium in Westerse ogen 1096–1204*. Assen, 1971.

Eckert, G., ed. *Wilhelm Liebknecht. Briefwechsel mit Karl Marx und Friedrich Engels*. The Hague, 1963.

Edwardes, M. *East–West passage. The travel of ideas, arts and inventions between Asia and the Western world*. London, 1971.

Eisner, K. *Der Geheimbund des Zaren*. Berlin, 1904.

Elm, A. von. 'Die Gewerkschaftsdebatte auf dem Mannheimer Parteitag'. *Sozialistische Monatshefte*, X (1906, 2) 831–9.

Elwood, R. C. *Russian social democracy in the underground*. Assen, 1974.

Elwood, R. C., ed. *Resolutions and decisions of the communist party of the Soviet Union*, I: *The Russian Social Democratic Party 1898–October 1917*. Toronto, 1974.

Elwood, R. C. 'Lenin and the Brussels "Unity" Conference of July 1914'. *Russian Review*, XXXIX (1980) 32–49.

Engelstein, L. 'Moscow in the 1905 revolution: a study in class conflict and political organisation'. Unpublished Ph.D diss., Stanford University, 1976.

Epstein, F. T. 'Der Komplex "Die russische Gefahr" und sein Einfluss auf die deutsch-russischen Beziehungen im 19. Jahrhundert' in: I. Geiss and B. J. Wendt, eds. *Deutschland in der Weltpolitik des 19. und 20. Jahrhunderts*. Düsseldorf, 1973.

Erlich, A. *The Soviet industrialisation debate*. Cambridge, Mass., 1960.

Eudin, X. J. and Fischer, H. H. *Soviet Russia and the West, 1920–1927. A documentary survey*. Stanford, Calif., 1957.

Eyck, E. *Geschichte der Weimarer Republik*. Erlenbach and Zürich, 1962.

Fainsod, M. *International socialism and the World War*. New York, 1966.

Fay, V., ed. *La révolution d'Octobre et le mouvement ouvrier européen*. Paris, 1967.

Ferro, M. *La révolution de 1917. La chute du tsarisme et les origines d'Octobre*. Paris, 1967.

*La révolution de 1917: Octobre. Naissance d'une société*. Paris, 1976.

*L'Occident devant la révolution soviétique. L'histoire et ses mythes*. Brussels, 1980.

Fischer, A. 'Lenin und die Technik des bewaffneten Aufstandes in der russischen Revolution von 1905'. *Wehrwissenschatiche Rundschau. Zeitschrift für die europäische Sicherheit* (1966, no. 7) 386–403.

*Russische Sozialdemokratie und bewaffneter Aufstand im Jahre 1905*. Wiesbaden, 1967.

Fischer, F. *Krieg der Illusionen. Die deutsche Politik von 1911 bis 1914*. Düsseldorf, 1969.

Fischer, L. *The Soviets in world affairs. A history of the relations between the Soviet Union and the rest of the world, 1917–1929*. New York, n.d.

*The life of Lenin*. New York, 1965.

Foner, P. S. *The Bolshevik revolution. Its impact on American radicals, liberals, and labor. A documentary study.* New York, 1967.

Footman, D. *Red prelude. A life of A. I. Zhelyabov.* London, 1968.

Frankel, J. 'Economism: a heresy exploited'. *Slavic Review,* XXII (1963) 263–84.

'Voluntarism, maximalism and the Group for the Emancipation of Labor' in: A. and J. Rabinowitch and L. K. D. Kristov, eds., *Revolution and politics in Russia. Essays in memory of B. I. Nicolaevsky.* Bloomington, Ind., 1972.

Frankel, J., ed. *Vladimir Akimov on the dilemmas of Russian Marxism 1895–1903.* Cambridge, 1969.

Freymond, J., ed. *La Première Internationale. Recueil de documents.* Geneva, 1962–71.

Futrell, M. *Northern underground. Episodes of Russian revolutionary transport and communications through Scandinavia and Finland 1863–1917.* London, 1963.

Galili, Z. *The Menshevik leaders in the Russian revolution. Social realities and political strategies.* Princeton, N.J., 1989.

Gankin, O. H. and Fisher, H. H., eds. *The Bolsheviks and the World War. The origin of the Third International.* Stanford, Calif., 1940.

Garvi, P. A. *Vospominanija socialdemokrata.* New York, 1946.

Geierhos, W. '*Der Sozialdemokrat* und die russischen Revolutionäre' in: U. Liszkowski, *Russland und Deutschland.* Kieler historische Studien, XXII. Stuttgart, 1974.

*Vera Zasulič und die russische revolutionäre Bewegung.* Munich, 1977.

Gercen, A. I. *Byloe i dumy.* Moscow, 1973.

Gerhard, D. *England und der Aufstieg Russlands. Zur Frage des Zusammenhanges der europäischen Staaten und ihres Ausgreifens in die aussereuropäische Welt in Politik und Wirtschaft des 18. Jahrhunderts.* Munich, 1933.

Gertler, J. 'Die deutsche Russlandpublizistik der Jahre 1853 bis 1870' in: *Forschungen zur osteuropäischen Geschichte,* VII. Berlin, 1959.

Getzler, I. *Martov. A political biography of a Russian social democrat.* Cambridge, 1967.

'Marxist revolutionaries and the dilemma of power' in: A. and J. Rabinowitch and L. K. D. Kristov, eds., *Revolution and politics in Russia. Essays in memory of B. I. Nicolaevsky.* Bloomington, Ind., 1972.

*Kronstadt 1917–1921. The fate of a Soviet democracy.* Cambridge, 1983.

Geyer, C. *Die revolutionäre Illusion. Zur geschichte des linken Flügels der USPD.* Stuttgart, 1976.

Geyer, D. 'Die russische Parteispaltung im Urteil der deutschen Sozialdemokratie 1903–1905'. *International Review of Social History* (1958) 195–219 and 418–44.

*Lenin in der russischen Sozialdemokratie. Die Arbeiterbewegung im Zaren-reich als Organisationsproblem der revolutionären Intelligenz, 1890–1903.* Cologne, 1962.

*Kautsky's russisches Dossier. Deutsche Sozialdemokraten als Treuhänder des russischen Parteivermögens.* Frankfurt, 1981.

Gleason, J. H. *The genesis of Russophobia in Great Britain. A study of the interaction of policy and opinion.* Cambridge, Mass., 1950.

Goehrke, C. *Die Theorien über die Entwicklung des 'Mir'.* Wiesbaden, 1964.

Goldschmidt, A. *Moskou 1920. Tagebuchblätter.* Berlin, 1920.

Gollwitzer, H. *Europabild und Europagedanke. Beiträge zur deutschen Geistesgeschichte des 18. und 19. Jahrhunderts.* Munich, 1951.

*Die gelbe Gefahr. Geschichte eines Schlagworts. Studien zum imperialis-tischen Denken.* Göttingen, 1962.

Gould, P. and White, R. *Mental maps.* New York, 1974.

Grass, M. *Friedensaktivität und Neutralität. Die scandinavische Sozial-demokratie und die neutrale Zusammenarbeit im Krieg, August 1914 bis Februar 1917.* Bonn, 1975.

Graubard, S. R. *British labour and the Russian revolution 1917–1924.* Cambridge, Mass., 1956.

Graus, F. 'Slavs and Germans' in: *Eastern and Western Europe in the Middle Ages.* London, 1970.

*Grecs et barbares.* Entretiens sur l'Antiquité classique, vol. VIII. Geneva, 1961.

Groh, D. *Russland und das Selbstverständnis Europas.* Neuwied, 1961.

Gruber, H., ed. *International communism in the era of Lenin. A documen-tary history.* New York, 1972.

Grunenberg, A., ed. *Die Massenstreikdebatte.* Frankfurt, 1970.

Guerrier, W. *Leibniz in seinen Beziehungen zu Russland und Peter dem Grossen.* n.p., 1873.

Guest, L. Haden. *The struggle for power in Europe 1917–1921.* London, 1921.

Gumplowicz, L. 'Das Russische Kaisertum und die Revolution'. *Sozialis-tische Monatshefte,* IX (1905, 1) 225–34.

Haar, J. M. 'The "Russian menace": Baltic German publicists and Russophobia in World War I Germany'. Unpublished Ph.D diss., University of Georgia, 1977.

Haimson, L. H. *The Russian Marxists and the origins of Bolshevism.* Cambridge, Mass., 1955.

'The problem of stability in urban Russia'. *Slavic Review,* XXIII (1964) 619–42 and XXIV (1965) 1–22. Also in: M. Cherniavsky, ed., *The structure of Russian history. Interpretive essays.* New York, 1970.

Haimson, L. H., ed. *The Mensheviks. From the revolution of 1917 to the Second World War.* Chicago, 1974.

Haimson, L. H. and Tilly, C., eds. *Strikes, wars and revolutions in an international perspective. Strike waves in the late nineteenth and early twentieth century.* Cambridge, 1989.

Hammen, O. J. 'Free Europe versus Russia, 1830–1854'. *American Slavic and Easteuropean Review,* XI (1952) 27–41.

Haney, B. M. 'Western reflections of Russia 1517–1812'. Unpublished Ph.D diss., University of Washington, 1971.

Harris, M. *The rise of anthropological theory. A history of theories of culture.* London, 1969.

Haupt, G., 'Lénine, les bolcheviks et la IIe Internationale'. *Cahiers du Monde Russe et Soviétique,* VII (1966) 378–407.

*Socialism and the Great War. The collapse of the Second International.* Oxford, 1972.

*Correspondance entre Lénine et Camille Huysmans 1905–1914.* Paris, 1963.

*Bureau Socialiste International. Comptes rendus des réunions, manifestes et circulaires,* I: *1900–1907.* Paris, 1969.

Hauser, O. *Deutschland und der englisch–russische Gegensatz.* Göttingen, 1958.

Hazard, P. *La crise de la conscience européenne 1680–1715.* Paris, 1935.

*La pensée européenne au XVIIIe siècle. De Montesquieu à Lessing.* Paris, 1963.

Hecker, H. *Die Tat und ihr Osteuropabild 1909–1939.* Cologne, 1974.

Heering, A. 'Filippo Turati e la II Internacionale (1891–1912)' in: *Filippo Turati e il socialismo europea.* Naples, 1985.

Hehn, V. *De moribus Ruthenorum. Zur Charakteristik der russischen Volksseele. Tagebuchblätter aus den Jahren 1857–1873.* Stuttgart, 1892.

Hemmings, F. W. J. *The Russian novel in France 1884–1914.* Oxford, 1950.

Henderson, W. O. *The life of Friedrich Engels.* London, 1976.

Herberstein, S. zu. *Reise zu den Moskovitern. 1526.* Munich, 1966.

Herod, C. C. *The nation in the history of Marxian thought. The concept of nations with history and without history.* The Hague, 1976.

Herzen, A. *From the other shore and The Russian people and socialism, an open letter to Jules Michelet.* Cleveland, 1963.

Hess, M. *Briefwechsel.* The Hague, 1959.

Hildermeier, M. *Die sozialrevolutionäre Partei Russlands. Agrarsozialismus und Modernisierung im Zarenreich (1900–1914).* Cologne, 1978.

Hilferding, R. 'Parlementarismus und Massenstreik'. *Die Neue Zeit,* XXIII (1904–5, 2) 804–17.

Hirsch, H., ed. *Eduard Bernsteins Briefwechsel mit Friedrich Engels.* Assen, 1970.

Hoffman, S. H. 'Scythianism. A cultural vision in revolutionary Russia'. Unpublished Ph.D diss., Columbia University, 1975.

Hollander, A. N. J. den. *Het andere volk. Een verkenning van groepsoordeel en groepsbeeld.* Leiden, 1946.

'Amerika in Europa's blikveld' in: A. N. J. den Hollander, *Visie en verwoording. Sociologische essays over het eigene en het andere.* Assen, 1968.

Hollander, P. *Political pilgrims. Travels of Western intellectuals to the Soviet Union, China and Cuba 1928–1978.* New York, 1981.

Holt, C. E. Jr. 'English liberals and Russia 1895–1907'. Unpublished Ph.D diss., University of Kentucky, 1976.

Honour, H. *Chinoiserie. The vision of Cathay.* London, 1961.

Hopper, B. 'Custine and Russia. A century after. A review essay'. *American Historical Review,* LVII (1952) 384–92.

Horowitz, I. L. *Radicalism and the revolt against reason. Peguy, Sorel, Barrès.* London, 1961.

Hueting, E., de Jong, F. and Neij, R. *Troelstra en het model van de nieuwe staat.* Assen, 1980.

Huggett, F. E. *The land question and European society.* London, 1975.

Hulst, H. van, Pleysier, A. and Scheffer, A. *Het Roode Vaandel volgen wij. Geschiedenis van de Sociaal-Democratische Arbeiders Partij van 1880 tot 1940.* The Hague, 1969.

Hussain, A. and Tribe, K. *Marxism and the agrarian question.* London, 1981, 1983.

Hyndman, H. M. *The record of an adventurous life.* London, 1911. *Further reminiscences.* London, 1912.

*Independent Labour Party. Report 1921.* London, 1921.

*L'Internationale socialiste et la Géorgie.* Paris, 1921.

*Iz istorii sozdanija partii novogo tipa. Doklad bol'ševikov meždunarodnomu socialističeskomu kongressu v 1904 g.* Moscow, 1963.

Ivanova, N. A. *V. I. Lenin o revoljucionoj massovoj stačke v Rossii.* Moskou, 1976.

Jahn, P. *Russophilie und Konservatismus. Die russophile Literatur in der deutschen Öffentlichkeit 1831–1852.* Stuttgart, 1980.

Jansen, M. *A show trial under Lenin. The trial of the socialist revolutionaries. Moscow 1922.* The Hague, 1982.

Jelen, C. *L'aveuglement. Les socialistes et la naissance du mythe soviétique.* Paris, 1984.

*Journey for our time. The journals of the Marquis de Custine.* New York, n.d.

Julliard, J. *Fernand Pelloutier et les origines du syndicalisme d'action directe.* Paris, 1971.

Jüthner, J. *Hellenen und Barbaren. Aus der Geschichte des Nationalbewustseins.* Leipzig, 1923.

Kahle, W. *Die Begegnung des baltischen Protestantismus mit der russischorthodoxen Kirche.* Leiden, 1959.

Kappeler, A. and Lemmenmeier, M. 'Die Schweizer Öffentlichkeit und die russische Revolution von 1905–1907'. *Jahrbücher für Geschichte Osteuropas,* n.s. XXI (1973) 392–418.

Karski, J. [Marschlevski]. 'Ein Missverständnis'. *Die Neue Zeit,* XXIX (1910–11, 1) 100–7.

Kaufman, W. *Nietzsche, philosopher, psychologist, antichrist.* Princeton, N.J., 1974.

Kautsky, J. H. 'Introduction' in: K. Kautsky, *The dictatorship of the proletariat.* Ann Arbor, Mich., 1964, 1971.

Kautsky, K. 'Finis Poloniae'. *Die Neue Zeit,* XIV (1895–6, 2) 484–91 and 513–25.

'Die neue Bewegung in Russland'. *Die Neue Zeit,* XIX (1900–1, 2) 123–7.

'Allerhand Revolutionäres'. *Die Neue Zeit,* XXII (1903–4, 1) 588–98, 620–7, 685–95 and 732–40.

'Wahlkreis und Partei'. *Die Neue Zeit,* XXII (1903–4, 2) 36–46.

'Die Differenzen unter den russischen Sozialisten'. *Die Neue Zeit,* XXIII (1904–5, 2) 68–79.

'Die Agrarfrage in Russland'. *Die Neue Zeit,* XXIV (1905–6, 1) 412–23.

'Die russische Duma'. *Die Neue Zeit,* XXIV (1905–6, 2) 241–5.

'Triebkräfte und Aussichten der russischen Revolution'. *Die Neue Zeit,* XXV (1906–7, 1) 284–90, 324–33.

'Was nun?'. *Die Neue Zeit,* XXVIII (1909–10, 2) 33–40, 68–80.

'Eine neue Strategie'. *Die Neue Zeit,* XXVIII (1909–10, 2) 332–41, 364–74, 412–21.

'Zwischen Baden und Luxemburg'. *Die Neue Zeit,* XXVIII (1909–10, 2) 652–67.

*Die Diktatur des Proletariats.* Vienna, 1918.

*Terrorismus und Kommunismus. Ein Beitrag zur Naturgeschichte der Revolution.* Berlin, 1919.

'Eine Schrift über den Bolschewismus'. *Der Kampf,* XIII (July 1920, no. 7) 260–5.

*Von der Demokratie zur Staats-Sklaverei. Eine Auseinandersetzung mit Trotzki.* Berlin, 1921.

*Aus der Frühzeit des Marxismus.* Prague, 1935.

*Sozialisten und Krieg. Ein Beitrag zur Ideengeschichte des Sozialismus von den Hussiten bis zum Völkerbund.* Prague, 1937.

*Erinnerungen und Erörterungen.* The Hague, 1960.

*The dictatorship of the proletariat.* Ann Arbor, Mich., 1964, 1971.

Kautsky, K. Jr. 'Vorwort' in: *August Bebels Briefwechsel mit Karl Kautsky.* Assen, 1971.

Keep, J. L. H. *The rise of social democracy in Russia.* Oxford, 1966. *The Russian revolution. A study in mass mobilisation.* London, 1976.

Kendall, W. *The revolutiᵤ ary movement in Britain 1900–1921. The origins of British communism.* London, 1969.

Kennan, G. F. *The Marquis de Custine and his Russia in 1839.* Princeton, N.J., 1971.

Kerensky, A. *The Kerensky memoirs. Russia and history's turning point.* London, 1965.

Kettle, M. *The Allies and the Russian collapse. March 1917–March 1918.* London, 1981.

Kindersley, R. *The first Russian revisionists. A study of 'Legal Marxism' in Russia.* Oxford, 1962.

Kirby, D. *War, peace and revolution. International socialism at the crossroads, 1914–1918.* Aldershot, 1986.

Kirchner, W. 'Die Bedeutung Narwas im 16.Jahrhundert. Ein Beitrag zum Studium der Beziehungen zwischen Russland und Europa'. *Historische Zeitschrift* (1951) 265–84.

Ključevskij, V. *Skazanija inostrancev o moskovskom gosudarstve.* Petrograd, 1918.

Koenker, D. *The Moscow workers and the 1917 revolution.* Princeton, N.J., 1981.

Kohn, H. 'Dostoyevsky and Danilevsky: Nationalist Messianism' in: E. J. Simmons, ed., *Continuity and change in Russian and Soviet thought.* New York, 1955.

*Internationaler Sozialisten-Kongress zu Paris 23. bis 27. September 1900.* Berlin, 1900.

*Internationaler Sozialisten-Kongress zu Amsterdam 14. bis 20. August 1904.* Berlin, 1904.

*Internationaler Sozialisten-Kongress zu Stuttgart 18. bis 24. August 1907.* Berlin, 1907.

Kool, F. and Oberländer, E. *Arbeiterdemokratie oder Parteidiktatur.* Dokumente der Weltrevolution, vol. II. Olten, 1967.

Koppelmann, H. L. *Nation, Sprache und Nationalismus.* Leiden, 1956.

Kossmann, E. H. *Politieke theorie in het zeventiende-eeuwse Nederland.* Verhandelingen der Koninklijke Nederlandse Akademie van Wetenschappen. Section Literature, n.s. LXVII, no. 2. Amsterdam, 1960.

Koz'min, B. P. *Russkaja sekcija Pervogo Internacionala.* Moscow, 1957.

Krabbo, H. 'Eine Schilderung der Elbslawen aus dem Jahre 1108' in: *Papsttum und Kaisertum. Festschrift Paul Kehr.* Munich, 1926, 1973.

Krader, L., ed. *The ethnological notebooks of Karl Marx.* Assen, 1972.

Krause, H. *Marx und Engels und das zeitgenössische Russland*. Marburger Abhandlungen zur Geschichte und Kultur Osteuropas, series II, vol. I. Giessen, 1958.

Krautheim, H. J. *Öffentliche Meinung und imperiale Politik. Das britische Russlandbild (1815–1844)*. Berlin, 1977.

Kriegel, A., ed. *Le congrès de Tours (décembre 1920). Naissance du Parti Communiste Français*. Mesnil-sur-l'Estrée, 1964.

Krispin, A. [Crispien, A.]. 'Pamjati Martova'. *Socialističeskij Vestnik*, 24 IV 1925.

Kritschewsky, B. 'Die russische revolutionäre Bewegung einst und jetzt'. *Die Neue Zeit*, IX (1891, 2) 642–9, 657–65, 701–8.

Prince Kropotkin. *The Terror in Russia. An appeal to the British nation*. London, 1909.

Kropotkin, P. *Memoirs of a revolutionist*. New York, 1962.

Krupskaya, N. *Memories of Lenin*. London, 1970.

Kučin, G. [Oranskij]. 'O našej partii'. *Socialističeskij Vestnik*, no. 18, 1922.

Kučin-Oranskij, G. 'Zapiski' in: B. Dvinov, *Ot legal'nosti k podpol'ju (1921–1922) (From legality to the underground (1921–1922))*. Stanford, Calif., 1968.

Kuskova, E. 'Mesjac "soglašatel'stva"'. *Volja Rossii*, nos. 3, 4 and 5, 1928, 50–69, 43–61 and 58–78.

*British Labour Delegation to Russia. Report*. London, 1920.

*The Labour Party. Report of the Executive Committee*. London, 1919.

*The Labour Party. Report of the Executive Committee*. London, 1920.

Lademacher, H., ed. *Die Zimmerwalder Bewegung. Protokolle und Korrespondenz*. The Hague, 1967.

Lafargue, P. 'Persönliche Erinnerungen an Friedrich Engels'. *Die Neue Zeit*, XXIII (1904–5, 2) 556–61.

Lagardell', G. *Vseobščaja stačka i socializm. Meždunarodnaja anketa. Mnenija i dokumenty*. St Petersburg, 1907.

Lagardelle, H. *La grève générale et le socialisme. Enquête internationale. Opinions et documents*. Paris, 1905.

Lambert, W. E. and Klineberg, O. *Children's views of foreign peoples. A cross-national study*. New York, 1967.

Lammig, M. *Das deutsche Osteuropabild in der Zeit der Reichsgründung*. Boppard on Rhein, 1977–8.

Lande, L. 'The Mensheviks in 1917' in: L. H. Haimson, ed., *The Mensheviks. From the revolution of 1917 to the Second World War*. Chicago, 1974.

Langlois, C. V. *La vie en France au moyen-âge au milieu du XIVe siècle. La connaissance de la nature et du monde d'après des écrits français à l'usage des laïcs*. Paris, 1927.

Laqueur, W. *Russia and Germany. A century of conflict.* London, 1965.

Larsson, R. *Theories of revolution. From Marx to the first Russian revolution.* Stockholm, 1970.

Lasch, C. *American liberals and the Russian revolution.* New York, 1962.

Laschitza, A. *Die deutsche Linke im Kampf für eine demokratische Republik.* Berlin, 1969.

Laslett, J. H. M. and Lipset, S. M., eds. *Failure of a dream. Essays in the history of American socialism.* New York, 1974.

Lassalle, F. *Reden und Schriften.* Munich, 1970.

Lauridzen, K. V. 'Revolution in Russia and response in France. Contemporary views from the French far left, 1905–1907'. Unpublished Ph.D diss., New York University, 1971.

Lavroff, P. 'Le socialisme en Russie'. *Revue Socialiste*, X (1889, 2) 276–83.

Lazitch, B. and Drachkovitch, M. M. *Lenin and the Comintern*, I. Stanford, Calif., 1972.

*Ein Leben für den Sozialismus. Erinnerungen an Karl Kautsky.* Hanover, 1954.

Lechner, K. 'Byzanz und die Barbaren'. *Speculum*, IV (1955) 292–306.

Lednicki, W. *Russia, Poland and the West. Essays in literary and cultural history.* London, 1954.

Legett, G. *The Cheka. Lenin's political police.* Oxford, 1981.

Lehning, A. et al., eds. *Archives Bakunine*: I, part 2: *Michel Bakounine et l'Italie 1871–1872.* Leiden, 1963. II: *Michel Bakounine et les conflits dans l'Internationale 1872.* Leiden, 1965. IV: *Michel Bakounine et les relations avec Sergej Nečaev 1870–1872.* Leiden, 1971.

Leib, B. *Rome, Kiev et Byzance à la fin du XIe siècle. Rapports religieux des latins et des Greco-russes sous le pontificat d'Urbain II (1088–1099).* Paris, 1924.

Leichter, O. *Otto Bauer.* Vienna, 1970.

Lenin, N. 'Predislovie k russkomu perevodu' in: K. Kautskij, *Dvižuščija sily i perspektivy russkoj revoljucii.* Moscow, 1907.

Lenin, V. I. *Keuze uit zijn werken*, III. Amsterdam, 1952.

*Polnoe sobranie sočinenija.* 5th edn. Moscow, 1963.

*Werke.* 40 vols. Berlin, 1963.

*Studienausgabe.* 2 vols. Frankfurt on Main, 1970.

Lenskij, 'K voprosu o formach proletarskoj bor'by' in: *Itogi i perspektivy.* Moscow, 1906.

LeVine, R. A. and Campbell, D. T. *Ethnocentrism. Theories of conflict, ethnic attitudes and group behavior.* London, 1972.

Lewin, M. *Political undercurrents in Soviet economic debates.* Princeton, N.J., 1974.

Lewitin, S. 'Das Jahr 1907' in: A. Tscherewanin, *Das Proletariat und die russische Revolution.* Stuttgart, 1908.

Lidtke, V. L. *The outlawed party. Social-democracy in Germany 1878–1890.* Princeton, N.J., 1966.

'Revisionismus' in: *Sowjetsystem und demokratische Gesellschaft. Eine vergleichende Enzyklopedie,* V. Freiburg, 1972.

Liebknecht, K. *Politische Aufzeichnungen aus seinem Nachlass. Geschrieben in den Jahren 1917/18.* Berlin, 1927.

Lindemann, A. S. *The 'red years'. European socialism vs. Bolshevism 1919–1921.* Berkeley, Calif., 1974.

'Socialist impressions of revolutionary Russia, 1920'. *Russian History,* I, no. 1 (1974).

Lipset, S. M. 'Whatever happened to the proletariat? An historic mission unfulfilled'. *Encounter* (June 1981) 18–34.

*Le livre de la description des pays de Gilles de Bouvier, dit Berry.* Paris, 1908.

Ljadov, M. *Iz žizni partii.* Moscow, 1956.

Locher, T. J. G. *Geschiedenis van ver en dichtbij.* Leiden, 1970.

Long, J. W. 'Organized protest against the 1906 Russian loan'. *Cahiers du Monde Russe et Soviétique,* XIII (1972) 24–39.

Longuet, J. and Silber, G. *Terroristes et policiers. Les dessous de la police russe. Asev, Harting et Cie. Etude historique et critique.* Paris, 1909.

Loopuit, J. *Het anarchisme in de arbeidersbeweging.* Amsterdam, 1905.

Lortholary, A. *Les 'philosophes' du XVIIIe siècle et la Russie. Le mirage russe en France au XVIIIe siècle.* Paris, 1948.

Lösche, P. *Der Bolschewismus im Urteil der deutschen Sozialdemokratie 1903–1920.* Berlin, 1967.

Lovejoy, A. O. *The great chain of being.* New York, 1965.

Lowe, C. J. and Marzari, F. *Italian foreign policy 1870–1940.* London, 1975.

Lozinsky, G. 'La Russie dans la littérature française du moyen âge: le pays'. *Revue des Etudes Slaves,* IX (1929) 71–89.

Lübbe, P., ed. *Kautsky gegen Lenin.* Berlin, 1981.

Luxemburg, R. 'Organisationsfragen der russischen Sozialdemokratie'. *Die Neue Zeit,* XXII (1903–4, 2) 484–92 and 529–35.

'Die Revolution in Russland'. *Die Neue Zeit,* XXIII (1904–5, 1) 572–7.

'Nach dem ersten Akt'. *Die Neue Zeit,* XXIII (1904–5, 1) 610–14.

'Ermattung oder Kampf'. *Die Neue Zeit,* XXVIII (1909–10, 2) 257–66, 291–305.

'Die Theorie und die Praxis'. *Die Neue Zeit,* XVIII (1909–10, 2) 564–78, 626–42.

*Die russische Revolution.* Frankfurt on Main, 1963.

*Gesammelte Werke.* 5 vols. Berlin, 1970–5.

*Briefe an Leon Jogiches.* Frankfurt on Main, 1971.

*Lettres à Léon Jogiches.* Paris, 1971.

Lydin, M. *Material zur Erlaüterung der Parteikrise in der Sozialdem. Arbeiterpartei Russlands.* Geneva, 1904.

McClellan, W. *Revolutionary exiles. The Russians in the First International and the Paris Commune.* London, 1979.

McDaniel, T. *Autocracy, capitalism, and revolution in Russia.* Berkeley, Calif., 1988.

McInnes, N. 'The labour movement, socialists, communists, trade-unions' in: *The impact of the Russian revolution 1917–1967. The influence of Bolshevism on the world outside Russia.* London. 1967.

Mackenzie Wallace, D. *Russia on the eve of war and revolution.* New York, 1961.

McNally, R. T. 'Das Russlandbild in der Publizistik Frankreichs zwischen 1814 und 1843'. *Forschungen zur osteuropäischen Geschichte,* VI (Berlin, 1958) 82–169.

Maitron, J. *Le mouvement anarchiste en France, I: Des origines à 1914.* Paris, 1975.

Maletzki, 'Der bürgerliche Liberalismus in der russischen Revolution'. *Die Neue Zeit,* XXVI (1907–8, 2) 551–7.

Malia, M. *Alexander Herzen and the birth of Russian socialism.* Cambridge, Mass., 1961.

Manacorda, G. *Rivoluzione borghese e socialismo. Studi e saggi.* Rome, 1975.

Manakorda, G. 'Otkliki v Italii na pervuju russkuju revoljuciju' in: *Pervaja Russkaja revoljucija 1905–1907 gg. i meždunarodnoe dviženie,* II. Moscow, 1956.

Man'kov, A. G., ed. *Inostrannye izvestija o vosstanii Stepana Razina. Materialy i issledovanija.* Leningrad, 1975.

Mann, G. *Deutsche Geschichte 1919–1945.* Frankfurt on Main, 1961.

Mann, T. 'Russische Anthologie' in: Thomas Mann, *Rede und Antwort. Gesammelte Abhandlungen und kleine Aufsätze.* Berlin, 1922.

*K. Marks i F. Engel's i revoljucionnaja Rossija.* Moscow, 1967.

Marquand, D. *Ramsay MacDonald.* London, 1977.

Martin, B. K. *The triumph of Lord Palmerston. A study of public opinion in England before the Crimean War.* London, 1963.

Martoff, L. 'Die erste Epoche der russischen Revolution'. *Die Neue Zeit,* XXIV (1905–6, 1) 18–23, 52–60.

'De eerste periode der Russische revolutie'. *Het Volk,* 21 and 24 X 1905.

'Der Staatsstreich in Russland'. *Die Neue Zeit,* XXV (1906–7, 2) 516–28.

'Die preussische Diskussion und die russische Erfahrung'. *Die Neue Zeit,* XXVIII (1909–10, 2) 907–19.

*Martov i ego blizkie. Sbornik.* New York, 1959.

Martov, J. *Le bolchevisme mondial.* Paris, 1934.

Martov, J. L. 'Das Problem der Internationale'. *Der Kampf*, XVI (Jan. 1923, no. 1) 1–9.

Martov, L. 'K. Kautskij [ i ] russkaja revoljucija' in: *Sbornik II*. Izd. 'Otkliki', St Petersburg, 1907.

*Spasiteli ili uprazdniteli? (Kto i kak razrušal R.S.D.R.P)*. Paris, 1911.

'Antwort an Zinoviev'. *Freiheit*, 15–16 XI 1920.

'K Venskoj konferencii'. *Socialističeskij Vestnik*, 18 III 1921.

'Nach dem Kronstadter Aufstand'. *Freiheit*, 1–2 IV 1921.

'Kronštadt'. *Socialističeskij Vestnik*, 5 IV 1921.

'Po povodu pis'ma tov. P. B. Aksel'roda'. *Socialističeskij Vestnik*, 20 V 1921, 3–6.

'Vosstanovlenie Internacionala'. *Socialističeskij Vestnik*, 5 VIII 1921, 3–8.

'Illjuzii i dejstvitel'nost''. *Socialističeskij Vestnik*, 16 IX 1921, 9–14.

'Problema Internacionala'. *Socialističeskij Vestnik*, 2 XI 1922, 5–9.

*Bol'ševizm v Rossii i v Internacional*. Berlin, 1923.

*Geschichte der russischen Sozialdemokratie*. Berlin, 1926. Reprint: Erlangen, 1973.

Marx, K. *Das Kapital*. Hamburg, 1867.

*La Russie et l'Europe*. Paris, 1954.

*Manuskripte über die polnische Frage (1863–1864)*. The Hague, 1961.

*Capital. A critique of political economy*. New York, 1967.

*Marx vs. Russia*. New York, 1962.

Marx, K. and Engels, F. *The Russian menace to Europe*. Glencoe, Ill., 1952.

*Werke*. 39 vols. Berlin, 1956-1970.

*Het communistisch manifest*. Amsterdam, 1967.

*Die russische Kommune. Kritik eines Mythos*. Munich, 1972.

*Marx/Bakounine: Socialisme autoritaire ou libertaire*. 2 vols. Paris, 1975.

*Marx–Engels Gesamtausgabe*. 4 vols. Berlin and Moscow, 1926–35.

*Marx–Engels Studienausgabe*. 4 vols. Frankfurt on Main, 1966.

Masaryk, T. G. *Sur le bolchevisme*. Geneva, 1920.

*Die Weltrevolution. Erinnerungen und Betrachtungen*. Berlin, 1925.

Massa, I. *A short history of the beginnings and origins of these present wars in Moscow under the reign of various sovereigns down to the year 1610*. Toronto, 1982.

Matthes, E. *Das veränderte Russland. Studien zum deutschen Russlandverständnis im 18. Jahrhundert zwischen 1725 und 1762*. Frankfurt on Main, 1981.

Matthias, E. 'Kautsky und der Kautskyanismus: die Funktion der Ideologie in der deutschen Sozialdemokratie vor dem Ersten Weltkriege'. *Marxismusstudien*, 2 (1957) 151–97.

Mayer, A. *Politics and diplomacy of peacemaking 1918–1919. Containment and counterrevolution at Versailles, 1918–1919*. New York, 1967.

Mayer, G. *Friedrich Engels. Eine Biographie.* Frankfurt on Main, 1975.

Mehringer, H. *Permanente Revolution und russische Revolution. Die Entwicklung der Theorie der permanenten Revolution im Rahmen der marxistischen Revolutionskonzeption 1848–1907.* Frankfurt on Main, 1978.

*Mémorandum présenté par la Délégation du parti socialiste révolutionnaire à l'étranger au Congrès des trois Unions internationales des partis socialistes et communistes.* Berlin, 1922.

Mendel, A. P. *Dilemmas of progress in tsarist Russia. Legal Marxism and legal populism.* Cambridge, Mass., 1961.

'Peasant and worker on the eve of the First World War'. *Slavic Review,* XXIV (1965) 23–3.

'On interpreting the fate of Imperial Russia' in: T. G. Stavrou, ed., *Russia under the last tsar.* Minneapolis, 1969.

Mervaud, M. 'Herzen et Proudhon'. *Cahiers du Monde Russe et Soviétique,* XII (1971) 110–88.

Mey, H. W. van der. *Rusland en het Nihilismus.* Haarlem, 1880.

Meyer, K. 'Die russische Revolution von 1905 im deutschen Urteil' in: U. Liszkowski, ed., *Russland und Deutschland.* Kieler historische Studien, XXII. Stuttgart, 1974.

Michelet, J. *Légendes démocratiques du Nord.* Paris, 1968.

Mihailovich, V. 'Hermann Hesse and Russia'. Unpublished Ph.D diss., University of California at Berkeley, 1966.

Mitchell, H. and Stearns, P. N. *The European labor movement, the working classes and the origins of social democracy 1890–1914.* Itasca, Ill., 1971.

'Mnenie Zapadno-evropeiskich socialistov o sovremennom obščestvennom dviženii v Rossii'. *Sovremennaja žizn'* (Nov. 1906) 206ff.

Mnuchina, R. S. 'Pod'em rabočego dviženija v Avstrii v 1905–1907gg' in: *Pervaja Russkaja Revoljucija 1905–1907gg i meždunarodnoe revoljucionnoe dviženie,* I. Moscow, 1955.

Mohrenschildt, D. S. von. *Russia in the intellectual life of eighteenth-century France.* New York, 1936, 1972.

Momigliano, A. *Alien wisdom. The limits of Hellenization.* London, 1975.

Moore, Barrington Jr. *Injustice. The social basis of obedience and revolt.* New York, 1978.

Moore, L. R. *European socialists and the American promised land.* n.p., 1970.

Muchnic, H. 'Dostoevsky's English reputation (1881–1936)'. *Smith College Studies in Modern Languages,* XX, nos. 1 and 2 (Oct. 1938, Jan. 1939).

Mühlpfordt, G. 'Zur Weltwirkung der russischen Revolution im 1905–1907' in: *Jahrbuch für Geschichte der deutsch-slawischen Beziehungen und Geschichte Ost- und Mitteleuropas,* I. Halle, 1956.

Murray, R. K. *Red-scare. A study in national hysteria.* Minneapolis, 1955.

Naarden, B. 'Een "verbael" van een reis naar Moskovië' in: E. H. Waterbolk, ed., *Proeven van Lieuwe van Aitzema, 1600–1669.* Leeuwarden, 1970.

'Was de revolutie onvermijdelijk?'. *Ruslandbulletin,* VIII, no. 2 (1984) 29–33.

'Nederlanders en het Westeuropese Ruslandbeeld' in: *Rusland in Nederlandse ogen. Een bundel opstellen.* Amsterdam, 1986.

'Revolution in Eastern Europe: the end of European despotism'. *Internationale Spectator,* XLIV, no. 11 (1990) 643–7.

*Filosofsko-literaturnoe nasledie G. V. Plechanova,* II: *G. V. Plechanov i meždunarodnoe rabočee dviženie.* Moscow, 1973.

Nettl, P. *Rosa Luxemburg.* Cologne, 1968.

Nettlau, M. *Die Vorfrühling der Anarchie. Ihre historische Entwicklung von den Anfängen bis zum Jahre 1864.* Glashütten in Taunus, 1925, 1972.

*Anarchisten und Sozialrevolutionäre. Die historische Entwicklung des Anarchismus in den Jahren 1880–1886.* Berlin, 1931; Glashütten in Taunus, 1972.

*Neudrucke marxistischer Seltenheiten,* III: *Die Briefe Karl Marx' und Friedrich Engels' an Danielson (Nikolai-on).* Leipzig, 1929.

Nicolaevsky, B. I. 'Stranicy prošlogo'. *Socialističeskij Vestnik,* July–Aug. 1958.

*Men'ševiki v dni oktjabr'skogo perevorota.* Inter-university project on the history of the Menshevik movement. Paper no. 8. New York, 1962.

*Power and the Soviet elite. 'The letter of an Old Bolshevik' and other essays.* Ann Arbor, Mich., 1975.

Nikolajewsky, B. *Asew. Die Geschichte eines Verrats.* Berlin, 1932.

Nicoll, G. D. 'Russian participation in the Second International 1889–1914'. Unpublished Ph.D diss., University of Boston, 1961.

Northcutt, W. B. 'Contemporary French evaluations of the Russian revolution of 1905'. Unpublished Ph.D diss., University of California at Irvine, 1974.

Oberländer, E. 'Zur Wirkungsgeschichte historischer Fälschungen: das 'Testament' Peters des Grossen'. *Jahrbücher für Geschichte Osteuropas,* n.s. XXI (1973) 46–60.

*Oeuvres de Ghillebert de Lannoy, voyageur, diplomate et moraliste.* Louvain, 1878.

'Otraženie sobytij 1905 g. za granicej' in: *Krasnyj Archiv,* II, no. 9 (1925) 32–55.

Pannekoek, A. *Herinneringen.* Amsterdam, 1982.

Parker, W. H. *An historical geography of Russia.* London, 1968.

*Aux partis socialistes du monde entier. Appel à l'Internationale de la Délégation Russe du parti socialdémocrate et du parti socialiste-révolutionnaire à l'étranger.* Stockholm, 1918.

Parvus [Helphand, A. I.]. 'Staatsstreich und politischer Massenstreik'. *Die Neue Zeit,* XIV (1895–6, 2) 199–206, 261–6, 304–11, 356–64, 389–95.

'Die gegenwärtige politische Lage Russlands und die Aussichten für die Zukunft'. *Die Neue Zeit,* XXIV (1905–6, 2) 108–20.

Peake, T. R. 'The impact of the Russian revolutions upon French attitudes and policies toward Russia 1917–1918'. Unpublished Ph.D. diss., University of North Carolina at Chapel Hill, 1974.

Pearce, B., ed. *1903. Second ordinary congress of the RSDLP. Complete text of the minutes.* London, 1978.

Pellenberg, P. H. *Bedrijfsrelokatie en ruimtelijke kognitie.* Sociaalgeografische reeks, no. 33. Diss., Groningen, 1985.

*Perepiska G. V. Plechanova i P. B. Aksel'roda.* Moscow, 1925.

Pipes, R. *Struve,* I: *Liberal on the left 1870–1905.* Cambridge, Mass., 1970.

*Struve,* II: *Liberal on the right 1905–1944.* Cambridge, Mass., 1980.

*Pis'ma P. B. Aksel'roda i Iu. O. Martova. Materialy po istorii russkogo revoljucionnogo dviženija,* I. Berlin, 1924.

Platzhoff, W. 'Das erste Auftauchen Russlands und der russischen Gefahr in der europäischen Politik'. *Historische Zeitschrift* (1916) 77–93.

Plechanow, G. 'Die sozialpolitischen Zustände Russlands im Jahre 1890'. *Die Neue Zeit,* IX (1890–1, 2) 661–8, 691–6, 731–9, 765–70, 791–800, 827–34.

'G. J. Uspenskij. Die Volksthümliche Belletristik und die moderne Entwicklung Russlands. Eine literarische Studie'. *Die Neue Zeit,* X (1892, 2) 678–83, 718–23, 786–94 and 819–22.

Plechanov, G. V. *Sočinenija.* XV, Moscow, 1926. XVI, Moscow, 1928.

Polevoj, I. Z. *Zaroždenie marksizma v Rossii 1893–1894 gg.* Moscow, 1959.

Poliakov, L. *Le mythe aryen.* Paris, 1971.

Pomper, P. *Peter Lavrov and the Russian revolutionary movement.* Chicago, 1972.

Preiswerk, R. and Perrot, D. *Ethnocentrism and history. Africa, Asia and Indian America in Western textbooks.* New York, 1978.

*Protokoll des internationalen Arbeiter-Congresses zu Paris. Abgehalten vom 14. bis 20. Juli 1889.* Nuremberg, 1890.

*Protokoll des internationalen Arbeiterkongresses in der Tonhalle Zürich von 6. bis 12. August 1893.* Zurich, 1894.

*Protokoll der internationalen Socialistischen Konferenz in Wien vom 22. bis 27. Februar.* Vienna, 1921.

*Protokoll der internationalen Konferenz der drei internationalen Executivkomitees in Berlin vom 2. bis 5. April 1922.* Vienna, 1922.

*Protokoll des Internationalen Sozialistischen Arbeiterkongresses in Hamburg vom 21. bis 25. Mai 1923.* Berlin, 1923.

*Protokoll über die Verhandlungen des Parteitages der Sozialdemokratischen Partei Deutschlands, abgehalten zu Bremen vom 18. bis 24. September 1904.* Berlin, 1904.

*Protokoll über die Verhandlungen des Parteitages der Sozialdemokratischen Partei Deutschlands, abgehalten zu Jena vom 17. bis 23. September 1905.* Berlin, 1905.

*Protokoll über die Verhandlungen des Parteitages der Sozialdemokratischen Partei Deutschlands, abgehalten zu Mannheim vom 23. bis 29. September 1906.* Berlin, 1906.

*Protokoll über die Verhandlungen des ausserordentlichen Parteitages in Halle vom 12. bis 17. Oktober 1920.* Berlin, n.d.

Rabinowitch, A. *Prelude to revolution. The Petrograd Bolsheviks and the July 1917 uprising.* Bloomington, Ind., 1968.

*The Bolsheviks come to power. The revolution of 1917 in Petrograd.* New York, 1978.

Radek, K. 'Erklärung'. *Die Neue Zeit*, XXIX (1909–10, 1) 27–8.

*Proletarian dictatorship and terrorism.* Detroit, n.d.

*Les questions de la révolution mondiale à la lumière du menchévisme.* Petrograd, 1921.

Radkey, O. H. *The agrarian foes of Bolshevism. Promise and defeat of the Russian socialist revolutionaries, February to October 1917.* New York, 1958.

*The sickle under the hammer. The Russian socialist revolutionaries in the early months of Soviet rule.* New York, 1963.

*The unknown civil war in Soviet Russia. A study of the Green movement in the Tambov region 1920–1921.* Stanford, Calif., 1976.

Randall, F. B. 'Introduction' in: B. Pares, *Between reform and revolution.* New York, 1962.

Ransome, A. *Russia in 1919.* New York, 1919.

*Rapport du Parti Socialiste Révolutionnaire de Russie au Congrès Socialiste International d'Amsterdam.* Paris, 1904.

*Raskol na II s'ezde. RSDRP i II Internacional. Sbornik dokumentov.* Moscow, 1933.

Rauch, G. von. 'Streiflichter zum russischen Deutschlandbilde des 19. Jahrhunderts'. *Jahrbücher für Geschichte Osteuropas*, n.s. XII (1964) 5–47.

*Studien über das Verhältnis Russlands zu Europa.* Darmstadt, 1964.

Read, C. *Religion, revolution and the Russian intelligentsia 1900–1912. The Vekhi debate and its intellectual backround.* London, 1979.

Reichard, R. W. 'The German working class and the Russian revolution of 1905'. *Journal of Central European Affairs*, XIII, no. 2 (1953) 136–53.

Reichwein, A. *China and Europe. Intellectual and artistic contacts in the eighteenth century.* London, 1968.

Reisberg, A. *Lenins Beziehungen zur deutschen Arbeiterbewegung.* Berlin, 1970.

Renaudel, P. *L'Internationale à Berne.* Paris, 1919.

*Report presented by the Russian Social-Democrats to the International Congress of the Socialist Workers and Trade-Unions.* London, 1896.

*Report of the 21st Annual Conference of the Labour Party.* London, 1921.

Resis, A. '*Das Kapital* comes to Russia'. *Slavic Review*, XXI (1970) 219–37.

Reuel', A. L. '*Kapitala' Karla Marksa v Rossii 1870-ch gg.* Moscow, 1939.

*Pervaja Russkaja revoljucija 1905–1907 gg. i meždunarodnoe revoljucionnoe dviženie*, II. Moscow, 1955.

Riasanovsky, N. V. *A history of Russia.* New York, 1963.

Riese, A. *Die Idealisierung der Naturvölker des Nordens in der griechischen und römischen Literatur.* Frankfurt on Main, 1975.

Riha, T. 'Constitutional developments in Russia' in: T. G. Stavrou, ed., *Russia under the last tsar.* Minneapolis, 1969.

*A Russian European. Paul Miliukov in Russian politics.* Notre Dame, Ind., 1969.

*Rainer Marie Rilke in Selbstzeugnissen und Bilddokumenten.* Hamburg, 1958.

Ritter, G. A., ed. *Die Zweite Internationale 1918/1919. Protokolle, Memoranden, Berichte und Korrespondenzen.* Berlin, 1980.

N. R. [Rjasanoff, N.]. 'Der Fall Asew und die russische Revolution'. *Die Neue Zeit*, XXVII (1908–9, 1) 796–808.

Rjasanoff, N. 'Karl Marx über den Ursprung der Vorherrschaft Russlands in Europa. Kritische Untersuchungen'. *Ergänzungshefte zur Neuen Zeit*, no. 5 (1908–9) 1–64.

'Marx als Verleumder'. *Die Neue Zeit*, XXIX (1910–11, 1) 278–86.

'Marx und seine russischen Bekannten in den vierziger Jahre'. *Die Neue Zeit*, XXXI (1912–13, 1) 715–21, 757–66.

'Die auswärtige Politik der alten Internationale und ihre Stellungnahme zum Krieg'. *Die Neue Zeit*, XXXIII (1914–15, 2) 329–35, 360–9, 438–43, 463–9, 509–19.

Roland Gol'st, G. *Vseobščaja stačka i social'-demokratija.* St Petersburg, 1906.

Roland Holst, H. *Algemeene Werkstaking en Sociaaldemokratie.* Rotterdam, 1906.

*Geschiedenis van den proletarischen klassenstrijd.* Rotterdam, 1909.

*Rosa Luxemburg. Haar leven en werken.* Rotterdam, 1935.

Roland Holst–Van der Schalk, H. *Het vuur brandde voort. Levensherinneringen.* Amsterdam, 1949.

Romein, J. M. *Dostojewsky in de Westersche kritiek. Een hoofdstuk uit de geschiedenis van den literairen roem.* Haarlem, 1924.

Roobol, W. H. *Tsereteli. A democrat in the Russian revolution.* The Hague, 1976.

Ropponen, R. *Die Kraft Russlands. Wie beurteilte die politische und militärische Führung der europäischen Grossmächte in der Zeit von 1905 bis 1914 die Kraft Russlands?* Helsinki, 1968.

*Die russische Gefahr. Das Verhalten der öffentlichen Meinung Deutschlands und Österreich-Ungarns gegenüber der Aussenpolitik Russlands in der Zeit zwischen dem Frieden von Portsmouth und dem Ausbruch des Ersten Weltkriegs.* Helsinki, 1976.

Rosdolsky, R. *Engels und das Problem der 'geschichtlosen Völker'.* Detroit, 1949.

Rosenberg, W. G. *Liberals in the Russian revolution. The Constitutional Democratic Party 1917–1921.* Princeton, N.J., 1974.

Rosenstone, R. A. *Romantic revolutionary. A biography of John Reed.* New York, 1975.

Rosmer, A. *Moscou sous Lénine,* II: *1921–1924.* Paris, 1970.

Rubanovič, R. *Inostrannaja pressa i russkoe dviženie.* Matériaux pour servir à l'histoire du mouvement socialiste révolutionnaire en Russie, XVI. Geneva, 1893.

Rubel, M. 'Les écrits de Karl Marx sur la Russie tsariste'. *Revue d'Histoire Economique et Sociale,* XXXIII, no. 1 (1953) 113–21.

Ruffmann, K. H. *Das Russlandbild im England Shakespeares.* Göttingen, 1952.

Rusanov, N. S. *V emigracii.* Moscow, 1929.

Russell, B. *The practice and theory of Bolshevism.* London, 1920.

*Russia. Report of the Russian Socialist Revolutionary Party to the International Socialist Congress, Amsterdam, 1904 by the Central Committee of the S.R. Party.* London, 1904.

Rüter, A. J. C. *De spoorwegstaking van 1903.* Leiden, 1935.

Salomé, Lou Andreas. *Lebensrückblick.* Frankfurt on Main, 1968, 1977.

Salvadori, M. *Karl Kautsky and the socialist revolution 1880–1938.* London, 1979.

Sapir, B. 'Petr Lavrov' in: J. Rougerie et al., eds., *1871. Jalons pour une histoire de la Commune de Paris.* Assen, 1973.

Sapir, B., ed. *Vpered 1873–1877.* Dordrecht, 1970.

*Lavrov. Years of emigration. Letters and documents.* Dordrecht, 1974.

*Theodore Dan. Letters (1899–1946).* Amsterdam, 1985.

*Sbornik resoljucij i tezisov Centr. K-ta R.S.D.R.P. i partijnych soveščanij.* Kharkov, 1920.

Schapiro, L. *The origin of communist autocracy. Political opposition in the Soviet state. First phase 1917-1922.* New York, 1965.

*The communist party of the Soviet Union.* London, 1970.

*Totalitarianism.* London, 1972.

*1917. The Russian revolutions and the origins of present-day communism.* Hounslow, 1984.

Schelting A. von. *Russland und Europa im russischen Geschichtsdenken.* Berne, 1948.

Schitlowsky, C. 'Die Polemik Plechanow contra Stern und Conrad Schmidt'. *Sozialistische Monatshefte,* III (1899) 277-83, 322-30.

Schorske, C. E. *German social democracy 1905-1917. The development of the great schism.* Cambridge, Mass., 1955.

Schultz, L. 'Das Verfassungsrecht Russlands' in: G. Katkov et al., eds., *Russlands Aufbruch ins 20. Jahrhunderts. Politik - Gesellschaft - Kultur 1894-1917.* Olten, 1970.

Schwarz, S. M. 'Populism and early Russian Marxism on ways of economic development of Russia (the 1880's and 1890's)' in: E. J. Simmons, ed., *Continuity and change in Russian and Soviet thought.* New York, 1955.

*The Russian revolution of 1905. The workers' movement and the formation of Bolshevism and Menshevism.* Chicago, 1967.

Schwierkott, H. J. 'Von Dostojewski zum Dritten Reich. Arthur Moeller van den Bruck und die "Konservative Revolution"'. *Politische Studien,* XX (1969) 184-200.

Senn, A. E. *The Russian revolution in Switzerland 1914-1917.* Madison, Wis., 1971.

Seredonin, S. M. *Sočinenie Džil'sa Fletčera 'Of the Russecommon wealth' kak istoričiskij istočnik.* St Petersburg, 1891.

Service, R. *The Bolshevik party in revolution. A study in organisational change 1917-1923.* London, 1979.

Seton-Watson, C. *Italy from liberalism to Fascism.* London, 1970.

Shaw, M. E. 'The Nashe Slovo Group and Russian social democracy during W.W.I: the search for unity'. Unpublished Ph.D diss., Indiana University, 1975.

Silberner, E. *Moses Hess. Geschichte seines Lebens.* Leiden, 1966.

Slice, A. van der. *International labor, diplomacy and peace 1914-1919.* Philadephia, Pa, 1941.

Smith, S. A. *Red Petrograd. Revolution in the factories 1917-1918.* Cambridge, 1983.

Snowden, Mrs P. *Through Bolshevik Russia.* London, 1920.

*Social-demokratičeskoe dviženie v Rossii. Materialy,* I. Moscow, 1928.

*Social-demokratija i revoljucija.* Odessa, 1920.

Sokolov, B. *Le voyage de Cachin et de Frossard dans la Russie des Soviets.* Paris, 1921.

Sola Pool, I. de. 'Effects of cross-national contact on national and international images' in: H. C. Kelman, ed., *International behavior. A social-psychological analysis.* New York, 1965.

Sombart, W. *Warum gibt es in den Vereinigten Staaten keinen Sozialismus?* Tübingen, 1906.

*Why is there no socialism in the United States?* London, 1976.

Sorel, G. *Réflexions sur la violence.* Paris, 1908.

*Réflexions sur la violence.* Paris, 1972.

Southern, R. W. *Western views of Islam in the Middle Ages.* Cambridge, Mass., 1962.

*Russkie sovremenniki o K. Markse i F. Engel'se.* Moscow, 1969.

Spector, I. *The first Russian revolution. Its impact on Asia.* Englewood Cliffs, N.J., 1962.

Stainbrook, R. D. 'La presse française et la révolution russe de 1905'. Unpublished diss., University of Paris, 1950.

Stammler, H. 'Wandlungen des deutschen Bildes vom russischen Menschen'. *Jahrbücher für Geschichte Osteuropas,* n.s. V (1957) 271–305.

Stampfer, F. *Erfahrungen und Erkenntnisse. Aufzeichnungen aus meinem Leben.* Cologne, 1957.

Starr, S. F. 'Introduction' in: A. von Haxthausen, *Studies on the interior of Russia.* Chicago, 1972.

Steenson, G. P. *Karl Kautsky 1854–1938. Marxism in the classical years.* Pittsburgh, Pa, 1978.

Stein, A. *Das Problem der Internationale.* Berlin, 1919.

Stepnjak, 'Der Terrorismus in Russland und Europa'. *Die Neue Zeit,* IX (1890–1, 1) 263–7 and 281–90.

Stepun, F. *Das Anlitz Russlands und das Gesicht der Revolution. Aus meinem Leben 1884–1922.* Munich, 1961.

Stern, L., ed. *Die Auswirkungen der ersten russischen Revolution von 1905–1907 auf Deutschland.* Berlin, 1955–6.

*Die russische Revolution von 1905–1907 im Spiegel der deutschen Presse.* Berlin, 1961.

Stillig, J. *Die russische Februarrevolution 1917 und die sozialistische Friedenspolitik.* Cologne, 1977.

Stoelinga, T. H. J. *Russische revolutie en vredesverwachtingen in de Nederlandse pers maart 1917–maart 1918.* Bussum, 1967.

Stökl, G. 'Russland und Europa vor Peter dem Grossen'. *Historische Zeitschrift* (1957) 531–54.

Stökl, G. 'Johannes Scherr und die Geschichte Russlands. Zur Popularisierung eines Feindbildes' in: U. Liszkowski, ed., *Russland und Deutschland.* Kieler historische Studien, XXII. Stuttgart, 1974.

Strobel, G. W. *Die Partei Rosa Luxemburgs, Lenin und die SPD. Der polnische 'europäische' Internationalismus in der russischen Sozialdemokratie.* Wiesbaden, 1974.

Surh, G. D. *1905 in St Petersburg. Labor, society and revolution.* Stanford, Calif., 1989.

Swain, G. *Russian social democracy and the legal labour movement, 1906–1914.* London, 1983.

Szamuely, T. *The Russian tradition.* London, 1974.

Szeftel, M. *The Russian constitution of April 23, 1906. Political institutions of the Duma monarchy.* Brussels, 1971.

Talmon, J. L. *The origins of totalitarian democracy.* London, 1961.

*Die Tätigkeit des Allgem. Jüdischen Arbeiterbundes in Littauen, Polen und Russland (Bund) nach seinem V. Parteitag. Bericht für den Internationalen Sozialistischen Kongress in Amsterdam.* Geneva, 1904.

'Erster Tätigkeitsbericht des Internationalen Gewerkschaftsbundes (Juli 1919–Dezember 1921) vorgelegt dem ordentlichen Kongress, Rom, April 1922' in: *Die internationale Gewerkschaftsbewegung. Organ des Internationalen Gewerkschaftsbundes,* Supp. V, April 1922.

*Tätigkeitsbericht des Internationalen Gewerkschaftsbundes über die Jahre 1922 und 1923 vorgelegt dem Dritten Ordentlichen Kongress, Wien, Juni 1922.* Amsterdam, n.d.

*Ternii bez roz. Sbornik.* Geneva, 1908.

Thalheim, K. C. 'Die wirtschaftliche Entwicklung Russlands' in: G. Katkov et al., eds., *Russlands Aufbruch im 20. Jahrhundert.* Olten, 1970.

*Theses, resolutions and manifestoes of the first four congresses of the Third International.* London, 1980.

Thomson, A. W. and Hart, R. A. *The uncertain crusade. America and the Russian revolution of 1905.* Amhurst, Mass., 1970.

Thul, M. 'Russland in den Augen Napoleons I'. *Jahrbücher für Geschichte Osteuropas,* n.s. XXI (1973) 531–59.

Tobias, H. J. *The Jewish Bund in Russia. From its origins to 1905.* Stanford, Calif., 1972.

Toynbee, A. J. 'Looking back fifty years' in: *The impact of the Russian revolution. The influence of Bolshevism on the world outside Russia.* London, 1967.

Trockij, N. A. *Carskie sudy protiv revoljucionnoj Rossii. Političeskie processy 1871–1880 gg.* Saratov, 1976.

Troelstra, P. J. *Gedenkschriften.* 4 vols. Amsterdam, 1930.

Trotnow, H. 'Karl Liebknecht und der "Deutsche Hilfsverein für die politischen Gefangenen und Verbannten Russlands"'. *Internationale wissenschaftliche Korrespondenz zur Geschichte der deutschen Arbeiterbewegung,* XII (1976) 353–67.

*Karl Liebknecht. Eine politische Biographie.* Cologne, 1980.

Trotzki, L. *Die Grundfragen der Revolution.* Hamburg, 1923.

*Mein Leben. Versuch einer Autobiographie.* Berlin, 1961.

Trotzki, N. 'Der Arbeiterdeputiertenrat und die Revolution'. *Die Neue Zeit,* XXV (1906–7, 2) 76–86.

'Die Duma und die Revolution'. *Die Neue Zeit,* XXV (1906–7, 2) 377–85.

'Über den Marxismus in Russland (Zum fünfundzwanzigjährigen Jubiläum der "Neuen Zeit")'. *Die Neue Zeit,* XXVI (1907–8, 1) 7–10.

'Das Proletariat und die russische Revolution'. *Die Neue Zeit,* XXVI (1907–8, 2) 782–91.

'Die verdorbene Suppe (Das Fazit der Asewaffäre)'. *Die Neue Zeit,* XXVII (1908–9, 1) 892–9.

'Die Entwicklungstendenzen der russischen Sozialdemokratie'. *Die Neue Zeit,* XXVIII (1909–10, 2) 860–71.

*Russland in der Revolution.* Dresden, n.d.

Trotsky, L. *Terrorism and communism. A reply to Karl Kautsky.* Ann Arbor, Mich., 1961.

Tscherewanin, A. *Das Proletariat und die russische Revolution.* Stuttgart, 1908.

Tschiżewskij, D. and Groh, D., eds. *Europa und Russland. Texte zum Problem des westeuropäischen und russischen Selbstverständnisses.* Darmstadt, 1959.

Ulam, A. B. *The Bolsheviks. The intellectual and political history of the triumph of communism in Russia.* Toronto, 1969.

Vandervelde, E. and Wauters, A. *Le procès des socialistes révolutionnaires à Moscou.* Brussels, 1922.

Venturi, F. *Roots of revolution. A history of the populist and socialist movements in nineteenth century Russia.* New York, 1966.

'Vil'gel'm II o russko-japonskoj vojne i revoljucii 1905 goda'. *Krasnyj Archiv,* II, no. 9 (1925) 56–65.

Vliegen, W. H. *Die onze kracht ontwaken deed. Geschiedenis der Sociaal-democratische Arbeiderspartij in Nederland gedurende de eerste 25 jaren van haar bestaan.* Amsterdam, n.d.

Vliet, E. C. L. van der. *Strabo over landen, volken en steden, bezien tegen de historische en sociale achtergronden van zijn leven en werken.* Assen, 1977.

*Les voyages du sieur Adam Olearius.* Tr. de Wicquefort. Amsterdam, 1727.

Vryonis, S. Jr. *Byzantium and Europe.* London, 1967.

Wade, R. A. *The Russian search for peace. February–October 1917.* Stanford, Calif., 1969.

Walicki, A. *The controversy over capitalism. Studies in the social philosophy of the Russian populists.* Oxford, 1969.

*The Slavophile controversy. History of a conservative utopia in nineteenth-century Russian thought.* Oxford, 1975.

Warth, R. D. *The Allies and the Russian revolution*. Durham, N.C., 1954.

Weber, H. [Bauer, O.]. *Die russische Revolution und das europäische Proletariat*. Vienna, 1917.

Weber, M. 'Zur Lage der bürgerlichen Demokratie in Russland'. *Archiv für Sozialwissenschaft und Sozialpolitik*, XXII (1906, no. 1, Supp.) 345ff.

'Russlands Übergang zum Scheinkonstitutionalismus'. *Archiv für Sozialwissenschaft und Sozialpolitik*, XXIII (1906, no. 1, Supp.) 249ff.

Webster, C. *The foreign policy of Palmerston*. London, 1951.

Weeks, A. L. *The first Bolshevik. A political biography of Peter Tkachev*. New York, 1968.

Weill, C. *Marxistes russes et social-démocratie allemande 1898–1904*. Paris, 1977.

Weissman, B. M. *Herbert Hoover and famine relief to Soviet Russia 1921–1923*. Stanford, Calif., 1974.

Wheeler, R. F. 'The Independent Social Democratic Party and the International'. Unpublished Ph.D diss., University of Pittsburgh, 1970.

*USPD und Internationale. Sozialistischer Internationalismus in der Zeit der Revolution*. Frankfurt, 1975.

Wiardi Beckman, H. B. *Het syndicalisme in Frankrijk*. Amsterdam, 1931.

Wibaut, F. M. *Levensbouw. Memoires*. Amsterdam, 1936.

Wieczynski, J. L. 'A. S. Khomyakov's "Foreigners opinions of Russia". A translation and historical commentary'. Unpublished Ph.D diss., Georgetown University, 1966.

Wijk, N. van. 'Over het Russische volkskarakter'. *De Tijdspiegel* (1907, 1) 155–180 and 294–310.

Wildman, A. *The making of a workers' revolution. Russian social democracy 1891–1903*. Chicago, 1967.

Winter, E. *Halle als Ausgangspunkt der deutschen Russlandkunde im 18. Jahrhundert*. Berlin, 1953.

Winter, P. J. van. *De Chinezen van Europa*. Groningen, 1965.

Wittram, R. *Peter I. Czar und Kaiser. Zur Geschichte Peter des Grossen in seiner Zeit*. Göttingen, 1964.

Wohl, R. *French communism in the making*. Stanford, Calif., 1966.

Wohl, R. *The generation of 1919*. Cambridge, Mass., 1979.

Wolfe, B. D. 'Introduction' in: J. Reed, *Ten days that shook the world*. New York, 1960.

*Three who made a revolution*. Harmondsworth, 1966.

*The bridge and the abyss. The troubled friendship of Maxim Gorky and V. I. Lenin*. London, 1967.

*Marxism. One hundred years in the life of a doctrine*. London, 1967.

*An ideology in power. Reflections on the Russian revolution*. New York, 1970.

Wollschläger, D. 'Lenins Verhältnis zur deutschen Sozialdemokratie 1898/99–1914'. Diss. Un. Cologne, 1971.

Woodcock, G. *Pierre Joseph Proudhon. His life and work.* New York, 1972.

Woytinsky, W. *La démocratie Georgienne.* Paris, 1921.

Zassulitsch, V. 'Die terroristische Strömung in Russland'. *Die Neue Zeit,* XXI (1902–3, 1) 324–30 and 361–70.

Zeman, Z. A. B. and Scharlau, W. B. *The merchant of revolution. The life of Alexander Israel Helphand (Parvus) (1867–1924).* London, 1965.

Zinov'ev, G. *Dvenadcat' dnej v Germanii.* Petrograd, 1920.

Zinoviev, G. *Douze jours en Allemagne.* Moscow, 1920.

# INDEX